Hockey Scouting Report 2003

SHERRY ROSS

GREYSTONE BOOKS

Douglas & McIntyre Publishing Group
Vancouver / Toronto / New York

In memory of John Cunniff:
a friend to this book, to this author and to the game of hockey.

Greystone Books
A division of Douglas & McIntyre Ltd.
2323 Quebec Street, Suite 201
Vancouver, British Columbia V5T 4S7
www.greystonebooks.com

National Library of Canada Cataloguing in Publication Data

Ross, Sherry
    Hockey scouting report

    Annual
    Continues: Brown, Frank, 1952- Hockey scouting report.
    ISSN 0836-5148

    1. Hockey.   2. National Hockey League.   I. Title.
GV847.8.N3B4   796.962'64   CS94-300970-7

Editing by Christine Kondo
Cover design by Peter Cocking
Cover photograph of Tomas Kaberle by Bruce Bennett/Bruce Bennett Studios
Typesetting by MicroMega Designs
Printed and bound in Canada

The publisher gratefully acknowledges the support of the Canada Council for the Arts and of the British Columbia Ministry of Tourism, Small Business and Culture. The publisher also wishes to acknowledge the financial support of the Government of Canada through the Book Publishing Industry Development Program (BPIDP) for its publishing activities.

CONTENTS

SHERRY ROSS

Yrs. of NHL service: 24
Born: Randolph, NJ
Position: press box
Height: no way
Weight: you gotta be kidding
Uniform no.: DKNJ
Shoots: straight

LAST SEASON
Ross is the hockey columnist for the *New York Daily News*. She lives in New Jersey with her cats Madam Marie and Candy, and horse Cody.

THE FINESSE GAME
The versatile Ross began her career in the 1978-79 season, covering the New York Rangers for the Morristown (N.J.) *Daily Record*. In addition to working as a sportswriter for the Bergen (N.J.) *Record*, *Newsday* and *The National*, she became the NHL's first female team broadcaster in 1992, when she was hired as a radio colour commentator by the New Jersey Devils. In 1994, she became the first woman to call a major professional men's sports championship as the radio colour analyst in the Stanley Cup Finals.

As a freelance writer, Ross has contributed to Sports *Illustrated*, the *Hockey News*, the *Sporting News* and *Beckett Hockey Monthly*. She is the secretary-treasurer for the Professional Hockey Writers Association. She also covers major horse racing events for the *Daily News*.

THE PHYSICAL GAME
Horseback riding, frequent trips to Walt Disney World and as many Bruce Springsteen concerts as possible helps shake off the rink rust.

THE INTANGIBLES
Although she has lost a step over the years, her character and enthusiasm keep Ross in the game.

ACKNOWLEDGEMENTS
Now that the hockey season seems to last 11 months, you would think the last thing hockey people would want to do is gab about their game in their precious time off. You don't know the people who love hockey.

Without the help of the anonymous people whose information and opinions fill these pages, this project would never make it to the bookshelves — the hockey equivalent of the Stanley Cup playoffs. I can't tell you their names, but if I did, you would recognize them. Scouts, players, ex-players, general managers, assistant GMs and analysts are always willing to share their insights when I call with a question. Or two. Or 20.

My thanks is hardly enough, but it's all I have to offer.

I hope this book will enhance fans' appreciation for the game and the people who play it. That has always been the main goal of the *HSR*, whether you are a pool player or a spectator who simply wants to learn more about this amazing sport. I have been told through the years that this book finds it way into the offices of a number of NHL teams. That is a gratifying thing to hear. I am just as happy when I hear from someone who has made a little cash with a fantasy or pool team, maybe because of some information from this book.

Because of the expected influx of a lot of young players, more rookies than usual have been added to this year's edition. Trying to anticipate in July which players will be in an NHL uniform in October is a tricky business, but it's a gamble we hope pays off.

Now for the people whose names I can mention.

NHL VP Frank Brown never hesitates to send useful information my way all season, along with corralling the much-needed team postseason guides (this year's Completely Unofficial Ross Postseason Guide Award Winners: The Ottawa Senators).

My rookie editor, Christine Kondo, has done a sensational job, one worthy of our version of the Calder Trophy.

As for my Masterton (sportsmanship, dedication and perseverance), that goes to Kelly Dresser, who makes editing miracles happen online, and provides directions that even I can understand.

My Bruce pal E.J. Hradek is always a source of help and encouragement when I seem to need it most.

I now owe my usual apologies to my family and friends, who are neglected during the season and especially during the assembly of this book. To them especially my parents, thank you for your love and understanding, without which I would have succeeded at nothing.

Player Index

POINT LEADERS

NHL Scoring Statistics 2001-2002

RANK	POS.	PLAYER	GP	G	A	PTS	+/-	PP	S	PCT
1.	R	JAROME IGINLA	82	52	44	96	27	16	311	16.7
2.	L	MARKUS NASLUND	81	40	50	90	22	8	302	13.3
3.	L	TODD BERTUZZI	72	36	49	85	21	14	203	17.7
4.	C	MATS SUNDIN	82	41	39	80	6	10	262	15.6
5.	R	JAROMIR JAGR	69	31	48	79	0	10	197	15.7
6.	C	JOE SAKIC	82	26	53	79	12	9	260	10.0
7.	R	PAVOL DEMITRA	82	35	43	78	13	11	212	16.5
8.	C	ADAM OATES	80	14	64	78	-4	3	102	13.7
9.	C	MIKE MODANO	78	34	43	77	14	6	219	15.5
10.	C	RON FRANCIS	80	27	50	77	4	14	165	16.4
11.	R	ALEXEI KOVALEV	67	32	44	76	2	8	266	12.0
12.	L	KEITH TKACHUK	73	38	37	75	21	13	244	15.6
13.	L	BRENDAN SHANAHAN	80	37	38	75	23	12	277	13.4
14.	C	ALEXEI YASHIN	78	32	43	75	-3	15	239	13.4
15.	C	CRAIG CONROY	81	27	48	75	24	7	146	18.5
16.	C	JASON ALLISON	73	19	55	74	2	5	139	13.7
17.	L	MIROSLAV SATAN	82	37	36	73	14	15	267	13.9
18.	C	ERIC LINDROS	72	37	36	73	19	12	196	18.9
19.	R	GLEN MURRAY	82	41	30	71	31	9	246	16.7
20.	R	DANIEL ALFREDSSON	78	37	34	71	3	9	243	15.2
21.	R	PETER BONDRA	77	39	31	70	-2	17	333	11.7
22.	L	ERIC DAZE	82	38	32	70	17	12	264	14.4
23.	L	SERGEI SAMSONOV	74	29	41	70	21	3	192	15.1
24.	C	RADEK BONK	82	25	45	70	3	6	170	14.7
25.	R	PAVEL BURE	68	34	35	69	-5	12	287	11.8
26.	R	SAMI KAPANEN	77	27	42	69	9	11	248	10.9
27.	L	ANDREW BRUNETTE	81	21	48	69	-4	10	106	19.8
28.	C	SERGEI FEDOROV	81	31	37	68	20	10	256	12.1
29.	C	JOE THORNTON	66	22	46	68	7	6	152	14.5
30.	L	MARIAN GABORIK	78	30	37	67	0	10	221	13.6
31.	L	*DANY HEATLEY	82	26	41	67	-19	7	202	12.9
32.	C	BRENDAN MORRISON	82	23	44	67	18	6	183	12.6
33.	C	ALEXEI ZHAMNOV	77	22	45	67	8	6	173	12.7
34.	C	JEREMY ROENICK	75	21	46	67	32	5	167	12.6
35.	R	BILL GUERIN	78	41	25	66	-1	10	355	11.6
36.	L	SIMON GAGNE	79	33	33	66	31	4	199	16.6
37.	R	MARIAN HOSSA	80	31	35	66	11	9	278	11.1
38.	R	TONY AMONTE	82	27	39	66	11	6	232	11.6
39.	R	OWEN NOLAN	75	23	43	66	7	8	217	10.6
40.	C	JEFF O'NEILL	76	31	33	64	-5	11	272	11.4
41.	R	MARK RECCHI	80	22	42	64	5	7	205	10.7
42.	R	BRETT HULL	82	30	33	63	18	7	247	12.1
43.	R	THEOREN FLEURY	82	24	39	63	0	7	267	9.0
44.	C	BRIAN ROLSTON	82	31	31	62	11	6	331	9.4
45.	R	ADAM DEADMARSH	76	29	33	62	8	12	139	20.9

GP = games played; G = goals; A = assists; PTS = points; +/- = goals-for minus goals-against while player is on ice; PP = power-play goals; S = no. of shots; PCT = percentage of goals to shots; * = rookie

RANK	POS.	PLAYER	GP	G	A	PTS	+/-	PP	S	PCT
46.	C	DAYMOND LANGKOW	80	27	35	62	18	6	171	15.8
47.	C	BRAD RICHARDS	82	20	42	62	-18	5	251	8.0
48.	L	PATRIK ELIAS	75	29	32	61	4	8	199	14.6
49.	L	RAY WHITNEY	67	21	40	61	-22	6	210	10.0
50.	C	MIKE YORK	81	20	41	61	7	3	218	9.2
51.	C	MICHAEL NYLANDER	82	15	46	61	28	6	158	9.5
52.	C	MIKE COMRIE	82	33	27	60	16	8	170	19.4
53.	C	DANIEL BRIERE	78	32	28	60	6	12	149	21.5
54.	R	MARK PARRISH	78	30	30	60	10	9	162	18.5
55.	R	ANSON CARTER	82	28	32	60	3	12	181	15.5
56.	C	MICHAEL PECA	80	25	35	60	19	3	168	14.9
57.	R	STEVE SULLIVAN	78	21	39	60	23	3	155	13.6
58.	R	ZIGMUND PALFFY	63	32	27	59	5	15	161	19.9
59.	D	SERGEI GONCHAR	76	26	33	59	-1	7	216	12.0
60.	C	DARCY TUCKER	77	24	35	59	24	7	124	19.4
61.	D	NICKLAS LIDSTROM	78	9	50	59	13	6	215	4.2
62.	C	JOE NIEUWENDYK	81	25	33	58	0	6	189	13.2
63.	C	VINCENT DAMPHOUSSE	82	20	38	58	8	7	172	11.6
64.	C	JOZEF STUMPEL	81	8	50	58	22	1	100	8.0
65.	L	PAUL KARIYA	82	32	25	57	-15	11	289	11.1
66.	R	ALEXANDER MOGILNY	66	24	33	57	1	5	188	12.8
67.	C	JAN HRDINA	79	24	33	57	-7	6	115	20.9
68.	C	YANIC PERREAULT	82	27	29	56	-3	6	156	17.3
69.	D	ROB BLAKE	75	16	40	56	16	10	229	7.0
70.	C	ROD BRIND'AMOUR	81	23	32	55	3	5	162	14.2
71.	C	VACLAV PROSPAL	81	18	37	55	-11	7	166	10.8
72.	D	BRIAN LEETCH	82	10	45	55	14	1	202	4.9
73.	R	TEEMU SELANNE	82	29	25	54	-11	9	202	14.4
74.	C	BOBBY HOLIK	81	25	29	54	7	6	270	9.3
75.	C	CLIFF RONNING	81	19	35	54	0	5	199	9.5
76.	C	MIKE RICCI	79	19	34	53	9	5	115	16.5
77.	C	KYLE CALDER	81	17	36	53	8	6	133	12.8
78.	R	ULF DAHLEN	69	23	29	52	-5	7	141	16.3
79.	C	SHAWN BATES	71	17	35	52	18	1	150	11.3
80.	D	SANDIS OZOLINSH	83	14	38	52	-7	3	172	8.1
81.	R	MIKAEL RENBERG	71	14	38	52	11	4	130	10.8
82.	R	*ILYA KOVALCHUK	65	29	22	51	-19	7	184	15.8
83.	L	JOHN LECLAIR	82	25	26	51	5	4	220	11.4
84.	R	MARIUSZ CZERKAWSKI	82	22	29	51	-8	6	169	13.0
85.	C	DEAN MCAMMOND	73	21	30	51	2	7	152	13.8
86.	C	ROBERT REICHEL	78	20	31	51	7	1	152	13.2
87.	L	LUC ROBITAILLE	81	30	20	50	-2	13	190	15.8
88.	R	MARTIN HAVLAT	72	22	28	50	-7	9	145	15.2
89.	C	TODD WHITE	81	20	30	50	12	4	147	13.6
90.	C	ROBERT LANG	62	18	32	50	9	5	175	10.3
91.	L	RYAN SMYTH	61	15	35	50	7	7	150	10.0
92.	C	ANDREW CASSELS	53	11	39	50	5	7	64	17.2
93.	R	JERE LEHTINEN	73	25	24	49	27	7	198	12.6
94.	R	SHANE DOAN	81	20	29	49	11	6	205	9.8
95.	R	ALEXEI MOROZOV	72	20	29	49	-7	7	162	12.4
96.	C	DOUG WEIGHT	61	15	34	49	20	3	131	11.4
97.	R	PETR SYKORA	73	21	27	48	12	4	194	10.8
98.	L	GARY ROBERTS	69	21	27	48	-4	6	122	17.2
99.	C	KEITH PRIMEAU	75	19	29	48	-3	5	151	12.6
100.	C	MATT CULLEN	79	18	30	48	-1	3	164	11.0

GP = games played; G = goals; A = assists; PTS = points; +/- = goals-for minus goals-against while player is on ice; PP = power-play goals; S = no. of shots; PCT = percentage of goals to shots; * = rookie

GOAL LEADERS

RANK	PLAYER	G
1.	JAROME IGINLA	52
2.	MATS SUNDIN	41
3.	GLEN MURRAY	41
4.	BILL GUERIN	41
5.	MARKUS NASLUND	40
6.	PETER BONDRA	39
7.	KEITH TKACHUK	38
8.	ERIC DAZE	38
9.	BRENDAN SHANAHAN	37
10.	MIROSLAV SATAN	37
11.	ERIC LINDROS	37
12.	DANIEL ALFREDSSON	37
13.	TODD BERTUZZI	36
14.	PAVOL DEMITRA	35
15.	MIKE MODANO	34
16.	PAVEL BURE	34
17.	SIMON GAGNE	33
18.	MIKE COMRIE	33
19.	ALEXEI KOVALEV	32
20.	ALEXEI YASHIN	32
21.	DANIEL BRIERE	32
22.	ZIGMUND PALFFY	32
23.	PAUL KARIYA	32
24.	JAROMIR JAGR	31
25.	SERGEI FEDOROV	31
26.	MARIAN HOSSA	31
27.	JEFF O'NEILL	31
28.	BRIAN ROLSTON	31
29.	MARIAN GABORIK	30
30.	BRETT HULL	30
31.	MARK PARRISH	30
32.	LUC ROBITAILLE	30
33.	SERGEI SAMSONOV	29
34.	ADAM DEADMARSH	29
35.	PATRIK ELIAS	29
36.	TEEMU SELANNE	29
37.	*ILYA KOVALCHUK	29
38.	ANSON CARTER	28
39.	RON FRANCIS	27
40.	CRAIG CONROY	27
41.	SAMI KAPANEN	27
42.	TONY AMONTE	27
43.	DAYMOND LANGKOW	27
44.	YANIC PERREAULT	27
45.	JOE SAKIC	26
46.	*DANY HEATLEY	26
47.	SERGEI GONCHAR	26
48.	SCOTT THORNTON	26
49.	RADEK BONK	25
50.	MICHAEL PECA	25

ASSIST LEADERS

PLAYER	A
ADAM OATES	64
JASON ALLISON	55
JOE SAKIC	53
MARKUS NASLUND	50
RON FRANCIS	50
NICKLAS LIDSTROM	50
JOZEF STUMPEL	50
TODD BERTUZZI	49
JAROMIR JAGR	48
CRAIG CONROY	48
ANDREW BRUNETTE	48
JOE THORNTON	46
JEREMY ROENICK	46
MICHAEL NYLANDER	46
RADEK BONK	45
ALEXEI ZHAMNOV	45
BRIAN LEETCH	45
JAROME IGINLA	44
ALEXEI KOVALEV	44
BRENDAN MORRISON	44
PAVOL DEMITRA	43
MIKE MODANO	43
ALEXEI YASHIN	43
OWEN NOLAN	43
SAMI KAPANEN	42
MARK RECCHI	42
BRAD RICHARDS	42
SERGEI SAMSONOV	41
*DANY HEATLEY	41
MIKE YORK	41
RAY WHITNEY	40
ROB BLAKE	40
BRIAN RAFALSKI	40
CHRIS PRONGER	40
MATS SUNDIN	39
TONY AMONTE	39
THEOREN FLEURY	39
STEVE SULLIVAN	39
ANDREW CASSELS	39
JANNE NIINIMAA	39
BRENDAN SHANAHAN	38
VINCENT DAMPHOUSSE	38
SANDIS OZOLINSH	38
MIKAEL RENBERG	38
SCOTT GOMEZ	38
JAROSLAV MODRY	38
KEITH TKACHUK	37
SERGEI FEDOROV	37
MARIAN GABORIK	37
VACLAV PROSPAL	37

P.I.M. LEADERS

RANK	PLAYER	MJR	PIM
1.	PETER WORRELL	34	354
2.	BRAD FERENCE	10	254
3.	*CHRIS NEIL	17	231
4.	KEVIN SAWYER	27	221
5.	THEOREN FLEURY	2	216
6.	ANDREI NAZAROV	31	215
7.	MATTHEW BARNABY	22	214
8.	DENNY LAMBERT	15	213
9.	ANDRE ROY	15	211
10.	*JODY SHELLEY	28	206
11.	ROB RAY	18	200
12.	DONALD BRASHEAR	17	199
13.	MATT JOHNSON	13	183
14.	JASON WIEMER	14	178
15.	BILLY TIBBETTS	8	178
16.	BRYAN MARCHMENT	6	178
17.	BOB PROBERT	18	176
18.	ERIC CAIRNS	14	176
19.	SEAN BROWN	12	174
20.	SANDY MCCARTHY	11	171
21.	BOB BOUGHNER	14	170
22.	CRAIG BERUBE	12	164
23.	REED LOW	18	160
24.	GEORGES LARAQUE	19	157
25.	PAUL LAUS	15	157

P-PLAY LEADERS

PLAYER	PP
PETER BONDRA	17
JAROME IGINLA	16
MIROSLAV SATAN	15
ZIGMUND PALFFY	15
ALEXEI YASHIN	15
RON FRANCIS	14
TODD BERTUZZI	14
LUC ROBITAILLE	13
KEITH TKACHUK	13
ERIC DAZE	12
BRENDAN SHANAHAN	12
ANSON CARTER	12
ADAM DEADMARSH	12
ERIC LINDROS	12
PAVEL BURE	12
DANIEL BRIERE	12
PAUL KARIYA	11
SAMI KAPANEN	11
JEFF O'NEILL	11
ANDY DELMORE	11
PAVOL DEMITRA	11
BILL GUERIN	10
ROB BLAKE	10
JASON ARNOTT	10
SERGEI FEDOROV	10

GOALIE WIN LEADERS

RANK	PLAYER	W
1.	DOMINIK HASEK	41
2.	MARTIN BRODEUR	38
3.	EVGENI NABOKOV	37
4.	BYRON DAFOE	35
5.	BRENT JOHNSON	34
6.	SEAN BURKE	33
7.	JOCELYN THIBAULT	33
8.	PATRICK ROY	32
9.	CHRIS OSGOOD	32
10.	OLAF KOLZIG	31
11.	FELIX POTVIN	31
12.	DAN CLOUTIER	31
13.	MARTIN BIRON	31
14.	ROMAN TUREK	30
15.	TOMMY SALO	30
16.	JOSE THEODORE	30
17.	CURTIS JOSEPH	29
18.	PATRICK LALIME	27
19.	JOHAN HEDBERG	25
20.	MIKE RICHTER	24
21.	NIKOLAI KHABIBULI	24
22.	ROMAN CECHMANEK	24
23.	MIKE DUNHAM	23
24.	ED BELFOUR	21
25.	ARTURS IRBE	20

GOALIE G.A.A. LEADERS

PLAYER	GAA
PATRICK ROY	1.94
ROMAN CECHMANEK	2.05
MARTY TURCO	2.09
JOSE THEODORE	2.11
J GIGUERE	2.13
MARTIN BRODEUR	2.15
DOMINIK HASEK	2.17
BRENT JOHNSON	2.18
BYRON DAFOE	2.21
TOMMY SALO	2.22
MARTIN BIRON	2.22
CURTIS JOSEPH	2.23
SEAN BURKE	2.29
EVGENI NABOKOV	2.29
FELIX POTVIN	2.31
NIKOLAI KHABIBULI	2.36
BRIAN BOUCHER	2.41
DAN CLOUTIER	2.43
PATRICK LALIME	2.48
JOCELYN THIBAULT	2.49
CHRIS OSGOOD	2.50
ROMAN TUREK	2.53
ARTURS IRBE	2.54
MIKE DUNHAM	2.61
TOM BARRASSO	2.62

ANAHEIM MIGHTY DUCKS

Players' Statistics 2001-2002

POS	NO.	PLAYER	GP	G	A	PTS	+/-	PIM	PP	SH	GW	GT	S	PCT
L	9	PAUL KARIYA	82	32	25	57	-15	28	11		8	1	289	11.1
C	17	MATT CULLEN	79	18	30	48	-1	24	3	1	4		164	11.0
L	12	MIKE LECLERC	82	20	24	44	-12	107	8		4		178	11.2
L	11	JEFF FRIESEN	81	17	26	43	-1	44	1	1			161	10.6
D	10	OLEG TVERDOVSKY	73	6	26	32	0	31	2		1		147	4.1
C	19	*ANDY MCDONALD	53	7	21	28	2	10	2		3		79	8.9
L	13	GERMAN TITOV	66	13	14	27	4	36	1		2		63	20.6
D	33	JASON YORK	74	5	20	25	-11	60	3		2		104	4.8
C	20	STEVE RUCCHIN	38	7	16	23	-3	6	4		1		57	12.3
C	26	SAMUEL PAHLSSON	80	6	14	20	-16	26	1	1			99	6.1
R	18	PATRIC KJELLBERG	77	8	11	19	-12	16	4				88	9.1
R	21	DAN BYLSMA	77	8	9	17	5	28			1	2	72	11.1
D	3	KEITH CARNEY	60	5	9	14	14	30			1		66	7.6
D	7	PAVEL TRNKA	71	2	11	13	-5	66	1				78	2.6
D	24	RUSLAN SALEI	82	4	7	11	-10	97			1		96	4.2
C	32	MARC CHOUINARD	45	4	5	9	2	10					40	10.0
L	27	DENNY LAMBERT	73	2	5	7	1	213					51	3.9
R	23	SERGEI KRIVOKRASOV	26	2	3	5	-2	36			1		51	3.9
D	28	NICLAS HAVELID	52	1	2	3	-13	40					45	2.2
D	5	VITALY VISHNEVSKI	74		3	3	-10	60					54	
L	29	*TIMO PARSSINEN	17		3	3	0	2					16	
L	25	KEVIN SAWYER	57	1	1	2	-4	221					29	3.5
D	37	ARIS BRIMANIS	5				-1	9					2	
D	36	DREW BANNISTER	1				0						1	
D	4	ANTTI-JUSSI NIEMI	1				-1							
G	31	STEVE SHIELDS	33				0	4						
G	35	J GIGUERE	53				0	28						
G	1	GREGG NAUMENKO				-	0							
G	30	ILJA BRYZGALOV	1				0							

GP = games played; G = goals; A = assists; PTS = points; +/- = goals-for minus goals-against while player is on ice; PIM = penalties in minutes; PP = power-play goals; SH = shorthanded goals; GW = game-winning goals; GT = game-tying goals; S = no. of shots; PCT = percentage of goals to shots; * = rookie

KEITH CARNEY

Yrs. of NHL service: 10
Born: Providence, R.I.; Feb. 3, 1970
Position: left defence
Height: 6-2
Weight: 211
Uniform no.: 3
Shoots: left

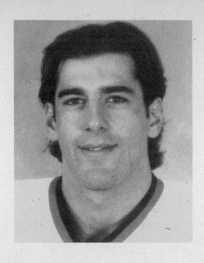

Career statistics:

GP	G	A	TP	PIM
648	32	119	151	635

1998-1999 statistics:

GP	G	A	TP	+/-	PIM	PP	SH	GW	GT	S	PCT
82	2	14	16	+15	62	0	2	0	0	62	3.2

1999-2000 statistics:

GP	G	A	TP	+/-	PIM	PP	SH	GW	GT	S	PCT
82	4	20	24	+11	87	0	0	1	0	73	5.5

2000-2001 statistics:

GP	G	A	TP	+/-	PIM	PP	SH	GW	GT	S	PCT
82	2	14	16	+15	86	0	0	0	0	65	3.1

2001-2002 statistics:

GP	G	A	TP	+/-	PIM	PP	SH	GW	GT	S	PCT
60	5	9	14	+14	30	0	0	1	0	66	7.6

LAST SEASON

Led team in plus-minus. Missed 17 games due to chipped bone in hand. Injury snapped his consecutive games-played streak at 262. Missed five games with elbow injury.

THE FINESSE GAME

Carney is quick and agile and he positions himself well defensively. He is a smart power-play point man who works on the second unit on the right side. He is among the NHL's better penalty killers, and he has good hockey sense and great anticipation. He reads the play well, is a fine skater and moves the puck smoothly and quickly out of the zone. He is a very good shot-blocker.

Carney was considered an offensive defenceman when he first tried to break into the NHL, but he lacked the elite skills to succeed on that style alone. He has turned his finesse skills to his defensive advantage and emphasizes play in his own zone, though he is capable of contributing some offence.

Carney compliments an offensive partner well. He is not strictly stay-at-home, though. He just picks his spots wisely and conserves energy.

THE PHYSICAL GAME

Carney is not a hitter, but he will get in the way of people; instead of punishing, he ties up his man effectively. A well-conditioned athlete, he is an honest worker who is the last one off the ice in practice. He can take a penalty at the worst time, or so it seems.

THE INTANGIBLES

Carney is a No. 4 or 5 defenceman on his best days. He was pretty much Anaheim's No. 1 defender last year, which was asking a lot. He is quiet and steady, but 20 minutes of ice time a night against other teams' top lines is a tall order, and he wears down late in the season if he is used in that way.

PROJECTION

His focus on defence will again limit Carney's total to around 20 points.

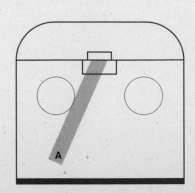

J. GIGUERE

Yrs. of NHL service: 2
Born: Montreal, Que., May 16, 1977
Position: goalie
Height: 6-0
Weight: 185
Uniform no.: 35
Shoots:

Career statistics:

GP	MIN	GA	SO	GAA	A	PIM
117	6742	283	8	2.52	2	28

1998-1999 statistics:

GP	MIN	GAA	W	L	T	SO	GA	S	SAPCT	PIM
15	860	3.21	6	7	1	0	46	447	.897	4

1999-2000 statistics:

GP	MIN	GAA	W	L	T	SO	GA	S	SAPCT	PIM
7	330	2.73	1	3	1	0	15	175	.914	2

2000-2001 statistics:

GP	MIN	GAA	W	L	T	SO	GA	S	SAPCT	PIM
34	2031	2.57	11	17	5	4	87	976	.911	8

2001-2002 statistics:

GP	MIN	GAA	W	L	T	SO	GA	S	SAPCT	PIM
53	3127	2.13	20	25	6	4	111	1384	.920	28

PROJECTION

Wins are still going to be hard to come by for Anaheim. The Ducks will probably want to keep his workload light (60 starts or so) and he should produce 20-22 wins.

LAST SEASON

Fifth in NHL in goals-against average with career best. Tied for fifth in NHL in save percentage. Tied career high in shutouts. Missed five games with groin injury.

THE PHYSICAL GAME

Giguere has bounced around in three different organizations since he was drafted in the first round by Hartford in 1995. It seems like he has finally landed on his (webbed?) feet as a Duck.

Giguere isn't a very tall goalie, so he's had to make an effort to keep his torso upright when he drops down to his knees. He is excellent down low. He is primarily a standup goalie, but he switches to the butterfly when the play is in close. Giguere is a good skater with quick post-to-post moves.

He's above average with both his blocker and glove hands. His puckhandling is okay. He's good with his stick for breaking up plays around the net.

THE INTANGIBLES

Giguere suffered groin injuries during his developmental years, which slowed his progress and may be a chronic problem. The Mighty Ducks thought enough of Giguere's performance that they traded away Steve Shields. Of course, they are also mighty cheap, so we don't know how much to read into that.

PAUL KARIYA

Yrs. of NHL service: 8
Born: North Vancouver, B.C.; Oct. 16, 1974
Position: left wing
Height: 5-10
Weight: 173
Uniform no.: 9
Shoots: left

Career statistics:

GP	G	A	TP	PIM
524	275	313	588	165

1998-1999 statistics:

GP	G	A	TP	+/-	PIM	PP	SH	GW	GT	S	PCT
82	39	62	101	+17	40	11	2	4	0	429	9.1

1999-2000 statistics:

GP	G	A	TP	+/-	PIM	PP	SH	GW	GT	S	PCT
74	42	44	86	+22	24	11	3	3	0	324	13.0

2000-2001 statistics:

GP	G	A	TP	+/-	PIM	PP	SH	GW	GT	S	PCT
66	33	34	67	-9	20	18	3	3	0	230	14.4

2001-2002 statistics:

GP	G	A	TP	+/-	PIM	PP	SH	GW	GT	S	PCT
82	32	25	57	-15	28	11	0	8	1	289	11.1

LAST SEASON

Led team in goals, points, power-play goals, game-winning goals and shots. Second on team in shooting percentage. One of three Ducks to appear in all 82 games.

THE FINESSE GAME

A magician with the puck, Kariya can make a play when it looks as if there are no possible options. He likes to use the net for protection, like his idol Wayne Gretzky, and make passes from behind the goal line. His release on his shot is excellent.

One of the best skaters in the NHL, Kariya is so smooth and fluid his movements appear effortless. He's also explosive, with a good change of direction; he can turn a defender inside out on a one-on-one rush. His speed is a weapon, since he forces defenders to play off him for fear of being burnt, and that opens the ice for his playmaking options. He combines his skating with no-look passes that are uncanny.

Kariya uses his speed defensively. He's quick on the backcheck to break up passes. He kills penalties by hounding the point men and pressuring them into making bad passes, which he then turns into scoring chances.

Kariya is a low-maintenance superstar. He has worked on his weaknesses, becoming stronger on the puck, less fancy in his passing and more willing to shoot.

THE PHYSICAL GAME

Kariya has powerful thighs and legs and has improved his upper-body strength. He is something of a workout nut — so much so that he actually has to scale back his off-season conditioning.

THE INTANGIBLES

Kariya was healthy all season yet finished with his lowest point total in four seasons, obviously suffering from the offensive void left when Teemu Selanne was traded in March 2001. It was obvious that the grind of playing for a hopeless franchise has worn him down. After playing without a true No. 1 centre for his entire eight-season Ducks career, Kariya finally gets one with the free agent signing of Adam Oates. Oates is a little long in the tooth, but his passing and playmaking skills haven't eroded much, and the trade for Petr Sykora adds a creative dash to the right wing.

PROJECTION

Kariya might be put back on the hockey map if Anaheim's roster tinkering pays off. A return to the 90-point range is likely if all of the parts fit and if Kariya can stay healthy again.

PATRIC KJELLBERG

Yrs. of NHL service: 4
Born: Falun, Sweden; June 17, 1969
Position: right wing
Height: 6-3
Weight: 210
Uniform no.: 18
Shoots: left

Career statistics:

GP	G	A	TP	PIM
318	56	85	141	68

1998-1999 statistics:

GP	G	A	TP	+/-	PIM	PP	SH	GW	GT	S	PCT
71	11	20	31	-13	24	2	0	2	0	103	10.7

1999-2000 statistics:

GP	G	A	TP	+/-	PIM	PP	SH	GW	GT	S	PCT
82	23	23	46	-11	14	9	0	3	0	129	17.8

2000-2001 statistics:

GP	G	A	TP	+/-	PIM	PP	SH	GW	GT	S	PCT
81	14	31	45	-2	12	5	0	2	0	139	10.1

2001-2002 statistics:

GP	G	A	TP	+/-	PIM	PP	SH	GW	GT	S	PCT
77	8	11	19	-12	16	4	0	0	0	88	9.1

Kjellberg will be on the bubble, and he may have to fight for his ice time.

PROJECTION

The most to expect out of Kjellberg is 15 goals, and that would be a career year.

LAST SEASON

Acquired from Nashville on November 1, 2001, for Petr Tenkrat. Tied for third on team in power-play goals. Missed five games with neck injury.

THE FINESSE GAME

Most of Kjellberg's goals come from in and around the crease. He's not flashy. He makes smart plays, though, and you really have to pay attention to notice the little things he does well. He's not a big offensive threat, but he has the finesse skills to maybe earn time on Anaheim's No. 2 line, since they don't have a lot of forwards with size.

He isn't quick, but Kjellberg is smart enough positionally to not get burned often defensively and he knows when to gamble in-deep. Kjellberg is not a bad choice to use in front of the net on a second-unit power play.

Kjellberg is a big, strong skater, but not a swift one. He is good along the wall and in the corners. He is a bigger Andreas Dackell.

THE PHYSICAL GAME

Kjellberg likes to get involved around the net. He will dig in for rebounds and garbage goals. Most of his goals come from five to ten feet out, in the dirty areas. He'll take a beating to get open. He has a very slow flash point and doesn't take bad penalties. He just takes the punishment.

THE INTANGIBLES

Kjellberg is hardly spectacular in any areas, but he is very steady. A coach can put Kjellberg in the lineup night after night and know exactly what he is going to get: a smart and honest effort from a modestly skilled player. As Anaheim upgrades its talent up front,

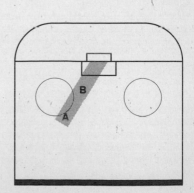

MIKE LECLERC

Yrs. of NHL service: 5
Born: Winnipeg, Man.; Nov. 10, 1976
Position: left wing
Height: 6-2
Weight: 204
Uniform no.: 12
Shoots: left

Career statistics:

GP	G	A	TP	PIM
224	44	56	100	213

1998-1999 statistics:

GP	G	A	TP	+/-	PIM	PP	SH	GW	GT	S	PCT
7	0	0	0	-2	4	0	0	0	0	1	0.0

1999-2000 statistics:

GP	G	A	TP	+/-	PIM	PP	SH	GW	GT	S	PCT
69	8	11	19	-15	70	0	0	2	0	105	7.6

2000-2001 statistics:

GP	G	A	TP	+/-	PIM	PP	SH	GW	GT	S	PCT
54	15	20	35	-1	26	3	0	3	2	130	11.5

2001-2002 statistics:

GP	G	A	TP	+/-	PIM	PP	SH	GW	GT	S	PCT
82	20	24	44	-12	107	8	0	4	0	178	11.2

LAST SEASON

Led team in shooting percentage. Second on team in goals, power-play goals and shots. Tied for second on team in game-winning goals. Third on team in assists and penalty minutes. One of three Ducks to appear in all 82 games.

THE FINESSE GAME

Leclerc showed some inconsistency, but given that last year was his first full, injury-free season, we're inclined to be a bit forgiving. Power forwards take a longer time to develop and Leclerc may have finally had his breakthrough.

Leclerc has a long reach with a lot of power on his shot, which is accurate and quickly released. He is unselfish and wants to dish the puck off, though his coaches want him to shoot. He has very good vision and is at his best in-tight.

Defensively aware, Leclerc works hard in all three zones. Skating is the only thing that might hold him back from becoming an elite power forward. He lacks quickness and acceleration, but has a long, strong stride once he gets in gear.

Leclerc's idol is Cam Neely, which is not a bad role model for a kid with size, touch and a bit of a temper, as Leclerc appears to have.

THE PHYSICAL GAME

He uses his body well, and Leclerc matches up well against other teams' rugged forwards, because he's not awed by them and he's certainly not afraid to drop his gloves. He is starting to make his reputation and doesn't need to spend as much time in the penalty box. He fights to get into the quality scoring zones around the net.

THE INTANGIBLES

The benefit in adding players like Adam Oates and Petr Sykora to the lineup is that it allows Leclerc to settle into a comfortable second-line role with other players while the two newcomers (with Paul Kariya) handle first-line duties.

Leclerc is intense and plays hard every night. He's a quiet kid and coachable; a good team player who will be an asset for years to come. Anaheim needs his physical presence up front.

PROJECTION

Last year we thought Leclerc was ready to make the 20-goal breakthrough, which he did — despite an 0-for-11 goalless streak near the end of the season. We'll up the ante slightly to 25 goals.

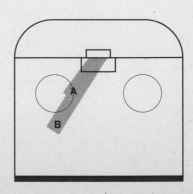

ADAM OATES

Yrs. of NHL service: 17
Born: Weston, Ont.; Aug. 27, 1962
Position: centre
Height: 5-11
Weight: 188
Uniform no.: 77
Shoots: right

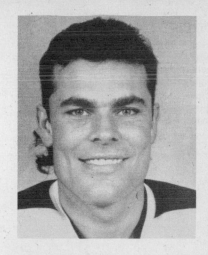

Career statistics:

GP	G	A	TP	PIM
1210	330	1027	1357	391

1998-1999 statistics:

GP	G	A	TP	+/-	PIM	PP	SH	GW	GT	S	PCT
59	12	42	54	-1	22	3	0	0	0	79	15.2

1999-2000 statistics:

GP	G	A	TP	+/-	PIM	PP	SH	GW	GT	S	PCT
82	15	56	71	+13	14	5	0	6	0	93	16.1

2000-2001 statistics:

GP	G	A	TP	+/-	PIM	PP	SH	GW	GT	S	PCT
81	13	69	82	-9	28	5	0	4	0	72	18.1

2001-2002 statistics:

GP	G	A	TP	+/-	PIM	PP	SH	GW	GT	S	PCT
80	14	64	78	-4	28	3	0	1	0	102	13.7

LAST SEASON

Signed as free agent on July 1, 2002. Acquired by Philadelphia from Washington on March 19, 2002, for Maxime Ouellet and a first, second and third round draft picks in 2002. Led NHL players in assists. Led Flyers in assists and points. Third on Flyers in shooting percentage. Eighth among NHL players in points. Tied for 10th among NHL players in power-play ponts (29). Missed three games with leg injury.

THE FINESSE GAME

Passing is Oates' first instinct, though he has a fine shot with a precise touch. Taking more shots makes him a less predictable player, since the defence can't back off and anticipate the pass. He is one of the NHL's best playmakers because of his passing ability and his creativity. He is most effective down low where he can open up more ice, especially on the power play. He has outstanding timing and vision.

Oates remains one of the elite playmakers in the NHL, defying age. He uses a shorter-than-average stick and a minimal curve on his blade, the result being exceptional control of the puck. Although he's a right-handed shooter, his right wings have always been his preferred receivers. He can pass on the backhand but also carries the puck deep. He shields the puck with his body and turns to make the pass to his right wing.

Use of the backhand gives Oates a tremendous edge against all but the rangiest NHL defencemen. He forces defenders to reach in and frequently draws penalties when he is hooked or tripped. If defenders don't harass him, he then has carte blanche to work his passing magic.

Oates is definitely not one of those players stubborn to a fault. He will also play a dump and chase game if he is being shadowed closely, throwing the puck smartly into the opposite corner with just the right velocity to allow his wingers to get in on top of the defence.

He was eighth in the NHL in face-offs (56.38 per cent), which makes him an asset on penalty killing; a successful draw eats up 10 to 15 seconds on the clock.

THE PHYSICAL GAME

Oates is not a physical player but he doesn't avoid contact. He plays in traffic and will take a hit to make the play, and he's smart enough at this stage of his career to avoid the garbage. He's an intense player with a wiry strength, but he tends to wear down late in the season as his line receives all the checking attention, and the Ducks don't appear to have much depth to lessen the checking pressure on him.

THE INTANGIBLES

Philadelphia paid a dear price for him for the stretch drive and playoff run, but the move was a bust. Now Oates gets a fresh start in the West, where he may be able to work some magic with Paul Kariya. He signed a two-year, $7 million (US) deal with Anaheim.

PROJECTION

If the chemistry is right with Kariya, Oates could lead the league in assists again.

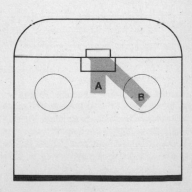

SAMI PAHLSSON

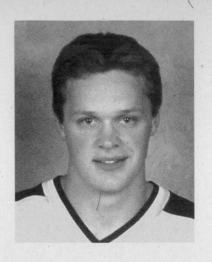

Yrs. of NHL service: 2
Born: Ornskoldsvik, Sweden; Dec. 17, 1977
Position: centre
Height: 5-11
Weight: 190
Uniform no.: 26
Shoots: left

Career statistics:

GP	G	A	TP	PIM
156	10	19	29	46

2000-2001 statistics:

GP	G	A	TP	+/-	PIM	PP	SH	GW	GT	S	PCT
76	4	5	9	-14	20	1	1	1	0	59	6.8

2001-2002 statistics:

GP	G	A	TP	+/-	PIM	PP	SH	GW	GT	S	PCT
80	6	14	20	-16	26	1	1	0	0	99	6.1

LAST SEASON

Missed one game with sprained ankle. Missed one game due to coach's decision.

THE FINESSE GAME

Pahlsson is a highly skilled centre with a hard edge. His primary attention is on his defence, but he has very good playmaking skills. He can make turnovers into points, and he churns up a lot of loose pucks with his forechecking. He won't be scoring the goals himself, but his partners will have plenty of good chances.

Pahlsson has a solid, gritty all-around game. He is positionally sound and he is excellent on draws. His skating is NHL-calibre. He isn't breakaway-quick, but his anticipation will buy him a few steps every time.

Pahlsson plays a sound game but has the skill level where he doesn't look out of place with better players. While he is not a logical top six forward, he could be a safety-valve player for two more offensive-minded partners.

THE PHYSICAL GAME

Pahlsson is average height but solid, and he plays even bigger. He seems to have a very long reach. He digs in the corners and is tough.

THE INTANGIBLES

Pahlsson was part of the Ray Bourque legacy in Boston, but the Bruins didn't waste much time before packing him off to Anaheim. The Ducks still believe Pahlsson has some offensive upside.

PROJECTION

Pahlsson has the potential of scoring 10 goals a season in a checking role. It doesn't sound like much, but once he adapts better to the NHL game, he will make Anaheim a harder team to fight your way through — and that is no small compliment.

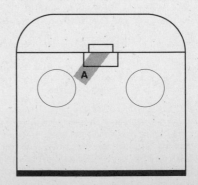

STEVE RUCCHIN

Yrs. of NHL service: 8
Born: Thunder Bay, Ont.; July 4, 1971
Position: centre
Height: 6-3
Weight: 212
Uniform no.: 20
Shoots: left

Career statistics:

GP	G	A	TP	PIM
452	113	218	331	116

1998-1999 statistics:

GP	G	A	TP	+/-	PIM	PP	SH	GW	GT	S	PCT
69	23	39	62	+11	22	5	1	5	1	145	15.9

1999-2000 statistics:

GP	G	A	TP	+/-	PIM	PP	SH	GW	GT	S	PCT
71	19	38	57	+9	16	10	0	2	2	131	14.5

2000-2001 statistics:

GP	G	A	TP	+/-	PIM	PP	SH	GW	GT	S	PCT
16	3	5	8	-5	0	2	0	0	0	19	15.8

2001-2002 statistics:

GP	G	A	TP	+/-	PIM	PP	SH	GW	GT	S	PCT
38	7	16	23	-3	6	4	0	1	0	57	12.3

LAST SEASON

Missed 44 games with stress fracture of tibia and surgery.

THE FINESSE GAME

Rucchin is one of the best little stories in the NHL, but injuries over the past two seasons have derailed the happy ending. A concussion and broken hand in 2000-01, and the leg injury last year kept this gritty small-college find (he was signed out of the University of Western Ontario in the 1994 Supplemental Draft) from being his effective self once again.

If Rucchin is healthy, he may finally be able to be used properly — as a third-line, checking centre with some offensive upside — rather than in the No. 1 role the Ducks tried to shoehorn him into (instead of spending the money on a bona fide No. 1 pivotman).

Rucchin has good size and range, and sharp hockey sense, which enables him to make the most of his above-average skating, passing and shooting skills. He grinds and digs the puck off the wall, and has the vision and the passing skills to find a breaking winger. He is patient and protects the puck well.

Rucchin is one of the best-kept secrets in the NHL when it comes to face-offs. He can win a draw outright, or if he fails, tie up the opposing centre to allow his teammates to get to the puck first.

THE PHYSICAL GAME

Rucchin can be a real force. He's strong and balanced, willing to forecheck hard and fight for the puck along the boards and in the corners. When he wins the puck, he's able to create a smart play with it. He has a long reach for holding off defenders and working the puck one handed, or reaching in defensively to knock the puck away from an attacker.

He often matches up against other teams' big centres.

THE INTANGIBLES

Rucchin is one of the important, underrated leaders on the team, and there is a big question mark about his health and how effective he will be coming back from another serious injury.

PROJECTION

When players start getting dinged up time after time, they never seem to fully recover. We would advise a wait and see on Rucchin. Even if he does come back at full strength, his 60-point days are a thing of the past. The Ducks would happily settle for 40 points from him in a two-way role.

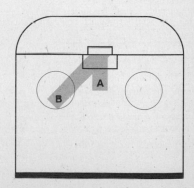

RUSLAN SALEI

Yrs. of NHL service: 6
Born: Minsk, Belarus; Nov. 2, 1974
Position: left defence
Height: 6-1
Weight: 207
Uniform no.: 24
Shoots: left

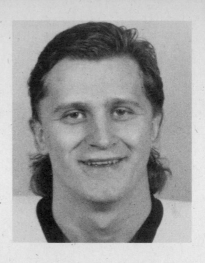

Career statistics:

GP	G	A	TP	PIM
373	17	42	59	433

1998-1999 statistics:

GP	G	A	TP	+/-	PIM	PP	SH	GW	GT	S	PCT
74	2	14	16	+1	65	1	0	0	0	123	1.6

1999-2000 statistics:

GP	G	A	TP	+/-	PIM	PP	SH	GW	GT	S	PCT
71	5	5	10	+3	94	1	0	0	0	116	4.3

2000-2001 statistics:

GP	G	A	TP	+/-	PIM	PP	SH	GW	GT	S	PCT
50	1	5	6	-14	70	0	0	0	0	73	1.4

2001-2002 statistics:

GP	G	A	TP	+/-	PIM	PP	SH	GW	GT	S	PCT
82	4	7	11	-10	97	0	0	1	0	96	4.2

PROJECTION

Anaheim's defence is going to suffer from the loss of Oleg Tverdovsky. Other guys will be asked to pick up some of the offensive slack. Salei isn't one of the guys who can do it.

LAST SEASON

Appeared in all 82 games.

THE FINESSE GAME

Salei is a fairly agile skater but he doesn't have great breakaway speed. He skates well backwards, is mobile and is not easy to beat one-on-one.

His defensive reads are very good, and he can kill penalties. There is a possibility he could see time on a second power-play unit, because he moves the puck well and appears to have an NHL-calibre point shot. He shoots well off the pass — and it's high-velocity.

Salei has become steadier and seems unfazed by the attention his controversial game brings with it. Now Salei has had a taste of his own medicine. Having received a concussion instead of giving one, it will be interesting to see how it affects his play.

THE PHYSICAL GAME

Salei, who made Mike Modano's list of dirtiest NHL players, managed to get through a season without being suspended. Salei is mature, solidly built and initiates a lot of contact. He is not afraid to hit anyone. He has a little nasty streak that results in some cheap hits, but he can play it hard and clean, too. He will sometimes start running around and lose track of his man.

THE INTANGIBLES

Salei is expected to be one of Anaheim's top four defencemen. He seems to have recovered fully from a concussion that affected him in 2000-01.

PETR SYKORA

Yrs. of NHL service: 7
Born: Plzen, Czech Republic; Nov. 19, 1976
Position: right wing
Height: 6-0
Weight: 190
Uniform no.: 17
Shoots: left

Career statistics:

GP	G	A	TP	PIM
445	145	205	350	182

1998-1999 statistics:

GP	G	A	TP	+/-	PIM	PP	SH	GW	GT	S	PCT
2	0	0	0	-1	0	0	0	0	0	2	0.0

1999-2000 statistics:

GP	G	A	TP	+/-	PIM	PP	SH	GW	GT	S	PCT
79	25	43	68	+24	26	5	1	4	0	222	11.3

2000-2001 statistics:

GP	G	A	TP	+/-	PIM	PP	SH	GW	GT	S	PCT
73	35	46	81	+36	32	9	2	3	0	249	14.1

2001-2002 statistics:

GP	G	A	TP	+/-	PIM	PP	SH	GW	GT	S	PCT
73	21	27	48	+12	44	4	0	4	0	194	10.8

LAST SEASON

Acquired from New Jersey on July 6, 2002, with Mike Commodore, J-F Damphousse and Igor Pohanka for Jeff Friesen, Oleg Tverdovsky and Maxim Balmochnykh. Third on Devils in shots. Missed five games with flu. Missed three games with virus. Missed one game with bruised ribs.

THE FINESSE GAME

Sykora has excellent hands in-tight, for passing or shooting. He defies the usual European stereotype of the reluctant shooter, because he's a goal-scorer, though he does tend to pass up a low-percentage shot to work for a better one. His wrist shot is excellent. He also has adequate snap and slap shots. He was one of the Devils' better power-play specialists.

There are only a few things Sykora doesn't do well technically, but what really sets him apart is his intelligence. Playing against men as a 17-year-old in the IHL in 1994-95 obviously spurred his development, and taught him how to survive as a smaller player in the mean NHL. Sykora is a creative player, and dares to do things that other players wouldn't try.

Sykora is a fine skater with a fluid stride, and he accelerates in a few steps. He is quick on a straight-away, with or without the puck, and is also agile in his turns. He picks his way through traffic well, and would rather try to outfox a defender and take the shortest path to the net than drive wide.

He sees the ice well and is a heads-up passer with a great touch. He needs to improve his face-offs. His defensive play has improved, though he blew a few key assignments at crucial points last season. He can

kill penalties because of his ability to read the play and his quickness, and is a penalty-killing regular.

THE PHYSICAL GAME

Sykora can't muck in the corners or along the boards, but don't expect him to be intimidated. He'll battle for the puck behind or in front of the net, but he is simply not a big, or mean, player. He is strong for his size and his skating provides him with good balance. His work ethic is strong.

THE INTANGIBLES

A lingering illness affected Sykora's play, as did the Devils' trade of his linemate Jason Arnott. It didn't help that New Jersey management felt Sykora was malingering. Whatever the mysterious ailment was, it took a lot of the zip out of Sykora's season. Sykora can play right wing or centre, and either position could be dynamite if he is paired with Paul Kariya.

PROJECTION

Some young players struggle when they are traded for the first time, and Sykora is a player whose confidence is fragile. But playing with Kariya could tap into Sykora's talent reservoir, and a return to the 70-point range should be expected.

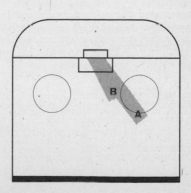

GERMAN TITOV

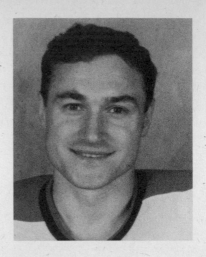

Yrs. of NHL service: 9
Born: Moscow, Russia; Oct. 16, 1965
Position: centre
Height: 6-1
Weight: 201
Uniform no.: 13
Shoots: left

Career statistics:

GP	G	A	TP	PIM
624	157	220	377	311

1998-1999 statistics:

GP	G	A	TP	+/-	PIM	PP	SH	GW	GT	S	PCT
72	11	45	56	+18	34	3	1	3	1	113	9.7

1999-2000 statistics:

GP	G	A	TP	+/-	PIM	PP	SH	GW	GT	S	PCT
70	17	29	46	-1	38	4	2	3	0	122	13.9

2000-2001 statistics:

GP	G	A	TP	+/-	PIM	PP	SH	GW	GT	S	PCT
71	9	11	20	-21	61	1	0	0	0	78	11.5

2001-2002 statistics:

GP	G	A	TP	+/-	PIM	PP	SH	GW	GT	S	PCT
66	13	14	27	+4	36	1	0	2	0	63	20.6

LAST SEASON

Third on team in plus-minus. Missed 16 games due to coach's decision.

THE FINESSE GAME

When a team as offence-starved as the Mighty Ducks makes a guy like Titov a healthy scratch for nearly a quarter of a season, you know there are problems.

The first, and major, concern is that Titov will not shoot. This is especially vexing (as new coach Mike Babcock will discover) because Titov skates well, works to get in a good scoring position and then tries to dish off. He averaged under a shot per game last season, which is unacceptable. He scored on 20 per cent of the shots he did take.

Using a short stick with which he does a lot of one-handed puckhandling gives Titov good control. It makes it harder for the defence to knock the puck loose without knocking him down and taking a penalty. It also gives him a quick release on his under-utilized wrister.

Titov shows great hockey sense in all zones. He is creative, but is a streaky scorer. He lacks consistency and doesn't step up on a nightly basis. He can play on the first power-play unit and is a solid two-way forward.

An agile skater, if not blazing fast, Titov is quick coming off the boards and driving to the circle for a shot. He has a good inside-out move and change of gears. Strong on his skates, he is tough to knock down. He has good hands on the draw. He kills penalties well and blocks shots.

THE PHYSICAL GAME

Titov uses his size well and is very solid. He takes a hit to make a play, blocks shots and sacrifices his body. He protects the puck in an unusual way, by getting his left leg out to kick away the stick of a defender so that he can't be sweep- or poke-checked. It's a move that requires superb balance.

THE INTANGIBLES

Titov has been through some tough times off the ice and he turns 37 this season — not a young man. He could have one decent season left in him if newcomers Adam Oates and Petr Sykora kick in big-time and relegate Titov to a supporting role. He'll get less ice time, but face less pressure.

PROJECTION

Maybe 30 points, but he is a risky prospect.

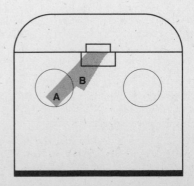

VITALY VISHNEVSKI

Yrs. of NHL service: 3
Born: Kharkov, Ukraine; Mar. 18, 1980
Position: left defence
Height: 6-2
Weight: 200
Uniform no.: 5
Shoots: left

Career statistics:

GP	G	A	TP	PIM
181	2	14	16	185

1999-2000 statistics:

GP	G	A	TP	+/-	PIM	PP	SH	GW	GT	S	PCT
31	1	1	2	0	26	1	0	0	0	17	5.9

2000-2001 statistics:

GP	G	A	TP	+/-	PIM	PP	SH	GW	GT	S	PCT
76	1	10	11	-1	99	0	0	0	0	49	2.0

2001-2002 statistics:

GP	G	A	TP	+/-	PIM	PP	SH	GW	GT	S	PCT
74	0	3	3	-10	60	0	0	0	0	54	0.0

LAST SEASON

Missed five games with sprained ankle. Missed two games due to suspension. Missed one game with back spasms.

THE FINESSE GAME

Vishnevski is an excellent skater with a long, powerful stride and good straightaway speed. He has good mobility and good balance. He has no trouble keeping pace with NHL-calibre skaters.

He has good size and strength, and plays a power game. He is a warrior around the crease and along the wall.

Vishnevski has to improve his defensive reads. He moves the puck extremely well and is poised and composed under pressure. He doesn't have much offensive upside — he just wants to get the puck out of his zone and knock the stuffing out of anyone who tries to skate back in with it. Opponents are going to be hurried into a lot of quick decisions when they come down his side of the ice.

THE PHYSICAL GAME

A solid 200 pounds, Vishnevski is a mean hitter Opponents hate him. He hits hard and he competes hard. He is an even better skater than Scott Stevens, so expect to see a lot of West Coast versions of those Stevens-style body bombs. He is confident in his checking ability and seeks out big hits at the blueline and in the neutral zone. He will hit anyone, regardless of name, number or salary rank. He is a bigger Darius Kasparaitis, and really gets under people's skin.

THE INTANGIBLES

Vishnevski got off to a slow start last season but improved greatly in the second half. He is only 22, and still needs coaching, but he made the big step to the NHL ahead of schedule and continues to progress. He makes his teammates play stronger and braver around him. He plays better with better players and is a nice fit with a high-risk offensive defenceman. The Mighty Ducks quickly signed him to a new contract in the off-season.

PROJECTION

Vishnevski is only going to grow in assurance and presence. His point totals will barely break into double digits, but he should have triple-digit PIM.

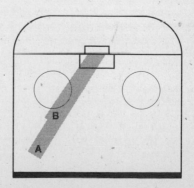

JASON YORK

Yrs. of NHL service: 8
Born: Ottawa, Ont.; May 20, 1970
Position: right defence
Height: 6-1
Weight: 200
Uniform no.: 33
Shoots: right

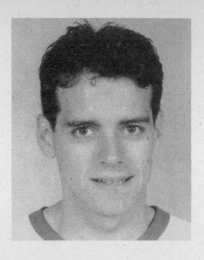

Career statistics:

GP	G	A	TP	PIM
567	35	152	187	473

1998-1999 statistics:

GP	G	A	TP	+/-	PIM	PP	SH	GW	GT	S	PCT
79	4	31	35	+17	48	2	0	0	1	177	2.3

1999-2000 statistics:

GP	G	A	TP	+/-	PIM	PP	SH	GW	GT	S	PCT
79	8	22	30	-3	60	1	0	1	0	159	5.0

2000-2001 statistics:

GP	G	A	TP	+/-	PIM	PP	SH	GW	GT	S	PCT
74	6	16	22	+7	72	3	0	2	0	133	4.5

2001-2002 statistics:

GP	G	A	TP	+/-	PIM	PP	SH	GW	GT	S	PCT
74	5	20	25	-11	60	3	0	2	0	104	4.8

LAST SEASON

Missed five games with shoulder injury. Missed three games due to coach's decision.

THE FINESSE GAME

York's finesse skills are fine. He is a good skater with a hard point shot, and he can handle the point on the second power-play unit — though he isn't quite good enough to step up to the first five. He's a fine penalty killer. He reads plays well (his offensive reads are far superior to his defensive reads) and has the skating ability to spring some shorthanded chances. He can be used in any game situation.

York is a smart, all-round defenceman who concentrated on learning the defensive part of the game first at the NHL level. Once he gained some confidence, his offensive contributions increased. He is never going to be the kind of player who can dominate a game but he is also fairly panic-proof. He's a low risk player, with moderate rewards.

York was bothered by a shoulder injury in January 2002, which affected his play the rest of the season.

THE PHYSICAL GAME

York made a conscious decision to add a physical element to his game. He plays with some zip now. He is not a big checker but employs positional play to angle attackers to the boards, using his stick to sweep-check or poke pucks. Once he gains control of the puck, he moves it quickly with no panicky mistakes. He doesn't have a polished defensive game but he does work hard. His shoulder injury made him less of a physical factor in the closing months of last season.

THE INTANGIBLES

York has shown gradual, steady improvement in his game over the past few seasons. While he will never be an elite NHL defenceman, he is a reliable blueliner who could fit into the top four on almost anyone's team. He does a lot of little things well and his energy and enthusiasm for the game are apparent.

PROJECTION

When healthy, York is capable of a 30-point season while losing nothing from his defensive game.

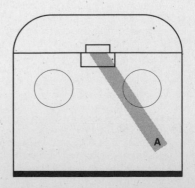

ATLANTA THRASHERS

Players' Statistics 2001-2002

POS.	NO.	PLAYER	GP	G	A	PTS	+/-	PIM	PP	SH	GW	GT	S	PCT
L	15	*DANY HEATLEY	82	26	41	67	-19	56	7		4		202	12.9
R	17	*ILYA KOVALCHUK	65	29	22	51	-19	28	7		4	1	184	15.8
C	12	TONY HRKAC	80	18	26	44	-12	12	5	1	2		101	17.8
R	18	LUBOS BARTECKO	71	13	14	27	-15	30	1				96	13.5
D	8	FRANTISEK KABERLE	61	5	20	25	-11	24	1				82	6.1
D	38	YANNICK TREMBLAY	66	9	15	24	-15	47	1		1	1	115	7.8
C	13	PATRIK STEFAN	59	7	16	23	-4	22	1				67	10.4
C	26	PASCAL RHEAUME	61	11	11	22	-4	29	6		2		80	13.8
L	14	TOMI KALLIO	60	8	14	22	-8	12	1				102	7.8
D	36	*DANIEL TJARNQVIST	75	2	16	18	-22	14	1				68	2.9
C	39	PER SVARTVADET	78	3	12	15	-12	24					80	3.8
D	25	ANDY SUTTON	43	2	8	10	-4	81	1				41	4.9
D	3	*BRIAN POTHIER	33	3	6	9	-19	22	1		1		65	4.6
R	20	JEFF ODGERS	46	4	4	8	-3	135			1		34	11.8
D	28	TODD REIRDEN	65	3	5	8	-25	82	1				85	3.5
C	24	ANDREAS KARLSSON	42	1	7	8	-8	20					41	2.4
L	16	JEFF COWAN	57	5	1	6	-14	90			2		64	7.8
D	4	CHRIS TAMER	78	3	3	6	-11	111		1			66	4.6
R	19	*BRAD TAPPER	20	2	4	6	-3	43					34	5.9
R	47	*JEAN-PIERRE VIGIER	15	4	1	5	-5	4					18	22.2
C	10	YURI BUTSAYEV	11	2		2	0	4					10	20.0
C	37	*DAN SNYDER	11	1	1	2	-3	30					7	14.3
D	6	DAVID HARLOCK	19	1	1	2	-2	18					12	
D	43	*MIKE WEAVER	16	1	1		0	10					9	
C	22	*KAMIL PIROS	8		1	1	-2	4					4	
C	45	*BENJAMIN SIMON	6				1	6					7	
C	9	*MARK HARTIGAN	2				-2	2					3	
D	6	*FRANCIS LESSARD	5				0	26					2	
D	29	*KIRIL SAFRONOV	3				-5	2					2	
L	23	*DEREK MACKENZIE	1				-1	2					1	
D	23	BRETT CLARK	2				-3							
D	40	*LUKE SELLARS	1				0	2						
G	1	DAMIAN RHODES	15				0							
G	33	MILAN HNILICKA	60				0	8						
G	35	FREDERIC CASSIVI	6				0							
G	34	NORM MARACLE	1				0							
G	30	SCOTT FANKHOUSER					0							
G	31	PASI NURMINEN	9				0							

GP = games played; G = goals; A = assists; PTS = points; +/- = goals-for minus goals-against while player is on ice; PIM = penalties in minutes; PP = power-play goals; SH = shorthanded goals; GW = game-winning goals; GT = game-tying goals; S = no. of shots; PCT = percentage of goals to shots; * = rookie

LUBOS BARTECKO

Yrs. of NHL service: 4
Born: Kezmarok, Czech.; July 14, 1976
Position: left wing
Height: 6-1
Weight: 200
Uniform no.: 18
Shoots: left

Career statistics:

GP	G	A	TP	PIM
220	39	56	95	99

1998-1999 statistics:

GP	G	A	TP	+/-	PIM	PP	SH	GW	GT	S	PCT
32	5	11	16	+4	6	0	0	1	0	37	13.5

1999-2000 statistics:

GP	G	A	TP	+/-	PIM	PP	SH	GW	GT	S	PCT
67	16	23	39	+25	51	3	0	3	0	75	21.3

2000-2001 statistics:

GP	G	A	TP	+/-	PIM	PP	SH	GW	GT	S	PCT
50	5	8	13	-1	12	0	0	3	0	51	9.8

2001-2002 statistics:

GP	G	A	TP	+/-	PIM	PP	SH	GW	GT	S	PCT
71	13	14	27	-15	30	1	0	0	0	96	13.5

LAST SEASON

Third on team in shooting percentage. Missed two games with heel injury.

THE FINESSE GAME

Bartecko has a stocky build and he's quick. Strong on his skates, he has the kind of skills that stamp him as a pure finisher. He has sure, soft hands and he is very willing to take the puck to the net for a strong wrist shot. He needs to be nagged to shoot more — a lot more.

Bartecko works well in the tough areas along the walls and in the corners. He applies himself more in the attacking zone than defensively. His two-way game still needs a lot of work, especially since he doesn't produce the numbers that would make a team be more tolerant of his defensive lapses.

THE PHYSICAL GAME

Bartecko has a solid frame. He won't initiate contact. He is pretty hard to knock off his feet, but it would be nice if he launched a pre-emptive strike now and then.

THE INTANGIBLES

Bartecko has had a hard time finding a role. He bounced around the St. Louis system for awhile and played his first full season last year in Atlanta. He didn't make much of an impact.

PROJECTION

Even on a Thrashers team that desperately needed someone to step up, Bartecko didn't. He is capable of a 20-goal season.

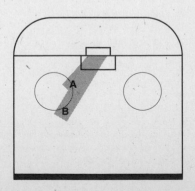

DANY HEATLEY

Yrs. of NHL service: 1
Born: Freiburg, Germany; Jan. 21, 1981
Position: left wing
Height: 6-2
Weight: 210
Uniform no.: 15
Shoots: left

Career statistics:

GP	G	A	TP	PIM
82	26	41	67	56

2001-2002 statistics:

GP	G	A	TP	+/-	PIM	PP	SH	GW	GT	S	PCT
82	26	41	67	-19	56	7	0	4	0	202	12.9

LAST SEASON

Won 2002 Calder Trophy. Led NHL rookies in points, assists, shots and power-play points (12). Tied for lead among NHL rookies in power-play goals. Second among NHL rookies in goals. Fourth among NHL rookies in shooting percentage. Led team in assists, points and shots. Tied for team lead in power-play goals and game-winning goals. Second on team in goals. Only Thrasher to appear in all 82 games.

THE FINESSE GAME

Heatley is not a very fast or smooth skater, and he probably has just enough speed to qualify as NHL-calibre. His chief assets are his willingness to shoot and his offensive instincts. He has a big point shot and is already a first-unit power-play man and a player who can take charge.

Heatley graduated to the NHL in a tough spot. The Thrashers didn't provide much support, so Heatley had to do everything himself. His all-around game is very advanced for a young player.

Heatley will produce even more if Atlanta can find a bona fide No. 1 centre for him. He is a pure goal-scorer, with an assortment of shots. He has learned to go get the puck and has to do a lot of the work himself. Just wait 'til he gets someone to get the puck to him. Heatley played well on a line with the flashier rookie, Ilya Kovalchuk, but the Thrashers will also split them up to divide the checking duty.

THE PHYSICAL GAME

Heatley needs to improve his strength and conditioning for the NHL wars. Heatley is rugged and likes to drive to the net.

THE INTANGIBLES

One really splendid thing about Heatley is that even with all his individual accolades, he hates losing. He won't just get used to it in Atlanta. He's going to try to change the culture.

Heatley and Kovalchuk are the first rookie teammates to finish 1-2 in team scoring since Alexandre Daigle and Alexei Yashin for the Ottawa Senators in 1993-94.

PROJECTION

We said that Heatley could be among the contenders for the Calder Trophy. He won it with a season that far exceeded our expectations.

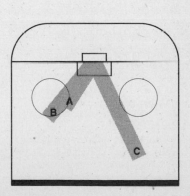

TOMI KALLIO

Yrs. of NHL service: 2
Born: Turku, Finland; Jan. 27, 1977
Position: left wing
Height: 6-0
Weight: 190
Uniform no.: 14
Shoots: left

Career statistics:

GP	G	A	TP	PIM
116	22	27	49	34

2000-2001 statistics:

GP	G	A	TP	+/-	PIM	PP	SH	GW	GT	S	PCT
56	14	13	27	-3	22	2	0	2	0	115	12.2

2001-2002 statistics:

GP	G	A	TP	+/-	PIM	PP	SH	GW	GT	S	PCT
60	8	14	22	-8	12	1	0	0	0	102	7.8

LAST SEASON

Missed 11 games with two concussions.

THE FINESSE GAME

Kallio is a fast skater with good offensive instincts and a lot of sandpaper in his game.

He plays his wing in a basic, up-and-down style. He likes to carry the puck and can make plays at high tempo. He will also crash the net for scoring chances, even though he isn't built like a power forward.

Kallio has a well-rounded game. He is sound defensively. Ask him to check and he will.

THE PHYSICAL GAME

Kallio relishes the physical North American style of play. You seldom see a night when he doesn't have his helmet askew from driving to the net and getting knocked around. He is solid and strong on his skates.

The concussions are a concern, though, especially for a player like Kallio who thrives on contact.

THE INTANGIBLES

Kallio might be another player whose career is lost to serious head injuries.

PROJECTION

If Kallio can return healthy and with his old vigour restored, he will play on one of Atlanta's top two lines and score 20 goals.

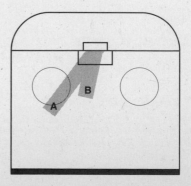

ILYA KOVALCHUK

Yrs. of NHL service: 1
Born: Tver, Russia; Apr. 15, 1983
Position: right wing
Height: 6-2
Weight: 202
Uniform no.: 17
Shoots: right

Career statistics:

GP	G	A	TP	PIM
65	29	22	51	28

2001-2002 statistics:

GP	G	A	TP	+/-	PIM	PP	SH	GW	GT	S	PCT
65	29	22	51	-19	28	7	0	4	1	184	15.8

LAST SEASON

Finalist for 2002 Calder Trophy. Led NHL rookies and team in goals. Second among NHL rookies in points and shooting percentage. Tied for lead among NHL rookies in power-play goals. Tied for second among NHL rookies in game-winning goals and power-play points (15). Tied for team lead in power-play goals and game-winning goals. Second on team in points and shooting percentage. Third on team in assists. Missed 17 games with shoulder injury.

THE FINESSE GAME

Kovalchuk is an explosive skater, a dynamic scorer and, did we mention, a gamebreaker?

Every offensive skill he possesses is world-class. Every time the puck is on his stick, he can make things happen. He has a very high confidence in his shot. Like the great snipers, he will shoot from angles that seem bizarre, and will usually get the shot on net. His release is quick, his selection varied, his aim accurate, his velocity rapid.

Kovalchuk's speed is intimidating. Defenders are forced to back off him, and that only opens up more ice for him to bust a move. He excels on the power play and in 4-on-4, and will become a penalty killer and shorthanded threat. Actually, it seems like the other team is shorthanded whenever he's on the ice.

THE PHYSICAL GAME

This kid's got attitude and an edge. He plays with a swagger. He's like that off the ice, too, which isn't exactly great news for his teammates. He's not the most lovable guy on the team.

THE INTANGIBLES

Think of a young Pavel Bure, with just a little more size and a lot more snarl. He is the most exciting young scoring star to come along since Mario Lemieux. Exaggeration? Just wait and watch.

PROJECTION

If it hadn't been for his shoulder injury, Kovalchuk would have flirted with 40 goals. Such a bump in a second year might seem a lot to ask, but Kovalchuk can do it. He will be scoring 60 soon.

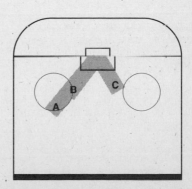

VYACHESLAV KOZLOV

Yrs. of NHL service: 9
Born: Voskresensk, Russia; May 3, 1972
Position: left wing
Height: 5-10
Weight: 180
Uniform no.: 13
Shoots: left

Career statistics:

GP	G	A	TP	PIM
645	211	226	437	392

1998-1999 statistics:

GP	G	A	TP	+/-	PIM	PP	SH	GW	GT	S	PCT
79	29	29	58	+10	45	6	1	4	2	209	13.9

1999-2000 statistics:

GP	G	A	TP	+/-	PIM	PP	SH	GW	GT	S	PCT
72	18	18	36	+11	28	4	0	3	0	165	10.9

2000-2001 statistics:

GP	G	A	TP	+/-	PIM	PP	SH	GW	GT	S	PCT
72	20	18	38	+9	30	4	0	5	1	187	10.7

2001-2002 statistics:

GP	G	A	TP	+/-	PIM	PP	SH	GW	GT	S	PCT
38	9	13	22	0	16	3	0	1	1	68	13.2

LAST SEASON

Acquired from Buffalo on June 22, 2002, with a second-round draft pick for second and third-round draft picks in 2002. Missed 43 games with torn Achilles tendon. Missed one game due to coach's decision.

THE FINESSE GAME

Kozlov has a very quick getaway step that allows him to jump into holes and openings. His darting style makes it impossible for defenders to chase him and easy for them to lose him.

Offensively, he can play as freewheeling as the team wants. He seems to materialize at the right place at the right time. He can split the defence if it plays him too close, or drive the defence back with his speed and use the open ice to find a teammate. He has great control of the puck at high speed and plays an excellent transition game. Kozlov does not have to be coaxed into shooting, and he has a quick release — generally to the top corners of the net.

That said, there are also times when Kozlov can be frustrating to watch. He will hold the puck past the point when he either should make a play with it or make a pass. He then either loses control of it or takes himself to lesser ice. The reasonable speculation is that by holding the puck he is buying time for teammates to break into open ice; other times, he simply appears incapable of making a decision about what to do or he is trying to make the perfect play instead of a good-enough play more quickly.

THE PHYSICAL GAME

Just as a defender comes to hit him, Kozlov gets rid of the puck. Usually it goes to a teammate, sometimes it simply goes up for grabs. It would be easy to say Kozlov is like a quarterback who gets rid of the ball rather than getting sacked. More likely, he's taking the hit to create space for someone else by allowing the defender to take himself — and Kozlov — out of the play. Kozlov is not tall but he is solidly built. He's got a little mean streak.

THE INTANGIBLES

Kozlov was on the move again (he came to the Sabres in the Dominik Hasek deal in 2001). He was playing all right before his injury. He needed surgery to repair his Achilles tendon.

PROJECTION

Kozlov should be a 30-goal scorer if he can return from his surgery. He will get a lot of ice time in Atlanta.

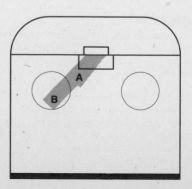

KARI LEHTONEN

Yrs. of NHL service: 0
Born: Helsinki, Finland; Nov. 16, 1983
Position: goaltender
Height: 6-3
Weight: 189
Uniform no.: n.a.
Catches: left

Career statistics:

GP	MIN	GA	SO	GAA	A	PIM
23	1242	37	4	1.79	0	0

2001-2002 European statistics:

GP	MIN	GAA	W	L	T	SO	GA	S	SAPCT	PIM
23	1242	1.79	13	5	3	4	37	n.a.	n.a.	2

LAST SEASON

Will be entering first NHL season. Drafted second overall in 2002.

THE PHYSICAL GAME

Lehtonen plays a hybrid standup/butterfly style with an emphasis on standup, and he has a good technical base. He is a good skater with quick feet for kick and pad saves and a quick glove. If he goes down, Lehtonen recovers quickly for the rebound.

Lehtonen is tall but he's reedy. He is built along athletic lines, racy like a Thoroughbred. Goalies can't put on too much weight too soon without having the gain affect their playing style. Lehtonen will have to make sure he can handle the pace of an NHL game and the grind of a long season — especially when you consider that Atlanta goalies faced 2,911 shots last season, the most of any team.

THE MENTAL GAME

Lehtonen is very mature for such a young player. He played well at the World Junior Championships for Finland, which has turned into something of a goalie nursery in the past few years.

Lehtonen is very composed. His winning attitude carries over to his teammates. He seldom looks flustered, even under pressure.

THE INTANGIBLES

There was conflicting information about whether Lehtonen had a military commitment to fulfill in his native Finland, or whether he would be free to join the Thrashers this season. He is widely considered the best goaltending prospect since Roberto Luongo. With Damian Rhodes on perennial IR, Milan Hnilicka not a legit No. 1 goalie and Pasi Nurminen waiting in the wings but less accomplished, the job is his if he can play here.

PROJECTION

Lehtonen will be 19 a month into the season, awfully young, especially for a bad team like Atlanta. If he wins the No. 1 role, 20 wins would be nothing short of a miracle (the team won only 19 all of last season).

SHAWN MCEACHERN

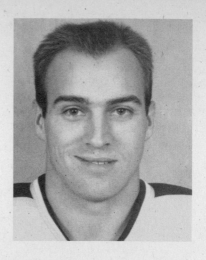

Yrs. of NHL service: 10
Born: Waltham, Mass.; Feb. 28, 1969
Position: centre / left wing
Height: 5-11
Weight: 193
Uniform no.: 15
Shoots: left

Career statistics:

GP	G	A	TP	PIM
755	227	263	490	380

1998-1999 statistics:

GP	G	A	TP	+/-	PIM	PP	SH	GW	GT	S	PCT
77	31	25	56	+8	46	7	0	4	1	223	13.9

1999-2000 statistics:

GP	G	A	TP	+/-	PIM	PP	SH	GW	GT	S	PCT
69	29	22	51	+2	24	10	0	4	1	219	13.2

2000-2001 statistics:

GP	G	A	TP	+/-	PIM	PP	SH	GW	GT	S	PCT
82	32	40	72	+10	62	9	0	1	1	231	13.9

2001-2002 statistics:

GP	G	A	TP	+/-	PIM	PP	SH	GW	GT	S	PCT
80	15	31	46	+9	52	5	0	3	0	196	7.7

LAST SEASON

Acquired from Ottawa on June 30, 2002, with a sixth-round draft pick in 2004 for Brian Pothier. Third on Senators in shots. Missed two games with groin injury.

THE FINESSE GAME

McEachern can shift speeds and direction smoothly without losing control of the puck. He can play both left wing and centre, but is better on the wing because he doesn't use his linemates as well as a centre should. An accurate shooter with a hard wrister, he has a quick release on his slap shot, which he lets go after using his outside speed. He is strong on face-offs and is a smart penalty killer who pressures the puck carrier.

McEachern isn't overly creative. He doesn't have to be. His dangerous acceleration is what gives him his edge. He suffers from some tunnel vision, which negates some of the advantage of his speed. He skates with his head down, looking at the ice instead of the play around him. He is strong and fast, with straight-away speed, but he tends to expend his energy almost carelessly and has to take short shifts.

At the start of his career, McEachern looked like he was going to be one of those speedy third-line checking types without much finish. Instead, he has worked hard to polish his game and likes his role as a scorer and go-to guy. Many of his goals result from beating the defenders to loose pucks around the net. He has decent hands in-tight.

THE PHYSICAL GAME

Generally an open-ice player, McEachern will also pursue the puck with some diligence in the attacking zone. He is light, and although he can sometimes build up momentum with his speed for a solid bump, he loses most of the close-in battles for the puck. He's a yapper; many nights he can distract opponents, who want to rip his head off. McEachern has some quiet grit and plays through injuries.

THE INTANGIBLES

McEachern is a versatile player who can fill a lot of roles with his speed. He isn't a true first-line winger, but fulfilled that role in Ottawa for several years. As a veteran with a very young Atlanta team, McEachern will add some savvy.

PROJECTION

McEachern will probably see a lot of ice time as well as power-play duty. Expect 50 points.

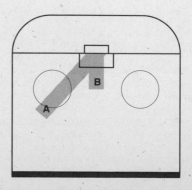

RICHARD SMEHLIK

Yrs. of NHL service: 9
Born: Ostrava, Czech Republic; Jan. 23, 1970
Position: right defence
Height: 6-4
Weight: 222
Uniform no.: 42
Shoots: left

Career statistics:

GP	G	A	TP	PIM
589	47	135	182	399

1998-1999 statistics:

GP	G	A	TP	+/-	PIM	PP	SH	GW	GT	S	PCT
72	3	11	14	-9	44	0	0	0	0	61	4.9

1999-2000 statistics:

GP	G	A	TP	+/-	PIM	PP	SH	GW	GT	S	PCT
64	2	9	11	+13	50	0	0	0	0	67	3.0

2000-2001 statistics:

GP	G	A	TP	+/-	PIM	PP	SH	GW	GT	S	PCT
56	3	12	15	+6	4	0	0	1	0	40	7.5

2001-2002 statistics:

GP	G	A	TP	+/-	PIM	PP	SH	GW	GT	S	PCT
60	3	6	9	-9	22	0	0	1	1	52	5.8

LAST SEASON

Signed by Atlanta as free agent on July 11, 2002. Missed 15 games with shoulder injury. Missed three games with groin injury. Missed four games due to coach's decision.

THE FINESSE GAME

Smehlik's skating is his strong suit, and the periodic groin problems he suffers affect his game. He is agile with good lateral movement and very solid on his skates. Because his balance is so good, he is tough to knock down.

He thinks defence, and his impressive finesse skills are dedicated to the defensive aspect of the game. If Smehlik takes more responsibility offensively, he can respond. He has good passing skills and fair hockey vision, and he can spot and hit the breaking forward. Most of his assists will be traced back to a headman feed out of the defensive zone. He plays well at the point and has a rocket shot, but isn't clever enough with the puck to be a really effective member of the power play.

Smehlik is vulnerable to a strong forecheck. Teams are aware of this and try to work his corner.

THE PHYSICAL GAME

Smehlik can use his body well but has to be more consistent and authoritative. He has to clean up his crease better, something he doesn't do well since he's not a mean hitter. It's not in his nature to be aggressive. He prefers to use his stick to break up plays, and he does that effectively. He has a long reach and is able to intercept passes, or reach in around a defender to pry the puck loose.

THE INTANGIBLES

Smehlik is a borderline No. 4 defenceman who will be asked to play in Atlanta's top pair. That's beyond his range but it's what is expected on a team that is only a few years removed from expansion.

PROJECTION

Smehlik has some decent skills, and his probable top level is in the 25- to 30-point range. He will continue to get plenty of ice time.

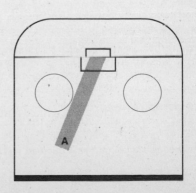

PATRIK STEFAN

Yrs. of NHL service: 3
Born: Pribham, Czech Republic; Sept. 16, 1980
Position: centre
Height: 6-3
Weight: 205
Uniform no.: 13
Shoots: left

Career statistics:

GP	G	A	TP	PIM
197	22	57	79	74

1999-2000 statistics:

GP	G	A	TP	+/-	PIM	PP	SH	GW	GT	S	PCT
72	5	20	25	-20	30	1	0	0	0	117	4.3

2000-2001 statistics:

GP	G	A	TP	+/-	PIM	PP	SH	GW	GT	S	PCT
66	10	21	31	-3	22	0	0	1	0	93	10.8

2001-2002 statistics:

GP	G	A	TP	+/-	PIM	PP	SH	GW	GT	S	PCT
59	7	16	23	-4	22	0	1	0	0	67	10.4

LAST SEASON

Missed nine games with elbow injury. Missed eight games with broken jaw.

THE FINESSE GAME

Stefan's progress in his first three NHL seasons is almost impossible to assess because of how often he is out of the lineup. Every so often, Stefan has one of those special nights that remind everyone of his abilities. He is a tall skater whose stance is upright, allowing him to keep his head up to see all of the ice and all of his options. He uses a long stick for a long reach to beat defenders one-on-one in open ice. He loves to carry the puck and has drawn comparisons to Jaromir Jagr for his end-to-end ability.

Stefan needs to use his speed more and take the shortest route to the net on an odd-man rush, instead of fanning himself to the outside. Even if he doesn't score, he can draw the attention of the goalie and defencemen and create room for his linemates.

An excellent passer who can thread a puck through a crowd, he shoots well forehand and backhand and isn't shy about using his shot. He is good on draws and can run a power play.

THE PHYSICAL GAME

Stefan needs to use his body better. His history of injuries may lead to his lack of interest in a physical game, but he has to step it up and play harder, to go through people to get to the net or the puck.

THE INTANGIBLES

Stefan may be better suited as a wing, but there is a gaping void in the middle and Atlanta seems intent on having Stefan fill it.

PROJECTION

Stefan's presence in the lineup is so unpredictable that we wouldn't advise him as a pool pick. Look at is this way: 15 goals would be a huge upgrade for Stefan.

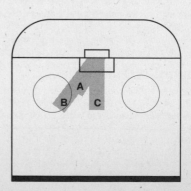

CHRIS TAMER

Yrs. of NHL service: 8
Born: Dearborn, Mich.; Nov. 17, 1970
Position: left defence
Height: 6 2
Weight: 205
Uniform no.: 4
Shoots: left

Career statistics:

GP	G	A	TP	PIM
534	18	50	68	1010

1998-1999 statistics:

GP	G	A	TP	+/-	PIM	PP	SH	GW	GT	S	PCT
63	1	5	6	-14	124	0	0	1	0	48	2.1

1999-2000 statistics:

GP	G	A	TP	+/-	PIM	PP	SH	GW	GT	S	PCT
69	2	8	10	-32	91	0	0	0	0	61	3.3

2000-2001 statistics:

GP	G	A	TP	+/-	PIM	PP	SH	GW	GT	S	PCT
82	4	13	17	-1	128	0	1	1	0	90	4.4

2001-2002 statistics:

GP	G	A	TP	+/-	PIM	PP	SH	GW	GT	S	PCT
78	3	3	6	-11	111	0	1	0	0	66	4.6

LAST SEASON
Second on team in penalty minutes.

THE FINESSE GAME
Tamer is a conservative, stay-at-home defenceman. He has limited skating and stick skills, but is smart enough to stay within his limitations and play a positional game.

He plays a poised game and learns from his mistakes. He does the little things well, chipping a puck off the boards or angling an attacker to the wall. He kills penalties, blocks shots and finishes his checks.

Tamer is smart enough when he is firing from the point to make sure his shot doesn't get blocked. He will take something off his shot, or put it wide so the forwards can attack the puck off the end boards.

THE PHYSICAL GAME
Tamer doesn't nail people, but he has some strength and will use it to push people out of the crease, and he'll battle in the corners. He doesn't have the good skating base to be a punishing open-ice hitter, but he defends himself and sticks up for his teammates. He doesn't have a serious nasty side, but is often guilty of late hits. Tamer is fearless in his shot-blocking and led the team in that category.

Tamer is a well-conditioned athlete and he can handle a lot of ice time (he averaged over 18 minutes last season), despite having to deal with asthma.

THE INTANGIBLES
Tamer was again the Thrashers' most consistent defenceman, and will be in Atlanta's top four. He will never be a star, but he gives solid support and can complement a more offensive player, like Frantisek Kaberle. His point production will be low, but he is an intelligent rearguard who will only get better. Tamer is a quiet leader who will continue to help the next generation of Thrashers build toward the future.

PROJECTION
Tamer's points are a bonus. What he gives that counts are his efforts in the defensive zone, his guts and, of course, his PIM.

BOSTON BRUINS

Players' Statistics 2001-2002

POS.	NO.	PLAYER	GP	G	A	PTS	+/-	PIM	PP	SH	GW	GT	S	PCT
R	27	GLEN MURRAY	82	41	30	71	31	40	9		9		246	16.7
L	14	SERGEI SAMSONOV	74	29	41	70	21	27	3		4		192	15.1
C	19	JOE THORNTON	66	22	46	68	7	127	6		5	1	152	14.5
R	13	BILL GUERIN	78	41	25	66	-1	91	10	1	7		355	11.6
C	12	BRIAN ROLSTON	82	31	31	62	11	30	6	9	7		331	9.4
C	16	JOZEF STUMPEL	81	8	50	58	22	18	1		3		100	8.0
R	20	MARTIN LAPOINTE	68	17	23	40	12	101	4		2	1	141	12.1
R	10	MARTY MCINNIS	79	11	17	28	-15	33	2		1		157	7.0
L	17	ROB ZAMUNER	66	12	13	25	6	24	1	2			98	12.2
D	21	SEAN O'DONNELL	80	3	22	25	27	89	1		2		112	2.7
L	11	P.J. AXELSSON	78	7	17	24	6	16		2			127	5.5
D	25	HAL GILL	79	4	18	22	16	77					137	2.9
D	44	*NICHOLAS BOYNTON	80	4	14	18	18	107			1		136	2.9
D	32	DON SWEENEY	81	3	15	18	22	35	1				70	4.3
R	26	MIKE KNUBLE	54	8	6	14	9	42			2		77	10.4
D	23	SEAN BROWN	73	6	5	11	7	174	3		1		64	9.4
D	18	KYLE MCLAREN	38		8	8	-4	19					57	
D	31	JAMIE RIVERS	66	4	2	6	3	49	1		1		51	7.8
D	33	JEFF NORTON	32		5	5	-5	10					15	
R	22	DENNIS BONVIE	23	1	2	3	3	84					5	20.0
D	64	JARNO KULTANEN	38		3	3	-1	33					31	
D	55	JONATHAN GIRARD	20		3	3	0	9					28	
C	42	P.J. STOCK	58		3	3	-2	122					12	
C	23	JOHN EMMONS	22		2	2	-4	16					20	
D	6	GORD MURPHY	15		2	2	2	13					10	
C	29	*ANDY HILBERT	6	1		1	-2	2					11	9.1
L	36	*IVAN HUML	1	1		1	2						2	
D	72	PAVEL KOLARIK	13				0	6					6	
D	43	RICHARD JACKMAN	2				-1	2					4	
C	57	ERIC MANLOW	3				0						2	
R	46	*TONY TUZZOLINO	2				-1						1	
D	48	CHRIS KELLEHER	1				0							
G	34	BYRON DAFOE	64				0	27						
G	47	JOHN GRAHAME	19				0	6						
G	1	ANDREW RAYCROFT	1				0							

GP = games played; G = goals; A = assists; PTS = points; +/- = goals-for minus goals-against while player is on ice; PIM = penalties in minutes; PP = power-play goals; SH = shorthanded goals; GW = game-winning goals; GT = game-tying goals; S = no. of shots; PCT = percentage of goals to shots; * = rookie

P. J. AXELSSON

Yrs. of NHL service: 5
Born: Kungalv, Sweden; Feb. 26, 1975
Position: left wing
Height: 6-1
Weight: 176
Uniform no.: 11
Shoots: left

Career statistics:

GP	G	A	TP	PIM
399	40	77	117	123

1998-1999 statistics:

GP	G	A	TP	+/-	PIM	PP	SH	GW	GT	S	PCT
77	7	10	17	-14	18	0	0	2	0	146	4.8

1999-2000 statistics:

GP	G	A	TP	+/-	PIM	PP	SH	GW	GT	S	PCT
81	10	16	26	+1	24	0	0	4	0	186	5.4

2000-2001 statistics:

GP	G	A	TP	+/-	PIM	PP	SH	GW	GT	S	PCT
81	8	15	23	-12	27	0	0	2	0	146	5.5

2001-2002 statistics:

GP	G	A	TP	+/-	PIM	PP	SH	GW	GT	S	PCT
78	7	17	24	+6	16	0	2	0	0	127	5.5

LAST SEASON

Missed three games with shoulder injury. Missed one game due to coach's decision.

THE FINESSE GAME

Axelsson is a role player but happily accepts that job. He is a very fast skater, yet unlike a lot of Swedes he is not strong on the puck. His hand skills are just about average, though he was a fairly decent scorer in the Swedish Elite League, and he doesn't fumble with the puck. His future in this league will be based less on his scoring than on his defensive ability. The Bruins keep expecting him to chip in more offensively, but it's not his game. Axelsson was used on the top line late last season. Axelsson could function as a safety-valve winger with two offensive-minded guys.

Killing penalties is where he excels. Axelsson is a smart player with a real head for the game. He has the skills (especially skating) that stamp him as a bona fide NHLer.

Axelsson's primary asset is his work ethic. He never stops skating, never stops fighting for the puck and he thrives on big checking assignments against other teams' top lines.

THE PHYSICAL GAME

Axelsson is competitive, a solid checker who will finish all of his hits. He will stand up to big power forwards and won't be intimidated, despite the fact that he is the kind of tall but scrawny player that some big guys could use as a toothpick. Axelsson is not fun to play against.

THE INTANGIBLES

Axelsson is a catalyst. Slotted correctly as a regular third-line left wing, he contributes an honest 16 minutes every night. He is a low-risk, high-energy performer. Scouts never soured on him.

PROJECTION

Axelsson may be able to score 10 to 15 goals, but not much more than that. However, he could earn Selke Trophy recognition further up the road.

NICHOLAS BOYNTON

Yrs. of NHL service: 1
Born: Nobleton, Ont.; Jan. 14, 1979
Position: right defence
Height: 6-2
Weight: 210
Uniform no.: 44
Shoots: right

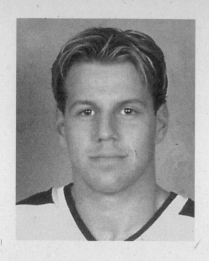

Career statistics:

GP	G	A	TP	PIM
86	4	14	18	107

1999-2000 statistics:

GP	G	A	TP	+/-	PIM	PP	SH	GW	GT	S	PCT
5	0	0	0	-5	0	0	0	0	0	6	-

2000-2001 statistics:

GP	G	A	TP	+/-	PIM	PP	SH	GW	GT	S	PCT
1	0	0	0	-1	0	0	0	0	0	1	0.0

2001-2002 statistics:

GP	G	A	TP	+/-	PIM	PP	SH	GW	GT	S	PCT
80	4	14	18	+18	107	0	0	1	0	136	2.9

LAST SEASON

First NHL season. Second among NHL rookies in plus-minus. Missed two games with food poisoning.

THE FINESSE GAME

He's no Ray Bourque, but Boynton is the most exciting defenceman the Bruins have developed in a long time. Boynton is an exceptional skater in all directions and he has good balance. It looked like Boynton was going to try to break in as a "offenceman," but he has dedicated himself to learning the defensive side of the game and is going to be a top pair, two-way defenceman for years to come.

Boynton is poised with the puck and makes crisp, calm outlet passes. He jumps up into the play intelligently. He doesn't have an elite shot but he has good lateral mobility along the blueline and that makes his slap shot more effective. Boynton is also clever enough to use the fake half-slap and pass.

Boynton just does everything well. He can separate the puck carrier from the puck. He makes the good first pass. With Kyle McLaren missing much of the season, Boynton took on a lot of ice time and saw assignments against other team's top lines. He stepped up big time and didn't show many weaknesses.

THE PHYSICAL GAME

Boynton has good size and coaches are going to expect him to be more aggressive. He isn't going to be a big banger, but he could develop along Wade Redden lines, and be a player who makes sure he stays between the attacker and the net with his body.

THE INTANGIBLES

Boynton was far and away the Bruins best defenceman in the postseason. He's going to get even better.

Boynton was diagnosed with diabetes two years ago and has had to learn how to balance that medical condition with trying to play at the pro level.

PROJECTION

Boynton will score around 30 points.

BYRON DAFOE

Yrs. of NHL service: 7
Born: Sussex, England; Feb. 25, 1971
Position: goaltender
Height: 5-11
Weight: 200
Uniform no.: 34
Catches: left

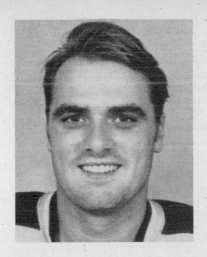

Career statistics:

GP	MIN	GA	SO	GAA	A	PIM
380	21610	935	26	2.60	9	66

1998-1999 statistics:

GP	MIN	GAA	W	L	T	SO	GA	S	SAPCT	PIM
68	4001	1.99	32	23	11	10	133	1800	.926	25

1999-2000 statistics:

GP	MIN	GAA	W	L	T	SO	GA	S	SAPCT	PIM
41	2307	2.96	13	16	0	3	114	1030	.889	0

2000-2001 statistics:

GP	MIN	GAA	W	L	T	SO	GA	S	SAPCT	PIM
45	2536	2.39	22	14	7	2	101	1076	.906	6

2001-2002 statistics:

GP	MIN	GAA	W	L	T	SO	GA	S	SAPCT	PIM
64	3827	2.21	35	26	3	4	141	1520	.907	27

At least it looks like Dafoe has gotten past his injury problems. He recovered well from knee surgery.

PROJECTION

At press time we weren't sure if Dafoe had a job. This is a 30-win goalie.

LAST SEASON

Fourth among NHL goalies in wins with career high. Missed one game due to personal reasons.

THE PHYSICAL GAME

Dafoe's game is technically sound and aggressive, sometimes overly so. He usually controls his rebounds well, but on nights when he doesn't his challenging style leaves him vulnerable on second shots. He can get scrambly, as if he doesn't trust his defence. Goalies for weaker teams tend to do too much. He plays a better game the less he tries to accomplish.

Dafoe is slightly smaller than many of today's goalies, but when he stands up and plays his angles, he is able to maximize his size.

He is quite average in a lot of areas, especially stickhandling. He thinks the game well, though, and he stays alert and doesn't beat himself.

THE MENTAL GAME

Dafoe has battled to get his playing chance and he handles adversity well. He always seems to be in a situation where he has to prove himself.

THE INTANGIBLES

If Dafoe hadn't blown up in the playoffs (3.18 goals-against average), his free agent excursion wouldn't have turned into the hockey version of the voyage of the *U.S.S. Minnow*. Fellow netminders Curtis Joseph, Ed Belfour and Mike Richter were inked in the first week of free agency, while the underrated Dafoe was stranded. Boston's acquisition of Steve Shields made it appear as if the Bruins were ready to move on.

HAL GILL

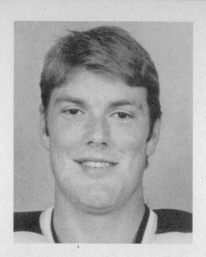

Yrs. of NHL service: 5
Born: Concord, Mass.; Apr. 6, 1975
Position: right defence
Height: 6-7
Weight: 230
Uniform no.: 25
Shoots: left

Career statistics:

GP	G	A	TP	PIM
388	13	48	61	309

1998-1999 statistics:

GP	G	A	TP	+/-	PIM	PP	SH	GW	GT	S	PCT
80	3	7	10	-10	63	0	0	2	0	102	2.9

1999-2000 statistics:

GP	G	A	TP	+/-	PIM	PP	SH	GW	GT	S	PCT
81	3	9	12	0	51	0	0	0	0	120	2.5

2000-2001 statistics:

GP	G	A	TP	+/-	PIM	PP	SH	GW	GT	S	PCT
80	1	10	11	-2	71	0	0	0	0	79	1.3

2001-2002 statistics:

GP	G	A	TP	+/-	PIM	PP	SH	GW	GT	S	PCT
79	4	18	22	+16	77	0	0	0	0	137	2.9

LAST SEASON

Career highs in goals, assists and points. Missed two games with shoulder/bicep injury. Missed one game with foot injury.

THE FINESSE GAME

Gill is a defenceman who can be used in any game situation. He is at his best under pressure, poised and calm with the puck, and he is a better outlet passer now than ever. Gill does not panic easily.

Gill was not much of a scorer at the college level and he won't be in the NHL either, but his finesse skills serve him well in a defensive role. He makes the first pass on the breakout or gets the puck and moves it out of the zone. He does possess a huge shot from the point, though his lack of mobility along the blueline makes it a less effective scoring weapon. His puck movement is advanced.

Gill's only drawback is his skating. He has slow feet, which may keep him from becoming an elite defenceman, but every other facet of his game is Grade A. Gill is one of the tallest players in the NHL, and he uses his reach well.

THE PHYSICAL GAME

Gill competes hard every night. He is not intimidated by some of the league's tough customers and is one of the few defencemen in the East who can stay on his feet after a hit by someone like Bobby Holik. Gill is solid and imposing, and can intimidate with his size. He is strong on the boards, strong in the corners and he clears out the front of his net. He doesn't fight — he doesn't have to. He has a pretty long fuse, but don't

confuse that with a lack of hockey courage. Gill is a gamer. The Bruins would like to see him initiate more, but that isn't his nature.

THE INTANGIBLES

How's this for a compliment? Jaromir Jagr called Gill the toughest player he competes against. Gill had to play a lot of minutes (he averaged 24:13) last season and was probably Boston's most consistent blueliner.

PROJECTION

Gill has matured into a top defencemen. He won't get much attention because, like Scott Stevens and Adam Foote, his point totals are minuscule. If the Bruins ever get truly competitive, Gill may finally receive the acclaim he deserves.

MARTIN LAPOINTE

Yrs. of NHL service: 9
Born: Ville Ste. Pierre, Que.; Sept. 12, 1973
Position: right wing
Height: 5-11
Weight: 200
Uniform no.: 20
Shoots: right

Career statistics:

GP	G	A	TP	PIM
620	125	145	270	989

1998-1999 statistics:

GP	G	A	TP	+/-	PIM	PP	SH	GW	GT	S	PCT
77	16	13	29	+7	141	7	1	4	0	153	10.5

1999-2000 statistics:

GP	G	A	TP	+/-	PIM	PP	SH	GW	GT	S	PCT
82	16	25	41	+17	121	1	1	2	1	127	12.6

2000-2001 statistics:

GP	G	A	TP	+/-	PIM	PP	SH	GW	GT	S	PCT
82	27	30	57	+3	127	13	0	8	0	181	14.9

2001-2002 statistics:

GP	G	A	TP	+/-	PIM	PP	SH	GW	GT	S	PCT
68	17	23	40	+12	101	4	0	2	1	141	12.1

LAST SEASON

Missed 12 games with hamstring injuries. Missed two games due to coach's decision.

THE FINESSE GAME

Everything about Lapointe's game stems more from what is between his ribs than what is between his ears. It all comes from the heart: the competitiveness, the drive that sends him to the net in the straightest line possible. If a defenceman or opposing forward — or goalie — happens to get knocked down in the process, that's their problem.

Lapointe's goals and assists result more from his acceleration than his speed. He doesn't have break-away speed, but his eagerness, his intensity and his willingness to compete make him seem faster than he actually is. He doesn't have a great shot, though he has a nice, quick release and uses a wrist or snap shot as opposed to a big windup. Most of his goals are scored in the hard areas around the crease. He screens goalies, tips shots and works for loose pucks.

Equally important, Lapointe does not let a stick-check slow him down. He'll pull a checker along like a boat tugging a water skier. He'll steam into the play to create an odd-man rush, and he creates lots of options with a nice passing touch that prevents goalies from overplaying him to shoot.

THE PHYSICAL GAME

Lapointe wants to play, wants to win and won't take an easy way out, which means a lot of opponents end up flat on the ice. He hits them all, big or small, and hits hard. He is low but wide, with a broad upper body and solid centre of gravity that powers his physical game. He can be a menace in the corners and a force in front of the net.

There is a snarl in Lapointe's game, a fire that always seems close to the fuse. He takes a good share of over-emotional penalties. He wakes things up, and never lets opponents take the easy way out. He never lets himself take the easy way, either. Lapointe was a flashy scorer in junior but dedicated himself to learning how to check. His approach is summarized in his statement, "I'd rather change my role and have the team win instead of being a one-man show."

THE INTANGIBLES

The Bruins spent a lot of money (uncharacteristically) to sign Lapointe as a free agent in 2001, and he was key in helping to change the culture of losing around the team.

PROJECTION

Lapointe's regular-season goal totals are likely to stay around 20 goals. His value goes way up in the post-season, although he had a fairly ordinary playoffs. His nagging hamstring injury, which affected him in the last half of the season, might have been a factor.

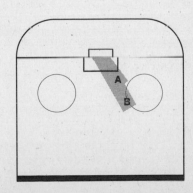

MARTY MCINNIS

Yrs. of NHL service: 10
Born: Hingham, Mass.; June 2, 1970
Position: left wing
Height: 5-11
Weight: 187
Uniform no.: 10
Shoots: right

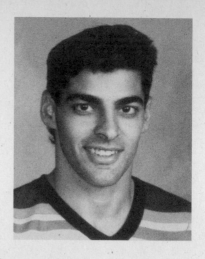

Career statistics:

GP	G	A	TP	PIM
719	161	240	401	292

1998-1999 statistics:

GP	G	A	TP	+/-	PIM	PP	SH	GW	GT	S	PCT
81	19	35	54	-15	42	11	1	5	0	146	13.0

1999-2000 statistics:

GP	G	A	TP	+/-	PIM	PP	SH	GW	GT	S	PCT
62	10	18	28	-4	26	2	1	2	0	129	7.8

2000-2001 statistics:

GP	G	A	TP	+/-	PIM	PP	SH	GW	GT	S	PCT
75	20	22	42	-21	40	10	0	1	0	136	14.7

2001-2002 statistics:

GP	G	A	TP	+/-	PIM	PP	SH	GW	GT	S	PCT
79	11	17	28	-15	33	2	0	1	0	157	7.0

LAST SEASON

Acquired from Anaheim on March 5, 2002, for third-round draft pick in 2002. Missed two games with wrist injury.

THE FINESSE GAME

The versatile McInnis does a lot of the little things well. He plays positionally, is smart and reliable defensively, and turns his checking work into scoring opportunities with quick passes and his work down low. He is a very patient shooter.

McInnis isn't fast but he is deceptive, with a quick first few strides to the puck. He seems to be more aware of where the puck is than his opponents are, so while they're looking for the puck he's already heading towards it. McInnis can handle some second-unit power-play time.

McInnis is a good penalty killer because of his tenacity and anticipation. He reads plays well on both offence and defence. Playing the off-wing opens up his shot for a quick release; he's always a shorthanded threat. He's an ideal third-line forward because he can check and provide some offensive counterpunch.

THE PHYSICAL GAME

McInnis is not big or tough, but he is sturdy and will use his body to bump and scrap for the puck. He always tries to get in the way, though he loses a lot of battles in-tight to larger forwards, because he is not that strong.

THE INTANGIBLES

McInnis finished up the season scoreless in 12 games, which only added to the pressure on the returning hometown boy. McInnis isn't asked to be a scorer. McInnis can be used in a lot of situations and with many different line combinations. He is a useful role player to have around.

PROJECTION

A healthy McInnis should be good for 15 goals.

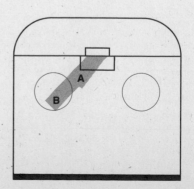

KYLE MCLAREN

Yrs. of NHL service: 7
Born: Humbolt, Sask.; June 18, 1977
Position: left defence
Height: 6-4
Weight: 230
Uniform no.: 18
Shoots: left

Career statistics:

GP	G	A	TP	PIM
417	34	90	124	370

1998-1999 statistics:

GP	G	A	TP	+/-	PIM	PP	SH	GW	GT	S	PCT
52	6	18	24	+1	48	3	0	0	0	97	6.2

1999-2000 statistics:

GP	G	A	TP	+/-	PIM	PP	SH	GW	GT	S	PCT
71	8	11	19	-4	67	2	0	3	0	142	5.6

2000-2001 statistics:

GP	G	A	TP	+/-	PIM	PP	SH	GW	GT	S	PCT
58	5	12	17	-5	53	2	0	0	1	91	5.5

2001-2002 statistics:

GP	G	A	TP	+/-	PIM	PP	SH	GW	GT	S	PCT
38	0	8	8	-4	19	0	0	0	0	57	0.0

LAST SEASON

Missed 31 games with torn wrist ligament and surgery. Missed 12 games with torn chest muscle. Missed one game with bruised knee.

THE FINESSE GAME

McLaren is big and mobile. His puckhandling is well above average, and he moves the puck out of the zone quickly and without panicking. He can rush with the puck or make the cautious bank off the boards to clear the zone. McLaren jumps eagerly into the play.

He can play either right or left defence, and his advanced defensive reads allow him to adapt, which is very hard to do for a young player.

McLaren is an effective penalty killer because he is fearless. He blocks shots and takes away passing lanes. He can also play on the power play, and probably will improve in this area because he plays heads-up and has a hard and accurate slap shot with a quick release. As he gains more confidence he will become more of an offensive factor, but frequently he puts the cart before the horse and goes on the attack — before he has taken care of his own end of the ice.

THE PHYSICAL GAME

McLaren is a mean, punishing hitter — witness his 2002 playoff hit on Richard Zednik. He is almost scary in his fierce checking ability. He is tough and aggressive, but he doesn't go looking for fights and doesn't take foolish penalties. When he does scrap, he can go toe-to-toe and has already earned some respect around the league as a player you don't want to tick off. He is strong on the puck, strong on the wall and doesn't allow loitering in front of his crease.

McLaren has a tendency to lose his edge and get too freewheeling and offensive. Every time he lapses into this bad habit, the coaching staff have to rein him in and bring him back to a simple game.

THE INTANGIBLES

McLaren's last two seasons have been savaged by injuries, and his playoff suspension (for the aforementioned high hit on Zednik) may play with his head as much as the injuries hurt his body. If McLaren recovers, physically and mentally, he is a cornerstone of a young defence crops in Boston with Nicholas Boynton and Hal Gill.

PROJECTION

The less McLaren thinks about getting points, the more easily he will score. Keep expectations low until you get a look at how McLaren starts off the season. Even in a good year, 25 points may be his max.

GLEN MURRAY

Yrs. of NHL service: 10
Born: Halifax, N.S.; Nov. 1, 1972
Position: right wing
Height: 6-3
Weight: 225
Uniform no.: 27
Shoots: right

Career statistics:

GP	G	A	TP	PIM
660	192	179	371	413

1998-1999 statistics:

GP	G	A	TP	+/-	PIM	PP	SH	GW	GT	S	PCT
61	16	15	31	-14	36	3	3	3	0	173	9.2

1999-2000 statistics:

GP	G	A	TP	+/-	PIM	PP	SH	GW	GT	S	PCT
78	29	33	62	+13	60	10	1	2	1	202	14.4

2000-2001 statistics:

GP	G	A	TP	+/-	PIM	PP	SH	GW	GT	S	PCT
64	18	21	39	+9	32	3	1	1	0	138	13.0

2001-2002 statistics:

GP	G	A	TP	+/-	PIM	PP	SH	GW	GT	S	PCT
82	41	30	71	+31	40	9	0	9	0	246	16.7

LAST SEASON

Acquired from Los Angeles on October 24, 2001, with Jozef Stumpel for Jason Allison and Mikko Eloranta. Led Bruins in assists, points, game-winning goals and shooting percentage. Tied for first on team in goals. Tied for third in NHL in goals and plus-minus. Second on team in power-play goals. Third on team in shots. One of two Bruins to appear in all 82 games.

THE FINESSE GAME

Who said there are no successful second acts? Murray turned what looked like a terribly lopsided trade in L.A.'s favour into a splashy comeback. Murray started his career with the Bruins and left in a 1995 trade. He carried a "next Cam Neely" tag for a long time. Now that he is playing more consistently, that tag is no longer a drag.

Murray is at his best on the right side, jamming in his forehand shots. He has good size and a top short game. He also has a quick release and, like a lot of great goal scorers, he just plain shoots. He doesn't even have to look at the net because he feels where the shot is going, and he protects the puck well with his body. Murray has also developed a wickedly fast slap shot and has developed confidence in this weapon. He is now more consistently using his speed and strength to get in better scoring position.

Murray is a lumbering skater who needs a good old dump-and-chase game, on a line with a playmaker who can get him the puck and set him up in the slot.

THE PHYSICAL GAME

On nights when he's playing well, Murray is leaning on people and making his presence felt. He'll bang, but on some nights he doesn't want to pay the price and prefers to rely on his shot. When he sleepwalks, he's useless. When he's ready to rock 'n' roll, he's effective. He is now more consistent at bringing his top game every night, and has made strides in becoming a solid power forward.

THE INTANGIBLES

Murray was able to shine as the No. 2 right wing in Boston behind Bill Guerin. Losing Guerin will heighten the defensive attention on Murray.

PROJECTION

Guerin's absence will hurt Murray, and probably slice 10 goals off his total from last season.

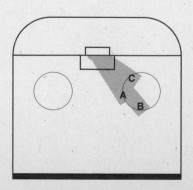

SEAN O'DONNELL

Yrs. of NHL service: 7
Born: Ottawa, Ont.; Oct. 13, 1971
Position: left defence
Height: 6-3
Weight: 230
Uniform no.: 21
Shoots: left

Career statistics:

GP	G	A	TP	PIM
541	19	94	113	1049

1998-1999 statistics:

GP	G	A	TP	+/-	PIM	PP	SH	GW	GT	S	PCT
80	1	13	14	+1	186	0	0	0	0	64	1.6

1999-2000 statistics:

GP	G	A	TP	+/-	PIM	PP	SH	GW	GT	S	PCT
80	2	12	14	+4	114	0	0	1	0	51	3.9

2000-2001 statistics:

GP	G	A	TP	+/-	PIM	PP	SH	GW	GT	S	PCT
80	4	13	17	0	161	1	0	2	0	67	6.0

2001-2002 statistics:

GP	G	A	TP	+/-	PIM	PP	SH	GW	GT	S	PCT
80	3	22	25	+27	89	1	0	2	0	112	2.7

LAST SEASON

Led team defencemen in points. Second on team in plus-minus. Missed two games with back spasms.

THE FINESSE GAME

O'Donnell has worked hard to rise above being a one-dimensional player, but his skating holds him back. He is not very good laterally and that results in him being beaten wide. He tries to line up someone and misses because he doesn't have the quickness to get there.

He has some offensive input because he is alert and tries so hard, but O'Donnell is really at his best when he can play a stay-at-home style. He makes a suitable partner for a high-risk defenceman, although he runs into spells where he starts taking high-risk runs at people. His hand skills are average at best. He can make a decent outlet pass, but he tends to get a bit panicky under pressure.

O'Donnell's defensive reads are adequate. He has become a decent shot-blocker.

THE PHYSICAL GAME

O'Donnell is fearless. He is a legitimate tough guy who fights anybody. He hits hard. He uses his stick. He's a nasty customer. O'Donnell sticks up for his teammates, but often overreacts. He has a penchant for taking bad penalties.

THE INTANGIBLES

O'Donnell is a serviceable third-pair defenceman, but injuries forced the Bruins to move him up and he performed well for long stretches. O'Donnell is a great team guy, and fit in well with the team's younger defencemen.

PROJECTION

O'Donnell will provide toughness, and 20-25 points.

BRIAN ROLSTON

Yrs. of NHL service: 8
Born: Flint, Mich.; Feb. 21, 1973
Position: left wing
Height: 6-2
Weight: 205
Uniform no.: 12
Shoots: left

Career statistics:

GP	G	A	TP	PIM
573	144	181	325	151

1998-1999 statistics:

GP	G	A	TP	+/-	PIM	PP	SH	GW	GT	S	PCT
82	24	33	57	+11	14	5	5	3	0	210	11.4

1999-2000 statistics:

GP	G	A	TP	+/-	PIM	PP	SH	GW	GT	S	PCT
77	16	15	31	-12	18	5	0	6	0	206	7.8

2000-2001 statistics:

GP	G	A	TP	+/-	PIM	PP	SH	GW	GT	S	PCT
77	19	39	58	+6	28	5	0	4	0	286	6.6

2001-2002 statistics:

GP	G	A	TP	+/-	PIM	PP	SH	GW	GT	S	PCT
82	31	31	62	+11	30	6	9	7	0	331	9.4

LAST SEASON

Led league in shorthanded goals. Second on team and third in NHL in shots. Tied for second on team in game-winning goals. Third on team in goals. Tied for third on team in power-play goals. Career highs in goals and points. One of two Bruins to appear in all 82 games.

THE FINESSE GAME

Rolston's game is speed. He is a fast, powerful skater who drives to the net and loves to shoot. He passes well on his forehand and backhand, and reads break-out plays by leading his man smartly.

The main difference in Rolston's game is that now he is converting the chances that he gets with his speed. Rolston has developed far more patience with his shot. He has a cannon from the top of the circles in, with a quick release. Where he once had a tendency to hurry his shots, now he waits. Rolston creates so many odd-man-rush opportunities, especially shorthanded ones, that not forcing the goalie to handle the puck is a sin. That is what was happening when he was pinging shots off the glass.

He is an aggressive penalty killer. He uses his quick getaway stride to pull away for shorthanded breaks. He takes some pride in this role, and works diligently. Although he doesn't like it, he has been shoehorned into the role of a defensive winger. He makes a highly effective shadow, as he is one of the few players with the size, skill and smarts to match strides with a Jaromir Jagr or Pavel Bure.

Rolston plays centre or wing, and plays the point well on the power play.

THE PHYSICAL GAME

Rolston will take a hit to make a play, and has taken the next step to start initiating fights for pucks. He can be intimidated, however, and lacks true grit. His better games come against skating clubs. He is durable; in part because he keeps himself out of areas where he can get hurt.

THE INTANGIBLES

Rolston's scoring was a surprise and a bonus last season. It will be a measure of his maturity to see how he plays this season with the bar raised.

PROJECTION

Quite honestly, we never thought Rolston would become a 30-goal scorer. A lot of things broke right for Boston and we're not so sure it will be a happy zone this year. For this reason, we'll bring Rolston back down to the 25-goal, 50-point range.

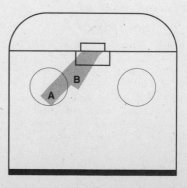

SERGEI SAMSONOV

Yrs. of NHL service: 5
Born: Moscow, Russia; Oct. 27, 1978
Position: left wing
Height: 5-8
Weight: 180
Uniform no.: 14
Shoots: right

Career statistics:

GP	G	A	TP	PIM
393	124	164	288	75

1998-1999 statistics:

GP	G	A	TP	+/-	PIM	PP	SH	GW	GT	S	PCT
79	25	26	51	-6	18	6	0	8	1	160	15.6

1999-2000 statistics:

GP	G	A	TP	+/-	PIM	PP	SH	GW	GT	S	PCT
77	19	26	45	-6	4	6	0	3	0	145	13.1

2000-2001 statistics:

GP	G	A	TP	+/-	PIM	PP	SH	GW	GT	S	PCT
82	29	46	75	+6	18	3	0	3	2	215	13.5

2001-2002 statistics:

GP	G	A	TP	+/-	PIM	PP	SH	GW	GT	S	PCT
74	29	41	70	+21	27	3	0	4	0	192	15.1

LAST SEASON

Second on team in points and shooting percentage. Third on team in assists. Tied career high in goals. Missed six games with knee injury.

THE FINESSE GAME

Samsonov has found an excellent linemate in Joe Thornton. It's like the quote about the pairing of Ginger Rogers and Fred Astaire — he gave them class and she gave them sex. Thornton provides the size and muscle and Samsonov brings the speed and touch.

Every time Samsonov has the puck, there is a buzz because he makes things happen. He tries stickhandling moves and shots that other players don't even dream of. Here's what's scary: he can be even better. He is an absolute treat to watch. He is an outstanding skater — the puck doesn't slow him down a hair. He performs the hockey equivalent of a between-the-legs dribble, putting pucks between the legs (his or the defenders') and executing cutbacks. Samsonov is as nifty in tight spaces as he is in open ice.

Although small, Samsonov has the ability to be an explosive game-breaker. Think Pavel Bure, although Samsonov isn't quite yet in that league. But he has the kind of speed and talent that can bring a crowd out of its seats or fake a defenceman out of his skates.

He has outstanding quickness and breakaway speed. He uses all of the ice. Samsonov can get too in love with his skating. When he slumps, it's because of the Alexei Kovalev syndrome, when his idea of a great play is to try to go the length of the ice and through all five defenders before taking a shot, as if hockey were some kind of obstacle course. When he keeps the game simple and uses his linemates better, he has more success. He is reliable enough defensively, and he is certainly no liability.

THE PHYSICAL GAME

Sturdily built, Samsonov is a little tank. He can't be scared off the play and he handles himself well in traffic and in tight spaces along the boards and corners. Samsonov digs into every scrum. Samsonov believes that a small man can star in the NHL if he is good enough. He is.

THE INTANGIBLES

Samsonov is recovered fully from a hip ailment and should continue to be an offensive force in Boston.

PROJECTION

Samsonov's assists will probably always be 10 higher than his goals. He should be a consistent 30-goal, 70-point player and will be ready soon to move to the next level.

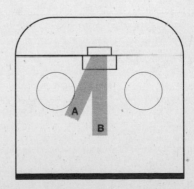

41

STEVE SHIELDS

Yrs. of NHL service: 4
Born: Toronto, Ont.; July 19, 1972
Position: goaltender
Height: 6-3
Weight: 215
Uniform no.: 31
Catches: left

Career statistics:

GP	MIN	GA	SO	GAA	A	PIM
189	10520	448	10	2.56	2	62

1998-1999 statistics:

GP	MIN	GAA	W	L	T	SO	GA	S	SAPCT	PIM
37	2162	2.22	15	11	8	4	80	1011	.921	6

1999-2000 statistics:

GP	MIN	GAA	W	L	T	SO	GA	S	SAPCT	PIM
67	3797	2.56	27	30	8	4	162	1826	.911	29

2000-2001 statistics:

GP	MIN	GAA	W	L	T	SO	GA	S	SAPCT	PIM
21	1135	2.48	6	8	5	2	47	531	.911	2

2001-2002 statistics:

GP	MIN	GAA	W	L	T	SO	GA	S	SAPCT	PIM
33	1777	2.67	9	20	2	0	79	850	.907	4

LAST SEASON

Acquired from Anaheim on June 25, 2002, for third-round draft pick in 2003. Missed four games with facial laceration and jaw contusions.

THE PHYSICAL GAME

Shields's game has some major hiccups, the primary one is that he can't catch the puck. He never seems to track the puck coming all the way to his body, which is why he doesn't watch the puck go into his glove. He also loses it after it hits him elsewhere on his body, which is why he is prone to many bad rebounds. This sounds so elementary, but no one seems to have tried to straighten him out, and it's going to be a major trip-up. It may be a habit he picked up from playing with Dominik Hasek years ago in Buffalo. The difference is that Hasek was always able to keep track of the puck and stop second and third tries.

Shields is mobile and competitive, but he is a big goalie who looks like Darren Pang (who was a small goalie) in the net because of his technical shortcomings. He has a lot of raw skills but needs a full-time goalie coach.

THE MENTAL GAME

Shields is able to shake off bad games and come right back. He needs to be more consistent on a nightly basis. He can win some big games on pure adrenaline when the team doesn't play well in front of him.

THE INTANGIBLES

Shields was a No.1 goalie in San Jose and may be asked to fill that role again in Boston if the Bruins are serious about using him to replace Byron Dafoe.

PROJECTION

Shields isn't in the top echelon of goaltenders. For Boston to go to him after Dafoe, if that is indeed the plan, it's a bad one. After all the progress Boston made last season, it would be a shame for them to get chintzy at such a key position.

JOZEF STUMPEL

Yrs. of NHL service: 9
Born: Nitra, Slovakia; June 20, 1972
Position: centre
Height: 6-3
Weight: 225
Uniform no.: 16
Shoots: right

Career statistics:

GP	G	A	TP	PIM
616	129	331	460	159

1998-1999 statistics:

GP	G	A	TP	+/-	PIM	PP	SH	GW	GT	S	PCT
64	13	21	34	-18	10	1	0	1	0	131	9.9

1999-2000 statistics:

GP	G	A	TP	+/-	PIM	PP	SH	GW	GT	S	PCT
57	17	41	58	+23	10	3	0	7	1	126	13.5

2000-2001 statistics:

GP	G	A	TP	+/-	PIM	PP	SH	GW	GT	S	PCT
63	16	39	55	+20	14	9	0	6	0	95	16.8

2001-2002 statistics:

GP	G	A	TP	+/-	PIM	PP	SH	GW	GT	S	PCT
81	8	50	58	+22	18	1	0	3	0	100	8.0

PROJECTION

Stumpel will score 50 assists, 60 points, but you may not be able to find him when you really need him.

LAST SEASON

Acquired from Los Angeles on October 24, 2001, with Glen Murray for Jason Allison and Mikko Eloranta. Led Bruins in assists. Tied for second on Bruins in plus-minus. Missed one game with groin injury.

THE FINESSE GAME

Stumpel is a setup man and he needs to play with a stone finisher. Stumpel has good hand skills, which allow him to compensate for his skating, up to a point. He also has a deft scoring touch and is a passer with a good short game. He is very patient. He uses his feet well to keep the puck alive, kick it up onto his stick or keep it in the attacking zone.

He also has keen hockey sense. But he does not shoot nearly enough, and that isn't likely to change at this point in his career.

Stumpel doesn't have much sand in his game and achieves everything with finesse.

THE PHYSICAL GAME

Stumpel is quite powerfully built, but he doesn't play to his size. He can be intimidated, and teams go after him early. He goes into the corners and bumps and protects the puck with his body, but when the action gets really fierce he backs off.

THE INTANGIBLES

Stumpel was unhappy with the trade, which separated him from his pal and linemate, Ziggy Palffy. He got over it well enough to put up some good (assist) numbers, but he is just not a crunch-time player and he came up empty in the playoffs.

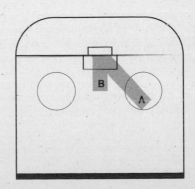

DON SWEENEY

Yrs. of NHL service: 14
Born: St. Stephen, N.B.; Aug. 17, 1966
Position: left defence
Height: 5-10
Weight: 186
Uniform no.: 32
Shoots: left

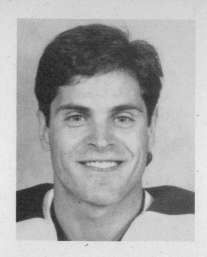

Career statistics:

GP	G	A	TP	PIM
985	49	205	254	639

1998-1999 statistics:

GP	G	A	TP	+/-	PIM	PP	SH	GW	GT	S	PCT
81	2	10	12	+14	64	0	0	0	0	79	2.5

1999-2000 statistics:

GP	G	A	TP	+/-	PIM	PP	SH	GW	GT	S	PCT
81	1	13	14	-14	48	0	0	0	0	82	1.2

2000-2001 statistics:

GP	G	A	TP	+/-	PIM	PP	SH	GW	GT	S	PCT
72	2	10	12	-1	26	1	0	1	0	60	3.3

2001-2002 statistics:

GP	G	A	TP	+/-	PIM	PP	SH	GW	GT	S	PCT
81	3	15	18	+22	35	1	0	0	0	70	4.3

LAST SEASON

Tied for third on team in plus-minus. Missed one game with flu.

THE FINESSE GAME

Sweeney is mobile, physical and greatly improved in the area of defensive reads. He has good hockey sense for recognizing offensive situations as well. Although he mostly stays at home and out of trouble, he is a good-enough skater to get involved in the attack and to take advantage of open ice. He is a good passer and has an adequate shot, and he has developed more confidence in his skills. He skates his way out of trouble and moves the puck well.

Sweeney is also a clever player who knows his strengths and weaknesses. Despite being a low draft pick (166th overall), he doesn't let anyone overlook him due to his effort and intelligence.

At 36, Sweeney is on the downside of his career, but Boston has done a good job of rebuilding its defence corps in the post-Ray Bourque years, and Sweeney can remain a veteran contributor.

THE PHYSICAL GAME

Sweeney is built like a little human Coke© machine. He is tough to play against and, while wear and tear is a factor, he never hides. He is always in the middle of physical play. He utilizes his lower-body drive and has tremendous leg power. He is also shifty enough to avoid a big hit when he sees it coming, and many a large forechecking forward has sheepishly picked himself up off the ice after Sweeney has scampered away from the boards with the puck.

The ultimate gym rat, Sweeney devotes a great deal of time to weightlifting and overall conditioning. Pound for pound, he is one of the strongest defencemen in the NHL. Of course, it doesn't hurt to pair him with a physical partner like Kyle McLaren.

THE INTANGIBLES

Sweeney is highly competitive. Despite his small size, a lot of teams would welcome him on their blueline.

PROJECTION

Sweeney's point totals won't go much higher than 20.

JOE THORNTON

Yrs. of NHL service: 5
Born: London, Ont.; July 2, 1979
Position: centre
Height: 6-4
Weight: 220
Uniform no.: 19
Shoots: left

Career statistics:

GP	G	A	TP	PIM
355	101	146	247	404

1998-1999 statistics:

GP	G	A	TP	+/-	PIM	PP	SH	GW	GT	S	PCT
81	16	25	41	+3	69	7	0	1	0	128	12.5

1999-2000 statistics:

GP	G	A	TP	+/-	PIM	PP	SH	GW	GT	S	PCT
81	23	37	60	-5	82	5	0	3	0	171	13.5

2000-2001 statistics:

GP	G	A	TP	+/-	PIM	PP	SH	GW	GT	S	PCT
72	37	34	71	-4	107	19	1	5	0	181	20.4

2001-2002 statistics:

GP	G	A	TP	+/-	PIM	PP	SH	GW	GT	S	PCT
66	22	46	68	+7	127	6	0	5	1	152	14.5

LAST SEASON

Second on team in assists and penalty minutes. Third on team in points and shooting percentage. Tied for third in power-play goals. Missed 13 games with shoulder injury. Missed three games due to suspension.

THE FINESSE GAME

Thornton was "discovered" last season during the Bruins' resurgence and because of his appearance at the NHL All-Star Game. He is a skating advertisement for not giving up on a high draft pick (first overall in 1997) when a kid doesn't become Mario Lemieux in his rookie season.

Thornton has played for some tough coaches — Pat Burns, Mike Keenan — and each one left his mark. A lot was demanded of Thornton, and once Jason Allison was traded to L.A., Thornto was ready to take over as Boston's No.1 centre.

Thornton's assets are his exceptional vision of the ice and the hand skills to make things happen. He is so adept at finding holes and passing lanes that teammates have to be alert when playing with him, because he will create something out of nothing. Sergei Samsonov was an ideal winger for him.

Thornton also loves to shoot and work the boards, corners and front of the net. He needs to be prodded to keep his feet moving, though, as he often drifts into a bad habit of standing and waiting for things to happen. He needs to make things happen. Thornton's skating could use some improvement, but it's NHL calibre. He is steadily improving his work on draws (last year's percentage was 49.1).

THE PHYSICAL GAME

Thornton plays with an edge and has a short fuse. He is a frequent target and he doesn't let too many misdeeds go unpunished. Opponents know it, and try to goad him. Thornton needs to learn how to play tough and stay out of the penalty box.

THE INTANGIBLES

Thornton may become one of the game's top five centres this season.

PROJECTION

Losing Bill Guerin might hurt, but Thornton should still account for 30 goals, 80 points.

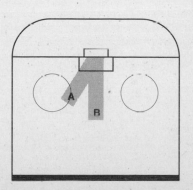

ROB ZAMUNER

Yrs. of NHL service: 10
Born: Oakville, Ont.; Sept. 17, 1969
Position: left wing
Height: 6-3
Weight: 203
Uniform no.: 17
Shoots: left

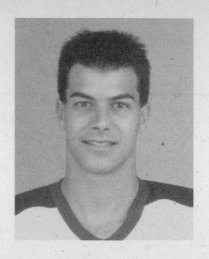

Career statistics:

GP	G	A	TP	PIM
686	125	161	286	433

1998-1999 statistics:

GP	G	A	TP	+/-	PIM	PP	SH	GW	GT	S	PCT
58	8	11	19	-15	24	1	1	2	0	89	9.0

1999-2000 statistics:

GP	G	A	TP	+/-	PIM	PP	SH	GW	GT	S	PCT
57	9	12	21	-6	32	0	1	0	0	103	8.7

2000-2001 statistics:

GP	G	A	TP	+/-	PIM	PP	SH	GW	GT	S	PCT
79	19	18	37	+7	52	1	2	4	1	123	15.4

2001-2002 statistics:

GP	G	A	TP	+/-	PIM	PP	SH	GW	GT	S	PCT
66	12	13	25	+6	24	1	2	0	0	98	12.2

LAST SEASON

Tied for team lead in shorthanded goals. Missed 14 games with chest injury. Missed two games with hip injury.

THE FINESSE GAME

Zamuner doesn't have great speed, but he compensates for it in other ways, including all-out effort, all the time. A complementary player, he is a grinder who can also handle the puck, and he has some hand skills. Lacking speed, he plays well positionally and takes away the attacker's angles to the net. He doesn't skate as well as many of today's third-line checking wingers, but he is smart enough.

Zamuner has pretty much become a penalty-killing specialist. He is a shorthanded threat because of his anticipation and work ethic, and he easily turns penalty-killing attempts into shorthanded counterattacks. He has a knack for scoring key goals.

Zamuner was a sniper at the minor-league level, but has not been able to have the same impact in the NHL. He has a decent touch for scoring or passing, but it's average at best.

THE PHYSICAL GAME

Zamuner had problems in the past with fitness, until he realized what a big edge he could have with better conditioning. He has good size and he uses it effectively; he is pesky and annoying to play against. On many nights he will be the most physically active forward, adding a real spark with his effort.

THE INTANGIBLES

There are a lot of things Zamuner can't do, but a coach who values what Zamuner can do will find him a valuable role player.

PROJECTION

Zamuner has become a checking winger who can provide a minimum of 15 goals a season.

BUFFALO SABRES

Players' Statistics 2001-2002

POS.	NO.	PLAYER	GP	G	A	PTS	+/-	PIM	PP	SH	GW	GT	S	PCT
L	81	MIROSLAV SATAN	82	37	36	73	14	33	15	5	5		267	13.9
C	41	STU BARNES	68	17	31	48	6	26	5		4	1	127	13.4
C	18	TIM CONNOLLY	82	10	35	45	4	34	3		3		126	7.9
R	17	JEAN-PIERRE DUMONT	76	23	21	44	-10	42	7		3	1	154	14.9
R	61	MAXIM AFINOGENOV	81	21	19	40	-9	69	3	1			234	9.0
C	77	CHRIS GRATTON	82	15	24	39	0	75	1		5		139	10.8
C	37	CURTIS BROWN	82	20	17	37	-4	32	4	1	5		171	11.7
D	44	ALEXEI ZHITNIK	82	1	33	34	-1	80	1				150	0.7
D	5	JASON WOOLLEY	59	8	20	28	-6	34	6		2		90	8.9
R	25	VACLAV VARADA	76	7	16	23	-7	82	1		1		138	5.1
L	13	VYACHESLAV KOZLOV	38	9	13	22	0	16	3		1	1	68	13.2
L	24	TAYLOR PYATT	48	10	10	20	4	35				1	61	16.4
C	9	ERIK RASMUSSEN	69	8	11	19	-1	34			2		89	9.0
D	3	JAMES PATRICK	56	5	8	13	3	16	1				45	11.1
D	45	DMITRI KALININ	58	2	11	13	-6	26					67	3.0
D	74	JAY MCKEE	81	2	11	13	18	43			1		50	4.0
D	4	RHETT WARRENER	65	5	5	10	15	113			1	1	66	7.6
D	42	RICHARD SMEHLIK	60	3	6	9	-9	22			1	1	52	5.8
C	29	BOB CORKUM	75	3	5	8	-32	20					80	3.8
R	55	DENIS HAMEL	61	2	6	8	-1	28					80	2.5
D	51	BRIAN CAMPBELL	29	3	3	6	0	12					30	10.0
R	32	ROB RAY	71	2	3	5	-3	200					23	8.7
L	26	ERIC BOULTON	35	2	3	5	-1	129			1		21	9.5
R	12	*ALES KOTALIK	13	1	3	4	-1	2					21	4.8
R	19	*NORMAN MILLEY	5		1	1	0						10	
D	10	*HENRIK TALLINDER	2				-1						4	
D	8	RORY FITZPATRICK	5				-2	4					2	
G	31	BOB ESSENSA	9				0							
G	43	MARTIN BIRON	72				0	8						
G	35	MIKA NORONEN	10				0	2						

GP = games played; G = goals; A = assists; PTS = points; +/- = goals-for minus goals-against while player is on ice; PIM – penalties in minutes; PP = power-play goals; SH = shorthanded goals; GW = game-winning goals; GT = game-tying goals; S = no. of shots; PCT = percentage of goals to shots; * = rookie

MAXIM AFINOGENOV

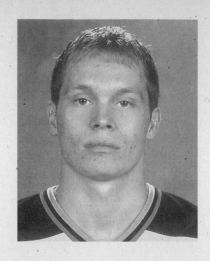

Yrs. of NHL service: 3
Born: Moscow, Russia; Sept. 4, 1979
Position: right wing
Height: 6-0
Weight: 195
Uniform no.: 61
Shoots: left

Career statistics:

GP	G	A	TP	PIM
224	51	59	110	150

1999-2000 statistics:

GP	G	A	TP	+/-	PIM	PP	SH	GW	GT	S	PCT
65	16	18	34	-4	41	2	0	2	0	128	12.5

2000-2001 statistics:

GP	G	A	TP	+/-	PIM	PP	SH	GW	GT	S	PCT
78	14	22	36	+1	40	3	0	5	0	190	7.4

2001-2002 statistics:

GP	G	A	TP	+/-	PIM	PP	SH	GW	GT	S	PCT
81	21	19	40	-9	69	3	1	0	0	234	9.0

PROJECTION

Afinogenov should be a consistent 25-goal scorer. He has to earn the ice time instead of thinking it is his due.

LAST SEASON

Second on team in shots. Third on team in goals. Missed one game with flu.

THE FINESSE GAME

Afinogenov is a powerful skater with explosive speed and excellent balance. He may have too much confidence in his puckhandling skills, because he likes to take the scenic Alexei Kovalev route to the net — that is, the longest way and through as many defenders as possible. Fun, maybe. Effective, no.

Afinogenov needs to use his linemates better and be more of a give-and-go player. His shot isn't great. It's his intimidating speed and the quickness of his shot that gives him the offensive edge.

Afinogenov is a poverty-stricken version of Pavel Bure, an NHL star who thinks he doesn't need his teammates. If Afinogenov scored 50 goals, that might be forgivable. He sees absolutely no need to concern himself with team defence, either. His plus-minus was among the worst.

THE PHYSICAL GAME

Afinogenov is not very big, but on the shifts where he turns on his intensity he can't be intimidated. He plays with determination in the attacking zone and has to learn to apply that to the rest of the ice.

THE INTANGIBLES

After a disappointing sophomore season, Afinogenov rallied with a slightly more productive season. If he is going to play such a high-risk game, though, he will need to score. It would better serve him to start learning how to help his team win when he's not scoring.

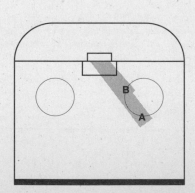

STU BARNES

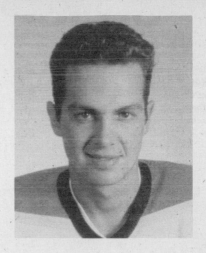

Yrs. of NHL service: 11
Born: Spruce Grove, Alta.; Dec. 25, 1970
Position: centre
Height: 5-11
Weight: 180
Uniform no.: 41
Shoots: right

Career statistics:

GP	G	A	TP	PIM
739	197	248	445	282

1998-1999 statistics:

GP	G	A	TP	+/-	PIM	PP	SH	GW	GT	S	PCT
81	20	16	36	-11	30	13	0	3	0	180	11.1

1999-2000 statistics:

GP	G	A	TP	+/-	PIM	PP	SH	GW	GT	S	PCT
82	20	25	45	-3	16	8	2	2	0	137	14.6

2000-2001 statistics:

GP	G	A	TP	+/-	PIM	PP	SH	GW	GT	S	PCT
75	19	24	43	-2	26	3	2	5	0	160	11.9

2001-2002 statistics:

GP	G	A	TP	+/-	PIM	PP	SH	GW	GT	S	PCT
68	17	31	48	+6	26	5	0	4	1	127	13.4

LAST SEASON

Second on team in points. Third on team in shooting percentage. Missed 14 games with a concussion.

THE FINESSE GAME

Barnes pursues the puck intelligently and finishes his checks. He employs these traits at even strength, killing penalties or on the power play. He reads the play coming out of the zone and uses his anticipation to pick off passes. He plays with great enthusiasm. He has sharply honed puck skills and offensive instincts, which he puts to effective use on the power play. He has good quickness and can control the puck in traffic. He uses a slap shot or a wrist shot in-tight.

Few of the quality chances that come Barnes's way get wasted. He has a quick release and is accurate with his shot. One of his favourite plays is using his right-handed shot for a one-timer on the power play.

Barnes has a good work ethic; his effort overcomes his deficiency in size. He's clever and plays a smart small-man's game. He plays all three forward positions. He tends to get into scoring slumps, but never quits working to try to snap out of them.

THE PHYSICAL GAME

Barnes is not big but he gets in the way. He brings a little bit of grit to the lineup, but what really stands out is his intensity and spirit. He can energize his team with one gutsy shift. He always keeps his feet moving and draws penalties. He gets outmuscled down low.

THE INTANGIBLES

Some players do not shoulder responsibility well. Barnes raises his game in the playoffs and responded well to the "C" being sewn on his sweater. He is the epitome of a player with a good work ethic. Tim Connolly, who, like Barnes, is on the small side, would do well to follow his example. His concussion was season-ending and has to concern the Sabres, who really need this guy in their lineup.

PROJECTION

Realistically, 20 goals is again the right target for Barnes, who is not really a No. 1 centre but will be asked to perform like one.

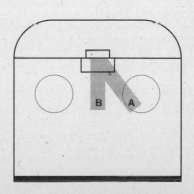

MARTIN BIRON

Yrs. of NHL service: 5
Born: Lac St. Charles, Que.; Aug. 15, 1977
Position: goaltender
Height: 6-2
Weight: 163
Uniform no.: 43
Catches: left

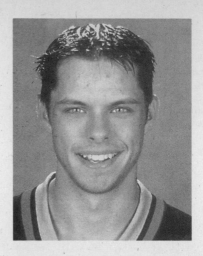

Career statistics:

GP	MIN	GA	SO	GAA	A	PIM
140	7632	300	11	2.36	1	14

1998-1999 statistics:

GP	MIN	GAA	W	L	T	SO	GA	S	SAPCT	PIM
6	281	2.14	1	2	1	0	10	120	.917	0

1999-2000 statistics:

GP	MIN	GAA	W	L	T	SO	GA	S	SAPCT	PIM
41	2229	2.42	19	18	2	5	90	988	.909	6

2000-2001 statistics:

GP	MIN	GAA	W	L	T	SO	GA	S	SAPCT	PIM
18	918	2.55	7	7	1	2	39	427	.909	0

2001-2002 statistics:

GP	MIN	GAA	W	L	T	SO	GA	S	SAPCT	PIM
72	4085	2.22	31	28	10	4	151	1781	.915	8

LAST SEASON

Third in NHL in minutes played.

THE PHYSICAL GAME

Biron was pretty much skin and bones when he was drafted, and has gradually built himself up to be able to handle the wear and tear of NHL goaltending. He is still on the ridiculously lean side, and will have to have his carbs on game days.

Like Martin Brodeur, whose personality Biron echoes, he is a hybrid goalie: not quite butterfly, not quite stand-up. His bent-over stance reminds onlookers of Mike Liut. His long legs taking away the lower portion of the net make the butterfly work well for him. His recovery time is good, and if he does go down, he recovers his feet quickly. He will be aggressive with his stick, taking a Bill Smith-like whack at someone in his crease. Biron is average handling the puck, although he is not quite in Brodeur's class.

THE MENTAL GAME

Having to take over for Dominik Hasek put a great strain on Biron and he struggled with it in the first half of the season. But his second-half goals-against (1.94) was much better than the first half (2.52), which is a promising sign.

Biron is very strong mentally. He is talkative with the press, with teammates, with opponents and the referees. If he weren't a goalie, he could be a captain. His teammates feed off his confidence.

THE INTANGIBLES

Biron is a student of the Francois Allaire school of goaltending, and seems ready to take the next step. It will be helpful to have a veteran goalie on hand as his backup, although the Sabres may be unwilling to spend the money. It might worry Biron that two of the organization's best prospects are goalies.

PROJECTION

Racking up 31 wins in a tumultuous season was a major accomplishment for Biron, who won't find things much easier this season.

CURTIS BROWN

Yrs. of NHL service: 6
Born: Unity, Sask.; Feb. 12, 1976
Position: centre
Height: 6-0
Weight: 196
Uniform no.: 37
Shoots: left

Career statistics:

GP	G	A	TP	PIM
400	85	115	200	218

1998-1999 statistics:

GP	G	A	TP	+/-	PIM	PP	SH	GW	GT	S	PCT
78	16	31	47	+23	56	5	1	3	3	128	12.5

1999-2000 statistics:

GP	G	A	TP	+/-	PIM	PP	SH	GW	GT	S	PCT
74	22	29	51	+19	42	5	0	4	1	149	14.8

2000-2001 statistics:

GP	G	A	TP	+/-	PIM	PP	SH	GW	GT	S	PCT
70	10	22	32	+15	34	2	1	0	0	105	9.5

2001-2002 statistics:

GP	G	A	TP	+/-	PIM	PP	SH	GW	GT	S	PCT
82	20	17	37	-4	32	4	1	5	0	171	11.7

PROJECTION

He will get a lot of ice time again; Brown should produce 40 points.

LAST SEASON

Tied for team lead in game-winning goals. Third on team in penalty minutes. One of five Sabres to appear in all 82 games.

THE FINESSE GAME

Brown is a little cannonball, strong and quick on his skates and unafraid to get involved around the net. He is an excellent penalty killer, with terrific reads and anticipation, and the jump to pick off passes and turn them into shorthanded chances.

A converted left wing, Brown makes an ideal third-line forward. The Sabres are so thin in talent that sometmes he is bumped up to a top six job. It's hard to fault a guy when he is playing out of position.

Brown has enough offensive skills to play on the top two lines, but his chief asset is his defensive ability. He is Selke Trophy calibre. Brown will create things with his speed on the forecheck and then use his skilled hands to make the tape-to-tape pass. He is a playmaker first. Brown's hockey sense and defensive awareness are exceptional.

THE PHYSICAL GAME

Brown is little, but plays with a bit of swagger. He isn't really tough — he just gives the impression that he won't back off. He is abrasive and annoying.

THE INTANGIBLES

As he continues to improve, Brown is gaining even more confidence. The Sabres need to guard against overusing him. Brown put on some weight in preseason, perhaps in anticipation of that, and all it did was slow him down.

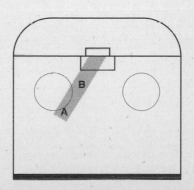

BRIAN CAMPBELL

Yrs. of NHL service: 2
Born: Strathroy, Ont.; May 23, 1979
Position: defense
Height: 6-0
Weight: 190
Uniform no.: 51
Shoots: left

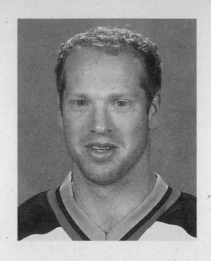

Career statistics:

GP	G	A	TP	PIM
49	4	7	11	18

1999-2000 statistics:

GP	G	A	TP	+/-	PIM	PP	SH	GW	GT	S	PCT
12	1	4	5	-2	4	0	0	0	0	10	10.0

2000-2001 statistics:

GP	G	A	TP	+/-	PIM	PP	SH	GW	GT	S	PCT
8	0	0	0	-2	2	0	0	0	0	7	0.0

2001-2002 statistics:

GP	G	A	TP	+/-	PIM	PP	SH	GW	GT	S	PCT
29	3	3	6	0	12	0	0	0	0	30	10.0

LAST SEASON

Appeared in 45 games with Rochester (AHL), scoring 2-35-37 with 13 PIM. Missed six games with shoulder injury. Missed six games due to coach's decision.

THE FINESSE GAME

Campbell is an offensive defenceman. At least, that was the case in junior hockey, but he has had a little more trouble adjusting to the pro game.

Campbell is a slick, speedy skater. He's a strong puckhandler with good hockey sense and vision. Campbell needs to improve his play in his own end. He is not going to have the kind of elite numbers that will allow teams to overlook his defensive lapses.

Campbell has gotten a lot smarter about his reads. He knows when to jump into the play and when to stay back. Because he's not very physical, he is going to have to continue to work on his positional play.

THE PHYSICAL GAME

The knock on Campbell is his lack of size. He's about Phil Housley-size, though, and that worked out just fine, didn't it?

THE INTANGIBLES

Campbell isn't a top four defenceman yet, but he could play his way onto the Sabres as a third-pair defender and pick up some second-unit power-play time. The loss of Richard Smehlik (to free agency) opens up a job slot.

PROJECTION

Campbell did okay in his quarter-season stint last season. He could start off with 25 points in his first full season.

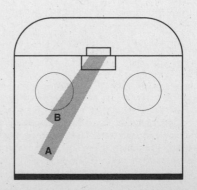

TIM CONNOLLY

Yrs. of NHL service: 3
Born: Syracuse, NY; May 7, 1980
Position: centre
Height: 6-0
Weight: 186
Uniform no.: 18
Shoots: right

Career statistics:

GP	G	A	TP	PIM
245	34	86	120	120

1999-2000 statistics:

GP	G	A	TP	+/-	PIM	PP	SH	GW	GT	S	PCT
81	14	20	34	-25	44	2	1	1	1	114	12.3

2000-2001 statistics:

GP	G	A	TP	+/-	PIM	PP	SH	GW	GT	S	PCT
82	10	31	41	-14	42	5	0	0	0	171	5.8

2001-2002 statistics:

GP	G	A	TP	+/-	PIM	PP	SH	GW	GT	S	PCT
82	10	35	45	+4	34	3	0	3	0	126	7.9

LAST SEASON

Second on team in assists. Third on team in assists. One of five Sabres to appear in all 82 games.

THE FINESSE GAME

Connolly has to learn that scoring goals is as important as making good plays. He is constantly looking to give his linemates a layup, but he has to realize that NHL teams are pretty smart and have him pegged as a passer. So he has to learn to shoot the puck. He sometimes overhandles the puck, probably a carryover from when he was able to dominate games at the junior level. Once he sheds that habit and learns to use his teammates better, he will be far more effective. He is an exceptional and exciting one-on-one player. He works the give-and-go well.

Connolly has reminded some scouts of Steve Yzerman because of his ability to make plays at a very high tempo. Connolly has great confidence in his abilities. He is creative and not afraid to try new moves. A quick and agile skater with a low centre of gravity, he maintains his control of the puck through traffic. He has a drive to succeed.

Connolly is a mainstay on the second-unit power play in Buffalo. He is smart and his anticipation is exceptional. As his game matures, he will also see more time killing penalties.

THE PHYSICAL GAME

Connolly needs to spend time in the weight room — he's still growing, too, so some natural maturing will help. He is pretty strong for his size already. Connolly has a bit of an attitude, which hasn't exactly endeared him to some veteran officials. He might not get the benefit of some penalty calls.

THE INTANGIBLES

Likely to be the No. 2 centre behind Stu Barnes, Connolly will get to avoid some checking attention. He struggled late in the season once all the injuries struck.

PROJECTION

Connolly can get into the 50-point range this season, with the accent on assists.

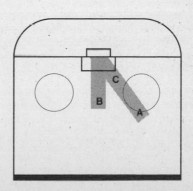

J. P. DUMONT

Yrs. of NHL service: 4
Born: Montreal, Que.; Apr. 1, 1978
Position: right wing
Height: 6-2
Weight: 202
Uniform no.: 17
Shoots: left

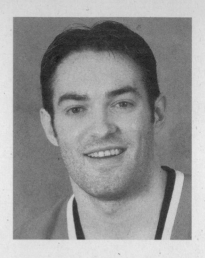

Career statistics:

GP	G	A	TP	PIM
227	65	63	128	124

1998-1999 statistics:

GP	G	A	TP	+/-	PIM	PP	SH	GW	GT	S	PCT
25	9	6	15	+7	10	0	0	2	0	42	21.4

1999-2000 statistics:

GP	G	A	TP	+/-	PIM	PP	SH	GW	GT	S	PCT
47	10	8	18	-6	18	0	0	1	0	86	11.6

2000-2001 statistics:

GP	G	A	TP	+/-	PIM	PP	SH	GW	GT	S	PCT
79	23	28	51	+1	54	9	0	5	0	156	14.7

2001-2002 statistics:

GP	G	A	TP	+/-	PIM	PP	SH	GW	GT	S	PCT
76	23	21	44	-10	42	7	0	3	1	154	14.9

LAST SEASON

Led team in shooting percentage. Second on team in assists and power-play goals. Missed six games with shoulder injury.

THE FINESSE GAME

Dumont has found the knack of being in the right place at the right time. He does a lot of his work around the front of the net. A lot of goal-scorers play on the perimeter, or look for the big, showy shot from somewhere. He's a guy that gets on the inside and doesn't mind the rough going.

He has all of the weapons needed to become a scorer in the NHL. Dumont is an instinctive shooter and playmaker who sees his options a step ahead of everyone else. He disguises his intentions well. Because he is unselfish with the puck, defenders may expect the pass. But he has an excellent wrist and slap shot, so you can't allow him to cruise to the net. He is pure hands.

Dumont goes through and around players like the breeze, with excellent puck control. His skating is NHL calibre. He has good acceleration for short bursts or rink-long sprints. He had to work on his conditioning and took power-skating lessons, so he is willing to work to improve his game. His hand-eye coordination for tip-ins and rebounds is outstanding.

As is typical with many slow-developing players, the knock on Dumont is his lack of intensity at times, but he is maturing. He is one of those rare players who finds the back of the net by any means possible.

THE PHYSICAL GAME

Dumont is tall but whippet-thin. He will need to fill out with some muscle now that he's no longer playing with boys, especially since he is going to make a living in the dirty areas around the net. He has an edge to his game, which shows he may thrive in the pros.

THE INTANGIBLES

Dumont can still be erratic. Because he has already been in three NHL organizations, it's easy to forget Dumont is only 24 and that power forwards take a longer time to develop. Buffalo, with all of its off-ice concerns, might not be the best lab for the Dumont experiment.

PROJECTION

Dumont should be a 30-goal scorer.

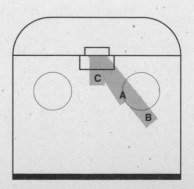

CHRIS GRATTON

Yrs. of NHL service: 9
Born: Brantford, Ont.; July 5, 1975
Position: centre
Height: 6-4
Weight: 226
Uniform no.: 77
Shoots: left

Career statistics:

GP	G	A	TP	PIM
690	146	247	393	1133

1998-1999 statistics:

GP	G	A	TP	+/-	PIM	PP	SH	GW	GT	S	PCT
78	8	26	34	-28	143	1	0	1	1	181	4.4

1999-2000 statistics:

GP	G	A	TP	+/-	PIM	PP	SH	GW	GT	S	PCT
72	15	34	49	-23	136	4	0	1	1	202	7.4

2000-2001 statistics:

GP	G	A	TP	+/-	PIM	PP	SH	GW	GT	S	PCT
82	19	21	40	0	102	5	0	5	1	156	12.2

2001-2002 statistics:

GP	G	A	TP	+/-	PIM	PP	SH	GW	GT	S	PCT
82	15	24	39	0	75	1	0	5	0	139	10.8

LAST SEASON

Tied for team lead in game-winning goals. One of five Sabres to appear in all 82 games.

THE FINESSE GAME

Gratton does a lot of things well, but not well enough or consistently enough to keep coaches and GMs from going grey. There are times when he can dominate a game, or step in to help an embattled teammate. And there are times when he takes shifts, nights and weeks off. For a player of his skill level and experience, those lapses are unforgivable. It's what keeps Gratton on the move from the fourth line to the first.

Of course, for a player of his size, much more is expected. He was supposed to be a power centre, and he is happier playing in the middle than when he is on the wing, but Gratton is clearly overmatched in the middle against other team's top units. One of the major reasons is his lack of foot speed, which hurts him despite a lot of coaching in this area.

Gratton's game is meat and potatoes. He's a grinder and needs to work hard every shift, every night, to make an impact. He has a hard shot, which he needs to use more. He gets his goals from digging around the net and there's some Cam Neely in him, but he lacks the long, strong stride Neely used in traffic. He has good hand-eye coordination and can pick passes out of midair for a shot. He has a big, noisy, but not always effective, slap shot.

An unselfish playmaker, Gratton is not the prettiest of passers, but he has some poise with the puck and he knows when to pass and when to shoot. He has shown an ability to win face-offs, and works diligently in his own end.

THE PHYSICAL GAME

On his good nights, Gratton is hard-working and doesn't shy from contact, but he has to initiate more. If his skating improves, he will be able to establish a more physical presence. He doesn't generate enough speed from leg drive to be much of a checker. He won't be an impact player in the NHL unless he does.

THE INTANGIBLES

Gratton's name always seem to pop up in trade rumours. The Sabres are desperate for his size, though they would make a deal if it comes along.

PROJECTION

Gratton is likely to score in the 20-goal range, and that appears to be his top end. Enough of the promise. That's the reality.

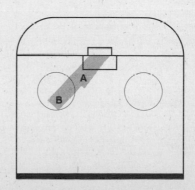

JOCHEN HECHT

Yrs. of NHL service: 3
Born: Mannheim, Germany; June 21, 1977
Position: centre
Height: 6-3
Weight: 196
Uniform no.: 20
Shoots: left

Career statistics:

GP	G	A	TP	PIM
220	48	70	118	136

1998-1999 statistics:

GP	G	A	TP	+/-	PIM	PP	SH	GW	GT	S	PCT
3	0	0	0	-2	0	0	0	0	0	4	0.0

1999-2000 statistics:

GP	G	A	TP	+/-	PIM	PP	SH	GW	GT	S	PCT
63	13	21	34	+20	28	5	0	1	0	140	9.3

2000-2001 statistics:

GP	G	A	TP	+/-	PIM	PP	SH	GW	GT	S	PCT
72	19	25	44	+11	48	8	3	1	2	208	9.1

2001-2002 statistics:

GP	G	A	TP	+/-	PIM	PP	SH	GW	GT	S	PCT
82	16	24	40	+4	60	5	0	3	1	211	7.6

LAST SEASON

Acquired from Edmonton for two draft picks in 2002. Second on Oilers in shots. One of five Oilers to appear in all 82 games.

THE FINESSE GAME

Hecht is a rangy forward who can handle all three forward positions. He is a good skater with a good passing touch, a playmaker more than a scorer. He plays with a straight-up stance that allows him to see everything. He stickhandles in close, and has a great move walking out from the corner or behind the net.

A very smart player with deceptive speed, Hecht will probably be a better winger since he isn't strong enough on draws to handle playing centre full-time. He is a tough read for opposing defencemen because he doesn't do the same thing every time. He is quite unpredictable: he might try to beat a defender one-on-one on one rush and the next time chip the puck into the corner or work a give-and-go. He uses a lot of play selections. Hecht is far from a reluctant shooter.

Hecht plays with drive. He doesn't quit. He's never going to be the big star on a team but he's going to be a big part of a team. Hecht was originally touted as a power forward when he broke in with the Blues but it's doubtful he will develop along those lines. Hecht is a guy who will show up to play every night. He can kill penalties and add depth to the Sabres.

THE PHYSICAL GAME

Physical play doesn't bother Hecht, but he doesn't initiate it. He has to get a lot stronger and learn to play in the dirty areas of the ice. He doesn't mind sticking his nose in. Hecht is well-conditioned and can handle 15-18 minutes of ice time a night.

THE INTANGIBLES

Hecht was part of the package that came to Edmonton in exchange for Doug Weight, which was pressure Hecht didn't need. He gets another fresh start in Buffalo. He's a underrated forward, the kind of guy you need to watch every night to appreciate.

PROJECTION

Hecht should consistently score in the 15 to 20-goal range and has some power-forward tendencies that could push him past that mark, if not this season then next.

DMITRI KALININ

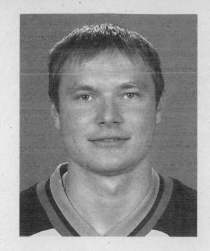

Yrs. of NHL service: 2
Born: Cheljabinsk, Russia; July 22, 1980
Position: defence
Height: 6-2
Weight: 198
Uniform no.: 45
Shoots: left

Career statistics:

GP	G	A	TP	PIM
58	2	11	13	26

2001-2002 statistics:

GP	G	A	TP	+/-	PIM	PP	SH	GW	GT	S	PCT
58	2	11	13	-6	26	0	0	0	0	67	3.0

LAST SEASON

Missed 18 games with thumb injury. Missed one game with flu; three games due to coach's decision.

THE FINESSE GAME

Kalinin is an excellent skater with good mobility and lateral movement. He has the ability to rush the puck out of the defensive zone, or make an outlet pass. Kalinin seems to make the right decision either way. He doesn't get panicky and is able to quickly make the proper decision.

Kalinin is smart and has a good grasp of the game. He is a hard worker, and he is consistent, especially for a younger player. Kalinin had to persevere through some injuries early in his junior career, and he seems to appreciate what it takes to hold an NHL job.

Kalinin has a decent shot from the point but he prefers to be a stay-at-home defenceman and it's not likely he will ever get too involved in the power play. He is a good penalty killer.

THE PHYSICAL GAME

Kalinin has good size and strength and is able to battle in a one-on-one situation. He takes the body well, but he isn't a huge hitter.

THE INTANGIBLES

Kalinin needs to become a little more consistent but he is assured a top four spot in Buffalo. Ideally, he will mature into a steady, everyday second-pair defenceman. He will probably have to beat out Jason Woolley for ice time.

PROJECTION

He should earn a full-time role and score 20 points.

JAY MCKEE

Yrs. of NHL service: 6
Born: Kingston, Ont.; Sept. 8, 1977
Position: left defence
Height: 6-4
Weight: 201
Uniform no.: 74
Shoots: left

Career statistics:

GP	G	A	TP	PIM
405	10	62	72	323

1998-1999 statistics:

GP	G	A	TP	+/-	PIM	PP	SH	GW	GT	S	PCT
72	0	6	6	+20	75	0	0	0	0	57	0.0

1999-2000 statistics:

GP	G	A	TP	+/-	PIM	PP	SH	GW	GT	S	PCT
78	5	12	17	+5	50	1	0	1	0	84	6.0

2000-2001 statistics:

GP	G	A	TP	+/-	PIM	PP	SH	GW	GT	S	PCT
74	1	10	11	+9	76	0	0	0	0	62	1.6

2001-2002 statistics:

GP	G	A	TP	+/-	PIM	PP	SH	GW	GT	S	PCT
81	2	11	13	+18	43	0	0	1	0	50	4.0

PROJECTION

McKee has become a regular as one of Buffalo's top two with Warrener, and he still has some upside. With a little more confidence, McKee is capable of a 20- to 25-point season.

LAST SEASON

Led team in plus-minus. Missed one game due to coach's decision.

THE FINESSE GAME

McKee has been studiously applying his skills to the defensive aspects of his game for so long now that the offensive part of the game — what little he had — has completely atrophied. He could be more of a two-way defenceman but seems to have found his comfort area in his own zone.

McKee is a strong skater, which powers his open-ice hits. He has good acceleration and quickness to carry the puck out of the zone. He gets involved in the attack because of his skating, but he doesn't have elite hands or playmaking skills.

He has sharp hockey sense and plays an advanced positional game. In Rhett Warrener, McKee has found a sympatico defence partner and this pair routinely handles the checking assignments against other teams' top forwards.

THE PHYSICAL GAME

McKee has good size and is wiry and tough, if a little on the lean side. He doesn't have much of a mean streak. McKee knows he has to hit to be effective. He just doesn't do it with much relish.

THE INTANGIBLES

McKee is never better than when he is paired with the fluid Warrener. McKee is one of the most valuable Sabres. He continues to mature as a player and as a leader.

TAYLOR PYATT

Yrs. of NHL service: 2
Born: Thunder Bay, Ont.; Aug. 19, 1981
Position: left wing
Height: 6-4
Weight: 220
Uniform no.: 24
Shoots: left

Career statistics:

GP	G	A	TP	PIM
126	14	24	38	74

2000-2001 statistics:

GP	G	A	TP	+/-	PIM	PP	SH	GW	GT	S	PCT
78	4	14	18	-17	39	1	0	2	0	86	4.7

2001-2002 statistics:

GP	G	A	TP	+/-	PIM	PP	SH	GW	GT	S	PCT
48	10	10	20	+4	35	0	0	0	1	61	16.4

LAST SEASON

Appeared in 27 games with Rochester (AHL), scoring 6-4-10 with 36 PIM.

THE FINESSE GAME

A powerful skater, Pyatt can without question skate at the NHL level.

He will be a goal-scorer — Pyatt has great hands. He is strong and he has a knack for the net. He has a good wrist and slap shot. Since Pyatt is usually so worried about the guy he was checking in his defensive role, he never felt very comfortable stretching himself offensively. He will.

Pyatt hustles and plays with energy. The Sabres liked him enough that at the end of the season he was sent out to protect a one-goal lead (on those rare occasions when the Sabres had one). He is strong along the wall and in the corners. He backchecks diligently.

THE PHYSICAL GAME

A willing hitter, Pyatt finishes his checks. He is very effective in traffic. Pyatt is very strong on his skates, well-balanced and tough to knock down. He will be a factor on the power play, since he willingly goes to the net to battle for rebounds, deflections and screens. He will fight if he has to.

THE INTANGIBLES

Pyatt was completely overmatched when the Islanders pushed him into the NHL right out of junior. Pyatt was still maturing physically and emotionally. The Sabres recognized this and sending him to the minors was a wise move. Pyatt is a good kid who was probably unsettled by the trade. It will probably work out best for him in the long run.

PROJECTION

Pyatt scored 10 goals in limited action last season. If he earns a full-time role, he should improve to 20 goals.

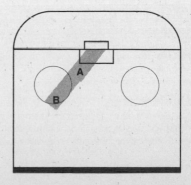

ERIK RASMUSSEN

Yrs. of NHL service: 4
Born: Minneapolis, Minn.; Mar. 28, 1977
Position: centre
Height: 6-3
Weight: 208
Uniform no.: 9
Shoots: left

Career statistics:

GP	G	A	TP	PIM
281	33	46	79	179

1998-1999 statistics:

GP	G	A	TP	+/-	PIM	PP	SH	GW	GT	S	PCT
42	3	7	10	+6	37	0	0	0	0	40	7.5

1999-2000 statistics:

GP	G	A	TP	+/-	PIM	PP	SH	GW	GT	S	PCT
67	8	6	14	+1	43	0	0	2	0	76	10.5

2000-2001 statistics:

GP	G	A	TP	+/-	PIM	PP	SH	GW	GT	S	PCT
82	12	19	31	0	51	1	0	3	0	95	12.6

2001-2002 statistics:

GP	G	A	TP	+/-	PIM	PP	SH	GW	GT	S	PCT
69	8	11	19	-1	34	0	0	2	0	89	9.0

PROJECTION

Rasmussen is losing ground to other Sabres prospects. If he doesn't pop with 40 points this season — production that is well within his scope — he may not get another chance.

LAST SEASON

Missed eight games with knee injuries. Missed three games with shoulder injury. Missed two games due to coach's decision.

THE FINESSE GAME

Big, tough and skilled, Rasmussen is the type of forward the Sabres have been waiting for. They're still waiting, because Rasmussen doesn't bring his "A" game to the ice every night, and injuries also chipped into his development.

Rasmussen doesn't have great hands, but he has good ones to complement a scoring instinct and a desire to drive to the net. He usually looks to make a play first; the Sabres will try to encourage him to make better use of his wrist shot. He also has a hard slap shot.

Rasmussen is a strong skater with a long stride. He has good balance and agility and is tough to knock off his feet. He needs to learn to play a full 60 minutes and not take any shifts off.

THE PHYSICAL GAME

Rasmussen is abrasive and annoying to play against. He isn't huge, but he is strong and willing to throw his weight around and get in people's faces. He competes hard and will lead by example. He is still learning that he has to play hard every night to stick.

THE INTANGIBLES

Rasmussen has been given every chance to win a top six job. He will turn 26 this season and isn't a kid anymore. This needs to be a breakthrough season for him.

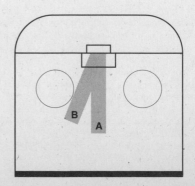

MIROSLAV SATAN

Yrs. of NHL service: 7
Born: Topolcany, Slovakia; Oct. 22, 1974
Position: left wing
Height: 6-3
Weight: 192
Uniform no.: 81
Shoots: left

Career statistics:

GP	G	A	TP	PIM
543	204	183	387	227

1998-1999 statistics:

GP	G	A	TP	+/-	PIM	PP	SH	GW	GT	S	PCT
81	40	26	66	+24	44	13	3	6	1	208	19.2

1999-2000 statistics:

GP	G	A	TP	+/-	PIM	PP	SH	GW	GT	S	PCT
81	33	34	67	+16	32	5	3	5	1	265	12.5

2000-2001 statistics:

GP	G	A	TP	+/-	PIM	PP	SH	GW	GT	S	PCT
82	29	33	62	+5	36	8	2	4	1	206	14.1

2001-2002 statistics:

GP	G	A	TP	+/-	PIM	PP	SH	GW	GT	S	PCT
82	37	36	73	+14	33	15	5	5	0	267	13.9

LAST SEASON

Led team in points for fifth season. Led team in goals, assists, power-play goals, shorthanded goals and shots. Tied for team lead in game-winning goals. Second on team in shooting percentage. Third on team in plus-minus. Third in NHL in shorthanded goals. Tied for third in NHL in power-play goals. One of five Sabres to appear in all 82 games.

THE FINESSE GAME

Satan has terrific breakaway speed, which allows him to pull away from many defenders. Satan will lapse into bad nights where he gambles and plays a riskier game, but he is a fairly conscientious two-way player.

Not shy about shooting, Satan keeps his head up and looks for his shooting holes, and is accurate with a wrist and snap shot. He sees his passing options and will sometimes make the play, but he is the sniper on whatever line he is playing and prefers to take the shot himself. One fault is his tendency to hold on to the puck too long.

Satan's biggest drawback is his lack of intensity, and with it, a lack of consistency. When he isn't scoring, he isn't doing much else to help his team win.

THE PHYSICAL GAME

Not being huge, and being the prime checking objective on a team that isn't exactly loaded with offensive options takes its toll on Satan at crunch time. With Buffalo's financial concerns, the burden is likely to get heavier on Satan before it gets lighter. Satan has a wiry strength, and shouldn't be as intimidated as he appears to be.

THE INTANGIBLES

Satan is still a bit moody and streaky to be thought of as a top-line sniper, and teams always seem to expect more out of him than they get. The big knock on Satan in the past was his playoff performance. The Sabres never got there last year. At $3.25 million (US), Satan would be a bargain anywhere else, and the strapped Sabres may find it worth it to ship him for some younger, cheaper players.

PROJECTION

Goals, goals, goals — forget playmaking. Satan wants to score. He was on the verge of another 40-goal season and if his teammates hadn't been decimated by injuries in the last quarter of the season he might have done it again.

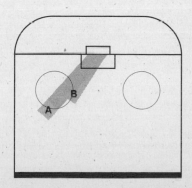

VACLAV VARADA

Yrs. of NHL service: 5
Born: Vsetin, Czech Republic; Apr. 26, 1976
Position: right wing
Height: 6-0
Weight: 214
Uniform no.: 25
Shoots: left

Career statistics:

GP	G	A	TP	PIM
332	39	94	133	303

1998-1999 statistics:

GP	G	A	TP	+/-	PIM	PP	SH	GW	GT	S	PCT
72	7	24	31	+11	61	1	0	1	0	123	5.7

1999-2000 statistics:

GP	G	A	TP	+/-	PIM	PP	SH	GW	GT	S	PCT
76	10	27	37	+12	62	0	0	0	0	140	7.1

2000-2001 statistics:

GP	G	A	TP	+/-	PIM	PP	SH	GW	GT	S	PCT
75	10	21	31	-2	81	2	0	2	0	112	8.9

2001-2002 statistics:

GP	G	A	TP	+/-	PIM	PP	SH	GW	GT	S	PCT
76	7	16	23	-7	82	1	0	1	0	138	5.1

LAST SEASON

Missed five games due to suspensions (three different incidents). Missed one game due to coach's decision.

THE FINESSE GAME

Varada seemed to be developing as a power forward, but he has yet to demonstrate the kind of scoring touch and desire to score that the role demands. When he is on, he plays with such intensity and reckless abandon that by the end of the game his face is cut and scraped, as if he had been attacked by crazed weasels.

With excellent size and great hands, Varada is wonderful with the puck — a superb stickhandler. He can also make plays, though his future is as a scorer. He has a good wrist and slap shot. He needs to be an involved player and not stay on the perimeter. He has a passion for scoring and drives to the net for his best chances. He handles himself well in traffic. He is a solidly balanced skater and an effective forechecker.

Varada has developed into a two-way forward with heavy emphasis on the defensive side of the puck.

THE PHYSICAL GAME

Varada is thick: thick arms, thick legs, thick thighs. He is much more powerful than he looks. He gives the Sabres some desperately needed size on the right side. He can be gritty and hard to play against. Varada needs to do that every night.

The biggest knock on Varada is his intensity level. If he brings his game up every night, he will be a star. There is plenty of room on this team for anyone who can put the puck in the net. Even a checking guy has to

score now and again. Varada hasn't found the same chemistry with any teammate since Michael Peca played his last game as a Sabre.

PROJECTION

Varada once looked like a 30-goal scorer but it looks as if even he has stopped believing that will happen. Ten to 15 goals would be an improvement.

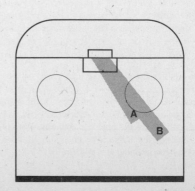

RHETT WARRENER

Yrs. of NHL service: 7
Born: Shaunavon, Sask.; Jan. 27, 1976
Position: left defence
Height: 6-1
Weight: 206
Uniform no.: 4
Shoots: right

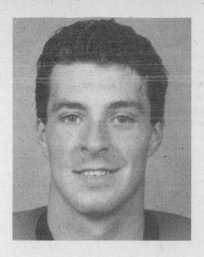

Career statistics:

GP	G	A	TP	PIM
433	13	47	60	597

1998-1999 statistics:

GP	G	A	TP	+/-	PIM	PP	SH	GW	GT	S	PCT
61	1	7	8	+2	84	0	0	0	0	44	2.3

1999-2000 statistics:

GP	G	A	TP	+/-	PIM	PP	SH	GW	GT	S	PCT
61	0	3	3	+18	89	0	0	0	0	68	0.0

2000-2001 statistics:

GP	G	A	TP	+/-	PIM	PP	SH	GW	GT	S	PCT
77	3	16	19	+10	78	0	0	2	0	103	2.9

2001-2002 statistics:

GP	G	A	TP	+/-	PIM	PP	SH	GW	GT	S	PCT
65	5	5	10	+15	113	0	0	1	1	66	7.6

LAST SEASON

Second on team in plus-minus. Third on team in penalty minutes. Missed 14 games with groin injury. Missed two games due to suspension. Missed one game due to coach's decision.

THE FINESSE GAME

Warrener's game is heavily slanted to defence. He has a foundation of good hockey sense, completed by his size and firm passing touch. He plays a simple game, wins a lot of the one-on-one battles, and sticks within his limitations. His defensive reads are quite good. He plays his position well and moves people out from in front of the net. He blocks shots, and he can start a quick transition with a breakout pass.

Warrener might struggle a bit with his foot speed. His turns and lateral movement are okay, but he lacks quickness and acceleration, which hampers him from becoming a more effective two-way defenceman.

He is smart. Warrener stepped up to become a reliable top-two defenceman last season, although he would probably be a second pair defenceman on a deeper team.

THE PHYSICAL GAME

He likes the aggressive game, but sometimes Warrener gets a little too rambunctious and gets out of position. However, that is to be expected from a player looking to make an impact. He's a solid hitter but doesn't make the open-ice splatters. Warrener is not a self-starter. He needs someone to stay on him about his conditioning and his effort.

THE INTANGIBLES

When Warrener is paired with a stay-at-home type like Jay McKee, he gets more involved in the attack. He can be the defensive partner, too, if he is teamed with a more offensive defenceman. Warrener doesn't seem to match up as well with any of the other Sabres blueliners as he does with McKee.

Warrener is an underrated player, one of those players who does so many little things well that you don't notice him until he's out of the lineup, which he was too frequently. He's a quiet leader for the Sabres and could be a future captain.

PROJECTION

Warrener won't win any Norris Trophies, but he can be a foundation defenceman who provides 20 points a year.

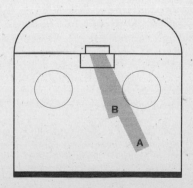

ALEXEI ZHITNIK

Yrs. of NHL service: 10
Born: Kiev, Ukraine; Oct. 10, 1972
Position: left defence
Height: 5-11
Weight: 215
Uniform no.: 44
Shoots: left

Career statistics:

GP	G	A	TP	PIM
744	74	273	347	843

1998-1999 statistics:

GP	G	A	TP	+/-	PIM	PP	SH	GW	GT	S	PCT
81	7	26	33	-6	96	3	1	2	0	185	3.8

1999-2000 statistics:

GP	G	A	TP	+/-	PIM	PP	SH	GW	GT	S	PCT
74	2	11	13	-6	95	1	0	0	0	139	1.4

2000-2001 statistics:

GP	G	A	TP	+/-	PIM	PP	SH	GW	GT	S	PCT
78	8	29	37	-3	75	5	0	1	1	149	5.4

2001-2002 statistics:

GP	G	A	TP	+/-	PIM	PP	SH	GW	GT	S	PCT
82	1	33	34	-1	80	1	0	0	0	150	0.7

LAST SEASON

Led team defencemen in points for second consecutive season. Third on team in assists. One of five Sabres to appear in all 82 games.

THE FINESSE GAME

Zhitnik has a bowlegged skating style that ex-coach Barry Melrose once compared to Bobby Orr's. Zhitnik is no Orr, but he was born with skates on. He has speed, acceleration and lateral mobility.

Zhitnik simply isn't an elite offensive defenceman, no matter how hard the Sabres try to pretend he is. It's like that Joan Cusack line from *Working Girl*. You can dance around in your underwear and sing, but it doesn't make you Madonna. Zhitnik's 34 points last season represented a pretty big contribution from him. One goal with all of the first-unit power-play time he gets is a little amazing, though.

Zhitnik needs to develop his lateral movement better, to use all of the blueline and stop his shots from getting blocked. He has a good, hard shot, and he keeps it low for deflections in front. He still likes to think about going on the attack before his own end is cleaned up, and will occasionally make the risky play. Overall, though, he plays defence reasonably well. He gets into position, takes away the passing lanes, and plays a strong transition game.

THE PHYSICAL GAME

Zhitnik plays sensibly and doesn't take bad penalties. His lower-body strength is impressive. He can really unload on some checks.

THE INTANGIBLES

With Richard Smehlik departed for Atlanta, Zhitnik will need to break in a new partner.

PROJECTION

Zhitnik's absolute top end is 40 points, but 35 (assist-heavy) is more reasonable.

CALGARY FLAMES

Players' Statistics 2001-2002

POS.	NO.	PLAYER	GP	G	A	PTS	+/-	PIM	PP	SH	GW	GT	S	PCT
R	12	JAROME IGINLA	82	52	44	96	27	77	16	1	7	2	311	16.7
C	22	CRAIG CONROY	81	27	48	75	24	32	7	2	4	1	146	18.5
C	37	DEAN MCAMMOND	73	21	30	51	2	60	7		4	1	152	13.8
D	53	DEREK MORRIS	61	4	30	34	-4	88	2		1		166	2.4
C	27	MARC SAVARD	56	14	19	33	-18	48	7		3	1	140	10.0
D	32	TONI LYDMAN	79	6	22	28	-8	52	1				126	4.8
D	25	IGOR KRAVCHUK	78	4	22	26	3	19	1		1		135	3.0
C	44	ROB NIEDERMAYER	57	6	14	20	-15	49	1	2	1	1	87	6.9
C	23	CLARKE WILM	66	4	14	18	-1	61		1			83	4.8
R	17	CHRIS CLARK	64	10	7	17	-12	79	2	1	4		109	9.2
C	40	SCOTT NICHOL	60	8	9	17	-9	107	2	1			49	16.3
L	18	JAMIE WRIGHT	44	4	12	16	6	20					64	6.3
L	10	DAVE LOWRY	62	7	6	13	-20	51	2	1	1	1	74	9.5
D	3	DENIS GAUTHIER	66	5	8	13	9	91		1	2		76	6.6
C	26	*STEVE BEGIN	51	7	5	12	-3	79	1			1	65	10.8
L	36	RONALD PETROVICKY	77	5	7	12	0	85	1		1		78	6.4
R	24	BLAKE SLOAN	67	2	9	11	-17	50					56	3.6
D	28	ROBYN REGEHR	77	2	6	8	-24	93					82	2.4
C	11	JEFF SHANTZ	40	3	3	6	-3	23	2				37	8.1
D	6	BOB BOUGHNER	79	2	4	6	9	170					58	3.5
L	16	CRAIG BERUBE	66	3	1	4	-2	164	1				34	8.8
D	8	PETR BUZEK	41	1	3	4	0	27					36	2.8
D	58	*STEVE MONTADOR	11	1	2	3	-2	26					10	10.0
L	20	JASON BOTTERILL	4	1		1	-3	2	1		1		4	25.0
C	15	*BLAIR BETTS	6	1		1	-1	2			1		4	25.0
C	19	OLEG SAPRYKIN	3				-2						9	
D	42	*MICKI DUPONT	2				0	2					2	
D	4	DALLAS EAKINS	3				1	4						
D	2	ALAN LETANG	2				-2							
L	39	*RYAN CHRISTIE	2				-1							
G	35	KAY WHITMORE	1				0							
G	29	MIKE VERNON	18				0							
G	1	ROMAN TUREK	69				0	4						

GP = games played; G = goals; A = assists; PTS = points; +/- = goals-for minus goals-against while player is on ice; PIM = penalties in minutes; PP = power-play goals; SH = shorthanded goals; GW = game-winning goals; GT = game-tying goals; S = no. of shots; PCT = percentage of goals to shots; * = rookie

STEVE BEGIN

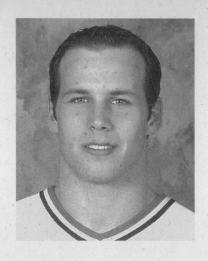

Yrs. of NHL service: 1
Born: Trois Rivieres, Que.; June 14, 1978
Position: centre
Height: 5-11
Weight: 190
Uniform no.: 26
Shoots: left

Career statistics:

GP	G	A	TP	PIM
73	8	6	14	141

1999-2000 statistics:

GP	G	A	TP	+/-	PIM	PP	SH	GW	GT	S	PCT
13	1	1	2	-3	18	0	0	0	0	3	33.3

2000-2001 statistics:

GP	G	A	TP	+/-	PIM	PP	SH	GW	GT	S	PCT
4	0	0	0	0	21	0	0	0	0	3	0.0

2001-2002 statistics:

GP	G	A	TP	+/-	PIM	PP	SH	GW	GT	S	PCT
51	7	5	12	-3	79	1	0	0	1	65	10.8

LAST SEASON

Missed nine games with shoulder injury. Missed six games with head injury.

THE FINESSE GAME

Begin is not overly skilled, but he is a team player first, and that may net him a roster spot on the Flames.

He could become a third-line player at best, although Begin will continue to be a fourth-line energy guy for the foreseeable future. He is versatile and can play any of the three forward positions.

Begin is strong in the corners. He will be one of those players who just skates up and down his wing. He will be a lot like Randy McKay was early in his career, although he doesn't have as much offensive upside as McKay because he is not as good a skater. His skating is NHL calibre but he lacks agility. He will get in on the forecheck and make his hits.

Begin doesn't have great hands or vision. He has a fairly heavy shot. Most of his goals will come from scaring people into giving him enough room and simply grinding it out around the net.

THE PHYSICAL GAME

A very rugged player, Begin is a throwback, a tough customer and a team man who will pay the price to win. He will come in and make his mark and keep other teams honest. His penalty minutes come from sticking up for teammates or to make a point. He is not an undisciplined player.

THE INTANGIBLES

Begin is a gritty depth guy.

PROJECTION

Players like Begin are an essential part of team chemistry. His points will be modest in a part-time role, but his penalty minutes are likely to be impressive.

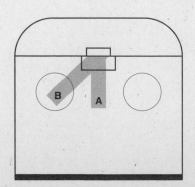

BOB BOUGHNER

Yrs. of NHL service: 7
Born: Windsor, Ont.; Mar. 8, 1971
Position: right defence
Height: 6-0
Weight: 203
Uniform no.: 6
Shoots: right

Career statistics:

GP	G	A	TP	PIM
466	11	32	43	1114

1998-1999 statistics:

GP	G	A	TP	+/-	PIM	PP	SH	GW	GT	S	PCT
79	3	10	13	-6	137	0	0	1	0	59	5.1

1999-2000 statistics:

GP	G	A	TP	+/-	PIM	PP	SH	GW	GT	S	PCT
73	3	4	7	-11	166	1	0	1	0	40	7.5

2000-2001 statistics:

GP	G	A	TP	+/-	PIM	PP	SH	GW	GT	S	PCT
58	1	3	4	+18	147	0	0	0	0	46	2.2

2001-2002 statistics:

GP	G	A	TP	+/-	PIM	PP	SH	GW	GT	S	PCT
79	2	4	6	+9	170	0	0	0	0	58	3.5

PROJECTION

Boughner will see third-pair ice time, add toughness and poise and maybe score a few points here and there.

LAST SEASON

Led team in penalty minutes.

THE FINESSE GAME

Boughner gets the most out of his talent. He's a defensive defenceman who plays a conservative game, but competes hard every night and maxes out his modest skills.

Boughner can still draw the occasional assignment against other teams' top lines, but Calgary has a good young starting four and Boughner gets to play in a comfortable role as a fifth or sixth defenceman. That puts him in a better position to succeed.

He doesn't have great hands, so Boughner doesn't get involved much in the offence. He doesn't (or shouldn't) try to make the first pass out of the zone. He has to be reminded to keep it simple and just bang the puck off the glass. Playing on a good-skating team like Calgary allows Boughner to make more low-risk passes and not try to do too much himself. He's a good fit here.

THE PHYSICAL GAME

Boughner is very aggressive and loves to hit. His teammates appreciate the way he pays the price and stands up for them.

THE INTANGIBLES

Boughner is surrounded by so many young defence-men that you have to hope his agent built a babysitting bonus into his contract. This is one of those steady, experienced character guys that always seem in such short supply and high demand. Boughner knows his role here and is willing to help.

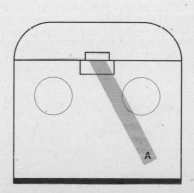

CRAIG CONROY

Yrs. of NHL service: 6
Born: Potsdam, N.Y.; Sept. 4, 1971
Position: centre
Height: 6-2
Weight: 197
Uniform no.: 22
Shoots: right

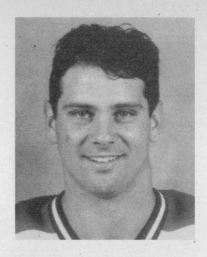

Career statistics:

GP	G	A	TP	PIM
467	88	146	234	257

1998-1999 statistics:

GP	G	A	TP	+/-	PIM	PP	SH	GW	GT	S	PCT
69	14	25	39	+14	38	0	1	1	0	134	10.4

1999-2000 statistics:

GP	G	A	TP	+/-	PIM	PP	SH	GW	GT	S	PCT
79	12	15	27	+5	36	1	2	3	0	98	12.2

2000-2001 statistics:

GP	G	A	TP	+/-	PIM	PP	SH	GW	GT	S	PCT
83	14	18	32	+2	60	0	4	2	0	133	10.5

2001-2002 statistics:

GP	G	A	TP	+/-	PIM	PP	SH	GW	GT	S	PCT
81	27	48	75	+24	32	7	2	4	1	146	18.5

LAST SEASON

Led team in assists. Tied for team lead in shorthanded goals. Second on team in goals, points and plus-minus. Tied for second on team in power-play goals and game-winning goals. Career highs in goals, assists and points.

THE FINESSE GAME

Conroy was a scorer at the minor-league level and college, but was pigeonholed as a defensive player when he got his first NHL break in the St. Louis system. He was so good at it that he became a Selke Trophy candidate, and it looked like he was doomed to being thought of as a one-dimensional player.

A trade to Calgary, a lot of confidence, and a guy named Jarome Iginla changed all that. Conroy's speed fit in well with Iginla (another good skater, Dean McAmmond, completes the trio). Conroy can play against other teams' top lines because he is so good defensively, but now he is also able to exploit top-line players whose own defensive awareness is far less keen than Conroy's.

Using his speed, size and anticipation, Conroy kills penalties well. He is a smart player who can make the little hook or hold to slow down an opponent without getting caught. He has quick hands and is good on draws. His hands are much better than the average checking centre's. He's reliable in all key situations: defending a lead, in the closing minutes of a period and killing penalties at crucial times.

THE PHYSICAL GAME

Conroy isn't mean, but he is tough in a quiet way. He uses his size well and accepts checking roles against elite players without being intimidated. He is relentless on every shift and has a great work ethic.

THE INTANGIBLES

Calgary coach Greg Gilbert coached Conroy in the minors and demanded a higher level of play from him. Conroy responded beyond anyone's expectations.

PROJECTION

Conroy went from 32 points in 2000-01 to 75 last season. We don't anticipate a 43-point improvement again. In fact, it might be hard for Conroy to come close to last year's numbers. Expectations will be higher, and Iginla has a contract to work out. Even so, 60 points would be a solid contribution.

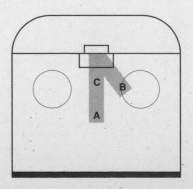

DENIS GAUTHIER

Yrs. of NHL service: 4
Born: Montreal, Que.; Oct. 1, 1976
Position: left defence
Height: 6-2
Weight: 210
Uniform no.: 3
Shoots: left

Career statistics:

GP	G	A	TP	PIM
232	11	19	30	303

1998-1999 statistics:

GP	G	A	TP	+/-	PIM	PP	SH	GW	GT	S	PCT
55	3	4	7	+3	68	0	0	0	0	40	7.5

1999-2000 statistics:

GP	G	A	TP	+/-	PIM	PP	SH	GW	GT	S	PCT
39	1	1	2	-4	50	0	0	0	0	29	3.4

2000-2001 statistics:

GP	G	A	TP	+/-	PIM	PP	SH	GW	GT	S	PCT
62	2	6	8	+3	78	0	0	0	0	33	6.1

2001-2002 statistics:

GP	G	A	TP	+/-	PIM	PP	SH	GW	GT	S	PCT
66	5	8	13	+9	91	0	1	2	0	76	6.6

LAST SEASON

Third on team in plus-minus. Missed six games with shoulder injury. Missed five games with strained oblique. Missed five games with facial injuries.

THE FINESSE GAME

Gauthier must be French for "keep your head up or I will take it off if you have it down." Gauthier is a powerful, fierce hitter. Anyone on the receiving end of a Gauthier check knows he has been rocked. He is especially good at catching people coming across the middle of the ice head down. Gauthier has the timing and the knack for it. One of his role models is Dave Manson. Another is Scott Stevens. Ouch. What Gauthier has to learn is to try not to kill someone on every rush, but to pick his spots better. There are times when a simple take-out is the right play.

A good skater, he is strong and balanced on his skates. Lower-body strength and speed power his hitting. He is capable of hitting in open ice because of his mobility. Gauthier doesn't mind hitting the big names, either.

Gauthier won't take off on many rushes. He prefers to skate the puck out of his zone or make the outlet pass or the bank off the boards. He is the epitome of a stay-at-home defenceman.

He is not quite as steady as he should be in terms of defensive reads and positioning, but he is maturing and improving.

THE PHYSICAL GAME

He doesn't fight, but Gauthier is a burr. He is always annoying people, always sticking his nose in and he'll be as snarly as David Spade while he does it. He is an agitator who always gets people worried about him, and he relishes going after other teams' stars. Gauthier is in excellent physical condition. He can handle a lot of ice time.

THE INTANGIBLES

Gauthier moved up into a top-four role with Calgary last season and is likely to stick there.

PROJECTION

Gauthier will have minor point totals and major penalty minutes.

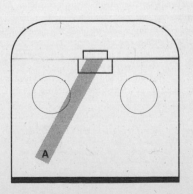

MARTIN GELINAS

Yrs. of NHL service: 13
Born: Shawinigan, Que.; June 5, 1970
Position: left wing
Height: 5-11
Weight: 195
Uniform no.: 23
Shoots: left

Career statistics:

GP	G	A	TP	PIM
895	231	237	468	563

1998-1999 statistics:

GP	G	A	TP	+/-	PIM	PP	SH	GW	GT	S	PCT
76	13	15	28	+3	67	0	0	2	2	111	11.7

1999-2000 statistics:

GP	G	A	TP	+/-	PIM	PP	SH	GW	GT	S	PCT
81	14	16	30	-10	40	3	0	0	0	139	10.1

2000-2001 statistics:

GP	G	A	TP	+/-	PIM	PP	SH	GW	GT	S	PCT
79	23	29	52	-4	59	6	1	4	0	170	13.5

2001-2002 statistics:

GP	G	A	TP	+/-	PIM	PP	SH	GW	GT	S	PCT
72	13	16	29	-1	30	3	0	1	1	121	10.7

LAST SEASON

Signed as free agent by Calgary on July 3, 2002. Missed seven games with a concussion. Missed three games with ankle injury.

THE FINESSE GAME

Gelinas plays a grinding game on the dump-and-chase. Much of his scoring is generated by his forechecking, with the majority of his goals tap-ins from about five feet out. He is strong along the boards and in front of the net. He is not a natural scorer, but he has good instincts and works hard for his chances. He is a good penalty killer.

Gelinas is ideally a third-line winger on a deeper team; with the Flames he will draw second-line duty. His lack of hockey sense and puckhandling prevent him from being a major factor in an expanded role.

Gelinas is an energetic player who provides momentum-changing shifts. He's not a goal-scorer, though, and gets into trouble when he starts thinking and playing like one. He can't help a power play much, although he will probably draw second-unit power-play time.

THE PHYSICAL GAME

Gelinas is a small player and seems to get himself into situations where he just gets flattened. He has very thick thighs, which power his skating and his body checks and his work in the corners. He isn't intimidated, but he does get wiped out of the play and he needs to be smarter about jumping in and out of holes, paying the price only when necessary.

THE INTANGIBLES

Gelinas left a Stanley Cup final team to sign with a team that has a long shot (at best) of even qualifying. Not all players grab for the bucks or the glory: Gelinas chose Calgary because his wife would be happiest with him playing there.

PROJECTION

Gelinas will certainly get the ice time, but 15 goals is about the best punch he can provide.

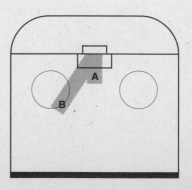

JAROME IGINLA

Yrs. of NHL service: 6
Born: Edmonton, Alberta; July 1, 1977
Position: right wing
Height: 6-1
Weight: 202
Uniform no.: 12
Shoots: right

Career statistics:

GP	G	A	TP	PIM
470	174	189	363	289

1998-1999 statistics:

GP	G	A	TP	+/-	PIM	PP	SH	GW	GT	S	PCT
82	28	23	51	+1	58	7	0	4	1	211	13.3

1999-2000 statistics:

GP	G	A	TP	+/-	PIM	PP	SH	GW	GT	S	PCT
77	29	34	63	0	26	12	0	4	0	256	11.3

2000-2001 statistics:

GP	G	A	TP	+/-	PIM	PP	SH	GW	GT	S	PCT
77	31	40	71	2	62	10	0	4	3	229	13.5

2001-2002 statistics:

GP	G	A	TP	+/-	PIM	PP	SH	GW	GT	S	PCT
82	52	44	96	+27	77	16	1	7	2	311	16.7

LAST SEASON

Won 2002 Art Ross Trophy as NHL's leading scorer. Won 2002 Rocket Richard Trophy as NHL's leading goal-scorer. Finalist for 2002 Hart Trophy. Led team and second in NHL in power-play goals. Tied for sixth in NHL in power-play points (30). Led team and fourth in NHL in shots. Led team in plus-minus and game-winning goals. Second on team in assists and shooting percentage. Only Flame to appear in all 82 games.

THE FINESSE GAME

There are breakout players, and then there is Iginla. His performance with the Flames was otherwordly. Opponents could focus all of their checking attention on Iginla, and this didn't stop him.

Iginla doesn't have great speed but he's smart and energetic. He is a savvy two-way forward, and made his way in the NHL on his defence first. The scoring touch came later, which is the reverse for most young players and is one of the reasons why he was able to step into the NHL with such success. He has a veteran's understanding of the game at a young age. We had our doubts that Iginla would become a great goal-scorer, but he proved us wrong.

Iginla does his best work in the corners and in front of the net. He is strong, and doesn't mind the trench warfare. In fact, he thrives on it. Iginla plays well in all three zones. He's a power forward who plays both ends of the rink, and there aren't many players with that description in the NHL.

Iginla played with Craig Conroy and Dean McAmmond as linemates last year. They're no all-stars, but they're swift and smart and they all clicked.

THE PHYSICAL GAME

Gritty, powerful and aggressive, Iginla will take a hit to make a play but, even better, he will initiate the hits. He has a mean streak and will have to control himself at the same time he is proving his mettle around the NHL — a fine line to walk, especially since teams target him now.

THE INTANGIBLES

Not only a terrific player, Iginla is cognizant of his duty as a role model. He conducts himself professionally off the ice as well as on. He is the best ambassador for the NHL since Wayne Gretzky.

PROJECTION

Iginla shot right past our expectations and now will face the burden of doing it all over again. Iginla was also a restricted free agent during the off-season. Calgary has to sign him, even if it means trading other players to afford him, and the Flames have to do it without having him miss training camp or the start of the season.

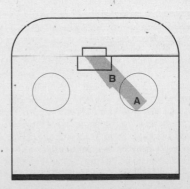

CHUCK KOBASEW

Yrs. of NHL service: 0
Born: Osoyoos, BC; Apr. 17, 1982
Position: right wing
Height: 5-11
Weight: 195
Uniform no.: n.a.
Shoots: right

Career statistics:

GP	G	A	TP	PIM
55	41	21	62	114

2001-2002 junior statistics:

GP	G	A	TP	PIM
55	41	21	62	114

LAST SEASON
Will be entering first NHL season. Appeared in 55 games with Kelowna (WHL), scoring 41-21-62 with 114 PIM.

THE FINESSE GAME
Kobasew is a two-way forward whose biggest asset is his brain. Anything else — his skating, hands, shot or size — fails to draw anyone's attention, but he's a smart player. His skating is NHL calibre, but not outstanding. Kobasew's effort is what will allow him to outskate lazier players.

Kobasew has decent hands in-tight around the net. He may turn into one of the most opportunistic scorers on the Flames. He is a dogged forechecker.

Few players this young step into the league (assuming Kobasew does this year) with as advanced an all-around game. He is sharp in all three zones. He knows what his defensive assignments are and finishes his checks. He will go into the corners.

Kobasew has been a good penalty killer in college and in junior. Calgary is likely to break him in gently, though, until he gets confidence in his NHL game.

THE PHYSICAL GAME
Kobasew isn't very big and he lacks a physical presence, but he's quietly tough. Kobasew wins a lot of puck battles simply because he wants it more than the other guy.

THE INTANGIBLES
The Flames are picturing Kobasew on a second line with Rob Niedermayer and free agent signee Martin Gelinas. Kobasew would have made the team out of training camp in 2001, but the Flames couldn't come to contract terms with him. Going for a year of junior (after playing for Boston College) was hardly the worst career move for him.

At every level he has played at so far, Kobasew has been a winner and a crunch-time player. You will notice him most in the last minutes of a game, whether his team needs to protect a lead or needs a goal. Scouts think he may develop along Jere Lehtinen lines, and he's got a little Adam Graves in him as well.

PROJECTION
If Kobasew can nab a top six job, it would be no shock to see him score 15 goals in his rookie season. He looks like a complete player.

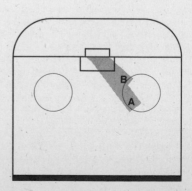

JORDAN LEOPOLD

Yrs. of NHL service: 0
Born: Golden Valley, Minn,; Aug. 3, 1980
Position: defence
Height: 6-0
Weight: 193
Uniform no.: n.a.
Shoots: left

Career statistics:

GP	G	A	TP	PIM
164	45	105	144	106

2001-2002 college statistics:

GP	G	A	TP	PIM
44	20	28	48	28

LAST SEASON

Will be entering first NHL season. Appeared in 44 games with University of Minnesota (WCHA), scoring 20-28-48 with 48 PIM.

THE FINESSE GAME

Leopold is a highly skilled offensive defenceman. He is a smooth skater with excellent balance and lateral movement. He has a small turning radius. Leopold likes to carry the puck but he will quickly learn he can't get away with the same things at the pro level that he did in college. The players here are more advanced, and the play happens much faster.

Leopold will adjust. He is poised and confident with the puck. If he doesn't rush it, he will be able to move it with an accurate pass. He has very good hockey vision and sense.

Leopold lacks a screaming point shot, but he has a quick release. He will probably develop into a point man who can quarterback a power play.

THE PHYSICAL GAME

Leopold does not have much of a physical presence. He plays a containment game and will outthink his opponents rather than outmuscle them.

THE INTANGIBLES

Leopold will start off the year in the minors, but with the Flames expected to move one of their top four defencemen at some point during the season, a slot is likely to open up soon. It will be hard for him to make the team with the defence that the Flames finished the season with. Calgary's top minor league coach is Jim Playfair, who has a sterling reputation as a teacher for young defencemen. Calgary would rather not put him in a sink or swim situation.

PROJECTION

The Flames are likely to start Leopold off conservatively, although within a few seasons he is likely to score in the 40-point range.

TONI LYDMAN

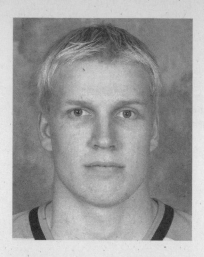

Yrs. of NHL service: 2
Born: Lahti, Finland; Sept. 25, 1977
Position: left defence
Height: 6-1
Weight: 200
Uniform no.: 32
Shoots: left

Career statistics:

GP	G	A	TP	PIM
141	9	38	47	82

2000-2001 statistics:

GP	G	A	TP	+/-	PIM	PP	SH	GW	GT	S	PCT
62	3	16	19	-7	30	1	0	0	0	80	3.8

2001-2002 statistics:

GP	G	A	TP	+/-	PIM	PP	SH	GW	GT	S	PCT
79	6	22	28	-8	52	1	0	0	0	126	4.8

LAST SEASON

Career highs in goals, assists and points.

THE FINESSE GAME

A good skater and puckhandler, Lydman should help make the Flames one of the most mobile defences in the league. He learned a lot from playing with Phil Housley when that veteran was with the Flames. Lydman is a very smart hockey player with good hockey sense and good positioning.

Lydman isn't exactly an offenceman. He is more of a two-way defenceman, more like ex-teammate Tommy Albelin — who has been one of the most underrated NHL journeymen — but Lydman is more highly skilled in all respects. He is very dependable both ways. He makes a good first pass. Lydman can jump into the play and has a good shot.

Occasionally Lydman tries to do too much, and the coaches have to remind him to get back to basics and make the simple plays.

Lydman seems to have the grit to compete on a nightly basis. He is a stronger, braver Calle Johansson.

THE PHYSICAL GAME

Lydman is a quiet competitor who won't run you over but won't get out of the way, either. He will battle until the end. He has decent size, is strong along the wall, and is a good enough skater to surprise an opponent with an open-ice body check, which he is not too timid to throw. Playing with Bob Boughner has inspired Lydman to add a physical element.

THE INTANGIBLES

Lydman initially had problems adjusting to North American hockey (smaller ice surface, the red line) but he has shown steady progress since recovering from a concussion. He can handle 20+ minutes a night as part of Calgary's young defence corps. You might not even notice him while he's getting the job done. Lydman will be an excellent complement to any high-risk offensive defenceman.

PROJECTION

Lydman can be a 30- to 35-point scorer this season.

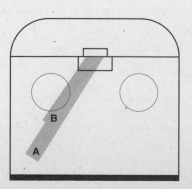

DEAN MCAMMOND

Yrs. of NHL service: 9
Born: Grand Cache, Alta.; June 15, 1973
Position: left wing
Height: 5-11
Weight: 200
Uniform no.: 37
Shoots: left

Career statistics:

GP	G	A	TP	PIM
540	108	171	279	326

1998-1999 statistics:

GP	G	A	TP	+/-	PIM	PP	SH	GW	GT	S	PCT
77	10	20	30	+8	38	1	0	1	0	138	7.2

1999-2000 statistics:

GP	G	A	TP	+/-	PIM	PP	SH	GW	GT	S	PCT
76	14	18	32	+11	72	1	0	1	0	118	11.9

2000-2001 statistics:

GP	G	A	TP	+/-	PIM	PP	SH	GW	GT	S	PCT
71	11	17	28	+3	43	2	0	1	0	112	9.8

2001-2002 statistics:

GP	G	A	TP	+/-	PIM	PP	SH	GW	GT	S	PCT
73	21	30	51	+2	60	7	0	4	1	152	13.8

LAST SEASON

Tied for second on team in power-play goals and game-winning goals. Third on team in goals, assists and point with career highs. Third on team in shots and shooting percentage. Missed eight games with rib injury. Missed one game with back injury.

THE FINESSE GAME

McAmmond's chief asset is his speed. He has excellent acceleration and quickness, and uses his speed to forecheck and force the play. He works the boards and the corners; he is effective in open ice as well because of his skating.

McAmmond is a give-and-go kind of player. He is most comfortable with forwards who like to play that style and not with forwards who like to hang on to the puck. Jarome Iginla and Craig Conroy made excellent partners. He uses his speed better when he doesn't have to try to figure out where his linemates are going with the puck.

McAmmond developed as a centre, so he uses all of the ice even when he is in his regular slot on left wing. He handles the puck well in traffic and has good vision to see developing plays. He is unselfish and passes well on the forehand and backhand. He also has a nice shot in-tight.

THE PHYSICAL GAME

McAmmond is feisty and aggressive. He isn't very big but he creates a ruckus in the offensive zone with his tenacity. He will stick his nose in just about anywhere and he can be irritating to play against. He drives to the net with authority, often right past bigger defenders.

THE INTANGIBLES

McAmmond was kicked around by a few teams (Edmonton, Chicago, Philadelphia). There were always forwards there better than him and, as a result, McAmmond was relegated to a third- or fourth-line role which he's really not good at.

PROJECTION

Last year we described McAmmond as a player destined to be on the move. It looks like he has finally found a home. He should score another 20 goals, 50 points.

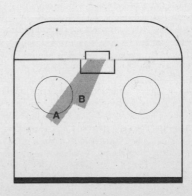

DEREK MORRIS

Yrs. of NHL service: 5
Born: Edmonton, Alta.; Aug. 24, 1978
Position: right defence
Height: 5-11
Weight: 200
Uniform no.: 53
Shoots: right

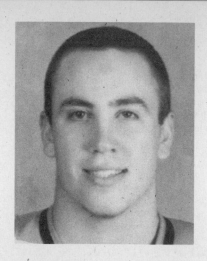

Career statistics:

GP	G	A	TP	PIM
343	34	129	163	385

1998-1999 statistics:

GP	G	A	TP	+/-	PIM	PP	SH	GW	GT	S	PCT
71	7	27	34	+4	73	3	0	2	2	150	4.7

1999-2000 statistics:

GP	G	A	TP	+/-	PIM	PP	SH	GW	GT	S	PCT
78	9	29	38	+2	80	3	0	2	0	193	4.7

2000-2001 statistics:

GP	G	A	TP	+/-	PIM	PP	SH	GW	GT	S	PCT
51	5	23	28	-15	56	3	1	4	0	142	3.5

2001-2002 statistics:

GP	G	A	TP	+/-	PIM	PP	SH	GW	GT	S	PCT
61	4	30	34	-4	88	2	0	1	0	166	2.4

LAST SEASON

Led team defencemen in points. Missed 21 games with wrist injury.

THE FINESSE GAME

Morris possesses all high-level skills, but what truly sets him apart from the other defencemen of his generation is his brain. For a young player, he has a real grasp of the technical part of the game. He is a thinker and understands hockey thoroughly. He could be a future All-Star.

Morris plays in all game situations, on the first penalty-killing unit and on the first power-play unit. He is a fan of Paul Coffey, and he possesses the kind of skating that brings to mind his role model. Morris is better defensively, however, and will become a better all-round player. He handles the puck well in an uptempo game and may develop into the kind of defenceman who can take over a game.

Morris needs only to improve his one-on-one play and get a little stronger to continue on the path to becoming an elite defenceman. He is occasionally prone to a defensive breakdown, but he learns from his mistakes.

THE PHYSICAL GAME

Morris has improved his stamina but needs to follow a serious strength and conditioning program. He is not very big, but he is strong. You can't run him over and he gets a lot of power from his legs for hitting and moving people out of the front of the net.

THE INTANGIBLES

Morris's name has been mentioned often in trade rumours. It had better be a sweet deal. Morris would be a top-two defenceman on almost any NHL team.

PROJECTION

As Morris continues to mature he will gain confidence in his offensive game without losing anything from his defence. There is a 60-point season in his not-too-distant future, if he can stay healthy.

ROB NIEDERMAYER

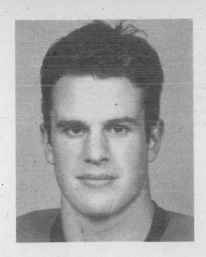

Yrs. of NHL service: 9
Born: Cassiar, B.C.; Dec. 28, 1974
Position: centre
Height: 6-2
Weight: 204
Uniform no.: 44
Shoots: left

Career statistics:

GP	G	A	TP	PIM
575	107	179	286	484

1998-1999 statistics:

GP	G	A	TP	+/-	PIM	PP	SH	GW	GT	S	PCT
82	18	33	51	-13	50	6	1	3	2	142	12.7

1999-2000 statistics:

GP	G	A	TP	+/-	PIM	PP	SH	GW	GT	S	PCT
81	10	23	33	-5	46	1	0	4	0	135	7.4

2000-2001 statistics:

GP	G	A	TP	+/-	PIM	PP	SH	GW	GT	S	PCT
67	12	20	32	-12	50	3	1	0	0	115	10.4

2001-2002 statistics:

GP	G	A	TP	+/-	PIM	PP	SH	GW	GT	S	PCT
57	6	14	20	-15	49	1	2	1	1	87	6.9

PROJECTION

Niedermayer's point totals will remain modest, probably around 40 points.

LAST SEASON

Tied for team lead in shorthanded goals. Missed 18 games with knee and ankle sprain. Missed four games with bruised hip.

THE FINESSE GAME

Niedermayer is an excellent skater, better even than older brother Scott (a defenceman for the New Jersey Devils). Big and strong, Niedermayer has the speed to stay with some of the league's best power centres, but he doesn't play a power game. Niedermayer has had some struggles with concussions, which were actually career-threatening, and it took away some of his inclination to play a physical style.

He is a strong passer and an unselfish player, probably too unselfish. He controls the puck well at tempo and can beat a defender one-on-one. He has started to finish better and play with much more authority.

Niedermayer is solid on face-offs. His speed and size down the middle are his biggest assets, especially down low in his team's defensive zone. He is a good two-way centre who needs to elevate his offensive game.

THE PHYSICAL GAME

Although not overly physical, Niedermayer has good size. He is an intelligent player and doesn't hurt his team by taking bad penalties.

THE INTANGIBLES

Niedermayer is a quiet team leader. The Flames didn't sour on him last season and he is likely to get the No. 2 centre's job.

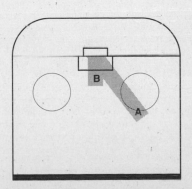

ROBYN REGEHR

Yrs. of NHL service: 3
Born: Recife, Brazil; Apr. 19, 1980
Position: left defence
Height: 6-2
Weight: 210
Uniform no.: 28
Shoots: left

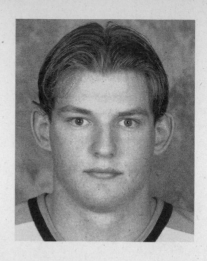

Career statistics:

GP	G	A	TP	PIM
205	8	16	24	209

1999-2000 statistics:

GP	G	A	TP	+/-	PIM	PP	SH	GW	GT	S	PCT
57	5	7	12	-2	46	2	0	0	0	64	7.8

2000-2001 statistics:

GP	G	A	TP	+/-	PIM	PP	SH	GW	GT	S	PCT
71	1	3	4	-7	70	0	0	0	0	62	1.6

2001-2002 statistics:

GP	G	A	TP	+/-	PIM	PP	SH	GW	GT	S	PCT
77	2	6	8	-24	93	0	0	0	0	82	2.4

LAST SEASON

Worst plus-minus on team.

THE FINESSE GAME

Regehr seems to have lost none of his skating ability after suffering past injuries to both of his legs. He has a good first step for a big guy; his skating is strong and well-balanced. He is defence-oriented, but with his heads-up passing and intelligence, he keys many breakouts that lead to scoring chances. He does not get involved in the rush himself. When parked on the point, he has a decent slap shot, but it is hardly his best skill, and it's not the reason why he's in the lineup.

Regehr seems to learn with each passing week about positioning, reads and dealing with the speed of the game. There are steps forward and back, and Regehr often had to sit out a game or a shift before finding his consistency again.

Regehr played in all defensive situations, five-on-five and killing penalties. He did not and will not see any power-play time. Regehr is still finding his way, and often plays like he's afraid to make mistakes instead of allowing his game to flow naturally.

THE PHYSICAL GAME

Regehr has NHL size. He's strong but not a fighter. He won't go out and try to beat people up, but he is tough to play against because he hits. He finishes his checks and pins players to the boards. He resembles a young Rod Langway. Regehr needs to be more aggressive, which will probably develop as he gains more confidence.

THE INTANGIBLES

Quite simply, Regehr is going to be a stud — a big, powerful, defensive defenceman and franchise foundation for years to come. He still needs polish and, at 22, is experiencing growing pains. He has the potential to be the next Adam Foote (coincidentally, Regehr was drafted by Colorado but went to Calgary in the 2000 Theo Fleury trade). If a trophy for the best defensive defenceman is ever created, Regehr will be an instant contender. Regehr is one of the first players opposing teams ask about when they come shopping in Calgary.

PROJECTION

Regehr will never score many goals. But he will prevent a lot of them from being scored. If he gets 10 points a season, that will be a high-end output.

MARC SAVARD

Yrs. of NHL service: 5
Born: Ottawa, Ont.; July 17, 1977
Position: centre
Height: 5-11
Weight: 184
Uniform no.: 27
Shoots: left

Career statistics:

GP	G	A	TP	PIM
309	69	133	202	192

1998-1999 statistics:

GP	G	A	TP	+/-	PIM	PP	SH	GW	GT	S	PCT
70	9	36	45	-7	38	4	0	1	0	116	7.8

1999-2000 statistics:

GP	G	A	TP	+/-	PIM	PP	SH	GW	GT	S	PCT
78	22	31	53	-2	56	4	0	3	1	184	12.0

2000-2001 statistics:

GP	G	A	TP	+/-	PIM	PP	SH	GW	GT	S	PCT
77	23	42	65	-12	46	10	1	5	2	197	11.7

2001-2002 statistics:

GP	G	A	TP	+/-	PIM	PP	SH	GW	GT	S	PCT
56	14	19	33	-18	48	7	0	3	1	140	10.0

LAST SEASON

Tied for second on team in power-play goals. Missed 15 games with knee injury. Missed 10 games with head injury.

THE FINESSE GAME

Savard's size and skating will prevent him from ever playing a dominating game. He is an intelligent play-maker whose points will always be heavier in assists than goals. He doesn't have a very quick or accurate shot.

Savard really has a knack for delivering the puck to a guy who can do something dangerous with it, instead of passing just because he's tired of carrying it. He possesses good vision and instincts for the power play. A left handed shot, he favours the attacking right-wing corner/half-boards for his "office." He will not even try one-on-one moves. He's a distributor.

Savard is not very quick off the mark and his speed is about average. He is pretty sturdy, well-balanced and strong on his skates, which makes his dives all the more comical. He is one of the most blatant actors in the game and draws a huge share of penalties. It's a wonder NHL referees haven't caught on to his act, because he's really terrible at it.

THE PHYSICAL GAME

Savard won't touch a soul with an intentional, clean hit. He is sneaky mean, however, and if he can, he'll pay you back. He is small and is targeted by a lot of bigger guys, so that's how he has learned to defend himself. He absorbs some pretty stiff hits without being the least bit intimidated. He is actually quite strong for his size. His defensive play will be limited to stick-checking.

THE INTANGIBLES

Injuries hurt Savard last season but his stock was already dropping in Calgary. He has lost a spot on the top three lines and might be traded.

PROJECTION

Savard won't get much playing time in Calgary, if he stays there. Best to think conservatively when assessing his production, although if he lands a job elsewhere and gets the ice time, he can score 50 points.

ROMAN TUREK

Yrs. of NHL service: 4
Born: Pisek, Czech. Republic; May 21, 1970
Position: goaltender
Height: 6-3
Weight: 215
Uniform no.: 1
Catches: right

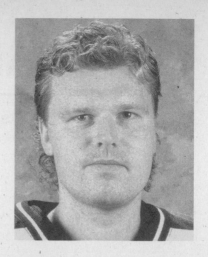

Career statistics:

GP	MIN	GA	SO	GAA	A	PIM
245	14242	530	20	2.23	7	16

1998-1999 statistics:

GP	MIN	GAA	W	L	T	SO	GA	S	SAPCT	PIM
26	1382	2.08	16	3	3	1	48	562	.915	0

1999-2000 statistics:

GP	MIN	GAA	W	L	T	SO	GA	S	SAPCT	PIM
67	3960	1.95	42	15	9	7	129	1470	.912	4

2000-2001 statistics:

GP	MIN	GAA	W	L	T	SO	GA	S	SAPCT	PIM
54	3232	2.28	24	18	10	6	123	1248	.901	6

2001-2002 statistics:

GP	MIN	GAA	W	L	T	SO	GA	S	SAPCT	PIM
69	4081	2.53	30	28	11	5	172	1839	.906	4

LAST SEASON

Fourth among NHL goalies in minutes played. Missed two games with knee injury.

THE PHYSICAL GAME

Turek not only gave his team a chance to win every night, but playing behind an inexperienced team, there were a lot of games when he had to win it himself.

Turek is one of the biggest, widest goalies in the NHL. And that's before he puts his pads on. Turek maximizes his size. He plays a hybrid half-butterfly, half-standup style. It's much like Martin Brodeur's, although Turek isn't quite as athletic as Brodeur. He is very good low, flaring out his legs to take away the bottom part of the net. And because he keeps his torso upright, he takes away the top part of the net. Turek doesn't have to go a mile out to cut down the angle on a shooter, and he is always confident he's in the right spot. He can play mind games with shooters as well as any goalie in the NHL.

He likes to handle the puck, and uses his stick very well. Turek takes away a shooter's options. He can get across the net quickly and use his flexibility and his big frame.

Turek seldom leaves bad rebounds. Pucks just seem to get absorbed in him. He is sometimes overly aggressive on plays around the net, though, so that when quick rebounds come, he is not always in position to recover well.

THE MENTAL GAME

Turek needs to feel like he is a No. 1 goalie, and Calgary gave him the chance. In fact, the Flames liked him well enough to sign him to a four-year contract extension just a few months into the season. That should reassure Turek.

THE INTANGIBLES

The Flames didn't find a suitable backup for Turek. Mike Vernon was used to being a top goalie and didn't care for the No. 2 role. Vernon didn't play well when he stepped in, and once Calgary lost confidence in him, Turek ended up being overplayed. Calgary needs to sign a goalie who is experienced, will be supportive, and will play well enough to get 20 starts but not make Turek feel threatened.

PROJECTION

Turek notched 30 wins with a Calgary team that got off to a hot start and then cooled off and missed the playoffs. Part of that had to do with Turek being worn down in the final quarter. He can get 30 wins again, and in fewer starts.

CAROLINA HURRICANES

Players' Statistics 2001-2002

POS.	NO.	PLAYER	GP	G	A	PTS	+/-	PIM	PP	SH	GW	GT	S	PCT
C	10	RON FRANCIS	80	27	50	77	4	18	14		5	2	165	16.4
R	24	SAMI KAPANEN	77	27	42	69	9	23	11		4	1	248	10.9
C	92	JEFF O'NEILL	76	31	33	64	-5	63	11		6	1	272	11.4
C	17	ROD BRIND'AMOUR	81	23	32	55	3	40	5	2	5	1	162	14.2
L	13	BATES BATTAGLIA	82	21	25	46	-6	44	5	1	2	3	167	12.6
L	26	*ERIK COLE	81	16	24	40	-10	35	3		2		159	10.1
D	22	SEAN HILL	72	7	26	33	0	89	4		2		145	4.8
C	63	JOSEF VASICEK	78	14	17	31	-7	53	3		3		117	12.0
L	23	MARTIN GELINAS	72	13	16	29	-1	30	3		1	1	121	10.7
D	5	MAREK MALIK	82	4	19	23	8	88					91	4.4
D	2	GLEN WESLEY	77	5	13	18	-8	56	1			1	88	5.7
C	15	KEVYN ADAMS	77	6	11	17	-5	43			2		108	5.6
D	6	BRET HEDICAN	57	5	11	16	-1	22			1		85	5.9
D	45	DAVID TANABE	78	1	15	16	-13	35					113	0.9
D	4	AARON WARD	79	3	11	14	0	74			2	1	69	4.3
L	11	JEFF DANIELS	65	4	1	5	-6	12		1			40	10.0
L	62	*JAROSLAV SVOBODA	10	2	2	4	0	2					12	16.7
L	20	DARREN LANGDON	58	2	1	3	2	106			1		12	16.7
D	7	NICLAS WALLIN	52	1	2	3	1	36					33	3.0
C	12	*CRAIG MACDONALD	12	1	1	2	-1						15	6.7
L	16	TOMMY WESTLUND	40		2	2	-8	6					29	
R	27	CRAIG ADAMS	33		1	1	2	38					17	
D	14	STEVEN HALKO	5		1	1	3	6						
C	21	JOSH HOLDEN	8				0	2					3	
D	48	*NIKOS TSELIOS	2				-2	6					3	
G	1	ARTURS IRBE	51				0	10						
G	80	KEVIN WEEKES	21				0							

GP = games played; G = goals; A = assists; PTS = points; +/- = goals-for minus goals-against while player is on ice; PIM = penalties in minutes; PP = power-play goals; SH = shorthanded goals; GW = game-winning goals; GT = game-tying goals; S = no. of shots; PCT = percentage of goals to shots; * = rookie

KEVYN ADAMS

Yrs. of NHL service: 3
Born: Washington, D.C.; Oct. 8, 1974
Position: centre
Height: 6-1
Weight: 195
Uniform no.: 15
Shoots: right

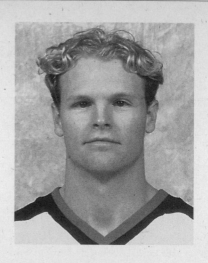

Career statistics:

GP	G	A	TP	PIM
213	22	37	59	143

1998-1999 statistics:

GP	G	A	TP	+/-	PIM	PP	SH	GW	GT	S	PCT
1	0	0	0	0	0	0	0	0	0	1	0.0

1999-2000 statistics:

GP	G	A	TP	+/-	PIM	PP	SH	GW	GT	S	PCT
52	5	8	13	-7	39	0	0	0	0	70	7.1

2000-2001 statistics:

GP	G	A	TP	+/-	PIM	PP	SH	GW	GT	S	PCT
78	11	18	29	+3	54	0	0	3	0	105	10.5

2001-2002 statistics:

GP	G	A	TP	+/-	PIM	PP	SH	GW	GT	S	PCT
77	6	11	17	-5	43	0	0	2	0	108	5.6

PROJECTION

Adams can contribute quality minutes as a third-line checking centre and role player. His top end is probably around 30 points.

LAST SEASON

Acquired from Florida on January 16, 2002, with Bret Hedican, Tomas Malec and a conditional second-round draft pick for Sandis Ozolinsh and Byron Ritchie. Missed one game due to travel (trade). Missed two games due to coach's decision.

THE FINESSE GAME

Originally a first-round draft pick by Boston (1993), Adams is a classic example of how time, patience — and expansion — can finally result in a pretty good living as an NHL journeyman. The Hurricanes, though, are Adams's fifth NHL team, which explains the "journey" part of that.

One of Adams's calling cards is as a good face-off man. The problem in Carolina is that they already have two top-five draw doctors in Rod Brind'Amour and Ron Francis, so he couldn't take over that specialist's role the way he has on other teams.

Strong on his skates, Adams gets involved in the high-traffic areas. He plays a very sound defensive game. He doesn't score much.

THE PHYSICAL GAME

Adams has good size but he is not imposing. He maximizes his strength by playing a quietly aggressive game, especially in his puck battles.

THE INTANGIBLES

Adams didn't click very well in Carolina in a third- and fourth-line role and could be on his way to NHL Team No. 6.

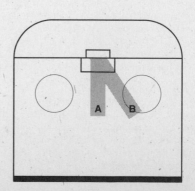

BATES BATTAGLIA

Yrs. of NHL service: 5
Born: Chicago, Ill.; Dec. 13, 1975
Position: left wing
Height: 6-2
Weight: 205
Uniform no.: 13
Shoots: left

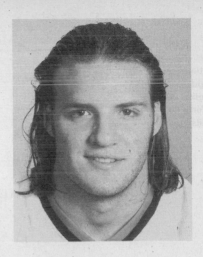

Career statistics:

GP	G	A	TP	PIM
332	58	73	131	191

1998-1999 statistics:

GP	G	A	TP	+/-	PIM	PP	SH	GW	GT	S	PCT
60	7	11	18	+7	22	0	0	0	2	52	13.5

1999-2000 statistics:

GP	G	A	TP	+/-	PIM	PP	SH	GW	GT	S	PCT
77	16	18	34	+20	39	3	0	3	0	86	18.6

2000-2001 statistics:

GP	G	A	TP	+/-	PIM	PP	SH	GW	GT	S	PCT
80	12	15	27	-14	76	2	0	3	0	133	9.0

2001-2002 statistics:

GP	G	A	TP	+/-	PIM	PP	SH	GW	GT	S	PCT
82	21	25	46	-6	44	5	1	2	3	167	12.6

LAST SEASON

Third on team in shots and shooting percentage. Career highs in goals, assists and points. One of two Hurricanes to appear in all 82 games.

THE FINESSE GAME

Battaglia is a good skater who is strong on the puck. He has had to drill hard to perfect most of his skills, because he is not a natural. His first strides are a bit sluggish, but he has a strong stride once he gets moving.

He goes hard to the net to create his scoring chances. He moves the puck alertly and plays smart positional hockey. He won't gamble or try to do anything fancy with the puck, which makes it easy for other grinders to play with him. He has a good head for the game, and the heart, too.

Battaglia is versatile and can play all three forward positions. He is a natural centre but will probably be used on the wing. He is skilled enough to take an occasional spin on one of the top lines with players like Ron Francis and Sami Kapanen, but he can't keep it up for long. A third-line role suits Battaglia just fine, although the 'Canes are a little weak on the left side and he may find himself in the top six.

THE PHYSICAL GAME

Battaglia has good size and is willing to use it. He works hard and his enthusiasm alone will bug other players. A Chicago native, he grew up emulating Jeremy Roenick. He'll never have Roenick's scoring touch, but he'll bring the nonstop work ethic of a young Roenick every night.

THE INTANGIBLES

Battaglia has a solid, 10-year NHL future in store as a third-line forward. He'll bring energy to every shift. He made a big jump going from college to the NHL and he is still finding his niche. He has relaxed into his role without assuming a comfort zone.

PROJECTION

Battaglia surpassed our 15-goal estimate for him last season. If he can provide 20 goals a season along with his customary spark, he will be one of the more valuable role players in the league.

ROD BRIND'AMOUR

Yrs. of NHL service: 13
Born: Ottawa, Ont.; Aug. 9, 1970
Position: centre / left wing
Height: 6-1
Weight: 202
Uniform no.: 17
Shoots: left

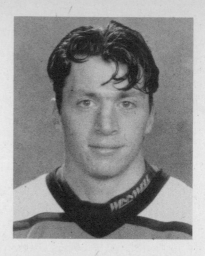

Career statistics:

GP	G	A	TP	PIM
983	325	511	836	811

1998-1999 statistics:

GP	G	A	TP	+/-	PIM	PP	SH	GW	GT	S	PCT
82	24	50	74	+3	47	10	0	3	2	191	12.6

1999-2000 statistics:

GP	G	A	TP	+/-	PIM	PP	SH	GW	GT	S	PCT
45	9	13	22	-13	26	4	1	1	0	87	10.3

2000-2001 statistics:

GP	G	A	TP	+/-	PIM	PP	SH	GW	GT	S	PCT
79	20	36	56	-7	47	5	1	5	0	163	12.3

2001-2002 statistics:

GP	G	A	TP	+/-	PIM	PP	SH	GW	GT	S	PCT
81	23	32	55	+3	40	5	2	5	1	162	14.2

LAST SEASON

Led team in shorthanded goals. Second on team in shooting percentage. Tied for second on team in game-winning goals. Missed one game with eye injury.

THE FINESSE GAME

Versatility and dependability are among Brind'Amour's trademarks. He is one of the best two-way centres in the league. He wins face-offs (he was second in the league according to NHL stats, with a winning percentage of 59.18). He checks. He has the strength, speed and stride to handle every defensive aspect of the game; the grit and desire to earn the loose pucks; the temperament and credibility to be on the ice in the last minute of a close game.

Brind'Amour may not beat many players one-on-one in open ice, but he outworks defenders along the boards and uses a quick burst of speed to drive to the net. He's a playmaker in the mucking sense, with scoring chances emerging from his commitment. He is a better player at centre than wing, and he likes playing the middle best, though he can handle either assignment.

Brind'Amour has a long, powerful stride with a quick first step to leave a defender behind; his hand skills complement the skating assets. He drives well into a shot on the fly, and has a quick-release snap shot and a strong backhand.

When Brind'Amour does not have the puck he works ferociously to get it back. An excellent penalty killer, and the centre the Hurricanes send out if they are two men short, Brind'Amour thinks nothing of blocking shots, despite the injury risk.

THE PHYSICAL GAME

A king in the weight room, Brind'Amour uses his size well and is a strong skater. He can muck with the best in the corners and along the boards. He will carry the puck through traffic in front of the net and battle for position for screens and tip-ins. He is among the hardest workers on the team, even in practice, and is always striving to improve his game. Brind'Amour isn't mean, but he is quietly tough.

THE INTANGIBLES

Brind'Amour is a coach's treasure because he can be deployed in any situation and will provide trustworthy work. He provides depth at centre behind the ageless wonder Ron Francis.

PROJECTION

Brind'Amour should again score in the 20-goal range.

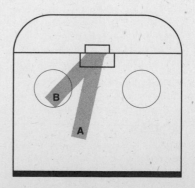

ERIK COLE

Yrs. of NHL service: 1
Born: Oswego, NY; Nov. 6, 1978
Position: left wing
Height: 6-0
Weight: 185
Uniform no.: 26
Shoots: left

Career statistics:

GP	G	A	TP	PIM
81	16	24	40	35

2001-2002 statistics:

GP	G	A	TP	+/-	PIM	PP	SH	GW	GT	S	PCT
81	16	24	40	-10	35	3	0	2	0	159	10.1

LAST SEASON

First NHL season. Tied for second among NHL rookies in assists. Fourth among NHL rookies in points and shots. Fifth among NHL rookies in goals. Missed one game with flu.

THE FINESSE GAME

Cole didn't get much attention in the Calder Trophy race. That's because, unlike Dany Heatley and Ilya Kovalchuk, Cole was able to save his best hockey for the most important time of the year — the postseason.

But even before the Hurricanes' magical run to the playoffs, Cole made an impact. He is a swift and sure skater with good agility. He goes into traffic with or without the puck. He is a good puckhandler.

Cole has a variety of shots, including an effective backhand. He works down low and behind the net and in all the dirty areas in order to score. Cole is versatile enough to play all three forward positions, although he is likely to succeed as a left winger. He can work both special teams.

The stats don't begin to tell the Cole story.

THE PHYSICAL GAME

Cole's greatest hits. No, it's not a CD, but the story of Cole's impressive rookie season. Until he wore down late in the playoffs, Cole was one of the most dynamic players on a largely veteran team. He needs to learn to improve his fitness level so that he can bring the same energy every night.

THE INTANGIBLES

Cole doesn't seem a likely candidate for a sophomore slump. Players who have a well-rounded game have a better chance getting through scoring slumps, since they can do many things to help their team win.

PROJECTION

Cole should move on up into the 20-goal range.

RON FRANCIS

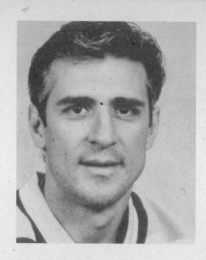

Yrs. of NHL service: 21
Born: Sault Ste. Marie, Ont.; Mar. 1, 1963
Position: centre
Height: 6-3
Weight: 200
Uniform no.: 10
Shoots: left

Career statistics:

GP	G	A	TP	PIM
1569	514	1187	1701	935

1998-1999 statistics:

GP	G	A	TP	+/-	PIM	PP	SH	GW	GT	S	PCT
82	21	31	52	-2	34	8	0	2	1	133	15.8

1999-2000 statistics:

GP	G	A	TP	+/-	PIM	PP	SH	GW	GT	S	PCT
78	23	50	73	+10	18	7	0	4	0	150	15.3

2000-2001 statistics:

GP	G	A	TP	+/-	PIM	PP	SH	GW	GT	S	PCT
82	15	50	65	-15	32	7	0	4	0	130	11.5

2001-2002 statistics:

GP	G	A	TP	+/-	PIM	PP	SH	GW	GT	S	PCT
80	27	50	77	+4	18	14	0	5	2	165	16.4

LAST SEASON

Led NHL in power-play points (42). Led team in assists, points, power-play goals and shooting percentage. Tied for second on team in goals and game-winning goals. Third on team in plus-minus. Tied for fourth in NHL in assists. Second in NHL in power-play assists (28). Missed two games due to coach's decision.

THE FINESSE GAME

Francis is a two-way centre who can still put some points on the board, especially with the manpower advantage. Technically, he is a choppy skater who gets where he has to be with a minimum amount of style. His understanding of the game is key because he has great awareness of his positioning. He gets loads of ice time, so he has learned to pace himself to conserve energy. There are few useless bursts of speed. He is one of the game's smartest players.

Francis is Dr. Draw. He ranked third in the NHL last season (59.18 per cent). On rare nights when he is struggling with an opposing centre, he'll tinker with his changes in the neutral zone, then save what he has learned for a key draw deep in either zone. Just as a great scorer never shows a goalie the same move twice in a row, Francis never uses the same technique twice in succession. He has good hand-eye coordination and uses his body well at the dot. Few players win their draws as outright as Francis does on a consistent basis.

When he focuses on a defensive role, Francis has the vision to come out of a scramble into an attacking rush. He anticipates passes, blocks shots, then springs an odd-man breakout with a smart play.

Francis doesn't have a screamingly hard shot, nor is he a flashy player. He works from the centre of the ice, between the circles, and has a quick release on a one-timer. He can kill penalties or work the point on the power play with equal effectiveness. He complements any kind of player.

THE PHYSICAL GAME

Not a big, imposing hitter, Francis will still use his body to get the job done. He will bump and grind and go into the trenches. Back on defence, he can function as a third defenceman; on offence, you will find him going into the corners or heading for the front of the net for tips and rebounds. He will be 40 this season. Francis keeps himself in great shape and is remarkably durable. The only two games Francis missed came when he was rested the last two days of the regular season. A wise move, considering the 'Canes' run to the finals.

THE INTANGIBLES

Francis could have peddled himself on the free agent market in the off-season. He decided to stay with Carolina.

PROJECTION

Just when you think that grey hair is a sign of age, Francis pops up with another +75-point season. We're going to lower the sights just a bit, to 65-70, since post-Cup hangover is likely to hit the Hurricanes.

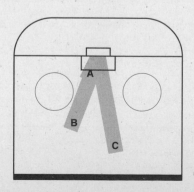

BRET HEDICAN

Yrs. of NHL service: 10
Born: St. Paul, Minn.; Aug. 10, 1970
Position: left defence
Height: 6-2
Weight: 205
Uniform no.: 6
Shoots: left

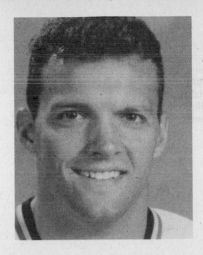

Career statistics:

GP	G	A	TP	PIM
645	37	156	193	554

1998-1999 statistics:

GP	G	A	TP	+/-	PIM	PP	SH	GW	GT	S	PCT
67	5	18	23	+5	51	0	2	1	1	90	5.6

1999-2000 statistics:

GP	G	A	TP	+/-	PIM	PP	SH	GW	GT	S	PCT
76	6	19	25	+4	68	2	0	1	0	58	10.3

2000-2001 statistics:

GP	G	A	TP	+/-	PIM	PP	SH	GW	GT	S	PCT
70	5	15	20	-7	72	4	0	1	0	104	4.8

2001-2002 statistics:

GP	G	A	TP	+/-	PIM	PP	SH	GW	GT	S	PCT
57	5	11	16	-1	22	0	0	1	0	85	5.9

LAST SEASON

Acquired from Florida on January 16, 2002, with Kevyn Adams, Tomas Malec and a conditional second-round draft pick for Sandis Ozolinsh and Byron Ritchie. Missed 14 games with fractured jaw. Missed seven games with back injury. Missed one game due to travel (trade).

THE FINESSE GAME

Hedican is among the best-skating defencemen in the NHL. He has a nice, deep knee bend and his fluid stride provides good acceleration; each stride eats up lots of ice. His steady balance allows him to go down to one knee and use his stick to challenge passes from the corners. He uses quickness, range and reach to make a confident stand at the blueline.

Hedican happily uses his speed with the puck to drive down the wing and create trouble in the offensive zone. He also varies the attack. He seems to prefer the left-wing boards, but will also take the right-wing route to try to make plays off the backhand.

He is a good enough stickhandler to try one-on-one moves. He is eager to jump into the play. He will never be a great point getter or playmaker because he doesn't think the game well enough, but he tries to help his team on the attack. He is a better player in the playoffs, when he doesn't think as much and lets his natural instincts rule.

Hedican knows that if an attacker beats him, he will be able to keep up with him and steer him to bad ice. He is the perfect guy to pick up the puck behind the net and get it to the redline and start the half-court game. He doesn't always just put his head down and go, either. He will move up the middle and look for a pass to a breaking wing, though he is guilty of some giveaways at the most inopportune times.

THE PHYSICAL GAME

Hedican has decent size but not a great deal of strength or toughness. He won't bulldoze in front of the net, but prefers to tie people up and go for the puck. He is more of a stick checker than a body checker, though he will sometimes knock a player off the puck at the blueline, control it and make a smart first pass. He prefers to use body positioning to nullify an opponent rather than initiate hard body contact.

THE INTANGIBLES

Injuries derailed Hedican last season, but he finished up well with Carolina after the trade and had a solid playoffs. Look for him in Carolina's top two pairing. His rebound came at the right time, since he was looking at free agency in the off-season and was rewarded with a new six-year deal with Carolina.

PROJECTION

Hedican hasn't taken the next step yet, and still has offensive upside. He should score around 30 points.

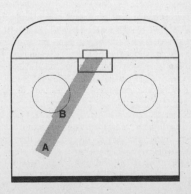

SEAN HILL

Yrs. of NHL service: 10
Born: Duluth, Minn.; Feb. 14, 1970
Position: right defence
Height: 6-0
Weight: 205
Uniform no.: 22
Shoots: right

Career statistics:

GP	G	A	TP	PIM
520	39	137	176	561

1998-1999 statistics:

GP	G	A	TP	+/-	PIM	PP	SH	GW	GT	S	PCT
54	0	10	10	+9	48	0	0	0	0	44	0.0

1999-2000 statistics:

GP	G	A	TP	+/-	PIM	PP	SH	GW	GT	S	PCT
62	13	31	44	+3	59	8	0	2	0	150	8.7

2000-2001 statistics:

GP	G	A	TP	+/-	PIM	PP	SH	GW	GT	S	PCT
48	1	10	11	+5	51	0	0	0	0	47	2.1

2001-2002 statistics:

GP	G	A	TP	+/-	PIM	PP	SH	GW	GT	S	PCT
72	7	26	33	0	89	4	0	2	0	145	4.8

LAST SEASON

Acquired from St. Louis on December 5, 2001, for Steve Halko and a fourth-round draft pick in 2002. Led Hurricanes defencemen in points. Second on Hurricanes in penalty minutes. Missed two games with groin injury. Missed two games due to travel (trade). Missed two games due to coach's decision.

THE FINESSE GAME

Some players just suit one team better than another. Hill was lured to St. Louis by free agent bucks in 2000, spent a frustrating season-and-a-half there, then was traded back to Carolina, where he's had his most success. In just 49 games with Carolina, he outscored every other defenceman on the team.

A good skater, Hill is agile, strong and balanced, if not overly fast. He can skate the puck out of danger or make a smart first pass. He learned defence in the Montreal system, but has since evolved into more of a specialty-team player. Hill couldn't get much power-play ice time in St. Louis behind Chris Pronger and Al MacInnis, but he does with Carolina.

Hill has a good point shot and good offensive sense. He likes to carry the puck and start things off a rush, or he will jump into the play. He can handle power-play time, but is not exceptional. He is more suited to a second-unit role, but he figures prominently in the 'Canes power play.

Hill's best quality is his competitiveness. He will hack and whack at puck carriers like an annoying terrier ripping and nipping your socks and ankles.

THE PHYSICAL GAME

For a smallish player, Hill gets his share of points by playing bigger than his size. He has a bit of a mean streak, and though he certainly can't overpower people, he is a solidly built player who doesn't get pushed around easily. Hill is a willing hitter.

THE INTANGIBLES

Hill was relatively injury-free after a few years when he was robbed of playing time, and that made a huge difference. He is a top-two defenceman in Carolina, which is way beyond his abilities.

PROJECTION

A poor-man's MacInnis, Hill brings a veteran's composure and an edge. He doesn't have elite skills, but he can chip in 25 points if he can manage to stay on ice most of the season.

ARTURS IRBE

Yrs. of NHL service: 9
Born: Riga, Latvia; Feb. 2, 1967
Position: goaltender
Height: 5-8
Weight: 190
Uniform no.: 1
Catches: left

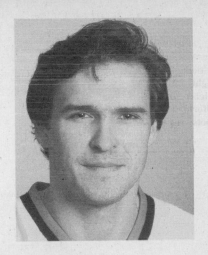

Career statistics:

GP	MIN	GA	SO	GAA	A	PIM
524	29618	1390	33	2.82	9	84

1998-1999 statistics:

GP	MIN	GAA	W	L	T	SO	GA	S	SAPCT	PIM
62	3643	2.22	27	20	12	6	135	1753	.923	10

1999-2000 statistics:

GP	MIN	GAA	W	L	T	SO	GA	S	SAPCT	PIM
75	4345	2.42	34	28	9	5	175	1858	.906	14

2000-2001 statistics:

GP	MIN	GAA	W	L	T	SO	GA	S	SAPCT	PIM
77	4406	2.45	37	29	9	6	180	1947	.908	6

2001-2002 statistics:

GP	MIN	GAA	W	L	T	SO	GA	S	SAPCT	PIM
51	2974	2.54	20	19	11	3	126	1282	.902	10

LAST SEASON

Highest goals-against average in four seasons.

THE PHYSICAL GAME

If you didn't know Irbe was a goalie, you might guess he was a gymnast — he has that kind of slender, muscular build. And if Mary Lou Retton played goal, she would probably play it as Irbe does: diving, rolling, scrambling and sticking the landing. Irbe is so flexible that when he does a split, he doesn't have to use his stick to cover what little five-hole is left. His, er, cup, is right on the ice. Teams have to try to beat him high.

Irbe is unbelievably quick. He has great confidence in his abilities and will challenge shooters by coming out well beyond his crease. He doesn't have great lateral movement, however. He does a lot of flailing, but like Dominik Hasek, Irbe never gives up on a puck until after it is in the net.

Irbe needs to improve on his work outside the net. He doesn't move the puck well and gets caught while he's making decisions. He can get mixed up with his defencemen.

Irbe has trouble picking up the puck through a crowd because of his small size. He will use his stick to whack some ankles. He is also vulnerable to crease-crashing, which is being called with less and less frequency.

THE MENTAL GAME

Irbe's unusual style matches his personality. He is quite outgoing and unpredictable. Irbe bounced back strongly after a couple of bad outings in the playoffs, when it seemed he would lose the No. 1 role to Kevin Weekes. Not a lot of goalies would be able to shake it off the way Irbe did.

THE INTANGIBLES

Irbe is not an elite goalie nor one who will take the 'Canes to the next level, but apparently Carolina is content to make do with him for now. Because of his age (36 in February), size and especially because of his active style, Irbe needs to be limited in his starts.

PROJECTION

Irbe's workload has been cut (wisely) — Weekes is a good backup. If last season and the playoffs were any indication, Irbe will get around 50 starts, 20 wins.

SAMI KAPANEN

Yrs. of NHL service: 7
Born: Vantaa, Finland; June 14, 1973
Position: right wing
Height: 5-10
Weight: 195
Uniform no.: 24
Shoots: left

Career statistics:

GP	G	A	TP	PIM
477	139	191	330	93

1998-1999 statistics:

GP	G	A	TP	+/-	PIM	PP	SH	GW	GT	S	PCT
81	24	35	59	-1	10	5	0	7	0	254	9.4

1999-2000 statistics:

GP	G	A	TP	+/-	PIM	PP	SH	GW	GT	S	PCT
76	24	24	48	+10	12	7	0	5	2	229	10.5

2000-2001 statistics:

GP	G	A	TP	+/-	PIM	PP	SH	GW	GT	S	PCT
82	20	37	57	-12	24	7	0	4	0	223	9.0

2001-2002 statistics:

GP	G	A	TP	+/-	PIM	PP	SH	GW	GT	S	PCT
77	27	42	69	+9	23	11	0	4	1	248	10.9

LAST SEASON

Led team in plus-minus. Second on team in assists, points and shots. Tied for second on team in goals and power-play goals. Career highs in goals, assists and points. Missed two games with back injury. Missed one game with hand injury. Missed two games due to coach's decision.

THE FINESSE GAME

Kapanen is one of the swiftest skaters in the league. He plays a smart small man's game. Kapanen is a skilled forward who is always moving. He handles the puck well while in motion, though like a lot of European forwards he tends to hold the puck a tad too long. He will shoot on the fly, however, and has an NHL shot when he does release it. He has a fine wrist shot and he can score off the rush.

Kapanen has quickness, good balance and good strength. He makes few mistakes. He knows where to be on the ice and how to use big players as picks and screens. He sticks to the perimeter until he darts into holes. He takes care of his defensive assignments, and even though he's too small to body check, he is able to harass opponents by lifting up a stick and swiping the puck. Kapanen is strong on the puck.

Kapanen uses a short stick to keep the puck in-close to his body. He loses a bit off his shot because of it, but he can create some great scoring chances with his passing because of his control. It also means defenders are forced to reach in for the puck, and that's when he's clever at drawing penalties.

THE PHYSICAL GAME

Kapanen plays without fear and draws a lot of penalties with his speed. He is lean without much muscle mass. He plays a spunky game and picks up the team on its quieter nights because he sprints to the pucks and tries on every shift.

THE INTANGIBLES

Kapanen is a clone of Montreal's Saku Koivu, except that Kapanen has been able to remain healthy. Kapanen is Carolina's most dangerous and most exciting player. His playoffs, though, were a major disappointment (one goal in 22 games). Except for that, Kapanen built a strong case to take into his off-season negotiations for his new contract (he was a restricted free agent after the season).

PROJECTION

If the Hurricanes ever get deeper to take some of the checking pressure off Kapanen, he could score 35 goals. Without it, his range is 25 to 30.

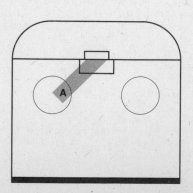

MAREK MALIK

Yrs. of NHL service: 5
Born: Ostrava, Czech.; June 24, 1975
Position: left defence
Height: 6-5
Weight: 215
Uniform no.: 5
Shoots: left

Career statistics:

GP	G	A	TP	PIM
307	17	58	75	275

1998-1999 statistics:

GP	G	A	TP	+/-	PIM	PP	SH	GW	GT	S	PCT
52	2	9	11	-6	36	1	0	0	0	36	5.6

1999-2000 statistics:

GP	G	A	TP	+/-	PIM	PP	SH	GW	GT	S	PCT
57	4	10	14	+13	63	0	0	1	0	57	7.0

2000-2001 statistics:

GP	G	A	TP	+/-	PIM	PP	SH	GW	GT	S	PCT
61	6	14	20	-4	34	1	0	1	0	72	8.3

2001-2002 statistics:

GP	G	A	TP	+/-	PIM	PP	SH	GW	GT	S	PCT
82	4	19	23	+8	88	0	0	0	0	91	4.4

LAST SEASON

Second on team in plus-minus. Third on team in penalty minutes. One of two Hurricanes to appear in all 82 games.

THE FINESSE GAME

Malik will never develop into the star the franchise once thought he could be, but at least he has progressed to becoming a top four defenceman, and for a time that was in doubt.

Malik is a good skater for his towering size, though he is a straight-legged skater and not quick. He uses his range mostly as a defensive tool and is not much involved in the attack. He has a fairly high skill level in all areas.

Malik is poised with the puck. He is a good passer and playmaker, and moves the puck out of his own end quickly. He won't try to do too much himself but will utilize his teammates well. He's big, but does a lot of little things well, which makes him a solid defensive player. He limits his offensive contributions to a shot from the point. However, he may yet develop better skills as a playmaker.

THE PHYSICAL GAME

Malik has begun to fill out his weedy frame to be able to handle some of the NHL's big boys one-on-one. Like Kjell Samuelsson, he takes up a lot of space with his arms and stick, and is more of an octopus-type defenceman than a solid hitter. He is strong in front of his net. He has some aggressiveness in him, but he is not a fighter.

THE INTANGIBLES

The biggest step Malik took last season was in his consistency. He took fewer nights off. He is starting to grasp the concept of the NHL game.

PROJECTION

Malik will be in the top four again and we would anticipate a slight improvement in production to the 25- to 30-point range, which is probably his top end.

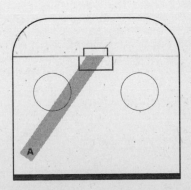

JEFF O'NEILL

Yrs. of NHL service: 7
Born: Richmond Hill, Ont.; Feb. 23, 1976
Position: centre
Height: 6-1
Weight: 190
Uniform no.: 92
Shoots: right

Career statistics:

GP	G	A	TP	PIM
524	154	167	321	454

1998-1999 statistics:

GP	G	A	TP	+/-	PIM	PP	SH	GW	GT	S	PCT
75	16	15	31	+3	66	4	0	2	0	121	13.2

1999-2000 statistics:

GP	G	A	TP	+/-	PIM	PP	SH	GW	GT	S	PCT
80	25	38	63	-9	72	4	0	7	0	189	13.2

2000-2001 statistics:

GP	G	A	TP	+/-	PIM	PP	SH	GW	GT	S	PCT
82	41	26	67	-18	106	17	0	5	2	242	16.9

2001-2002 statistics:

GP	G	A	TP	+/-	PIM	PP	SH	GW	GT	S	PCT
76	31	33	64	-5	63	11	0	6	1	272	11.4

LAST SEASON

Led team in goals for second consecutive season. Led team in game-winning goals and shots. Tied for second on team in plus-minus. Third on team in assists and points. Missed four games with back spasms. Missed two games due to coach's decision.

THE FINESSE GAME

O'Neill continues to be a study in frustration. Following his career year in 2000-01, there was great optimism that O'Neill had put all the pieces of the puzzle together. But still his intensity slacks off at times and he doesn't maintain an involved game.

An excellent skater, with balance, speed, acceleration and quickness, he has a good sense of timing and is patient with his passes. He doesn't have a big-time release but he has a decent one-timer. Now he has confidence in his shots, and is taking more one-timers and looking to shoot more, when in past seasons he thought "pass" first. O'Neill continues to improve in that area.

O'Neill likes to carry the puck down the left-wing boards to protect the puck, and with his speed he is able to blow by defencemen. He does not follow this move up by driving to the net. Defensively, he has to remind himself not to leave the zone before the puck does. He is often too anxious to counterattack before his team has control.

THE PHYSICAL GAME

O'Neill could always be in better shape. He is considered something of a soft player, whose effort and intensity don't come up to his skill level. O'Neill has been inspired by teammate Ron Francis to be a more consistent and dedicated player.

THE INTANGIBLES

O'Neill was taken off the top line when he started to slump in the playoffs. To his credit, he found chemistry with a new linemate, Josef Vasicek, and responded to the challenge. There is just something about O'Neill that makes you feel there's some gas left in the tank. Carolina liked what they saw, though, and re-signed him for two years.

PROJECTION

O'Neill is a consistent 30-goal scorer who could be a consistent 40-goal scorer. It's up to him.

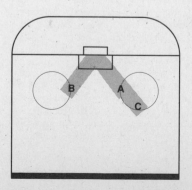

DAVID TANABE

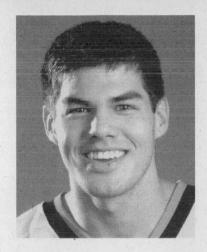

Yrs. of NHL service: 3
Born: Minneapolis, Minn.; July 19, 1980
Position: right defence
Height: 6-1
Weight: 190
Uniform no.: 45
Shoots: right

Career statistics:

GP	G	A	TP	PIM
183	12	37	49	91

1999-2000 statistics:

GP	G	A	TP	+/-	PIM	PP	SH	GW	GT	S	PCT
31	4	0	4	-4	14	3	0	0	0	28	14.3

2000-2001 statistics:

GP	G	A	TP	+/-	PIM	PP	SH	GW	GT	S	PCT
74	7	22	29	-9	42	5	0	1	0	130	5.4

2001-2002 statistics:

GP	G	A	TP	+/-	PIM	PP	SH	GW	GT	S	PCT
78	1	15	16	-13	35	0	0	0	0	113	0.9

LAST SEASON

Missed one game with flu. Missed three games due to coach's decision.

THE FINESSE GAME

Tanabe is a terrific skater who may turn into one of the best-skating defencemen of his generation. The only question mark is his hockey sense, because he doesn't seem to be able to make as many good things happen as he should. Tanabe is still young, but for the second straight season he was benched in the second half. Not being selected for the U.S. Olympic team was an additional distraction.

He can make a good first pass out of his zone or rush the puck end-to-end. He has a hard shot from the point. His defensive reads need a lot of work. Tanabe looks good on the power play, but he has to make a living at working five-on-five.

Tanabe has taken a page out of Scott Niedermayer's book. Like the highly skilled Devils' defenceman, Tanabe hustles back on defence after he has made an offensive-zone play. One thing Tanabe has to remember is never to lose momentum. When he keeps his feet moving, he can cover the entire ice surface effortlessly.

THE PHYSICAL GAME

Tanabe needs to improve his conditioning and his strength. He is built on the lean side, and is easily muscled off the puck. Tanabe has to be tougher to play through. He battles asthma and has to use an inhaler during games.

THE INTANGIBLES

Tanabe left college (Wisconsin) early for financial reasons, but in the long run it might hurt his hockey career. It would be a different story if he had been able to break into the league at 22 after three or four years in college. He is still getting past the shock of adjusting to the pro life.

Tanabe seems to want to be one of the best offensive defencemen of the next generation, but the development will not be instantaneous. There are growing pains still to come.

PROJECTION

With Sandis Ozolinsh traded to Florida, more offensive pressure was put on Tanabe and he didn't handle it well. Tanabe will be a top four defenceman with the Hurricanes and possibly a 35-point scorer.

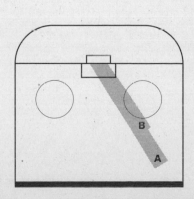

JOSEF VASICEK

Yrs. of NHL service: 2
Born: Havlickuv Brod, Czech Republic; Sept. 12, 1980
Position: centre
Height: 6-4
Weight: 200
Uniform no.: 63
Shoots: left

Career statistics:

GP	G	A	TP	PIM
154	22	30	52	106

2001-2002 statistics:

GP	G	A	TP	+/-	PIM	PP	SH	GW	GT	S	PCT
78	14	17	31	-7	53	3	0	3	0	117	12.0

LAST SEASON
Missed four games with knee injury.

THE FINESSE GAME
Vasicek is still in pursuit of consistency. Maybe you could just chalk it up to a sophomore slump. Or maybe it's a sign that someone needs to light a fire under him.

Vasicek is a good skater with good balance. He has good acceleration for a big guy and can get in quickly on the forecheck.

He has terrific hockey instincts, especially on offence. He has good passing skills and is more of a playmaker than a scorer. He doesn't shoot enough.

THE PHYSICAL GAME
Vasicek is tall and still filling out. He needs to use his body better because he could be much more of a physical factor. He doesn't initiate enough, and he can be intimidated.

THE INTANGIBLES
Vasicek is a quiet leader. He was named captain of his team in junior, which is a pretty rare honour for a European player.

PROJECTION
A slump, or the start of a negative trend? Vasicek wasn't much of a factor in the playoffs, so we're going to keep our prediction for Vasicek modest: 40 points, with an emphasis on assists.

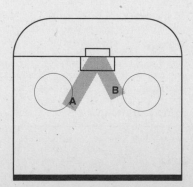

GLEN WESLEY

Yrs. of NHL service: 15
Born: Red Deer, Alta.; Oct. 2, 1968
Position: left defence
Height: 6-1
Weight: 205
Uniform no.: 2
Shoots: left

Career statistics:

GP	G	A	TP	PIM
1103	123	366	489	815

1998-1999 statistics:

GP	G	A	TP	+/-	PIM	PP	SH	GW	GT	S	PCT
74	7	17	24	+14	44	0	0	2	1	112	6.3

1999-2000 statistics:

GP	G	A	TP	+/-	PIM	PP	SH	GW	GT	S	PCT
78	7	15	22	-4	38	1	0	0	2	99	7.1

2000-2001 statistics:

GP	G	A	TP	+/-	PIM	PP	SH	GW	GT	S	PCT
71	5	16	21	-2	42	3	0	0	0	92	5.4

2001-2002 statistics:

GP	G	A	TP	+/-	PIM	PP	SH	GW	GT	S	PCT
77	5	13	18	-8	56	1	0	0	1	88	5.7

LAST SEASON

Missed five games with shoulder injury.

THE FINESSE GAME

Wesley simply isn't the 40-point player he was years ago in Boston. He is at best a No. 4 defenceman at this stage of his career. He has toiled in the one to two slot for Carolina because the team is so thin defensively, but if some of the younger plays like David Tanabe and Marek Malik continue to progess, it will allow Wesley to slide back in a lesser role and put him in a position to succeed.

Wesley has solid, but not elite, skills. He is very good with the puck. He clicks on the power play because he knows when to jump into the holes. He has good but not great offensive instincts, which means he thinks rather than reacts when gauging when to pinch, rush, pass the puck and back off. He is a decent skater who is not afraid to veer into the play deep; he seldom gets trapped there. He has a good slap shot from the point and snap shot from the circle.

You could count on two hands the number of times Wesley has been beaten one-on-one during his career, and there are very few defencemen you can say that about. He makes defensive plays with confidence and is poised even when outnumbered in the rush. He has to keep his feet moving.

THE PHYSICAL GAME

Wesley is not a bone-crunching defenceman, but neither was Jacques Laperriere, and he's in the Hall of Fame. We're not suggesting that Wesley is in that class, only that you don't have to shatter glass to be a solid checker, which he is. He's not a mean hitter, but he will execute a takeout check and not let his man get back into the play.

He is also sly about running interference for his defence partner, allowing him time to move the puck and giving him confidence that he won't get hammered by a forechecker.

THE INTANGIBLES

Wesley is a more relaxed player in Carolina, and is helping to break in some of the younger defencemen. He makes a steady partner for the more offensive-minded kids like Tanabe. Wesley is reliable and does his job with a minimum of fuss.

PROJECTION

At 34, Wesley is beginning his downward slide. He can be expected to score in the 20-point range.

CHICAGO BLACKHAWKS

Players' Statistics 2001-2002

POS.	NO.	PLAYER	GP	G	A	PTS	+/-	PIM	PP	SH	GW	GT	S	PCT
L	55	ERIC DAZE	82	38	32	70	17	36	12		5	1	264	14.4
C	13	ALEXEI ZHAMNOV	77	22	45	67	8	67	6		3		173	12.7
R	10	TONY AMONTE	82	27	39	66	11	67	6	1	4		232	11.6
C	92	MICHAEL NYLANDER	82	15	46	61	28	50	6		2		158	9.5
R	26	STEVE SULLIVAN	78	21	39	60	23	67	3		8	2	155	13.6
C	19	KYLE CALDER	81	17	36	53	8	47	6		3		133	12.8
D	6	PHIL HOUSLEY	80	15	24	39	-3	34	8		6	1	218	6.9
C	22	IGOR KOROLEV	82	9	20	29	-5	20		1	1		78	11.5
L	28	*MARK BELL	80	12	16	28	-6	124	1		1		120	10.0
R	12	TOM FITZGERALD	78	8	12	20	-7	39		2			125	6.4
D	42	JON KLEMM	82	4	16	20	-3	42	2		1		111	3.6
D	2	BORIS MIRONOV	64	4	14	18	15	68			1		129	3.1
D	7	LYLE ODELEIN	77	2	16	18	-28	93					86	2.3
L	32	STEVE THOMAS	34	11	4	15	0	17	3				66	16.7
D	25	ALEXANDER KARPOVTSEV	65	1	9	10	10	40		1			40	2.5
D	23	JOE REEKIE	55	2	6	8	-5	69					33	6.1
D	8	STEVE POAPST	56	1	7	8	6	30					48	2.1
L	17	MIKE PELUSO	37	4	2	6	-3	19			1	1	45	8.9
C	11	PETER WHITE	48	3	3	6	-8	10	1		1		21	14.3
C	39	*TYLER ARNASON	21	3	1	4	-3	4					19	15.8
L	24	BOB PROBERT	61	1	3	4	-9	176			1		33	3.0
R	14	RYAN VANDENBUSSCHE	50	1	2	3	-10	103					22	4.6
D	4	CHRIS MCALPINE	40		3	3	8	36					40	
R	15	JIM CAMPBELL	9	1	1	2	-3	4					12	8.3
D	45	VLAD CHEBATURKIN	13		2	2	0	6					8	
R	44	AARON DOWNEY	36	1		1	-2	76			1		10	10.0
L	16	MATT HENDERSON	4		1	1	-1						3	
D	5	STEVE MCCARTHY	3				-1	2					2	
L	20	*CASEY HANKINSON	3				-2						1	
G	29	STEVE PASSMORE	23				0	2						
G	41	JOCELYN THIBAULT	67				0	2						

GP = games played; G = goals; A = assists; PTS = points; +/- = goals-for minus goals-against while player is on ice; PIM = penalties in minutes; PP = power-play goals; SH = shorthanded goals; GW = game-winning goals; GT = game-tying goals; S = no. of shots; PCT = percentage of goals to shots; * = rookie

MARK BELL

Yrs. of NHL service: 1
Born: St. Paul's, Ont.; Aug. 5, 1980
Position: centre/left wing
Height: 6-3
Weight: 198
Uniform no.: 28
Shoots: left

Career statistics:

GP	G	A	TP	PIM
93	12	17	29	128

2000-2001 statistics:

GP	G	A	TP	+/-	PIM	PP	SH	GW	GT	S	PCT
13	0	1	1	0	4	0	0	0	0	14	0.0

2001-2002 statistics:

GP	G	A	TP	+/-	PIM	PP	SH	GW	GT	S	PCT
80	12	16	28	-6	124	1	0	1	0	120	10.0

LAST SEASON

First NHL season. Seventh among NHL rookies in goals. Tied for ninth among NHL rookies in assists. Second on team in penalty minutes. Missed two games with bruised hip.

THE FINESSE GAME

Bell experienced the expected growing pains in his first full NHL season. He was mentioned among the early Calder Trophy candidates before Christmas, but his play tailed off late in the season. He scored only two goals in the last 23 games. But there was still a lot to like.

Bell is all finesse. He is a terrific puckhandler and passer, a natural point-producer who is always looking to make things happen in the offensive zone. He has a hard slap shot and a strong wrister. He has good hand-eye coordination for tipping pucks in front of the net. He also has good hockey sense, good vision and good instincts — there is almost nothing negative about his offensive game.

Bell is a smooth, fluid skater who is very strong on his skates. He can put on a good burst of speed to beat a defender wide. He uses his speed to establish an aggressive forechecking game, and he can quickly make a turnover into a scoring chance.

His defensive game will need work, as will his proficiency on face-offs. He can be used to kill penalties.

THE PHYSICAL GAME

Bell was noted as a physical player in juniors. He is tall and strong and is still adding muscle. Last season he began playing with an edge again. He suffered two concussions several years ago and it might have taken him time to regain confidence in his physical play.

THE INTANGIBLES

Bell is coach Brian Sutter's kind of guy. Sutter will ride him hard when Bell doesn't deliver, but he will emerge a tougher, better player for it. Bell has a very bright future.

PROJECTION

Bell will probably continue to see most of his time on the third or fourth line, but he is projected as a top-two centre in the near future. He did well in his first season and should improve to 30-35 points.

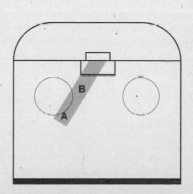

KYLE CALDER

Yrs. of NHL service: 2
Born: Mannville, Alta.; Jan. 5, 1979
Position: centre
Height: 5-11
Weight: 180
Uniform no.: 19
Shoots: left

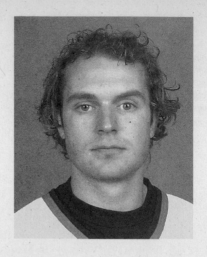

Career statistics:

GP	G	A	TP	PIM
132	23	47	70	63

1999-2000 statistics:

GP	G	A	TP	+/-	PIM	PP	SH	GW	GT	S	PCT
8	1	1	2	-3	2	0	0	0	0	5	20.0

2000-2001 statistics:

GP	G	A	TP	+/-	PIM	PP	SH	GW	GT	S	PCT
43	5	10	15	-4	14	0	0	1	0	63	7.9

2001-2002 statistics:

GP	G	A	TP	+/-	PIM	PP	SH	GW	GT	S	PCT
81	17	36	53	+8	47	6	0	3	0	133	12.8

LAST SEASON

Second on team in shooting percentage. Tied for third on team in power-play goals. Career highs in goals, assists and points. Missed one game with concussion.

THE FINESSE GAME

Calder has good offensive instincts. He is a heady player, too, and the defensive part of his game is pretty well advanced for such a young player.

He sees the ice well and finds the open man. Calder has a very nice scoring touch and has a lot of confidence in his shot. It's an accurate shot with a quick release, and he works hard to get to the high-percentage scoring areas.

Calder's skating is not great. It's NHL calibre, but it's something he is still going to have to work on. He is slippery, though, and a defender who thinks he has Calder corralled may be surprised when he wriggles his way out and finds open space for a shot.

THE PHYSICAL GAME

Calder is tough along the boards. He is small and needs to get a little thicker in his upper body to win puck battles and not get shoved out of the crease easily. He is gritty and has become more consistent in his effort, which was one of the knocks on him early in his career.

THE INTANGIBLES

Calder stepped up big time into the top six forwards for most of the season. Now he had to work to stay there. Tony Amonte's departure opens the door a little bit wider for him. Calder has a terrific work ethic and is a favourite with the coaches.

PROJECTION

Calder continues to progress and should retain his job on one of the top two lines. Calder should break through to 20-goal territory this season.

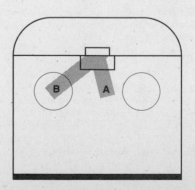

ERIC DAZE

Yrs. of NHL service: 7
Born: Montreal, Que.; July 2, 1975
Position: left wing
Height: 6-6
Weight: 234
Uniform no.: 55
Shoots: left

Career statistics:

GP	G	A	TP	PIM
527	200	143	343	160

1998-1999 statistics:

GP	G	A	TP	+/-	PIM	PP	SH	GW	GT	S	PCT
72	22	20	42	-13	22	8	0	2	3	189	11.6

1999-2000 statistics:

GP	G	A	TP	+/-	PIM	PP	SH	GW	GT	S	PCT
59	23	13	36	-16	28	6	0	1	1	143	16.1

2000-2001 statistics:

GP	G	A	TP	+/-	PIM	PP	SH	GW	GT	S	PCT
79	33	24	57	+1	16	9	1	8	2	205	16.1

2001-2002 statistics:

GP	G	A	TP	+/-	PIM	PP	SH	GW	GT	S	PCT
82	38	32	70	+17	36	12	0	5	1	264	14.4

LAST SEASON

Led team in goals, points, power-play goals, shots and shooting percentage. Career highs in goals, assists and points. Second on team in game-winning goals. Third on team in plus-minus. One of only five Blackhawks to appear in all 82 games.

THE FINESSE GAME

Although the most impressive thing about Daze is his size, it is his skating ability that sets him apart from other lumbering big men. He isn't a speed demon, but he skates well enough to not look out of place with faster linemates.

Daze keeps his hands close together on his stick and is able to get a lot on his shot with very little backswing. Daze's best weapon is his one-timer, which may be one of the most unstoppable shots in the NHL. Daze keeps his stick on the ice and always seems to be poised to take the shot. He has excellent hands for shooting or scoring, and is an adept stickhandler who can draw defenders to him and then slip a pass through to a teammate. He sets screens on the power play. He has good hockey vision and an innate understanding of the game. His defensive game has improved dramatically. He is now a very solid two-way forward.

Daze excels when he drives wide, protects the puck and takes it to the net. Very few defencemen can handle him when he does, but he frequently stops working and moving his feet. When he stands around rooted to one spot on the power play, he is useless. Daze played left wing most of the season and that is his preferred side, although he can play the right.

THE PHYSICAL GAME

Daze doesn't back down, but he doesn't show much initiative either. He is not a typical power forward. There will be the occasional night when he tries to run guys over, but those games are infrequent. He doesn't have the strength or the taste for it. Daze has a long reach — he can pass or shoot the puck even when a defenceman thinks he has him all wrapped up and under control. He doesn't have much of a mean streak.

THE INTANGIBLES

Of all of the players who will be affected by Tony Amonte's departure, Daze's name will be at the top of the list. He will draw nearly all of the checking attention now, and it will make his job that much harder.

Daze had a coming-out party of sorts at the NHL All-Star Game, where he was named MVP. For a player who hasn't gotten to enjoy much glory in his career, it made for a pleasant pat on the back.

PROJECTION

Daze could be a 40-goal scorer if he had a better supporting cast. That won't happen unless he is traded (which is quite likely to happen).

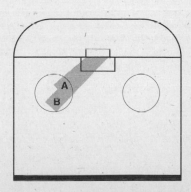

PHIL HOUSLEY

Yrs. of NHL service: 20
Born: St. Paul, Minn.; Mar. 9, 1964
Position: right defence
Height: 5-10
Weight: 185
Uniform no.: 6
Shoots: left

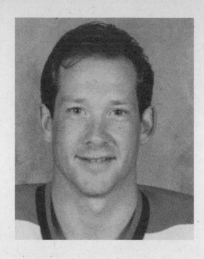

Career statistics:

GP	G	A	TP	PIM
1437	332	871	1203	796

1998-1999 statistics:

GP	G	A	TP	+/-	PIM	PP	SH	GW	GT	S	PCT
79	11	43	54	+14	52	4	0	1	0	193	5.7

1999-2000 statistics:

GP	G	A	TP	+/-	PIM	PP	SH	GW	GT	S	PCT
78	11	44	55	-12	24	5	0	2	1	176	6.3

2000-2001 statistics:

GP	G	A	TP	+/-	PIM	PP	SH	GW	GT	S	PCT
69	4	30	34	-15	24	0	0	0	0	115	3.5

2001-2002 statistics:

GP	G	A	TP	+/-	PIM	PP	SH	GW	GT	S	PCT
80	15	24	39	-3	34	8	0	6	1	218	6.9

LAST SEASON

Led team defencemen in points for fourth consecutive season. Second on team in power-play goals and game-winning goals. Third on team in shots. Became only fourth defenceman in NHL history to score 1,200 career points. Missed two games with concussion.

THE FINESSE GAME

If you have good wheels, you can last in the NHL forever, and Housley's skating fuels his game. He can accelerate in a heartbeat and his edges are deep and secure, giving him the ability to avoid checks with gravity-defying moves. Everything he does is at high tempo. He intimidates with his speed and skills, forcing defenders back and opening up more ice for himself and his teammates. He can continue to be an effective offensive weapon because he has barely lost a step over the years.

This is a player with an excellent grasp of the ice. On the power play he is a huge threat. His shots are low, quick and heavy, either beating the goalie outright or setting up a rebound for the forwards down deep. He also sets up low on the power play, and he isn't shy about shooting from an impossible angle that can catch a goalie napping on the short side.

Housley has great anticipation and can break up a rush by picking off a pass and turning the play into a counterattack. He is equally adept with a long headman or short cup-and-saucer pass over a defender's stick.

Defence remains this defenceman's weakness.

THE PHYSICAL GAME

Housley is not the least bit physical. He is not strong enough to shove anyone out of the zone, so his defensive play is based on his pursuit of the puck. He is likely to avoid traffic areas unless he feels he can get in and out with the puck quickly enough.

Success on a rush, even a two-on-one, against Housley is not guaranteed, since he is a good enough skater to position himself properly and break up the play with his stick.

THE INTANGIBLES

Housley is a power-play specialist and was brought back for another season because the 'Hawks would be offence-starved without him. They probably will be anyway. Housley was the chief reason why Chicago made the playoffs for the first time since 1998.

PROJECTION

Housley is as ageless as Ron Francis, and considerably less grey. He will continue to see first-unit power-play time and should reach 40 points again.

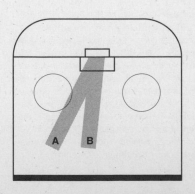

ALEXANDER KARPOVTSEV

Yrs. of NHL service: 9
Born: Moscow, Russia; Feb. 25, 1974
Position: left defence
Height: 6-3
Weight: 215
Uniform no.: 25
Shoots: left

Career statistics:

GP	G	A	TP	PIM
523	30	136	166	396

1998-1999 statistics:

GP	G	A	TP	+/-	PIM	PP	SH	GW	GT	S	PCT
58	3	25	28	+39	52	1	0	1	0	65	4.6

1999-2000 statistics:

GP	G	A	TP	+/-	PIM	PP	SH	GW	GT	S	PCT
69	3	14	17	+9	54	3	0	0	0	51	5.9

2000-2001 statistics:

GP	G	A	TP	+/-	PIM	PP	SH	GW	GT	S	PCT
53	2	13	15	-4	39	1	0	0	0	52	3.8

2001-2002 statistics:

GP	G	A	TP	+/-	PIM	PP	SH	GW	GT	S	PCT
65	1	9	10	+10	40	0	1	0	0	40	2.5

LAST SEASON

Missed seven games with arthoscopic knee surgery. Missed three games with bruised ribs. Missed three games with groin injury. Missed two games with sprained knee. Missed one game with sprained ankle. Missed one game due to personal reasons.

THE FINESSE GAME

Ask Karpovtsev, "What did you have for dinner last night, Alex?" and he is likely to answer, "Pucks." If there were a shot-blocking contest at the NHL All-Star Game, Karpovtsev would be reigning champ. It's one of the reasons why he misses so much playing time — many of his injuries result from his shot-blocking attempts.

Karpovtsev has decent puck-carrying skills and the good sense to move the puck quickly, but displays the defensive defenceman's mindset of getting to the redline and dumping the puck into the corner or making a short outlet pass. Under pressure behind his net, he tends to whack the puck around the boards, a play that often gets picked off.

The strength of Karpovtsev's skating game is best reflected in his terrific lateral movement. He covers acres of ground with a huge stride and a long reach, has excellent balance, turns nicely in both directions and boasts a fair amount of quickness and agility. He has a quick first step to the puck.

Karpovtsev does show, at times, a good instinct for seeing a better passing option than the obvious in the attacking zone. He has an effective, hard shot from the point, and his accuracy has improved.

THE PHYSICAL GAME

A crease clearer and shot-blocker, Karpovtsev is far more comfortable and poised in front of his net than when he chases to the corners or sideboards. Once he gets away from the slot, with or without the puck, he loses either confidence or focus or both, which can lead to unforced errors or turnovers. Still, he is an effective weapon against a power forward. He can tie up the guy in front, lean on him, and hit and skate.

Karpovtsev has become increasingly fragile and less willing to throw his body at other people. He still seems perfectly willing to hurl himself in front of shots, but he's either very unlucky or not very good at timing his slides. The puck is supposed to hit his equipment, not bone or a vital organ.

THE INTANGIBLES

Karpovtsev is useful enough when he plays, but his attitude and his tendency to miss so many games would put him atop our "To Trade" list.

PROJECTION

Here is a prediction: Karpovtsev's number of games missed will be higher than his points scored.

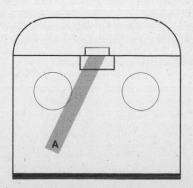

JON KLEMM

Yrs. of NHL service: 7
Born: Cranbrook, B.C.; Jan. 8, 1970
Position: right defence
Height: 6-3
Weight: 200
Uniform no.: 42
Shoots: right

Career statistics:

GP	G	A	TP	PIM
490	33	72	105	254

1998-1999 statistics:

GP	G	A	TP	+/-	PIM	PP	SH	GW	GT	S	PCT
39	1	2	3	+4	31	0	0	0	0	28	3.6

1999-2000 statistics:

GP	G	A	TP	+/-	PIM	PP	SH	GW	GT	S	PCT
73	5	7	12	+26	34	0	0	0	0	64	7.8

2000-2001 statistics:

GP	G	A	TP	+/-	PIM	PP	SH	GW	GT	S	PCT
78	4	11	15	+22	54	2	0	2	0	97	4.1

2001-2002 statistics:

GP	G	A	TP	+/-	PIM	PP	SH	GW	GT	S	PCT
82	4	16	20	-3	42	2	0	1	0	111	3.6

LAST SEASON

One of five Blackhawks to appear in all 82 games.

THE FINESSE GAME

Who could have guessed that the smartest off-season signing of 2001 wouldn't be one of the glossy star free agents available, but this quiet, underrated defenceman out of the powerful Colorado organization? Klemm is hardly a No. 1 defenceman, but that is how the 'Hawks utilized him, and Klemm was able to provide stability and instill confidence in his teammates from his first game with his new team.

Klemm's finesse skills are good enough that he can be used up front in a pinch. His defensive skills are good enough that he can be paired with a high-risk offensive defenceman, either a young kid or a more experienced roamer.

Klemm is an all-purpose defenceman who does everything the team asks of him. His skating is average, but he plays within his limitations. When he's moved up front, he fills the role of a grinding winger. On defence, he is as steady and low-risk as they come, without doing anything truly special.

THE PHYSICAL GAME

Klemm doesn't go looking for hits. He eliminates his man but doesn't have the explosive drive from his legs to make powerful highlight hits. Klemm stays in good condition and handled a lot of ice time last season (he averaged 23:50) without breaking down.

THE INTANGIBLES

Klemm is a sportswriter's nightmare because he's so quiet, yet he's appreciated by his coaches and teammates for his willingness to do anything for the team. It looked like Klemm was going to be in over his head on the Blackhawks, but he never looked fazed by the challenge.

PROJECTION

Klemm can give you a reliable performance on defence game after game and produce 20 points.

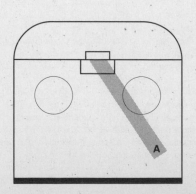

BORIS MIRONOV

Yrs. of NHL service: 10
Born: Moscow, Russia; March 21, 1972
Position: right defence
Height: 6-3
Weight: 223
Uniform no.: 2
Shoots: right

Career statistics:

GP	G	A	TP	PIM
585	67	208	275	749

1998-1999 statistics:

GP	G	A	TP	+/-	PIM	PP	SH	GW	GT	S	PCT
75	11	38	49	+13	131	5	0	4	1	173	6.4

1999-2000 statistics:

GP	G	A	TP	+/-	PIM	PP	SH	GW	GT	S	PCT
58	9	28	37	-3	72	4	2	1	1	144	6.3

2000-2001 statistics:

GP	G	A	TP	+/-	PIM	PP	SH	GW	GT	S	PCT
66	5	17	22	-14	42	3	0	0	0	143	3.5

2001-2002 statistics:

GP	G	A	TP	+/-	PIM	PP	SH	GW	GT	S	PCT
64	4	14	18	+15	68	0	0	1	0	129	3.1

LAST SEASON

Missed nine games with dislocated shoulder. Missed five games with groin injury. Missed three games with pulled muscle in side.

THE FINESSE GAME

Mironov has a huge slap shot and is a good puckhandler as well, so he can start a rush out of his own zone and finish things up at the other end. He has improved the release on his shot and sets things up well from the point with his passing.

Mironov has improved his defensive play to the stage where he belongs as part of a team's top defence against other teams' top lines. He uses his size well to protect the puck. He has made his game easier by allowing the play to come to him, instead of trying to make too many things happen by himself.

He helps his team most with his ability to carry or pass the puck out of his own zone. Attacking teams have to back off their forecheck, because he will start his team on a breakout and jump into the play to create an odd-man rush.

The major problem with Mironov is that there are too many nights where he's not in the mood to do any or all of the above.

THE PHYSICAL GAME

Mironov is big and mobile. He isn't a thumper, but he's strong and eliminates people. He handles a lot of minutes (averaged 22:43 last season). Mironov also gets hurt a lot. In the last three seasons, he has failed to play more than 66 games a year.

THE INTANGIBLES

Mironov is far too inconsistent to play the kind of prominent role Chicago needs him for. Mironov had a nice recovery season and, if the Blackhawks are smart, they will deal him before he gets hurt again or before a rival GM reads this book.

PROJECTION

Mironov has the skills to score in the 60-point range. We're not sure he has the desire. He seems to be much happier scoring 20 points and not raising people's expectations.

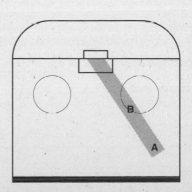

MICHAEL NYLANDER

Yrs. of NHL service: 9
Born: Stockholm, Sweden; Oct. 3, 1972
Position: centre
Height: 6-1
Weight: 195
Uniform no.: 92
Shoots: left

Career statistics:

GP	G	A	TP	PIM
550	122	251	373	232

1998-1999 statistics:

GP	G	A	TP	+/-	PIM	PP	SH	GW	GT	S	PCT
33	4	10	14	-9	8	1	0	0	0	33	12.1

1999-2000 statistics:

GP	G	A	TP	+/-	PIM	PP	SH	GW	GT	S	PCT
77	24	30	54	+6	30	5	0	2	0	122	19.7

2000-2001 statistics:

GP	G	A	TP	+/-	PIM	PP	SH	GW	GT	S	PCT
82	25	39	64	+7	32	4	0	5	0	176	14.2

2001-2002 statistics:

GP	G	A	TP	+/-	PIM	PP	SH	GW	GT	S	PCT
82	15	46	61	+28	50	6	0	2	0	158	9.5

LAST SEASON

Led team in assists and plus-minus. Career high in assists. Tied for third on team in game-winning goals. One of five Blackhawks to appear in all 82 games.

THE FINESSE GAME

Nylander's point production has never reflected his high skill level: he can do things with the puck that are magical. He knows all about time and space. If anything, he is guilty of hanging on to the puck too long and passing up quality shots, as he tries to force a pass to a teammate who is in a worse scoring position than Nylander is.

An open-ice player, Nylander is an excellent skater and composed with the puck. He's strictly a one-way forward. He needs to play with finishers, but also needs a safety-valve winger who is defensively alert.

Nylander was probably Chicago's best forward from after the Olympic break through the playoff stretch drive. He has established good rapport with the overachieving Steve Sullivan.

THE PHYSICAL GAME

Nylander is on the small side and plays even smaller. He uses his body to protect the puck but he won't fight hard for possession.

THE INTANGIBLES

Nylander is the No. 2 centre by default in Chicago, which really doesn't even have a true No. 1. He is streaky and moody, but he responded well to the coaching change to tough taskmaster Brian Sutter.

Nylander won't dominate games. He is a very capable player who can complement any star. Too bad the Blackhawks don't have any.

PROJECTION

Nylander has been an erratic player but now he has put together two pretty good back-to-back seasons. Another 60-point season is doable, and the 'Hawks could sure use his production.

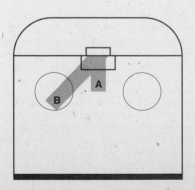

LYLE ODELEIN

Yrs. of NHL service: 12
Born: Quill Lake, Sask.; July 21, 1968
Position: right defence
Height: 5-11
Weight: 210
Uniform no.: 7
Shoots: left

Career statistics:

GP	G	A	TP	PIM
879	39	185	224	2096

1998-1999 statistics:

GP	G	A	TP	+/-	PIM	PP	SH	GW	GT	S	PCT
70	5	26	31	+6	114	1	0	0	1	101	5.0

1999-2000 statistics:

GP	G	A	TP	+/-	PIM	PP	SH	GW	GT	S	PCT
73	2	22	24	-9	123	1	0	1	0	89	2.2

2000-2001 statistics:

GP	G	A	TP	+/-	PIM	PP	SH	GW	GT	S	PCT
81	3	14	17	-16	118	1	0	0	0	104	2.9

2001-2002 statistics:

GP	G	A	TP	+/-	PIM	PP	SH	GW	GT	S	PCT
77	2	16	18	-28	93	0	0	0	0	86	2.3

LAST SEASON

Acquired from Columbus on March 19, 2002, for Jaroslav Spacek and a second-round draft pick in 2003. Missed three games with back spasms. Missed one game due to travel (trade).

THE FINESSE GAME

Defence is Odelein's forte. He is very calm with the puck and able to wait until a player is on top of him, then carry the puck or find an open man. His skating is average at best, but he keeps himself out of trouble by playing a conservative game and not getting caught out of position. An attacker who comes into Odelein's piece of the ice will have to pay the price by getting through him.

Odelein's finesse skills are modest at best, but he has developed sufficient confidence to get involved in the attack if needed. He prefers to limit his contribution to shots from the point.

Odelein deserves credit for having moulded himself into more than an overachieving goon. Odelein remains an utterly fearless shot-blocker.

THE PHYSICAL GAME

Odelein is a banger, a limited player who knows what his limits are, stays within them, and plays effectively as a result. He's rugged and doesn't take chances. He takes the man at all times in front of the net and he plays tough. Heavy but not tall, he gives the impression of being a much bigger man. He will fight, but not very well.

Odelein can be taken off his game easily and gets caught up in yapping matches, which does his game no good. Odelein has become less of an impact player over the past several seasons.

THE INTANGIBLES

Odelein was picked up by the Blackhawks for the stretch drive and playoff run, but his arrival didn't have the kind of impact Chicago hoped for.

PROJECTION

Odelein will give you minutes on the ice and in the box. He won't give you points, but that's not what he's there for.

TUOMO RUUTU

Yrs. of NHL service: 0
Born: Vantaa, Finland; Feb. 16, 1983
Position: centre
Height: 6-1
Weight: 201
Uniform no.: n.a.
Shoots: left

Career statistics:

GP	G	A	TP	PIM
98	18	27	45	155

2001-2002 European statistics:

GP	G	A	TP	PIM
51	7	16	23	69

LAST SEASON

Will be entering first NHL season. Appeared in 45 games with Jokerit (Finland), scoring 4-20-24 with 24 penalty minutes.

THE FINESSE GAME

Ruutu is a power forward with exceptional finesse skills. He is abrasive and intense, and thinks the game well in all areas.

Skating may be the only negative on his plus-minus sheet. Ruutu has a choppy stride, and has worked on his leg strength in the off-season to generate more speed and power. He has already shown improvement but he can stand to get better.

Ruutu works hard around the net for his goals. Although he's not a great finisher, he will get more than his share through effort.

Ruutu has a very advanced game defensively.

THE PHYSICAL GAME

Talk about making an impact. Ruutu will not arrive meekly in the NHL. Ruutu plays a very mature game. He is gritty and aggressive. He is mentally tough and he will do all of the little things to help his team win.

THE INTANGIBLES

All right, 'Hawks fans. You lost Tony Amonte. But you might be getting the next Peter Forsberg. Chicago thinks Ruutu is ready. He was considered to be the best player not in the NHL last year.

PROJECTION

Ruutu may not light it up just yet. Forsberg scored 15 goals in his first season. We'd take that as a jumping-off point.

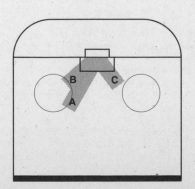

JAROSLAV SPACEK

Yrs. of NHL service: 4
Born: Rokycany, Czech Republic; Feb. 11, 1974
Position: left defence
Height: 5-11
Weight: 198
Uniform no.: 3
Shoots: left

Career statistics:

GP	G	A	TP	PIM
281	25	70	95	162

1998-1999 statistics:

GP	G	A	TP	+/-	PIM	PP	SH	GW	GT	S	PCT
63	3	12	15	+15	28	2	1	0	0	92	3.3

1999-2000 statistics:

GP	G	A	TP	+/-	PIM	PP	SH	GW	GT	S	PCT
82	10	26	36	+7	53	4	0	1	0	111	9.0

2000-2001 statistics:

GP	G	A	TP	+/-	PIM	PP	SH	GW	GT	S	PCT
62	7	19	26	+3	28	3	0	1	0	106	6.6

2001-2002 statistics:

GP	G	A	TP	+/-	PIM	PP	SH	GW	GT	S	PCT
74	5	13	18	-4	53	1	1	2	0	93	5.4

LAST SEASON

Missed eight games with broken finger. Missed two additional games with injury.

THE FINESSE GAME

Spacek is an agile skater. He is good one-on-one and even defending against a two-on-one. He moves the puck very well and has some offensive upside.

Spacek uses his finesse skills in a defensive manner, positioning himself intelligently and anticipating plays. He kills penalties, and can handle some second-unit power-play chores. He is a smart passer and executes the give-and-go well. He has even more offensive upside than he has shown.

Spacek broke into the league as an older rookie and was able to make a quick transition to the North American style of play. He is asked to shoulder much more responsibility in Columbus than he should for his level of ability.

THE PHYSICAL GAME

Spacek is not a big hitter, and he isn't very large, but his positional play is good and he steps up to stop people in the neutral zone.

THE INTANGIBLES

Spacek will be part of a defence corps that will include some marginal veterans (Luke Richardson, Scott Lachance) as well as a budding star in Rostislav Klesla.

PROJECTION

Spacek's production last season was a disappointment, but injuries were a factor. He should provide 25-30 points.

STEVE SULLIVAN

Yrs. of NHL service: 6
Born: Timmins, Ont.; July 6, 1974
Position: centre/right wing
Height: 5-9
Weight: 160
Uniform no.: 26
Shoots: right

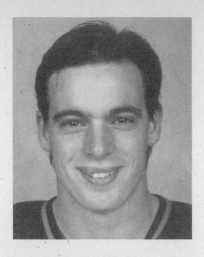

Career statistics:

GP	G	A	TP	PIM
435	125	190	315	290

1998-1999 statistics:

GP	G	A	TP	+/-	PIM	PP	SH	GW	GT	S	PCT
63	20	20	40	+12	28	4	0	5	0	110	18.2

1999-2000 statistics:

GP	G	A	TP	+/-	PIM	PP	SH	GW	GT	S	PCT
80	22	43	65	+19	56	2	1	6	0	180	12.2

2000-2001 statistics:

GP	G	A	TP	+/-	PIM	PP	SH	GW	GT	S	PCT
81	34	41	75	+3	54	6	8	3	1	204	16.7

2001-2002 statistics:

GP	G	A	TP	+/-	PIM	PP	SH	GW	GT	S	PCT
78	21	39	60	+23	67	3	0	8	2	155	13.6

LAST SEASON

Led team and tied for fourth in NHL in game-winning goals. Second on team in plus-minus. Third on team in assists. Missed four games with separated shoulder.

THE FINESSE GAME

Sullivan brings a centre's vision to the right-wing position he played almost exclusively again last season. He has terrific speed, hands, sense and anticipation. Playing wing, he doesn't have to be down low on defensive-zone coverage, and the trade-off of using a smaller player along the boards still works out in his and Chicago's favour.

One advantage to being as small as Sullivan is that you are closer to the puck than a lot of your rivals. Sullivan complicates matters by using a short stick — short even by his standards — to keep the puck in his feet. He draws penalties by protecting the puck so well; foes usually have to foul him to get it. He is able to maintain control of the puck because it is so close to his body. He wants the puck and likes to shoot. He will scrap around the net for loose pucks.

Sullivan is quick and smart enough to get himself out of pending jams, but he does not have elite skills and has to apply himself constantly. He is strictly an offensive threat, almost a specialty player. This is particularly true on the penalty-killing unit. The one really mystifying aspect of Sullivan's season is how he went from leading the league in shorthanded goals in 2000-01 with eight but had none last year.

THE PHYSICAL GAME

You can't survive in the NHL if you are small and soft. Sullivan has to play with fire. If he gets bounced around he has to get back up, and get his stick up. His effort has to be more consistent. Over the past three seasons he has done a good job of keeping his intensity level high.

THE INTANGIBLES

Sullivan wore down again late in the season, and his decline was complicated by his shoulder injury. Sullivan also signed a new contract late in the year and we would hate to think a lack of hunger was the result.

PROJECTION

Sullivan came back to earth a little, and should be regarded realistically as a 20-goal, 60-point guy.

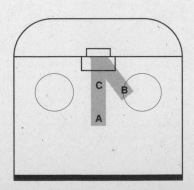

JOCELYN THIBAULT

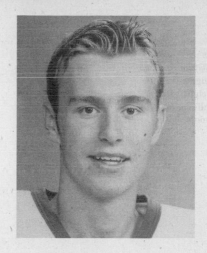

Yrs. of NHL service: 8
Born: Montreal, Que.; Jan. 12, 1975
Position: goaltender
Height: 5-11
Weight: 170
Uniform no.: 41
Catches: left

Career statistics:

GP	MIN	GA	SO	GAA	A	PIM
460	26006	1185	27	2.73	3	12

1998-1999 statistics:

GP	MIN	GAA	W	L	T	SO	GA	S	SAPCT	PIM
52	3014	2.71	21	26	5	4	136	1435	.905	2

1999-2000 statistics:

GP	MIN	GAA	W	L	T	SO	GA	S	SAPCT	PIM
60	3438	2.76	25	26	7	3	158	1679	.906	2

2000-2001 statistics:

GP	MIN	GAA	W	L	T	SO	GA	S	SAPCT	PIM
66	3844	2.81	27	32	7	6	180	1711	.895	2

2001-2002 statistics:

GP	MIN	GAA	W	L	T	SO	GA	S	SAPCT	PIM
67	3838	2.49	33	23	9	6	159	1626	.902	2

LAST SEASON

Career high in wins. Tied career high in shutouts.

THE PHYSICAL GAME

Thibault is a small netminder whose technique makes him look even smaller. He is a butterfly-style goalie, but when he goes to his knees he doesn't keep his torso upright (as Patrick Roy does so splendidly), and that costs Thibault a big chunk of net.

Because he plays deep in his net, Thibault does not challenge shooters. He relies on his reflexes, which, happily for him, happen to be excellent. He is a battler and doesn't give up on a puck, but he creates problems for himself by making the easy saves more difficult than they would be if his fundamentals were better. He has a good glove hand and quick feet, and he is a good skater with lateral mobility.

Thibault has improved his stickhandling, and how he directs his rebounds. He is not very strong on his stick, which means he fails to make key poke-checks or knock-away, cross-crease passes.

THE MENTAL GAME

The Blackhawks let Thibault's workload creep up and that's not recommended. He weighs about 160 pounds after an all-you-can-eat buffet, and his athletic style takes a lot out of him. He seemed to wear down in the late months of the season. Mentally and physically, Thibault is not an elite No. 1 goalie and probably never will be, but he is all the Blackhawks have for now and he works extremely hard.

THE INTANGIBLES

Thibault needs to start in around 58-60 games, so the Blackhawks should spend the money on a veteran backup who can take some of the pressure off and not make Thibault feel threatened. Oh, wait, Blackhawks...spend money? What was I thinking?

PROJECTION

The Hawks had a surprisingly good season and Thibault was able to post a career-best 33 wins. Expect a slide downgrade to 25-28 wins since the team will probably come back down to earth a little this season.

ALEXEI ZHAMNOV

Yrs. of NHL service: 10
Born: Moscow, Russia; Oct. 1, 1970
Position: centre
Height: 6-1
Weight: 200
Uniform no.: 13
Shoots: left

Career statistics:

GP	G	A	TP	PIM
666	222	393	615	540

1998-1999 statistics:

GP	G	A	TP	+/-	PIM	PP	SH	GW	GT	S	PCT
76	20	41	61	-10	50	8	1	2	1	200	10.0

1999-2000 statistics:

GP	G	A	TP	+/-	PIM	PP	SH	GW	GT	S	PCT
71	23	37	60	+7	61	5	0	7	0	175	13.1

2000-2001 statistics:

GP	G	A	TP	+/-	PIM	PP	SH	GW	GT	S	PCT
63	13	36	49	-12	40	3	1	3	0	117	11.1

2001-2002 statistics:

GP	G	A	TP	+/-	PIM	PP	SH	GW	GT	S	PCT
77	22	45	67	+8	67	6	0	3	0	173	12.7

LAST SEASON

Second on team in assists and points. Third on team in goals and shooting percentage. Tied for third on team in power-play goals. Missed four games with hip injury.

THE FINESSE GAME

Zhamnov's game is puck control: he can carry it at top speed or work the give-and-go. The Russian is a crafty playmaker and is not too unselfish. He has an accurate if not overpowering shot. He gets his wrist shot away quickly, and he shoots it with his feet still moving, which few players can do. As well, he can blast off the pass, or manoeuvre until he has a screen and then wrist it. He will try to score from "bad" angles. He is cool and patient with the puck, and he turns harmless-looking plays into dangerous scoring chances. On the power play, he works the left point or, if used low, can dart in and out in front of the goalie, using his soft hands for a tip.

Defensively, Zhamnov is sound and is frequently used against other teams' top forward lines. He is a dedicated backchecker and never leaves the zone too quickly.

Zhamnov came back well after an injury-plagued 2000-01 season. He simply isn't an elite player, no matter how much the 'Hawks pretend.

THE PHYSICAL GAME

Zhamnov will bump to prevent a scoring chance or go for a loose puck, but body work is not his forte. The knock on Zhamnov is his lack of physical play, but he works hard and competes. He is strong and fights his way through traffic in front of the net to get to a puck when he wants to. He needs to do a better job of tying up the opposing centre on face-offs, since he wins few draws cleanly.

THE INTANGIBLES

Zhamnov just doesn't have the presence or the drive to be a true No. 1 centre under these circumstances, but that's where he stands on the team's depth chart.

PROJECTION

Checking pressure and a generally glum atmosphere in Chicago will probably mean a 20-goal, 60-point season for Zhamnov.

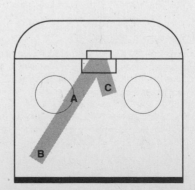

COLORADO AVALANCHE

Players' Statistics 2001-2002

POS	NO.	PLAYER	GP	G	A	PTS	+/-	PIM	PP	SH	GW	GT	S	PCT
C	19	JOE SAKIC	82	26	53	79	12	18	9	1	4	1	260	10.0
D	4	ROB BLAKE	75	16	40	56	16	58	10		2		229	7.0
L	40	ALEX TANGUAY	70	13	35	48	8	36	7		2		90	14.4
C	18	CHRIS DRURY	82	21	25	46	1	38	5		6		236	8.9
C	28	STEVEN REINPRECHT	67	19	27	46	14	18	4		3	1	111	17.1
R	23	MILAN HEJDUK	62	21	23	44	0	24	7	1	5	1	139	15.1
D	41	MARTIN SKOULA	82	10	21	31	-3	42	5		1		100	10.0
R	17	*RADIM VRBATA	52	18	12	30	7	14	6		3		112	16.1
D	52	ADAM FOOTE	55	5	22	27	7	55	1	1			85	5.9
D	7	GREG DE VRIES	82	8	12	20	18	57	1	1	3		148	5.4
L	12	MIKE KEANE	78	6	11	17	-4	38	1			1	73	8.2
C	26	STEPHANE YELLE	73	5	12	17	1	48		1	1		71	7.0
L	29	ERIC MESSIER	74	5	10	15	-5	26			3		84	5.9
R	50	*BRIAN WILLSIE	56	7	7	14	4	14	2		1	1	66	10.6
D	11	DARIUS KASPARAITIS	80	2	12	14	0	142					81	2.5
D	3	PASCAL TREPANIER	74	4	9	13	4	59	2				87	4.6
R	13	DAN HINOTE	58	6	6	12	8	39		1	3		75	8.0
L	9	*BRAD LARSEN	50	2	7	9	4	47	1				38	5.3
C	32	*RIKU HAHL	22	2	3	5	1	14			1		17	11.8
R	27	SCOTT PARKER	63	1	4	5	0	154					32	3.1
C	22	*VACLAV NEDOROST	25	2	2	4	-4	2	1				22	9.1
D	5	TODD GILL	36		4	4	3	25					26	
C	20	KELLY FAIRCHILD	10	2		2	1	2					6	33.3
D	2	BRYAN MUIR	22	1	1	2	1	9					26	3.8
L	37	*JORDAN KRESTANOVICH	8		2	2	1						6	
C	45	JEFF DAW	1		1	1	0						2	
C	36	*STEVE MOORE	8				-4	4					5	
D	43	*JAROSLAV OBSUT	3				0						3	
C	21	PETER FORSBERG					0							
G	33	PATRICK ROY	63				0	26						
G	1	DAVID AEBISCHER	21				0	4						

GP = games played; G = goals; A = assists; PTS = points, +/- = goals-for minus goals-against while player is on ice; PIM = penalties in minutes; PP = power-play goals; SH = shorthanded goals; GW = game-winning goals; GT = game-tying goals; S = no. of shots; PCT = percentage of goals to shots; * = rookie.

ROB BLAKE

Yrs. of NHL service: 12
Born: Simcoe, Ont.; Dec. 10, 1969
Position: right defence
Height: 6-4
Weight: 227
Uniform no.: 4
Shoots: right

Career statistics:

GP	G	A	TP	PIM
750	156	339	495	1117

1998-1999 statistics:

GP	G	A	TP	+/-	PIM	PP	SH	GW	GT	S	PCT
62	12	23	35	-7	128	5	1	2	0	216	5.6

1999-2000 statistics:

GP	G	A	TP	+/-	PIM	PP	SH	GW	GT	S	PCT
77	18	39	57	+10	112	12	0	5	0	327	5.5

2000-2001 statistics:

GP	G	A	TP	+/-	PIM	PP	SH	GW	GT	S	PCT
67	19	40	59	+3	77	10	0	2	1	267	7.1

2001-2002 statistics:

GP	G	A	TP	+/-	PIM	PP	SH	GW	GT	S	PCT
75	16	40	56	+16	58	10	0	2	0	229	7.0

LAST SEASON

Led team defencemen and third among NHL defencemen in points. Second on team in assists, points and plus-minus. Third on team in shots. Missed four games with groin injury. Missed two games with knee injury. Missed one game with flu.

THE FINESSE GAME

Lower-body strength is the key to Blake's open-ice hitting, along with, of course, his skating. Blake is one of the best open-ice hitting defencemen in the league. Blake is a powerful skater, quick and agile, with good balance. He steps up and challenges at the blueline, and has great anticipation. He's also quite bold, forcing turnovers at the blueline with his body positioning and quick stickwork. He is brave but not brash in his decision making.

Blake has finesse skills that make an impact in any zone on the ice. He works the point on the power play and has a good, low shot, which he rifles off the pass. He has quality hand skills and is not afraid to skip in deep to try to make something happen. He is confident about attempting to force the play deep in the offensive zone, and has sharp enough passing skills to use a backhand pass across the goalmouth.

Blake rarely goes a game without getting at least one shot on goal, and he had two 10-shot games last season. Not only does he take shots, he blocks them as well. Blake is also among the best in the league at that painful skill.

THE PHYSICAL GAME

Blake is among the hardest hitters in the league. He has a nasty streak and will bring up his gloves and stick them into the face of an opponent when he thinks the referee isn't watching. He can dominate with his physical play — when he does, he opens up a lot of ice for himself and his teammates. Blake sees the major checking duties against other teams' top lines.

Blake sees a ridiculous amount of ice time. He was fourth in the NHL at 27:34 last season.

THE INTANGIBLES

Have to wonder what the Avs were thinking by not signing rental Darius Kasparaitis after the playoffs. Blake might average 32 minutes this season.

PROJECTION

Blake should still score in the 50-point range, although Colorado needs to develop a little more depth on defence to take some of the stress off him.

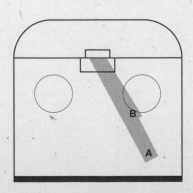

CHRIS DRURY

Yrs. of NHL service: 4
Born: Trumbull, Conn.; Aug. 20, 1976
Position: centre
Height: 5-10
Weight: 180
Uniform no.: 18
Shoots: right

Career statistics:

GP	G	A	TP	PIM
314	85	137	222	189

1998-1999 statistics:

GP	G	A	TP	+/-	PIM	PP	SH	GW	GT	S	PCT
79	20	24	44	+9	62	6	0	3	1	138	14.5

1999-2000 statistics:

GP	G	A	TP	+/-	PIM	PP	SH	GW	GT	S	PCT
82	20	47	67	+8	42	7	0	2	0	213	9.4

2000-2001 statistics:

GP	G	A	TP	+/-	PIM	PP	SH	GW	GT	S	PCT
71	24	41	65	+6	47	11	0	5	1	204	11.8

2001-2002 statistics:

GP	G	A	TP	+/-	PIM	PP	SH	GW	GT	S	PCT
82	21	25	46	+1	38	5	0	6	0	236	8.9

LAST SEASON

Led team in game-winning goals. Tied for second on team in goals. One of four Avs to appear in all 82 games.

THE FINESSE GAME

Drury was another of the Avs who was affected by Peter Forsberg's season-long absence. You just can't take a major asset like Forsberg out of the lineup and not expect it to drag down everyone's point totals.

Drury has a wealth of assets, starting with his skating. He gets in on top of a goalie very quickly — and we mean right on top, because he is probably the best on the team at crease-crashing. He is able to control the puck while charging in. He knows where the net is and isn't afraid to get there by the shortest route possible, even though he isn't the biggest guy in the world.

Drury has quick and soft hands, and is a steady scorer. His effort is so consistent and that's what produces his points. He already has an advanced defensive side to his game; even on nights when he isn't scoring, he is doing something to help his team win. He is a clever playmaker, but linemates can also pick up goals by following him to the net and feasting on the rebounds his efforts create.

He is capable of playing wing or centre and was used extensively at both positions, though centre is his natural position. Drury is a smart player who quickly grasps any concepts the coaching staff pitch him.

THE PHYSICAL GAME

Small but sturdy, Drury doesn't back down an inch and is usually the player who makes the pre-emptive hit. He sure doesn't play little. Drury plays hard and competes every shift, whether it's the first minute of the game or the last.

THE INTANGIBLES

Remarkably poised and mature, with excellent leadership skills, Drury is probably a future captain.

PROJECTION

Drury should be good for 25-30 goals if Forsberg is back. If not, subtract five goals.

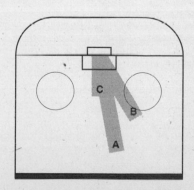

ADAM FOOTE

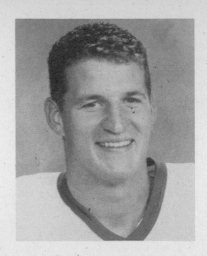

Yrs. of NHL service: 11
Born: Toronto, Ont.; July 10, 1971
Position: right defence
Height: 6-2
Weight: 215
Uniform no.: 52
Shoots: right

Career statistics:

GP	G	A	TP	PIM
648	36	137	173	965

1998-1999 statistics:

GP	G	A	TP	+/-	PIM	PP	SH	GW	GT	S	PCT
64	5	16	21	+20	92	3	0	0	0	83	6.0

1999-2000 statistics:

GP	G	A	TP	+/-	PIM	PP	SH	GW	GT	S	PCT
59	5	13	18	+5	98	1	0	2	0	63	7.9

2000-2001 statistics:

GP	G	A	TP	+/-	PIM	PP	SH	GW	GT	S	PCT
35	3	12	15	+6	42	1	1	1	0	59	5.1

2001-2002 statistics:

GP	G	A	TP	+/-	PIM	PP	SH	GW	GT	S	PCT
55	5	22	27	+7	55	1	1	0	0	85	5.9

LAST SEASON

Career highs in assists and points. Missed 16 games with shoulder surgery. Missed six games with knee injury. Missed two games with finger injury. Missed one game with groin injury. Missed two games due to suspension.

THE FINESSE GAME

Foote has great foot speed and quickness, especially for a player considered a big, tough guy. Defensively, he's strong in his coverage as a stay-at-home type, but he's not creative with the puck, probably his major deficiency. Still, all of the Avalanche defencemen are encouraged to jump into the attack and Foote eagerly does so when given the chance. He is wise in his pinches and knows when to drive to the slot, and he has a useful shot. He won't take wild chances.

The Avalanche would like to wring just a little more offensive production out of him, but at this stage of his career it is not likely to happen. Foote believes his job is to concentrate on defence, though he can handle some second-unit power-play time.

Foote usually skates the puck out of his zone and is less likely to find the man for an outlet pass. There are few defencemen in the league who can match him in getting the first few strides in and jumping out of the zone. He is an excellent penalty killer.

THE PHYSICAL GAME

Foote is big, solid and uses his body well. He plays the man, not the puck. He is highly aggressive in his defensive zone; anyone trying to get to the net through Foote will pay a price. He plays it smart and takes few bad penalties. In recent seasons, he has stepped up his physical play and he dishes out some powerful checks. He has good lower-body strength and drives his body upwards, resulting in a heavy impact with his unfortunate target. Foote can fight when provoked and stands up for his teammates. Foote is the Avs' most physically dominant defenceman.

THE INTANGIBLES

Foote is a warrior, an excellent two-way defenceman whose offensive skills are a few notches below elite class. He is one of the more underrated blueliners around. What sets him apart is his competitiveness. He thrives on the challenge of playing against other teams' top forwards. The downside is that Foote plays so hard he gets dinged up a lot. If he were a car, he would be covered with those mismatched patches of primer paint. If a team needs to protect a lead late in the game, it couldn't do much better than having Foote digging in.

PROJECTION

Foote plays a defence-heavy game but can still score 25 to 30 points.

PETER FORSBERG

Yrs. of NHL service: 7
Born: Örnsköldsvik, Sweden; July 20, 1973
Position: centre
Height: 6 0
Weight: 205
Uniform no.: 21
Shoots: left

Career statistics:

GP	G	A	TP	PIM
466	169	411	580	444

1998-1999 statistics:

GP	G	A	TP	+/-	PIM	PP	SH	GW	GT	S	PCT
78	30	67	97	+27	108	9	2	7	0	217	13.8

1999-2000 statistics:

GP	G	A	TP	+/-	PIM	PP	SH	GW	GT	S	PCT
49	14	37	51	+9	52	3	0	2	0	105	13.3

2000-2001 statistics:

GP	G	A	TP	+/-	PIM	PP	SH	GW	GT	S	PCT
73	27	62	89	+23	54	12	2	5	0	178	15.2

2001-2002 statistics:

Did not play in NHL in 2001-02

LAST SEASON

Missed entire 2001-02 regular season.

THE FINESSE GAME

Forsberg is an amazingly strong skater. When he has the puck, any time he falls down a penalty should probably be called. He's that solid on his feet. Forsberg is a smooth skater with explosive speed and can accelerate while carrying the puck. He has excellent vision of the ice and is a sublime playmaker. One of the few knocks on him is that he doesn't shoot enough. He works most effectively down between the circles with a wrist or backhand shot off the rush, and does his best work in traffic. There's a lot of Gordie Howe about him.

Forsberg protects the puck as well as anybody in the league. He is so strong he can control the puck with one arm while fending off a checker, and still make an effective pass. His passing is nearly as good as teammate Joe Sakic's. He can be off-balance with his head down, digging the puck out of his skates, yet still put a pass on a teammate's stick. The Swede seems to be thinking a play or two ahead of everyone else on the ice and has an amazing sense of every player's position.

Forsberg is used in all game situations: power play, penalty killing and four-on-four. His skill level is world class in every department.

THE PHYSICAL GAME

Forsberg is better suited for the North American style than most Europeans — or many North Americans, for that matter. He is tough to knock down. He loves contact and dishes out more than he receives. He has a wide skating base and great balance. He can be cross-checked when he's on his backhand and still not lose control of the puck. Jaromir Jagr may be the only other player who can do that.

Forsberg has a cockiness that many great athletes carry like an aura; he dares people to try to intimidate him. His drive to succeed helps him handle the cheap stuff and keep going. He's got a mean streak too: bringing his stick up into people's faces. He also takes abuse and is a frequent target of cheap hits. He plays equally hard on any given inch of the ice. His physical game sometimes goes over the top and robs him of his offensive game, which is why rivals are so eager to engage him.

THE INTANGIBLES

Forsberg took the first half of last season to mend physically and mentally from the hockey wars of the past few seasons. When he was ready to return to the Avalanche just before the Olympics, a medical exam revealed an ankle injury that required surgery and delayed his return until the playoffs. Up until the Avs were eliminated in the Western Conference Finals, Forsberg was a leading Conn Smythe Trophy candidate. That is how amazing this guy is.

PROJECTION

Forsberg is a proud and fierce competitor who should be back in the 90-point range this season. If you had one player to pick to build a team around, this would be the one.

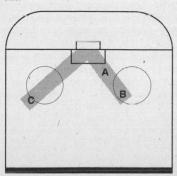

MILAN HEJDUK

Yrs. of NHL service: 4
Born: Usti-nad-Labem, Czech Republic; Feb. 14, 1976
Position: right wing
Height: 5-11
Weight: 185
Uniform no.: 23
Shoots: right

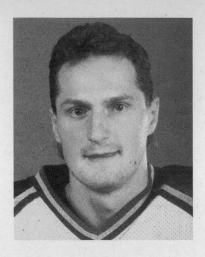

Career statistics:

GP	G	A	TP	PIM
306	112	131	243	102

1998-1999 statistics:

GP	G	A	TP	+/-	PIM	PP	SH	GW	GT	S	PCT
82	14	34	48	+8	26	4	0	5	0	178	7.9

1999-2000 statistics:

GP	G	A	TP	+/-	PIM	PP	SH	GW	GT	S	PCT
82	36	36	72	+14	16	13	0	9	2	228	15.8

2000-2001 statistics:

GP	G	A	TP	+/-	PIM	PP	SH	GW	GT	S	PCT
80	41	38	79	+32	36	12	1	9	0	213	19.3

2001-2002 statistics:

GP	G	A	TP	+/-	PIM	PP	SH	GW	GT	S	PCT
62	21	23	44	0	24	7	1	5	1	139	15.1

LAST SEASON

Second on team in shorthanded goals. Tied for second on team in goals. Third on team in shooting percentage. Tied for third on team in power-play goals. Missed 20 games with abdominal strain.

THE FINESSE GAME

No less an authority than Joe Sakic has declared that Hejduk has the best hands on the Avs. Hejduk is a finisher. His release is deadly quick and accurate. Hejduk rarely shoots the puck wide of the net. Most importantly, he is willing to pay the price around the net to score. He has excellent speed, hockey sense and vision, and he is outstanding on the power play. He has great stamina and can handle of lot of ice time.

Playing most of the season with Sakic forces Hejduk to keep his game uptempo. Sakic plays so hard every night that a young player needs to make sure he doesn't let up, or he will waste the scoring chances that Sakic creates.

Hejduk is built for speed, not abuse, but the Avs are not very big up front, and Hejduk has tried to compensate by driving to the front of the net for screens and rebounds. He can't plant himself there since he lacks the size, but he will jump in and out of holes and takes the pounding.

Hejduk's skating is probably underrated. It took him some time, early in his career, to adjust to the quickness of the NHL game, but he has evolved.

THE PHYSICAL GAME

Hejduk is small but has a solid build; he doesn't stay out of the high-traffic areas. He won't be intimidated. He plays the game with great gusto and determination. His injury was a definite concern last season, since the abdominal muscles affect skating and strength so much.

THE INTANGIBLES

Hejduk's upbeat attitude makes him popular in the Avs' dressing room. He has earned his respect as one of the quiet leaders.

PROJECTION

If Hejduk comes back at 100 per cent, he should hit the 35-goal mark.

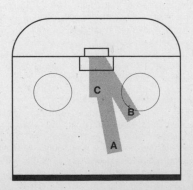

MIKE KEANE

Yrs. of NHL service: 14
Born: Winnipeg, Man.; May 28, 1967
Position: left wing
Height: 6-0
Weight: 185
Uniform no.: 12
Shoots: right

Career statistics:

GP	G	A	TP	PIM
1032	155	288	443	827

1998-1999 statistics:

GP	G	A	TP	+/-	PIM	PP	SH	GW	GT	S	PCT
81	6	23	29	-2	62	1	1	1	0	106	5.7

1999-2000 statistics:

GP	G	A	TP	+/-	PIM	PP	SH	GW	GT	S	PCT
81	13	21	34	+9	41	0	4	3	0	85	15.3

2000-2001 statistics:

GP	G	A	TP	+/-	PIM	PP	SH	GW	GT	S	PCT
67	10	14	24	+4	35	1	0	1	0	64	15.6

2001-2002 statistics:

GP	G	A	TP	+/-	PIM	PP	SH	GW	GT	S	PCT
78	6	11	17	-4	38	1	0	0	1	73	8.2

LAST SEASON

Acquired from St. Louis on February 11, 2002, for Shjon Podein.

THE FINESSE GAME

Keane is one of the NHL's most valuable role players. That may sound like a backhanded compliment, but Keane is well aware of his status and takes great pride in it.

There are few better on the boards and in the corners, and he's the perfect linemate for a finisher. If you want the puck, he'll get it. Not only will he win the battle for it, he'll make a pass and then set a pick or screen. His game is skewed more to defence, but he can still contribute with a big goal.

Keane's chief assets are his intelligence and desire. He doesn't waste energy. He's a good skater and will use his speed to forecheck or create short-handed threats when killing penalties. He can play all three forward positions, but is most effective on the right side. He is a smart player who can be thrust into almost any playing situation.

THE PHYSICAL GAME

Keane is a physical catalyst; he is constantly getting in someone's way. He always finishes his checks in all three zones, stands up for his teammates and is aggressive, though he is not a fighter.

THE INTANGIBLES

At 35, Keane might be less of an impact player on the ice, but he is still an asset as a role player and leader. It was strange that his move to St. Louis failed to work out the way the Blues had hoped.

PROJECTION

As a checking forward Keane probably won't score more than 10 goals a year, but since he prevents more than that, it's not the worst trade-off. If injuries hit he can step in almost anywhere but in the net. Keane even scored a power-play goal last season.

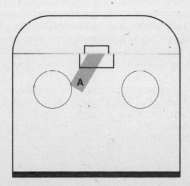

PATRICK ROY

Yrs. of NHL service: 17
Born: Quebec City, Que.; Oct. 5, 1965
Position: goaltender
Height: 6-2
Weight: 192
Uniform no.: 33
Catches: left

Career statistics:

GP	MIN	GA	SO	GAA	A	PIM
966	56458	2409	61	2.56	45	242

1998-1999 statistics:

GP	MIN	GAA	W	L	T	SO	GA	S	SAPCT	PIM
61	3648	2.29	32	19	8	5	139	1673	.917	28

1999-2000 statistics:

GP	MIN	GAA	W	L	T	SO	GA	S	SAPCT	PIM
63	3704	2.28	32	21	8	2	141	1640	.914	10

2000-2001 statistics:

GP	MIN	GAA	W	L	T	SO	GA	S	SAPCT	PIM
62	3585	2.21	40	13	7	4	132	1513	.913	10

2001-2002 statistics:

GP	MIN	GAA	W	L	T	SO	GA	S	SAPCT	PIM
63	3773	1.94	32	23	8	9	122	1629	.925	26

LAST SEASON

Led NHL in goals-against average and shutouts with career bests. Second in NHL in save percentage. Twelfth season with 30 or more wins. Missed two games with hip injury.

THE PHYSICAL GAME

Roy is the butterfly goalie by whom all others are judged. He tempts shooters with a gaping hole between his pads, then, when he has the guy suckered, he snaps the pads closed at the last second to deny the goal. There is no one in the NHL better at this tantalizing technique.

Tall but not broad, Roy uses his body well. He plays his angles, stays at the top of his crease and squares his body to the shooter. He is able to absorb the shot and deaden it, so there are few juicy rebounds left on his doorstep.

He goes down much sooner than he did earlier in his career. The book on Roy is to try to beat him high. But usually there isn't much net there and it's a small spot for a shooter to hit, so opponents try to get too fine. He gets into slumps when he allows wide-angle shots taken from the blueline to the top of the circle, but those lapses are seldom prolonged.

Roy comes back to the rest of the pack in his puck-handling, where he is merely average, although he tends to think he is much better than he is. Roy tries risky passes that Martin Brodeur can do in his sleep, but it usually gives the Avs nightmares. Roy also gets into trouble because he moves back and forth in the crease on his knees rather than trying to regain his feet. His glove hand is good, but he prefers to use his body. If he is under a strong forecheck, he isn't shy about freezing the puck for a draw, especially since he plays with excellent face-off men in Colorado.

THE MENTAL GAME

Roy is still considered one of the best money goalies in the game, but his 2002 playoffs may have indicated the run is coming to an end. There were just enough Statue of Liberty plays — his flamboyant but failed glove saves — to make one wonder if the aura of invincibility has been pierced.

Roy is also capable of losing his cool in a game and blowing up at a referee's call.

THE INTANGIBLES

Roy probably has two elite seasons left in him. The Avs are pretty good about watching his minutes and are not likely to overuse him at age 37.

Roy skipped the Olympics, which didn't make him a big favourite in his native Canada.

PROJECTION

Thirty wins are pretty much a lock.

JOE SAKIC

Yrs. of NHL service: 14
Born: Burnaby, B.C.; July 7, 1969
Position: centre
Height: 5-11
Weight: 185
Uniform no.: 19
Shoots: left

Career statistics:

GP	G	A	TP	PIM
1016	483	774	1257	416

1998-1999 statistics:

GP	G	A	TP	+/-	PIM	PP	SH	GW	GT	S	PCT
73	41	55	96	+23	29	12	5	6	1	255	16.1

1999-2000 statistics:

GP	G	A	TP	+/-	PIM	PP	SH	GW	GT	S	PCT
60	28	53	81	+30	28	5	1	5	0	242	11.6

2000-2001 statistics:

GP	G	A	TP	+/-	PIM	PP	SH	GW	GT	S	PCT
82	54	64	118	+45	30	19	3	12	2	332	16.3

2001-2002 statistics:

GP	G	A	TP	+/-	PIM	PP	SH	GW	GT	S	PCT
82	26	53	79	+12	18	9	1	4	1	260	10.0

LAST SEASON

Led team in goals, assists, points and shots. Third in NHL in assists. Tied for fifth in NHL in points. Second on team in power-play goals. One of four Avs to appear in all 82 games. Has appeared in 194 consecutive games.

THE FINESSE GAME

First Sakic carried the Avs to a 2001 Cup after Peter Forsberg was injured, then he carried them through the entire regular season. With Forsberg gone until the 2002 playoffs, all of the checking attention was focused on Sakic. That's why his numbers were off. His effort never was.

Sakic is one of the game's best playmakers. It's not a secret that he has also become one of the game's best shooters, and he isn't shy about it. How do you defend against him? Try to keep the puck far, far away. Sakic's ability to visualize while speeding through the offensive zone is exceptional. He is slippery, and will spin off a defender and get a shot away.

Sakic has one of the most explosive first steps in the league. He finds and hits the holes in a hurry — even with the puck — to create his chances. He uses a stick shaft with a little "whip" in it that makes his shots more lethal. He has a terrific wrist shot and snap shot and one of the quickest releases in the game.

Sakic's most impressive gift, however, is his great patience with the puck. He will hold it until the last minute, when he has drawn the defenders to him and opened up ice, creating time and space for his linemates. This makes him a gem on the power play, where he works down low and just off the half-boards on the right wing. He can also play the point.

Sakic is a scoring threat whenever he is on the ice because he can craft a dangerous scoring chance out of a situation that looks innocent. He is lethal trailing the rush. He takes a pass in full stride without slowing, then dekes and shoots before the goalie can even flinch. He is smart defensively, and is a good face-off man, too. Even if he's tied up, he uses his skates to kick the puck free.

THE PHYSICAL GAME

Sakic is not a physical player, but he is stronger than he looks. He uses his body to protect the puck when he is carrying deep; you have to go through him to get it. He will try to keep going through traffic or along the boards with the puck, and often squirts free with it because he is able to maintain control and balance. He creates turnovers with his quickness and hands, not by initiating contact. Sakic was able to stay healthy last season.

THE INTANGIBLES

Sakic is 33 and has played a lot of hockey over the past few seasons (long playoff runs take a toll). He just hasn't shown any signs of hitting the wall yet.

PROJECTION

If Forsberg is back at 100 per cent for the full season, Sakic will get the support he needs and should get back into the 90-point range.

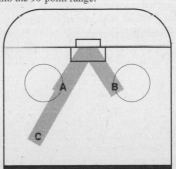

MARTIN SKOULA

Yrs. of NHL service: 3
Born: Litvinov, Czech Republic; Oct. 28, 1979
Position: defence
Height: 6-2
Weight: 195
Uniform no.: 41
Shoots: left

Career statistics:

GP	G	A	TP	PIM
244	21	51	72	100

1999-2000 statistics:

GP	G	A	TP	+/-	PIM	PP	SH	GW	GT	S	PCT
80	3	13	16	+5	20	2	0	0	0	66	4.5

2000-2001 statistics:

GP	G	A	TP	+/-	PIM	PP	SH	GW	GT	S	PCT
82	8	17	25	+8	38	3	0	2	0	108	7.4

2001-2002 statistics:

GP	G	A	TP	+/-	PIM	PP	SH	GW	GT	S	PCT
82	10	21	31	-3	42	5	0	1	0	100	10.0

LAST SEASON

Career highs in goals, assists and points. One of four Avs to appear in all 82 games.

THE FINESSE GAME

Skoula still has some learning to do, especially on the defensive end of his game. He has become a much more productive player offensively, but his defensive lapses are often spectacular.

Skoula has the skills to excel in his own end. He is reliable and poised with the puck. Skoula's problems emerge when he doesn't have the puck. He will lapse into the bad habit of chasing behind the net and losing his checking assignment.

Skoula's natural offensive instincts are excellent. He reacts quickly to plays and understands game situations well. Skoula is a wonderful skater both forwards and backwards. He has a long, smooth, natural stride. He is quick and efficient. He handles the puck well and has nice hands for making or receiving passes. He has good hockey vision, and is a heads-up player. He plays a good transition game.

Skoula picked up the power-play ice time after Ray Bourque's retirement in 2001, and he should continue to get it.

THE PHYSICAL GAME

Skoula is big and well-built. He isn't a mean hitter, but he registers meaningful takeouts. He wore down a bit late in the season, especially in the playoffs, and needs to improve his stamina to stay in the top four.

THE INTANGIBLES

Calgary took Robyn Regehr instead of Skoula in the Theo Fleury deal in 1999. It will be interesting to watch both of these two young defencemen in the coming seasons.

PROJECTION

Skoula made the move into the 30-point range, as projected last season. Colorado is going to be a little thick on defence this season, which might make the overall game more difficult for Skoula. Offensively, though, there is no reason why he can't continue to improve on his numbers.

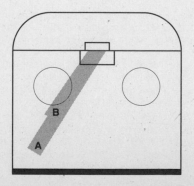

ALEX TANGUAY

Yrs. of NHL service: 3
Born: Ste-Justine, Que.; Nov. 21, 1979
Position: centre/left wing
Height: 6 0
Weight: 190
Uniform no.: 40
Shoots: left

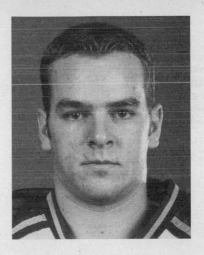

Career statistics:

GP	G	A	TP	PIM
228	57	119	176	95

1999-2000 statistics:

GP	G	A	TP	+/-	PIM	PP	SH	GW	GT	S	PCT
76	17	34	51	+6	22	5	0	3	1	74	23.0

2000-2001 statistics:

GP	G	A	TP	+/-	PIM	PP	SH	GW	GT	S	PCT
82	27	50	77	+35	37	7	1	3	0	135	20.0

2001-2002 statistics:

GP	G	A	TP	+/-	PIM	PP	SH	GW	GT	S	PCT
70	13	35	48	+8	36	7	0	2	0	90	14.4

LAST SEASON

Third on team in assists and points. Tied for third on team in power-play goals. Missed six games with sinus injury. Missed four games with ankle injury. Missed two games with hip injury.

THE FINESSE GAME

Tanguay is a strong skater with breakaway speed. He can embarrass a defenceman who doesn't realize how quick Tanguay is. He is nearly as fast with the puck as without it. He is absolutely dynamic. He loves to have the puck but he isn't selfish and is a good playmaker. Tanguay has to continually be urged by his coaches to shoot more. It's frustrating to have a guy with this much ability not even average two shots a game.

Tanguay has the natural sixth sense of scoring that cannot be taught. He finds the open space in front of the net, or the loose puck seems to materialize on his stick. He has played the wing for most of his first two NHL seasons, but he is a natural centre, and his playmaking skill complements that of Joe Sakic, his usual centre.

Like any young player, Tanguay needs to develop the defensive aspect of his game, but he has pretty good awareness of his responsibility and it won't take him long to become proficient. He likes his team to rely on him and will develop into a player who can be used in all game situations.

THE PHYSICAL GAME

Tanguay goes willingly into the combat zones. He is aggressive and creative, a combination that gives him the hockey courage to play in the dirty areas of the ice and the vision and hands to make something good happen for his team. Tanguay isn't big but he is highly competitive and will do what it takes to win. He is in good shape and handles a lot of minutes.

THE INTANGIBLES

Tanguay still needs to develop confidence in his shot. He had some nagging injuries in the first half of the season but was strong down the stretch and again had a good playoffs. He is becoming a money player.

PROJECTION

Tanguay is capable of a 70-point season. He is about to hit his best stride.

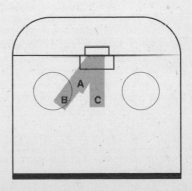

RADIM VRBATA

Yrs. of NHL service: 1
Born: Mlada Boleslav, Czech Republic; June 13, 1981
Position: right wing
Height: 6-0
Weight: 175
Uniform no.: 17
Shoots: right

Career statistics:

GP	G	A	TP	PIM
52	18	12	30	14

2001-2002 statistics:

GP	G	A	TP	+/-	PIM	PP	SH	GW	GT	S	PCT
52	18	12	30	+7	14	6	0	3	0	112	16.1

LAST SEASON

First NHL season. Led NHL rookies in shooting percentage. Fourth among NHL rookies in goals. Seventh among NHL rookies in points. Tied for third among NHL rookies in power-play goals. One of only three NHL rookies to record a hat trick. Missed eight games with rib injury. Missed one game with flu. Appeared in 20 games with Hershey (AHL), scoring 8-14-22.

THE FINESSE GAME

Vrbata started last season in the minors and was promoted in November. The Avs liked what they saw.

Vrbata certainly has the skills to play in the NHL. He is an excellent skater. Vrbata has a goal-scorer's mentality and a goal-scorer's shot.

Vrbata got his playing chance last year due to some injuries. He will have a harder time working his way into the lineup if the top guns stay healthy, but he is a first-rate understudy for the time being. Vrbata got a little taste of the Stanley Cup playoffs, which will only help his development.

THE PHYSICAL GAME

Vrbata needs to get stronger and grittier.

THE INTANGIBLES

Vrbata registered a higher goals-per-game average in his rookie season than several big Avs stars, including Joe Sakic, Peter Forsberg and Chris Drury. The Colorado scouting system continues to unearth gems.

PROJECTION

Assuming Vrbata can get decent ice time in 60-65 games, he should be in the 20 to 25-goal range.

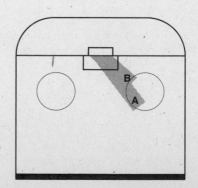

STEPHANE YELLE

Yrs. of NHL service: 7
Born: Ottawa, Ont.; May 9, 1974
Position: centre
Height: 6-1
Weight: 190
Uniform no.: 26
Shoots: left

Career statistics:

GP	G	A	TP	PIM
505	54	89	143	252

1998-1999 statistics:

GP	G	A	TP	+/-	PIM	PP	SH	GW	GT	S	PCT
72	8	7	15	-8	40	1	0	0	0	99	8.1

1999-2000 statistics:

GP	G	A	TP	+/-	PIM	PP	SH	GW	GT	S	PCT
79	8	14	22	+9	28	0	1	1	0	90	8.9

2000-2001 statistics:

GP	G	A	TP	+/-	PIM	PP	SH	GW	GT	S	PCT
50	4	10	14	-3	20	0	1	0	0	54	7.4

2001-2002 statistics:

GP	G	A	TP	+/-	PIM	PP	SH	GW	GT	S	PCT
73	5	12	17	+1	48	0	1	1	0	71	7.0

THE INTANGIBLES

Yelle is a smart player and works diligently, which compensates for some of his other flaws. He's one of those players you don't notice much until he's out of the lineup.

PROJECTION

Yelle's absolute top end is 15 goals, though he is more likely to score goals in single digits. His value is as a defensive forward.

LAST SEASON

Missed one game with ankle injury. Missed one game with flu. Missed one game with bruised foot. Missed one game with bruised knee. Missed five games with shoulder injury.

THE FINESSE GAME

Yelle is an intelligent player who reads the play extremely well; it's his knowledge of the game that has made him an NHL player. His other skills are average: he's a good skater, but he sees the ice in terms of his defensive role. Yelle just doesn't think offence. He's a player you want on the ice to kill penalties or to protect a lead, or sometimes just to go out and play a smart shift to settle a team down.

Yelle doesn't have quick hands, and as a result, has a lot of off-nights on draws. He doesn't have the hands to get involved in the offence. He isn't even a real shorthanded threat because he doesn't have breakaway speed and will make the safe play instead of the prettier high-risk one. He kills penalties but has to be paired with a better-skating partner.

On a team of glamorous forwards, Yelle is blue collar. His nightly effort is consistently strong.

THE PHYSICAL GAME

Yelle is a tall and stringy-looking athlete with toothpicks for legs. He handles himself well, because even though he doesn't look strong he finds a way to get the puck out. He is usually pretty durable although he had a nightmare year with injuries last season.

COLUMBUS BLUE JACKETS

Players' Statistics 2001-2002

POS	NO.	PLAYER	GP	G	A	PTS	+/-	PIM	PP	SH	GW	GT	S	PCT
L	14	RAY WHITNEY	67	21	40	61	-22	12	6		3		210	10.0
C	16	MIKE SILLINGER	80	20	23	43	-35	54	8		5		150	13.3
C	21	ESPEN KNUTSEN	77	11	31	42	-28	47	5	2	1		102	10.8
R	29	GRANT MARSHALL	81	15	18	33	-20	86	6		4	1	152	9.9
R	9	DAVID VYBORNY	75	13	18	31	-14	6	6		2		103	12.6
D	7	DERON QUINT	75	7	18	25	-34	26	3		1		169	4.1
C	28	TYLER WRIGHT	77	13	11	24	-40	100	4		1	1	120	10.8
D	3	JAROSLAV SPACEK	74	5	13	18	-4	53	1	1	2		93	5.4
L	8	GEOFF SANDERSON	42	11	5	16	-15	12	5		2		112	9.8
D	44	*ROSTISLAV KLESLA	75	8	8	16	-6	74	1			1	102	7.8
L	10	SERGE AUBIN	71	8	8	16	-20	32	1		1		86	9.3
R	18	ROBERT KRON	59	4	11	15	-14	4	1				92	4.3
C	42	BRETT HARKINS	25	2	12	14	-5	8	2				9	22.2
R	11	KEVIN DINEEN	59	5	8	13	-6	62					73	6.8
D	37	MATTIAS TIMANDER	78	4	7	11	-34	44	1				68	5.9
D	34	J-LUC GRAND-PIERRE	81	2	6	8	-28	90					62	3.2
L	45	*JODY SHELLEY	52	3	3	6	1	206					35	8.6
D	32	RADIM BICANEK	60	1	5	6	-15	34					43	2.3
R	22	CHRIS NIELSEN	23	2	3	5	-3	4			1		28	7.1
C	12	SEAN PRONGER	26	3	1	4	-4	4					25	12.0
D	6	JAMIE HEWARD	28	1	2	3	-9	7					38	2.6
R	41	*MATT DAVIDSON	17	1	2	3	-11	10					18	5.6
L	19	*MATHIEU DARCHE	14	1	1	2	-5	6					15	6.7
D	33	JAMIE ALLISON	44		2	2	-7	52					16	
C	26	*ANDREJ NEDOROST	7		2	2	-3	2					12	
L	20	*MARTIN SPANHEL	4	1		1	-2	2					6	16.7
D	23	*DERRICK WALSER	2	1		1	-2						2	50.0
C	38	*BLAKE BELLEFEUILLE	2		1	1	1						2	
R	43	DAVID LING	5				-1	7					5	
D	40	*DUVIE WESTCOTT	4				-2	2					3	
C	40	*BRAD MORAN	3				0						2	
G	1	JEAN LABBE	3				0							
G	31	RON TUGNUTT	44				0							
G	30	MARC DENIS	42				0	2						

GP = games played; G = goals; A = assists; PTS = points; +/- = goals-for minus goals-against while player is on ice; PIM = penalties in minutes; PP = power-play goals; SH = shorthanded goals; GW = game-winning goals; GT = game-tying goals; S = no. of shots; PCT = percentage of goals to shots; * = rookie

RADIM BICANEK

Yrs. of NHL service: 3
Born: Uherkke Hradiste, Czech Republic; Jan. 18, 1975
Position: defence
Height: 6-1
Weight: 212
Uniform no.: 32
Shoots: left

Career statistics:

GP	G	A	TP	PIM
122	1	11	12	62

1998-1999 statistics:

GP	G	A	TP	+/-	PIM	PP	SH	GW	GT	S	PCT
14	0	0	0	-4	10	0	0	0	0	13	0.0

1999-2000 statistics:

GP	G	A	TP	+/-	PIM	PP	SH	GW	GT	S	PCT
11	0	3	3	+7	4	0	0	0	0	8	-

2000-2001 statistics:

GP	G	A	TP	+/-	PIM	PP	SH	GW	GT	S	PCT
9	0	2	2	+1	6	0	0	0	0	11	0.0

2001-2002 statistics:

GP	G	A	TP	+/-	PIM	PP	SH	GW	GT	S	PCT
60	1	5	6	-15	34	0	0	0	0	43	2.3

LAST SEASON

Missed 22 games due to coach's decision.

THE FINESSE GAME

Bicanek has been up and down like a yo-yo in the Ottawa, Chicago and Columbus organizations. Last season represented his first big chance to grab a full-time NHL job. He didn't exactly grab it as much as he did toy with it.

Bicanek has been a successful scorer at the minor-league level, mostly with assist-heavy totals, but he was neither a playmaker nor a scorer nor much of a presence at all with the Blue Jackets last season.

Bicanek was drafted (27th overall in 1993) on the strength of his excellent shot, which hasn't been on display at all in the NHL. He was projected as a future power-play quarterback. That future has never arrived.

THE PHYSICAL GAME

Bicanek remains a project in the defensive zone. And, oh yeah, he's not very physical, either.

THE INTANGIBLES

The Blue Jackets gave Bicanek a one-way contract a year ago. Don't know what they were thinking.

PROJECTION

One goal in 122 NHL games? Steer clear.

MARC DENIS

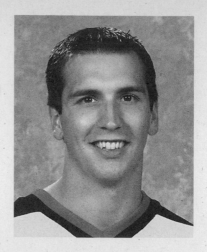

Yrs. of NHL service: 2
Born: Montreal, Que.; Aug. 1, 1977
Position: goaltender
Height: 6-0
Weight: 188
Uniform no.: 30
Catches: left

Career statistics:

GP	MIN	GA	SO	GAA	A	PIM
102	5645	283	4	3.01	1	2

1998-1999 statistics:

GP	MIN	GAA	W	L	T	SO	GA	S	SAPCT	PIM
4	217	2.49	1	1	1	0	9	110	.918	0

1999-2000 statistics:

GP	MIN	GAA	W	L	T	SO	GA	S	SAPCT	PIM
23	1203	2.54	9	8	3	3	51	618	.917	6

2000-2001 statistics:

GP	MIN	GAA	W	L	T	SO	GA	S	SAPCT	PIM
32	1830	3.25	6	20	4	0	99	940	.895	2

2001-2002 statistics:

GP	MIN	GAA	W	L	T	SO	GA	S	SAPCT	PIM
42	2335	3.11	9	24	5	1	121	1197	.899	2

LAST SEASON

Missed four games with groin injury.

THE PHYSICAL GAME

Denis is a good standup goalie whose technique has improved in the past two seasons. Denis made his most dramatic advance in his positioning. Denis now anticipates the shot, so he's not meeting the puck at a certain point, he's already there when the puck arrives.

With all the practice time he's devoted, Denis thinks less and is more in the flow of the game. He is less robotic. There were times he seemed almost lackadaisical because he was doing everything so textbook. Now he's not afraid to hit the ice and scramble his arms and legs all over to make a save. Denis is now not afraid to let his natural ability take over.

Sound and reliable, Denis has also improved his quickness and flexibility with the pads. That's important, because tall golies have a tendency to be a little clumsy and vulnerable low. He is in better position to make the second saves. He moves well and is well-balanced. Denis keeps his knees bent instead of playing straight-legged as he used to, when he was slower and more predictable. Now he has a good base to react and get power from.

THE MENTAL GAME

Denis is confident but coachable. He shows a hunger and a desire to get better and better. Columbus has a good goalie coach in Rick Wamsley (all teams should invest so wisely). Having Ron Tugnutt around as a few seasons as a mentor was also a plus.

THE INTANGIBLES

Columbus felt confident enough in Denis to trade away Tugnutt. Denis was once in Colorado's system and considered the successor to Patrick Roy. He isn't in that elite class yet, but he's done nothing wrong.

PROJECTION

If Denis were playing behind a better team, we would feel confident in predicting 25 wins in his first full season. But since the Blue Jackets won only 22 games all of last year, he should be good for 20 wins. Columbus plays a good defensive style, so if your pool includes goals-against average and save percentage, Denis might make a smart sleeper pick.

JEAN-LUC GRAND-PIERRE

Yrs. of NHL service: 3
Born: Montreal, Que.; Feb. 2, 1977
Position: right defence
Height: 6 3
Weight: 207
Uniform no.: 34
Shoots: right

Career statistics:

GP	G	A	TP	PIM
172	3	11	14	195

1998-1999 statistics:

GP	G	A	TP	+/-	PIM	PP	SH	GW	GT	S	PCT
16	0	1	1	0	17	0	0	0	0	11	0.0

1999-2000 statistics:

GP	G	A	TP	+/-	PIM	PP	SH	GW	GT	S	PCT
11	0	0	0	-1	15	0	0	0	0	10	0.0

2000-2001 statistics:

GP	G	A	TP	+/-	PIM	PP	SH	GW	GT	S	PCT
64	1	4	5	-6	73	0	0	0	0	33	3.0

2001-2002 statistics:

GP	G	A	TP	+/-	PIM	PP	SH	GW	GT	S	PCT
81	2	6	8	-28	90	0	0	0	0	62	3.2

PROJECTION

Grand-Pierre will make sure the Blue Jackets don't get pushed around, but he won't pick up many points in the process.

LAST SEASON

Third on team in penalty minutes. Career hghs in goals, assists and points. Missed one game due to coach's decision.

THE FINESSE GAME

Grand-Pierre is big and can skate, and that's a dandy start for an NHL defence prospect. Where Grand-Pierre has come up short at the NHL level are in his hand skills and his ability to adjust to the big-league pace. He has trouble with defensive reads.

Grand-Pierre has a long, powerful stride. He has good speed and acceleration for a big man. His pivots and lateral quickness are also good.

Grand-Pierre is a determined penalty killer. He has a long reach for picking off passes in the lanes and he blocks shots. His trouble lies in getting the puck out of the zone. He has to learn to make the quick, safe plays.

The knock on him is turnovers and a need for more intelligent play.

THE PHYSICAL GAME

The only thing Grand-Pierre has to learn is to pick his spots better. He's a legitimate tough guy who will stand up for his teammates. He can't afford to take dumb penalties. On the flip side, he can't afford to take nights off and play soft.

THE INTANGIBLES

Grand-Pierre was shuttled between defence and forward, which doesn't help his attempts to become a more reliable player on defence. He should be a No. 6 defenceman with the Blue Jackets this season. Or a fourth-line forward. Pick one.

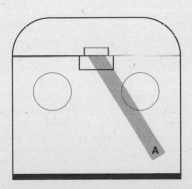

ROSTISLAV KLESLA

Yrs. of NHL service: 1
Born: Novy Jicin, Czech Republic; Mar. 21, 1982
Position: left defence
Height: 6-2
Weight: 198
Uniform no.: 44
Shoots: left

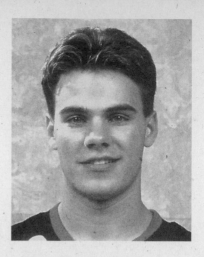

Career statistics:

GP	G	A	TP	PIM
83	10	8	18	80

2000-2001 statistics:

GP	G	A	TP	+/-	PIM	PP	SH	GW	GT	S	PCT
8	2	0	2	-1	6	0	0	0	0	10	20.0

2001-2002 statistics:

GP	G	A	TP	+/-	PIM	PP	SH	GW	GT	S	PCT
75	8	8	16	-6	74	1	0	0	1	102	7.8

LAST SEASON

First NHL season. Missed seven games with shoulder sprain.

THE FINESSE GAME

Klesla didn't attract much attention in his rookie season in Columbus, but don't mistake the silence for disappointment. Klesla had a quietly effective freshman campaign, and was better in the second half than the first, which is always a positive sign.

Klesla learned something every day, and he paid close attention to the veterans on the team and his coaches. Early on, Klesla was too aggressive, and he tried plays he could make with ease in junior but which smart NHL players were just waiting to pounce on. So Klesla stopped trying to force fancy plays, adjusted to major-league speed, and steeled himself for the physical battles.

Klesla isn't a pure offensive defenceman. He uses his finesse skills in a defensive role, taking away passing lanes and playing well positionally. It will be impossible to confine Klesla to a role on a trapping team, and it's likely the Blue Jackets will learn simply to design their game plan around him.

Klesla will be a threat on the power play and especially four-on-four. He is considered the closest thing to a "rover" since Bobby Orr revolutionized the defenceman's role. He is an effortless skater, with a smooth change of direction, tight turning radius and acceleration. He has excellent breakaway speed with or without the puck.

THE PHYSICAL GAME

Klesla is never going to be a punishing hitter, but he could develop along the lines of a Scott Niedermayer, who uses his secure skating to make his take-out hits. Like Niedermayer, Klesla has a long fuse but when provoked, will show a surprising mean streak. Klesla handled a lot of ice time for a first-year player, averaging over 18 minutes a game.

THE INTANGIBLES

You can hang his sweater in the locker now, because he's here to stay. There will still be a lot of growing pains. Columbus added veterans Luke Richardson and Scott Lachance to help in Klesla's education. He will be in the Blue Jackets' top four this season and for years to come.

PROJECTION

Klesla didn't put up the numbers that attract Calder Trophy votes but consider this: veteran Columbus defencemen Mattias Timander and Deron Quint each were -34. Klesla was -6. His offensive numbers should improve to 25-30 points.

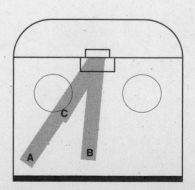

ESPEN KNUTSEN

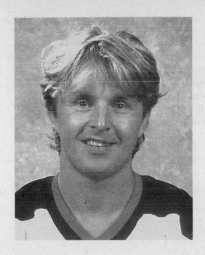

Yrs. of NHL service: 2
Born: Oslo, Norway; Jan. 12, 1972
Position: centre
Height: 5-11
Weight: 180
Uniform no.: 21
Shoots: left

Career statistics:

GP	G	A	TP	PIM
143	22	73	95	77

2000-2001 statistics:

GP	G	A	TP	+/-	PIM	PP	SH	GW	GT	S	PCT
66	11	42	53	-3	30	2	0	0	0	62	17.7

2001-2002 statistics:

GP	G	A	TP	+/-	PIM	PP	SH	GW	GT	S	PCT
77	11	31	42	-28	47	5	2	1	0	102	10.8

LAST SEASON

Second on team in assists. Third on team in points. Tied for third on team in shooting percentage. Missed three games with hip pointer. Missed one game with flu. Missed one game with knee injury.

THE FINESSE GAME

Knutsen has proven he has the skills to play at the NHL level. Now he has to show he can play with intensity on a nightly basis, especially at even strength.

Knutsen is something of a power-play specialist, which is a luxury for a developing team like Columbus. He is a good skater and is creative. At times he played as the team's No. 1 centre and there were games when he was the Blue Jackets' best player. He has terrific hockey vision.

Knutsen has improved in doing the dirty work in his own end of the ice, taking hits to make plays, and recognizing that his defence can be just as important as his offence.

He excels as a power-play quarterback. He doesn't shoot much. He is the brains of the outfit, alert to Geoff Sanderson or another willing sniper and able to thread them a pass.

THE PHYSICAL GAME

Knutsen is small and needs to get a bit thicker for the battles along the wall and in front of the net. He wants the puck and works harder for it in the offensive zone than in his own end. Knutsen is very secure on his skates and is tough to knock off the puck.

Knutsen is tough mentally and physically. He shakes off injuries like rainwater and almost always returns to the lineup faster than expected. Knutsen was the player whose shot was deflected into the stands, killing a young girl. He was blameless, but still had to face media pressure because of it and he handled it gracefully.

THE INTANGIBLES

On nights when Knutsen "gets it," he can be an effective two-way player. He missed Sanderson last season (Sanderson was limited to 42 games) otherwise Knutsen's numbers would have been better.

PROJECTION

Knutsen should stay on one of the top two lines in Columbus, see plenty of ice time (especially on the power play), and top 50 points.

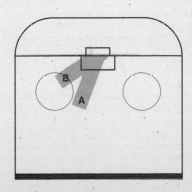

RICK NASH

Yrs. of NHL service: 0
Born: Brampton, Ont.; June 16, 1984
Position: left wing
Height: 6-3
Weight: 188
Uniform no.: n.a.
Shoots: left

Career statistics:

GP	G	A	TP	PIM
112	63	75	138	144

2001-2002 junior statistics:

GP	G	A	TP	PIM
54	32	40	72	88

LAST SEASON
Will be entering first NHL season. Selected first overall in 2002 draft.

THE FINESSE GAME
Nash is a power forward in the making. His skating, though, is the question mark. It may be marginally NHL calibre, but no one thought Luc Robitaille was a great skater either (600 goals later, it's still a deficiency).

What makes Nash seem faster is that he wants to get to where the puck is. Nash forechecks aggressively. He is able to get in on the puck carrier and happily wades into the wars in the corners, along the boards and in front of the net.

Nash is a combination of finesse and power. He has a great wrist shot, accurate and with a quick release. Nash can also shoot off the fly (as fast as he flies, anyway). He is also fairly aware defensively.

THE PHYSICAL GAME
Nash has shown up when the game is on the line. He is competitive and intense. Some scouts have compared him to a young Brendan Shanahan.

THE INTANGIBLES
It takes an exceptional 18-year-old to step in and make an impact in his first NHL season. Nash might just be that good. And he is lucky to be going to a team with a coach (Dave King) who has a reputation of also being a teacher.

PROJECTION
Columbus is a very small team up front and Nash is likely to land a job on the top six. We're going to go with the optimistic feeling and ask him to score 35 points in his first season.

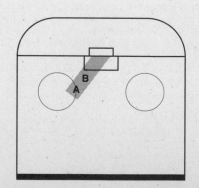

CHRIS NIELSEN

Yrs. of NHL service: 2
Born: Moshi, Tanzania; Feb. 16, 1980
Position: centre
Height: 6-2
Weight: 185
Uniform no.: 22
Shoots: right

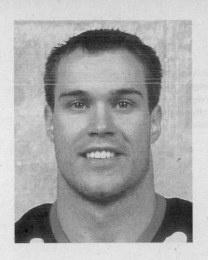

Career statistics:

GP	G	A	TP	PIM
52	6	8	14	8

2000-2001 statistics:

GP	G	A	TP	+/-	PIM	PP	SH	GW	GT	S	PCT
29	4	5	9	+4	4	0	0	1	1	36	11.1

2001-2002 statistics:

GP	G	A	TP	+/-	PIM	PP	SH	GW	GT	S	PCT
23	2	3	5	-3	4	0	0	1	0	28	7.1

LAST SEASON

Appeared in 47 games with Syracuse (AHL), scoring 12-12-24 with 18 penalty minutes. Missed 14 games with groin injury.

THE FINESSE GAME

Injuries and inconsistent play conspired to keep Nielsen from making the big step the Blue Jackets have been waiting (and waiting) for. Nielsen won a job out of training camp, but just three games into the season, suffered the groin injury that required surgery and sidelined him until late November. He struggled when he returned and was shipped off to the minors.

Nielsen has to be more consistent. He is a strong skater with a good stride, shows a good change of pace in his skating, and is effective coming in off the wing.

Nielsen can be used on the point on the power play. Confidence is a big factor for a scorer, and when Nielsen gets on a roll, he can really have a hot hand. When he loses that confidence, he turns into a tentative player. Then it's back on the bus.

THE PHYSICAL GAME

Nielsen can intimidate with his speed, but he has to get stronger in his upper body and add a little more grit to his game.

THE INTANGIBLES

Nielsen was called up again late in the season, so the Blue Jackets haven't forgotten him. This has to be the season he puts it all together. While the team isn't improving drastically, there are some prospects who are gaining on Nielsen.

PROJECTION

Nielsen needs to play a better all-round game to win a full-time role. If he does, he should see some power-play time and could score between 15 and 20 goals.

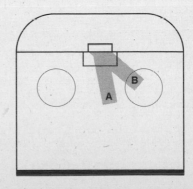

DERON QUINT

Yrs. of NHL service: 7
Born: Durham, NH; March 12, 1976
Position: left defence
Height: 6-2
Weight: 219
Uniform no.: 7
Shoots: left

Career statistics:

GP	G	A	TP	PIM
356	35	80	115	128

1998-1999 statistics:

GP	G	A	TP	+/-	PIM	PP	SH	GW	GT	S	PCT
60	5	8	13	-10	20	2	0	0	0	94	5.3

1999-2000 statistics:

GP	G	A	TP	+/-	PIM	PP	SH	GW	GT	S	PCT
54	4	7	11	-2	24	0	0	1	0	94	4.3

2000-2001 statistics:

GP	G	A	TP	+/-	PIM	PP	SH	GW	GT	S	PCT
57	7	16	23	-19	16	3	0	0	0	148	4.7

2001-2002 statistics:

GP	G	A	TP	+/-	PIM	PP	SH	GW	GT	S	PCT
75	7	18	25	-34	26	3	0	1	0	169	4.1

LAST SEASON

Led team defencemen in points. Second on team in shots. Missed one game with bruised thigh. Missed six games due to coach's decision.

THE FINESSE GAME

Quint has some NHL-level skills, starting with his skating. He has very good speed with a change of gears and can shift directions in a fluid motion. He also possesses a fine, accurate slap shot with a quick release. He can rush the puck end-to-end or start a rush with a smart pass and then join the attack.

The problem isn't Quint's hands or feet, but his head. There's a big question about his desire to excel in the NHL or just show up and collect a paycheque.

Quint would probably thrive if he were paired with a defence-minded partner who would feel comfortable in just telling Quint to go. He doesn't read the rush well and overcommits to plays. He has to learn to tune in to odd-man rushes.

THE PHYSICAL GAME

Quint is in good physical shape and can handle a lot of ice time. He played 33:18 in one game against Detroit. He doesn't have great size for an NHL defenceman but he is big enough to bump and get in the way of people, though he's inconsistent with his body work. He also has a problem picking the right man to eliminate.

THE INTANGIBLES

Quint was very immature when he was initially brought into the NHL, and his problems were complicated by bad off-ice habits. He seems to have straightened himself out, but the coaching staff remains a little wary. Quint could be on the bubble because of the addition of free agent veterans Scott Lachance and Luke Richardson.

PROJECTION

Quint may have a 30-point season in him if the Blue Jackets improve even a little bit offensively.

LUKE RICHARDSON

Yrs. of NHL service: 15
Born: Ottawa, Ont.; Mar. 26, 1969
Position: left defence
Height: 6-3
Weight: 210
Uniform no.: 22
Shoots: left

Career statistics:

GP	G	A	TP	PIM
1101	31	129	160	1804

1998-1999 statistics:

GP	G	A	TP	+/-	PIM	PP	SH	GW	GT	S	PCT
78	0	6	6	-3	106	0	0	0	0	49	0.0

1999-2000 statistics:

GP	G	A	TP	+/-	PIM	PP	SH	GW	GT	S	PCT
74	2	5	7	+14	140	0	0	1	0	50	4.0

2000-2001 statistics:

GP	G	A	TP	+/-	PIM	PP	SH	GW	GT	S	PCT
82	2	6	8	+23	131	0	1	0	0	75	2.7

2001-2002 statistics:

GP	G	A	TP	+/-	PIM	PP	SH	GW	GT	S	PCT
72	1	8	9	+18	102	0	0	0	0	65	1.5

LAST SEASON

Signed as free agent by Columbus on July 4, 2002. Missed 10 games with fractured right foot.

THE FINESSE GAME

Richardson is a good skater with lateral mobility and balance, but not much speed. He overcomes his skating flaws by taking up as much space as he can with his size. Richardson has learned to play a more conservative style as he has gotten older and it has made him less of a liability. There were actually stretches with the Flyers last season where he was among their best defenders on a nightly basis.

Richardson can't carry the puck and doesn't jump up into the rush well. He is best paired with a puck-carrying partner so he can just make the dish and play stay-at-home. He seldom uses his point shot, which is merely adequate.

Richardson doesn't always know when to stay in front of his net and when to challenge in the corners. The less he tries to do, the better. Richardson has become less of a headhunter and doesn't run around looking for the big hit. He is a smart and willing shot-blocker.

THE PHYSICAL GAME

Richardson is the kind of player you hate to play against but love to have on your side. He hits to hurt and is an imposing presence on the ice. He scares people. When he checks, he separates the puck carrier from the puck and doesn't let the man back into the play. When he is on the ice, his teammates play a bit bigger and braver. He also plays hurt. Richardson isn't shy about dropping his gloves, either.

THE INTANGIBLES

Richardson finished out his Flyers career putting together two back-to-back seasons which were very serviceable. He was rewarded with a free agent contract. Columbus will be a different story. Richardson will be asked to step into the role vacated by Lyle Odelein, who was traded to Minnesota. He will get a lot more minutes than he was seeing with the Flyers and he will be asked to help bring kids like Rostislav Klesla along. We weren't the biggest Richardson fans, but in the last few years he has shown us some pretty good character.

PROJECTION

Richardson's role is as a physical stay-at-home defender; his point totals will remain low (10 to 15 points), even with the increased ice time.

GEOFF SANDERSON

Yrs. of NHL service: 11
Born: Hay River, N.W.T.; Feb. 1, 1972
Position: left wing
Height: 6-0
Weight: 190
Uniform no.: 8
Shoots: left

Career statistics:

GP	G	A	TP	PIM
766	266	243	509	321

1998-1999 statistics:

GP	G	A	TP	+/-	PIM	PP	SH	GW	GT	S	PCT
75	12	18	30	+8	22	1	0	1	0	155	7.7

1999-2000 statistics:

GP	G	A	TP	+/-	PIM	PP	SH	GW	GT	S	PCT
67	13	13	26	+4	22	4	0	3	0	136	9.6

2000-2001 statistics:

GP	G	A	TP	+/-	PIM	PP	SH	GW	GT	S	PCT
68	30	26	56	+4	46	9	0	7	0	199	15.1

2001-2002 statistics:

GP	G	A	TP	+/-	PIM	PP	SH	GW	GT	S	PCT
42	11	5	16	-15	12	5	0	2	0	112	9.8

LAST SEASON

Missed 24 games with hernia surgery. Missed 10 games with back injury. Missed six games with concussion.

THE FINESSE GAME

Maybe it's age, maybe it's wisdom, maybe it's just the fact that he needs to catch his breath now and again, but the result is that Sanderson has learned how to vary the pace of his skating instead of going full-tilt every time. When he plays a pure speed game, Sanderson is too far ahead of the game and his teammates. With his better sense of timing and his ability to accelerate into holes, Sanderson revived what had been a flagging career.

Sanderson takes a lot of shots. He can drive wide on a defenceman or open up space by forcing the defence to play back off him. He doesn't score often off the rush because he doesn't have a heavy shot. He can create chaos off the rush, though, and finish up by getting open in the slot for a pass.

He has a superb one-timer on the power play, where he likes to score on his off-wing in the deep right slot. Sanderson has become a better all-round player: he is more intelligent in his own end and his checking is more consistent. He can also kill penalties. His speed makes him a shorthanded threat.

THE PHYSICAL GAME

Sanderson is wiry but gets outmuscled, and although his speed keeps him clear of a lot of traffic, he has to battle when the room isn't there.

THE INTANGIBLES

Sanderson couldn't have had worse luck last season. He worked his way back into action following mid-season hernia surgery, then suffered a season-ending concussion after two months.

PROJECTION

Sanderson is subject to missing lots of games due to injuries. He is a hero in Columbus, but we're hesitant to pencil him in for much more than 30 points the way things are going for him.

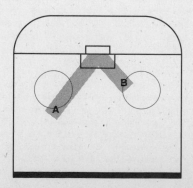

MIKE SILLINGER

Yrs. of NHL service: 10
Born: Regina, Sask.; June 29, 1971
Position: centre
Height: 5-10
Weight: 191
Uniform no.: 16
Shoots: right

Career statistics:

GP	G	A	TP	PIM
678	135	196	331	387

1998-1999 statistics:

GP	G	A	TP	+/-	PIM	PP	SH	GW	GT	S	PCT
79	8	5	13	-29	36	0	2	0	0	92	8.7

1999-2000 statistics:

GP	G	A	TP	+/-	PIM	PP	SH	GW	GT	S	PCT
80	23	29	52	-30	102	8	3	2	0	146	15.8

2000-2001 statistics:

GP	G	A	TP	+/-	PIM	PP	SH	GW	GT	S	PCT
68	16	25	41	-11	48	1	0	2	0	119	13.4

2001-2002 statistics:

GP	G	A	TP	+/-	PIM	PP	SH	GW	GT	S	PCT
80	20	23	43	-35	54	8	0	5	0	150	13.3

LAST SEASON

Led team in power-play goals, game-winning goals and shooting percentage. Second on team in goals and points. Third on team in assists. Missed one game with concussion. Missed one game with knee injury.

THE FINESSE GAME

One of the drawbacks to this veteran's career is his size, but Sillinger is not without his assets. He is a clever player with a knack for positioning himself in the attacking zone. And he has a good shot with a quick release.

Sillinger is an energetic skater with speed and balance. His one-step acceleration is good. He plays well in traffic, using his sturdy form to protect the puck, and he has sharp hand-eye coordination. He is a smart penalty killer and a shorthanded threat, as well as an ace on face-offs. Sillinger was seventh in the NHL (57.01 per cent) on draws last season.

Expansion was tailor-made for guys like Sillinger. He has worked hard to make the most of what might be a last chance, and could be in a position to be picked up by a contender come playoff time.

THE PHYSICAL GAME

Sillinger is small but burly. He is tough to budge from in front of the net because of his low centre of gravity. He is not feisty or aggressive. He keeps himself in good condition and over the past few seasons has missed very few games due to injuries.

THE INTANGIBLES

Sillinger is a special-teams specialist. He kills penalties, is a shorthanded threat, works the open ice on the power play and can fill in (short-term) on the top two lines in a pinch. He is a grinder, a role player and a leader by example. In short, a nice fit on a team that is trying to mould its future.

PROJECTION

Sillinger hit our 20-goal prediction on the nose. He is likely to continue in a similar role for the Blue Jackets and match that number. Until Columbus gets better, Sillinger will be among its front-line forwards.

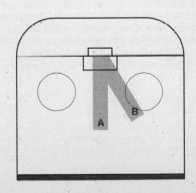

RAY WHITNEY

Yrs. of NHL service: 10
Born: Fort Saskatchewan, Alta.; May 8, 1972
Position: left wing / centre
Height: 5-10
Weight: 175
Uniform no.: 14
Shoots: right

Career statistics:

GP	G	A	TP	PIM
552	167	249	416	175

1998-1999 statistics:

GP	G	A	TP	+/-	PIM	PP	SH	GW	GT	S	PCT
81	26	38	64	-3	18	7	0	6	1	193	13.5

1999-2000 statistics:

GP	G	A	TP	+/-	PIM	PP	SH	GW	GT	S	PCT
81	29	42	71	+16	35	5	0	3	2	198	14.6

2000-2001 statistics:

GP	G	A	TP	+/-	PIM	PP	SH	GW	GT	S	PCT
46	10	24	34	-17	30	5	0	0	0	120	8.3

2001-2002 statistics:

GP	G	A	TP	+/-	PIM	PP	SH	GW	GT	S	PCT
67	21	40	61	-22	12	6	0	3	0	210	10.0

LAST SEASON

Led team in goals, assists, points and shots. Tied for second on team in power-play goals. Third on team in game-winning goals. Missed 11 games with chest injury. Mised two games with food poisoning. Missed one game with back injury. Missed two games for personal reasons.

THE FINESSE GAME

Whitney is not a fast skater, but he is shifty in tight quarters and that makes him very tough to check. He likes to cut to the middle of the ice and use his forehand. He is dangerous every shift.

Savvy and determined, Whitney compensates for his lack of speed with a keen sense of anticipation. He jumps into the right spot simply by knowing before his checker does that it's the right place to be. That makes him appear quicker than he really is.

Whitney is poised in traffic and well-balanced on his feet. He has exceptionally good hands for passing and shooting. He can lift a backhand shot when he is practically on top of the goalie. And he has a deceptive shot because he does not telegraph whether he is going to pass or shoot.

Because he can't win the battles on the boards, Whitney needs to play with a grinder on his wing.

THE PHYSICAL GAME

Whitney is small, but he plays a wily game. A centre of his ability needs to be protected with a tough winger and defenceman, but Whitney brings so much to the game that a team can make room for him. He is remarkably durable for his size.

THE INTANGIBLES

Whitney's bad back continued to bother him, even though he only sat one game because of it.

PROJECTION

Whitney has the ability to be a consistent 25-goal scorer in the right circumstances. If healthy, he will continue as a top-line player in Columbus.

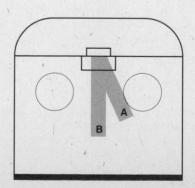

TYLER WRIGHT

Yrs. of NHL service: 7
Born: Canora, Sask.; Apr. 6, 1973
Position: centre
Height: 6-0
Weight: 185
Uniform no.: 28
Shoots: right

Career statistics:

GP	G	A	TP	PIM
432	49	44	93	627

1998-1999 statistics:

GP	G	A	TP	+/-	PIM	PP	SH	GW	GT	S	PCT
61	0	0	0	-2	90	0	0	0	0	16	0.0

1999-2000 statistics:

GP	G	A	TP	+/-	PIM	PP	SH	GW	GT	S	PCT
50	12	10	22	+4	45	0	0	1	0	68	17.6

2000-2001 statistics:

GP	G	A	TP	+/-	PIM	PP	SH	GW	GT	S	PCT
76	16	16	32	-9	140	4	1	2	1	141	11.4

2001-2002 statistics:

GP	G	A	TP	+/-	PIM	PP	SH	GW	GT	S	PCT
77	13	11	24	-40	100	4	0	1	1	120	10.8

PROJECTION

Wright has developed a scoring touch to complement his feisty game. He is a likely 15-goal, 30-point candidate.

LAST SEASON

Second on team in penalty minutes. Tied for third on team in shooting percentage. Missed five games with concussion.

THE FINESSE GAME

Wright brings to mind the prototypical agitators like Keith Acton and Ken Linseman. Playing in his third-line capacity, Wright will stir things up but be on the outside of the pile after everyone else has jumped in, admiring what he started. Wright is consistent in his effort, too. It's rare when he takes a night, or a shift, off.

Wright doesn't have a lot of finish around the net. He is not a natural goal-scorer. He has to work hard for everything he gets.

He's a quick and shifty skater, and handles the puck fine, but he does not have a big-league shot. His added dimension is as a penalty killer.

THE PHYSICAL GAME

Always in someone's face, Wright loves to try to distract other teams' top players — even from the bench. Yap, yap, yap. He's started to back up some of his chatter with points now, which is even more infuriating for opponents. He'll get slapped around a little because he's not much of a fighter. He's the human equivalent of a Jack Russell terrier.

THE INTANGIBLES

Wright is an enthusiastic and energetic player who adds something to a team's chemistry. He is a good leader for a team that is just a few years away from expansion, and is probably a future captain (he wore an "A" last season).

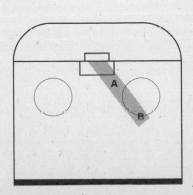

DALLAS STARS

Players' Statistics 2001-2002

POS.	NO.	PLAYER	GP	G	A	PTS	+/-	PIM	PP	SH	GW	GT	S	PCT
C	9	MIKE MODANO	78	34	43	77	14	38	6	2	5		219	15.5
R	26	JERE LEHTINEN	73	25	24	49	27	14	7	1	4	2	198	12.6
C	77	PIERRE TURGEON	66	15	32	47	-4	16	7		1	1	121	12.4
C	44	JASON ARNOTT	73	25	20	45	2	65	10		3		197	12.7
D	56	SERGEI ZUBOV	80	12	32	44	-4	22	8		2		198	6.1
L	10	BRENDEN MORROW	72	17	18	35	12	109	4		3		102	16.7
D	5	DARRYL SYDOR	78	4	29	33	3	50	2				183	2.2
L	22	KIRK MULLER	78	10	20	30	-12	28	4		1		111	9.0
D	2	DERIAN HATCHER	80	4	21	25	12	87	1			2	111	3.6
D	24	RICHARD MATVICHUK	82	9	12	21	11	52	4		2		109	8.3
R	16	PAT VERBEEK	64	7	13	20	-4	72	3		1		81	8.6
R	12	RANDY MCKAY	69	7	11	18	4	72	3		1		73	9.6
C	27	MANNY MALHOTRA	72	8	6	14	-4	47		1	1		60	13.3
L	33	SCOTT PELLERIN	68	4	10	14	-11	21					63	6.3
R	18	ROB DIMAIO	61	6	6	12	-2	25		2	2		63	9.5
L	41	BRENT GILCHRIST	45	3	6	9	-9	14			1		53	5.7
D	37	BRAD LUKOWICH	66	1	6	7	-1	40				1	56	1.8
R	51	JOHN MACLEAN	20	3	3	6	-1	17			1		40	7.5
C	14	JONATHAN SIM	26	3		3	-3	10	1				43	7.0
D	4	DAVE MANSON	47		2	2	2	33					36	
C	32	JIM MONTGOMERY	8		2	2	-1						8	
D	3	*JOHN ERSKINE	33		1	1	-8	62					16	
C	39	*NIKO KAPANEN	9		1	1	-1	2					3	
L	43	*STEVE GAINEY	5		1	1	-1	7					1	
D	6	SAMI HELENIUS	39				-4	58					18	
D	28	GREG HAWGOOD	2				0	2					1	
G	20	ED BELFOUR	60				0	12						
G	35	MARTY TURCO	31				0	10						

GP = games played; G = goals; A = assists; PTS = points; +/- = goals-for minus goals-against while player is on ice; PIM = penalties in minutes; PP = power-play goals; SH = shorthanded goals; GW = game-winning goals; GT = game-tying goals; S = no. of shots; PCT = percentage of goals to shots; * = rookie

JASON ARNOTT

Yrs. of NHL service: 9
Born: Collingwood, Ont.; Oct. 11, 1974
Position: centre
Height: 6 4
Weight: 225
Uniform no.: 44
Shoots: right

Career statistics:

GP	G	A	TP	PIM
598	200	264	464	780

1998-1999 statistics:

GP	G	A	TP	+/-	PIM	PP	SH	GW	GT	S	PCT
74	27	27	54	+10	79	8	0	3	1	200	13.5

1999-2000 statistics:

GP	G	A	TP	+/-	PIM	PP	SH	GW	GT	S	PCT
76	22	34	56	+22	51	7	0	4	0	244	9.0

2000-2001 statistics:

GP	G	A	TP	+/-	PIM	PP	SH	GW	GT	S	PCT
54	21	34	55	+23	75	8	0	3	2	138	15.2

2001-2002 statistics:

GP	G	A	TP	+/-	PIM	PP	SH	GW	GT	S	PCT
73	25	20	45	+2	65	10	0	3	0	197	12.7

LAST SEASON

Acquired from New Jersey on March 19, 2002, with Randy McKay and a first-round draft pick in 2002 for Joe Nieuwendyk and Jamie Langenbrunner. Led Stars in power-play goals. Tied for second on Stars in assists. Third on Stars in shooting percentage. Missed five games with back injury. Missed two games with groin injury. Missed two games with flu.

THE FINESSE GAME

What a weird scenario it was when Arnott, whose double-overtime goal defeated the Stars in the 2001 Stanley Cup Finals, arrived in Dallas. For whatever reason, Arnott never fit in comfortably after his late-season move. He was injured, and scored three goals in his 10 games with Dallas.

For a player of his size, Arnott has tremendous skills. As a skater he has speed, balance, a long stride, plus agility in turning to either side. He has also added muscle to his frame, without losing any edge in his skating. He has one of the hardest shots on the team, which is why the Devils used him on the point on their first power-play unit. He has a booming cannon of a shot. Arnott also smartly switches off with a winger on the half-boards and has a great one-timer from the circles.

Arnott's major flaw is that he is so skilled for a big guy that some nights he likes to take the easy way out. He should be a more effective power forward than he is, but he is easily sucked into a perimeter game. Arnott is a decent passer, though he is better getting the puck late and deep. His timing with passes is fine, as he holds onto the puck until a teammate is in the open. He is average on draws on a good night, and some nights really struggles. The Stars will probably want to play him on the wing, but he is not as effective, nor as happy, there. Arnott can be undisciplined in his positioning defensively.

THE PHYSICAL GAME

Arnott has shown that he's willing to pay a physical price, but the Devils thought he had a low pain threshold, which was among the reasons for the trade.

THE INTANGIBLES

Arnott may never achieve anywhere near the harmony he had with Patrik Elias and Petr Sykora in their two great seasons in New Jersey. Dallas was quietly inviting trade offers during the off-season.

PROJECTION

Arnott is tough to predict since it's impossible to know where he will fit in with the Stars. He is capable of being a point-a-game player, but we would hazard a prediction on the lower side, say 60 points.

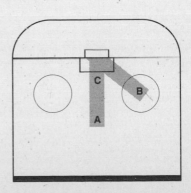

JOHN ERSKINE

Yrs. of NHL service: 1
Born: Ajax, Ont.; June 26, 1980
Position: defence
Height: 6-4
Weight: 215
Uniform no.: 3
Shoots: left

Career statistics:

GP	G	A	TP	PIM
33	0	1	1	62

2001-2002 statistics:

GP	G	A	TP	+/-	PIM	PP	SH	GW	GT	S	PCT
33	0	1	1	-8	62	0	0	0	0	16	0.0

LAST SEASON

First NHL season. Appeared in 39 games with Utah (AHL), scoring 2-6-8 with 118 PIM. Missed 13 games with fractured foot.

THE FINESSE GAME

Erskine has been described as a poor man's Derian Hatcher. Given Hatcher's years of service for the Stars, that's pretty rich. Erskine is built along Hatcher lines. He's tall and lanky and a little raw.

Erskine's skating is serviceable. He could stand to work with a skating coach to improve his foot speed.

Erskine makes a smart first pass out of the zone. He wants to keep the game simple and he will develop into a stay-at-home defenceman and a solid anchor for a more mobile and offensive-minded partner.

THE PHYSICAL GAME

Erskine will need to fill out a bit more for the NHL battles but he's got the right frame, and the right frame of mind. He is naturally aggressive. Erskine loves to hit and he's good at it.

THE INTANGIBLES

Erskine's positive first impression was formed by the high energy level he brought to the ice in his stint with the Stars last season. He'll get a shot to play on the third pair this season.

PROJECTION

Erskine has never been much of a point-getter at any level and his offensive production is bound to be minimal. He could reap some penalty minutes for you, if your pool includes that stat.

BILL GUERIN

Yrs. of NHL service: 10
Born: Wilbraham, Mass.; Nov. 9, 1970
Position: right wing
Height: 6-2
Weight: 210
Uniform no.: 13
Shoots: right

Career statistics:

GP	G	A	TP	PIM
733	256	248	504	1036

1998-1999 statistics:

GP	G	A	TP	+/-	PIM	PP	SH	GW	GT	S	PCT
80	30	34	64	+7	133	13	0	2	1	261	11.5

1999-2000 statistics:

GP	G	A	TP	+/-	PIM	PP	SH	GW	GT	S	PCT
70	24	22	46	+4	123	11	0	2	0	188	12.8

2000-2001 statistics:

GP	G	A	TP	+/-	PIM	PP	SH	GW	GT	S	PCT
85	40	45	85	+7	140	11	1	5	0	289	13.8

2001-2002 statistics:

GP	G	A	TP	+/-	PIM	PP	SH	GW	GT	S	PCT
78	41	25	66	-1	91	10	1	7	0	355	11.6

LAST SEASON

Signed as free agent on July 3, 2002. Led NHL in shots on goal. Led Bruins in power-play goals. Tied for first on Bruins in goals with career high. Tied for second in NHL in goals. Tied for second on Bruins in game-winning goals. Missed three games due to suspension. Missed one game with charley horse.

THE FINESSE GAME

Guerin has a terrifying slap shot, a wicked screamer that he unleashes off the wing in full flight. He has gotten smarter about mixing up his shots, using a wrister or snap shot for a one-timer instead of going into a full windup.

Guerin becomes ineffective when he stops playing like a power forward and dances on the perimeter, playing an east-west instead of north-south game. His speed and power are potent weapons; but he needs to drive down the right wing and force the defence back with his speed. When he backs off and takes the easier route to the off-wing, his scoring chances decrease drastically in quality.

Hockey sense and creativity are lagging a tad behind his other attributes, but Guerin is a conscientious player. He is aware defensively and has worked hard at that part of the game, though he will still lose his checking assignments and start running around in the defensive zone. On a sound Bruins defensive team, he was the only regular among the forwards who was a minus player last season. It would be a great idea to play him on a line with a good two-way player like Jere Lehtinen.

THE PHYSICAL GAME

The more physical the game is, the more Guerin gets involved. He is big, strong and tough in every sense of the word; he's useless when he plays otherwise.

The kind of game Guerin is going to have can usually be judged in the first few shifts. He can play it clean or mean, with big body checks or the drop of a glove. He will move to the puck carrier and battle for control until he gets it, and he's hard to knock off his skates.

In front of the net, Guerin digs hard. He works to establish position and has the hand skills to make something happen when the puck gets to his stick. He is durable, in great shape and can routinely handle 20 minutes a night.

THE INTANGIBLES

Guerin achieved his career high in goals despite more shake-ups (losing centre Jason Allison). He has been traded and managed to create chemistry wherever has has moved, so the change of scene to Dallas shouldn't hinder him.

PROJECTION

With a big-money contract comes added pressure. Guerin has shown in the past few years he can handle it, and he should top 40 goals again.

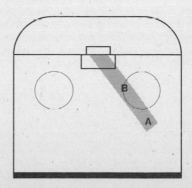

DERIAN HATCHER

Yrs. of NHL service: 11
Born: Sterling Heights, Mich.; June 4, 1972
Position: left defence
Height: 6-5
Weight: 230
Uniform no.: 2
Shoots: left

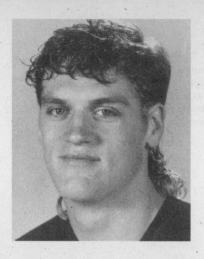

Career statistics:

GP	G	A	TP	PIM
745	63	201	264	1274

1998-1999 statistics:

GP	G	A	TP	+/-	PIM	PP	SH	GW	GT	S	PCT
80	9	21	30	+21	102	3	0	2	0	125	7.2

1999-2000 statistics:

GP	G	A	TP	+/-	PIM	PP	SH	GW	GT	S	PCT
57	2	22	24	+6	68	0	0	0	0	90	2.2

2000-2001 statistics:

GP	G	A	TP	+/-	PIM	PP	SH	GW	GT	S	PCT
80	2	21	23	+5	77	1	0	2	0	97	2.1

2001-2002 statistics:

GP	G	A	TP	+/-	PIM	PP	SH	GW	GT	S	PCT
80	4	21	25	+12	87	1	0	0	2	111	3.6

LAST SEASON

Second on team in penalty minutes. Tied for third on team in plus-minus. Missed two games with hamstring injury.

THE FINESSE GAME

Hatcher is among the game's most underrated defencemen. He plays in all key situations and has developed confidence in his decision-making process. His skating is laboured, so he lets the play come to him. He is sturdy and well-balanced, though the fewer strides he has to take the better.

He has very good hands for a big man, and has a good head for the game. Hatcher is fairly effective from the point on the power play — not because he has a big, booming slap shot, but because he has a good wrist shot and will get the puck on net quickly. He will join the rush eagerly once he gets into gear (his first few strides are sluggish), and he handles the puck nicely.

Hatcher plays hard in every zone, every night. His skills are just a shade below elite level but he takes steps forward every season as a leader. He is a character player, one his teammates look to for setting the tempo and seizing control of a game.

THE PHYSICAL GAME

This man is a big force. Hatcher has a mean streak when provoked and is a punishing hitter who relishes the physical aspect of the game. But he is also smart enough to realize that he's a target and opponents want to take him off his game. It's a huge detriment to the Stars when he is in the box, and not just because he is one of their key penalty killers. He plays physically every night and demands respect and room. He's fearless. He's also a big horse and eats up all the ice time Dallas gives him. Last season he was sixth in the NHL in average ice time (26:40). The more work he gets, the better.

THE INTANGIBLES

Hatcher will not put up big numbers, but he and Mike Modano are the cornerstones of the franchise. Hatcher is the kind of player the team looks to for consistent effort and intensity. He is a fine role model for the younger Stars, and has grown into a mature veteran. He is a quiet player who wants to make a big impact.

PROJECTION

Hatcher is the defenceman you want on your team when you have to win a clutch game. He can provide 30 points and invaluable leadership.

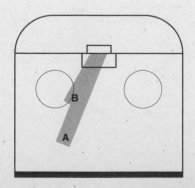

JERE LEHTINEN

Yrs. of NHL service: 7
Born: Espoo, Finland; June 24, 1973
Position: left wing
Height: 6-0
Weight: 200
Uniform no.: 26
Shoots: right

Career statistics:

GP	G	A	TP	PIM
430	113	154	267	94

1998-1999 statistics:

GP	G	A	TP	+/-	PIM	PP	SH	GW	GT	S	PCT
74	20	32	52	+29	18	7	1	2	0	173	11.6

1999-2000 statistics:

GP	G	A	TP	+/-	PIM	PP	SH	GW	GT	S	PCT
17	3	5	8	+1	0	0	0	1	0	29	10.3

2000-2001 statistics:

GP	G	A	TP	+/-	PIM	PP	SH	GW	GT	S	PCT
74	20	25	45	+14	24	7	0	1	1	148	13.5

2001-2002 statistics:

GP	G	A	TP	+/-	PIM	PP	SH	GW	GT	S	PCT
73	25	24	49	+27	14	7	1	4	2	198	12.6

LAST SEASON

Led team in plus-minus. Second on team in points and game-winning goals. Tied for second on team in goals and shots. Career high in goals. Missed eight games with ankle injury. Missed one game with knee surgery.

THE FINESSE GAME

Lehtinen is the smartest positional player on the Stars. He is remarkably astute and so honest and reliable that other players, almost through osmosis, have to come on-board.

As much as Mike Modano did on his own to become a more complete centre, much of that progress can be traced to his teaming with Lehtinen. Modano returned the favour by enhancing the Finn's latent offensive ability. Both players are more complete because of the other, and they've had some of their best games as linemates. It was a natural move to keep Lehtinen on the top line with Modano as the safety-valve winger, but Lehtinen never hurts the line offensively, either. He always plays with his head up.

Lehtinen's skating is well above adequate. He's not really top flight, but he has enough quickness and balance to play with highly skilled people. He controls the puck well and is an unselfish playmaker.

Lehtinen struggles only in his finishing. He appears to have a good shot with a quick release, but at times is reluctant to shoot. He is gaining more confidence.

THE PHYSICAL GAME

Is there a loose puck that Lehtinen ever loses a battle for? He is so strong on the puck: he protects it and won't be intimidated, and he competes along the boards. He completes his checks and never stops trying. He can handle a good amount of ice time and averaged just under 20 minutes last season.

THE INTANGIBLES

Lehtinen is as reliable a forward as there is in the league. You have to figure the Stars will give him and Modano a look with Bill Guerin, which could turn out to be a great line.

PROJECTION

Lehtinen will always concentrate more on the defensive aspect of the game and sacrifice scoring if he has to. For that reason, his point totals will never be gaudy. You should plan on 55-60 points if he stays healthy.

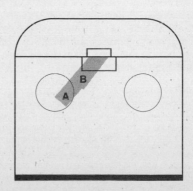

MANNY MALHOTRA

Yrs. of NHL service: 4
Born: Mississauga, Ont.; May 18, 1980
Position: centre/left wing
Height: 6-2
Weight: 210
Uniform no.: 27
Shoots: left

Career statistics:

GP	G	A	TP	PIM
222	20	22	42	95

1998-1999 statistics:

GP	G	A	TP	+/-	PIM	PP	SH	GW	GT	S	PCT
73	8	8	16	-2	13	1	0	2	0	61	13.1

1999-2000 statistics:

GP	G	A	TP	+/-	PIM	PP	SH	GW	GT	S	PCT
27	0	0	0	-6	4	0	0	0	0	18	-

2000-2001 statistics:

GP	G	A	TP	+/-	PIM	PP	SH	GW	GT	S	PCT
50	4	8	12	-10	31	0	0	2	0	46	8.7

2001-2002 statistics:

GP	G	A	TP	+/-	PIM	PP	SH	GW	GT	S	PCT
72	8	6	14	-4	47	0	1	1	0	60	13.3

LAST SEASON

Acquired from N.Y. Rangers on March 12, 2002, with Barrett Heisten for Martin Rucinsky and Roman Lyashenko. Missed 10 games due to coach's decision.

THE FINESSE GAME

Malhotra is a versatile player who may turn into a young Rod Brind'Amour — able to check, work on the power play, centre or wing, give a team a lead or protect it. Malhotra brings so many things to a team.

Malhotra is a two-way centre. He will never be a big-time scorer — his shot is not an awesome weapon — but by working to get in position and dig for short-range chances he will get his share. Malhotra also has a terrific first step and reads offensive plays well. He gets more than his fair share of breakaways. He has to read plays better defensively. He has a very young game yet. He is going to make his niche on the defensive side and has to develop his offence a bit more.

Malhotra's play is fuelled by will and determination. In fact, he might need to become a little less intense in practices and games, in order to relax and get a better feel for the game. Few recent young players have been so highly ranked in terms of character. He is highly coachable.

THE PHYSICAL GAME

Malhotra is big and strong and likes to play a physical game, but he needs to bulk up a bit more to play against the big boys, against whom he still looks a bit coltish. He makes big hits and churns up pucks on the forecheck. He has been described as an ultimate team player and a kid who thrives on hard work and improving himself. He's a low-maintenance player. He will not take a night, or a shift, off.

THE INTANGIBLES

Malhotra needed the changed of scene. He lost two years of development in a shameful tug-of-war between a coach who wouldn't play him (John Muckler) and a GM who refused to send him back to juniors (Neil Smith). Then, with the arrival of a new GM, he was one of the players drafted by the old GM, and therefore doomed to leave.

Malhotra seems back on the right track but is still finding a way. This has to be the season when he puts things together and wins a full-time job on the third line. He gets yet another fresh start with a new coach.

PROJECTION

Muckler once dismissively called Malhotra nothing better than a third-line player. Couched in more diplomatic terms, that's accurate. What Malhotra should become is an excellent third-line forward, but he is probably two or three seasons away from becoming a defensive forward who can also produce 20 goals. At least he's now with a team that will value his assets.

RICHARD MATVICHUK

Yrs. of NHL service: 10
Born: Edmonton, Alta.; Feb. 5, 1973
Position: left defence
Height: 6-2
Weight: 215
Uniform no.: 24
Shoots: left

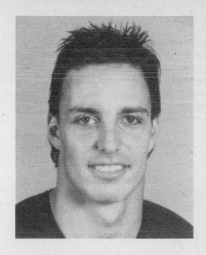

Career statistics:

GP	G	A	TP	PIM
590	36	104	140	490

1998-1999 statistics:

GP	G	A	TP	+/-	PIM	PP	SH	GW	GT	S	PCT
64	3	9	12	+23	51	1	0	0	0	54	5.6

1999-2000 statistics:

GP	G	A	TP	+/-	PIM	PP	SH	GW	GT	S	PCT
70	4	21	25	+7	42	0	0	1	0	73	5.5

2000-2001 statistics:

GP	G	A	TP	+/-	PIM	PP	SH	GW	GT	S	PCT
78	4	16	20	+5	62	2	0	1	0	85	4.7

2001-2002 statistics:

GP	G	A	TP	+/-	PIM	PP	SH	GW	GT	S	PCT
82	9	12	21	+11	52	4	0	2	0	109	8.3

LAST SEASON

Only Star to appear in all 82 games. Career high in goals.

THE FINESSE GAME

Matvichuk has found his niche as a mobile, two-way defenceman. He is a good skater with a long stride, who skates well backwards and pivots in either direction. He has started to get involved more in the attack, and is capable of doing that to a degree. He has the hand skills and instincts to play with the offensive players to a point, but that is not a high priority for him. He uses his hockey skills defensively. If his partner wants to go, Matvichuk will make sure to stay at home.

He has a low, hard, accurate shot from the point. Matvichuk makes smart, crisp passes and uses other players well. He can play either side defensively.

Matvichuk wants the ice time when the team needs a calm, defensive presence on the ice. He kills penalties and is one of the Stars' best shot-blockers.

THE PHYSICAL GAME

Matvichuk knows the importance of strength and aerobic training and wants to add even more muscle to stay competitive, since he was a little light by today's NHL standards. He's a hack-and-whack kind of mean guy, not a fighter. He occasionally gets into a mode where he starts fishing for the puck and has to be reminded to take the body. Matvichuk did this on a much more consistent basis last season, maybe because he was able to stay healthy.

Because he plays so hard and blocks so many shots, Matvichuk is subject to great wear and tear. He is tough, though, and plays through injuries.

THE INTANGIBLES

Matvichuk is part of a solid four-man corps in Dallas.

PROJECTION

Matvichuk has become a confident and capable defenceman. He may have slightly more offensive upside, though 20 to 25 points is a reliable range.

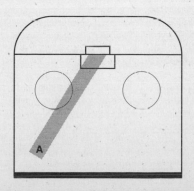

MIKE MODANO

Yrs. of NHL service: 13
Born: Livonia, Mich.; June 7, 1970
Position: centre
Height: 6-3
Weight: 205
Uniform no.: 9
Shoots: left

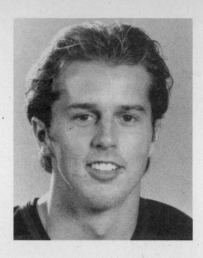

Career statistics:

GP	G	A	TP	PIM
946	416	561	977	634

1998-1999 statistics:

GP	G	A	TP	+/-	PIM	PP	SH	GW	GT	S	PCT
77	34	47	81	+29	44	6	4	7	1	224	15.2

1999-2000 statistics:

GP	G	A	TP	+/-	PIM	PP	SH	GW	GT	S	PCT
77	38	43	81	0	48	11	1	8	3	188	20.2

2000-2001 statistics:

GP	G	A	TP	+/-	PIM	PP	SH	GW	GT	S	PCT
81	33	51	84	+26	52	8	3	7	1	208	15.9

2001-2002 statistics:

GP	G	A	TP	+/-	PIM	PP	SH	GW	GT	S	PCT
78	34	43	77	+14	38	6	2	5	0	219	15.5

LAST SEASON

Led team in goals, assists, points, game-winning goals and shots. Tied for ninth in NHL in points. Tied for team lead in shorthanded goals. Second on team in plus-minus and shooting percentage. Missed two games with back injury. Missed one game with thigh injury. Missed one game due to personal reasons.

THE FINESSE GAME

Modano is one of the game's most well-rounded players. He has world-class skills that match those of just about any player in the NHL. Modano is not a physical player, but he isn't soft. When there is a lot of open ice, he's a thrilling player to watch. He has outstanding offensive instincts and great hands, and he is a smooth passer and a remarkable skater in all facets.

Modano makes other players around him better, which is the mark of a superstar. His speed and agility with the puck leave defenders mesmerized and open up ice for his linemates. He is the pivot for one of the best lines in the game, with Jere Lehtinen and possibly newcomer (and fellow U.S. Olympian) Bill Guerin as his right wing.

Modano has become a top penalty killer. His anticipation and quick hands help him intercept passes. By going to a straighter stickblade he has improved his face-offs, and become so reliable defensively that he is thrown onto the ice in the closing minutes of a period or game. He won about 53 per cent of his draws last season.

Like Steve Yzerman, Modano learned that flirting with 100-point seasons was fun, but to become a champion one has to sacrifice some of the offensive spark to play a better all-round game. Modano has done so.

THE PHYSICAL GAME

He plays through injuries, and in his own way Modano is strong and tough — maybe not aggressive and feisty, but questions about his hockey courage have been quelled forever. He is a gamer.

THE INTANGIBLES

Joe Nieuwendyk's departure placed more pressure on Modano, but Guerin's addition should help both on the ice and in the dressing room. Missing the playoffs for the first time since 1996 had to sting, and Modano has had a long off-season to think about how to fix it.

PROJECTION

Have to think the Guerin chemistry will fire. If Dallas can assemble a solid second line, Modano could get back in the 90-point range.

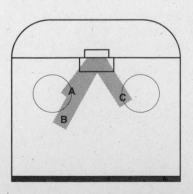

BRENDEN MORROW

Yrs. of NHL service: 3
Born: Carlyle, Sask.; Jan. 16, 1979
Position: left wing
Height: 5-11
Weight: 200
Uniform no.: 10
Shoots: left

Career statistics:

GP	G	A	TP	PIM
218	51	61	112	318

1999-2000 statistics:

GP	G	A	TP	+/-	PIM	PP	SH	GW	GT	S	PCT
64	14	19	33	+8	81	3	0	3	0	113	12.4

2000-2001 statistics:

GP	G	A	TP	+/-	PIM	PP	SH	GW	GT	S	PCT
82	20	24	44	+18	128	7	0	6	0	121	16.5

2001-2002 statistics:

GP	G	A	TP	+/-	PIM	PP	SH	GW	GT	S	PCT
72	17	18	35	+12	109	4	0	3	0	102	16.7

LAST SEASON

Led team in penalty minutes for second consecutive season. Led team in shooting percentage. Tied for third on team in plus-minus. Missed 10 games with knee injury.

THE FINESSE GAME

This is Dallas, so we have to start with defence. No kid in the Stars' system gets a chance to play with the big boys unless he has good defensive awareness and yes, it will probably remain the same after the coaching change to Dave Tippett. Morrow was smart enough to understand that and built his game with a solid defensive foundation.

Now it's time to raise the roof. Morrow isn't very tall, but he is stocky and very strong on his skates and tough to knock off-balance. He is a very crafty, creative and skillful puckhandler.

Morrow is a dedicated forechecker. Offensively, he will plunge into the slot and force a defender to take him down. In his own zone, he backchecks and positions himself well. He works well with the extra space on the power play and has a knack for scoring the big goal.

Morrow is growing along power forward lines, and he will have a good veteran to learn from in Bill Guerin.

THE PHYSICAL GAME

Morrow isn't afraid to play with a little edge. He can be annoying, and he will often have other players chasing him and trying to slap him down like a bug.

THE INTANGIBLES

A hard worker, Morrow is a nice two-way forward who can have a long and steady career in his role. He wants to stay here and will do what it takes.

PROJECTION

Morrow will never put up spectacular numbers, but he works hard enough and is skilled enough to start getting into the 50-point range on a consistent basis.

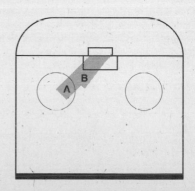

DARRYL SYDOR

Yrs. of NHL service: 10
Born: Edmonton, Alta.; May 13, 1972
Position: right defence
Height: 6-1
Weight: 205
Uniform no.: 5
Shoots: left

Career statistics:

GP	G	A	TP	PIM
782	77	292	369	558

1998-1999 statistics:

GP	G	A	TP	+/-	PIM	PP	SH	GW	GT	S	PCT
74	14	34	48	-1	50	9	0	2	1	163	8.6

1999-2000 statistics:

GP	G	A	TP	+/-	PIM	PP	SH	GW	GT	S	PCT
74	8	26	34	+6	32	5	0	1	0	132	6.1

2000-2001 statistics:

GP	G	A	TP	+/-	PIM	PP	SH	GW	GT	S	PCT
81	10	37	47	+5	34	8	0	1	0	140	7.1

2001-2002 statistics:

GP	G	A	TP	+/-	PIM	PP	SH	GW	GT	S	PCT
78	4	29	33	+3	50	2	0	0	0	183	2.2

THE INTANGIBLES

Sydor was rewarded with a five-year contract extension in February. He is a top-four defenceman on one of the best defensive teams in the league.

PROJECTION

Sydor should score in the 35-40 points range.

LAST SEASON

Missed three games with a concussion.

THE FINESSE GAME

Sydor's offensive game can kick in at any time. He has a fine shot from the point and can handle power-play time. He has good sense for jumping into the attack and controls the puck ably when carrying it, though he doesn't always protect it well with his body. He makes nice outlet passes and has good vision of the ice. He can rush with the puck or play dump-and-chase. In his own zone, he has developed into a safe, reliable defender.

Sydor is yet another player whose game was offence-heavy before joining a defensively-conscious organization. As a result, he has become a more well-rounded player.

A very strong skater with balance and agility and excellent lateral movement, Sydor can accelerate well and changes directions easily. Not a dynamic defenceman, but better than average, he can be used up front during injury emergencies.

A converted forward, Sydor can be used up front in a pinch by the Stars, and saw a little time at left wing last season.

THE PHYSICAL GAME

Sydor wants and needs to establish more of a physical presence. He is intense and has to be reined in. He has learned that sometimes going nowhere is better than trying to go everywhere. He competes hard and could still get stronger.

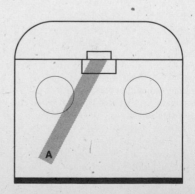

PIERRE TURGEON

Yrs. of NHL service: 15
Born: Rouyn, Que.; Aug. 28, 1969
Position: centre
Height: 6-1
Weight: 199
Uniform no.: 77
Shoots: left

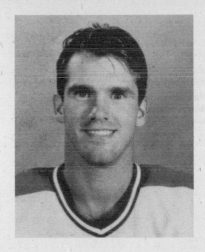

Career statistics:

GP	G	A	TP	PIM
1074	468	724	1192	372

1998-1999 statistics:

GP	G	A	TP	+/-	PIM	PP	SH	GW	GT	S	PCT
67	31	34	65	+4	36	10	0	5	2	193	16.1

1999-2000 statistics:

GP	G	A	TP	+/-	PIM	PP	SH	GW	GT	S	PCT
52	26	40	66	+30	8	8	0	3	0	139	18.7

2000-2001 statistics:

GP	G	A	TP	+/-	PIM	PP	SH	GW	GT	S	PCT
79	30	52	82	+14	37	11	0	6	1	171	17.5

2001-2002 statistics:

GP	G	A	TP	+/-	PIM	PP	SH	GW	GT	S	PCT
66	15	32	47	-4	16	7	0	1	1	121	12.4

LAST SEASON

Tied for second on team in assists. Third on team in points. Tied for third on team in power-play goals. Missed 12 games with ankle injury. Missed four games with shoulder injury.

THE FINESSE GAME

What looked like a no-brainer free agent move by Dallas in 2001 was a disaster on the ice. Maybe with Joe Nieuwendyk around (before he was dealt to the Devils in March 2002), there were just too many centres. Turgeon never made a case to get more ice time.

Turgeon is a better player than we saw last season. His skills are amazing. He never seems to be looking at the puck, yet he is always in perfect control of it. Turgeon has a style unlike just about anyone else in the NHL. He's not a fast skater, but he can deke a defender or make a sneaky-Pete surprise pass. He is tough to defend against, because if you aren't aware of where he is on the ice or don't deny him the pass, he can kill a team with several moves.

Turgeon can slow or speed up the tempo of a game. He lacks breakout speed, but because he is slippery and can change speeds so smoothly, he's deceptive. His control with the puck down low is remarkable. He protects the puck well with the body and has good anticipation; he reads plays well and is patient with the puck. Turgeon is fairly good on draws (around 48 per cent last season).

Although best known for his playmaking, Turgeon has an excellent shot. He will curl out from behind the net with a wrist shot, shoot off the fly from the right wing (his preferred side of the ice) or stand off to the side of the net on a power play and reach for a redirection of a point shot. He doesn't have a bazooka shot, but he uses quick, accurate wrist and snap shots. He has to create odd-man rushes — this is when he is at his finest.

THE PHYSICAL GAME

Though he isn't very aggressive or big, Turgeon battles hard. He doesn't play a perimeter game and he gets hurt because of it.

THE INTANGIBLES

There is no question that Dallas signed free agent Scott Young (who had a subpar year of his own in St. Louis) to revive Turgeon.

PROJECTION

Turgeon should be a point-a-game player or better, but if he doesn't get off to a quick start this season, the heat will be on him early. He makes too much money to play this poorly.

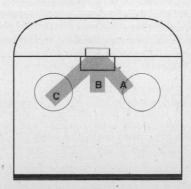

SCOTT YOUNG

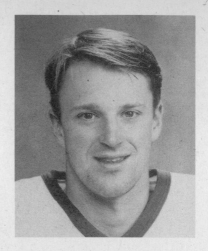

Yrs. of NHL service: 13
Born: Clinton, Mass.; Oct. 1, 1967
Position: right wing
Height: 6-1
Weight: 200
Uniform no.: 48
Shoots: right

Career statistics:

GP	G	A	TP	PIM
970	293	357	650	352

1998-1999 statistics:

GP	G	A	TP	+/-	PIM	PP	SH	GW	GT	S	PCT
75	24	28	52	+8	27	8	0	4	0	205	11.7

1999-2000 statistics:

GP	G	A	TP	+/-	PIM	PP	SH	GW	GT	S	PCT
75	24	15	39	+12	18	6	1	7	1	244	9.8

2000-2001 statistics:

GP	G	A	TP	+/-	PIM	PP	SH	GW	GT	S	PCT
81	40	33	73	+15	30	14	3	7	1	321	12.5

2001-2002 statistics:

GP	G	A	TP	+/-	PIM	PP	SH	GW	GT	S	PCT
67	19	22	41	+11	26	5	0	1	0	210	9.1

LAST SEASON

Signed by Dallas as free agent on July 6, 2002. Missed 11 games with eye injury. Missed four games with back spasms.

THE FINESSE GAME

Young is a hockey machine. He has a very heavy shot that surprises a lot of goalies, and he loves to fire it off the wing. He can also one-time the puck low on the face-off, or he'll battle for pucks and tips in front of the net. He's keen to score and always goes to the net with his stick down, ready for the puck, though he is not a great finisher. Young has a bit of tunnel vision, and doesn't really see his teammates or use them as well as he might. But he has tremendous confidence in his ability to score.

With all of that in mind, his defensive awareness is even more impressive. He reads plays in all zones equally well and has good anticipation. He played defence in college, so he is well-schooled.

Young is a fast skater, which, combined with his reads, makes him a sound forechecker. He will often outrace defencemen to get pucks and avoid icings, and his speed allows him to recover when he gets over-zealous in the attacking zone.

THE PHYSICAL GAME

Young's lone drawback is that he is not a physical player. He will do what he has to do in battles along the boards in the defensive zone, but he's more of a defensive force with quickness and hand skills. He's not a pure grinder, but will bump and get in the way.

THE INTANGIBLES

Injuries to both Young and centre Doug Weight — as well as Young's inability to click with the new forward — added up to a disappointing farewell season in St. Louis. In Dallas, Young is expected to reunite with Pierre Turgeon, another veteran who will be looking to redeem himself after an off year.

Young is the kind of player who will want to prove the Stars didn't make a mistake by signing him. He is a character person as well as an ultra-reliable performer. Players with great wheels like Young tend to last a long time, so expect him to flash his ability for another season or two.

PROJECTION

Young is due for a bounce-back season and we would make a guess at 25 goals if he stays healthy.

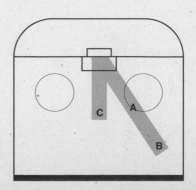

SERGEI ZUBOV

Yrs. of NHL service: 10
Born: Moscow, Russia; July 22, 1970
Position: right defence
Height: 6-1
Weight: 200
Uniform no.: 56
Shoots: right

Career statistics:

GP	G	A	TP	PIM
697	105	405	510	207

1998-1999 statistics:

GP	G	A	TP	+/-	PIM	PP	SH	GW	GT	S	PCT
81	10	41	51	+9	20	5	0	3	0	155	6.5

1999-2000 statistics:

GP	G	A	TP	+/-	PIM	PP	SH	GW	GT	S	PCT
77	9	33	42	-2	18	3	1	3	0	179	5.0

2000-2001 statistics:

GP	G	A	TP	+/-	PIM	PP	SH	GW	GT	S	PCT
79	10	41	51	+22	24	6	0	1	1	173	5.8

2001-2002 statistics:

GP	G	A	TP	+/-	PIM	PP	SH	GW	GT	S	PCT
80	12	32	44	-4	22	8	0	2	0	198	6.1

LAST SEASON

Led team defencemen in points for fifth consecutive season. Second on team in power-play goals. Tied for second on team in assists and shots. Missed two games with shoulder injury.

THE FINESSE GAME

The overly patient Zubov is so close to being an elite NHL "offenceman," except for his tendency to hold the puck and look for a pass when the shot is his. He continually improves in this category, but there are still times when his failure to shoot is frustrating.

Zubov has some world-class skills. He skates with good balance and generates power from his leg drive. He is agile in his stops and starts, even backwards. He also has a good slap shot and one-times the puck with accuracy — when he deigns to shoot. He masks his intentions well, faking a shot and finding the open man with a slick pass. He's not afraid to come in deep, either. Zubov will occasionally frustrate his teammates when he slows things down with the puck on a rush or breakout while the rest of the team has already taken off like racehorses.

He has strong lateral acceleration, but Zubov is also educated enough to keep his skating stride for stride with the wing trying to beat him to the outside. So many other defencemen speed up a couple of strides, then try to slow their men with stick-checks. Zubov will use his reach, superior body positioning or his agility to force the play and compel the puck carrier to make a decision. However, he doesn't always search out the right man or, when he does, he doesn't always eliminate the right man. A team has to live with that because Zubov's offensive upside is huge.

THE PHYSICAL GAME

Zubov is not physical, but he is solidly built and will take a hit to make a play. He can give a team a lot of minutes (he was fifth in the NHL with 26:46 minutes last season) and not wear down physically.

His boyhood idol was Viacheslav Fetisov, and that role model should give you some idea of Zubov's style. He gets his body in the way with his great skating, then strips the puck when the attacker finds no path to the net. He doesn't initiate much, but doesn't mind getting hit to make a play.

THE INTANGIBLES

Mentally, Zubov will still lose his focus and is capable of the most astounding giveaways. He can often atone with a terrific offensive play, but his lapses keep him from being rated among the league's best. Trade rumours have been swirling around Zubov, but offensive defencemen like him are rare. The Stars will continue to put up with his defensive lapses for at least another season.

PROJECTION

As the Stars' reigning offensive defenceman, Zubov should score between 50 and 60 points this season.

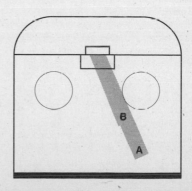

DETROIT RED WINGS

Players' Statistics 2001-2002

POS.	NO.	PLAYER	GP	G	A	PTS	+/-	PIM	PP	SH	GW	GT	S	PCT
L	14	BRENDAN SHANAHAN	80	37	38	75	23	118	12	3	7	3	277	13.4
C	91	SERGEI FEDOROV	81	31	37	68	20	36	10		6		256	12.1
R	17	BRETT HULL	82	30	33	63	18	35	7	1	4	2	247	12.1
D	5	NICKLAS LIDSTROM	78	9	50	59	13	20	6				215	4.2
L	20	LUC ROBITAILLE	81	30	20	50	-2	38	13		5	2	190	15.8
C	19	STEVE YZERMAN	52	13	35	48	11	18	5	1	5		104	12.5
C	8	IGOR LARIONOV	70	11	32	43	-5	50	4		1		50	22.0
D	24	CHRIS CHELIOS	79	6	33	39	40	126	1		1		128	4.7
C	13	*PAVEL DATSYUK	70	11	24	35	4	4	2		1		79	13.9
C	33	KRIS DRAPER	82	15	15	30	26	56		2	3		137	10.9
L	96	TOMAS HOLMSTROM	69	8	18	26	-12	58	6		1		79	10.1
C	21	BOYD DEVEREAUX	79	9	16	25	9	24			2		116	7.8
L	18	KIRK MALTBY	82	9	15	24	15	40		1	5		108	8.3
D	11	MATHIEU DANDENAULT	81	8	12	20	-5	44	2		3		97	8.3
D	28	STEVE DUCHESNE	64	3	15	18	3	28	1		2		70	4.3
D	27	FREDRIK OLAUSSON	47	2	13	15	9	22	1	1	1		61	3.3
R	25	DARREN MCCARTY	62	5	7	12	2	98			1	2	74	6.8
C	29	*JASON WILLIAMS	25	8	2	10	2	4	4				32	25.0
D	2	JIRI FISCHER	80	2	8	10	17	67			1		103	1.9
D	71	JIRI SLEGR	46	3	6	9	-20	59	1				67	4.5
C	42	*SEAN AVERY	36	2	2	4	1	68			1		30	6.7
D	32	*MAXIM KUZNETSOV	39	1	2	3	0	40					27	3.7
D	4	UWE KRUPP	8		1	1	-1	8					9	
D	3	*JESSE WALLIN	15		1	1	-1	13					8	
R	15	LADISLAV KOHN	4				0	4					2	
G	39	DOMINIK HASEK	65				0	8						
G	34	MANNY LEGACE	20				0							

GP = games played; G = goals; A = assists; PTS = points; +/- = goals-for minus goals-against while player is on ice; PIM = penalties in minutes; PP = power-play goals; SH = shorthanded goals; GW = game-winning goals; GT = game-tying goals; S = no. of shots; PCT = percentage of goals to shots; * = rookie

CHRIS CHELIOS

Yrs. of NHL service: 18
Born: Chicago, Ill.; Jan. 25, 1962
Position: right defence
Height: 6-1
Weight: 190
Uniform no.: 24
Shoots: right

Career statistics:

GP	G	A	TP	PIM
1260	174	700	874	2556

1998-1999 statistics:

GP	G	A	TP	+/-	PIM	PP	SH	GW	GT	S	PCT
75	9	27	36	+1	93	3	1	1	1	187	4.8

1999-2000 statistics:

GP	G	A	TP	+/-	PIM	PP	SH	GW	GT	S	PCT
81	3	31	34	+48	103	0	0	0	0	135	2.2

2000-2001 statistics:

GP	G	A	TP	+/-	PIM	PP	SH	GW	GT	S	PCT
24	0	3	3	+4	45	0	0	0	0	26	0.0

2001-2002 statistics:

GP	G	A	TP	+/-	PIM	PP	SH	GW	GT	S	PCT
79	6	33	39	+40	126	1	0	1	0	128	4.7

LAST SEASON

Led team and NHL in plus-minus. Led team in penalty minutes.

THE FINESSE GAME

Whatever the team needs, Chelios will bleed to give. He can become a top offensive defenceman, pinching boldly at every opportunity. Or he can create offence off the rush, make a play through the neutral zone or quarterback the power play from the point. He has a good, low, hard slap shot. He is not afraid to skate in-deep, where he can handle the puck well and use a snap shot or wrist shot with a quick release.

If defence is needed, Chelios will rule in his own zone. He is extremely confident and poised with the puck and doesn't overhandle it, though he is slowing down a step. He wants to get the puck away from his net by the most expedient means possible. He is aggressive in forcing the puck carrier to make a decision by stepping up. He also steps up in the neutral zone to break up plays with his stick.

Chelios is an instinctive player. When he is on his game, he reacts and makes plays few other defencemen can. When he struggles, which is seldom, he is back on his heels. He tries to do other people's jobs and becomes undisciplined.

Chelios has excellent anticipation and is a strong penalty killer. He's a mobile, smooth skater with good lateral movement. He is seldom beaten one on one, and he's even tough facing a two-on-one. In his mind, he can do anything. He usually does.

THE PHYSICAL GAME

At age 41, Chelios should not be handling the ice time and demands of a No. 2 defenceman. That he is still able to do so, and perform at such a high calibre of play, gives you an idea of how dedicated Chelios is to his conditioning. Chelios is not that big but plays like an enormous defenceman. He is mean, tough and physical, strong and solid on his skates, and fearless.

THE INTANGIBLES

Chelios was a free agent during the off-season and could have gone to a lesser team, but chose to stay in Detroit. It was a smart decision, because even if he earned more money with a team like the Rangers, the wear and tear on him would be considerable. Staying with a strong team in Detroit will add a season or two to his career.

PROJECTION

Chelios did not ease into the Detroit lineup the way we thought he would, but came on full-throttle and doubled the number of points we had projected for him. The way he looked last season, he certainly seems capable of returning with a 30-point season.

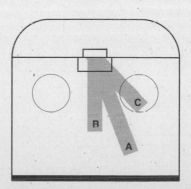

PAVEL DATSYUK

Yrs. of NHL service: 1
Born: Sverdlovsk, Russia; July 20, 1978
Position: centre
Height: 5-11
Weight: 180
Uniform no.: 13
Shoots: left

Career statistics:

GP	G	A	TP	PIM
70	11	24	35	4

2001-2002 statistics:

GP	G	A	TP	+/-	PIM	PP	SH	GW	GT	S	PCT
70	11	24	35	+4	4	2	0	1	0	79	13.9

LAST SEASON
First NHL season. Missed one game with flu.

THE FINESSE GAME
Just when it seemed like Detroit would have to discover the fountain of youth to revive its aging roster, along came this dynamic kid last season.

Datsyuk is a terrific skater. He has the best lateral movement on the team, and when the team includes forwards such as Sergei Fedorov and Steve Yzerman, that is high praise. He is a great one-on-one player.

Datsyuk is a better playmaker than scorer. He will probably always have about a 1:2 ratio between his goals and assists, and he barely averaged a shot per game last season. Datsyuk reminds scouts of a smaller and less cerebral Igor Larionov.

Datsyuk can develop into an effective penalty killer.

THE PHYSICAL GAME
Datsyuk is on the small side and doesn't have much of a physical presence. He needs to get stronger to survive in the NHL.

THE INTANGIBLES
Some players have trouble worming their way into a lineup laced with veterans who have won Cups. It's an ideal situation for Datsyuk, who found a nice chemistry with Brett Hull.

PROJECTION
Datsyuk played well enough to earn a full-time role, and with Yzerman slated to miss the first few months of the season, Datsyuk should win a top six job. He should score 50 points.

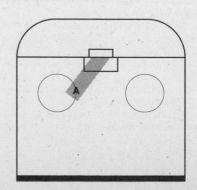

SERGEI FEDOROV

Yrs. of NHL service: 12
Born: Pskov, Russia; Dec. 13, 1969
Position: centre
Height: 6-1
Weight: 200
Uniform no.: 91
Shoots: left

Career statistics:

GP	G	A	TP	PIM
828	364	507	871	535

1998-1999 statistics:

GP	G	A	TP	+/-	PIM	PP	SH	GW	GT	S	PCT
77	26	37	63	+9	66	6	2	3	0	224	11.6

1999-2000 statistics:

GP	G	A	TP	+/-	PIM	PP	SH	GW	GT	S	PCT
68	27	35	62	+8	22	4	4	7	0	263	10.3

2000-2001 statistics:

GP	G	A	TP	+/-	PIM	PP	SH	GW	GT	S	PCT
75	32	37	69	+12	40	14	2	7	1	268	11.9

2001-2002 statistics:

GP	G	A	TP	+/-	PIM	PP	SH	GW	GT	S	PCT
81	31	37	68	+20	36	10	0	6	0	256	12.1

LAST SEASON

Second on team in goals, points, game-winning goals and shots. Third on team in assists and power-play goals.

THE FINESSE GAME

Fedorov likes to gear up from his own defensive zone, using his acceleration and balance to drive wide to his right, carrying the puck on his backhand and protecting it with his body. If the defenceman lets up at all, Fedorov is by him, pulling the puck quickly to his forehand. Nor is he by any means selfish. He has 360-degree vision of the ice and makes solid, confident passes right under opponents' sticks and smack onto the tape of his teammates'. His skating is nothing short of phenomenal; he can handle the puck while dazzling everyone with his blades.

Versatility is a Fedorov hallmark. In his career he has played left wing, centre and even defence. He fuels a power play and kills penalties. With his enormous package of offensive and defensive skills, he can go from checking his opponent's top centre to powering the power play from shift to shift. Fedorov may be Detroit's top defensive centre and he contributes big numbers offensively.

Fedorov will swing behind the opposing net from left to right, fooling the defence into thinking he is going to continue to curl around, but he can quickly reverse with the puck on his backhand, shake his shadow and wheel around for a shot or goalmouth pass. He does it all in a flash, and skating with the puck doesn't slow him down one whit.

THE PHYSICAL GAME

When you are as gifted as Fedorov, opponents will do all they can to hit you and hurt you. Although the wiry Fedorov is reluctant to absorb big hits or deliver any, he will leave the relative safety of open ice and head to the trenches when he is getting punished.

Much of his power is generated from his strong skating. For the most part, his defence is dominated by his reads, anticipation and quickness in knocking down passes and breaking up plays. He is not much of a body checker, and he gets most of his penalties from stick and restraining fouls.

THE INTANGIBLES

Fedorov will be among the players asked to pick up the slack with Steve Yzerman expected to miss half the season. This is when Fedorov's versatility really pays off.

PROJECTION

Expect 65-70 points from Fedorov.

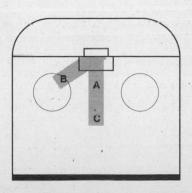

JIRI FISCHER

Yrs. of NHL service: 3
Born: Horovice, Czech Republic; July 31, 1980
Position: left defence
Height: 6-5
Weight: 225
Uniform no.: 2
Shoots: left

Career statistics:

GP	G	A	TP	PIM
187	3	24	27	171

1999-2000 statistics:

GP	G	A	TP	+/-	PIM	PP	SH	GW	GT	S	PCT
52	0	8	8	+1	45	0	0	0	0	41	0.0

2000-2001 statistics:

GP	G	A	TP	+/-	PIM	PP	SH	GW	GT	S	PCT
55	1	8	9	+3	59	0	0	0	0	64	1.6

2001-2002 statistics:

GP	G	A	TP	+/-	PIM	PP	SH	GW	GT	S	PCT
80	2	8	10	+17	67	0	0	1	0	103	1.9

LAST SEASON

Career high in games played.

THE FINESSE GAME

For such a tall skater, Fischer doesn't look a bit gangly. He is strong on his skates and has a long stride. It doesn't take him long to get into stride, either. He is well-coordinated and agile in his turns.

Fischer has a low panic point and is confident with the puck. Soft hands for giving or receiving make him a good passer. He has some faith in his ability to skate the puck out and is willing to get involved in the rush, though he can be expected to focus on the defensive part of the game as he continues to break in.

Fischer will get some second-unit power-play and penalty-killing stints. His reach makes him a natural shorthanded threat, since he takes up a lot of ice. He has a decent point shot, though his release isn't quick. One-on-one he is just about impossible to best, because a skater has to go a long way to get around him.

Fischer has often drawn comparisons to Rob Blake, but he may not have Blake's scoring touch.

THE PHYSICAL GAME

Fischer is very tall but not thick or heavy. He needs to develop more muscle for the battles along the wall and in front of the net. He can use his long reach to wrap up and neutralize an attacker. He has a latent mean streak; opponents will quickly learn not to take liberties with him. Fischer works hard.

THE INTANGIBLES

Fischer remains a work in progress, but he should be the No. 3 defenceman this season. Fischer is a long-term investment for Detroit, which expects him to be one of its core defencemen for years to come. Patience has been the key word, and even this season the Wings won't rush him. Fischer has a good relationship with the veteran defencemen on the team and they have been willing to help him learn his craft.

PROJECTION

Fischer does not have a lot of offensive upside. Twenty points would be a peak year.

TOMAS HOLMSTROM

Yrs. of NHL service: 6
Born: Pitea, Sweden; Jan 23, 1973
Position: left wing
Height: 6-0
Weight: 200
Uniform no.: 96
Shoots: left

Career statistics:

GP	G	A	TP	PIM
400	61	105	166	287

1998-1999 statistics:

GP	G	A	TP	+/-	PIM	PP	SH	GW	GT	S	PCT
82	13	21	34	-11	69	5	0	4	0	100	13.0

1999-2000 statistics:

GP	G	A	TP	+/-	PIM	PP	SH	GW	GT	S	PCT
72	13	22	35	+4	43	4	0	1	0	71	18.3

2000-2001 statistics:

GP	G	A	TP	+/-	PIM	PP	SH	GW	GT	S	PCT
73	16	24	40	-12	40	9	0	2	0	74	21.6

2001-2002 statistics:

GP	G	A	TP	+/-	PIM	PP	SH	GW	GT	S	PCT
69	8	18	26	-12	58	6	0	1	0	79	10.1

LAST SEASON

Missed five games with wrist injury. Missed three games with flu. Missed two games with back injury.

THE FINESSE GAME

Holmstrom has a toothless grin and a gutsy game. He plays in the hard five feet outside the crease, sometimes inside it, and drives goalies wild. He has such a good shooting percentage because he takes most of his scoring chances from inside a very tight perimeter.

With the desire and work ethic of every low draft pick to ever make it to the NHL (257th in 1994), Holmstrom is a rough-cut stone. That makes him even more important, because he provides an element of grit along the wall and in front of the net.

This Swede has style, too, and can score in the clutch. He has an excellent close-range shot. If anything, he needs to shoot more. He is also a smart passer. Holmstrom doesn't have great hands but he doesn't quit digging for loose pucks. He is a power-play mainstay because of his ability to screen and distract defencemen.

Defensively, though, Holmstrom is something of a liability. For the second year in a row, he had the worst plus-minus (-12) among team forwards. He is usually trapped so deep inside the offensive zone that his teammates are left playing a man down at the other end of the ice.

THE PHYSICAL GAME

Stocky and strong on his skates, Holmstrom can take a bloody pounding and get right back in the trenches to position himself for a pass. What is most impressive is how he is able to provoke the attacks without getting penalized himself. He rarely takes a bad penalty. The fact that he bounces back with a jack-o'-lantern smile is especially infuriating to opponents.

THE INTANGIBLES

Holmstrom tied for second on the Red Wings in playoff goals with eight, which matched his goal output for the entire season. The postseason is his time of year. Not a lot of teams can afford to carry a postseason specialist through 82 games, but the Red Wings do have that luxury.

PROJECTION

Don't expect much more than 15-20 goals from Holmstrom in the regular season. His value increases dramatically in April and May.

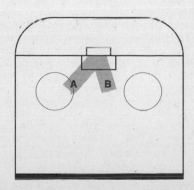

BRETT HULL

Yrs. of NHL service: 15
Born: Belleville, Ont.; Aug. 9, 1964
Position: right wing
Height: 5-11
Weight: 203
Uniform no.: 17
Shoots: right

Career statistics:

GP	G	A	TP	PIM
1101	679	567	1246	424

1998-1999 statistics:

GP	G	A	TP	+/-	PIM	PP	SH	GW	GT	S	PCT
60	32	26	58	+19	30	15	0	11	0	192	16.7

1999-2000 statistics:

GP	G	A	TP	+/-	PIM	PP	SH	GW	GT	S	PCT
79	24	35	59	-21	43	11	0	3	0	223	10.8

2000-2001 statistics:

GP	G	A	TP	+/-	PIM	PP	SH	GW	GT	S	PCT
79	39	40	79	+10	18	11	0	8	1	219	17.8

2001-2002 statistics:

GP	G	A	TP	+/-	PIM	PP	SH	GW	GT	S	PCT
82	30	33	63	+18	35	7	1	4	2	247	12.1

LAST SEASON

Third on team in points and shots. Tied for third on team in goals. One of three Red Wings to appear in all 82 games.

THE FINESSE GAME

Funny that after all those years of whining about playing a defensive system, the free agent Hull would choose to sign with another team that demands a high degree of accountability from its players. Hull delivered nicely on both fronts. He killed penalties for the Red Wings, scored 30 goals and popped in some key scores as the Red Wings won the Stanley Cup.

All those handcuffed years in Dallas made Hull a better all-around player. Make no mistake, though, scoring goals is what Hull still does best and enjoys most. He remains a shooter first. His shot is seldom blocked — he gets it away so quickly the defence doesn't have time to react — and his shots have tremendous velocity, especially his one-timers from the tops of the circles in.

Hull is always working to get himself in position for a pass but doesn't look like he's working. He sort of drifts into open ice and before a defender can react, he is firing off any kind of shot accurately. He usually moves to his off-wing on the power play. He can play the point but is a better asset down low.

An underrated playmaker who can thread a pass through traffic right onto the tape, Hull will find the open man because he has soft hands and good vision. When the opponent overplays him, he makes smart decisions about whether to shoot or pass.

Hull plays well in all three zones and has excellent instincts that serve him well in whatever he desires to apply them.

THE PHYSICAL GAME

Hull is compact and when he wants to hit, it's a solid check. He was healthy last season, and that makes a huge difference in his play. He is not as physically involved as he was when he was scoring goals at an absurd rate, but he will bump people.

THE INTANGIBLES

Detroit proved a nice fit for Hull. It's a veteran team of winners, and he didn't have to be the centre (or right wing) of attention.

PROJECTION

Hull is still a big-time player and a big asset to a team in the right spot. We would expect 55-60 points.

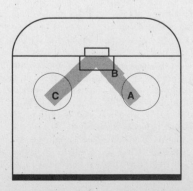

CURTIS JOSEPH

Yrs. of NHL service: 11
Born: Keswick, Ont.; Apr. 29, 1967
Position: goaltender
Height: 5-11
Weight: 190
Uniform no.: 31
Catches: left

Career statistics:

GP	MIN	GA	SO	GAA	A	PIM
706	41122	1908	36	2.78	29	86

1998-1999 statistics:

GP	MIN	GAA	W	L	T	SO	GA	S	SAPCT	PIM
67	4001	2.56	35	24	7	3	171	1903	.910	6

1999-2000 statistics:

GP	MIN	GAA	W	L	T	SO	GA	S	SAPCT	PIM
63	3801	2.49	36	20	7	4	158	1854	.915	14

2000-2001 statistics:

GP	MIN	GAA	W	L	T	SO	GA	S	SAPCT	PIM
68	4100	2.39	33	27	8	6	163	1907	.915	8

2001-2002 statistics:

GP	MIN	GAA	W	L	T	SO	GA	S	SAPCT	PIM
51	3065	2.23	29	17	5	4	114	1210	.906	10

LAST SEASON

Signed as free agent by Detroit on July 2, 2002. Career-best goals-against average. Missed 21 games with broken hand.

THE PHYSICAL GAME

Maybe it was the Olympics. Maybe it was his impending free agency. Maybe it was the injury. Whatever the reasons, Joseph looked like a fairly ordinary goalie last season. That didn't matter to the Red Wings, who locked up Joseph shortly after he came on the free agent market.

Nothing Joseph does is by the book. He always looks unorthodox and off-balance, but he is one of those hybrid goalies whose success can't be argued with. Fortunately, the Red Wings had another unorthodox goalie to play with last season, Dominik Hasek, so there should be little adjustment needed.

Joseph positions himself well, angling out to challenge the shooter. He is one of the best goalies against the breakaway in the NHL. He goes to his knees quickly, but bounces back to his skates fast for the rebound. He tends to keep rebounds in front of him. His glove hand is outstanding.

A strong, if bizarre, stickhandler, Joseph has to move his hands on the stick, putting the butt-end into his catching glove and lowering his blocker. His favourite move is a weird backhand whip off the boards. He is a good skater who moves out of his cage confidently to handle the puck.

He needs to improve his lateral movement. He uses his stick to harass anyone who camps on his doorstep. He's not Billy Smith, but he's aggressive with his whacks. Joseph gets into technical slumps, which seem to sprout from fatigue. You can judge this by the way he starts to play too deep in his net.

THE MENTAL GAME

Joseph is accustomed to a lot of work, but cutting back his games to under 65 would result in a fresher netminder for the playoffs. The only reason his workload was trimmed last season was because of his hand injury. He is never fazed by facing a ton of shots in a night. Playing behind a rock-solid defensive team should mean less work for Joseph.

THE INTANGIBLES

The problem with Joseph, as it once was with Hasek, is that you're never a winner until you win the big prize. That's the big reason why he jumped to Detroit.

PROJECTION

Hasek won 41 games with the Red Wings last season, and Joseph will probably match that.

NICKLAS LIDSTROM

Yrs. of NHL service: 11
Born: Vasteras, Sweden; Apr. 28, 1970
Position: left defence
Height: 6-2
Weight: 185
Uniform no.: 5
Shoots: left

Career statistics:

GP	G	A	TP	PIM
853	145	481	626	220

1998-1999 statistics:

GP	G	A	TP	+/-	PIM	PP	SH	GW	GT	S	PCT
81	14	43	57	+14	14	6	2	3	0	205	6.8

1999-2000 statistics:

GP	G	A	TP	+/-	PIM	PP	SH	GW	GT	S	PCT
81	20	53	73	+19	18	9	4	3	0	218	9.2

2000-2001 statistics:

GP	G	A	TP	+/-	PIM	PP	SH	GW	GT	S	PCT
82	15	56	71	+9	18	8	0	0	0	272	5.5

2001-2002 statistics:

GP	G	A	TP	+/-	PIM	PP	SH	GW	GT	S	PCT
78	9	50	59	+13	20	6	0	0	0	215	4.2

LAST SEASON

Won 2002 Norris Trophy. Won 2002 Conn Smythe Trophy. Named to NHL First All-Star Team. Tied for first among NHL defencemen in points. Led team and tied for fourth in NHL in assists. Tied for sixth in NHL in power-play points (30). Missed three games with groin injury.

THE FINESSE GAME

Lidstrom is an excellent skater with good vision of the ice. He prefers to look for the breakout pass, rather than carry the puck, and he has a superb point shot that stays low and accurate. His work at the point on the power play has improved significantly. His rink management is solid, his decision-making is better and his passing — especially to set up one-timers — is tape-to-tape.

Defensively, he uses exceptional anticipation to position himself perfectly. He is almost impossible to beat one-on-one, even two-on-one, in open ice. He neatly breaks up passes with a quick stick. He kills penalties and willingly blocks shots. He also plays either side — an underrated asset — and is dependable in the closing minutes of a tight period or game.

Lidstrom has added enough muscle to become a wiry, strong athlete who can handle an astounding amount of quality ice time. He was third in the NHL in average ice time last season with 28:48. He wastes little energy and his innate talent maximizes his stamina.

THE PHYSICAL GAME

Lidstrom truly perseveres. He does not take the body much and depends on his wits more than hard hits. But on the other side of the puck, he has little fear of contact and will accept a hit to make a play. It is a tribute to his style that he can play with quiet toughness and still be a Lady Byng candidate. This is how the game is meant to be played.

Although not a physical player, Lidstrom plays smart. With body positioning and stick positioning, he leaves opposing puck carriers no place to go and no alternative but to give up the puck — usually to him. He finds a way to tie up the opponent's stick. He has stepped up his physical play. He's not a punishing hitter, but puck carriers are wary of him because he makes them pay a price. He won't be intimidated; many teams have tried and failed with that tactic.

THE INTANGIBLES

Lidstrom has matured into the best two-way defenceman in the NHL.

PROJECTION

We made a "conservative" estimate of 60 points last season, and he would have made it if he hadn't been injured. He should be in the 55-point range again.

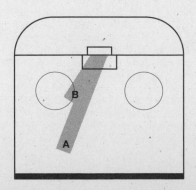

KIRK MALTBY

Yrs. of NHL service: 9
Born: Guelph, Ont.; Dec. 22, 1972
Position: left wing
Height: 6-0
Weight: 180
Uniform no.: 18
Shoots: right

Career statistics:

GP	G	A	TP	PIM
556	74	67	141	474

1998-1999 statistics:

GP	G	A	TP	+/-	PIM	PP	SH	GW	GT	S	PCT
53	8	6	14	-6	34	0	1	2	0	76	10.5

1999-2000 statistics:

GP	G	A	TP	+/-	PIM	PP	SH	GW	GT	S	PCT
41	6	8	14	+1	24	0	2	1	0	71	8.5

2000-2001 statistics:

GP	G	A	TP	+/-	PIM	PP	SH	GW	GT	S	PCT
79	12	7	19	+16	22	1	3	3	0	119	10.1

2001-2002 statistics:

GP	G	A	TP	+/-	PIM	PP	SH	GW	GT	S	PCT
82	9	15	24	+15	40	0	1	5	0	108	8.3

LAST SEASON

One of three Red Wings to appear in all 82 games.

THE FINESSE GAME

Maltby's skating helps keep him in position defensively; he seldom is caught up-ice. He plays well without the puck, understands the game and is coachable. He kills penalties effectively and blocks shots.

Maltby isn't overly creative, but he works tirelessly along the boards and in the corners to keep the puck alive. He has an average wrist and snap shot, yet has enough moves to be a threat when his team is shorthanded. Most of his goals are of the opportunistic type; he jumps on loose pucks and creates turnovers with his forechecking.

Astute hockey sense stamps Maltby as a two-way winger. He plays a key role for the Red Wings on the Grind Line.

THE PHYSICAL GAME

There are few nights when you don't notice Maltby is on the ice. He has good speed and he loves to flatten people with clean, hard hits. He is not very big, but he is solid and won't back down from a challenge. He draws more than his fair share of penalties, either by forcing opponents to pull him down or by aggravating them enough that they take a whack at him.

Maltby's power emanates from his lower-body drive. He is strong and balanced and will punish with his hits. His work ethic and conditioning are strong. He wants to win the races for loose pucks.

THE INTANGIBLES

Maltby is a role player who takes great pride in that designation. He provides jump, energy and intelligence to any lineup. He is one of the depth guys that makes a good team into a Cup-winning one.

PROJECTION

Maltby should score 10-12 goals if he can enjoy another healthy season.

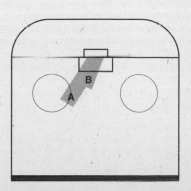

DARREN MCCARTY

Yrs. of NHL service: 9
Born: Burnaby, B.C.; April, 1972
Position: right wing
Height: 6-1
Weight: 210
Uniform no.: 25
Shoots: right

Career statistics:

GP	G	A	TP	PIM
527	100	140	240	1087

1998-1999 statistics:

GP	G	A	TP	+/-	PIM	PP	SH	GW	GT	S	PCT
69	14	26	40	+10	108	6	0	1	1	140	10.0

1999-2000 statistics:

GP	G	A	TP	+/-	PIM	PP	SH	GW	GT	S	PCT
24	6	6	12	+1	48	0	0	1	0	40	15.0

2000-2001 statistics:

GP	G	A	TP	+/-	PIM	PP	SH	GW	GT	S	PCT
72	12	10	22	-5	123	1	1	3	1	118	10.2

2001-2002 statistics:

GP	G	A	TP	+/-	PIM	PP	SH	GW	GT	S	PCT
62	5	7	12	+2	98	0	0	1	2	74	6.8

LAST SEASON

Third on team in penalty minutes. Missed 11 games with knee injury; two games with shoulder injury.

THE FINESSE GAME

McCarty has worked to make himself a suitable linemate for a skilled player like Sergei Fedorov. It's a pretty easy formula: give Fedorov the puck and get to the net. McCarty also stirs things up in the corners to dig the puck out for his centre's playmaking. McCarty reads off his linemates and reacts well to situations.

McCarty isn't the greatest skater. He has an awkward stride and his first few steps are rather slow, but he is strong on his skates and his acceleration is serviceable. He has decent finishing skills to go with a physical aspect. His balance is underrated. He absorbs (or delivers) hard hits from (to) some of the biggest skaters in the league, but hardly ever staggers.

McCarty has the poise to execute the consummate pro move: follow up a great play with a good one. He can deke a defender with an inside-outside move, then go backhand-forehand to finish the play with a huge goal — providing a huge boost to his team while utterly deflating the opposition.

McCarty has decent hands and will score the majority of his goals in-tight. He is not terribly creative but stays with a basic power game and is solid on the forecheck.

THE PHYSICAL GAME

Mean, big, strong, tough and fearless — all the ingredients are there, along with the desire to throw his body at any player or puck he can reach. If a game is off to a quiet start, look for McCarty to wake everyone up. He forechecks and backchecks fiercely, and tries to go through players, not just to them.

McCarty is not a great fighter but he is willing. He's intelligent in picking his spots. His teammates know he is always there to back them up, which is why McCarty gets to play with some of Detroit's top players when he's not on the Grind Line.

THE INTANGIBLES

McCarty is a valuable player on team full of MVPs. He plays with huge heart and brings an edge to the rink every night. The Red Wings are a smaller team in many ways when he is out of the lineup.

PROJECTION

He plays so hard and has become a little brittle in recent years, though, so we wouldn't expect much more than 70 games — and 20 points — out of him. We still want him on our side in the playoffs.

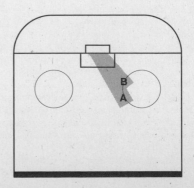

LUC ROBITAILLE

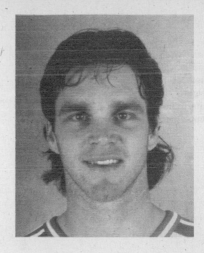

Yrs. of NHL service: 16
Born: Montreal, Que.; Feb. 17, 1966
Position: left wing
Height: 6-1
Weight: 215
Uniform no.: 20
Shoots: left

Career statistics:

GP	G	A	TP	PIM
1205	620	668	1288	1019

1998-1999 statistics:

GP	G	A	TP	+/-	PIM	PP	SH	GW	GT	S	PCT
82	39	35	74	-1	54	11	0	7	0	292	13.4

1999-2000 statistics:

GP	G	A	TP	+/-	PIM	PP	SH	GW	GT	S	PCT
71	36	38	74	+11	68	13	0	7	0	221	16.3

2000-2001 statistics:

GP	G	A	TP	+/-	PIM	PP	SH	GW	GT	S	PCT
82	37	31	88	+10	66	16	1	4	1	235	15.7

2001-2002 statistics:

GP	G	A	TP	+/-	PIM	PP	SH	GW	GT	S	PCT
81	30	20	50	-2	38	13	0	5	2	190	15.8

LAST SEASON

Led team in power-play goals. Tied for third on team in goals and game-winning goals.

THE FINESSE GAME

Robitaille gets the most done when he determines one course of action and follows through on it, because he simply does not have the quickness of hand, foot or mind to do multiple tasks. Slow on his feet to begin with, his problems are magnified by questionable balance. It doesn't take much to knock him off his feet.

Carrying the puck slows Robitaille even more, because it requires him to read a defence and identify a passing option. He is far better getting the puck, moving it and moving his feet to the holes.

Tracking those deficiencies makes you appreciate how much Robitaille wants to score goals. He has become one of the game's great scorers because of his goal-scoring instincts and fabulous shot. When he works to an opening in the front of the net and shoots off the pass, he can be devastatingly effective: the shot is accurate and the release too quick for defencemen to block. Robitaille might not win many skills contests, but somehow the puck ends up in the net a majority of the time.

THE PHYSICAL GAME

Although he's considered a finesse player, the physical aspect is an under-noticed part of Robitaille's game. He's among the first to avenge any cheap shot against one of his teammates. He isn't a fighter, but his sense of team is significant.

Robitaille goes to the grungy parts of the ice; he mucks for the puck. He also pays a physical price, absorbing a fair amount of hits because he isn't quick enough to get out of the way. And, because he does not think or act quickly, he gets whacked while making up his mind. Still, Robitaille has such great upper-body strength that a defender will think he has him wrapped up, only to see the puck in the net after Robitaille has somehow gotten his hands free.

THE INTANGIBLES

Robitaille chose Detroit to sign with in 2001 to get a chance at winning the Cup. Now the question is what will keep him hungry this season?

PROJECTION

Robitaille should be good for 25 goals. He is 36, but shows no signs of wear and tear.

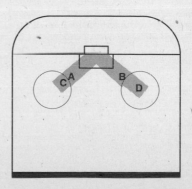

BRENDAN SHANAHAN

Yrs. of NHL service: 15
Born: Mimico, Ont.; Jan. 23, 1969
Position: left wing
Height: 6-3
Weight: 218
Uniform no.: 14
Shoots: right

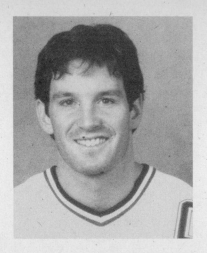

Career statistics:

GP	G	A	TP	PIM
1108	503	527	1030	2053

1998-1999 statistics:

GP	G	A	TP	+/-	PIM	PP	SH	GW	GT	S	PCT
81	31	27	58	+2	123	5	0	5	0	288	10.8

1999-2000 statistics:

GP	G	A	TP	+/-	PIM	PP	SH	GW	GT	S	PCT
78	41	37	78	+24	105	13	1	9	1	283	14.5

2000-2001 statistics:

GP	G	A	TP	+/-	PIM	PP	SH	GW	GT	S	PCT
81	31	45	76	+9	81	15	1	7	1	278	11.1

2001-2002 statistics:

GP	G	A	TP	+/-	PIM	PP	SH	GW	GT	S	PCT
80	37	38	75	+23	118	12	3	7	3	277	13.4

LAST SEASON

Led team in goals, points, shorthanded goals, game-winning goals and shots. Second on team in assists, power-play goals, penalty minutes and shooting percentage. Third on team in plus-minus. Tied for ninth in NHL in goals.

THE FINESSE GAME

Shanahan is as good as he is because he works hard at it. The release on his shot is instantaneous, and he practises his one-timers religiously to maintain that touch. Shanahan can convert shots from imperfect feeds because of his drills. He beats goaltenders from a distance, and a lot of players can't because they don't have enough velocity on their shot. Shanahan works to get into a high-percentage scoring area and shoots with power and accuracy. He has wonderfully soft hands for nifty goalmouth passes.

On the power play, he is one of the best at staying just off the crease, waiting for a shot to come from the point, then timing his arrival at the front of the net for the moving screen, the tip or the rebound. He can get a lot on his shot even when the puck is near his feet, because of a short backswing and strong wrists.

Skating is one of Shanahan's few flaws. He isn't quick, isn't agile and he often looks awkward with the puck. Most of the time he's better off making the hit that frees the puck, then passing it to a teammate and breaking to a spot, because he can score from anywhere. Shanahan doesn't skate very well backwards, and that gives him some defensive problems with Detroit's left-wing lock system. It's possible he will play more at centre this season with Steve Yzerman expected to miss a good chunk of playing time.

THE PHYSICAL GAME

The dilemma for rival teams: If you play Shanahan aggressively, it brings out the best in him; if you lay off and give him room, he will kill you with his skills. Shanahan spent his formative NHL years establishing his reputation by dropping his gloves with anybody who challenged him, but he has gotten smarter without losing his tough edge. Shanahan may have a longer fuse, but players around the league are aware of his reputation and know he is capable of snapping on any given night.

He takes or makes a hit to create a play. He's willing to eat glass to make a pass, but would rather strike the first blow. He does that by using his strength to fight through checks to get himself in position to score. He sees the puck, goes and gets it and puts it towards the front of the net.

THE INTANGIBLES

With all due respect to Yzerman, Shanahan is the behind-the-scenes captain of the Red Wings. He will be asked to carry a big share of the load during the regular season because of Yzerman's knee surgery. Scotty Bowman's retirement will be a change for Shanahan, who often sparred with the legendary coach.

Other than his willingness to hit or to scrap, no aspect of his game is elite. But Shanahan is there when you need him to make a play that will win for you, to say the right thing in the dressing room or to orchestrate the Stanley Cup hand-off. And he's always there for the fans; Shanahan is one of the NHL's most popular players.

PROJECTION

Shanahan rose to the occasion last season with Yzerman struggling with injuries, and we expect the same, and a probably 70 points, from him this season.

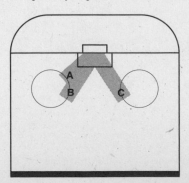

JESSE WALLIN

Yrs. of NHL service: 1
Born: Saskatoon, Sask.; Mar. 10, 1978
Position: defence
Height. 6-2
Weight: 190
Uniform no.: 3
Shoots: left

Career statistics:

GP	G	A	TP	PIM
17	0	1	1	15

1999-2000 statistics:

GP	G	A	TP	+/-	PIM	PP	SH	GW	GT	S	PCT
1	0	0	0	-2	0	0	0	0	0	0	-

2000-2001 statistics:

GP	G	A	TP	+/-	PIM	PP	SH	GW	GT	S	PCT
1	0	0	0	0	2	0	0	0	0	1	0.0

2001-2002 statistics:

GP	G	A	TP	+/-	PIM	PP	SH	GW	GT	S	PCT
15	0	1	1	-1	13	0	0	0	0	8	0.0

LAST SEASON

Entering first full NHL season. Appeared in five games with Cincinnati (AHL), scoring 1-1-2 with 2 PIM.

THE FINESSE GAME

Wallin is another case for creating a defensive defenceman award. He's never going to attract a lot of attention because his offensive contributions will be minimal, but people will appreciate him for the way he plays the other side of the game.

Wallin is a steady, stay-at-home, low risk blueliner. He is strong and is a pretty good skater for his size, although he needs to improve his backwards skating.

Any other team would have rushed Wallin to the majors. Allowing him to mature in the minors was the best route for Wallin. He has been described as a complementary player, a Greg de Vries type.

THE PHYSICAL GAME

Wallin indicates he will do what it takes to win games for his team. He is solid and strong but not mean.

THE INTANGIBLES

Wallin made a good impression in his 15-game tryout last season and should get more playing time on the third defensive pair. He has good leadership potential.

PROJECTION

This could be the blue chipper among Detroit's next generation. He might need one more year to get his game in full swing. Once he does, he'll be a 10-year player. He might only be a 10-points-a-year player because defence is his game.

JASON WILLIAMS

Yrs. of NHL service: 1
Born: London, On.; Aug. 11, 1980
Position: centre
Height: 5-11
Weight: 188
Uniform no.: 29
Shoots: right

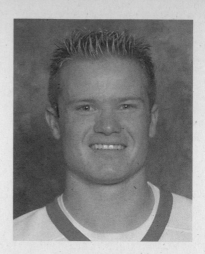

Career statistics:

GP	G	A	TP	PIM
30	8	5	13	6

2001-2002 statistics:

GP	G	A	TP	+/-	PIM	PP	SH	GW	GT	S	PCT
25	8	2	10	+2	4	4	0	0	0	32	25.0

LAST SEASON

Will be entering first full NHL season. Appeared in 52 games with Cincinnati (AHL), scoring 23-27-50 with 27 PIM.

THE FINESSE GAME

Williams is a smaller, less talented version of Detroit's own Steve Yzerman. Let's make that the post-100 points-era Yzerman.

Williams is undersized but he does everything fairly well. He is not outstanding in any one area. Williams's offensive skills are average, but he's a savvy player. He is defensively aware, and also has some creativity.

Williams is likely to get his start on the fourth line but there are signs he could win a future job on a second line.

THE PHYSICAL GAME

Have we mentioned Williams is on the small side? We have. At least Williams's work ethic is exemplary. He was a free agent signing in 2000, so he is accustomed to having to work for what he wants.

THE INTANGIBLES

Williams made the squad after training camp last fall but struggled and was sent back to the minors. His confidence might be a little shaken. This is a veteran team and under normal circumstances, it's a tough lineup to crack.

PROJECTION

There's room up the middle, as long as Yzerman is on the sidelines, but Williams will have to show more consistency if he wants the gig. He can also play right wing, which might be where his future is. He is likely to get a part-time role and score 20 points.

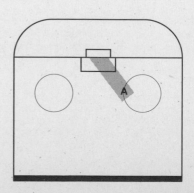

STEVE YZERMAN

Yrs. of NHL service: 19
Born: Cranbrook, B.C.; May 9, 1965
Position: centre
Height: 5-11
Weight: 185
Uniform no.: 19
Shoots: right

Career statistics:

GP	G	A	TP	PIM
1362	658	1004	1662	852

1998-1999 statistics:

GP	G	A	TP	+/-	PIM	PP	SH	GW	GT	S	PCT
80	29	45	74	+8	42	13	2	4	0	231	12.6

1999-2000 statistics:

GP	G	A	TP	+/-	PIM	PP	SH	GW	GT	S	PCT
78	35	44	79	+28	34	15	2	6	1	234	15.0

2000-2001 statistics:

GP	G	A	TP	+/-	PIM	PP	SH	GW	GT	S	PCT
54	18	34	52	14	18	5	0	7	0	155	11.6

2001-2002 statistics:

GP	G	A	TP	+/-	PIM	PP	SH	GW	GT	S	PCT
52	13	35	48	+11	18	5	1	5	0	104	12.5

LAST SEASON

Third on team in shooting percentage. Tied for third on team in game-winning goals. Missed 25 games with knee injuries; three games with ankle injury.

THE FINESSE GAME

Yzerman went to play for Canada in the Olympics on a bad knee, winning a gold medal. He played on a bad knee through the playoffs for Detroit, winning a Stanley Cup. Now we'll find out how much that dedication cost him, because Yzerman underwent reconstructive knee surgery in the off-season and is expected to miss the first two months of 2002-03.

The impact on the Red Wings may be dramatic. Yzerman is one of the three most complete forwards in the NHL, with Peter Forsberg and Mike Modano. Yzerman is outstanding on draws and ranked fifth in the NHL in face-off wins (58.37 per cent). He is a great penalty killer because of his speed and anticipation.

A sensational skater, Yzerman zigs and zags all over the ice, spending very little time in the middle. He has great balance and quick feet, and is adroit at kicking the puck up onto his blade for a shot in one seamless motion. He's also strong for an average-sized forward. He protects the puck well with his body and has the arm strength for wraparound shots and off-balance shots through traffic.

Yzerman prefers to stickhandle down the right side of the ice. In addition to using his body to shield the puck, he uses the boards to protect it. If a defender starts reaching in with his stick, he usually ends up pulling Yzerman down for a penalty.

THE PHYSICAL GAME

Yzerman sacrifices his body in the right circumstances and thinks nothing of diving to block a shot. He pays the price along the boards and around the net, and he's deceptively strong. Yzerman knows he isn't big enough to be an intimidating hitter, but he gets his body and stick in the way and at least makes the puck carrier change direction abruptly. He simply does not give up on a play, and he plays all 200 feet of the rink.

THE INTANGIBLES

The Red Wings are simply a different team when Yzerman is out of the lineup. And players sometimes are simply different when they return from serious knee surgery. At 37, Yzerman's recovery might not be too quick.

PROJECTION

We red-flagged Yzerman's injury potential in last year's edition. It's no knock on him — Yzerman has simply played a lot of hockey over the years and it catches up at some point. Yzerman may still be a point-a-game player when he returns, but odds are he will try to peak for the playoffs and not come back ahead of schedule.

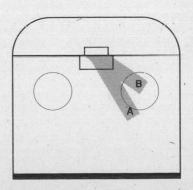

EDMONTON OILERS

Players' Statistics 2001-2002

POS.	NO.	PLAYER	GP	G	A	PTS	+/-	PIM	PP	SH	GW	GT	S	PCT
C	16	MIKE YORK	81	20	41	61	7	16	3		6	1	218	9.2
C	89	MIKE COMRIE	82	33	27	60	16	45	8		5	3	170	19.4
R	22	ANSON CARTER	82	28	32	60	3	25	12		6		181	15.5
L	94	RYAN SMYTH	61	15	35	50	7	48	7	1	5	1	150	10.0
D	44	JANNE NIINIMAA	81	5	39	44	13	80	1		2		119	4.2
C	20	JOCHEN HECHT	82	16	24	40	4	60	5		3	1	211	7.6
C	26	TODD MARCHANT	82	12	22	34	7	41		3	1		124	9.7
R	7	DANIEL CLEARY	65	10	19	29	-1	51	2	1	1		75	13.3
R	25	MIKE GRIER	82	8	17	25	1	32		2	3		112	7.1
D	2	ERIC BREWER	81	7	18	25	-5	45	6		2		165	4.2
C	10	SHAWN HORCOFF	61	8	14	22	3	18					57	14.0
R	27	GEORGES LARAQUE	80	5	14	19	6	157	1		1		95	5.3
D	21	JASON SMITH	74	5	13	18	14	103		1	1		85	5.9
L	18	ETHAN MOREAU	80	11	5	16	4	81		2	1	1	129	8.5
L	12	JOSH GREEN	61	10	5	15	9	52	1		1		78	12.8
C	15	MARTY REASONER	52	6	5	11	0	41	3		2		66	9.1
D	24	STEVE STAIOS	73	5	5	10	10	108			1		101	4.9
C	14	DOMENIC PITTIS	22		6	6	-2	8					18	
D	32	SCOTT FERGUSON	50	3	2	5	11	75					27	11.1
C	37	*BRIAN SWANSON	8	1	1	2	-1						7	14.3
C	28	*JASON CHIMERA	3	1		1	-3						3	33.3
D	19	SVEN BUTENSCHON	14				0	4					8	
D	45	ALES PISA	2				0	2					3	
R	46	*JANI RITA	1				0							
G	30	JUSSI MARKKANEN	14				0							
G	35	TOMMY SALO	69				0	2						
G	1	TY CONKLIN	4				0							

GP = games played; G = goals; A = assists; PTS = points; +/- = goals-for minus goals-against while player is on ice; PIM = penalties in minutes; PP = power-play goals; SH = shorthanded goals; GW = game-winning goals; GT = game-tying goals; S = no. of shots; PCT = percentage of goals to shots; * = rookie

ERIC BREWER

Yrs. of NHL service: 4
Born: Vernon, B.C.; Apr. 17, 1979
Position: left defence
Height: 6-3
Weight: 220
Uniform no.: 2
Shoots: left

Career statistics:

GP	G	A	TP	PIM
247	19	40	59	150

1998-1999 statistics:

GP	G	A	TP	+/-	PIM	PP	SH	GW	GT	S	PCT
63	5	6	11	-14	32	2	0	0	0	63	7.9

1999-2000 statistics:

GP	G	A	TP	+/-	PIM	PP	SH	GW	GT	S	PCT
26	0	2	2	-11	20	0	0	0	0	30	0.0

2000-2001 statistics:

GP	G	A	TP	+/-	PIM	PP	SH	GW	GT	S	PCT
77	7	14	21	+13	33	2	0	2	0	91	7.7

2001-2002 statistics:

GP	G	A	TP	+/-	PIM	PP	SH	GW	GT	S	PCT
81	7	18	25	-5	45	6	0	2	0	165	4.2

LAST SEASON

Career highs in goals, assists and points. Missed one game with shoulder injury.

THE FINESSE GAME

Brewer has a little cockiness to him that shows an innate awareness of his skill level. It will get him in trouble sometimes, but it will also encourage him to try some of the high-risk moves that only elite players make. Brewer can make them, and the Oilers encourage him to.

Brewer can be used in all game situations. He can control games the way Scott Niedermayer does with the Devils. He has the skating and puck control to dominate. He's an excellent skater with quick acceleration and lateral movement. And like Niedermayer, the bigger the games are, the more Brewer steps up his game. He might have been Edmonton's top playoff performer.

Being selected to play for Canada's Olympic team was another step in Brewer's development.

THE PHYSICAL GAME

Brewer is very strong in the defensive zone. He has good size — he will fill out more as he matures — and he likes to hit. He's smart in his own end. He's durable and in great condition, and averaged around 24 minutes a game last season. Brewer is the complete package.

THE INTANGIBLES

The Oilers staff put great faith in Brewer, and coach Craig MacTavish has said openly he thinks Brewer can be a "spectacular" defenceman. Maybe that show of faith is just what Brewer needed.

Brewer is a laid-back kid by nature, so coaches need to learn how to coax a better effort out of him on a nightly basis. Brewer was a restricted free agent during the off-season.

PROJECTION

Brewer has more offensive upside. His next step up should be to 40 points.

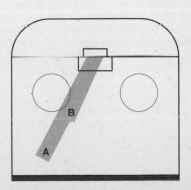

ANSON CARTER

Yrs. of NHL service: 6
Born: Toronto, Ont.; June 6, 1974
Position: right wing
Height: 6-1
Weight: 200
Uniform no.: 22
Shoots: right

Career statistics:

GP	G	A	TP	PIM
373	117	133	250	124

1998-1999 statistics:

GP	G	A	TP	+/-	PIM	PP	SH	GW	GT	S	PCT
55	24	16	40	+7	22	6	0	6	0	123	19.5

1999-2000 statistics:

GP	G	A	TP	+/-	PIM	PP	SH	GW	GT	S	PCT
59	22	25	47	+8	14	4	0	1	1	144	15.3

2000-2001 statistics:

GP	G	A	TP	+/-	PIM	PP	SH	GW	GT	S	PCT
61	16	26	42	+1	23	7	1	4	0	102	15.7

2001-2002 statistics:

GP	G	A	TP	+/-	PIM	PP	SH	GW	GT	S	PCT
82	28	32	60	+3	25	12	0	6	0	181	15.5

PROJECTION

Carter would have hit the 30-goal mark we targeted for him last season without that second-half slide. He'll do it this season.

LAST SEASON

Led team in power-play goals. Tied for second on team in game-winning goals. Second on team in goals and shooting percentage. Tied for second on team in points. Third on team in shots. Career highs in goals, assists and points. One of five Oilers to appear in all 82 games.

THE FINESSE GAME

Carter is a deceptive skater with a long, rangy, loping stride, but he isn't a bit awkward in turns. What really sets him apart, though, is his hockey intelligence. He thinks the game well in all zones. He is capable of playing centre but is better utilized as a winger.

Carter has pushed himself hard to improve his skating and shooting, and both skills are now polished. He is worthy of handling key ice time on the top two forward lines and now he has the production to match his effort.

Carter drives to the net well. He has good balance and is hard to knock off his skates. He isn't a power forward per se, but he goes into the high-traffic areas and has soft hands for receiving passes and releasing a quick shot.

THE PHYSICAL GAME

A late bloomer physically, Carter still needs to add some muscle but he is not afraid to hit, not afraid to take a hit and, like Peter Forsberg, will make a pre-emptive hit while carrying the puck. He's not dirty or mean, just honestly tough.

THE INTANGIBLES

Carter hit the wall around January and went into a two-month slump with only one goal.

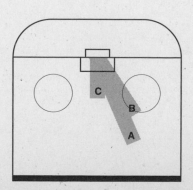

DANIEL CLEARY

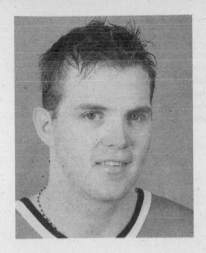

Yrs. of NHL service: 4
Born: Carbonear, Nfld.; Dec. 19, 1978
Position: right wing
Height: 6-0
Weight: 203
Uniform no.: 7
Shoots: left

Career statistics:

GP	G	A	TP	PIM
204	31	47	78	120

1998-1999 statistics:

GP	G	A	TP	+/-	PIM	PP	SH	GW	GT	S	PCT
35	4	5	9	-1	24	0	0	0	0	49	8.2

1999-2000 statistics:

GP	G	A	TP	+/-	PIM	PP	SH	GW	GT	S	PCT
17	3	2	5	-1	8	0	0	1	0	18	16.7

2000-2001 statistics:

GP	G	A	TP	+/-	PIM	PP	SH	GW	GT	S	PCT
81	14	21	35	+5	37	2	0	2	1	107	13.1

2001-2002 statistics:

GP	G	A	TP	+/-	PIM	PP	SH	GW	GT	S	PCT
65	10	19	29	-1	51	2	1	1	0	75	13.3

LAST SEASON

Missed 14 games with knee surgery.

THE FINESSE GAME

Just when the message was sinking in that Cleary would have to supplement his talent with a better work ethic, Cleary had to struggle through a knee injury and surgery.

Cleary has a smooth stride and he accelerates quickly. He can handle the puck at a high pace (perfect for the Oilers' system) and is very good one-on-one in open ice. He has a decent scoring touch but has to be reminded to work consistently to get into the high-percentage scoring areas. He has a tendency to be overanxious and rush his shots.

Cleary has good hockey sense and an awareness of where his teammates are. He saw some power-play time last season and should earn more this year on the second unit. Cleary will also see penalty-killing shifts.

THE PHYSICAL GAME

Once he begins to consistently play with passion and aggression, Cleary is one of the best Oilers along the wall. Cleary isn't huge, but he has good power. He is feisty and doesn't mind taking his minutes when he is able to aggravate the other team. Cleary can be very annoying to play against. He blocks shots, hits, carries the puck and is smart defensively.

THE INTANGIBLES

Cleary should get a second chance on the Oilers' second line.

PROJECTION

Cleary's production was disappointing last season but the injury was probably a factor. If he is healthy and returns with the right attitude, he should take the next step and score 20 goals.

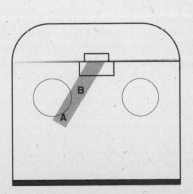

MIKE COMRIE

Yrs. of NHL service: 2
Born: Edmonton, Alta.; Sept. 11, 1980
Position: centre
Height: 5-9
Weight: 172 .
Uniform no.: 89
Shoots: left

Career statistics:

GP	G	A	TP	PIM
123	41	41	82	59

2000-2001 statistics:

GP	G	A	TP	+/-	PIM	PP	SH	GW	GT	S	PCT
41	8	14	22	+6	14	3	0	1	0	62	12.9

2001-2002 statistics:

GP	G	A	TP	+/-	PIM	PP	SH	GW	GT	S	PCT
82	33	27	60	+16	45	8	0	5	3	170	19.4

LAST SEASON

Led team in goals, plus-minus and shooting percentage. Second on team in power-play goals. Tied for second on team in points and game-winning goals. Career highs in goals, assists and points. One of five Oilers to appear in all 82 games.

THE FINESSE GAME

Doug Weight? Who was Doug Weight again? After trading their top forward to St. Louis in 2001, the Oilers could have been expected to collapse, but Comrie was one of the players who stepped up to the challenge of replacing him. True, Comrie couldn't carry them into the playoffs, but he couldn't be blamed.

Comrie has to get a lot of ice time to be effective, and with Weight gone, he got it. He has a terrific instinct and passion for the game on top of good puckhandling, skating and passing skills. Comrie is a natural goal-scorer and a confident one, who wants the puck in key situations. He doesn't have a big shot, but it's a deceptive one, and a goalie never knows if Comrie will pass or shoot because he is equally adept at both. Comrie stars on the power play, but he's not all offence. He has an advanced defensive game.

Comrie anticipates well. The puck always seems to be around him, and nothing on the ice ever seems to catch him by surprise. He's a very good positional player, which a little guy has to be.

THE PHYSICAL GAME

He's small, but spunky. Comrie gets back up even faster than he's knocked down. He isn't intimidated. He knows how to pick his spots while darting in and out of traffic, but he is fearless in going into the corners or in front of the net. Other teams singled him out for punishment a lot last season, and Comrie often battled back with his own shots. He will even jump in to stick up for a teammate.

THE INTANGIBLES

Comrie arrived much sooner than anticipated. His work ethic is exemplary.

PROJECTION

Comrie more than doubled our prediction for him last season. He has positioned himself as a 30-goal scorer now, and we expect him to duplicate that this season.

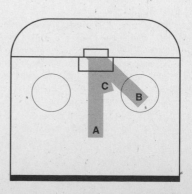

MIKE GRIER

Yrs. of NHL service: 6
Born: Detroit, Mich.; Jan. 5, 1975
Position: right wing
Height: 6-1
Weight: 227
Uniform no.: 25
Shoots: right

Career statistics:

GP	G	A	TP	PIM
448	81	102	183	292

1998-1999 statistics:

GP	G	A	TP	+/-	PIM	PP	SH	GW	GT	S	PCT
82	20	24	44	+5	54	3	2	1	0	143	14.0

1999-2000 statistics:

GP	G	A	TP	+/-	PIM	PP	SH	GW	GT	S	PCT
65	9	22	31	+9	68	0	3	2	0	115	7.8

2000-2001 statistics:

GP	G	A	TP	+/-	PIM	PP	SH	GW	GT	S	PCT
74	20	16	36	+11	20	2	3	2	1	124	16.1

2001-2002 statistics:

GP	G	A	TP	+/-	PIM	PP	SH	GW	GT	S	PCT
82	8	17	25	+1	32	0	2	3	0	112	7.1

LAST SEASON

Tied for second on team in shorthanded goals. One of five Oilers to appear in all 82 games.

THE FINESSE GAME

Grier is a hockey player in a football player's body — an aggressive forechecker who bores in on the unfortunate puck carrier with all the intensity of a lineman blitzing a quarterback. But Grier doesn't waste energy. He is intelligent about when to come in full-tilt or when to back off a bit and pick off a hasty pass. He frightens a lot of people into mistakes, and the savvier he gets at reading their reactions, the better he'll be.

Grier definitely believes that the most direct route to the net is the best path to choose. He won't hesitate to bull his way through two defencemen to get there.

The knock on Grier has always been his skating, but it's getting much better. He has a slow first couple of strides, but he then gets into gear and is strong and balanced with fair agility. He scores his goals like Adam Deadmarsh does, by driving to the net after loose pucks. Grier was a scorer at the collegiate level and has decent hands. Since he always keeps his legs pumping, he draws a good share of penalties. He is also a sound penalty killer and a shorthanded scoring threat.

THE PHYSICAL GAME

Grier can't be too bulky or he won't be agile enough for his pursuit. Grier underwent reconstructive shoulder surgery prior to the 2000-01 season, and he continued to struggle with it all season. Grier is tough but he isn't a fighter. It takes a lot to provoke him. He's just an honest, tough, physical winger.

THE INTANGIBLES

Grier is the unsung hero of the Oilers.

PROJECTION

Grier's production suffered because of his shoulder problems. For now, it's best to consider him a defensive forward and expect 10-12 goals instead of 20.

TODD MARCHANT

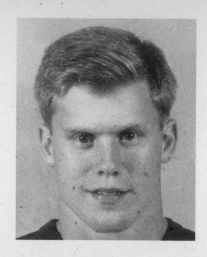

Yrs. of NHL service: 8
Born: Buffalo, N.Y.; Aug. 12, 1973
Position: centre
Height: 5-10
Weight: 178
Uniform no.: 26
Shoots: left

Career statistics:

GP	G	A	TP	PIM
602	116	167	283	442

1998-1999 statistics:

GP	G	A	TP	+/-	PIM	PP	SH	GW	GT	S	PCT
82	14	22	36	+3	65	3	1	2	0	183	7.7

1999-2000 statistics:

GP	G	A	TP	+/-	PIM	PP	SH	GW	GT	S	PCT
82	17	23	40	+7	70	0	1	0	2	170	10.0

2000-2001 statistics:

GP	G	A	TP	+/-	PIM	PP	SH	GW	GT	S	PCT
71	13	26	39	+1	51	0	4	2	1	113	11.5

2001-2002 statistics:

GP	G	A	TP	+/-	PIM	PP	SH	GW	GT	S	PCT
82	12	22	34	+7	41	0	3	1	0	124	9.7

LAST SEASON

Led team in power-play goals. One of five Oilers to appear in all 82 games.

THE FINESSE GAME

A speed merchant, Marchant is a strong one-on-one player with zippy outside speed. His quick hand skills keep pace with his feet, and he is particularly adept at tempting the defender with the puck, then dragging it through the victim's legs. He then continues to the net for his scoring chances.

Marchant is opportunistic, and, with his pace, reminds scouts of a young Theo Fleury. However, he has a long way to go to match Fleury's scoring touch. He will never be an elite scorer because he doesn't have the hands.

Marchant is smart, sees the ice well and is a solid playmaker as well as shooter. He is no puck hog. He is an excellent penalty killer and a shorthanded threat because of his speed.

THE PHYSICAL GAME

Teammates have nicknamed him "Mighty Mouse," as Marchant is fearless in the face of bigger, supposedly tougher, opposition. He hurls his body at larger foes. He is irritating to play against, because a big lug like Derian Hatcher looks foolish trying to chase down and swat a little-bitty guy like Marchant.

Marchant is average size but his grit makes him look bigger. He sacrifices his body, but you wonder how long his body will last under the stress he puts it through. He is well-conditioned and can handle a lot of ice time. The mental toughness is there, too. He will take a hit to make a play but has to get smarter about

picking his spots in order to survive. Edmonton is a very mobile team and Marchant's lack of size is not as much of a detriment as it could be on other teams.

THE INTANGIBLES

Marchant is a key component of Edmonton's run-and-gun team.

PROJECTION

Marchant is a role player with a big heart. His top end is 20 goals, which he probably would have achieved last season but for a sluggish start.

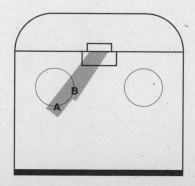

ETHAN MOREAU

Yrs. of NHL service: 6
Born: Huntsville, Ont.; Sept. 22, 1975
Position: left wing
Height: 6-2
Weight: 211
Uniform no.: 18
Shoots: left

Career statistics:

GP	G	A	TP	PIM
445	71	62	133	525

1998-1999 statistics:

GP	G	A	TP	+/-	PIM	PP	SH	GW	GT	S	PCT
80	10	11	21	-3	92	0	0	2	0	96	10.4

1999-2000 statistics:

GP	G	A	TP	+/-	PIM	PP	SH	GW	GT	S	PCT
73	17	10	27	+8	62	1	0	3	0	106	16.0

2000-2001 statistics:

GP	G	A	TP	+/-	PIM	PP	SH	GW	GT	S	PCT
68	9	10	19	-6	90	0	1	3	0	97	9.3

2001-2002 statistics:

GP	G	A	TP	+/-	PIM	PP	SH	GW	GT	S	PCT
80	11	5	16	+4	81	0	2	1	1	129	8.5

PROJECTION

Moreau seems stuck in the third-line role, and unless he shows something better in training camp, he should score around 10-15 goals.

LAST SEASON

Tied for second on team in shorthanded goals.

THE FINESSE GAME

Moreau is an intelligent, safe player with good hockey sense. He can also play centre, though his future is clearly at left wing. He is not a natural scorer but has to work for his goals. His scoring touch improves with effort (funny how that works).

A long reach and a long stick allow Moreau to get his strong wrist shots away around a defenceman who may think he has Moreau tied up. Defensively, he's on his way because he has an understanding of positional play. He's a budding power forward who goes to the net hard. Moreau worked well with the spunky Todd Marchant on Edmonton's third line.

Moreau is a solid penalty killer.

THE PHYSICAL GAME

Moreau has good size and strength and is starting to develop more of a presence. He finishes his checks, especially around the net. There may be a latent aggressive streak that will emerge with more ice time and confidence. He works hard, is strong in the corners and will take a hit to make a play.

THE INTANGIBLES

Former coach Craig Hartsburg compared Moreau to a young Bob Gainey, both for his playing style and budding leadership ability. Moreau is very well-liked and he has some good leadership qualities.

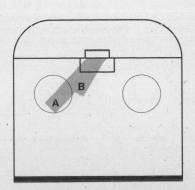

JANNE NIINIMAA

Yrs. of NHL service: 6
Born: Raahe, Finland; May 22, 1975
Position: right defence
Height: 6-1
Weight: 220
Uniform no.: 44
Shoots: left

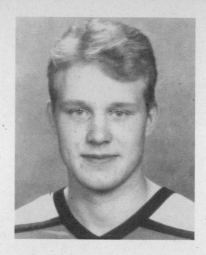

Career statistics:

GP	G	A	TP	PIM
479	37	201	238	467

1998-1999 statistics:

GP	G	A	TP	+/-	PIM	PP	SH	GW	GT	S	PCT
81	4	24	28	+7	88	2	0	1	0	142	2.8

1999-2000 statistics:

GP	G	A	TP	+/-	PIM	PP	SH	GW	GT	S	PCT
81	8	25	33	+14	89	2	2	0	0	133	6.0

2000-2001 statistics:

GP	G	A	TP	+/-	PIM	PP	SH	GW	GT	S	PCT
82	12	34	46	+6	90	8	0	1	0	122	9.8

2001-2002 statistics:

GP	G	A	TP	+/-	PIM	PP	SH	GW	GT	S	PCT
81	5	39	44	+13	80	1	0	2	0	119	4.2

LAST SEASON

Led team defence in points. Second on team in assists. Third on team in plus-minus.

THE FINESSE GAME

The best news about Niinimaa's play in the last few seasons is his consistency. He makes fewer of the boneheaded decisions that marred his early career. He remains a gambler at heart, though, which will pay off with his creative offensive moves.

In the past, Niinimaa would get too active in a confined area. In his own end, he would sometimes get a guy pinned and there would be too much movement. He had to learn to be patient and just pin the guy. Once he works the puck free, he is good at jumping into the play and getting up-ice. He sometimes gets impatient. He wants to create things offensively and when there isn't anything there, he gets into trouble.

A nimble, agile player, Niinimaa sets his feet wide apart for outstanding drive, power and balance, and uses a long stride and long reach to win races to the puck. He can turn the corners at near top speed and doesn't have to slow down when carrying the puck. When the opportunity to jump into the play presents itself, he is gone in a vapour trail.

Niinimaa is a dynamic player with elite skills. A left-handed shot who plays the right side, he has excellent skating and puckhandling skills, which allow him to handle the amount of body shifting necessary to open his body to the rink and keep the forehand available as often as possible. He has become Edmonton's top power-play quarterback and puck carrier.

Like Paul Kariya, Niinimaa does a great job of "framing" his stick and giving his teammates a pass-

ing target. He keeps the blade on the ice and available, his body position saying, "Put it here, so I can do something with it." Niinimaa knows he can create just as much offensive danger by merely flipping a puck towards the net instead of taking the full-windup slap shot every time. Although his one-timers can be blistering, he doesn't always shoot to score; sometimes he shoots to create a rebound or possible deflection. He does a good job of looking for lanes to get the puck through to the net instead of just blasting away with shots than can be blocked.

THE PHYSICAL GAME

Niinimaa plays a fairly physical game, though he is not aggressive. He bumps and jolts, and makes opponents pay a price for every inch of important ice gained. He seems to relish one-on-one battles. He wants the puck and does whatever is necessary to win control of it. He is in very good physical shape and was Edmonton's ice-time leader last season, averaging around 26 minutes per game.

THE INTANGIBLES

Niinimaa is just a cut below the game's elite defencemen.

PROJECTION

Niinimaa moved into 40-point territory last season and we think he will stay there.

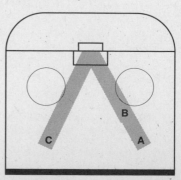

MARTY REASONER

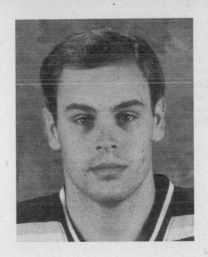

Yrs. of NHL service: 3
Born: Rochester, NY; Feb. 26, 1977
Position: centre
Height: 6-1
Weight: 203
Uniform no.: 15
Shoots: left

Career statistics:

GP	G	A	TP	PIM
147	23	35	58	83

1998-1999 statistics:

GP	G	A	TP	+/-	PIM	PP	SH	GW	GT	S	PCT
22	3	7	10	+2	8	1	0	0	0	33	9.1

1999-2000 statistics:

GP	G	A	TP	+/-	PIM	PP	SH	GW	GT	S	PCT
32	10	14	24	+9	20	3	0	0	0	51	19.6

2000-2001 statistics:

GP	G	A	TP	+/-	PIM	PP	SH	GW	GT	S	PCT
41	4	9	13	-5	14	0	0	0	0	65	6.2

2001-2002 statistics:

GP	G	A	TP	+/-	PIM	PP	SH	GW	GT	S	PCT
52	6	5	11	0	41	3	0	2	0	66	9.1

LAST SEASON

Missed four games with knee injury.

THE FINESSE GAME

Reasoner is a playmaker, and most effective when he attacks in straight lines. When he starts to zig-zag, he slows down and loses his speed as a weapon. He has such good hands and vision that he is able to bring the puck in with his deceptive speed and force the defenders to commit.

He has terrific hockey sense. Reasoner may not possess all the tools to be a top-six forward, though. Reasoner can handle power-play duty, but his five-on-five play usually doesn't earn him that right. And he doesn't do a lot of things to help his team win when he's not scoring.

THE PHYSICAL GAME

Reasoner is average size and has never shown a knack for the physical part of the game. He can't afford to be a perimeter player. He could afford to work on his upper-body strength and his skating.

THE INTANGIBLES

Reasoner had a sluggish training camp last year, made a bad impression with the coaches and never seemed to be able to recover as the season wore on.

PROJECTION

Reasoner is mostly a set-up guy. He might not be setting up Oilers, though. Reasoner can score 25 points if he gets moved, but he's running out of chances.

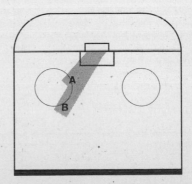

TOMMY SALO

Yrs. of NHL service: 6
Born: Surahammar, Sweden; Feb. 1, 1971
Position: goaltender
Height: 5-11
Weight: 173
Uniform no.: 35
Catches: left

Career statistics:

GP	MIN	GA	SO	GAA	A	PIM
412	23831	1005	30	2.53	6	61

1998-1999 statistics:

GP	MIN	GAA	W	L	T	SO	GA	S	SAPCT	PIM
51	3018	2.62	17	26	7	5	132	1368	.904	12

1999-2000 statistics:

GP	MIN	GAA	W	L	T	SO	GA	S	SAPCT	PIM
70	4164	2.33	27	28	3	2	162	1875	.914	8

2000-2001 statistics:

GP	MIN	GAA	W	L	T	SO	GA	S	SAPCT	PIM
73	4364	2.46	36	25	12	8	179	1856	.904	4

2001-2002 statistics:

GP	MIN	GAA	W	L	T	SO	GA	S	SAPCT	PIM
69	4035	2.22	30	28	10	6	149	1713	.913	2

LAST SEASON

Career best goals-against average.

THE PHYSICAL GAME

Salo has improved at coming out to the top of his crease and beyond to challenge shooters, and it has made him a much more effective goalie, because he looks so much larger in the net. When the action is in-tight, he is excellent on low shots. He has adjusted to playing with traffic, which is one of the biggest adjustments for European goalies. He has quick feet but is not a great skater; he needs to continually work on his lateral movement. He does have a problem with being bumped. He is out of the paint a lot and he's not very big, so on nights when the referees are lenient about calling goalie interference, Salo can be at a distinct disadvantage.

Salo has a bad habit of not holding his stick at a proper angle. When he gets into this slump he might as well not bother playing with a stick at all. He has a quick glove and tends to try and catch everything instead of using other parts of his body. Since he doesn't use his stick well, he will try to cover up on every loose puck for face-offs. Better stickhandling work would elevate his game a notch.

Salo's reflexes are outstanding. Few goalies in the league use their stick-side blocker better than Salo.

THE MENTAL GAME

The big knock on Salo was always his lack of concentration, but he has matured over the years and allows fewer bad goals (except for in the Olympics). His effort is far more consistent. Salo has great confidence in his abilities.

THE INTANGIBLES

Salo allowed a bad goal in the Olympics that had his whole native country of Sweden up in arms, and it took several weeks for that to die down. The negative attention affected his play.

PROJECTION

Salo is among the middle of the pack of NHL goalies, but fits in well with the Oilers. He plays behind a wide-open offence and knows he will face a lot of shots. He should pick up 30 wins again.

JASON SMITH

Yrs. of NHL service: 9
Born: Calgary, Alta.; Nov. 2, 1973
Position: right defence
Height: 6-3
Weight: 210
Uniform no.: 21
Shoots: right

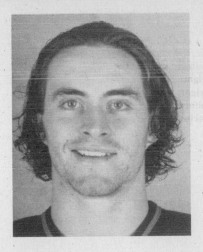

Career statistics:

GP	G	A	TP	PIM
574	22	77	99	617

1998-1999 statistics:

GP	G	A	TP	+/-	PIM	PP	SH	GW	GT	S	PCT
72	3	12	15	-9	51	0	0	0	0	68	4.4

1999-2000 statistics:

GP	G	A	TP	+/-	PIM	PP	SH	GW	GT	S	PCT
80	3	11	14	+16	60	0	0	1	0	96	3.1

2000-2001 statistics:

GP	G	A	TP	+/-	PIM	PP	SH	GW	GT	S	PCT
82	5	15	20	+14	120	1	1	0	0	140	3.6

2001-2002 statistics:

GP	G	A	TP	+/-	PIM	PP	SH	GW	GT	S	PCT
74	5	13	18	+14	103	0	1	1	0	85	5.9

LAST SEASON

Second on team in plus-minus. Third on team in penalty minutes. Missed six games with back injury. Missed two games with elbow injury.

THE FINESSE GAME

Smith has a low-key personality and will never be the kind of defenceman who can control a game. He can, however, keep a game from getting out of hand with his cool work in the defensive zone. He has improved his defensive reads greatly, and is better at moving the puck. His panic point seems to improve every season.

Smith has gained confidence and has more poise and presence. He sacrifices his body to make hits and block shots, and was again the Oilers' leader in both of those categories. He doesn't give himself enough credit. He is the kind of player who needs to have the coaches give him a pat on the back or he will worry he's not doing enough.

Offensively, Smith won't make anyone forget Brian Leetch. He has a fairly heavy shot but it has little movement on it. He's not very creative, and he doesn't gamble. However, he can kill penalties, though he'll get into trouble against a team that cycles well down low.

THE PHYSICAL GAME

Smith is a solid hitter with a latent mean streak; his takeouts are effective along the boards and in front of the net. He's not as good in open ice because his mobility is not exceptional. He has a fairly long fuse but is a capable fighter. He has a high pain threshold and consistently plays hurt. He is fit and capable of handling a lot of minutes.

THE INTANGIBLES

Smith is emerging as a quiet leader. He's a little insecure, but wants to learn and will work hard to improve. The insecurity part might be a drawback, since Smith opted for salary arbitration in the off-season, which can be a painful experience for a player. He is very coachable. He will work best paired with an offensive defenceman, and appreciates it when he is given the task of trying to stop the other team's top line. He has developed into a reliable top-four defenceman and penalty killer.

PROJECTION

Smith is evolving into a reliable crunch-time player, but his numbers will never be gaudy. He can get 20 points a season, which seems to be his max.

RYAN SMYTH

Yrs. of NHL service: 7
Born: Banff, Alta.; Feb. 21, 1976
Position: left wing
Height: 6-1
Weight: 195
Uniform no.: 94
Shoots: left

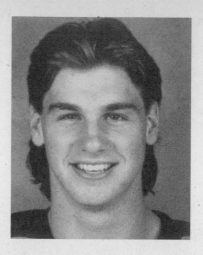

Career statistics:

GP	G	A	TP	PIM
494	148	162	310	374

1998-1999 statistics:

GP	G	A	TP	+/-	PIM	PP	SH	GW	GT	S	PCT
71	13	18	31	0	62	6	0	2	2	161	8.1

1999-2000 statistics:

GP	G	A	TP	+/-	PIM	PP	SH	GW	GT	S	PCT
82	28	26	54	-2	58	11	0	4	1	238	11.8

2000-2001 statistics:

GP	G	A	TP	+/-	PIM	PP	SH	GW	GT	S	PCT
82	31	39	70	+10	58	11	0	6	1	245	12.6

2001-2002 statistics:

GP	G	A	TP	+/-	PIM	PP	SH	GW	GT	S	PCT
61	15	35	50	+7	48	7	1	5	1	150	10.0

LAST SEASON

Third on team in assists, power-play goals and shooting percentage. Tied for third on team in game-winning goals. Missed 21 games with fractured right ankle and surgery.

THE FINESSE GAME

Smyth is not a great, fluid skater, so he has to keep his feet moving. He does, with great energy that lifts his bench, his fans and gets him behind the opponent's defence. Smyth does so with great consistency, driving to the net on a nightly basis and never more determined than when the stakes are high, as in the playoffs.

Smyth possesses little subtlety. Most of his goals come from the hash marks in, and probably half of them aren't the result of his shots, but tip-ins and body bounces. That's an art in itself, because Smyth has a knack for timing his moves to the net, along with a shooter's release. He has a long reach for getting to rebounds and is strong on his stick for deflections. He gets himself in the right place and is always aware of where the pass or the point shot is coming from. He has an advantage because his instincts and his reaction time are usually quicker than anyone else's.

Smyth is at a disadvantage when he is forced to shoot or make a play because he doesn't have a quick release. When he carries the puck, he doesn't have much sense of what to do with it.

THE PHYSICAL GAME

Smyth isn't built like a power forward, but when he is playing with confidence he sure tries to play like one. Smyth is one of the best forwards in the league along the wall. He uses his feet well to keep the puck alive. He is a pesky net-crasher and can be an irritating presence. He doesn't throw bombs, but he is a willing thrasher along the boards and gets good leg drive for solid hits. He's not a fighter, yet he won't back down.

THE INTANGIBLES

Likely as a result of Olympic fever, Smyth pushed himself to come back too quickly from his ankle surgery.

PROJECTION

The full summer off will help Smyth get back to his range of 25-30 goals.

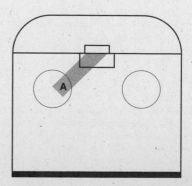

MICHAEL YORK

Yrs. of NHL service: 3
Born: Pontiac, Mich.; Jan. 3, 1978
Position: centre
Height: 5-10
Weight: 185
Uniform no.: 16
Shoots: right

Career statistics:

GP	G	A	TP	PIM
242	60	82	142	54

1999-2000 statistics:

GP	G	A	TP	+/-	PIM	PP	SH	GW	GT	S	PCT
82	26	24	50	-17	18	8	0	4	2	177	14.7

2000-2001 statistics:

GP	G	A	TP	+/-	PIM	PP	SH	GW	GT	S	PCT
79	14	17	31	+1	20	3	2	4	0	171	8.2

2001-2002 statistics:

GP	G	A	TP	+/-	PIM	PP	SH	GW	GT	S	PCT
81	20	41	61	+7	16	3	0	6	1	218	9.2

LAST SEASON

Acquired from N.Y. Rangers on March 19, 2002, with a fourth-round draft pick in 2002 for Tom Poti and Rem Murray. Led Oilers in assists, points and shots. Tied for first on Oilers in game-winning goals. Third on Oilers in goals. Career high in assists and points. Missed one game with flu.

THE FINESSE GAME

Let's be honest. Most of those numbers in the preceding paragraph were accumulated with the Rangers. York was jarred by the trade, and struggled with only two goals and two assists in four games.

Much better is expected of York this season, and the Oilers weren't down on him at all despite his lack of production down the stretch. One thing readily apparent to the Edmonton coaching staff is that York makes players around him better, and that doesn't show up in his stats.

York is reliable and can be used in every conceivable game situation with the possible exception of a bench-clearing brawl.

York is small but he finds a way to get the job done. He is fast enough to be first on the puck and will take a hit to make a play. He has good hands and vision. York finds a way to get the puck on net. He doesn't have a dangerous shot. He has a decent wrister that he releases quickly and accurately, and a soft passing touch. Plus he's smart.

THE PHYSICAL GAME

York is small and needs to play a smarter small-man's game. He is a high-energy player and forechecks hard every shift, which tends to wear him out. He is remarkably durable but and plays through a lot of dings without a complaint. He's a quiet guy, and well-respected by his teammates.

THE INTANGIBLES

York is not a star by any means, but he is a 10-year NHLer and a complementary player who can fit in on any hockey team. His size is his only drawback.

PROJECTION

Despite that post-trade hiccup, York fits well into the Oilers' team concept and another 60-point season should follow.

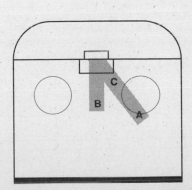

FLORIDA PANTHERS

Players' Statistics 2001-2002

POS	NO.	PLAYER	GP	G	A	PTS	+/-	PIM	PP	SH	GW	GT	S	PCT
D	44	SANDIS OZOLINSH	83	14	38	52	-7	58	3		1		172	8.1
R	22	*KRISTIAN HUSELIUS	79	23	22	45	-4	14	6	1	3		169	13.6
L	18	MARCUS NILSON	81	14	19	33	-14	55	6	1	2		147	9.5
C	28	JASON WIEMER	70	11	20	31	-4	178	5	1	1		115	9.6
R	39	IVAN NOVOSELTSEV	70	13	16	29	-10	44	1	1	5		109	11.9
C	12	OLLI JOKINEN	80	9	20	29	-16	98	3	1		1	153	5.9
D	24	ROBERT SVEHLA	82	7	22	29	-19	87	3				119	5.9
L	14	*NIKLAS HAGMAN	78	10	18	28	-6	8		1	2		134	7.5
C	25	VIKTOR KOZLOV	50	9	18	27	-16	20	6		1		143	6.3
R	20	VALERI BURE	31	8	10	18	-3	12	2		1		100	8.0
D	45	BRAD FERENCE	80	2	15	17	-13	254					65	3.1
L	26	*PIERRE DAGENAIS	42	10	4	14	-10	8	3		1	2	77	13.0
C	43	BYRON RITCHIE	35	5	6	11	-2	36	2			1	60	8.3
D	55	IGOR ULANOV	53		10	10	-7	64					26	
L	8	PETER WORRELL	79	4	5	9	-15	354			1		65	6.2
D	3	PAUL LAUS	45	4	3	7	1	157		1			39	10.3
D	49	LANCE WARD	68	1	4	5	-20	131					39	2.6
C	17	RYAN JOHNSON	29	1	3	4	-5	10					24	4.2
L	38	*ERIC BEAUDOIN	8	1	3	4	-2	4			1		11	9.1
R	21	DENIS SHVIDKI	8	1	2	3	-4	2					11	9.1
D	2	LANCE PITLICK	35	1	1	2	-14	12					15	6.7
C	19	*STEPHEN WEISS	7	1	1	2	0		1				15	6.7
L	42	BRAD NORTON	22		2	2	-2	45					6	
L	32	*RYAN JARDINE	8		2	2	0	2					6	
D	36	JOEY TETARENKO	38	1		1	-5	123					10	10.0
D	29	LUKAS KRAJICEK	5				0						3	
C	41	*NICK SMITH	15				-1						2	
R	33	DAVID MORISSET	4				-7	5					2	
C	42	MATTHEW HERR	3				-2						1	
D	23	ROCKY THOMPSON	6				0	12					1	
D	23	*KYLE ROSSITER	2				-1	2						
G	37	TREVOR KIDD	33				0							
G	31	WADE FLAHERTY	4				0							
G	1	ROBERTO LUONGO	58				0	2						

GP = games played; G = goals; A = assists; PTS = points; +/- = goals-for minus goals-against while player is on ice; PIM = penalties in minutes; PP = power-play goals; SH = shorthanded goals; GW = game-winning goals; GT = game-tying goals; S = no. of shots; PCT = percentage of goals to shots; * = rookie

JAY BOUWMEESTER

Yrs. of NHL service: 0
Born: Edmonton, Alta.; Sept. 27, 1983
Position: defence
Height: 6 3
Weight: 206
Uniform no.: n.a.
Shoots: left

Career statistics:

GP	G	A	TP	PIM
156	39	109	148	96

2001-2002 junior statistics:

GP	G	A	TP	PIM
61	12	49	61	42

LAST SEASON

Will be entering first NHL season. Selected third overall in 2002 Entry Draft. Appeared in 61 games with Medicine Hat (OHL), scoring 12-49-61.

THE FINESSE GAME

At various times, Bouwmeester has been compared to Bobby Orr, Rob Blake, Paul Coffey and Chris Pronger. So why did two teams pass on him?

In part because some scouting systems weigh "upside" heavily, and Bouwmeester is already so good that some analysts think he has already peaked.

Those teams (Columbus and Atlanta) might regret the decision. For openers, Bouwmeester is an outstanding skater, one of the fastest in junior hockey last year. He can carry the puck, jump into the play and dominate at both ends of the ice.

He has a cannon point shot, either a slapper or a one-timer, and a nice passing touch. His hockey sense and vision are very advanced. On defence, Bouwmeester is poised and has an instinctive feel for being in the right place at the right time.

THE PHYSICAL GAME

Bouwmeester is already six-foot-four and he will fill out his frame, which was already pretty solid and had him looking like a men among boys in junior. But now he'll be a boy among men, and he has to be willing to pay the physical price. He is not a punishing hitter. Bouwmeester isn't overly tough, and he doesn't fight. He is exceptionally fit.

THE INTANGIBLES

Bouwmeester gets to step into a thin defence corps in Florida. It's hardly ideal. He would probably be better off back in junior. Bouwmeester has a very low-key personality. How he will get along with Mike Keenan is anybody's guess, but his junior coaches have considered him coachable. His modesty, which seems genuine, should help him blend in with older teammates, but Keenan might want him to be more assertive. His quiet demeanour has some detractors saying Bouwmeester lacks a passion for the game.

PROJECTION

Expectations are so sky-high that anything less than a Calder Trophy might be a disappointment. Let's let Bouwmeester grow into the role. Twenty points would make for a nice debut season.

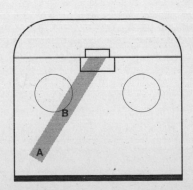

VALERI BURE

Yrs. of NHL service: 7
Born: Moscow, Russia; June 13, 1974
Position: right wing
Height: 5-10
Weight: 185
Uniform no.: 20
Shoots: right

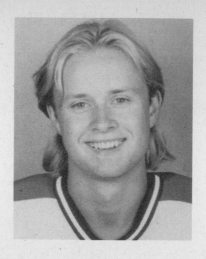

Career statistics:

GP	G	A	TP	PIM
502	147	173	320	185

1998-1999 statistics:

GP	G	A	TP	+/-	PIM	PP	SH	GW	GT	S	PCT
80	26	27	53	0	22	7	0	4	0	260	10.0

1999-2000 statistics:

GP	G	A	TP	+/-	PIM	PP	SH	GW	GT	S	PCT
82	35	40	75	-7	50	13	0	6	1	308	11.4

2000-2001 statistics:

GP	G	A	TP	+/-	PIM	PP	SH	GW	GT	S	PCT
78	27	28	55	-21	26	16	0	2	0	276	9.8

2001-2002 statistics:

GP	G	A	TP	+/-	PIM	PP	SH	GW	GT	S	PCT
31	8	10	18	-3	12	2	0	1	0	100	8.0

LAST SEASON

Missed 37 games with knee surgery. Missed 14 games with second knee surgery.

THE FINESSE GAME

The grand experiment to unite the Bure brothers disintegrated like the meniscus in Valeri Bure's right knee. His brother Pavel was packed off to the Rangers, making it a completely wasted season.

While still a dynamic player, Bure struggles with the team concept. Bure has a great sense of anticipation and wants the puck every time he's on the ice. And he can make things happen, though he sometimes tries to force the action rather than let the game flow naturally. He gets carried away in his pursuit of the puck and gets caught out of position, whereas if he just showed patience the puck would come to him.

Bure works well down low on the power play, but will also switch off and drop back to the point. He shows supreme confidence in his shot and scoring ability, and is very tough to defend against one-on-one.

He has good hands to go along with his speed and seems to get a shot on goal or a scoring chance on every shift. He is smart and creative, and can make plays as well as finish. Where Bure has to raise his game most is in the clutch, which is something he has never done.

THE PHYSICAL GAME

Bure is strong for his size and has to be more willing to pay the price. He has to keep a little grit in his game to succeed.

THE INTANGIBLES

Bure's attitude may be affected by his brother's trade and the Panthers could be looking to shop him.

PROJECTION

Bure seems to be the kind of player who needs everything to go right for him to have a big season. Even assuming he fully recovers from his knee surgeries, we'll keep our estimation low, around 40 points.

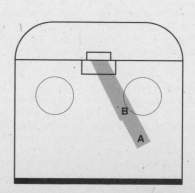

BRAD FERENCE

Yrs. of NHL service: 2
Born: Calgary, Alta.; Apr. 2, 1979
Position: right defence
Height: 6-3
Weight: 196
Uniform no.: 45
Shoots: right

Career statistics:

GP	G	A	TP	PIM
107	2	18	20	314

1999-2000 statistics:

GP	G	A	TP	+/-	PIM	PP	SH	GW	GT	S	PCT
13	0	2	2	+2	46	0	0	0	0	10	-

2000-2001 statistics:

GP	G	A	TP	+/-	PIM	PP	SH	GW	GT	S	PCT
14	0	1	1	-10	14	0	0	0	0	5	0.0

2001-2002 statistics:

GP	G	A	TP	+/-	PIM	PP	SH	GW	GT	S	PCT
80	2	15	17	-13	254	0	0	0	0	65	3.1

LAST SEASON

Second on team in penalty minutes. Missed two games due to suspension.

THE FINESSE GAME

Ference is one tough customer, but when he's not in the penalty box, he can be a different kind of force. One of the best skills Ference possesses is his shot from the point. He's not Al MacInnis, but he's pretty smart with the puck on the point. He hardly ever has his shot blocked. He makes sure that if he doesn't get the puck on net, at least he gets it deep.

Ference was a little on the lean side when he broke into the pros, but he has added a lot of useful muscle.

Ference is a good skater. He shows an ability to get involved in the offensive side of the game. He handles the puck and passes fairly well. Ference has an upbeat attitude and wants to learn, wants to improve.

THE PHYSICAL GAME

Ference is mean and his short fuse can get him into trouble — with the refs, with the league and with his own coach. Ference's minor penalties aren't for holding or tripping. They're for cross-checking and roughing. He is not intimidated by other team's top lines. Ference needs to learn to keep his composure. He already has a pretty fierce reputation around the NHL. Ference doesn't have to uphold it every night.

THE INTANGIBLES

Ference has a long way to go, but he's been compared to Chris Pronger. In fact, Pronger had Panthers coach Mike Keenan as one of his early teachers.

PROJECTION

Ference has an upside and should get enough ice time to make the most of it. He could score 25 points, and accumulate more than 250 PIM.

NIKLAS HAGMAN

Yrs. of NHL service: 1
Born: Espoo, Finland; Dec. 5, 1979
Position: left wing
Height: 6-0
Weight: 190
Uniform no.: 14
Shoots: left

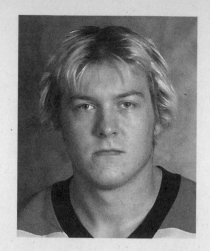

Career statistics:

GP	G	A	TP	PIM
78	10	18	28	8

2001-2002 statistics:

GP	G	A	TP	+/-	PIM	PP	SH	GW	GT	S	PCT
78	10	18	28	-6	8	0	1	2	0	134	7.5

LAST SEASON

First NHL season. Tied for eighth among NHL rookies in points. Missed four games due to coach's decision.

THE FINESSE GAME

Hagman is coach Mike Keenan's type of player. He is quick on the forecheck and he finishes all of his hits, even though he isn't all that big. Hagman simply gives you everything he has.

Hagman has great hockey sense. Add that to his good skating ability and a really nice set of hands, and the possibilities await. Florida might try to play him as a third-liner again, but he is really too undersized for that. He deserves a shot with the top six forwards.

Hagman is a very good penalty killer, but he shouldn't be pegged as a mere defensive forward.

THE PHYSICAL GAME

Hagman's major drawback is his lack of size, but he doesn't let that interfere with his style of play.

THE INTANGIBLES

Hagman should not suffer through a sophomore slump because his energy level is so consistent. He has second-line potential, although he might not ever be a huge scorer. Hagman is a character guy. Think of a slightly less physical Dallas Drake, with better hands. He had a terrific World Championships, which should provide a nice confidence boost for him after the kind of season the Panthers had.

PROJECTION

Hagman could score in the 15 to 20-goal range. There is a lot to like here.

OLLI JOKINEN

Yrs. of NHL service: 4
Born: Kuopio, Finland; Dec. 5, 1978
Position: centre
Height: 6-3
Weight: 208
Uniform no.: 12
Shoots: left

Career statistics:

GP	G	A	TP	PIM
314	35	52	87	334

1998-1999 statistics:

GP	G	A	TP	+/-	PIM	PP	SH	GW	GT	S	PCT
66	9	12	21	-10	44	3	1	1	0	87	10.3

1999-2000 statistics:

GP	G	A	TP	+/-	PIM	PP	SH	GW	GT	S	PCT
82	11	10	21	0	80	1	2	3	0	138	8.0

2000-2001 statistics:

GP	G	A	TP	+/-	PIM	PP	SH	GW	GT	S	PCT
78	6	10	16	-22	106	0	0	0	0	121	5.0

2001-2002 statistics:

GP	G	A	TP	+/-	PIM	PP	SH	GW	GT	S	PCT
80	9	20	29	-16	98	3	1	0	1	153	5.9

LAST SEASON

Third on team in shots. Missed two games due to coach's decision.

THE FINESSE GAME

Jokinen never struck a balance between producing enough points to be forgiven his defensive flaws, or playing well enough as a checker to be forgiven his lack of production. In short, he was one of the few young players traded away by the Islanders in recent years who got even worse once he was traded.

Jokinen certainly has enough skills to be better than he has shown during his three NHL stops. He has some creativity and power, but while he has performed well in international events, he lacks the confidence or drive to thrive at the NHL level.

Jokinen has played some wing but he is better at centre. He is a better playmaker than scorer. He has good vision and a wonderful sense of timing with his passes. He is probably too unselfish and will need to develop a shot he has confidence in, because he has the ability to score.

THE PHYSICAL GAME

Jokinen was not very consistent in his efforts again last season. He has a tendency to play too soft, which is inexcusable for someone his size and the reason why he gets benched. When he chooses to play hard, he uses his solid build and won't be intimidated. He has a slightly nasty side that he needs to let loose more often. He can be chippy and annoying to play against.

THE INTANGIBLES

You would think Jokinen would have ended up in coach Mike Keenan's doghouse from the first pratise, but Keenan made a project out of Jokinen after his arrival last season and Jokinen did wake up a little. Jokinen had one goal and one assist in 24 games and was benched twice prior to Keenan's arrival. Keenan gave him more ice time and Jokinen played regularly with 8-19-27 in the remaining 56 games.

PROJECTION

Jokinen was handed a top-six forward role. Maybe that's the problem, because he has never had to earn it. Jokinen will be assist-heavy. If he continues to play the same way he did after Keenan took over, Jokinen could improve to a 40-point season. It would be a long overdue step up.

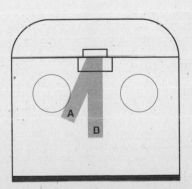

VIKTOR KOZLOV

Yrs. of NHL service: 7
Born: Togliatti, Russia; Feb. 14, 1975
Position: centre
Height: 6-5
Weight: 232
Uniform no.: 25
Shoots: right

Career statistics:

GP	G	A	TP	PIM
466	97	180	277	134

1998-1999 statistics:

GP	G	A	TP	+/-	PIM	PP	SH	GW	GT	S	PCT
65	16	35	51	+13	24	5	1	1	0	209	7.7

1999-2000 statistics:

GP	G	A	TP	+/-	PIM	PP	SH	GW	GT	S	PCT
80	17	53	70	+24	16	6	0	2	0	223	7.6

2000-2001 statistics:

GP	G	A	TP	+/-	PIM	PP	SH	GW	GT	S	PCT
51	14	23	37	-4	10	6	0	2	0	139	10.1

2001-2002 statistics:

GP	G	A	TP	+/-	PIM	PP	SH	GW	GT	S	PCT
50	9	18	27	-16	20	6	0	1	0	143	6.3

LAST SEASON

Tied for team lead in game-winning goals. Missed seven games with hip/groin injury. Missed 25 games with sports hernia surgery.

THE FINESSE GAME

Kozlov is a beautiful skater for his size. He has the moves of a 150-pounder, with quickness and agility. He holds his own faster linemates, but playing on a line with power wingers would probably suit his game better. Too bad the Panthers don't have any.

Kozlov has learned to come off the boards much quicker. As a huge right-handed shooter attacking the left side, he has a move that — dare we say it — makes him look like Mario Lemieux. He can undress a defender with his stickhandling and create a scoring chance down low. He has a keen sense of timing and pace, and is one of the top stickhandlers in the league.

Kozlov had two injury-plagued seasons which set back his development and confidence. He usually loves to shoot and wasn't able to do it as often or as well. He has an accurate wrist shot with a quick release. It is so strong that he can beat a goalie with an unscreened wrister from 40 feet out and the netminder won't be to blame. Kozlov is strong on the puck and strong shooting the puck. The defence sags off him and opens up room for Bure as well as himself.

He won't float and he has defensive principles. He won't hang at the redline, but he is an attentive backchecker. With deceptively quick acceleration for a player of his size, he excels at the transition game. Kozlov needs to learn to protect the puck better by keeping it closer to his feet. He often makes it too easy for a defender to strip the puck from him.

THE PHYSICAL GAME

Kozlov's physique makes him sturdy in contact, and when he goes down on a hook or a hold, nine times out of ten it's a dive. Although he has a long reach, Kozlov doesn't care to play the body defensively, though offensively he will work with the puck to get in front of the net and into scoring position. He handles the puck well in traffic. He has added some muscle but it would help to add more, since he is Florida's No. 1 centre.

THE INTANGIBLES

It's often hard to predict what kind of players will become coach Mike Keenan's type. Right now Kozlov looks like Keenan's most important project.

PROJECTION

Kozlov has 80-point skill and usually displays 40-point desire.

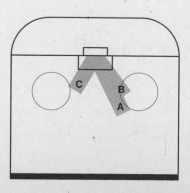

LUKAS KRAJICEK

Yrs. of NHL service: 0
Born: Prostejov, Czech Republic; Mar. 11, 1983
Position: defence
Height: 6 2
Weight: 182
Uniform no.: 29
Shoots: left

Career statistics:

GP	G	A	TP	PIM
5	0	0	0	0

2001-2002 statistics:

GP	G	A	TP	+/-	PIM	PP	SH	GW	GT	S	PCT
5	0	0	0	0	0	0	0	0	0	3	0.0

LAST SEASON

Will be entering first NHL season. Appeared in 55 games with Peterborough (AHL), scoring 10-32-42 with 56 PIM.

THE FINESSE GAME

You don't have to look very far on the Panthers' current roster to see the type of player Krajicek might become: Sandis Ozolinsh. Krajicek has world-class offensive skills. His skating and hand skills are exceptional. Krajicek is developing into a second-pair defenceman who will always be high-risk.

Krajicek is poised with the puck, intelligent and has good vision. All of his efforts though are concentrated on creating scoring chances.

Everything about Krajicek's game is attractive, except for his gambling passes, his ill-advised pinches and his tendency to get trapped deep while the other team skates back on an odd-man rush.

THE PHYSICAL GAME

Krajicek isn't the least bit physical. He nearly made the Panthers' team last season, but he proved entirely overmatched by NHL players and, wisely, was sent back to junior.

THE INTANGIBLES

Right now, Krajicek looks like a power-play specialist. The Panthers don't have the luxury of carrying a player like that on their roster. He won't make the club unless he rounds out his game.

PROJECTION

Krajicek has a lot of offensive promise, but he's a defensive project. If he makes the team, he could score 30 points. He could also be -30.

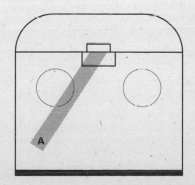

ROBERTO LUONGO

Yrs. of NHL service: 2
Born: Montreal, Que.; Apr. 4, 1979
Position: goaltender
Height: 6-3
Weight: 198
Uniform no.: 1
Catches: left

Career statistics:

GP	MIN	GA	SO	GAA	A	PIM
129	6950	317	10	2.74	1	4

1999-2000 statistics:

GP	MIN	GAA	W	L	T	SO	GA	S	SAPCT	PIM
24	1292	3.25	7	14	1	1	70	730	.904	0

2000-2001 statistics:

GP	MIN	GAA	W	L	T	SO	GA	S	SAPCT	PIM
47	2628	2.44	12	24	7	5	107	1333	.920	2

2001-2002 statistics:

GP	MIN	GAA	W	L	T	SO	GA	S	SAPCT	PIM
58	3030	2.77	16	33	4	4	140	1653	.915	2

LAST SEASON

Career high in wins. Missed four games with lacerated forearm. Missed 13 games with ankle injury.

THE PHYSICAL GAME

Luongo is very tall and plays a butterfly style that completely takes away the top part of the net from shooters. So they try to go five-hole. Guess what? Luongo has really, really big pads (whatever happened to that NHL crackdown?), fast legs and good flexibility.

Luongo has a tendency to try to use his feet too much to kick out the puck, and he can leave some bad rebounds. Improved confidence in using his stick and controlling the puck for his defencemen will be a help. Luongo doesn't have to be Martin Brodeur. He just needs to give his defence a chance to play the puck.

Luongo's one glaring weakness is his lack of lateral movement. He needs to concentrate on improving his footwork, because it won't take NHL shooters very long to figure out how to jerk him from post to post. Luongo has to avoid staying deep in his net. He is a terrific athlete.

THE MENTAL GAME

Luongo won the No. 1 goalie job from Trevor Kidd and, at only 23, is beginning to carry himself like a No. 1 goalie should. Luongo is very likable and has a great deal of presence and poise. He is starting to handle the mental ups and downs of the game better, staying competitive but on an even keel.

THE INTANGIBLES

Luongo backstopped a really confused team that should be in better shape starting the season under Mike Keenan (rather than having Keenan step in midway through the year). Luongo suffered a season-ending injury in March (torn ankle ligaments) that prevented the Panthers from making even a feeble playoff push.

PROJECTION

We were counting on 20 wins from Luongo last season, but injuries kept him from attaining that target. Florida doesn't look to be much improved, and we would keep Luongo's win estimate around 20-22.

MARCUS NILSON

Yrs. of NHL service: 3
Born: Balstå, Sweden; Mar 1, 1978
Position: left wing
Height: 6-2
Weight: 193
Uniform no.: 18
Shoots: right

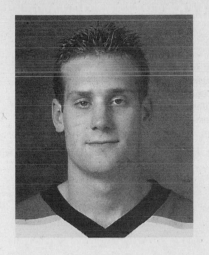

Career statistics:

GP	G	A	TP	PIM
176	27	46	73	136

1998-1999 statistics:

GP	G	A	TP	+/-	PIM	PP	SH	GW	GT	S	PCT
8	1	1	2	+2	5	0	0	1	0	7	14.3

1999-2000 statistics:

GP	G	A	TP	+/-	PIM	PP	SH	GW	GT	S	PCT
9	0	2	2	+2	2	0	0	0	0	6	-

2000-2001 statistics:

GP	G	A	TP	+/-	PIM	PP	SH	GW	GT	S	PCT
78	12	24	36	-3	74	0	0	2	0	141	8.5

2001-2002 statistics:

GP	G	A	TP	+/-	PIM	PP	SH	GW	GT	S	PCT
81	14	19	33	-14	55	6	1	2	0	147	9.5

LAST SEASON

Tied for team lead in goals. Tied for second on team in power-play goals. Third on team in points. Missed one game due to suspension.

THE FINESSE GAME

Nilson helped ease Kristian Huselius's entry into the NHL, but the talented rookie was also instrumental in bringing Nilson out of his shell a bit more. Nilson is a two-way player who has concentrated more on his defence, but he can produce more than he has thus far.

Nilson has very good hockey sense, a good passing touch and is a playmaker first. It behoves him to play with a finisher like Huselius.

Nilson's chief flaw is his skating. He is pretty awkward and doesn't have great speed. We tend to think of all Europeans as being great skaters. Nilson is a glaring exception.

THE PHYSICAL GAME

Nilson is on the quiet side, not aggressive, but he's actually pretty gritty. He has improved his strength somewhat, but could always do more.

THE INTANGIBLES

This season may be the one that finally determines whether Nilson can play on the top two lines or whether he will be a third-line checker and penalty killer at best.

PROJECTION

Until he proves otherwise, Nilson's max is probably 30 points.

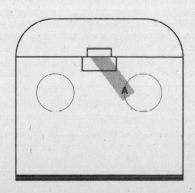

IVAN NOVOSELTSEV

Yrs. of NHL service: 2
Born: Golitsino, Russia; Jan. 23, 1979
Position: left wing
Height: 6-1
Weight: 202
Uniform no.: 39
Shoots: left

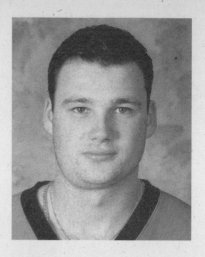

Career statistics:

GP	G	A	TP	PIM
122	18	23	41	68

1999-2000 statistics:

GP	G	A	TP	+/-	PIM	PP	SH	GW	GT	S	PCT
14	2	1	3	-3	8	2	0	0	0	8	25.0

2000-2001 statistics:

GP	G	A	TP	+/-	PIM	PP	SH	GW	GT	S	PCT
38	3	6	9	-5	16	0	0	0	0	34	8.8

2001-2002 statistics:

GP	G	A	TP	+/-	PIM	PP	SH	GW	GT	S	PCT
70	13	16	29	-10	44	1	1	5	0	109	11.9

LAST SEASON

Led team in game-winning goals. Second on team in shooting percentage. Missed five games with back injuries. Missed seven games due to coach's decision.

THE FINESSE GAME

Novoseltsev is a left-handed shot who plays the right wing. This opens up his forehand for one-timers. He plays a reckless style and is always looking for the net. He also has blinding speed and the ability to pick up the puck behind his own net and go end-to-end. He intimidates with his speed, driving defencemen back on their heels before he cuts inside or outside. His wrist shot is his favourite weapon. He needs to work to get into position to take more and better shots.

The usual red flag attached to Novoseltsev is his lack of defensive awareness. He can also be a bit selfish with the puck and doesn't always use his teammates well. He was coached to concentrate on his defensive duties last season in the minors, and took an important first step towards becoming a better two-way forward.

Expectations were extremely high for Novoseltsev early in his career, but they have been scaled back drastically.

THE PHYSICAL GAME

Novoseltsev doesn't get overly involved in physical play. For one thing, you can't hit what you can't catch. He will drive to the crease for a scoring chance.

THE INTANGIBLES

Novoseltsev is maddeningly inconsistent. This will be his last chance to prove himself with the team that drafted him.

PROJECTION

The only thing Novoseltsev does is score, and if he's not doing that, he's worthless in the lineup. If he doesn't break the 20-goal barrier this season, you can be assured his days are done in Florida, and maybe in the NHL.

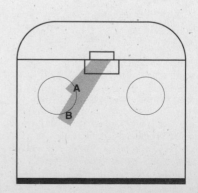

SANDIS OZOLINSH

Yrs. of NHL service: 10
Born: Riga, Latvia; Aug. 3, 1972
Position: left defence
Height: 6 3
Weight: 205
Uniform no.: 44
Shoots: left

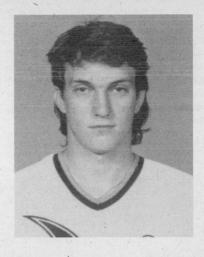

Career statistics:

GP	G	A	TP	PIM
661	141	324	465	498

1998-1999 statistics:

GP	G	A	TP	+/-	PIM	PP	SH	GW	GT	S	PCT
39	7	25	32	+10	22	4	0	3	0	81	8.6

1999-2000 statistics:

GP	G	A	TP	+/-	PIM	PP	SH	GW	GT	S	PCT
82	16	36	52	+17	46	6	0	1	0	210	7.6

2000-2001 statistics:

GP	G	A	TP	+/-	PIM	PP	SH	GW	GT	S	PCT
72	12	32	44	-25	71	4	2	2	0	145	8.3

2001-2002 statistics:

GP	G	A	TP	+/-	PIM	PP	SH	GW	GT	S	PCT
83	14	38	52	-7	58	3	0	1	0	172	8.1

LAST SEASON

Acquired from Carolina on January 16, 2002, with Byron Ritchie for Bret Hedican, Kevyn Adams, Tomas Malec and a conditional second-round draft pick. Led Panthers in points, assists and shots. Fifth among NHL defencemen in points. Tied for third on Panthers in goals. Missed three games with sprained knee. Appeared in 83 games due to trade.

THE FINESSE GAME

Ozolinsh has good straightaway speed, but he can't make a lot of agile, pretty moves. Because he can't weave his way through a number of defenders, he has to power his way into open ice with the puck and drive the defenders back through intimidation. His speed often allows him to get back and help out on the odd-man rushes that he helps create — though as his plus-minus will attest, Ozolinsh is more apt to simply quit after his mistakes.

Ozolinsh is a pure "offenceman," but one who doesn't always recognize when it's safe to go. He sees only one traffic light, and it's stuck on green. He likes to start things by pressing in the neutral zone, where he will gamble and try to intercept cross-ice passes. His defence partner and the forwards will always have to be alert to guard against odd-man rushes back, because he doesn't recognize when it's a good time to be aggressive or when to back off.

He will start the breakout play with his smooth skating, then spring a teammate with a crisp pass. He can pass on his forehand or backhand, which is a good thing because he is all over the ice. He will follow up the play to create an odd-man rush, trail in for a drop pass or drive to the net for a rebound.

Ozolinsh sometimes hangs on to the puck too long. He has a variety of shots, with his best being a one-timer from the off side on the power play, where he slides into the back door on the weak side. He is not as effective when he works down low.

THE PHYSICAL GAME

Ozolinsh goes into areas of the ice where he gets hit a lot, but he is stronger than he looks. He is all business on the ice and pays the price to get the puck, but doesn't really have a taste for hitting, or the desire to keep his crease clean.

THE INTANGIBLES

How do you score 52 points and be -7? Ozolinsh is a bad fit on a bad team, which the Panthers figure to be again this season. Coach Mike Keenan has received a lot of credit for moulding a young Chris Pronger. Let's see what he can do with this guy.

PROJECTION

This is what we said last year, and we're not changing a word for this season: Ozolinsh gets a big chunk of ice time, especially on the power play, and is due for another 50 points and another humiliating plus-minus.

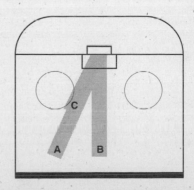

STEPHEN WEISS

Yrs. of NHL service: 0
Born: Toronto, On.; Apr. 3, 1983
Position: centre
Height: 6-0
Weight: 183
Uniform no.: 19
Shoots: left

Career statistics:

GP	G	A	TP	PIM
7	1	1	2	0

2001-2002 statistics:

GP	G	A	TP	+/-	PIM	PP	SH	GW	GT	S	PCT
7	1	1	2	0	0	1	0	0	0	15	6.7

LAST SEASON

Will be entering first NHL season. Appeared in 46 games with Plymouth (OHL), scoring 25-45-70 with 69 PIM.

THE FINESSE GAME

Weiss has posted nice numbers in junior, but he's going to be more than just a one-way centre. He has some flair, but he's no prima donna. He backchecks diligently and will likely turn into one of Florida's better face-off guys once he adapts to the NHL.

Scouts think he might develop into a Steve Yzerman-type, a player who has the skill level to score 100 points but who will settle for 80 because he will dedicate himself to a two-way game. He has the heads and the hands for the game.

Weiss has a fluid skating stride, very efficient and with good acceleration.

THE PHYSICAL GAME

Weiss will need to improve his upper-body strength. He will probably never get bulky, but he can be wiry-tough. Weiss must also keep up his conditioning for the NHL grind.

THE INTANGIBLES

Weiss did OK in his seven-game trial with the big club and that sets him up for a strong training camp. He seems to have desire and a good attitude. Weiss was a captain of his junior team. He missed some playing time with his junior team because of an elbow injury suffered at the World Junior Championships.

PROJECTION

Weiss has the potential to be a No. 1 centre in Florida in a few seasons. If he wins a full-time role this year, it would be no shock to see him score 35 points.

LOS ANGELES KINGS

Players' Statistics 2001-2002

POS.	NO.	PLAYER	GP	G	A	PTS	+/-	PIM	PP	SH	GW	GT	S	PCT
C	41	JASON ALLISON	73	19	55	74	2	68	5		2	2	139	13.7
R	28	ADAM DEADMARSH	76	29	33	62	8	71	12		5		139	20.9
R	33	ZIGMUND PALFFY	63	32	27	59	5	26	15	1	6	1	161	19.9
C	7	CLIFF RONNING	81	19	35	54	0	32	5			2	199	9.5
D	44	JAROSLAV MODRY	80	4	38	42	-4	65	4				119	3.4
C	21	BRYAN SMOLINSKI	80	13	25	38	7	56	4	1		2	187	6.9
R	57	STEVE HEINZE	73	15	16	31	-15	46	8		4	1	123	12.2
D	43	PHILIPPE BOUCHER	80	7	23	30	0	94	4		2		198	3.5
D	10	MATHIEU SCHNEIDER	55	7	23	30	3	68	4				123	5.7
L	23	CRAIG JOHNSON	72	13	14	27	14	24	4	1	3	1	102	12.8
C	25	ERIC BELANGER	53	8	16	24	2	21	2	1	1		67	11.9
C	22	IAN LAPERRIERE	81	8	14	22	5	125			3		89	9.0
D	17	LUBOMIR VISNOVSKY	72	4	17	21	-5	14	1		2		95	4.2
L	42	MIKKO ELORANTA	77	9	9	18	-1	56	1		2		136	6.6
D	3	AARON MILLER	74	5	12	17	14	54		1	3		75	6.7
R	29	BRAD CHARTRAND	46	7	9	16	5	40			1		49	14.3
R	9	KELLY BUCHBERGER	74	6	7	13	-13	105			1		39	15.4
D	14	MATTIAS NORSTROM	79	2	9	11	-2	38					42	4.8
R	19	NELSON EMERSON	41	5	2	7	-8	25			1		40	12.5
C	27	*JAROSLAV BEDNAR	22	4	2	6	-4	8	1		2		20	20.0
D	6	ANDREAS LILJA	26	1	4	5	3	22	1				12	8.3
L	12	KEN BELANGER	43	2		2	-5	85					22	9.1
C	24	ADAM MAIR	18	1	1	2	1	57					10	10.0
R	38	ROBERT VALICEVIC	17	1	1	2	-4	8					9	11.1
C	11	STEVE KELLY	8		1	1	-1	2						
L	49	*RYAN FLINN	10				0	51					2	
D	53	JASON HOLLAND	3				-1						1	
D	37	*KIP BRENNAN	4				1	22						
G	39	FELIX POTVIN	71				0	19						
G	1	JAMIE STORR	19				0	4						

GP = games played; G = goals; A = assists; PTS = points; +/- = goals-for minus goals-against while player is on ice; PIM = penalties in minutes; PP = power-play goals; SH = shorthanded goals; GW = game-winning goals; GT = game-tying goals; S = no. of shots; PCT = percentage of goals to shots; * = rookie

JASON ALLISON

Yrs. of NHL service: 9
Born: North York, Ont.; May 29, 1975
Position: centre
Height: 6-3
Weight: 218
Uniform no.: 41
Shoots: right

Career statistics:

GP	G	A	TP	PIM
460	131	266	397	343

1998-1999 statistics:

GP	G	A	TP	+/-	PIM	PP	SH	GW	GT	S	PCT
82	23	53	76	+5	68	5	1	3	0	158	14.6

1999-2000 statistics:

GP	G	A	TP	+/-	PIM	PP	SH	GW	GT	S	PCT
37	10	18	28	+5	20	3	0	1	1	66	15.2

2000-2001 statistics:

GP	G	A	TP	+/-	PIM	PP	SH	GW	GT	S	PCT
82	36	59	95	-8	85	11	3	6	0	185	19.5

2001-2002 statistics:

GP	G	A	TP	+/-	PIM	PP	SH	GW	GT	S	PCT
73	19	55	74	+2	68	5	0	2	2	139	13.7

LAST SEASON

Acquired from Boston on October 24, 2001, with Mikko Eloranta for Glen Murray and Jozef Stumpel. Second in NHL and led Kings in assists. Led NHL in power-play assists (32) and second in power-play points (37). Led Kings in points. Third on Kings in shooting percentage. Tied for third on Kings in goals. Missed nine games in contract dispute.

THE FINESSE GAME

Allison is among the best players in the league from the top of the circles in. He isn't flashy, he isn't brawny, but he is savvy, resolute and highly skilled. Allison is a player capable of dominating games. He is strong on the puck, skates well, has excellent vision and sure, soft hands to put passes where they need to go. He is the complete package offensively.

Allison faces top checkers every shift and still excels. He makes players on his line better, and seems to adjust to whatever linemates are on his flanks. He moved from East Coast to West and didn't miss a beat. Allison is, night in and night out, one of the best forwards on the ice, especially on the power play. He excels with his down-low playmaking.

The puck follows Allison around the rink. He has great patience, uncanny hockey sense and is one of the top ten centres in the league when he is at the top of his game. Although his impact is predominantly on offence, he is often put on the ice to protect leads late in games, so his defence is hardly suspect.

He wants to get even better, and he continually works with skating instructors in the off-season to step up his foot speed.

Not only that, but he was in the top 10 in the league in draws (54.47 per cent, 10th overall).

THE PHYSICAL GAME

Allison hates to lose, and that gives him his great competitive edge. Allison is not quite as strong or tough as some of the league's best power forwards, but he goes through traffic and makes plays despite the checking attention focused on him. He is hungry to score and will pay the price to do so.

THE INTANGIBLES

Allison was the Kings' MVP but suffers from the team's lack of depth at centre. Adding a solid No. 2 centre would take a lot of the heat off Allison. That is what Bryan Smolinski was supposed to do, but he had a woeful season.

PROJECTION

A 100-point season beckons. Allison will be much heavier on assists, it could be something like a 25-goal, 75-assist year.

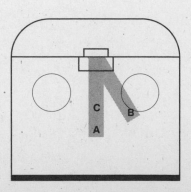

JAROSLAV BEDNAR

Yrs. of NHL service: 0
Born: Prague, Czech Republic; Nov. 8, 1976
Position: centre
Height: 6-0
Weight: 198
Uniform no.: 27
Shoots: right

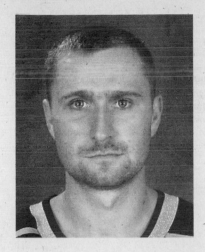

Career statistics:

GP	G	A	TP	PIM
22	4	2	6	8

2001-2002 statistics:

GP	G	A	TP	+/-	PIM	PP	SH	GW	GT	S	PCT
22	4	2	6	-4	8	1	0	2	0	20	20.0

LAST SEASON

First NHL season. Appeared in 48 games with Manchester (AHL), scoring 16-21-37 with 16 PIM. Missed five games due to coach's decision.

THE FINESSE GAME

Bednar could soon work his way into the Kings' top six forwards. He makes some beautiful goals and passes. His finesse moves have been compared to Martin Rucinsky, but this guy's got more determination to his game.

Bednar has an excellent wrist shot. He is a sleek, fast, well-balanced skater with speed and acceleration.

Bednar plays more of a traditional North American game — less of an East-West game than a lot of Europeans. Bednar needs to improve his defensive play and his consistency.

THE PHYSICAL GAME

Bednar doesn't initiate hits but he will fight his way through checks. He can be very strong along the boards, when he plays with determination — which isn't every night.

THE INTANGIBLES

Bednar was an overage draft pick in 2001; the Kings hoped he could have moved right into their lineup last year. However, he had to be dispatched to the minors to develop his all-around game.

PROJECTION

So far, Bednar's best work has come in the minors, but the Kings still think he can make the jump this season. He has future 30-goal potential, but that may be a season or two away, if it comes at all.

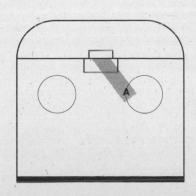

KELLY BUCHBERGER

Yrs. of NHL service: 14
Born: Langenburg, Sask.; Dec. 2, 1966
Position: right wing
Height: 6-2
Weight: 210
Uniform no.: 9
Shoots: left

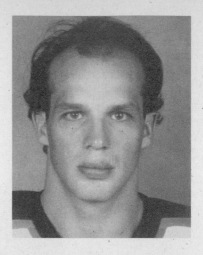

Career statistics:

GP	G	A	TP	PIM
1032	101	192	293	2079

1998-1999 statistics:

GP	G	A	TP	+/-	PIM	PP	SH	GW	GT	S	PCT
52	4	4	8	-6	68	0	2	1	0	29	13.8

1999-2000 statistics:

GP	G	A	TP	+/-	PIM	PP	SH	GW	GT	S	PCT
81	7	13	20	-36	152	0	0	0	0	76	9.2

2000-2001 statistics:

GP	G	A	TP	+/-	PIM	PP	SH	GW	GT	S	PCT
82	6	14	20	-10	75	0	0	1	0	66	9.1

2001-2002 statistics:

GP	G	A	TP	+/-	PIM	PP	SH	GW	GT	S	PCT
74	6	7	13	-13	105	0	0	1	0	39	15.4

LAST SEASON

Signed by Phoenix as free agent on July 7, 2002. Second on Kings in penalty minutes. Missed seven games with ankle injury, ending consecutive games-played ironman streak at 234. Missed one game due to coach's decision.

THE FINESSE GAME

Buchberger is an ideal role player. Night in and out, he faces other teams' top forwards and does a terrific shadow job, harassing without taking bad penalties.

Buchberger works hard and provides a consistent effort. He will grind, go to the net, kill penalties — all of the grunt work. He can finish off some plays now and then, but that is not his objective. The biggest change in Buchberger in the waning years of his career is that he has developed a degree of confidence in his finesse moves and is now willing to try something that looks too difficult for a "defensive" player. Sometimes it works, sometimes it doesn't, but he can surprise opponents.

Buchberger has some straight-ahead speed and will go to the net and muck, but this kind of player needs some luck to get goals. He has earned a great deal of respect for his work ethic. He doesn't quit. He has notched five playoff-overtime goals simply because he's a gamer.

THE PHYSICAL GAME

Buchberger is a legitimately tough customer. Honest and gritty, he won't get knocked around and is a solid hitter who likes the physical part of the game. He is a very disciplined player. He's also very determined. He keeps his legs moving constantly, and a player who lets up on this winger will be sorry, because Buchberger will keep plugging with the puck or go to the net. Buchberger keeps himself in excellent condition.

THE INTANGIBLES

Buchberger played with Wayne Gretzky in Edmonton and now plays for him. Gretzky obviously understands what an asset Buchberger can be on a young team. He can still produce 20 points and be the kind of player who can teach the next generation about being a winner and a leader.

PROJECTION

Point totals in this case are minimal and meaningless.

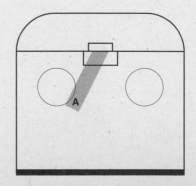

ADAM DEADMARSH

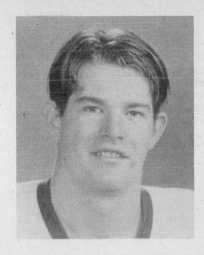

Yrs. of NHL service: 8
Born: Trail, B.C.; May 10, 1975
Position: right wing
Height: 6-0
Weight: 195
Uniform no.: 28
Shoots: right

Career statistics:

GP	G	A	TP	PIM
547	171	185	356	798

1998-1999 statistics:

GP	G	A	TP	+/-	PIM	PP	SH	GW	GT	S	PCT
66	22	27	49	-2	99	10	0	3	1	152	14.5

1999-2000 statistics:

GP	G	A	TP	+/-	PIM	PP	SH	GW	GT	S	PCT
71	18	27	45	-10	106	5	0	4	0	153	11.8

2000-2001 statistics:

GP	G	A	TP	+/-	PIM	PP	SH	GW	GT	S	PCT
57	17	13	32	+1	63	7	0	2	1	126	13.5

2001-2002 statistics:

GP	G	A	TP	+/-	PIM	PP	SH	GW	GT	S	PCT
76	29	33	62	+8	71	12	0	5	0	139	20.9

LAST SEASON

Led team and tied for second in NHL in shooting percentage. Second on team in goals, points, game-winning goals and power-play goals. Career highs in assists and points. Third on team in plus-minus. Missed one game with groin injury. Missed five games with upper body/abdominal injury.

THE FINESSE GAME

Deadmarsh is feisty, tough and can work in a checking role, but he can also play on a top line — as he did with the Kings last season — and score off the chances he creates with his defence and not look out of place. His game is incredibly mature. He is reliable enough to be put out on the ice to protect a lead in the late minutes of a game, because he'll do what it takes to win.

Deadmarsh is capable of playing in every situation. He's not as skilled as many top NHL forwards, but he has a meanness and a toughness about him. He's relentless in finishing his checks. He's very strong on the puck, very strong on the boards, and he's one of the faster players in the NHL in a power package. Deadmarsh doesn't have the same touch around the net as Keith Tkachuk or John LeClair, but he should be a bona fide 30-goal scorer. Although better at centre than wing, he is versatile enough to handle either role.

Deadmarsh doesn't have to be the glamour guy, but that doesn't mean he provides unskilled labour. He has dangerous speed and quickness, and a nice scoring touch to convert the chances he creates off his forechecking. He can play centre as well as both wings, so he's versatile. He doesn't play a complex game. He's a basic up-and-down winger; he excels as a dedicated penalty killer.

THE PHYSICAL GAME

Deadmarsh always finishes his checks. He has a strong work ethic with honest toughness. He never backs down from a challenge and issues some of his own. He isn't a dirty player, but he will fight when challenged or stand up for his teammates.

THE INTANGIBLES

Deadmarsh has a smirk on his face all the time. Either you want to kiss it or punch it. No one knows whether that's just the way his face is, or if he's laughing at you, and that can be really irritating. He runs you over with that little smile and you think, "Are you serious? Are you pulling my leg?"

Deadmarsh will never be a star, but he is the kind of player who will help his team find a way to win.

PROJECTION

Deadmarsh lacks the fine touch to be an elite scorer, but he should consistently score in the 30-goal, 60-point range.

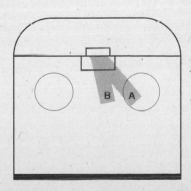

ALEXANDER FROLOV

Yrs. of NHL service: 0
Born: Moscow, Russia; June 19, 1982
Position: left wing
Height: 6-4
Weight: 191
Uniform no.: n.a.
Shoots: right

Career statistics:

GP	G	A	TP	PIM
88	38	31	69	55

2001-2002 European statistics:

GP	G	A	TP	PIM
43	18	12	30	16

LAST SEASON
Will be entering first NHL season. Appeared in 43 games with Soviet Wings (Russia), scoring 18-12-30 with 16 penalty minutes.

THE FINESSE GAME
Frolov is going to develop into a solid two-way power forward. He can play either left wing or centre.

Frolov is a finisher by nature. He has a goal-scorer's mentality. Put the puck on Frolov's stick anywhere near the net and a high-percentage scoring opportunity will result.

He protects the puck well. He is a tough guy to take off the puck. Frolov is strong one-on-one.

THE PHYSICAL GAME
Frolov has the size and strength to play the pro game. There is a slight question as to whether he has the mental toughness.

THE INTANGIBLES
Frolov was so impressive in training camp in 2001 that the Kings wanted to sign him and put him right into their lineup, but they couldn't come to contract terms with their top prospect.

PROJECTION
Assuming he can fit onto one of the Kings' top two lines, Frolov should start off with 25-30 points in his rookie season.

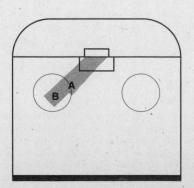

IAN LAPERRIERE

Yrs. of NHL service: 8
Born: Montreal, Que.; Jan. 19, 1974
Position: centre
Height: 6-1
Weight: 201
Uniform no.: 22
Shoots: right

Career statistics:

GP	G	A	TP	PIM
560	61	102	163	1062

1998-1999 statistics:

GP	G	A	TP	+/-	PIM	PP	SH	GW	GT	S	PCT
72	3	10	13	-5	138	0	0	1	0	62	4.8

1999-2000 statistics:

GP	G	A	TP	+/-	PIM	PP	SH	GW	GT	S	PCT
79	9	13	22	-14	185	0	0	1	0	87	10.3

2000-2001 statistics:

GP	G	A	TP	+/-	PIM	PP	SH	GW	GT	S	PCT
79	8	10	18	+5	141	0	0	0	0	60	13.3

2001-2002 statistics:

GP	G	A	TP	+/-	PIM	PP	SH	GW	GT	S	PCT
81	8	14	22	+5	125	0	0	3	0	89	9.0

LAST SEASON

Led team in penalty minutes. Missed one game due to personal reasons.

THE FINESSE GAME

Laperriere has always played hard. Now he plays smart. Laperriere grew up watching Guy Carbonneau in Montreal, and he studied well. Laperriere knows how to win a draw between his feet. He uses his stick and his body to make sure the opposing centre doesn't get the puck. He gets his bottom hand way down on the stick and tries to win draws on his backhand. He gets very low to the ice on draws.

The knock on Laperriere earlier in his career was his skating, but he has improved tremendously in that department. Although he'll never be a speed demon, he doesn't look out of place at the NHL level. He always tries to take the extra stride when he is backchecking so he can make a clean check, instead of taking the easy way out and committing a lazy hooking foul. He wins his share of races for the loose puck.

Laperriere is ever willing to use the backhand, either for shots or to get the puck deep. He is reliable defensively. He has little offensive instinct. He can play on a third line as a checker or on a fourth line as a tempo-changer.

THE PHYSICAL GAME

Laperriere is an obnoxious player who really battles for the puck. Although smallish, he has absolutely no fear of playing in the "circle" that extends from the lower inside of the face-off circles to behind the net. He will pay any price. He's a momentum changer. He thrives on being the first man in on the forecheck.

Laperriere has suffered some serious head injuries but remains a soldier undaunted.

He shows a ton of heart. He is essential to team chemistry. Laperriere channels his aggressions and takes few cheap penalties. He knows he can hurt his team by taking unnecessary calls.

THE INTANGIBLES

Laperriere adds true grit to the lineup despite his small size, which is his major flaw and the only one he can't do anything to change. His nightly effort puts a lot of bigger guys to shame. He is one of L.A.'s most consistent and popular forwards.

PROJECTION

Laperriere is best suited as a third- or fourth-line centre. His skills are limited, but what he does, he does very well. His top range appears to be 25 points.

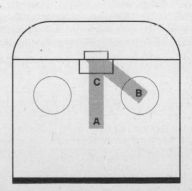

MATTIAS NORSTROM

Yrs. of NHL service: 8
Born: Mora, Sweden; Jan. 2, 1972
Position: left defence
Height: 6-2
Weight: 220
Uniform no.: 14
Shoots: left

Career statistics:

GP	G	A	TP	PIM
528	9	85	94	422

1998-1999 statistics:

GP	G	A	TP	+/-	PIM	PP	SH	GW	GT	S	PCT
78	2	5	7	-10	36	0	1	0	0	61	3.3

1999-2000 statistics:

GP	G	A	TP	+/-	PIM	PP	SH	GW	GT	S	PCT
82	1	13	14	+22	66	0	0	0	0	62	1.6

2000-2001 statistics:

GP	G	A	TP	+/-	PIM	PP	SH	GW	GT	S	PCT
82	0	18	18	+10	60	0	0	0	0	59	0.0

2001-2002 statistics:

GP	G	A	TP	+/-	PIM	PP	SH	GW	GT	S	PCT
79	2	9	11	-2	38	0	0	0	0	42	4.8

LAST SEASON

Missed three games with bruised ribs.

THE FINESSE GAME

Norstrom has started to establish himself as a major physical presence and seems to rise to every challenge the Kings give him. He's a good skater, though he is still working on his pivots and turns. He does have straight-ahead speed, to a degree, thanks to a long stride. Along the boards he delivers strong, and frequent, hits.

Norstrom's foot skills outdistance his hand skills. He can make a decent pass but mostly he'll keep things simple with the puck — smacking it around the boards if he gets into trouble, rather than trying to make a play.

For so large a player, Norstrom uses a surprisingly short stick that cuts down on his reach defensively and limits some of his offensive options. However, he feels his responsibility is to break down the play, rather than create it. He will pinch down the boards occasionally, but only to drive the puck deeper, not to take the puck and make a play; he won't jump into the play on offence.

THE PHYSICAL GAME

Norstrom lives inside his opponent's jersey. He is hard-nosed — when he hits, you feel it. He is willing to do what it takes to help his team win. He is solidly built and likes to throw big, loud hits. He sacrifices his body by blocking shots. When Norstrom misses a game because of an injury, then he is really hurt, because he plays through a lot of pain.

He knows what he's good at. Norstrom has tremendously powerful legs and is strong on his skates. He has confidence in his power game and has developed a great enthusiasm for the physical aspect. Norstrom does it all without spending a lot of time in the box, which is pretty amazing when you watch how hard he plays.

THE INTANGIBLES

Norstrom was named the Kings captain, which means a lot to him, especially as a European player. Maybe it's because he plays like a North American.

Norstrom is a hard-working athlete who loves to practise, a player valued more for his character than for his abilities, which are average. He is a defensive-style defenceman who will give his coach what's asked for, but won't try to do things that will put the puck, or the team, in trouble. He is a steady player who routinely draws assignments against other teams' top lines. He's a real throwback.

PROJECTION

Norstrom will continue to get a large chunk of ice time, but his lack of offensive skills limit him to 15 to 20 points at best.

ZIGMUND PALFFY

Yrs. of NIIL service: 8
Born: Skalica, Slovakia; May 5, 1972
Position: left wing
Height: 5-10
Weight: 183
Uniform no.: 33
Shoots: left

Career statistics:

GP	G	A	TP	PIM
531	265	280	545	251

1998-1999 statistics:

GP	G	A	TP	+/-	PIM	PP	SH	GW	GT	S	PCT
50	22	28	50	-6	34	5	2	1	0	168	13.1

1999-2000 statistics:

GP	G	A	TP	+/-	PIM	PP	SH	GW	GT	S	PCT
64	27	39	66	+18	32	4	0	3	1	186	14.5

2000-2001 statistics:

GP	G	A	TP	+/-	PIM	PP	SH	GW	GT	S	PCT
73	38	51	89	+22	20	12	1	8	0	217	17.5

2001-2002 statistics:

GP	G	A	TP	+/-	PIM	PP	SH	GW	GT	S	PCT
63	32	27	59	+5	26	15	1	6	1	161	19.9

LAST SEASON

Led team in goals, power-play goals and game-winning goals. Tied for third in NHL in power-play goals. Second on team and fourth in NHL in shooting percentage. Third on team in points. Missed 14 games with fractured ribs. Missed five games with back spasms.

THE FINESSE GAME

Palffy has elite, intellectual instincts with the puck and great vision. He has the confidence — and the arrogance — to try moves that only world-class players can execute. He is a game-breaker.

He has deceptive quickness. An elusive skater with a quick first step, he is shifty and can handle the puck while dancing across the ice. He won't burn around people, but when there's an opening he can get to it in a hurry. Sometimes a defender will let up on him for a fraction of a second, and when he does, Palffy has gained a full stride. His anticipation is what sets him apart.

Palffy has excellent hands for passing or shooting. Early in his career he would look to make a play before shooting, but he has since become a bona fide sniper. He is an aggressive penalty killer, always gambling for the shorthanded break, and is a constant threat.

THE PHYSICAL GAME

Palffy has a little bit of an edge to him. He's got the magic ingredient that sets the superior smaller players apart from the little guys who can't make the grade. He's not exactly a physical specimen, either. One player said of Palffy, "He's as unathletic a superstar as you'll ever find."

There are a lot of nights when Palffy coasts, and he has to be reminded by his coaches to produce more of a two-way effort. It has a magical effect on the Kings bench when he does.

Decidedly on the small side, Palffy can't afford to get into any battles in tight areas where he'll get crunched. He can jump in and out of holes and pick his spots, and he often plays with great spirit. He never puts himself in a position to get bowled over, but he has become less of a perimeter player and is more willing to take the direct route to the net, which has paid off in more quality scoring chances. He's not really a soft player. He won't go into the corner if he's going to get massacred, but he's not against hacking an opponent because he wants the puck.

THE INTANGIBLES

Injuries took a big toll on Palffy. His pal, Jozef Stumpel, was traded, too. You could day Ziggy zagged last season.

PROJECTION

Palffy has 50-goal potential, and playing with the great Jason Allison might help him get there.

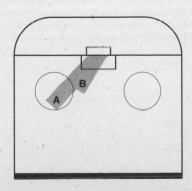

FELIX POTVIN

Yrs. of NHL service: 10
Born: Anjou, Que.; June 23, 1971
Position: goaltender
Height: 6-1
Weight: 190
Uniform no.: 39
Catches: left

Career statistics:

GP	MIN	GA	SO	GAA	A.	PIM
565	32792	1522	25	2.78	16	68

1998-1999 statistics:

GP	MIN	GAA	W	L	T	SO	GA	S	SAPCT	PIM
11	606	3.66	2	7	1	0	37	345	.893	0

1999-2000 statistics:

GP	MIN	GAA	W	L	T	SO	GA	S	SAPCT	PIM
34	1966	2.59	12	13	7	0	85	906	.906	2

2000-2001 statistics:

GP	MIN	GAA	W	L	T	SO	GA	S	SAPCT	PIM
58	3416	2.62	27	22	8	6	149	1485	.900	4

2001-2002 statistics:

GP	MIN	GAA	W	L	T	SO	GA	S	SAPCT	PIM
71	4071	2.31	31	27	8	6	157	1686	.907	19

LAST SEASON

Career-best goals-against average. Tied career high in shutouts. Fifth among NHL goalies in minutes played. Recorded 30 or more wins for third time in career.

THE PHYSICAL GAME

Potvin has a habit of playing deep in his net. He prefers to keep his skates in the paint at all times, but seems to be honestly trying to play at the top of his crease instead of back on his goal line. It's a constant battle getting Potvin to leave his comfort zone.

Excellent on low shots, Potvin's style is similar to that of his idol, Patrick Roy: he likes to butterfly and flirt with leaving a five-hole for shooters. The best place to beat Potvin is high, but shooters see that tempting gap between the pads and go for it, and he snaps the pads shut.

Potvin does a good job of keeping himself square to the shooter, and he knows where the puck is. He allows very few bad rebounds. He either controls them into the corners or deadens them in front of him. He is a poor stickhandler. He doesn't use his stick well around the net to break up passes, and hates to come out of his net to try to move the puck. Potvin prefers to leave the puck work to his defencemen.

THE MENTAL GAME

Players love to play for him because of his unruffled temperament. He is a leader in the dressing room and never alibis his mistakes.

THE INTANGIBLES

The Kings liked Potvin enough to re-sign him for another season. Potvin has stabilized the Kings' goaltending but he is not the guy to take a team to the next level. Potvin will at least keep them competitive, and at 31 is still in his goalie prime.

PROJECTION

Potvin reached our 30-win target (after a slow start) and should do it again.

MATHIEU SCHNEIDER

Yrs. of NHL service: 13
Born: New York, N.Y.; June 12, 1969
Position: left defence
Height: 5-10
Weight: 192
Uniform no.: 10
Shoots: left

Career statistics:

GP	G	A	TP	PIM
836	138	318	456	834

1998-1999 statistics:

GP	G	A	TP	+/-	PIM	PP	SH	GW	GT	S	PCT
75	10	24	34	-19	71	5	0	2	0	159	6.3

1999-2000 statistics:

GP	G	A	TP	+/-	PIM	PP	SH	GW	GT	S	PCT
80	10	20	30	-6	78	3	0	1	1	228	4.4

2000-2001 statistics:

GP	G	A	TP	+/-	PIM	PP	SH	GW	GT	S	PCT
73	16	35	51	0	56	7	1	2	2	183	8.7

2001-2002 statistics:

GP	G	A	TP	+/-	PIM	PP	SH	GW	GT	S	PCT
55	7	23	30	+3	68	4	0	0	0	123	5.7

LAST SEASON

Missed 23 games with hernia surgery. Missed two games with shoulder injury. Missed one game due to personal reasons. Missed one game due to coach's decision.

THE FINESSE GAME

Schneider is an excellent skater, plus he's deceptively strong for his size. He sees the ice and moves the puck well coming out of his own end, and is capable of controlling the pace. He has developed into a good two-way defenceman with the offensive skills to get involved in the attack and to work the point on the power play. A major concern has always been his positional play, but he's learned to make fewer high-risk plays as he has gained more experience. He blocks a lot of shots.

Strong, balanced and agile, Schneider lacks breakaway speed but is quick with his first step and changes directions smoothly. He can carry the puck but does not lead many rushes. He gets the puck out of the corner quickly. He makes good defensive decisions.

Schneider has improved his point play, doing more with the puck than just drilling shots, though he has a tendency to get his shots blocked when he is slow on the release. He handles the puck well and looks for the passes down low. Given the green light, he is likely to get involved down low more often. He has the skating ability to recover quickly when he takes a chance.

THE PHYSICAL GAME

Schneider is a poor-man's version of Chris Chelios, and plays with a lot more intensity than people tend to give him credit for. He is not a big hitter, because he is rather small by today's NHL-defenceman standards.

Schneider will battle the opposition's big forwards. He's extremely strong on his feet. He's also great at making the first pass, but he is not flashy, so he doesn't stand out. Schneider does have a knack for taking dumb penalties, often at the most inopportune moments.

Schneider's goal is to play a containment game and move the puck quickly and intelligently out of the zone. He is often matched against other teams' top scoring lines and always tries to do the job. He is best when paired with a physical defenceman. He has a tendency to hit high and gets penalties because of it.

THE INTANGIBLES

Schneider's major problem has to do with confidence. He's one of those guys you have to tell, all the time, when he's doing well, and then he'll respond. Conversely, criticism from a coach can get Schneider into a funk. He doesn't react well to being ridden hard, even though, like all players, he needs it sometimes. Schneider's pleasantly goofy personality fools people into thinking he doesn't care. He does.

Schneider's hernia surgery took place in November and took a lot out of his season. He was tied for third in scoring among NHL defencemen at the time of the injury.

PROJECTION

Schneider gets a lot of power-play time in L.A. and should net 40 points over a full season.

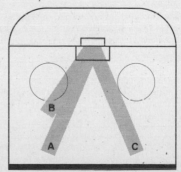

BRYAN SMOLINSKI

Yrs. of NHL service: 9
Born: Toledo, Ohio; Dec. 27, 1971
Position: centre / right wing
Height: 6-1
Weight: 208
Uniform no.: 21
Shoots: right

Career statistics:

GP	G	A	TP	PIM
681	191	251	442	434

1998-1999 statistics:

GP	G	A	TP	+/-	PIM	PP	SH	GW	GT	S	PCT
82	16	24	40	-7	49	7	0	3	0	223	7.2

1999-2000 statistics:

GP	G	A	TP	+/-	PIM	PP	SH	GW	GT	S	PCT
79	20	36	56	+2	48	2	0	0	2	160	12.5

2000-2001 statistics:

GP	G	A	TP	+/-	PIM	PP	SH	GW	GT	S	PCT
78	27	32	59	+10	40	5	3	5	0	183	14.8

2001-2002 statistics:

GP	G	A	TP	+/-	PIM	PP	SH	GW	GT	S	PCT
80	13	25	38	+7	56	4	1	0	2	187	6.9

LAST SEASON

Third on team in shots on goal. Missed one game with flu. Missed one game with back spasms.

THE FINESSE GAME

Smolinski is the No. 2 centre (behind Jason Allison) in L.A., and it's the right spot for him, but it just didn't work for him last season. It might have been the trade that hurt Smolinski the most, since he had shown a knack alongside Glen Murray, and Murray was dealt to Boston in the Allison trade.

Smolinski has been shuffled from centre to wing during his career, but works much better in the middle, where he makes good use of the open ice. Smolinski has a quick release and an accurate shot, and, on nights when he brings his "A" game, he works to get himself into quality shooting areas. Confidence is a big factor; he has a history of being a streaky, slumpy player, although the droughts aren't supposed to last 30 games the way his did last season.

Smolinski's skating is adequate, but it could improve with some lower-body work. He has good balance and lateral movement but he is not quick. He has a railroad-track skating base and is tough to knock over.

Smolinski has the smarts to be an asset on both specialty teams, and he has really stepped up as a penalty killer. He has good defensive awareness — his play away from the puck is sound. He is good in-tight with the puck.

THE PHYSICAL GAME

Smolinski has a thick, blocky build, and he can be a solid hitter. He doesn't have much of an aggressive nature on a nightly basis, but it shows up sporadically, and on those nights he is at his most effective.

THE INTANGIBLES

Smolinski has a lot going for him physically, but he's rather easy-going and needs a fire lit under him from time to time. Teams get frustrated with him because of his lack of drive and intensity.

PROJECTION

Smolinski's production was well off last year. He's not a big goal producer, but anything under 20 for a full season is unacceptable.

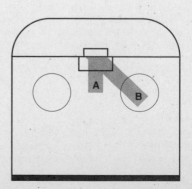

LUBOMIR VISNOVSKY

Yrs. of NHL service: 2
Born: Topolcany, Slovakia; Aug. 11, 1976
Position: left defence
Height: 5-10
Weight: 183
Uniform no.: 17
Shoots: left

Career statistics:

GP	G	A	TP	PIM
153	11	49	60	50

2000-2001 statistics:

GP	G	A	TP	+/-	PIM	PP	SH	GW	GT	S	PCT
81	7	32	39	+16	36	3	0	3	0	105	6.7

2001-2002 statistics:

GP	G	A	TP	+/-	PIM	PP	SH	GW	GT	S	PCT
72	4	17	21	-5	14	1	0	2	0	95	4.2

LAST SEASON
Missed 10 games due to coach's decision.

THE FINESSE GAME
Visnovsky is an undersized defenceman with over-sized offensive skills. He will never be an elite scoring defenceman, although there have been several small blueliners who have been able to have a major impact. He doesn't have quite the skating level for that. Visnovsky is a poor man's Brian Rafalski.

He moves the puck very well and is smart and agile enough to keep himself out of high-risk areas where he could get steamrolled.

Visnovsky has a good shot from the point but is better used as a set-up man. He has good lateral mobility along the blueline and that increases his options.

THE PHYSICAL GAME
Visnovsky looks a lot smaller than advertised. Again, to make a Rafalski comparison, the New Jersey defenceman is very thick through his torso and can absorb some punishment, while Visnovsky is more slender. He is surrounded by some physical defence mates which makes his small stature less detrimental than it could be on some other teams. But when he gets in one-on-one situations he is simply swamped.

THE INTANGIBLES
After making the All-Rookie team in 2001, Visnovsky was hit with the sophomore jinx. All of his games missed were due to benchings, and he lost some power-play time to more veteran players. With Philippe Boucher gone, however, Visnovsky should get some of that time back.

PROJECTION
Visnovsky should be able revert to his rookie form and repeat in the 35-point range.

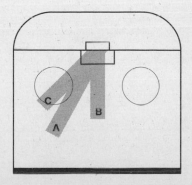

MINNESOTA WILD

Players' Statistics 2001-2002

POS	NO	PLAYER	GP	G	A	PTS	+/-	PIM	PP	SH	GW	GT	S	PCT
L	15	ANDREW BRUNETTE	81	21	48	69	-4	18	10		2	1	106	19.8
L	10	MARIAN GABORIK	78	30	37	67	0	34	10		4	1	221	13.6
C	34	JIM DOWD	82	13	30	43	-14	54	5		1		111	11.7
R	33	SERGEI ZHOLTOK	73	19	20	39	-10	28	10		2	1	146	13.0
L	24	ANTTI LAAKSONEN	82	16	17	33	-5	22			1		104	15.4
C	37	WES WALZ	64	10	20	30	0	43		2	5		97	10.3
L	11	*PASCAL DUPUIS	76	15	12	27	-10	16	3	2			154	9.7
C	18	RICHARD PARK	63	10	15	25	-1	10	2	1	2		115	8.7
L	9	HNAT DOMENICHELLI	67	9	16	25	-23	44	1		1	1	144	6.3
C	14	DARBY HENDRICKSON	68	9	15	24	-22	50	2	2	1		79	11.4
D	17	FILIP KUBA	62	5	19	24	-6	32	3		1		101	4.9
D	77	LUBOMIR SEKERAS	69	4	20	24	-7	38	4		1		82	4.9
R	22	STACY ROEST	58	10	11	21	-3	8	1	4	2	1	98	10.2
C	44	AARON GAVEY	71	6	11	17	-21	38	1				75	8.0
D	2	WILLIE MITCHELL	68	3	10	13	-16	68			1		67	4.5
D	23	JASON MARSHALL	80	5	6	11	-8	148	1				73	6.8
D	55	*NICK SCHULTZ	52	4	6	10	0	14	1		1		47	8.5
D	3	LADISLAV BENYSEK	74	1	7	8	-12	28					44	2.3
R	26	TONY VIRTA	8	2	3	5	0						15	13.3
L	12	MATT JOHNSON	60	4		4	-13	183			1		23	17.4
D	4	BRAD BROWN	51		4	4	-11	123					23	
D	5	BRAD BOMBARDIR	28	1	2	3	-6	14	1				24	4.2
C	31	ROMAN SIMICEK	6	2		2	1	8					4	50.0
L	36	SYLVAIN BLOUIN	43		2	2	-11	130					28	
D	19	*DAVID CULLEN	17				-8	6					3	
D	39	TRAVIS ROCHE	4				-1	2					1	
D	6	MIKE MATTEUCCI	3				1	2						
G	35	EMMANUEL FERNANDEZ	44				0	4						
G	30	DWAYNE ROLOSON	45				0	8						
G	31	DEREK GUSTAFSON	1				0							

GP = games played; G = goals; A = assists; PTS = points; +/- = goals-for minus goals-against while player is on ice; PIM = penalties in minutes; PP = power-play goals; SH = shorthanded goals; GW = game-winning goals; GT = game-tying goals; S = no. of shots; PCT = percentage of goals to shots; * = rookie

ANDREW BRUNETTE

Yrs. of NHL service: 7
Born: Sudbury, Ont.; Aug. 24, 1973
Position: left wing
Height: 6-1
Weight: 210
Uniform no.: 15
Shoots: left

Career statistics:

GP	G	A	TP	PIM
378	88	161	249	124

1998-1999 statistics:

GP	G	A	TP	+/-	PIM	PP	SH	GW	GT	S	PCT
77	11	20	31	-10	26	7	0	1	0	65	16.9

1999-2000 statistics:

GP	G	A	TP	+/-	PIM	PP	SH	GW	GT	S	PCT
81	23	27	50	-32	30	9	0	2	1	107	21.5

2000-2001 statistics:

GP	G	A	TP	+/-	PIM	PP	SH	GW	GT	S	PCT
77	15	44	59	-5	26	6	0	4	1	104	14.4

2001-2002 statistics:

GP	G	A	TP	+/-	PIM	PP	SH	GW	GT	S	PCT
81	21	48	69	-4	18	10	0	2	1	106	19.8

LAST SEASON

Led team in assists, points and shooting percentage. Tied for team lead in power-play goals. Second on team in goals. Fifth in NHL in shooting percentage. Career highs in assists and points. Missed one game with shoulder injury.

THE FINESSE GAME

Brunette has an excellent short game, from the hash marks down. He has very good hands. He is able to make a pass in a small space.

Although Brunette is not an NHL-calibre skater, he is able to prove that he is an NHL-calibre scorer. Brunette is like a Dave Andreychuk in miniature. He has excellent soft hands for flicking in pucks out of midair, making deflections, scooping up rebounds. Brunette will not be scoring goals off the rush.

The problem with being a smaller Andreychuk is that Brunette does not have the same reach the big 500-goal scorer does. And he will not be able to stretch around defencemen or lean on his stick in front of the net the way Andreychuk did in his prime.

Brunette possesses a goal-scorer's mentality and expansion has given him the chance to prove it in Atlanta and now in Minnesota. Brunette has good hockey vision and excels on the power play.

THE PHYSICAL GAME

Brunette is not afraid to take his lumps around the net. Brunette has a power-forward's build and has a little bit of an edge to him. To use an Andreychuk comparison again, he has a pretty long fuse and he has to be provoked before he'll snap. He is tough along the boards and is willing to fight for the puck in all the dirty areas of the ice.

THE INTANGIBLES

Brunette will be Minnesota's No. 1 left wing again.

PROJECTION

Brunette will continue to see prime ice time with Minnesota, and should score another 20 goals and 70 points.

HNAT DOMENICHELLI

Yrs. of NHL service: 5
Born: Edmonton, Alberta; Feb. 17, 1976
Position: centre / left wing
Height: 6-0
Weight: 194
Uniform no.: 9
Shoots: left

Career statistics:

GP	G	A	TP	PIM
266	52	61	113	104

1998-1999 statistics:

GP	G	A	TP	+/-	PIM	PP	SH	GW	GT	S	PCT
23	5	5	10	-4	11	3	0	0	0	45	11.1

1999-2000 statistics:

GP	G	A	TP	+/-	PIM	PP	SH	GW	GT	S	PCT
59	11	18	29	-21	16	1	0	1	0	125	8.8

2000-2001 statistics:

GP	G	A	TP	+/-	PIM	PP	SH	GW	GT	S	PCT
63	15	12	27	-9	18	4	0	1	0	150	10.0

2001-2002 statistics:

GP	G	A	TP	+/-	PIM	PP	SH	GW	GT	S	PCT
67	9	16	25	-23	44	1	0	1	1	144	6.3

LAST SEASON

Acquired from Atlanta on January 22, 2002, for Andy Sutton. Missed five games due to coach's decision.

THE FINESSE GAME

Domenichelli's size is a big drawback. He's of average height but very, very slender and easy to knock off the puck. But he is quick enough to jump in and out of holes and he has great hands and a good shot.

His best asset is his hockey sense, and he can play centre or wing. He is a creative playmaker with good vision, but won't pass up a good shot if he has it. Domenichelli saw a lot of power-play time towards the end of last season and needs to earn his way onto the top unit this year, where he can make an impact.

He is a good skater with quickness and agility, but doesn't possess real breakaway speed.

THE PHYSICAL GAME

Domenichelli tries, but he's just not going to win one-on-one battles. He has strength more than size, but doesn't yet seem to have the appetite for battling in the high-traffic areas. Another smallish guy, Theo Fleury, excelled because he did pay the price, and Domenichelli must learn to do the same.

THE INTANGIBLES

Domenichelli scored only 1-5-6 in 27 games with Minnesota after the trade.

PROJECTION

Domenichelli is capable of a 25/25 season (goals/assists), but he has to stay healthy and maintain a consistent effort instead of just playing well in bursts.

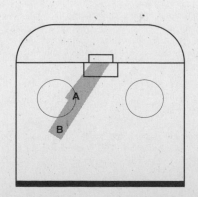

EMMANUEL FERNANDEZ

Yrs. of NHL service: 2
Born: Etobicoke, Ont.; Aug. 27, 1974
Position: goaltender
Height: 6-0
Weight: 185
Uniform no.: 35
Catches: left

Career statistics:

GP	MIN	GA	SO	GAA	A	PIM
119	6714	291	6	2.60	2	12

1998-1999 statistics:

GP	MIN	GAA	W	L	T	SO	GA	S	SAPCT	PIM
1	60	2.00	0	1	0	0	2	29	.931	0

1999-2000 statistics:

GP	MIN	GAA	W	L	T	SO	GA	S	SAPCT	PIM
24	1353	2.13	11	8	3	1	48	603	.920	2

2000-2001 statistics:

GP	MIN	GAA	W	L	T	SO	GA	S	SAPCT	PIM
42	2461	2.24	19	17	4	4	92	1147	.920	6

2001-2002 statistics:

GP	MIN	GAA	W	L	T	SO	GA	S	SAPCT	PIM
44	2463	3.05	12	24	5	1	125	1157	.892	4

LAST SEASON

Missed two games with ankle sprain.

THE PHYSICAL GAME

Fernandez plays an athletic, scrambling style that is a good fit for an inexperienced club. He is a very active goalie out of his net, and that takes some of the heat off his defencemen. Minnesota's top pair would be No. 6 and 7 on a good team, so the more help they can get from their goalie, the better.

He has uncanny flexibility and quick reactions. His lateral movement is exceptional. Fernandez is one of the best goalies in the league at pushing off to get across from post to post.

Fernandez has a quirky personality. But he worked hard during his many years as backup to Ed Belfour in Dallas to earn the respect of his teammates, who might otherwise not have been eager to follow him into battle.

THE MENTAL GAME

Fernandez took a step backwards last season after his first year in the No. 1 role in 2000-01. He has to assert himself this season or the job might slip away.

THE INTANGIBLES

Dwayne Roloson actually appeared in one more game than Fernandez did last season. A No. 1 goalie has to play in more than 44 games.

PROJECTION

This season might be Fernandez's last chance to be a No. 1 goalie. That's a lot of pressure, but that's the nature of his job. Fernandez needs to shave at least .7 off his GAA and win 25 games or the Wild will be auditioning for his replacement. Being coach Jacques Lemaire's nephew won't help.

MARIAN GABORIK

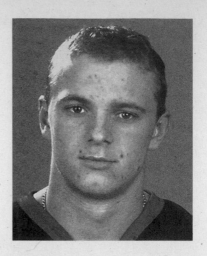

Yrs. of NHL service: 2
Born: Trencin, Slovakia; Feb. 14, 1982
Position: left wing
Height: 6-1
Weight: 183
Uniform no.: 10
Shoots: left

Career statistics:

GP	G	A	TP	PIM
149	48	55	103	66

2000-2001 statistics:

GP	G	A	TP	+/-	PIM	PP	SH	GW	GT	S	PCT
71	18	18	36	-6	32	6	0	3	0	179	10.1

2001-2002 statistics:

GP	G	A	TP	+/-	PIM	PP	SH	GW	GT	S	PCT
78	30	37	67	0	34	10	0	4	1	221	13.6

LAST SEASON

Led team in goals and shots. Tied for team lead in power-play goals. Second on team in assists, points and game-winning goals. Career highs in goals, assists and points. Missed three games with thigh injury. Missed one game recovering from off-season sports hernia surgery.

THE FINESSE GAME

Gaborik is a dynamic player. He has all the tools: skating, hands, a quick release on his shot. And he has the brains to make it all work.

Gaborik may never be an elite goal-scorer but he is a threat every time he has the puck. He can have a pretty successful career scoring consistently in the 30-goal range. Consistency is the issue, but he is only 20. Gaborik works hard on his flaws, like one-timers, which have improved. Coach Jacques Lemaire cut him some slack defensively to let him gain confidence in his offensive game. He doesn't need much work anyway — Gaborik's game is pretty complete and mature. He and two other Wild players were the only three who weren't minus players last season.

The NHL game is played on a smaller rink, it's more physical, and happens a lot faster that Gaborik was used to, but he has adjusted quickly.

Gaborik is very smart and is always looking to break a linemate out of the zone for a scoring rush.

THE PHYSICAL GAME

Young and still filling out, Gaborik will never be a power player, but he is sturdy enough to stand up under everyday NHL abuse.

THE INTANGIBLES

Gaborik wasn't hit by the sophomore jinx. In fact, his second season was an improvement over his solid first.

PROJECTION

Gaborik progressed much faster than we expected. He should become a consistent 65-70 point scorer, with totals that will go higher when (if) the Wild get better.

DARBY HENDRICKSON

Yrs. of NHL service: 7
Born: Richfield, Minn.; Aug. 28, 1972
Position: centre
Height: 6-1
Weight: 195
Uniform no.: 14
Shoots: left

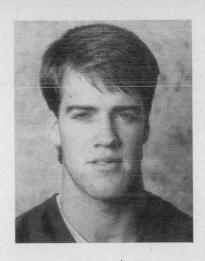

Career statistics:

GP	G	A	TP	PIM
456	62	56	118	350

1998-1999 statistics:

GP	G	A	TP	+/-	PIM	PP	SH	GW	GT	S	PCT
62	4	5	9	-19	52	1	0	0	0	70	5.7

1999-2000 statistics:

GP	G	A	TP	+/-	PIM	PP	SH	GW	GT	S	PCT
40	5	4	9	-3	14	0	1	1	0	39	12.8

2000-2001 statistics:

GP	G	A	TP	+/-	PIM	PP	SH	GW	GT	S	PCT
72	18	11	29	+1	36	3	1	1	1	114	15.8

2001-2002 statistics:

GP	G	A	TP	+/-	PIM	PP	SH	GW	GT	S	PCT
68	9	15	24	-22	50	2	2	1	0	79	11.4

LAST SEASON

Tied for second on team in shorthanded goals. Missed six games with eye injury. Missed four games with back spasms. Missed three games with sinus infection. Missed one game with flu.

THE FINESSE GAME

Hendrickson is a two-way forward with better-than-average skills for a checking role. He is a good, quick skater in small areas. He is clever with the puck and will look to make a pass rather than shoot.

He is defensively alert, and has pretty much lost confidence in his offensive game. He's coachable and can play any forward position, which is a plus.

Hendrickson works hard and gives an honest effort that maximizes his modest skills. He is an in-between forward, since he isn't big enough to play an effective power game, but his skills aren't elite enough for him to be considered a pure finesse play-maker. Hendrickson is an efficient penalty killer.

THE PHYSICAL GAME

Hendrickson has a feisty side, and isn't afraid to get involved with some of the league's tougher players (like Keith Tkachuk), if not the heavyweights. When he's not dinged up, he digs in and plays in-your-face hockey, which gets him more ice time.

THE INTANGIBLES

Hendrickson is an honest third-line centre or winger on his best night. He is Jacques Lemaire's kind of player. He loves playing in his home state.

PROJECTION

Hendrickson can probably get 30 points in a full season, but that's his top end.

FILIP KUBA

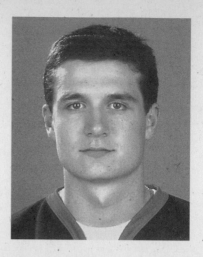

Yrs. of NHL service: 2
Born: Ostrava, Czech Republic; Dec. 29, 1976
Position: left defence
Height: 6-3
Weight: 205
Uniform no.: 17
Shoots: left

Career statistics:

GP	G	A	TP	PIM
155	15	46	61	62

1998-1999 statistics:

GP	G	A	TP	+/-	PIM	PP	SH	GW	GT	S	PCT
5	0	1	1	+2	0	0	0	0	0	5	0.0

1999-2000 statistics:

GP	G	A	TP	+/-	PIM	PP	SH	GW	GT	S	PCT
13	1	5	6	-3	2	1	0	1	0	16	6.3

2000-2001 statistics:

GP	G	A	TP	+/-	PIM	PP	SH	GW	GT	S	PCT
75	9	21	30	-6	28	4	0	4	1	141	6.4

2001-2002 statistics:

GP	G	A	TP	+/-	PIM	PP	SH	GW	GT	S	PCT
62	5	19	24	-6	32	3	0	1	0	101	4.9

LAST SEASON

Led team defencemen in points for second consecutive season. Missed 20 games with fractured right hand.

THE FINESSE GAME

The Wild have given Kuba plenty of chances to fail and, more often than not, he hasn't. Coach Jacques Lemaire showed faith in him by putting him back out even after he had a bad shift, and the result is that Kuba has cut back on his bad nights.

Kuba is a defensive defencemen, but he can make at least a modest contribution offensively. He would have slightly bettered his previous season's numbers if he hadn't missed nearly a quarter of a season with his hand injury. Kuba has a very hard shot from the point, but he's got a "wild thing" in him and he is frequently wide off the glass. He would do better to take a little velocity off the shot and just make sure it's on target.

He handles all game situations with the Wild: five-on-five, four-on-four, power play and penalty killing.

THE PHYSICAL GAME

Kuba is a very well-conditioned athlete. Last season he led the Wild in average ice time (25:30) and logged over 32 minutes in one game. Kuba does not play the body much. He has a big wingspan, though, and makes good use of the poke-check. He also blocks shots.

THE INTANGIBLES

The Wild coaches loved Kuba's attitude; he will be on one of their top defence pairings next season. He is Minnesota's best and most consistent defenceman.

PROJECTION

Kuba could improve to 35 points, but it's a mistake to think he can carry much more of an offensive load than that.

ANTTI LAAKSONEN

Yrs. of NHL service: 3
Born: Tammela, Finland; Oct. 3, 1973
Position: left wing
Height: 6-0
Weight: 180
Uniform no.: 24
Shoots: left

Career statistics:

GP	G	A	TP	PIM
202	35	38	73	50

1998-1999 statistics:

GP	G	A	TP	+/-	PIM	PP	SH	GW	GT	S	PCT
11	1	2	3	-1	2	0	0	0	0	8	12.5

1999-2000 statistics:

GP	G	A	TP	+/-	PIM	PP	SH	GW	GT	S	PCT
27	6	3	9	+3	2	0	0	1	0	23	26.1

2000-2001 statistics:

GP	G	A	TP	+/-	PIM	PP	SH	GW	GT	S	PCT
82	12	16	28	-7	24	0	2	1	0	129	9.3

2001-2002 statistics:

GP	G	A	TP	+/-	PIM	PP	SH	GW	GT	S	PCT
82	16	17	33	-5	22	0	0	1	0	104	15.4

LAST SEASON

Third on team in shooting percentage. Career highs in goals, assists and points. One of two Minnesota players to appear in all 82 games.

THE FINESSE GAME

Laaksonen became acclimated to North American life by playing college hockey, and spent an apprenticeship in the minors before expansion provided him with a shot at his first full-time NHL job.

He has average skills and above-average intelligence. Laaksonen is a role player with good defensive awareness. He can be given a checking assignment against other teams' top lines and will do the job.

Laaksonen rarely makes a bad decision with the puck. He did nice work with Wes Walz on the checking line and kills penalties.

THE PHYSICAL GAME

Laaksonen is average-sized, but is willing to get his body in the way.

THE INTANGIBLES

Laaksonen is coach Jacques Lemaire's kind of player: an intelligent and diligent checking forward and penalty killer. Laaksonen has appeared in every Wild game from day one.

PROJECTION

Laaksonen should again be a mainstay on the third line and can chip in 15-18 goals in a largely defensive role.

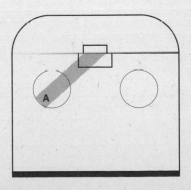

JASON MARSHALL

Yrs. of NHL service: 7
Born: Cranbrook, B.C.; Feb. 22, 1971
Position: right defence
Height: 6-2
Weight: 200
Uniform no.: 23
Shoots: right

Career statistics:

GP	G	A	TP	PIM
434	14	36	50	875

1998-1999 statistics:

GP	G	A	TP	+/-	PIM	PP	SH	GW	GT	S	PCT
72	1	7	8	-5	142	0	0	0	0	63	1.6

1999-2000 statistics:

GP	G	A	TP	+/-	PIM	PP	SH	GW	GT	S	PCT
55	0	3	3	-10	88	0	0	0	0	41	-

2000-2001 statistics:

GP	G	A	TP	+/-	PIM	PP	SH	GW	GT	S	PCT
55	3	4	7	-13	122	2	1	1	0	43	7.0

2001-2002 statistics:

GP	G	A	TP	+/-	PIM	PP	SH	GW	GT	S	PCT
80	5	6	11	-8	148	1	0	0	0	73	6.8

PROJECTION

Marshall will be hard-pressed to get points in the double digits, but his PIM will be close to 150 if he gets the ice time he did last season.

LAST SEASON

Second on team in penalty minutes. Missed two games due to coach's decision.

THE FINESSE GAME

Marshall is big and mobile with good puck skills. He has been slow to come to hand, mostly from having to learn the mental discipline of playing his position, and odds are we've seen the best of what he has to offer.

He will never be involved much offensively. He lacks the instincts to be much of a factor from the point and his shot is only average. He is a good skater for his size.

Marshall can be his own worst enemy. If he makes a mistake he is very hard on himself. He doesn't have much confidence in his game and doesn't take well to benchings or to challenges to his job.

THE PHYSICAL GAME

Marshall is big and likes to play a physical game. He sticks up for his teammates and will take the initiative to set a physical tone. He is a hard worker and shows up most nights. He can have games where he gets headstrong and starts running around out of position, committing sins of commission rather than omission.

THE INTANGIBLES

Marshall fits well into coach Jacques Lemaire's defensive system and he plays hard every night. He would be a third-pair defenceman on a good team, but will continue to play as a top four in Minnesota until the team gets deeper at the position. That doesn't look like it will happen anytime soon.

WILLIE MITCHELL

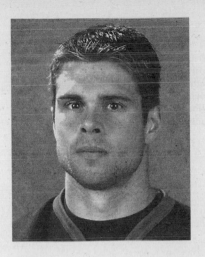

Yrs. of NHL service: 2
Born: Fort McNeill, B.C.; Apr. 23, 1977
Position: defense
Height: 6-3
Weight: 205
Uniform no.: 2
Shoots: left

Career statistics:

GP	G	A	TP	PIM
103	4	19	23	108

1999-2000 statistics:

GP	G	A	TP	+/-	PIM	PP	SH	GW	GT	S	PCT
2	0	0	0	+1	0	0	0	0	0	2	-

2000-2001 statistics:

GP	G	A	TP	+/-	PIM	PP	SH	GW	GT	S	PCT
33	1	9	10	+4	40	0	0	0	0	30	3.3

2001-2002 statistics:

GP	G	A	TP	+/-	PIM	PP	SH	GW	GT	S	PCT
68	3	10	13	-16	68	0	0	1	0	67	4.5

LAST SEASON

Missed five games with shoulder injury. Missed five games with bruised wrist. Missed three games with groin injury. Missed one game due to coach's decision.

THE FINESSE GAME

Mitchell is yet another product of the deep New Jersey Devils defensive system, but wasn't good enough to crack their mostly veteran lineup as a youngster, and was traded to Minnesota for veteran playoff help (Sean O'Donnell) in 2001.

Mitchell is a decent skater for his size. He is strong on his skates but has only average speed and agility. He has to continue to learn the art of positioning.

Mitchell has a hard slap shot from the point, but doesn't have much hockey sense or vision to do much with it other than put his head down and shoot. There isn't one outstanding aspect of Mitchell's game, but there are a lot of little things that add up.

THE PHYSICAL GAME

Mitchell needs to become more consistent in his physical game. He is a brave shot-blocker as well. He's a strong guy and can become more of a presence.

THE INTANGIBLES

Defencemen like Mitchell take a few years to develop. He's 25 and about to hit his prime. Mitchell showed more consistency last season even while battling through nagging injuries. Mitchell should be in the Wild's top four.

PROJECTION

Mitchell won't get more than 20 points, and he remains a project.

BILL MUCKALT

Yrs. of NHL service: 4
Born: Surrey, B.C.; July 15, 1974
Position: right wing
Height: 6-1
Weight: 200
Uniform no.: 17
Shoots: right

Career statistics:

GP	G	A	TP	PIM
248	35	54	89	198

1998-1999 statistics:

GP	G	A	TP	+/-	PIM	PP	SH	GW	GT	S	PCT
73	16	20	36	-9	98	4	2	1	0	119	13.4

1999-2000 statistics:

GP	G	A	TP	+/-	PIM	PP	SH	GW	GT	S	PCT
45	8	11	19	+11	21	1	0	1	1	79	10.1

2000-2001 statistics:

GP	G	A	TP	+/-	PIM	PP	SH	GW	GT	S	PCT
60	11	15	26	-4	33	1	0	2	1	90	12.2

2001-2002 statistics:

GP	G	A	TP	+/-	PIM	PP	SH	GW	GT	S	PCT
70	0	8	8	-3	46	0	0	0	0	73	0.0

PROJECTION

Until Muckalt rediscovers the joy of scoring, we will scale back our expectations to 20 points. He should see more ice time with the Wild than he did with the Senators.

LAST SEASON

Signed a free agent by Minnesota on July 3, 2002. Missed nine games with right leg injury. Missed three games due to coach's decision.

THE FINESSE GAME

Muckalt has all the skills, but only in moderate doses. His biggest asset is his understanding of the game. Muckalt plays well positionally and has good hockey sense.

Muckalt's scoring touch, which was once adequate, has all but disappeared. It is absolutely mystifying that he could play 70 games last season — in a reduced role, averaging about 10 minutes of ice time — and not score a single goal even by accident. What goals may come for him will result from his grit and determination around the net.

Muckalt is an average playmaker. His skating is just a touch above average.

THE PHYSICAL GAME

He is of average size, but Muckalt is fairly strong and willing to do the work along the boards.

THE INTANGIBLES

Muckalt had two seasons interrupted by serious injuries, and last year did not go well for him in Ottawa where he was behind a large group of forwards far more talented than he. Minnesota wants Muckalt for his strength and to provide some leadership on a young team.

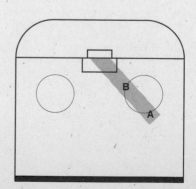

CLIFF RONNING

Yrs. of NHL service: 15
Born: Vancouver, B.C.; Oct. 1, 1965
Position: centre
Height: 5-8
Weight: 165
Uniform no.: 7
Shoots: left

Career statistics:

GP	G	A	TP	PIM
1017	280	517	797	427

1998-1999 statistics:

GP	G	A	TP	+/-	PIM	PP	SH	GW	GT	S	PCT
79	20	40	60	-3	42	10	0	4	0	257	7.8

1999-2000 statistics:

GP	G	A	TP	+/-	PIM	PP	SH	GW	GT	S	PCT
82	26	36	62	-13	34	7	0	2	0	248	10.5

2000-2001 statistics:

GP	G	A	TP	+/-	PIM	PP	SH	GW	GT	S	PCT
80	19	43	62	+4	28	6	0	4	0	237	8.0

2001-2002 statistics:

GP	G	A	TP	+/-	PIM	PP	SH	GW	GT	S	PCT
81	19	35	54	0	32	5	0	0	2	199	9.5

LAST SEASON

Acquired by Minnesota on June 22, 2002, from Los Angeles for a fourth-round draft pick in 2002. Acquired by Los Angeles on March 16, 2002, from Nashville for Jere Karalahti and a conditional draft pick in 2003. Led Kings in shots. Third on Kings in assists. Tied for third on Kings in goals.

THE FINESSE GAME

Ronning's forte is not scoring goals but creating chances for his wingers. He lets bigger linemates attract defenders so that he can dipsy-doodle with the puck He's quick, shifty and smart (he has to be smart, otherwise he'll be flattened along the boards like an advertisement). Ronning might make a nice linemate for the skilled young Wild winger, Marian Gaborik.

Ronning likes to work from behind the net, using the cage as a shield and daring defenders to chase him. Ronning plays hockey like a game of chicken. He is a tempting target, and even smaller-sized defencemen fantasize about smashing him to the ice, but he keeps himself out of trouble by dancing in and out of openings and finding free teammates. He also works well off the half-boards on the power play.

A quick thinker and unpredictable, Ronning can curl off the wall into the slot, pass to the corners or the point and jump to the net, or beat a defender wide at the top of the circle and feed a teammate coming into the play late. He's not afraid of going into traffic. And as good a passer and playmaker as he is, Ronning isn't shy about pulling the trigger.

Ronning puts a lot of little dekes into a compact area and opens up the ice with his bursts of speed and his fakes. Unless the defence can force him along the wall and contain him, he's all over the ice trying to make things happen. He has not yet lost a step in his skating.

THE PHYSICAL GAME

No one asks jockeys to tackle running backs. Ronning is built for speed and deception. He is smart enough to avoid getting crunched and talented enough to compensate for his lack of strength. He has skills and a huge heart and competes hard every night.

Ronning is so small that usually the best he can do is tug at an opponent like a pesky little brother. He gets involved with his stick, hooking at a puck carrier's arm and worrying at the puck in a player's skates. He keeps the puck in his skates when he protects it, so that a checker will often have to pull Ronning down to get at the puck, which creates a power play. He is pretty durable for a small guy, and pays great attention to his physical fitness.

THE INTANGIBLES

Poor Ronning. He finally gets traded from an expansion to team a contender, only to be traded to another expansion team. Maybe that one goal in 14 games with the Kings had something to do with it, although L.A. played him on the wing, which isn't his prime position. At least he has had experience in playing with younger guys and marginal talent. He should have a positive impact in Minnesota.

PROJECTION

Ronning has been terrifically consistent, with four consecutive seasons of 55 or more points, heavier on the assists than the goals. He will get a lot of ice time again with the Wild as the probable No. 1 centre, and can be expected to repeat those numbers.

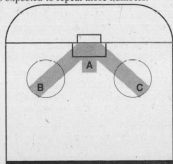

WES WALZ

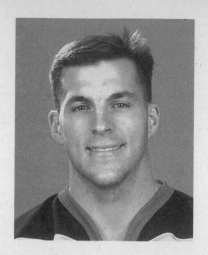

Yrs. of NHL service: 9
Born: Calgary, Alta.; May 15, 1970
Position: centre
Height: 5-10
Weight: 185
Uniform no.: 37
Shoots: right

Career statistics:

GP	G	A	TP	PIM
315	55	83	138	151

2000-2001 statistics:

GP	G	A	TP	+/-	PIM	PP	SH	GW	GT	S	PCT
82	18	12	30	-8	37	0	7	3	0	152	11.8

2001-2002 statistics:

GP	G	A	TP	+/-	PIM	PP	SH	GW	GT	S	PCT
64	10	20	30	0	43	0	2	5	0	97	10.3

LAST SEASON

Led team in game-winning goals. Tied for second on team in shorthanded goals. Missed 10 games with shoulder injury. Missed eight games with sprained ankle.

THE FINESSE GAME

Walz has a lot of ability in a little package. His best asset is his speed (he won the team's fastest skating competition). It gives him one-step quickness on a defender and a head start on breakaways. His shot is not scary, but it's accurate and he has a quick release.

He is a better playmaker than scorer, but with a lack of finishers on a second-year expansion team, he took advantage of his chances. He keeps the puck alive in corners and threads a pass to teammates. Most of his scoring chances come in-tight.

Defensive play was a Walz weakness early in his career. Now it's helping him earn his paycheque. He pursues pucks instead of turning away, and doesn't break out of the zone prematurely. He is consistent in his effort. Walz likes the checking part of the game, but he also has a knack for scoring timely goals.

THE PHYSICAL GAME

It was his size that handicapped him in winning a full-time NHL job with better teams. With the game expanding and opening to more finesse-oriented players, Walz can now survive.

THE INTANGIBLES

Walz spent four years playing in Switzerland waiting for a chance to break back into the NHL and he has made the most of it.

PROJECTION

Minnesota doesn't figure to get much deeper this season. Walz will again figure in as the third-line centre for the Wild and can score 15-20 goals in his checking role.

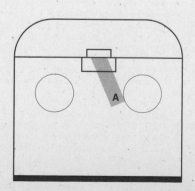

MONTREAL CANADIENS

Players' Statistics 2001-2002

POS.	NO.	PLAYER	GP	G	A	PTS	+/-	PIM	PP	SH	GW	GT	S	PCT
C	94	YANIC PERREAULT	82	27	29	56	-3	40	6		7	2	156	17.3
R	20	RICHARD ZEDNIK	82	22	22	44	-3	59	4		3		249	8.8
R	14	OLEG PETROV	75	24	17	41	-4	12	3	1	6		152	15.8
C	93	DOUG GILMOUR	70	10	31	41	-7	48	5		2		78	12.8
C	90	JOE JUNEAU	70	8	28	36	-3	10	1		1	1	96	8.3
R	24	ANDREAS DACKELL	79	15	18	33	-3	24	2	3	2		83	18.1
D	43	PATRICE BRISEBOIS	71	4	29	33	9	25	2	1	1		95	4.2
L	95	SERGEI BEREZIN	70	11	15	26	2	8	4		5		200	5.5
D	52	CRAIG RIVET	82	8	17	25	1	76					90	8.9
D	79	ANDREI MARKOV	56	5	19	24	-1	24	2		1		73	6.8
L	25	CHAD KILGER	75	8	15	23	-7	27		1	2		87	9.2
C	27	SHAUN VAN ALLEN	73	8	13	21	0	26		1	1		48	16.7
C	38	JAN BULIS	53	9	10	19	-2	8	1		3		87	10.3
C	71	*MIKE RIBEIRO	43	8	10	18	-11	12	3				48	16.7
R	82	DONALD AUDETTE	33	5	13	18	3	20	3		3		82	6.1
D	5	STEPHANE QUINTAL	75	6	10	16	-7	87	1		1		85	7.1
L	22	BILL LINDSAY	76	5	10	15	-11	140			1		77	6.5
D	28	KARL DYKHUIS	80	5	7	12	16	32			1		85	5.9
D	56	STEPHANE ROBIDAS	56	1	10	11	-25	14	1				68	1.5
C	45	ARRON ASHAM	35	5	4	9	7	55					30	16.7
L	29	GINO ODJICK	36	4	4	8	3	104					40	10.0
D	44	SHELDON SOURAY	34	3	5	8	-5	62	1			1	56	5.4
D	54	PATRICK TRAVERSE	25	2	3	5	-7	14	2				24	8.3
D	51	FRANCIS BOUILLON	28		5	5	-5	33					24	
L	37	PATRICK POULIN	28		5	5	6	6					15	
C	36	*MARCEL HOSSA	10	3	1	4	2	2					20	15.0
C	11	SAKU KOIVU	3		2	2	0						2	
C	46	BENOIT GRATTON	8	1		1	-1	8					8	12.5
C	78	ERIC LANDRY	2		1	1	2							
C	63	CRAIG DARBY	2					0						
D	59	MARTTI JARVENTIE	1					2						
G	35	STEPHANE FISET	2					0						
G	31	JEFF HACKETT	15					0	2					
G	30	MATHIEU GARON	5					0						
G	60	JOSE THEODORE	67					0	2					
G	95	OLIVIER MICHAUD	1					0						

GP = games played; G = goals; A = assists; PTS = points; +/- = goals-for minus goals-against while player is on ice; PIM = penalties in minutes; PP = power-play goals; SH = shorthanded goals; GW = game-winning goals; GT = game-tying goals; S = no. of shots; PCT = percentage of goals to shots; * = rookie

DONALD AUDETTE

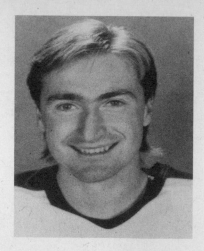

Yrs. of NHL service: 11
Born: Laval, Que.; Sept. 23, 1969
Position: right wing
Height: 5-8
Weight: 190
Uniform no.: 82
Shoots: right

Career statistics:

GP	G	A	TP	PIM
630	240	225	465	527

1998-1999 statistics:

GP	G	A	TP	+/-	PIM	PP	SH	GW	GT	S	PCT
49	18	18	36	+7	51	6	0	2	0	152	11.8

1999-2000 statistics:

GP	G	A	TP	+/-	PIM	PP	SH	GW	GT	S	PCT
63	19	24	43	+2	57	1	1	4	0	162	11.7

2000-2001 statistics:

GP	G	A	TP	+/-	PIM	PP	SH	GW	GT	S	PCT
76	34	45	79	+1	76	14	1	3	2	159	15.1

2001-2002 statistics:

GP	G	A	TP	+/-	PIM	PP	SH	GW	GT	S	PCT
33	5	13	18	+3	20	3	0	3	0	82	6.1

LAST SEASON

Acquired from Dallas on November 20, 2001, with Shaun Van Allen for Martin Rucinsky and Benoit Brunet. Missed 49 games with forearm injury.

THE FINESSE GAME

A bustling forward who barrels to the net at every opportunity, Audette is eager and feisty down low and has good hand skills. He also has keen scoring instincts, along with the quickness to make good things happen. His feet move so fast (with a choppy stride) that he doesn't look graceful, but he can really get moving and he has good balance.

A scorer first, Audette has a great top-shelf shot, which he gets away quickly and accurately. He can also make a play, but he will do this at the start of a rush. Once he is inside the offensive zone and low, he wants the puck. Considering his scoring touch, though, his selfishness can be forgiven.

Audette is at his best on the power play. He is savvy enough not to just stand around and take punishment. He times his jumps into the space between the left post and the bottom of the left circle. Audette is not very big, yet he makes his living around the net by smartly jumping in and out of the holes.

Audette steps up his game with the pressure.

THE PHYSICAL GAME

Opponents hate Audette, which he takes as a great compliment. He runs goalies, yaps and takes dives — then goes out and scores on the power play after the opposition has taken a bad penalty.

Though he isn't as diligent coming back, Audette will forecheck and scrap for the puck. He's not very big, but around the net he plays like he's at least a six-footer. He keeps jabbing and working away until he is bowled over by an angry defender.

THE INTANGIBLES

Audette suffered a gruesome forearm/wrist injury that required delicate surgery to repair. He did return for the end of the regular season and the playoffs. His six playoff goals (in 12 games) showed he has regained his touch.

PROJECTION

You can't help but be impressed with Audette's perseverance. His comeback saga was understandably overshadowed by Saku Koivu's. Don't sell Audette short. He can return to 30-goal status.

PATRICE BRISEBOIS

Yrs. of NHL service: 11
Born: Montreal, Que.; Jan. 27, 1971
Position: right defence
Height: 6-1
Weight: 203
Uniform no.: 43
Shoots: right

Career statistics:

GP	G	A	TP	PIM
647	71	211	282	447

1998-1999 statistics:

GP	G	A	TP	+/-	PIM	PP	SH	GW	GT	S	PCT
54	3	9	12	-8	28	1	0	1	0	90	3.3

1999-2000 statistics:

GP	G	A	TP	+/-	PIM	PP	SH	GW	GT	S	PCT
54	10	25	35	-1	18	5	0	2	2	88	11.4

2000-2001 statistics:

GP	G	A	TP	+/-	PIM	PP	SH	GW	GT	S	PCT
77	15	21	36	-31	28	11	0	4	0	178	8.4

2001-2002 statistics:

GP	G	A	TP	+/-	PIM	PP	SH	GW	GT	S	PCT
71	4	29	33	+9	25	2	1	1	0	95	4.2

LAST SEASON

Led team defencemen in points for third consecutive season. Second on team in goals and plus-minus. Missed 10 games with neck injury.

THE FINESSE GAME

Brisebois has some nice offensive skills, but he doesn't have the hockey sense to combine them in a complete package so he can be an elite-level defence-man. He has a decent first step to the puck, plus a good stride with some quickness, though he won't rush end-to-end. He carries the puck with authority but will usually take one or two strides and look for a pass, or else make the safe dump out of the zone. He steps up in the neutral zone to slow an opponent's rush. He is a good outlet passer and is getting steadier under pressure.

Brisebois plays the point well enough to be on the first power-play unit, but his goal production fell off sharply considering the amount of time he saw there. He lacks the rink vision and lateral movement that mark truly successful point men. He has a good point shot, though, with a sharp release, and he keeps it low and on target. He doesn't often venture to the circles on offence — when he does he has the passing skills and the shot to make something happen. And grant him this, he is always trying to make something good happen.

Brisebois has become less undisciplined and plays his position more calmly.

THE PHYSICAL GAME

Brisebois continues to pay the price physically. Although not a punishing hitter, he is strong and will make take-outs. He doesn't have a mean streak, so he has to dedicate himself to taking the body.

THE INTANGIBLES

Brisebois has worked hard to develop better defensive presence and has become a legitimate No. 3 defence-man, although he is asked to function as a top two, which is beyond his ability.

PROJECTION

When he stays healthy, Brisebois can contribute 40 points, but we would like to see him dedicate himself more in his own end.

JAN BULIS

Yrs. of NHL service: 5
Born: Paradubice, Czech Republic; Mar. 18, 1978
Position: centre
Height: 6-1
Weight: 208
Uniform no.: 38
Shoots: left

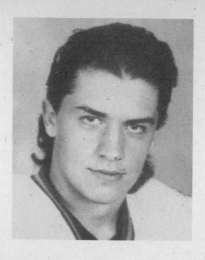

Career statistics:

GP	G	A	TP	PIM
246	35	77	112	88

1998-1999 statistics:

GP	G	A	TP	+/-	PIM	PP	SH	GW	GT	S	PCT
38	7	16	23	+3	6	3	0	3	0	57	12.3

1999-2000 statistics:

GP	G	A	TP	+/-	PIM	PP	SH	GW	GT	S	PCT
56	9	22	31	+7	30	0	0	1	0	92	9.8

2000-2001 statistics:

GP	G	A	TP	+/-	PIM	PP	SH	GW	GT	S	PCT
51	5	18	23	-1	26	1	0	0	0	61	8.2

2001-2002 statistics:

GP	G	A	TP	+/-	PIM	PP	SH	GW	GT	S	PCT
53	9	10	19	-2	8	1	0	3	0	87	10.3

PROJECTION

The injuries make him a risky pool pick. He is capable of scoring 40 points over a full season. Pro-rate accordingly.

LAST SEASON

Missed 20 games with knee injury.

THE FINESSE GAME

Bulis has decent size, skating and skills to stamp him as a future top forward. He handles the puck well through traffic and in the open at high tempo.

More of a playmaker than a scorer, Bulis is not a pure passer. He has a quick release on his wrist shot and will take the shot if that is his better option, rather than try to force the pass. He has a good slap shot, too. His shot was clocked at close to 90 m.p.h. in his first year of junior.

Bulis plays a smart positional game and will not need too much tutoring to learn the defensive aspects of the NHL game. He is a well-conditioned athlete and has a lot of stamina to handle the ice time and travel. He is very good on draws.

THE PHYSICAL GAME

Bulis brings an infectious enthusiasm, whether it's to a game or a practice session. He is one of those players who looks like he is simply having a great time playing hockey, but he is also serious about the sport. Bulis has a work ethic that has earned him the respect of the veterans. He isn't aggressive, but he is stocky and strong on his skates. He can compete in a physical game and he likes to hit.

THE INTANGIBLES

In each of his last four NHL seasons, Bulis has missed significant playing time due to injury. The potential is still there, but he has to coordinate body and mind to get his game together.

MARIUSZ CZERKAWSKI

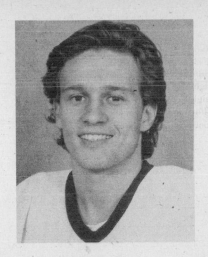

Yrs. of NHL service: 8
Born: Radomsko, Poland; Apr. 13, 1972
Position: right wing
Height: 6-0
Weight: 195
Uniform no.: 21
Shoots: left

Career statistics:

GP	G	A	TP	PIM
586	177	185	362	232

1998-1999 statistics:

GP	G	A	TP	+/-	PIM	PP	SH	GW	GT	S	PCT
78	21	17	38	-10	14	4	0	1	2	205	10.2

1999-2000 statistics:

GP	G	A	TP	+/-	PIM	PP	SH	GW	GT	S	PCT
79	35	35	70	-16	34	16	0	4	1	276	12.7

2000-2001 statistics:

GP	G	A	TP	+/-	PIM	PP	SH	GW	GT	S	PCT
82	30	32	62	-24	48	10	1	0	0	287	10.4

2001-2002 statistics:

GP	G	A	TP	+/-	PIM	PP	SH	GW	GT	S	PCT
82	22	29	51	-8	48	6	0	6	1	169	13.0

LAST SEASON

Acquired from N.Y. Islanders on June 22, 2002, for Arron Asham and a fifth-round draft pick. Tied for team lead on Islanders in game-winning goals. Tied for third on Islanders in shots. One of two Islanders to appear in all 82 games.

THE FINESSE GAME

A quick wrist shot is Czerkawski's best weapon. With the extra room on the power play, he is at his best. He has soft hands for passes and good vision. He needs to play with someone who will get him the puck since he will not go into the corners for it.

Czerkawski is superb in open ice, with great one-on-one moves and a phenomenal shot. He likes to use all of the ice, and will cut across the middle or to the right side to make the play. He is a shifty skater, not one with great straightaway speed, but he puts the slip on a defender with a lateral move and is off.

With all of those assets, Czerkawski's subpar season was a mystery. He never clicked with Alexei Yashin and with the other top line set, and was often relegated to third or fourth line duty. Instead of 18-20 minutes a game, he was seeing between 10-15 by the end of the season, and the sulk set in. Once he stopped scoring, he stopped being a factor.

THE PHYSICAL GAME

Czerkawski has to get better at protecting the puck and perform at least a willing game along the boards. He uses his body in the offensive zone, but in a perfunctory manner, and he doesn't like to get involved too much in the defensive zone. He can be intimidated physically. He is quick enough to peel back and help out with backchecking, since he is very smart at anticipating passes, but he will rarely knock anyone off the puck.

THE INTANGIBLES

Czerkawski's funk might be lifted by the trade to the Canadiens, who have a flock of small, skilled forwards who may provide the right mix of linemates for him. Czerkawski also went through a divorce, so the fresh start in Montreal might be a needed change.

PROJECTION

As the Islanders got better, Czerkawski got worse. With his new cast in Montreal, Czerkawski should return to the rank of 30-goal scorers.

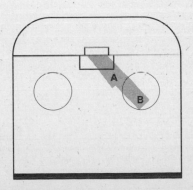

ANDREAS DACKELL

Yrs. of NHL service: 6
Born: Gavle, Sweden; Dec. 29, 1972
Position: right wing
Height: 5-11
Weight: 195
Uniform no.: 24
Shoots: right

Career statistics:

GP	G	A	TP	PIM
480	80	133	213	128

1998-1999 statistics:

GP	G	A	TP	+/-	PIM	PP	SH	GW	GT	S	PCT
77	15	35	50	+9	30	6	0	3	0	107	14.0

1999-2000 statistics:

GP	G	A	TP	+/-	PIM	PP	SH	GW	GT	S	PCT
82	10	25	35	+5	18	0	0	1	1	99	10.1

2000-2001 statistics:

GP	G	A	TP	+/-	PIM	PP	SH	GW	GT	S	PCT
81	13	18	31	+7	24	1	0	3	0	72	18.1

2001-2002 statistics:

GP	G	A	TP	+/-	PIM	PP	SH	GW	GT	S	PCT
79	15	18	33	-3	24	2	3	2	0	83	18.1

LAST SEASON

Led team in shorthanded goals and shooting percentage. Missed one game with virus.

THE FINESSE GAME

Dackell has good hockey sense and is sound defensively. He does a lot of subtle things well. Tapes of his game could be used to illustrate hustling on backchecks to knock the puck away from an attacker, attacking in the neutral zone without committing yourself, playing strong along the wall and keeping your man out of the play. Dackell is a last-minute man, one of the guys put on the ice in the final minute of a period or game to protect a lead. He kills penalties and protects the puck well.

He has a decent, accurate shot that he could utilize more. He seems to score timely goals, and is a short-handed threat on the penalty kill.

Dackell doesn't have blazing speed but works hard to be where he's supposed to be. He's very smart and hard to knock off the puck.

THE PHYSICAL GAME

Dackell isn't very big and he's not a banger, but he'll make checks and won't be intimidated. He could be the toughest 30-PIM-a-year player in the NHL.

THE INTANGIBLES

Much of what Dackell contributes to a team is subtle, but he is a valuable role player on the Canadiens. He gives his team an honest 14 minutes a night. Dackell is the kind of player you won't notice until he's missing from the lineup, and he was an important role player in the Habs' playoff drive.

PROJECTION

Dackell can handle a second-line role as a safety-valve winger, but because of his lack of scoring touch, he is better suited as a third-line checking forward who can provide a steady 12 to 15 goals a season.

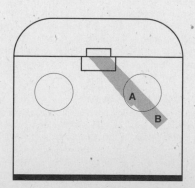

KARL DYKHUIS

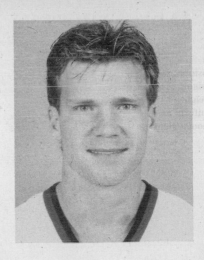

Yrs. of NHL service: 9
Born: Sept-Iles, Que.; July 8, 1972
Position: right defence
Height: 6-3
Weight: 214
Uniform no.: 28
Shoots: left

Career statistics:

GP	G	A	TP	PIM
570	41	87	128	459

1998-1999 statistics:

GP	G	A	TP	+/-	PIM	PP	SH	GW	GT	S	PCT
78	4	5	9	-23	50	1	0	0	0	88	4.5

1999-2000 statistics:

GP	G	A	TP	+/-	PIM	PP	SH	GW	GT	S	PCT
72	7	13	20	-5	46	3	1	0	0	69	10.1

2000-2001 statistics:

GP	G	A	TP	+/-	PIM	PP	SH	GW	GT	S	PCT
67	8	9	17	+9	44	2	0	1	0	66	12.1

2001-2002 statistics:

GP	G	A	TP	+/-	PIM	PP	SH	GW	GT	S	PCT
80	5	7	12	+16	32	0	0	1	0	85	5.9

LAST SEASON

Led team in plus-minus.

THE FINESSE GAME

Dykhuis has learned the importance of keeping his feet moving, because it helps him stay up with the play. His game edges towards the offensive side, but he also uses his finesse skills well in his own end. He keeps the passes short, accurate and crisp, and banks the puck off the boards or glass if that's the only option available to clear the zone.

He is a natural for penalty killing and four-on-four play because he has fine mobility and quickness, with a quick shift of gears that allows him to get up the ice in a hurry. Smart, with good hands for passing or drilling shots from the point, Dykhuis also leans towards conservatism. He won't venture down low unless the decision to pinch is a sound one.

THE PHYSICAL GAME

Although tall and rangy, Dykhuis isn't a heavyweight. But he goes out of his way to screen off opposing forecheckers and to buy time for his partner. There are times, on a regular basis, when his physical aspect is almost non-existent. He is strong and makes solid contact on those occasions when he does hit, though. He's also such a good skater that he can break up a play; dig out the loose puck and be off in just a stride or two to start an odd-man rush. He also uses his reach to break up plays.

THE INTANGIBLES

Dykhuis is the most reliable defender on Montreal's blueline. That +16 is pretty impressive compared to the rest of his teammates.

PROJECTION

Dykhuis will not score many points (10 to 15), although he will provide sensible defence.

MARCEL HOSSA

Yrs. of NHL service: 0
Born: Ilava, Slovenia; Oct. 12, 1981
Position: centre
Height: 6-1
Weight: 200
Uniform no.: 36
Shoots: left

Career statistics:

GP	G	A	TP	PIM
10	3	1	4	2

2001-2002 statistics:

GP	G	A	TP	+/-	PIM	PP	SH	GW	GT	S	PCT
10	3	1	4	+2	2	0	0	0	0	20	15.0

LAST SEASON

Will be entering first full NHL season. Appeared in 50 games with Quebec (AHL), scoring 17-15-32 with 24 penalty minutes. Missed seven games with wrist injury. Missed two games due to coach's decision.

THE FINESSE GAME

Hossa is a good skater who is strong and balanced. He is clever with the puck and has good hockey vision. He is more of a playmaker than a passer at this point, but he has a good array of shots. Hossa needs to shoot more and also be more determined in battling his way into the hard areas of the ice.

Hossa is the younger brother of Ottawa's Marian, and talent runs in the family. Several scouts don't think he will become the same elite player Marian is, but this kid brother is very skilled. Hossa's likely future is as a second-line set-up man. Montreal played him on the left wing mostly in his brief audition but he is a natural centre and that is where he will end up.

As is the case with a lot of young players, Hossa needs to improve his consistency on a nightly basis.

THE PHYSICAL GAME

Hossa has good size but doesn't use it in an authoritative manner. The Habs would like to see a little more fire in his game.

THE INTANGIBLES

Hossa was called up at mid-season and made a splashy impression, scoring twice in four games and suffering a wrist injury. He had a strong training camp and if he can repeat that this fall, he has a great chance to stick.

PROJECTION

Hossa could score 30 points if he wins a job.

JOE JUNEAU

Yrs. of NHL service: 10
Born: Pont-Rouge, Que.; Jan. 5, 1968
Position: centre
Height: 6-0
Weight: 195
Uniform no.: 90
Shoots: left

Career statistics:

GP	G	A	TP	PIM
686	145	390	535	232

1998-1999 statistics:

GP	G	A	TP	+/-	PIM	PP	SH	GW	GT	S	PCT
72	15	28	43	-4	22	2	1	3	0	150	10.0

1999-2000 statistics:

GP	G	A	TP	+/-	PIM	PP	SH	GW	GT	S	PCT
65	13	24	37	+3	22	2	0	2	0	126	10.3

2000-2001 statistics:

GP	G	A	TP	+/-	PIM	PP	SH	GW	GT	S	PCT
69	10	23	33	-2	28	5	0	3	1	100	10.0

2001-2002 statistics:

GP	G	A	TP	+/-	PIM	PP	SH	GW	GT	S	PCT
70	8	28	36	-3	10	1	0	1	1	96	8.3

LAST SEASON

Missed eight games with knee injury. Missed two games with back injury. Missed one game with virus.

THE FINESSE GAME

A natural centre, Juneau gravitates to the left wing and generates most of his scoring chances from there. He varies his play selection. He will take the puck to the net on one rush, then pull up at the top of the circle and hit the trailer late on the next rush.

Although the circles are his office, Juneau is not just a perimeter player. He will go into traffic, and is bigger than he looks on-ice. His quick feet and light hands make him seem smaller because he is so crafty with the puck. Laterally, Juneau is among the best skaters in the NHL. He has an extra gear that allows him to pull away from people. He does not have breakaway speed, but he has great anticipation and gets the jump on a defender with his first few steps.

Juneau doesn't shoot the puck enough and gets a little intimidated when there is a scramble for a loose puck in front of the net. He is not always willing to sacrifice his body that way. He shoots a tad prematurely. When he could wait and have the goalie down and out, he unloads quickly, because he hears footsteps. His best shot is a one-timer from the left circle. Juneau is a better playmaker than scorer.

Juneau is fine on draws and kills penalties. His game has become more weighted defensively.

THE PHYSICAL GAME

Juneau has improved his toughness and willingness to take a hit to make a play, but he is still a featherweight. You can almost see him psych himself up to make or take a hit. It doesn't come naturally to him.

THE INTANGIBLES

Juneau had the usual array of nagging injuries.

PROJECTION

We wouldn't expect much more than 40 points from Juneau, especially since he has missed from 12 to 26 games in each of the last four seasons.

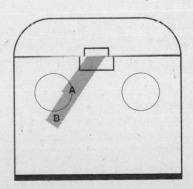

CHAD KILGER

Yrs. of NHL service: 7
Born: Cornwall, Ont.; Nov. 27, 1976
Position: centre
Height: 6-3
Weight: 215
Uniform no.: 25
Shoots: left

Career statistics:

GP	G	A	TP	PIM
399	54	69	123	187

1998-1999 statistics:

GP	G	A	TP	+/-	PIM	PP	SH	GW	GT	S	PCT
77	15	12	27	-4	34	2	1	1	1	81	18.5

1999-2000 statistics:

GP	G	A	TP	+/-	PIM	PP	SH	GW	GT	S	PCT
40	3	2	5	-6	18	0	0	0	0	32	9.4

2000-2001 statistics:

GP	G	A	TP	+/-	PIM	PP	SH	GW	GT	S	PCT
77	14	18	32	-8	51	2	1	1	0	103	13.6

2001-2002 statistics:

GP	G	A	TP	+/-	PIM	PP	SH	GW	GT	S	PCT
75	8	15	23	-7	27	0	1	2	0	87	9.2

PROJECTION

Kilger needs to have a regular role and not be a part-timer. To become a regular, he has to prove he's worthy of the minutes. Anything less than a 15-goal season is unacceptable.

LAST SEASON

Missed seven games with neck injury.

THE FINESSE GAME

Kilger plays an intelligent, poised, unexceptional game. He sees the ice well and is a good passer. The release on his shot is too slow for him to be much of an impact scorer in the NHL. He has a long reach, which works to his advantage in dangling the puck away from defenders.

His size and skating ability are just NHL calibre. Few big players skate as well as Kilger. He is at his best when he accelerates through the neutral zone. When he gets the puck, if he wants it, he can get a lot of chances by busting through.

Kilger has bounced around a lot. He's 26 and Montreal is his fifth team. The damage done by rushing him into the league at 18 has never been completely undone, but he is an okay depth forward for a team like Montreal.

THE PHYSICAL GAME

Big and physical, Kilger has developed a better knack for getting involved, but it takes a concerted effort on his part and does not come naturally. He needs to consistently exhibit a better work ethic and finish his checks, playing well at both ends of the ice.

THE INTANGIBLES

Kilger can't seem to put a full season together. He had a terrible start, a better finish, but the whole wasn't very encouraging.

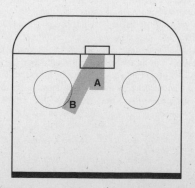

SAKU KOIVU

Yrs. of NHL service: 7
Born: Turku, Finland; Nov. 23, 1974
Position: centre
Height: 5-10
Weight: 181
Uniform no.: 11
Shoots: left

Career statistics:

GP	G	A	TP	PIM
347	85	187	272	218

1998-1999 statistics:

GP	G	A	TP	+/-	PIM	PP	SH	GW	GT	S	PCT
65	14	30	44	-7	38	4	2	0	0	145	9.7

1999-2000 statistics:

GP	G	A	TP	+/-	PIM	PP	SH	GW	GT	S	PCT
24	3	18	21	+7	14	1	0	0	1	53	5.7

2000-2001 statistics:

GP	G	A	TP	+/-	PIM	PP	SH	GW	GT	S	PCT
54	17	30	47	+2	40	7	0	3	2	113	15.0

2001-2002 statistics:

GP	G	A	TP	+/-	PIM	PP	SH	GW	GT	S	PCT
3	0	2	2	0	0	0	0	0	0	2	0.0

LAST SEASON

Won 2002 Masterton Trophy. Missed 79 games recovering from treatment for non-Hodgkin's lymphoma.

THE FINESSE GAME

Koivu has overcome a lot of challenges to make it to the NHL. It was nothing compared to what he did to make it back. Diagnosed during training camp with a form of cancer, Koivu underwent surgery, radiation and chemotherapy to return in time to help Montreal make the playoffs.

A highly skilled, versatile player, Koivu brings brilliance and excitement to every shift. Considered one of the world's best playmakers, he makes things happen with his speed and intimidates by driving the defence back, then uses the room to create scoring chances.

He has great hands and can handle the puck at a fast pace. He stickhandles through traffic and reads plays well. He is intelligent and involved. Not a pure goal-scorer, he needs to distribute the puck more to be a more effective centre.

Koivu has a variety of shots. He has a slick backhand for shooting or passing. He also has a strong wrist shot and is deadly accurate. At the top of his game, he is one of the most dazzling players in the league. And one of the bravest.

THE PHYSICAL GAME

The lone knock on Koivu is his lack of size. He loves to play a physical game, but he just can't. He takes a beating, gets shoved around and frequently broken. He plays through pain, but the Habs need to keep him from getting so damaged. He won't be intimidated, though, and uses his stick as an equalizer.

THE INTANGIBLES

Gritty, gifted and determined, Koivu is well-respected by his teammates. You can't help but root for this guy.

PROJECTION

If he can stand up under the ordeal of a full season, there is no reason why Koivu can't be a 25-goal, 60-assist man next season.

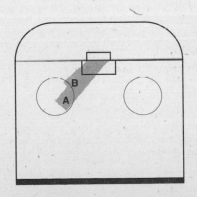

RANDY MCKAY

Yrs. of NHL service: 13
Born: Montreal, Que.; Jan. 25, 1967
Position: right wing
Height: 6-2
Weight: 210
Uniform no.: 21
Shoots: right

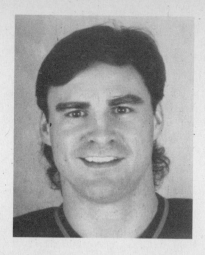

Career statistics:

GP	G	A	TP	PIM
857	156	188	344	1659

1998-1999 statistics:

GP	G	A	TP	+/-	PIM	PP	SH	GW	GT	S	PCT
70	17	20	37	+10	143	3	0	5	0	136	12.5

1999-2000 statistics:

GP	G	A	TP	+/-	PIM	PP	SH	GW	GT	S	PCT
67	16	23	39	+8	80	3	0	4	0	116	13.8

2000-2001 statistics:

GP	G	A	TP	+/-	PIM	PP	SH	GW	GT	S	PCT
77	23	20	43	+3	50	12	0	5	0	120	19.2

2001-2002 statistics:

GP	G	A	TP	+/-	PIM	PP	SH	GW	GT	S	PCT
69	7	11	18	+4	72	3	0	1	0	73	9.6

LAST SEASON

Signed by Montreal as free agent on July 3, 2002. Acquired by Dallas from New Jersey with Jason Arnott and a first-round draft pick in 2002 for Joe Nieuwendyk and Jamie Langenbrunner. Tied for third on Stars in penalty minutes. Missed 10 games with hip injury. Missed one game with rib injury.

THE FINESSE GAME

This is a switch: a player leaves a fat-wallet U.S. team to sign as a free agent with a Canadian one. McKay, a native Montrealer, wasted little time in choosing the Canadiens, and he could play a valuable role on a team that needs his size and grit.

There is never a lack of effort on McKay's part. His reputation earns him extra ice and extra time, and he makes use of both. He is one of those rare tough guys who has enough skills to make himself a useful player in other areas, including the power play. And he has the ability to beat a defender one-on-one by setting his skates wide, dangling the puck, then drawing it through the defenceman's legs and blowing past him for a shot.

McKay is alert enough to find a linemate with a pass. He doesn't have great hockey vision, but he doesn't keep his eyes glued to the puck either. Still, most of his points come from driving to the net. He's smarter about this, too, especially on the power play. Instead of just planting himself in front, McKay has learned to slide in and out of the slot, à la Dave Andreychuk, and that makes him harder to defend.

The problem for McKay comes in the assessments of him as an overachieving fourth-liner, which is how he made his name, or weighing him as the second-line winger on the team.

THE PHYSICAL GAME

Even though McKay is an absolutely ferocious fighter, don't expect to see him duking it out many nights. That doesn't mean McKay is any less intense, however. He is astoundingly strong on his skates, tough to knock down and nearly impossible to knock out. His problems arise when he plays too fancy and thinks about being a goal-scorer instead of working for his chances.

THE INTANGIBLES

Injuries — shoulder, hand, and hip — robbed McKay's effectiveness over the past three seasons. He claims to be physically healed, but at 36, injuries must remain a concern. Like the rest of us, McKay just doesn't heal as quickly anymore. McKay will be an excellent leader by example in the Habs' room.

PROJECTION

McKay could maybe get 20 goals in Montreal, where he is likely to play the power forward role on the power play.

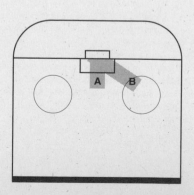

YANIC PERREAULT

Yrs. of NHL service: 8
Born: Sherbrooke, Que.; Apr. 4, 1971
Position: centre
Height: 5-10
Weight: 185
Uniform no.: 94
Shoots: left

Career statistics:

GP	G	A	TP	PIM
529	155	175	330	244

1998-1999 statistics:

GP	G	A	TP	+/-	PIM	PP	SH	GW	GT	S	PCT
76	17	25	42	+7	42	4	3	3	0	141	12.1

1999-2000 statistics:

GP	G	A	TP	+/-	PIM	PP	SH	GW	GT	S	PCT
58	18	27	45	+3	22	5	0	4	0	114	15.8

2000-2001 statistics:

GP	G	A	TP	+/-	PIM	PP	SH	GW	GT	S	PCT
76	24	28	52	0	52	5	0	2	0	134	17.9

2001-2002 statistics:

GP	G	A	TP	+/-	PIM	PP	SH	GW	GT	S	PCT
82	27	29	56	-3	40	6	0	7	2	156	17.3

LAST SEASON

Led team in goals, points, power-play goals and game-winning goals. Second on team in shooting percentage. Tied for second on team in assists. Third on team in shots. Career high in points. One of three Canadiens to appear in all 82 games.

THE FINESSE GAME

Perreault is the NHL's face-off king, leading his fellow centremen for the second consecutive season with 61.27 per cent. That's nothing. Some nights he wins 70 or even 80 or 90 per cent of his draws.

Perreault's skating speed is marginal for the NHL level. He tries to compensate with his intelligence, and that alone will keep earning him NHL jobs on third and fourth lines until he decides to pack it in. What Perreault did last season was nothing short of amazing as he helped keep the Habs' playoff hopes alive until Saku Koivu's emotional return.

Perreault has very good hands and always has his head up, looking for openings. While he doesn't have open-ice speed, he works hard to put on a quick burst in the offensive zone, to gain a half-step on a defender. Once he is open for the shot he waits for the goalie to commit, or he makes a patient pass.

Tricky and solid on his feet, Perreault works the half-boards on the power play. He has an accurate shot with a quick release, and he slithers around to get in the best position for the shot.

THE PHYSICAL GAME

Perreault lacks the size for one-on-one battles in the attacking zone. Defensively, he can't do much except harass a puck carrier with his stick. He is an in-betweener, and if forced to carry the play in any zone his flaws become apparent.

THE INTANGIBLES

Perreault should be a complementary player, not a star. He overachieved last season. Perreault seemed to have a difference of opinion with coach Michel Therrien in the playoffs, a situation that may bear watching.

PROJECTION

Perreault should be able to back off his top line role, so expect fewer goals and points. But 20-25 points and 45-50 points would still be a successful season for a player who does as much as he does.

OLEG PETROV

Yrs. of NHL service: 9
Born: Moscow, Russia; Apr. 18, 1971
Position: right wing
Height: 5-9
Weight: 171
Uniform no.: 14
Shoots: left

Career statistics:

GP	G	A	TP	PIM
312	63	97	160	83

1999-2000 statistics:

GP	G	A	TP	+/-	PIM	PP	SH	GW	GT	S	PCT
44	2	24	26	+10	8	1	0	0	1	96	2.1

2000-2001 statistics:

GP	G	A	TP	+/-	PIM	PP	SH	GW	GT	S	PCT
81	17	30	47	-11	24	4	2	1	2	158	10.8

2001-2002 statistics:

GP	G	A	TP	+/-	PIM	PP	SH	GW	GT	S	PCT
75	24	17	41	-4	12	3	1	6	0	152	15.8

LAST SEASON

Second on team in goals and game-winning goals. Third on team in shooting percentage. Tied for third on team in points. Career high in goals. Missed six games with shoulder injury.

THE FINESSE GAME

Anytime Petrov is around the puck, Montreal has a chance to make something good happen. He is a little guy who is fun to watch. He makes the pretty plays; the energetic dashes up ice, the passes that look impossible yet somehow connect. He even puts on a show in warm-ups, dipsy-doodling with the puck with a display that is as much about warming up as it is about showing off. He has an obvious joy for the game.

Petrov works hard at both ends of the ice. His defensive play is underrated. His game has matured since his first stint (1993-96), after which he returned to play in Europe for three years. Petrov regained the confidence he had lost since getting only part-time roles with the Habs.

Petrov works with another highly skilled, dynamic, small player in Saku Koivu.

THE PHYSICAL GAME

Petrov is slightly built and can't take much abuse.

THE INTANGIBLES

Petrov wore down a little in the last third of the season. He had 16 goals in the first 45 games, but only eight thereafter.

PROJECTION

Petrov should score 20 goals, more if he gets to play with a healthy Koivu all season.

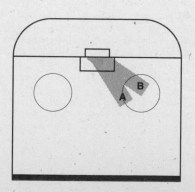

STEPHANE QUINTAL

Yrs. of NHL service: 14
Born: Boucherville, Que.; Oct. 22, 1968
Position: right defence
Height: 6-3
Weight: 228
Uniform no.: 5
Shoots: right

Career statistics:

GP	G	A	TP	PIM
897	55	170	225	1168

1998-1999 statistics:

GP	G	A	TP	+/-	PIM	PP	SH	GW	GT	S	PCT
82	8	19	27	-23	84	1	1	4	0	159	5.0

1999-2000 statistics:

GP	G	A	TP	+/-	PIM	PP	SH	GW	GT	S	PCT
75	2	14	16	-10	77	0	0	1	0	102	2.0

2000-2001 statistics:

GP	G	A	TP	+/-	PIM	PP	SH	GW	GT	S	PCT
72	1	18	19	-9	60	0	0	0	0	109	0.9

2001-2002 statistics:

GP	G	A	TP	+/-	PIM	PP	SH	GW	GT	S	PCT
75	6	10	16	-7	87	1	0	1	0	85	7.1

LAST SEASON

Missed three games with shoulder injury. Missed one game with tooth injury.

THE FINESSE GAME

Quintal's game is limited by his lumbered skating. He has some nice touches, including a decent point shot, and a good head and hands for passing, but his best moves have to be executed at a virtual standstill. He needs to be paired with a quick skater or his shifts will be spent solely in the defensive zone.

Fortunately, Quintal is aware of his flaws. He plays a smart positional game and doesn't get involved in low-percentage plays in the offensive zone. He won't step up in the neutral zone to risk an interception but will fall back into a defensive mode. He takes up a lot of ice with his body and stick, and when he doesn't overcommit, he reduces the space available to a puck carrier. Quintal should not carry the puck. He tends to get a little panicky under pressure.

Although he can exist as an NHL regular in the five-on-five mode, Quintal is a risky proposition for any specialty-team play.

THE PHYSICAL GAME

Strong on his skates, Quintal thrives on contact and works hard along the boards and in front of the net. He hits hard without taking penalties and is a tough and willing fighter if he has to do it. He has the strength to clear the crease and is a good skater for his size.

THE INTANGIBLES

Quintal is thrilled to be back playing in his native Montreal and it shows in his play.

PROJECTION

Quintal can score 20 to 25 points and he is a serviceable, third-pairing defenceman if he is paired with a mobile partner. He had to play in the top four with Montreal, and that's a stretch for him.

CRAIG RIVET

Yrs. of NHL service: 6
Born: North Bay, Ont.; Sept. 13, 1974
Position: right defence
Height: 6-2
Weight: 207
Uniform no.: 52
Shoots: right

Career statistics:

GP	G	A	TP	PIM
355	15	52	67	460

1998-1999 statistics:

GP	G	A	TP	+/-	PIM	PP	SH	GW	GT	S	PCT
66	2	8	10	-3	66	0	0	0	0	39	5.1

1999-2000 statistics:

GP	G	A	TP	+/-	PIM	PP	SH	GW	GT	S	PCT
61	3	14	17	+11	76	0	0	1	1	71	4.2

2000-2001 statistics:

GP	G	A	TP	+/-	PIM	PP	SH	GW	GT	S	PCT
26	1	2	3	-8	36	0	0	0	0	22	4.6

2001-2002 statistics:

GP	G	A	TP	+/-	PIM	PP	SH	GW	GT	S	PCT
82	8	17	25	+1	76	0	0	0	0	90	8.9

LAST SEASON

Career highs in goals, assists and points. One of three Canadiens to appear in all 82 games.

THE FINESSE GAME

There is little that Rivet does not do well. His primary asset is his hockey sense. It has been slow to develop at the NHL level, but gradually Rivet has become an extremely reliable player in his own zone. He is a willing shot-blocker. He is an efficient skater. He passes well and moves the puck quickly out of his zone with low-risk plays.

Rivet's offensive upside is high. He has been concentrating on the defensive end of the game more, but he has the skating ability, the hands and the shot to get more involved in the attack. He is a smart offensive player. He could become a poor-man's Ray Bourque.

Rivet also kills penalties well. He competes hard and is a natural leader.

THE PHYSICAL GAME

The physical part of the game comes naturally to Rivet. He is a willing hitter, not necessarily mean, but he takes his man out with authority. He has good size and knows how to use it. Rivet is strong on his skates and finishes his checks. Not many opposing forwards relish coming into his corner.

THE INTANGIBLES

While he will never be an elite defenceman, he could be a No. 2 on anyone's team except for the league's half-dozen teams now, and he might not be far from that rank soon. He is a sleeper. Rivet shows up in the big spots. He enjoyed a healthy season last year, and that gave a better indication of the kind of player Rivet truly is. He's a great team guy who helped keep the team together during Saku Koivu's illness.

PROJECTION

Rivet is coming into his own. He can continue to contribute more offensively, possibly in the 25- to 30-point range.

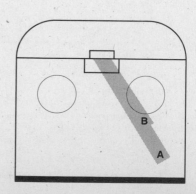

SHELDON SOURAY

Yrs. of NHL service: 5
Born: Elk Point, Alta.; July 7, 1976
Position: right defence
Height: 6-4
Weight: 223
Uniform no.: 44
Shoots: left

Career statistics:

GP	G	A	TP	PIM
287	13	35	48	466

1998-1999 statistics:

GP	G	A	TP	+/-	PIM	PP	SH	GW	GT	S	PCT
70	1	7	8	+5	110	0	0	0	0	101	1.0

1999-2000 statistics:

GP	G	A	TP	+/-	PIM	PP	SH	GW	GT	S	PCT
71	3	8	11	+1	114	0	0	0	0	113	2.7

2000-2001 statistics:

GP	G	A	TP	+/-	PIM	PP	SH	GW	GT	S	PCT
52	3	8	11	-11	95	0	0	2	0	103	2.9

2001-2002 statistics:

GP	G	A	TP	+/-	PIM	PP	SH	GW	GT	S	PCT
34	3	5	8	-5	62	1	0	0	1	56	5.4

LAST SEASON

Missed 44 games with wrist injury. Missed three games with groin injury. Missed one game with hip injury.

THE FINESSE GAME

Souray has worked hard on his skating, but still needs improvement in his turns and lateral movement. He has good straightaway speed once he gets going. Souray is very strong on his skates for corner and board work, which he relishes.

He plays a high-risk game. It could have a big pay-off in Souray's offensive contributions, but he isn't a good enough skater to recover from his mistakes; he has to be wiser about his decisions when he pinches or forces the play in the attacking zone. He can't play too staid a game, though, since he can get involved in the rush. He has a heavy slap shot and he loves to unleash it. He is likely to see some tail-end power-play time. It's not likely he will become a top-notch point man.

Souray blocks shots and plays a fairly sound positional game, though he will get rattled in his coverage now and then and start running around. Experience and confidence are the only things lacking in his game, and they should come with increased ice time.

THE PHYSICAL GAME

Souray is an imposing physical specimen and an all-round athlete. He is a little too hair-trigger in coming to the aid of his teammates, but that beats the opposite reaction. He is a good fighter and excels in a physical game. He has a major-league mean streak, and he gives a rather small Montreal team some important physical presence.

THE INTANGIBLES

Every time Souray gets healthy and into a good playing groove, he gets another injury. It has to be discouraging, but he remains an upbeat player who loves being a Canadien.

PROJECTION

Souray could score 20 points in a full-time role, although his major asset is his physical play.

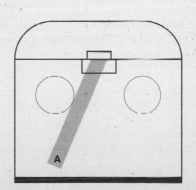

JOSE THEODORE

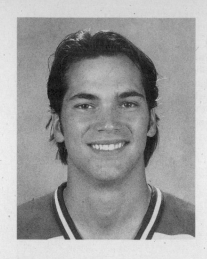

Yrs. of NHL service: 4
Born: Laval, Que.; Sept. 13, 1976
Position: goaltender
Height: 5-11
Weight: 182
Uniform no.: 60
Catches: right

Career statistics:

GP	MIN	GA	SO	GAA	A	PIM
191	10560	439	15	2.49	3	8

1998-1999 statistics:

GP	MIN	GAA	W	L	T	SO	GA	S	SAPCT	PIM
18	913	3.29	4	12	0	1	50	406	.877	0

1999-2000 statistics:

GP	MIN	GAA	W	L	T	SO	GA	S	SAPCT	PIM
30	1655	2.10	12	13	2	5	58	717	.919	0

2000-2001 statistics:

GP	MIN	GAA	W	L	T	SO	GA	S	SAPCT	PIM
59	3298	2.57	20	29	5	2	141	1546	.909	6

2001-2002 statistics:

GP	MIN	GAA	W	L	T	SO	GA	S	SAPCT	PIM
67	3864	2.11	30	24	10	7	136	1972	.931	6

PROJECTION

Assuming Montreal stays just a little healthier this season, Theodore should repeat his 30 victories.

LAST SEASON

Won 2002 Hart Trophy and Vezina Trophy. Fourth in goals-against average. Tied for second in NHL in shutouts. Missed four games with a concussion.

THE PHYSICAL GAME

Theodore is "technically" a very sound goalie. One of his best assets is his ability to control rebounds. He doesn't just try to kick the puck away, but he is able to deaden the shot, absorb the shock and have it land in a spot where he is better able to control it.

It also helps Theodore to be a lefty goalie. There aren't many in the NHL, and for shooters it's like having to face a lefty tennis player. The stick side and glove side of Theodore are opposite to what shooters are accustomed to seeing.

Theodore has excellent reflexes. While he is not quite as extreme as Dominik Hasek, his flexibility and tenacity in not giving up on a shot are very similar. Theodore's stickhandling is better than average.

THE MENTAL GAME

Even when he was Jeff Hackett's backup, Theodore exhibited a certain assurance — close to cockiness — that you just have to love in a young goalie. His teammates believe in him. He was instrumental in keeping the team in the playoff race all season. Theodore had a tough playoffs, though he might have been physically worn out at the end of a long season.

THE INTANGIBLES

Theodore had an unbelievable season that will be tough to top.

RICHARD ZEDNIK

Yrs. of NHL service: 5
Born: Bystrica, Slovakia; Jan. 6, 1976
Position: left wing
Height: 6-0
Weight: 199
Uniform no.: 20
Shoots: left

Career statistics:

GP	G	A	TP	PIM
351	88	81	169	266

1998-1999 statistics:

GP	G	A	TP	+/-	PIM	PP	SH	GW	GT	S	PCT
49	9	8	17	-6	50	1	0	2	0	115	7.8

1999-2000 statistics:

GP	G	A	TP	+/-	PIM	PP	SH	GW	GT	S	PCT
69	19	16	35	+6	54	1	0	2	3	179	10.6

2000-2001 statistics:

GP	G	A	TP	+/-	PIM	PP	SH	GW	GT	S	PCT
74	19	25	44	-4	71	5	0	3	1	178	10.7

2001-2002 statistics:

GP	G	A	TP	+/-	PIM	PP	SH	GW	GT	S	PCT
82	22	22	44	-3	59	4	0	3	0	249	8.8

LAST SEASON

Led team in shots. Second on team in points. Third on team in goals. Tied for third on team in power-play goals. Career high in goals. One of three Canadiens to appear in all 82 games.

THE FINESSE GAME

Zednik has the skating speed and hand skills to mark him as a top six forward, and with the trade to a team where the jobs are wide open, he has a chance for a fresh start. Lucky for him, Bulis came along in the deal; the two had established on-ice chemistry in Washington.

Very good down low, Zednik can control the game and go to the net; he has nice hands and is not shy about shooting. Zednik has a very low crouch and gets a lot on his shot. He is a dynamic player.

Zednik is not as effective on the power play as he should be and needs to capitalize more, since he can expect to get a lot of ice time with the man advantage in Montreal. When his goal slumps occur, he works hard to snap out of his drought.

THE PHYSICAL GAME

Although he is not big, Zednik is strong. Coming off the wing, he just about carries defenders on his back. Solid and sturdy on his skates, he likes to get involved and isn't rattled by physical play, though he does not initiate contact.

THE INTANGIBLES

Zednik may remain a frustrating player. There always seems to be something left in the tank. Unfortunately, Zednik's most memorable moment last season was when he was concussed by Kyle McLaren in the playoffs.

PROJECTION

Zednik should score in the range of 25-30 goals. He will score in the range of 20 to 25 goals.

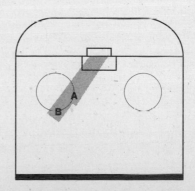

NASHVILLE PREDATORS

Players' Statistics 2001-2002

POS.	NO.	PLAYER	GP	G	A	PTS	+/-	PIM	PP	SH	GW	GT	S	PCT
C	22	GREG JOHNSON	82	18	26	44	-14	38	3		2	1	145	12.4
L	25	DENIS ARKHIPOV	82	20	22	42	-18	16	7		6	1	118	17.0
D	44	KIMMO TIMONEN	82	13	29	42	2	28	9		1		154	8.4
L	17	SCOTT HARTNELL	75	14	27	41	5	111	3		4		162	8.6
D	5	ANDY DELMORE	73	16	22	38	-13	22	11		3		175	9.1
R	33	VLADIMIR ORSZAGH	79	15	21	36	-15	56	5		3		113	13.3
L	19	*MARTIN ERAT	80	9	24	33	-11	32	2		2		84	10.7
C	11	DAVID LEGWAND	63	11	19	30	1	54	1	1	1		121	9.1
L	43	VITALI YACHMENEV	75	11	16	27	-16	14	1	2			103	10.7
R	15	PETR TENKRAT	67	8	16	24	-10	34		1	2	1	95	8.4
D	3	KARLIS SKRASTINS	82	4	13	17	-12	36			1	1	84	4.8
C	9	GREG CLASSEN	55	5	6	11	1	30		1			32	15.6
D	26	*ANDY BERENZWEIG	26	3	7	10	-3	14			1		27	11.1
R	27	JUKKA HENTUNEN	38	4	5	9	-9	4	1		1		50	8.0
R	24	SCOTT WALKER	28	4	5	9	-13	18	1				46	8.7
C	14	STEVE DUBINSKY	29	6	2	8	-1	14			1		48	12.5
D	4	MARK EATON	58	3	5	8	-12	24					52	5.8
D	23	BILL HOULDER	82		8	8	-1	40					44	
L	12	REID SIMPSON	51	6	1	7	-1	132			1		22	27.3
R	39	MARIAN CISAR	10	1	2	3	-3	8	1				16	6.3
R	20	*NATHAN PERROTT	22	1	2	3	-1	74			1		7	14.3
R	18	MARK MOWERS	14	1	2	3	-2	2					5	20.0
L	8	STU GRIMSON	30	1	1	2	0	76					5	20.0
D	32	CALE HULSE	63		2	2	-18	121					70	
D	13	JERE KARALAHTI	45		2	2	-6	41					27	
R	34	ADAM HALL	1	1		1	0						2	
R	48	*JONAS ANDERSSON	5				-2	2					4	
D	14	BRETT HAUER	3				-3	6					2	
D	14	RICHARD BRENNAN	4				0	2						
C	12	YVES SARAULT	1				0							
L	28	JEREMY STEVENSON	4				0	9						
R	40	DAVID GOSSELIN	3				-1	5						
D	42	PAVEL SKRBEK	3				-2	2						
D	42	*ROBERT SCHNABEL	1				0							
G	1	MIKE DUNHAM	58				0	2						
G	29	TOMAS VOKOUN	29				0	2						
G	30	CHRIS MASON					0							
G	35	JAN LASAK	3				0	2						

GP = games played; G = goals; A = assists; PTS = points; +/- = goals-for minus goals-against while player is on ice; PIM = penalties in minutes; PP = power-play goals; SH = shorthanded goals; GW = game-winning goals; GT = game-tying goals; S = no. of shots; PCT = percentage of goals to shots; * = rookie

DENIS ARKHIPOV

Yrs. of NHL service: 2
Born: Kazan, Russia; May 19, 1979
Position: left wing
Height: 6-3
Weight: 195
Uniform no.: 25
Shoots: left

Career statistics:

GP	G	A	TP	PIM
122	26	29	55	20

2000-2001 statistics:

GP	G	A	TP	+/-	PIM	PP	SH	GW	GT	S	PCT
40	6	7	13	0	4	0	0	0	0	42	14.3

2001-2002 statistics:

GP	G	A	TP	+/-	PIM	PP	SH	GW	GT	S	PCT
82	20	22	42	-18	16	7	0	6	1	118	17.0

LAST SEASON

Led team in goals with career high. Led team in shooting percentage. Tied for second on team in points. Third on team in power-play goals. One of five Predators to appear in all 82 games.

THE FINESSE GAME

Arkhipov is a power player with a very nice scoring touch. He has stepped up his game every time the bar has been raised. Nashville played him at centre and he took some of the pressure off of David Legwand and allowed Nashville to trade Cliff Ronning.

He plays so hard and with so much presence that you will come away from the rink thinking Arkhipov is a much bigger player. He isn't short, but he's not very thick. He doesn't look imposing. He simply plays a determined style. Arkhipov was entrusted with playing against some of the league's power centres, like Bobby Holik, last season.

Arkhipov possesses good size, very good hands, good vision and passing skills. He clicked with Vladimir Orszagh and Martin Erat and that became Nashville's No. 1 line. He has good speed and lateral mobility.

THE PHYSICAL GAME

He needs to get a little stronger, but Arkhipov shows the willingness to play an involved game and that bodes well. He is very competitive.

THE INTANGIBLES

Arkhipov is one of the foundation players for Nashville's future. He has gained a lot of confidence over the past two seasons.

PROJECTION

Arkhipov hit the 20 goals we predicted for him last season. He has a lot of upside. An improvement to 25-30 goals would not be out of line.

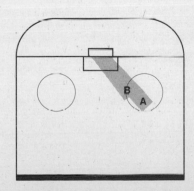

ANDY DELMORE

Yrs. of NHL service: 3
Born: LaSalle, Ont.; Dec. 26, 1976
Position: right defence
Height: 6-1
Weight: 192
Uniform no.: 5
Shoots: right

Career statistics:

GP	G	A	TP	PIM
168	23	37	60	46

1998-1999 statistics:

GP	G	A	TP	+/-	PIM	PP	SH	GW	GT	S	PCT
2	0	1	1	-1	0	0	0	0	0	2	0.0

1999-2000 statistics:

GP	G	A	TP	+/-	PIM	PP	SH	GW	GT	S	PCT
27	2	5	7	-1	8	0	0	1	0	55	3.6

2000-2001 statistics:

GP	G	A	TP	+/-	PIM	PP	SH	GW	GT	S	PCT
66	5	9	14	+2	16	2	0	0	0	119	4.2

2001-2002 statistics:

GP	G	A	TP	+/-	PIM	PP	SH	GW	GT	S	PCT
73	16	22	38	-13	22	11	0	3	0	175	9.1

LAST SEASON

Led team in power-play goals and shots. Third on team in goals. Led NHL defencemen in power-play goals.

THE FINESSE GAME

Delmore is an excellent skater with a booming slap shot. That might be good enough to keep him in the league as a forward, but Delmore is a defenceman whose defensive reads are barely adequate. He needs a lot of work on his defensive game and needs to be paired with a reliable, stay-at-home defenceman who can almost act as an on-ice coach. Delmore has potential because of his offensive ability, but he is high, high risk.

Delmore can't be sent out to protect a lead late in a tight game because he is a defensive liability. But high risks can mean high rewards; he will use his blazing speed to rush the puck when other, more sensible, defencemen wouldn't. If it pays off with a goal, then Delmore is a hero. If not, he's a minus.

Delmore has a hard, accurate shot with a quick release, and is totally unafraid to gamble in-deep. He should be very afraid.

THE PHYSICAL GAME

Delmore has average size for an NHL defenceman, but is not in any way physical. He needs to be willing to use his body to at least tie up an opposing forward. Delmore has to get stronger and learn better body positioning. He will block shots.

THE INTANGIBLES

The Predators would be happy to see Delmore sacrifice some points and apply his finesse skills more to the defensive part of the game. Nashville isn't a strong enough team to carry a power-play specialist. Delmore must become a more complete player if he wants a long NHL career.

PROJECTION

Delmore's points were impressive but he needs to be less high-risk. Delmore can score 35 points and trim his plus-minus.

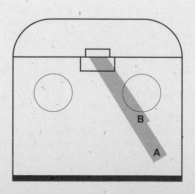

MIKE DUNHAM

Yrs. of NHL service: 6
Born: Johnson City, N.Y.; June 1, 1972
Position: goaltender
Height: 6-3
Weight: 200
Uniform no.: 1
Catches: left

Career statistics:

GP	MIN	GA	SO	GAA	A	PIM
243	13461	596	11	2.66	3	16

1998-1999 statistics:

GP	MIN	GAA	W	L	T	SO	GA	S	SAPCT	PIM
44	2472	3.08	16	23	3	1	127	1387	.908	4

1999-2000 statistics:

GP	MIN	GAA	W	L	T	SO	GA	S	SAPCT	PIM
52	3077	2.85	19	27	6	0	146	1584	.908	6

2000-2001 statistics:

GP	MIN	GAA	W	L	T	SO	GA	S	SAPCT	PIM
48	2810	2.28	21	21	4	4	107	1381	.923	2

2001-2002 statistics:

GP	MIN	GAA	W	L	T	SO	GA	S	SAPCT	PIM
58	3316	2.61	23	24	9	3	144	1525	.906	2

PROJECTION

Dunham should reach the 25-win mark in a full, healthy season with the Predators.

LAST SEASON

Career high in wins. Missed two games with concussion.

THE PHYSICAL GAME

Dunham is built well for the stand-up style he favours. He injects some butterfly elements, but for the most part he makes the best use of his size by staying upright and letting the puck hit him. He has to stay on his feet or his knees since he does not have great reflexes for close-in scrambles.

Dunham handles the puck fairly well. He is no Martin Brodeur, but he has obviously learned a great deal from being Brodeur's teammate for two years in New Jersey, and he helps out his defence by moving the puck. He also uses his stick well to break up passes around the crease.

Dunham has some streaks of inconsistency, which may be more due to his frequent injuries than inexperience, since he is a rather seasoned goalie. He gives his young team a chance to win every night by not allowing very many soft goals. That is saying something for a recent expansion team.

THE MENTAL GAME

Dunham has become a more poised performer, less quick to jump on teammates for their mistakes and more willing to handle criticism himself. He is very competitive and his years as Nashville's No. 1 goalie have given him the confidence that he can handle the job at the NHL level until the team is ready to take its next competitive step.

Nashville is worried about Dunham's fragility. He was distracted by the Olympics last season; at least he won't have to deal with that this year.

MARTIN ERAT

Yrs. of NHL service: 1
Born: Trebic, Czech Repulic; Aug. 29, 1981
Position: left wing
Height: 5-11
Weight: 176
Uniform no.: 19
Shoots: left

Career statistics:

GP	G	A	TP	PIM
80	9	24	33	32

2001-2002 statistics:

GP	G	A	TP	+/-	PIM	PP	SH	GW	GT	S	PCT
80	9	24	33	-11	32	2	0	2	0	84	10.7

LAST SEASON

First NHL season. Tied for second among NHL rookies in assists. Fifth among NHL rookies in shooting percentage. Sixth among NHL rookies in points.

THE FINESSE GAME

Erat is an average-sized winger, but his skating and his high-energy maximize all of his assets. He is very determined in his puck pursuit. He is strong on the puck.

Erat played for Brent Sutter in junior, and that is one teacher who demands a great deal from his pupils. Erat could develop into a Brent Sutter-type of player. Erat might not ever post huge numbers, but he will do a lot of little things to try to help his team win.

Erat's scoring touch is erratic. It looks like he is going to be one of those scorers who is either on a streak or in a slump. It means Erat will have to keep working on the other parts of his game, so that he is never just a scratch in a sweater in games where the points don't come.

THE PHYSICAL GAME

Erat is an intense player. He will lose some puck battles because of his size, but few from lack of effort.

THE INTANGIBLES

Erat ended up the season playing left wing on Nashville's liveliest line (with Denis Arkhipov and Vladimir Orszagh). He was probably the most pleasant surprise for the Predators last season.

PROJECTION

Expect an upgrade to 15-20 goals for Erat.

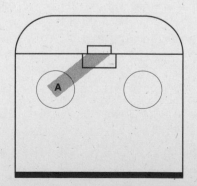

BRENT GILCHRIST

Yrs. of NHL service: 14
Born: Moose Jaw, Sask.; Apr. 3, 1967
Position: centre / left wing
Height: 5-11
Weight: 180
Uniform no.: 41
Shoots: left

Career statistics:

GP	G	A	TP	PIM
751	134	168	302	386

1998-1999 statistics:

GP	G	A	TP	+/-	PIM	PP	SH	GW	GT	S	PCT
5	1	0	1	-1	0	0	0	1	0	4	25.0

1999-2000 statistics:

GP	G	A	TP	+/-	PIM	PP	SH	GW	GT	S	PCT
24	4	2	6	+1	24	0	0	0	0	33	12.1

2000-2001 statistics:

GP	G	A	TP	+/-	PIM	PP	SH	GW	GT	S	PCT
60	1	8	9	-8	41	0	0	0	0	75	1.3

2001-2002 statistics:

GP	G	A	TP	+/-	PIM	PP	SH	GW	GT	S	PCT
45	3	6	9	-9	14	0	0	1	0	53	5.7

PROJECTION

Gilchrist was buried on two strong organizations last year. Nashville will give him an expanded role, but anything over 20 points would be a bonus.

LAST SEASON

Signed by Nashville as free agent on July 11, 2002. Clamied by Dallas off waivers from Detroit on February 13, 2002. Missed three games with eye injury.

THE FINESSE GAME

Gilchrist is a dependable forward who can play any position up front, and play in any game situation. In a way, his versatility hurt him early in his career because he was never able to establish himself in any one position or any one role. Now that he is late into his career, the same quality helps him find a job.

Gilchrist can play on the top line alongside scorers in a pinch, but not for long. He was a scorer at the minor league level but that never translated into NHL success on the scoreboard. He is best cast as a third-line checker.

What Gilchrist will do best is help a team win. He does all of the little things. He's smart and works hard in every zone. He is a very good penalty killer. Gilchrist has good balance and quickness but no breakaway speed.

THE PHYSICAL GAME

Gilchrist is a strong player for his size, but despite his most intense efforts, he gets batted around quite a bit. He won't back down from a challenge.

THE INTANGIBLES

After the Predators traded Cliff Ronning and Tom Fitzgerald, most of their top forwards were under 25. Gilchrist has had injury problems, but his leadership ability is prized. Gilchrist is a player's player.

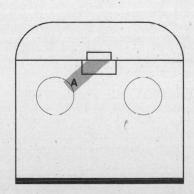

SCOTT HARTNELL

Yrs. of NHL service: 2
Born: Regina, Sask.; Apr. 18, 1982
Position: right wing
Height: 6-3
Weight: 192
Uniform no.: 17
Shoots: left

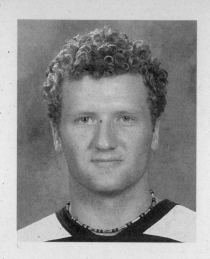

Career statistics:

GP	G	A	TP	PIM
150	16	41	57	159

2000-2001 statistics:

GP	G	A	TP	+/-	PIM	PP	SH	GW	GT	S	PCT
75	2	14	16	-8	48	0	0	0	0	92	2.2

2001-2002 statistics:

GP	G	A	TP	+/-	PIM	PP	SH	GW	GT	S	PCT
75	14	27	41	+5	111	3	0	4	0	162	8.6

LAST SEASON

Led team in plus-minus. Second on team in assists, game-winning goals and shots. Third on team in penalty minutes. Missed two games with concussion.

THE FINESSE GAME

Hartnell is a prototypical power forward. He can play with finesse players — his junior linemates were Milan Kraft and Michal Sivek — and he adds character and heart to a squad.

The knock on Hartnell is his skating speed, but he has good power. And here's the main thing about his skating: he wants to get there. He is always digging hard and keeping his feet in motion. He is an up-and-down winger who crashes and gets inside. He is strong on the forecheck and plays with a lot of energy.

Hartnell has very good hockey sense. He has good hands, can make plays with the puck, can drive the net and have the poise to pull up and find an open man.

THE PHYSICAL GAME

Hartnell plays a hard-nosed game. He is gritty around the net. He hits and, when he has to, he will fight.

THE INTANGIBLES

Hartnell is a natural leader who is respected by his peer group as well as veteran players. The Predators believe he will be their future captain. Hartnell's progress hasn't been entirely smooth. There are stretches where his game takes a step backwards. He will become more consistent and is part of the Preds' core group of young players

PROJECTION

The goals won't always be pretty or come easy. Hartnell will earn his way on to one of the top two lines and may flirt with 20 goals.

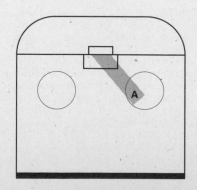

BILL HOULDER

Yrs. of NHL service: 15
Born: Thunder Bay, Ont.; Mar. 11, 1967
Position: left defence
Height: 6-2
Weight: 215
Uniform no.: 23
Shoots: left

Career statistics:

GP	G	A	TP	PIM
764	57	187	244	366

1998-1999 statistics:

GP	G	A	TP	+/-	PIM	PP	SH	GW	GT	S	PCT
76	9	23	32	+8	40	7	0	5	0	115	7.8

1999-2000 statistics:

GP	G	A	TP	+/-	PIM	PP	SH	GW	GT	S	PCT
71	3	14	17	-9	26	2	0	1	0	89	3.4

2000-2001 statistics:

GP	G	A	TP	+/-	PIM	PP	SH	GW	GT	S	PCT
81	4	12	16	-7	40	0	1	1	1	78	5.1

2001-2002 statistics:

GP	G	A	TP	+/-	PIM	PP	SH	GW	GT	S	PCT
82	0	8	8	-1	40	0	0	0	0	44	0.0

LAST SEASON

One of five Predators to appear in all 82 games.

THE FINESSE GAME

Houlder has a big shot, but otherwise his overall skills are average. Although he struggles as a skater, especially with his turns, he has a decent first step with the puck and is strong on his skates.

A calm and cerebral player, Houlder makes smart options with his passes and does not like to carry the puck. He prefers to dish off to a teammate or chip the puck out along the wall, rather than try to carry it past a checker.

He works well on the penalty kill despite his lack of foot speed. When in danger, he just gets the puck out. Nothing fancy; he is not a risk taker. His attack is mostly limited to point shots, though he will get brave once in a while and gamble to the top of the circle. Most of his goals come from 60 feet out with some traffic in front.

THE PHYSICAL GAME

Houlder is a gentle giant. There is always the expectation with bigger players that they will make monster hits, but we have the feeling that a lot of them were big as youngsters and were told by their parents not to go around picking on smaller kids. Houlder is definitely among the big guys who don't hit to hurt. If he did get involved he would be a dominating defenceman, but that's not about to happen at this stage of his career.

Still, Houlder will take out his man with quiet efficiency. He has to angle the attacker to the boards because of his lack of agility. He is vulnerable to out-side speed when he doesn't close off the lane. At 35, Houlder still logs a lot of ice time (averaging 21:34 last season) and he blocks shots.

THE INTANGIBLES

Houlder would be a No. 6 defenceman for a better team, but he has played top four (sometimes top two) with the Predators. Nashville continues to work some inexperienced, offensive-minded defencemen into the lineup, and Houlder makes a solid partner.

PROJECTION

Houlder will provide solid defence and 10.

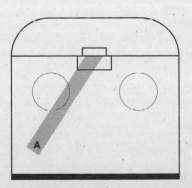

CALE HULSE

Yrs. of NHL service: 6
Born: Edmonton, Alberta; Nov. 10, 1973
Position: right defence
Height: 6-3
Weight: 220
Uniform no.: 32
Shoots: right

Career statistics:

GP	G	A	TP	PIM
418	11	52	63	693

1998-1999 statistics:

GP	G	A	TP	+/-	PIM	PP	SH	GW	GT	S	PCT
73	3	9	12	-8	117	0	0	0	0	83	3.6

1999-2000 statistics:

GP	G	A	TP	+/-	PIM	PP	SH	GW	GT	S	PCT
47	1	6	7	-11	47	0	0	0	0	41	2.4

2000-2001 statistics:

GP	G	A	TP	+/-	PIM	PP	SH	GW	GT	S	PCT
82	1	7	8	-5	128	0	0	1	0	93	1.1

2001-2002 statistics:

GP	G	A	TP	+/-	PIM	PP	SH	GW	GT	S	PCT
63	0	2	2	-18	121	0	0	0	0	70	0.0

LAST SEASON

Second on team in penalty minutes. Missed 19 games with broken hand. Missed one game with knee injury.

THE FINESSE GAME

Hulse has worked hard during past off-seasons on speed drills, and he is now among the fastest straight-ahead skaters on the Predators defence. This has helped him improve his puck movement and he is able to lug the puck out of the zone if needed.

Now a better-than-average skater, Hulse has a long, strong stride with good balance. He is sound in the defensive aspects of the game, but is reluctant to get involved even modestly in the attack. His only goal of the season was a game-winner, in overtime.

Hulse has a good shot from the point. Once he comprehends he can actually cross the far blueline once in a while, he could work on a second power-play unit with more experience, although his future is as a defensive mainstay. Intelligent and steady, he has also become a mainstay on the penalty-killing squad.

THE PHYSICAL GAME

Hulse is tough, an outstanding fighter who doesn't go looking for trouble but won't back down from a challenge either. Hulse isn't mean by nature. He understands, however, that he has a job in the NHL because of his physical ability.

He will hit hard along the boards and in the corners. He's not a strong open-ice hitter, but he plays well positionally and makes attackers pay the price for coming onto his piece of the ice.

THE INTANGIBLES

Hulse's chief flaw is a lack of intensity. This is one of those players who needs a kick in the butt now and then. He usually responds.

PROJECTION

Hulse is one of Nashville's top four defencemen, for now. His point totals will be barely in double digits. Hulse is a physical complement to a more offensive partner.

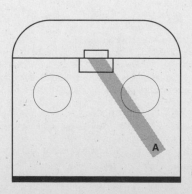

GREG JOHNSON

Yrs. of NHL service: 7
Born: Thunder Bay, Ont.; Mar. 16, 1971
Position: centre
Height: 5-11
Weight: 202
Uniform no.: 22
Shoots: left

Career statistics:

GP	G	A	TP	PIM
597	112	189	301	280

1998-1999 statistics:

GP	G	A	TP	+/-	PIM	PP	SH	GW	GT	S	PCT
68	16	34	50	-8	24	2	3	0	0	120	13.3

1999-2000 statistics:

GP	G	A	TP	+/-	PIM	PP	SH	GW	GT	S	PCT
82	11	33	44	-15	40	2	0	1	0	133	8.3

2000-2001 statistics:

GP	G	A	TP	+/-	PIM	PP	SH	GW	GT	S	PCT
82	15	17	32	-6	46	1	0	4	0	97	15.5

2001-2002 statistics:

GP	G	A	TP	+/-	PIM	PP	SH	GW	GT	S	PCT
82	18	26	44	-14	38	3	0	2	1	145	12.4

PROJECTION

With Johnson's speed and decent hands, he should be a 20-goal scorer. History says he isn't likely to score many more than 15. But if you want assists, he's your man in Nashville.

LAST SEASON

Led team in points. Second on team in goals with career high. Third on team in assists and shooting percentage. One of five Predators to appear in all 82 games. Has appeared in 246 consecutive games.

THE FINESSE GAME

Johnson can be used in many playing situations thanks to his speed, which is explosive. A small centre, he has fine finesse skills. He's also a smart and creative passer, though he doesn't shoot enough, especially given the amount of ice time he receives. When he chooses, he has an accurate wrist shot. He isn't a hard player but he competes well.

On a stronger team, Johnson might be pegged as a checking forward, but he has more ice time and more responsibility with Nashville.

Johnson can play four-on-four, kill penalties and work on the power play. He has been increasing his shot totals but needs to improve yet in that area.

THE PHYSICAL GAME

Johnson is small and gets bounced around a lot. Being one of the faster skaters in the league allows him to avoid some situations where he can be outmuscled. He keeps himself in great shape and led Nashville forwards in average ice time (19:50) last season.

THE INTANGIBLES

Johnson has been very durable for a smaller player. He is one of the players opposing teams ask about most when looking for a deal at deadline time.

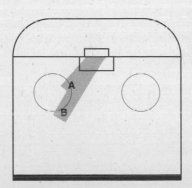

JERE KARALAHTI

Yrs. of NHL service: 3
Born: Helsinki, Finland; Mar. 25, 1975
Position: right defence
Height: 6-2
Weight: 210
Uniform no.: 13
Shoots: right

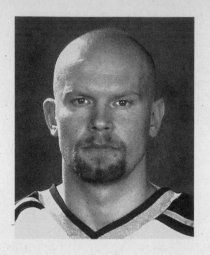

Career statistics:

GP	G	A	TP	PIM
149	8	19	27	97

1999-2000 statistics:

GP	G	A	TP	+/-	PIM	PP	SH	GW	GT	S	PCT
48	6	10	16	+3	18	4	0	1	0	69	8.7

2000-2001 statistics:

GP	G	A	TP	+/-	PIM	PP	SH	GW	GT	S	PCT
56	2	7	9	+8	38	0	0	0	0	26	7.7

2001-2002 statistics:

GP	G	A	TP	+/-	PIM	PP	SH	GW	GT	S	PCT
45	0	2	2	-6	41	0	0	0	0	27	0.0

LAST SEASON

Acquired from Los Angeles on March 16, 2002, with a conditional draft pick for Cliff Ronning.

THE FINESSE GAME

When Karalahti puts all the pieces together, he shows signs of being a special two-way defenceman. When he doesn't, he's a puzzle.

Karalahti has fine offensive skills. He is a good passer who can work the point on the power play or make the smart outlet pass out of his own zone. He is a fine skater. He also has good size and strength and can move guys out from the slot.

His biggest focus has to be maintaining his intensity from shift to shift, night to night. On nights when he is interested, he is a willing hitter and shot-blocker.

THE PHYSICAL GAME

Karalahti is big and strong and is willing to use his size to his advantage. He has to be hounded to keep up his conditioning. He isn't a self-motivator.

Karalahti underwent treatment for drug addiction in his native Finland several years ago, and since coming to the NHL has had a relapse of a substance-abuse problem which required counselling. This will obviously be a lifelong battle.

PROJECTION

Some good signs, some warning flags. Karalahti is a very good defenceman, certainly a top-four in Nashville. He has been frequent healthy scratch over the past few seasons.

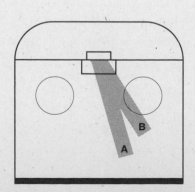

DAVID LEGWAND

Yrs. of NHL service: 3
Born: Detroit, Mich.; Aug. 17, 1980
Position: centre
Height: 6-2
Weight: 190
Uniform no.: 11
Shoots: left

Career statistics:

GP	G	A	TP	PIM
216	37	62	99	122

1998-1999 statistics:

GP	G	A	TP	+/-	PIM	PP	SH	GW	GT	S	PCT
1	0	0	0	0	0	0	0	0	0	2	0.0

1999-2000 statistics:

GP	G	A	TP	+/-	PIM	PP	SH	GW	GT	S	PCT
71	13	15	28	-6	30	4	0	2	0	111	11.7

2000-2001 statistics:

GP	G	A	TP	+/-	PIM	PP	SH	GW	GT	S	PCT
81	13	28	41	+1	38	3	0	3	0	172	7.6

2001-2002 statistics:

GP	G	A	TP	+/-	PIM	PP	SH	GW	GT	S	PCT
63	11	19	30	+1	54	1	1	1	0	121	9.1

LAST SEASON

Third on team in plus-minus. Missed 19 games with back injuries.

THE FINESSE GAME

Legwand's all-around game continues to improve, helping him become a better player even if he doesn't put up the splashy number to draw attention. Think of him as a young Steve Yzerman, without the history of the 100-point seasons.

Legwand handles the puck well in traffic and shoots well in stride. He wants the puck when the game is on the line, because he has that goal-scorer's mentality that the team is better off when the puck is on his stick rather than anyone else's. He isn't totally unselfish and is a good passer, but his first option will always be to take the shot. Legwand is very strong on the puck. He just has to find his shot and utilize his outside speed better.

Legwand is an absolutely dynamic skater. So much is expected of him (he was the second player drafted after Vincent Lecavalier in 1998) that his improvement must seem painfully slow, but it must be remembered that he is only 21 years old and will be entering his fourth NHL season playing on a team that is very young.

He needs to learn the defensive part of the game better. He especially has a long way to go on face-offs. To Legwand's credit, he works extensively on these aspects of his game with the assistant coaches.

THE PHYSICAL GAME

He has been compared to Mike Modano in style, but physically and mentally Legwand is years away from being a Modano-type of player. Legwand is still boyish in build and needs to get a lot stronger to be able to compete in the NHL. He has to improve his battle skills. He has a strong lower body and must develop the upper body to go along with it. Remember, it took Modano years to become the all-round player and leader he is now.

THE INTANGIBLES

Legwand's crabby back is a concern. Legwand needs to show more consistency and commitment. This could be the season that determines his future.

PROJECTION

Legwand scored a pro-rated 39 points last season. We won't ask for a huge bump from him — but 45 points over a full season doesn't seem too much of a burden.

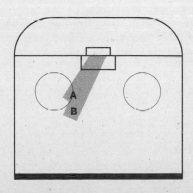

VLADIMIR ORSZAGH

Yrs. of NHL service: 3
Born: Banska Bystrica, CZE
Position: right wing
Height: 5-11
Weight: 173
Uniform no.: 33
Shoots: left

Career statistics:

GP	G	A	TP	PIM
113	18	23	41	68

1998-1999 statistics:

GP	G	A	TP	+/-	PIM	PP	SH	GW	GT	S	PCT
12	1	0	1	+2	6	0	0	0	0	5	20.0

1999-2000 statistics:

GP	G	A	TP	+/-	PIM	PP	SH	GW	GT	S	PCT
11	2	1	3	+1	4	0	0	0	0	16	12.5

2000-2001 statistics:

Did not play in NHL

2001-2002 statistics:

GP	G	A	TP	+/-	PIM	PP	SH	GW	GT	S	PCT
79	15	21	36	-15	56	5	0	3	0	113	13.3

PROJECTION

Orszagh figures prominently in Nashville's top-six forward plans. A jump to 45 points is logical.

LAST SEASON

Second on team in shooting percentage. Tied for third on team in game-winning goals. Career highs in goals, assists and points. Missed two games with charley horse.

THE FINESSE GAME

Orszagh is a left-handed shot who plays the right wing. Last year he finished up with Martin Erat and Denis Arkhipov, a compatible trio. Playing the off-wing opens up one-timers for Orszagh. Once he gets over the blueline he won't be looking to force a pass. He won't back up and make a play. Orszagh will shoot. He has a good selection of shots.

Orszagh is a good skater. He doesn't have blazing speed but is quick and he's strong on his feet. He can hold off a defender with one arm and keep advancing the puck. He battles for his patch of ice.

He thinks the game well and has good hockey sense.

THE PHYSICAL GAME

Even though he isn't very big, Orszagh is a tough customer. He plays with an edge and he is unfazed by matchups against bigger, stronger, more famous players. He made a memorable impact on the Rangers' Eric Lindros in New York last season. Orszagh could always stand to add some muscle, which can be done, and height, which can't.

THE INTANGIBLES

Orszagh was a free agent find, after starting in the Islanders organization and then returning to Europe to play for a season.

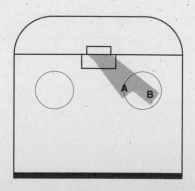

KARLIS SKRASTINS

Yrs. of NHL service: 3
Born: Riga, Latvia; July 9, 1974
Position: left defence
Height: 6-1
Weight: 208
Uniform no.: 3
Shoots: left

Career statistics:

GP	G	A	TP	PIM
225	10	31	41	86

1998-1999 statistics:

GP	G	A	TP	+/-	PIM	PP	SH	GW	GT	S	PCT
2	0	1	1	0	0	0	0	0	0	0	0.0

1999-2000 statistics:

GP	G	A	TP	+/-	PIM	PP	SH	GW	GT	S	PCT
59	5	6	11	-7	20	1	0	2	0	51	9.8

2000-2001 statistics:

GP	G	A	TP	+/-	PIM	PP	SH	GW	GT	S	PCT
82	1	11	12	-12	30	0	0	1	0	66	1.5

2001-2002 statistics:

GP	G	A	TP	+/-	PIM	PP	SH	GW	GT	S	PCT
82	4	13	17	-12	36	0	0	1	1	84	4.8

PROJECTION

Skrastins isn't likely to score more than 20 points.

LAST SEASON

One of five Predators to appear in all 82 games.

THE FINESSE GAME

Skrastins has a future as a steady, stay-at-home defenceman. He is a good penalty killer and worked on the Predators' top unit. He blocks a lot of shots and plays a sound positional game. Skrastins is the player you want on the ice to help protect a lead, in the few games when the Preds have a lead.

He is strong, mobile and has decent hockey sense. His offensive upside is minimal, though he handles the puck well and is poised. He concentrates on the defensive aspects of his game.

On a better team, Skrastins would be on the third pairing, but he gets assignments on a top pair with Nashville and seems to relish the challenge. He is very underrated because he doesn't have the flashy point totals.

THE PHYSICAL GAME

Skrastins is a horse. He plays a lot of minutes against other teams' top players, and does so aggressively. Skrastins averaged 20.30 of ice time last season. He takes the body, blocks a lot of shots and takes away a lot of passing and shooting lanes. Skrastins plays hurt. He hasn't missed a game in two seasons but that doesn't mean he never felt ouchy.

THE INTANGIBLES

The coaches love his energy and attitude, and he has progressed faster than expected, although his play levelled off a bit last season.

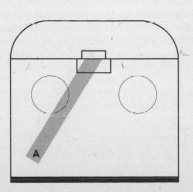

KIMMO TIMONEN

Yrs. of NHL service: 4
Born: Kuopio, Finland; Mar. 18, 1975
Position: left defence
Height: 5-10
Weight: 196
Uniform no.: 44
Shoots: left

Career statistics:

GP	G	A	TP	PIM
265	37	75	112	134

1998-1999 statistics:

GP	G	A	TP	+/-	PIM	PP	SH	GW	GT	S	PCT
50	4	8	12	-4	30	1	0	0	0	75	5.3

1999-2000 statistics:

GP	G	A	TP	+/-	PIM	PP	SH	GW	GT	S	PCT
51	8	25	33	-5	26	2	1	2	0	97	8.2

2000-2001 statistics:

GP	G	A	TP	+/-	PIM	PP	SH	GW	GT	S	PCT
82	12	13	25	-6	50	6	0	3	0	151	7.9

2001-2002 statistics:

GP	G	A	TP	+/-	PIM	PP	SH	GW	GT	S	PCT
82	13	29	42	+2	28	9	0	1	0	154	8.4

LAST SEASON

Led team defencemen in points for third consecutive season. Led team in assists with career high. Second on team in plus-minus. Tied for second on team in points with career high. Third on team in shots. One of five Predators to appear in all 82 games.

THE FINESSE GAME

Timonen has good quickness and adds a lot of skill to the Nashville backline, which doesn't have much in that department. He has been their best defenceman for the past few seasons. He is not a defensive liability, and has worked to improve the defensive aspects of his game.

Adding Andy Delmore to the roster took some of the scoring pressure off Timonen, so teams are unable to concentrate solely on him to shut down Nashville's attack. He has good ability in all offensive areas. He is not elite class, but he moves the puck and sees the ice well. Timonen has excellent hockey sense. He gets first-unit power-play time. He could also kill penalties, but Nashville does need to give him a breather now and then.

Timonen is one of the smaller defencemen in the league, and in Finland several seasons ago was the partner of New Jersey's Brian Rafalski. Timonen is a lot like Rafalski, although he lacks his ex-teammate's explosive speed. He does have quickness, however. He reads and jumps into the rush well to create offence.

THE PHYSICAL GAME

Somewhat on the small side, Timonen is not very strong. He isn't going to get bigger, so he has to try to get stronger. He has a powerful lower body.

THE INTANGIBLES

Timonen is one of the first players other teams ask about when seeking a deal with Nashville, but he is quite valuable in this spot. While he would be a complementary player elsewhere, he is pretty close to a No. 1 defenceman here. Timonen had a good Olympic tournament, which was another boost to his confidence.

PROJECTION

Timonen graduated to the 40-point ranks last season. That is probably close to his top end. If he can produce 40-45 points a season on a consistent basis, he will have a successful career.

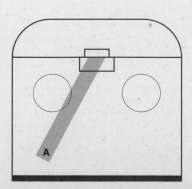

SCOTT WALKER

Yrs. of NHL service: 7
Born: Montreal, Que.; July 19, 1973
Position: right wing
Height: 5-10
Weight: 195
Uniform no.: 24
Shoots: right

Career statistics:

GP	G	A	TP	PIM
439	61	114	175	743

1998-1999 statistics:

GP	G	A	TP	+/-	PIM	PP	SH	GW	GT	S	PCT
71	15	25	40	0	103	0	1	2	0	96	15.6

1999-2000 statistics:

GP	G	A	TP	+/-	PIM	PP	SH	GW	GT	S	PCT
69	7	21	28	-16	90	0	1	0	1	98	7.1

2000-2001 statistics:

GP	G	A	TP	+/-	PIM	PP	SH	GW	GT	S	PCT
74	25	29	54	-2	66	9	3	1	1	159	15.7

2001-2002 statistics:

GP	G	A	TP	+/-	PIM	PP	SH	GW	GT	S	PCT
28	4	5	9	-13	18	1	0	0	0	46	8.7

LAST SEASON

Missed 54 games with concussion.

THE FINESSE GAME

Few players have reinvented themselves so thoroughly, or successfully, as Walker has done. Walker played defence in junior and seemed to be on the fast track to becoming an enforcer type, but he was switched to right wing in his early days with Vancouver. He continues to develop along power forward lines.

He can still be dropped back on defence in an emergency. Walker is actually versatile enough to play all three forward positions, too. No one's asked him to try goal yet.

Walker has very good speed. He is an excellent penalty killer. He grinds and gets his nose in and doesn't quit on the puck. He doesn't have great hands, but he works hard for his scoring chances and creates off the forecheck. He gets involved in traffic.

THE PHYSICAL GAME

His game is feisty, but instead of just stirring things up, Walker has concentrated on being more of a hockey player, so his penalty minutes have dropped. He wants to stay on the ice. Walker can be a pain to play against. He is courageous and gritty, and he fights. When he does drop the gloves, it's against the big guys, and he holds his own.

THE INTANGIBLES

Walker's season was a washout due to his concussion. Walker is a role player who can add energy and flexibility to a lineup. He was missed by the Predators last season. Walker would be an excellent third-line player elsewhere. For Nashville, he is a key top six forward.

PROJECTION

Players recovering from a concussion always make us leery, even more so when it involves someone who has to play physical the way that Walker does. He could score 25 goals if he returns healthy.

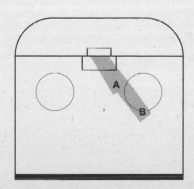

CLARKE WILM

Yrs. of NHL service: 4
Born: Central Butte, Sask.; Oct. 24, 1976
Position: centre
Height: 6-0
Weight: 202
Uniform no.: 23
Shoots: left

Career statistics:

GP	G	A	TP	PIM
303	31	42	73	250

1998-1999 statistics:

GP	G	A	TP	+/-	PIM	PP	SH	GW	GT	S	PCT
78	10	8	18	+11	53	2	2	0	0	94	10.6

1999-2000 statistics:

GP	G	A	TP	+/-	PIM	PP	SH	GW	GT	S	PCT
78	10	12	22	-6	67	1	3	0	0	81	12.3

2000-2001 statistics:

GP	G	A	TP	+/-	PIM	PP	SH	GW	GT	S	PCT
81	7	8	15	-11	69	2	0	0	0	85	8.2

2001-2002 statistics:

GP	G	A	TP	+/-	PIM	PP	SH	GW	GT	S	PCT
66	4	14	18	-1	61	0	1	0	0	83	4.8

PROJECTION

Wilm's absolute top end is 20 points.

LAST SEASON

Signed as free agent by Nashville on July 11, 2002. Missed 12 games with ankle injury.

THE FINESSE GAME

Wilm is one of those players who will always be on the bubble, but will almost always find a job with a team because of his effort.

Primarily a defensive specialist and role player, Wilm will kill penalties, take draws and pretty much adapt to whatever role the team asks of him.

Wilm was known as a scorer in junior, but that touch hasn't translated well to the NHL, probably because of his skating. It is marginally NHL calibre, but Wilm just plugs along until he gets to where he has to be. He simply can't get there fast enough to make much happen. Wilm has decent hands but he can't carry the puck anywhere, so he has to be right on top of the crease in order to score.

Wilm was smart enough to realize his NHL ticket would be his defensive play, so he modeled his game after Brian Skrudland, becoming a hard worker who can chip in the odd goal here or there.

THE PHYSICAL GAME

Wilm competes hard and blocks shots. He is tough but not a fighter. He goes into the dirty areas of the ice and takes his licks.

THE INTANGIBLES

Wilm gives everything he has every game. He is a fourth-line centre, who can be used defensively or be put out on an energy line when a team needs a little wake-up call.

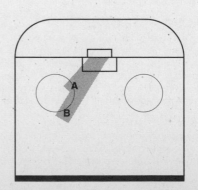

VITALI YACHMENEV

Yrs. of NHL service: 7
Born: Chelyabinsk, Russia; Jan. 8, 1975
Position: left wing
Height: 5-11
Weight: 195
Uniform no.: 43
Shoots: left

Career statistics:

GP	G	A	TP	PIM
425	78	118	196	76

1998-1999 statistics:

GP	G	A	TP	+/-	PIM	PP	SH	GW	GT	S	PCT
55	7	10	17	-10	10	0	1	2	0	83	8.4

1999-2000 statistics:

GP	G	A	TP	+/-	PIM	PP	SH	GW	GT	S	PCT
68	16	16	32	+5	12	1	1	3	0	120	13.3

2000-2001 statistics:

GP	G	A	TP	+/-	PIM	PP	SH	GW	GT	S	PCT
78	15	19	34	-5	10	4	1	4	1	123	12.2

2001-2002 statistics:

GP	G	A	TP	+/-	PIM	PP	SH	GW	GT	S	PCT
75	11	16	27	-16	14	1	2	0	0	103	10.7

PROJECTION

Yachmenev is a steady, if unspectacular, forward who can net 15 goals a season.

LAST SEASON

Led team in shorthanded goals. Missed three games with back spasms.

THE FINESSE GAME

When Yachmenev first broke into the league, his centre was a guy by the name of Wayne Gretzky, and many attributed Yachmenev's strong rookie season to his linemate. But you have to be a smart player to click with Gretzky, and Yachmenev is.

After a few seasons, Yachmenev has regained his game and his confidence. His shot is what got him to the NHL. He has a sniper's touch and he has to score because he doesn't bring much else to the table. He has a tendency to hang on to the puck too long. He has some quickness but no real speed, or he would have a better scoring upside.

Yachmenev is an intelligent player with good hockey sense who can be used to kill penalties and shadow opposing forwards. He is a left-handed shot who plays the right wing; defensively he makes the right play on the wall. He is reliable no matter where he plays. He reminds people of Andreas Dackell.

THE PHYSICAL GAME

Yachmenev isn't very big, but he is strong on his skates and solidly built. He protects the puck well and is strong along the boards.

THE INTANGIBLES

Yachmenev has become a favourite with fans and the coaching staff in Nashville for bringing intelligence and energy to the ice every night. His versatility makes him a useful role player.

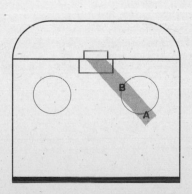

NEW JERSEY DEVILS

Players' Statistics 2001-2002

POS.	NO.	PLAYER	GP	G	A	PTS	+/-	PIM	PP	SH	GW	GT	S	PCT
L	26	PATRIK ELIAS	75	29	32	61	4	36	8	1	8		199	14.6
C	25	JOE NIEUWENDYK	81	25	33	58	0	22	6		6	1	189	13.2
C	16	BOBBY HOLIK	81	25	29	54	7	97	6		3	2	270	9.3
R	17	PETR SYKORA	73	21	27	48	12	44	4		4		194	10.8
C	23	SCOTT GOMEZ	76	10	38	48	-4	36	1		1		156	6.4
D	28	BRIAN RAFALSKI	76	7	40	47	15	18	2		4	1	125	5.6
C	18	SERGEI BRYLIN	76	16	28	44	21	10	5		3		133	12.0
D	27	SCOTT NIEDERMAYER	76	11	22	33	12	30	2		6		129	8.5
R	15	JAMIE LANGENBRUNNER	82	13	19	32	-9	77		1	4		163	8.0
R	44	STEPHANE RICHER	68	14	14	28	-9	14	1		2		123	11.4
C	11	JOHN MADDEN	82	15	8	23	6	25			2	1	170	8.8
L	22	VALERI KAMENSKY	54	7	14	21	1	20			1		72	9.7
D	4	SCOTT STEVENS	82	1	16	17	15	44			1		121	0.8
L	20	JAY PANDOLFO	65	4	10	14	12	15		1			72	5.6
R	14	*BRIAN GIONTA	33	4	7	11	10	8					58	6.9
L	12	SERGEI NEMCHINOV	68	5	5	10	-9	10			1		49	10.2
L	21	ANDREAS SALOMONSSON	39	4	5	9	-12	22	1		1		58	6.9
C	10	*CHRISTIAN BERGLUND	15	2	7	9	-3	8					22	9.1
L	19	JIM MCKENZIE	67	3	5	8	0	123	1				33	9.1
D	3	KEN DANEYKO	67		6	6	2	60					44	
D	5	COLIN WHITE	73	2	3	5	6	133					81	2.5
D	7	ANDREI ZYUZIN	47	1	4	5	-5	31	1				61	1.6
D	6	TOMMY ALBELIN	42	1	3	4	0	4			1		33	3.0
R	9	BRUCE GARDINER	7	2	1	3	-1	2	1				10	20.0
R	24	TURNER STEVENSON	21		2	2	-3	25					33	
D	2	*MIKE COMMODORE	37	1	1	1	-12	30					22	
D	29	JOEL BOUCHARD	1		1	1	1							
L	9	*JIRI BICEK	1				-1						2	
G	34	JOHN VANBIESBROUCK	5				0	4						
G	30	MARTIN BRODEUR	73				0	8						
G	1	J-F DAMPHOUSSE	6				0							
G	40	SCOTT CLEMMENSEN	2				0							

GP = games played; G = goals; A = assists; PTS = points; +/- = goals-for minus goals-against while player is on ice; PIM = penalties in minutes; PP = power-play goals; SH = shorthanded goals; GW = game-winning goals; GT = game-tying goals; S = no. of shots; PCT = percentage of goals to shots; * = rookie

CHRISTIAN BERGLUND

Yrs. of NHL service: 0
Born: Orebro, Sweden; Mar. 12, 1980
Position: right wing
Height: 5-11
Weight: 195
Uniform no.: 10
Shoots: left

Career statistics:

GP	G	A	TP	PIM
15	2	7	9	8

2001-2002 statistics:

GP	G	A	TP	+/-	PIM	PP	SH	GW	GT	S	PCT
15	2	7	9	-3	8	0	0	0	0	22	9.1

LAST SEASON

Will be entering first full NHL season. Appeared in 60 games with Albany (AHL), scoring 21-26-47 with 69 penalty minutes. Missed three games due to coach's decision.

THE FINESSE GAME

Berglund has a very wide skating stance for good balance and a sprinter's acceleration. He will probably never be a great scorer, but we could see him sneaking into the 25-goal range in the future, because he combines a heavy shot with a quick release.

Berglund has good passing skills and hockey vision; he's an unselfish player. He will drive to the net and created some havoc for screens and tips.

Berglund needs to improve his defensive play. He tends to get wrapped up in the fun of trying to score goals (and he sure does seem to have a lot of fun when he plays).

THE PHYSICAL GAME

Berglund reminds a lot of scouts of Tomas Sandstrom. He can beat you in a lot of ways. He is tough, abrasive and high-energy. Berglund isn't very tall but he has a muscular, stocky build and he's willing to plow into people along the boards and in front of the net. He is really annoying to play against. Berglund will draw his share of penalties, but he also has to guard against taking them, which is something he did at inopportune times during his New Jersey audition last season.

THE INTANGIBLES

We don't understand why Berglund didn't get more ice time last season, especially since so many of his teammates seemed disinterested. There have been a lot of personnel shake-ups in the off-season, and a good training camp could earn Berglund a job.

PROJECTION

Berglund is more likely to start the season in the minors, but if he gets the promotion, look for 10-12 goals in what will probably be a part-time role at first. He should be a fixture on the third line soon and has second-line potential.

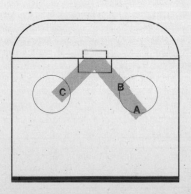

MARTIN BRODEUR

Yrs. of NHL service: 9
Born: Montreal, Que.; May 6, 1972
Position: goaltender
Height: 6-2
Weight: 205
Uniform no.: 30
Catches: left

Career statistics:

GP	MIN	GA	SO	GAA	A	PIM
592	34583	1272	55	2.21	23	40

1998-1999 statistics:

GP	MIN	GAA	W	L	T	SO	GA	S	SAPCT	PIM
70	4239	2.29	39	21	10	4	162	1728	.906	4

1999-2000 statistics:

GP	MIN	GAA	W	L	T	SO	GA	S	SAPCT	PIM
72	4312	2.24	43	20	8	6	161	1797	.910	16

2000-2001 statistics:

GP	MIN	GAA	W	L	T	SO	GA	S	SAPCT	PIM
72	4297	2.32	42	17	11	9	166	1762	.906	14

2001-2002 statistics:

GP	MIN	GAA	W	L	T	SO	GA	S	SAPCT	PIM
73	4347	2.15	38	26	9	4	156	1655	.906	8

LAST SEASON

Recorded 35 or more wins for sixth consecutive season. Second among NHL goalies in wins. Led NHL goalies in minutes played.

THE PHYSICAL GAME

Brodeur makes the most of his generous size. He stands upright in the net and squares himself so well to the shooter that he looks enormous. He is probably the best in the game at using his stick around the net. He breaks up passes and will make a quick jab to knock the puck off an opponent's stick. He will also whack players in the ankles or jab them behind the knees to protect his turf.

Opponents want to get Brodeur's feet moving — wraparound plays, rebounds, anything involving his skates exposes his weaknesses. Because of his puck control, he prevents a lot of scrambles and minimizes his flaws. When he falls into bad streaks, it is usually because of his footwork.

Brodeur has improved his play out of the net — if the league ever legislates against goalies handling the puck it will have to be known as the Brodeur Rule. He has to guard against cockiness, though. He gets carried away with clearing shots through the middle of the ice. Most of the time he handles the puck intelligently and is effective on the penalty kill, sending the puck up-ice, acting as a third defenceman and thoroughly frustrating the opponents' power play.

THE MENTAL GAME

Bad games and bad goals don't rattle Brodeur for long. Although he has a tendency to show his frustration on-ice, he also bounces back quickly with strong efforts. He concentrates and doesn't lose his intensity throughout a game. Brodeur exudes confidence and even a bit of defiance through the layers of padding and his mask. When he is on, his glove saves are snappy and he bounces on his feet with flair.

Last season, for the first time, Brodeur was publicly critical of his teammates' play on occasion. He could stand to play a little less, but thrives on the work; the Devils generally let him dictate his own schedule.

THE INTANGIBLES

Brodeur's individual reputation suffers from playing for a strong team, but he is one of the game's elite no matter what the stats say. Winning a gold medal in the Olympics was a big morale boost after the disappointment of the 2001 playoffs. Brodeur wasn't very sharp in the 2002 first-round playoff loss to Carolina, but his 1.42 GAA in the series meant the defeat was not the fault of the goalie.

PROJECTION

Brodeur's streak of 35-win seasons could be in jeopardy as the Devils don't figure to be as deep in front of him as they used to be.

KEN DANEYKO

Yrs. of NHL service: 17
Born: Windsor, Ont.; Apr. 17, 1964
Position: left defence
Height: 6-1
Weight: 215
Uniform no.: 3
Shoots: left

Career statistics:

GP	G	A	TP	PIM
1214	34	135	169	2481

1998-1999 statistics:

GP	G	A	TP	+/-	PIM	PP	SH	GW	GT	S	PCT
82	2	9	11	+27	63	0	0	0	0	63	3.2

1999-2000 statistics:

GP	G	A	TP	+/-	PIM	PP	SH	GW	GT	S	PCT
78	0	6	6	+13	98	0	0	0	0	74	-

2000-2001 statistics:

GP	G	A	TP	+/-	PIM	PP	SH	GW	GT	S	PCT
77	0	4	4	+8	87	0	0	0	0	50	0.0

2001-2002 statistics:

GP	G	A	TP	+/-	PIM	PP	SH	GW	GT	S	PCT
67	0	6	6	+2	60	0	0	0	0	44	0.0

LAST SEASON

Missed seven games with shoulder injury. Missed eight games due to coach's decision.

THE FINESSE GAME

Break down Daneyko's game — average skater, average passer, below-average shooter — and he looks like someone who would have trouble getting ice time. But Daneyko's edge is his competitive drive: he will do anything to win a hockey game. Add to that his strength and sound hockey sense, and the result is a powerful defensive defenceman.

Despite his slow footwork, Daneyko has evolved into one of his team's top penalty killers. He is a good shot-blocker, though he could still use some improvement. When he goes down and fails to block a shot, he does little more than screen his goalie with his burly body.

A Daneyko rush is a rare thing. He's smart enough to recognize his limitations and he seldom joins the play or gets involved deep in the attacking zone. His offensive involvement is usually limited to a smart, safe breakout pass.

At this stage of his career, Daneyko has to be paired with a mobile partner.

THE PHYSICAL GAME

Daneyko is powerful, with great upper and lower-body strength. His legs give him drive when he's moving opposing forwards out from around the net. He is a punishing hitter; when he makes a take-out the opponent stays out of the play. He is smart enough not to get beaten by superior skaters and will force an attacker to the perimeter. He has cut down on his bad penalties. Emotions still sometimes get the better of him, but he will usually get his two or five minutes' worth.

Daneyko is a formidable fighter, a player few are willing to tangle with. That means he now has to prove himself less frequently. If somebody wants a scrap, though, he's willing and extremely able, and he stands up for his teammates.

THE INTANGIBLES

Daneyko is a classic, a throwback to an era when guys dragged themselves onto the ice and played on fractured ankles. Despite his age, however, he is in exceptional shape. He truly takes the game of hockey to heart.

PROJECTION

Now 38 and no longer a top-four defenceman, Daneyko has survived challenges from young studs before; he now mentors those who might be taking his job away. This could be his final season — of course, we said that last year, too.

PATRIK ELIAS

Yrs. of NHL service: 5
Born: Trebic, Czech Republic; Apr. 13, 1976
Position: left wing
Height: 6-1
Weight: 200
Uniform no.: 26
Shoots: left

Career statistics:

GP	G	A	TP	PIM
396	141	180	321	209

1998-1999 statistics:

GP	G	A	TP	+/-	PIM	PP	SH	GW	GT	S	PCT
74	17	33	50	+19	34	3	0	2	0	157	10.8

1999-2000 statistics:

GP	G	A	TP	+/-	PIM	PP	SH	GW	GT	S	PCT
72	35	37	72	+16	58	9	0	9	1	183	19.1

2000-2001 statistics:

GP	G	A	TP	+/-	PIM	PP	SH	GW	GT	S	PCT
82	40	56	96	+45	51	8	3	6	1	220	18.2

2001-2002 statistics:

GP	G	A	TP	+/-	PIM	PP	SH	GW	GT	S	PCT
75	29	32	61	+4	36	8	1	8	0	199	14.6

LAST SEASON

Led team in points for third consecutive season. Led team in goals, power-play goals, game-winning goals and shooting percentage. Second on team in shots. Third on team in assists. Tied for fourth among NHL players in game-winning goals. Missed five games with finger infection. Missed two games with flu.

THE FINESSE GAME

Elias is one of the best transition forwards in the game. He is quick enough to be in a defensive posture when the opponent has the puck, and savvy enough to read the play, knock down a pass or sprint when one of his teammates gains control and looks to send him flying.

Elias has become increasingly confident in his shot. He has a quick, low release, especially on his wrist shot, and can shoot on the fly or fake a shot and stickhandle in close for a backhander. He is not quite a power forward, though he is strong enough to muscle his way into traffic areas for scoring chances. He has superb hockey vision and brings a centre's vision and passing skills to the wing. The Devils played him at centre on occasion last season, and with the loss of Bobby Holik, may do so again. Elias is really much better suited as a winger, but he also likes centre because he gets to control the puck more.

Elias falls into slumps where he fails to get shots away on net. This is either a by-product of his tendency to look for a pass first, or a lapse in his confidence.

Elias works both special teams. He is reliable defensively, enjoys killing penalties and is a threat to create scoring chances off shorthanded rushes. He takes draws on the PK and holds his own. Elias wants the puck when the game is on the line.

THE PHYSICAL GAME

Elias has good upper-body strength for work along the boards and good lower-body strength for skating speed and balance. He is tough to knock off his skates and plays with controlled aggression. He doesn't take many bad penalties, but will bring his stick up or take a swing if he believes he is being taken advantage of. Elias can't be intimidated. He never backs down and frequently initiates. He plays with attitude and is as quietly tough a forward as you can find in the NHL.

THE INTANGIBLES

Despite some upheavals (primarily, the loss of his regular pivotman, Jason Arnott), Elias remained the Devils' top forward. The Devils were able to sign him to a contract extension on the eve of salary arbitration. Elias was gratified by the deal, and is eager to assume a new leadership role on and off the ice. He will miss his pal and linemate, Petr Sykora (traded to Anaheim), but has all of the off-season to get over it.

PROJECTION

Elias can score in the 40-goal, 80-point range if he is motivated — and it sounds like he will be.

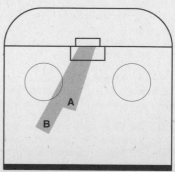

JEFF FRIESEN

Yrs. of NHL service: 8
Born: Meadow Lake, Sask.; Aug. 5, 1976
Position: left wing
Height: 6-0
Weight: 205
Uniform no.: 11
Shoots: left

Career statistics:

GP	G	A	TP	PIM
608	168	237	405	370

1998-1999 statistics:

GP	G	A	TP	+/-	PIM	PP	SH	GW	GT	S	PCT
78	22	35	57	+3	42	10	1	3	1	215	10.2

1999-2000 statistics:

GP	G	A	TP	+/-	PIM	PP	SH	GW	GT	S	PCT
82	26	35	61	2	47	11	3	7	0	191	13.6

2000-2001 statistics:

GP	G	A	TP	+/-	PIM	PP	SH	GW	GT	S	PCT
79	14	34	48	+5	66	4	0	1	0	149	9.4

2001-2002 statistics:

GP	G	A	TP	+/-	PIM	PP	SH	GW	GT	S	PCT
81	17	26	43	-1	44	1	1	0	0	161	10.6

LAST SEASON

Acquired from Anaheim on July 6, 2002, with Oleg Tverdovsky and Maxim Balmochnykh for Petr Sykora, Mike Commodore, J-F Damphousse and Igor Pohanka. Tied for second on Ducks in assists. Missed one game with sprained left ankle.

THE FINESSE GAME

Friesen is a fast, strong skater who handles the puck well and has the size to go with those qualities. He is a better finisher than playmaker. He needs to play with linemates who have a lot of patience and the ability to hold on to the puck for a long time. Friesen can get into holes with his speed for the pass. He has a quick, strong release on his snap or wrist shot, and is shifty with a smooth change of speed. Carrying the puck doesn't slow him down. He is not a natural goal-scorer and probably will never be an elite one, but he works hard and earns his goals.

Friesen never seems to get rattled or forced into making bad plays. In fact, he's the one who forces opponents into panic moves with his pressure. He draws penalties by keeping his feet moving as he drives to the net or digs for the puck along the boards. He is strong on face-offs.

A pure goal-scorer in junior, Friesen developed first as a checking-line winger in his rookie year before becoming a complete player. He deserves a lot of credit for making himself into an all-around player.

THE PHYSICAL GAME

Friesen has dedicated himself to his strength and conditioning. He doesn't have much of a mean streak, but he plays tough and honest.

THE INTANGIBLES

Friesen was lost after the deal to Anaheim. He wasn't a good fit with Paul Kariya, and the talent drops off so precariously after that name that Friesen never found his role. He was taken off special teams duty and relegated to a part-timer. Friesen is excited about the move to New Jersey. The Devils have little depth at centre, so he might be moved back to that position.

PROJECTION

We correctly predicted that Friesen's goal total would drop down to around 20. This season, we don't expect that much of an upgrade — maybe he can be a 25/50 man (goals and points) since the Devils figure to play a defensive system under new coach Pat Burns.

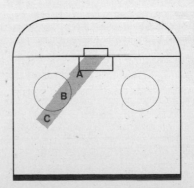

BRIAN GIONTA

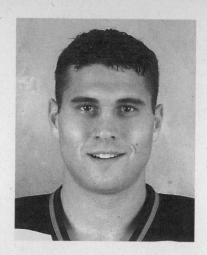

Yrs. of NHL service: 1
Born: Rochester, NY; Jan. 18, 1979
Position: right wing
Height: 5-7
Weight: 160
Uniform no.: 14
Shoots: right

Career statistics:

GP	G	A	TP	PIM
33	4	7	11	8

2001-2002 statistics:

GP	G	A	TP	+/-	PIM	PP	SH	GW	GT	S	PCT
33	4	7	11	+10	8	0	0	0	0	58	6.9

LAST SEASON

First NHL season. Tied for third among NHL rookies in plus-minus. Missed four games due to coach's decision. Appeared in 37 games with Albany (AHL), scoring 9-16-25.

THE FINESSE GAME

Gionta is too small to play in the NHL. Just try saying that to his face, even if you have to bend down a little to look him in the eye. Listed at a generous five-foot-seven, Gionta is a smart, slick forward who made an impact with the Devils last season. Playing in the NHL is something people have been telling him he couldn't do ever since he was a little(r) guy.

Gionta was a standout player in college (Boston College) and in junior competitions at the international level. One of his frequent linemates in tournament play was Scott Gomez, a Devils' teammate. They were drafted in the same year (1998).

Gionta is a natural goal-scorer. He reads very well off of other players (especially Gomez). He is an instinctive player, and is usually one mental step ahead of most of the other players on the ice. Gionta beats his man off the boards frequently. He wins puck battles against bigger players by getting good body position. Gionta is a nifty skater. He doesn't have great breakaway speed but he is agile and quick. He has excellent hand skills for shooting or passing.

Gionta can be used to kill penalties and excels on the power play. He was +10 in only 33 games.

THE PHYSICAL GAME

Gionta competes hard. He won't bowl people over — well, maybe Jason Blake or Andy McDonald — but he won't be intimidated. He has a little cockiness to his game, which is a good thing. Size doesn't always matter. Gionta plays with a big heart.

THE INTANGIBLES

Gionta plays like he doesn't know he's a shrimp.

PROJECTION

Gionta made great strides in his first pro season, and should earn a spot on the Devils' second line. Based on his limited NHL showing, a full season should yield 10-15 goals and 25-30 points.

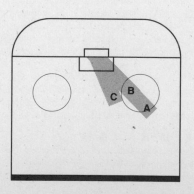

SCOTT GOMEZ

Yrs. of NHL service: 3
Born: Anchorage, AK; Dec. 23, 1979
Position: centre
Height: 5-11
Weight: 200
Uniform no.: 23
Shoots: left

Career statistics:

GP	G	A	TP	PIM
234	43	138	181	160

1999-2000 statistics:

GP	G	A	TP	+/-	PIM	PP	SH	GW	GT	S	PCT
82	19	51	70	+14	78	7	0	1	2	204	9.3

2000-2001 statistics:

GP	G	A	TP	+/-	PIM	PP	SH	GW	GT	S	PCT
76	14	49	63	-1	46	2	0	4	0	155	9.0

2001-2002 statistics:

GP	G	A	TP	+/-	PIM	PP	SH	GW	GT	S	PCT
76	10	38	48	-4	36	1	0	1	0	156	6.4

LAST SEASON

Second on team in assists. Missed six games with fractured hand.

THE FINESSE GAME

Gomez's ability to use the space behind the net to shield himself from defenders and set up plays is almost Wayne Gretzky-like. He has terrific vision and patience with the puck, and can thread a pass through what seems like the eye of a needle to find a teammate. Anyone playing with Gomez has to be alert, because he is adept at finding seams that others don't even know exist.

He has a very good wrist shot, not a heavy one, but accurate. You might think with his assists-to-goals ratio that Gomez doesn't shoot enough, but he isn't shy about letting it go. He is just not as gifted a goal-scorer as he is a passer. However, he makes excellent use of the extra room on a power play. The Devils frequently used him as a winger instead of a centre last season because of his defensive shortcomings. This is a mistake. Gomez needs to be in the middle of the ice. He is not as effective along the boards.

Gomez is not a good skater. He needs to be constantly reminded to keep his feet moving and not to glide. He is strong on his skates, though, tough to knock off his feet and willing to work in the dirty areas for pucks. He lacks outside speed but can put on a short burst to get a jump on the defence. His plus-minus is awful for a good defensive team, and he needs to work more diligently in his own zone. Face-offs also continue to be a weak area for Gomez.

THE PHYSICAL GAME

As easy-going as Gomez is off-ice, he is just as competitive on it, except he has not brought that itensity to the ice on a nightly basis. At his best, Gomez is like a young Claude Lemeiux: chippy, chirpy, tough around the net and picking up clutch points. When he is in that zone, he is irritating to play against. He won't back down from a scuffle and isn't shy about starting one. He is solid and durable.

THE INTANGIBLES

Gomez is still a work in progress. He had an accelerated start, a slump and was playing well down the stretch when he suffered the hand injury. Gomez still has some rough edges, but his raw talent and desire to succeed are evident, even if he has to be benched now and then to get his attention. The Devils lack serious size up the middle with the departures of Jason Arnott and Bobby Holik. Gomez will get more playing time but the going will be tougher. He was a restricted free agent during the off-season.

PROJECTION

With Lemieux and Mogilny gone, Gomez never found chemistry with any linemates last season. He needs to take a big step in maturity this season and take his place among team leaders. If he does, he should score 60 points, with a heavy emphasis on assists.

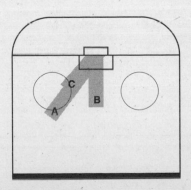

JAMIE LANGENBRUNNER

Yrs. of NHL service: 7
Born: Duluth, Minn.; July 24, 1975
Position: right wing
Height: 6-1
Weight: 200
Uniform no.: 15
Shoots: right

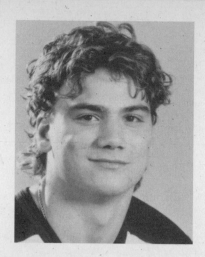

Career statistics:

GP	G	A	TP	PIM
446	93	148	241	384

1998-1999 statistics:

GP	G	A	TP	+/-	PIM	PP	SH	GW	GT	S	PCT
75	12	33	45	+10	62	4	0	1	0	145	8.3

1999-2000 statistics:

GP	G	A	TP	+/-	PIM	PP	SH	GW	GT	S	PCT
65	18	21	39	+16	68	4	2	6	0	153	11.8

2000-2001 statistics:

GP	G	A	TP	+/-	PIM	PP	SH	GW	GT	S	PCT
53	12	18	30	+4	57	3	2	4	0	104	11.5

2001-2002 statistics:

GP	G	A	TP	+/-	PIM	PP	SH	GW	GT	S	PCT
82	13	19	32	-9	77	0	1	4	0	163	8.0

LAST SEASON

Acquired from Dallas on March 19, 2002, with Joe Nieuwendyk for Jason Arnott, Randy McKay and a first-round draft pick in 2002. One of three Devils to appear in all 82 games.

THE FINESSE GAME

An average skater, Langenbrunner won't be coming in with speed and driving a shot off the wing. He is not dynamic at all. But he does have a strong short game; his offence is generated within 15 to 20 feet of the net and he has a quick release on his shot. Any deficiencies he may have are offset by his desire to compete and succeed.

Langenbrunner is a plumber, but one who is talented enough to play with the likes of Joe Nieuwendyk. Nieuwendyk's creativity has also helped Langenbrunner's awareness that a pass may come at any time, and that a scoring chance may evolve at any moment. He is an aggressive forechecker who creates turnovers for his linemates.

Langenbrunner has very good hand skills. He is intelligent and poised with the puck, and can play as a centre or right wing, though his style of play makes him more suitable as a winger. He has good hockey vision and can pick his spots for shots. He is also a smart passer on either his forehand or backhand.

THE PHYSICAL GAME

Langenbrunner plays an intense game, bigger than his size allows. He will wear down physically. Last season he managed to stay intact, but that isn't always the case, and he did get banged up in the playoffs. He competes hard in the hard areas of the ice, to either get a puck or get himself into a space to get the puck. He lacks the size to be a power forward, but he is one of the gritty types who are annoying to play against. He won't just hang on the perimeter and won't back down — he'll even try to stir things up.

THE INTANGIBLES

Langenbrunner is one of the game's most significant unsung heroes, not just for his talent but for his smarts, his energy and his attitude. The Devils' core team is changing, and Langenbrunner can be a significant part of that in his first full season in New Jersey.

PROJECTION

Langenbrunner fell well short of the 20 goals he should produce. He will see increased ice time and should hit that mark in a second-line role.

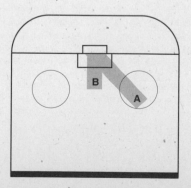

JOHN MADDEN

Yrs. of NHL service: 3
Born: Barrie, Ont.; May 4, 1975
Position: centre
Height: 5-11
Weight: 195
Uniform no.: 11
Shoots: left

Career statistics:

GP	G	A	TP	PIM
240	54	33	87	43

1998-1999 statistics:

GP	G	A	TP	+/-	PIM	PP	SH	GW	GT	S	PCT
4	0	1	1	-2	0	0	0	0	0	4	0.0

1999-2000 statistics:

GP	G	A	TP	+/-	PIM	PP	SH	GW	GT	S	PCT
74	16	9	25	+7	6	0	6	3	0	115	13.9

2000-2001 statistics:

GP	G	A	TP	+/-	PIM	PP	SH	GW	GT	S	PCT
80	23	15	38	+24	12	0	3	4	1	163	14.1

2001-2002 statistics:

GP	G	A	TP	+/-	PIM	PP	SH	GW	GT	S	PCT
82	15	8	23	+6	25	0	0	2	1	170	8.8

LAST SEASON

One of three Devils to appear in all 82 games.

THE FINESSE GAME

Madden was +24 with 23 goals (two shorthanded) when he won the 2001 Selke Trophy. He went to +6 and 15 goals (no shorties) last season.

Madden doesn't have a lot of finesse. His goals come through hard work and his quick burst of speed. Madden's acceleration is exceptional in his first few strides. He can also stop and change direction and put on another skating burst. He is an aggressive forechecker. When he kills penalties, which he does often and well, he puts the heat on the point men and knocks down a lot of point-to-point passes.

Madden lacks creativity and doesn't have a great scoring touch.

Madden needs to improve his work on face-offs. He works hard at it, but his hands just aren't quick enough.

THE PHYSICAL GAME

Madden is a blocky, stocky guy. On the short side, he can be outmuscled by bigger opposing forwards, which is why Bobby Holik often drew the top checking assignments against other teams' No. 1 centres like Eric Lindros. Holik is gone now, and Madden will be tested in that role — maybe even against Holik himself.

Madden plays with an edge. He is always yapping and getting players to retaliate, but he has to guard against taking bad penalties himself.

THE INTANGIBLES

Madden put a lot of pressure on himself to duplicate his Selke Trophy season, and it looked like he was trying too hard. He is often his own worst enemy because he is so critical of his own play.

PROJECTION

A checking centre who can produce 15-20 goals a season is worth his weight in shorthanded goals.

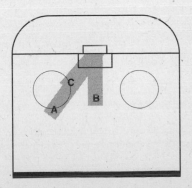

SCOTT NIEDERMAYER

Yrs. of NHL service: 10
Born: Edmonton, Alta.; Aug. 31, 1973
Position: right defence
Height: 6-1
Weight: 200
Uniform no.: 27
Shoots: left

Career statistics:

GP	G	A	TP	PIM
730	87	296	383	372

1998-1999 statistics:

GP	G	A	TP	+/-	PIM	PP	SH	GW	GT	S	PCT
72	11	35	46	+16	26	1	1	3	0	161	6.8

1999-2000 statistics:

GP	G	A	TP	+/-	PIM	PP	SH	GW	GT	S	PCT
71	7	31	38	+19	48	1	0	0	0	109	6.4

2000-2001 statistics:

GP	G	A	TP	+/-	PIM	PP	SH	GW	GT	S	PCT
57	6	29	35	+14	22	1	0	5	0	87	6.9

2001-2002 statistics:

GP	G	A	TP	+/-	PIM	PP	SH	GW	GT	S	PCT
76	11	22	33	+12	30	2	0	6	0	129	8.5

LAST SEASON

Second among team defencemen in points. Tied for second on team in game-winning goals. Missed three games due to neck injury. Missed two games with back injury. Missed one game due to coach's decision.

THE FINESSE GAME

Niedermayer is an exceptional skater, one of the best-skating defencemen in the NHL. He has it all: speed, balance, agility, mobility, lateral movement and strength. Plus he has an unbelievable edge for turns and eluding pursuers. Yet Niedermayer doesn't seem to have the vision the great ones have, or the snaky lateral movement that makes a point shot so danger-ous. The missing component may be more mental than physical. He has nights when he is "on," and he is spectacular. Those nights tend to come against high-profile teams, or in the playoffs, when he is more interested in his surroundings. But he takes a lot of nights off, when the challenge fails to excite him.

Those lapses have prevented Niedermayer from joining the ranks of the league's elite "offencemen." While it's true he also has had to heel to the Devils' defensive system, which may have cut into his point production, Niedermayer doesn't have the fire or the flair of a Paul Coffey or Brian Leetch. It's time to stop faulting him for that.

Niedermayer is a far better defensive player than many of the other top scorers at his position. Even when he makes a mistake in the offensive zone, he can get back so quickly his partner is seldom outnumbered. He is simply one of the best two-way defencemen in the game...when he chooses to be.

THE PHYSICAL GAME

An underrated body checker because of the focus on the glitzier aspects of his game, Niedermayer has continued to improve his strength and is a willing, if not vicious, hitter. Niedermayer's skating ability helps him tremendously, giving more impetus to his open-ice checks. He makes rub-outs along the wall. He would rather be in open ice, but will pay the price in the trenches. He knows the defensive game well. He has a quiet toughness and won't be intimidated, although it took him time to recover mentally and physically from the concussion caused by Tie Domi's cheap-shot elbow in the 2001 playoffs.

THE INTANGIBLES

Niedermayer had a terrible start to the season, and while he never used it as an excuse, it's possible the concussion he suffered in the 2001 playoffs had some lingering effects. He was a far better player in the last quarter of the season, and turned it on when it mattered most — in the playoffs.

PROJECTION

Niedermayer continues to mature into an excellent all-round defenceman, but he will not be among the league's leading defenceman scorers. His range is around 40 points.

JOE NIEUWENDYK

Yrs. of NHL service: 15
Born: Oshawa, Ont.; Sept. 10, 1966
Position: centre
Height: 6 1
Weight: 205
Uniform no.: 25
Shoots: left

Career statistics:

GP	G	A	TP	PIM
1033	494	473	967	545

1998-1999 statistics:

GP	G	A	TP	+/-	PIM	PP	SH	GW	GT	S	PCT
67	28	27	55	+11	34	8	0	8	1	157	17.8

1999-2000 statistics:

GP	G	A	TP	+/-	PIM	PP	SH	GW	GT	S	PCT
48	15	19	34	-1	26	7	0	2	0	110	13.6

2000-2001 statistics:

GP	G	A	TP	+/-	PIM	PP	SH	GW	GT	S	PCT
69	29	23	52	+5	30	12	0	4	0	166	17.5

2001-2002 statistics:

GP	G	A	TP	+/-	PIM	PP	SH	GW	GT	S	PCT
81	25	33	58	0	22	6	0	6	1	189	13.2

LAST SEASON

Acquired from Dallas on March 19, 2002, with Jamie Langenbrunner for Jason Arnott, Randy McKay and a first-round draft pick in 2002. Second on team in points and shooting percentage. Tied for second on team in goals, power-play goals and game-winning goals. Missed one game with flu.

THE FINESSE GAME

Hands down, Nieuwendyk has the best hands in the NHL for tipping pucks in front of the net. This skill is priceless on power plays. He has fantastic hand-eye coordination; he not only gets his blade on the puck, he acts as if he knows where he's directing it. He also has a long, powerful reach for snaring loose pucks around the crease. Those same hand skills make Nieuwendyk one of the league's best in the face-off department. He was fourth in the NHL on draws last season (58.82 per cent).

He is aggressive, tough and aware around the net. He can finish or make a play down low. He has the vision, poise and hand skills to make neat little passes through traffic. He's a better playmaker than finisher, but he never doubts that he will convert his chances. He has good anticipation and uses his long stick to break up passes.

One of his best moves comes on the rush, when Nieuwendyk cuts wide to the right-wing boards then pulls the puck to his forehand for a dangerous shot.

THE PHYSICAL GAME

Nieuwendyk does not initiate, but he will take punishment around the net and stand his ground. He won't be intimidated — but he won't scare anyone, either. Last season was one of his healthiest in several years, and his 81 games played marked a career high.

THE INTANGIBLES

Nieuwendyk needs to play with grinding, energy wingers (like Langenbrunner, who came along with him in the deal from the Stars) to do the dirty work he is physically incapable of doing. Teammates need to be alert enough to polish off a pass that can come anytime, from anywhere. Nieuwendyk was nearly a point a game player after the trade to New Jersey (2 9 11 in 14 games), but he had a disappointing playoffs.

PROJECTION

Losing Bobby Holik to free agency has weakened the Devils up the middle and places more pressure on Nieuwendyk. Expect his numbers to decline.

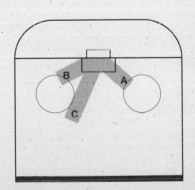

JAY PANDOLFO

Yrs. of NHL service: 4
Born: Winchester, Mass.; Dec. 27, 1974
Position: left wing
Height: 6-1
Weight: 190
Uniform no.: 20
Shoots: left

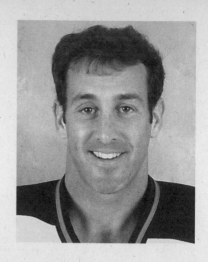

Career statistics:

GP	G	A	TP	PIM
338	36	54	90	55

1998-1999 statistics:

GP	G	A	TP	+/-	PIM	PP	SH	GW	GT	S	PCT
70	14	13	27	+3	10	1	1	4	0	100	14.0

1999-2000 statistics:

GP	G	A	TP	+/-	PIM	PP	SH	GW	GT	S	PCT
71	7	8	15	0	4	0	0	0	0	86	8.1

2000-2001 statistics:

GP	G	A	TP	+/-	PIM	PP	SH	GW	GT	S	PCT
63	4	12	16	+3	16	0	0	0	0	57	7.0

2001-2002 statistics:

GP	G	A	TP	+/-	PIM	PP	SH	GW	GT	S	PCT
65	4	10	14	+12	15	0	1	0	0	72	5.6

PROJECTION

He's the glue, not the glitter. Pandolfo has never scored more than 27 points in an NHL season. We doubt he's going to improve on that much.

LAST SEASON

Missed 10 games with hip injury. Missed six games with rib injury.

THE FINESSE GAME

It's hard to believe Pandolfo led the Hockey East League in goals when he played for Boston University back in 1995-96. Pandolfo is like Brian Rolston, but with worse hands.

Of course, there was a time when the speedy Rolston looked like he would never develop into more than a 20-goal scorer, and he popped home 31 for Boston this season. So maybe the same bolt of lightning will strike Pandolfo some day.

For the time being, though, it looks like Pandolfo is not going to break his defensive mould. He is a terrific penalty killer, usually working in tandem with 2001 Selke Trophy winner John Madden. Pandolfo has good speed — both in short bursts and on the long straightaway — to create shorthanded chances, but he just can't finish.

THE PHYSICAL GAME

Pandolfo always gets involved. He has a little bit of an edge, but mostly it's his willingness to pay the price to help his team win that has Pandolfo bruised and bloodied much of the season.

THE INTANGIBLES

Pandolfo does a lot of the little things to help a team win, especially defensively, and he's a solid team guy.

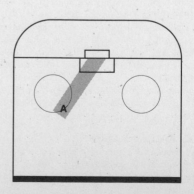

BRIAN RAFALSKI

Yrs. of NHL service: 3
Born: Dearborn, MI; Sept. 28, 1973
Position: right defence
Height: 5-9
Weight: 195
Uniform no.: 28
Shoots: right

Career statistics:

GP	G	A	TP	PIM
229	21	110	131	72

1999-2000 statistics:

GP	G	A	TP	+/-	PIM	PP	SH	GW	GT	S	PCT
75	5	27	32	+21	28	1	0	1	0	128	3.9

2000-2001 statistics:

GP	G	A	TP	+/-	PIM	PP	SH	GW	GT	S	PCT
78	9	43	52	+36	26	6	0	1	1	142	6.3

2001-2002 statistics:

GP	G	A	TP	+/-	PIM	PP	SH	GW	GT	S	PCT
76	7	40	47	+15	18	2	0	4	1	125	5.6

LAST SEASON

Led team is assists. Led team defencemen in point for second consecutive season. Eighth among NHL defencemen in points. Tied for second on team in plus-minus. Missed one game with groin injury. Missed four games with knee injury. Missed one game due to coach's decision.

THE FINESSE GAME

Rafalski's greatest asset is his ability to get the puck out of the zone. It sounds so simple, but watch other teams' defences struggle with clearing the puck and you'll appreciate what Rafalski can do by skating the puck out of danger, making a smart pass or just hanging it off the boards. He doesn't look for the highlight play. He makes the smart one, which usually turns into a highlight.

Rafalski is an excellent skater. He's not quite in the class of teammate Scott Niedermayer, but he is darned close, and he allows the Devils the luxury of placing one smooth-skating, puckhandling defenceman with a slower, physical partner. In Rafalski's case, that is usually captain Scott Stevens, and Stevens benefits as much from Rafalski's presence as Rafalski does in playing alongside one of the league's premier defensive defencemen.

He has the speed and the hands to get involved in the attack, and does so willingly. Knowing he has Stevens as a backup, Rafalski is confident when he pinches or joins the rush. He has a good shot from the point and sees significant power-play time.

THE PHYSICAL GAME

The downside to being Stevens's partner is that teams want to stay away from the right wing on the attack (Stevens plays left defence) and will overload on the left side, meaning Rafalski has to fight more than his share of physical battles. He is small and makes the best use of his finesse skills in a defensive mode, but he will also get his body in the way. He is durable and strong on his skates. Rafalski is very thick through his upper body and shoulders, so his small appearance can be deceptive.

THE INTANGIBLES

Rafalski is intelligent, poised and utterly unflappable. His panic point is minuscule. Along with Stevens, he routinely handles matchups against other teams' best forwards and relishes the assignments. He is confident in his ability to tackle a challenge and is usually at his peak at crunch time.

PROJECTION

Despite an overall down season for the Devils, Rafalski threatened the 50-point mark and should do so again.

SCOTT STEVENS

Yrs. of NHL service: 20
Born: Kitchener, Ont.; Apr. 1, 1964
Position: left defence
Height: 6-1
Weight: 215
Uniform no.: 4
Shoots: left

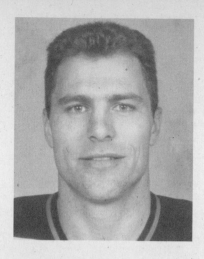

Career statistics:

GP	G	A	TP	PIM
1516	189	687	876	2722

1998-1999 statistics:

GP	G	A	TP	+/-	PIM	PP	SH	GW	GT	S	PCT
75	5	22	27	+29	64	0	0	1	0	111	4.5

1999-2000 statistics:

GP	G	A	TP	+/-	PIM	PP	SH	GW	GT	S	PCT
78	8	21	29	+30	103	0	1	1	0	133	6.0

2000-2001 statistics:

GP	G	A	TP	+/-	PIM	PP	SH	GW	GT	S	PCT
81	9	22	31	+40	71	3	0	2	0	171	5.3

2001-2002 statistics:

GP	G	A	TP	+/-	PIM	PP	SH	GW	GT	S	PCT
82	1	16	17	+15	44	0	0	1	0	121	0.8

LAST SEASON

One of three Devils to appear in all 82 games.

THE FINESSE GAME

Stevens has a tremendous work ethic that more than makes up for some of his shortcomings (most of those are sins of commission rather than omission). He is a bear on penalty killing because he just won't quit, and a fearless shot-blocker. Stevens occasionally gets suckered into chasing the puck carrier behind the net at inopportune moments.

Stevens is secure and strong in his skating, capable both forwards and backwards and with good lateral mobility. He is not overly nimble, though, and more and more players on the rush are able to beat him one-on=one in open ice. He has a tendency to over-handle the puck in the defensive zone. Instead of quickly banging the puck off the boards to clear the zone, it seems to take him an unusual amount of time to get the puck teed up, and it's often kept in by the attacking team. Stevens then digs in twice as hard to win the puck back, but he often creates more work for himself.

Opponents used to delight in goading a young, immature Stevens into taking bad penalties. The tactic can still be effective, but only occasionally. Stevens is a smart player who recognizes the challenges presented to him every night and rarely fails to meet them. He works best paired with a mobile partner. Brian Rafalski is an especially complementary player, although Stevens also meshes well with Scott Niedermayer.

THE PHYSICAL GAME

Stevens is one of the most punishing open-ice hitters. He has the skating ability to line up the puck carrier, and the size and strength to explode on impact.

Stevens is also effective in small spaces. He shovels most opponents out from in front of the net and crunches them along the boards. He prides himself on his conditioning and can handle a lot of minutes, although the Devils are wise not to overuse him. Amazing turnaround stat for Stevens last season: he was -11 on December 30 but finished the season +15.

THE INTANGIBLES

Stevens plays in as many games as possible, even when the Devils have healthy leads in the standings. Now that he is 38 — he will be a remarkably fit 39 by the 2003 playoffs — he needs to take the occasional breather. Stevens isn't a rah-rah, speechmaking kind of guy, but leads by example. He works harder than almost anyone on the team in practice. Attention to nutrition and fitness has helped Stevens maintain his peak, but the clock eventually winds down for everyone, and Stevens's time is coming.

PROJECTION

Stevens is all defence now. Don't expect his point totals to be much above 20.

TURNER STEVENSON

Yrs. of NHL service: 8
Born: Prince George, B.C.; May 18, 1972
Position: right wing
Height: 6-3
Weight: 225
Uniform no.: 24
Shoots: right

Career statistics:

GP	G	A	TP	PIM
475	53	86	139	733

1998-1999 statistics:

GP	G	A	TP	+/-	PIM	PP	SH	GW	GT	S	PCT
69	10	17	27	+6	88	0	0	2	1	102	9.8

1999-2000 statistics:

GP	G	A	TP	+/-	PIM	PP	SH	GW	GT	S	PCT
64	8	13	21	-1	61	0	0	2	0	94	8.5

2000-2001 statistics:

GP	G	A	TP	+/-	PIM	PP	SH	GW	GT	S	PCT
69	8	18	26	+11	97	2	0	1	1	92	8.7

2001-2002 statistics:

GP	G	A	TP	+/-	PIM	PP	SH	GW	GT	S	PCT
21	0	2	2	-3	25	0	0	0	0	33	0.0

LAST SEASON

Missed 61 games due to knee injury and surgery.

THE FINESSE GAME

Effort is never an issue, because Stevenson would love to be more of a contributor. He doesn't shoot enough and has to take the puck to the net with more authority. He is strong along the offensive boards, especially below the goal line. When he gets into a situation, he always makes the opposition player pay the price. The Devils sometimes give him some power-play time when they need muscle in front of the net.

Stevenson's main flaw is his lack of foot speed, though he is a fair skater for his size. He has a good, long stride and is balanced and agile. Stevenson has slow hand speed to go along with his slow foot speed.

Stevenson has a variety of shots and uses all of them with power and accuracy, but his release needs improvement. He will follow the puck to the net and not give up on shots. He is also a decent passer and possesses some vision and creativity. He plays a short power game.

THE PHYSICAL GAME

Stevenson isn't tall but he is solidly built and thick through his trunk. He can lay on some serious hits. It's too bad he doesn't have more of a mean streak. He seems to have no idea what kind of physical presence he could add to the team on a consistent basis.

THE INTANGIBLES

Stevenson was more a rumour than a factor last year because of his knee injury. With Randy McKay gone, the Devils could use Stevenson to step into his role, although it's unlikely Stevenson will ever develop the scoring touch McKay did. Stevenson adds quiet toughness and leadership when he is healthy enough to contribute. He can give a team an honest 8 to 12 minutes a night as a fourth-liner, and be a positive influence in the room.

PROJECTION

Stevenson is a role player who can contribute some energy shifts, but his top end is 10 to 12 goals.

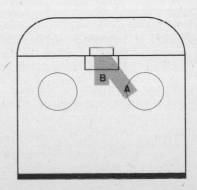

OLEG TVERDOVSKY

Yrs. of NHL service: 8
Born: Donetsk, Ukraine; May 18, 1976
Position: left defence
Height: 6-0
Weight: 200
Uniform no.: 10
Shoots: left

Career statistics:

GP	G	A	TP	PIM
565	69	208	277	222

1998-1999 statistics:

GP	G	A	TP	+/-	PIM	PP	SH	GW	GT	S	PCT
82	7	18	25	+11	32	2	0	2	0	117	6.0

1999-2000 statistics:

GP	G	A	TP	+/-	PIM	PP	SH	GW	GT	S	PCT
82	15	36	51	+5	30	5	0	5	0	153	9.8

2000-2001 statistics:

GP	G	A	TP	+/-	PIM	PP	SH	GW	GT	S	PCT
82	14	39	53	-11	32	8	0	3	2	188	7.4

2001-2002 statistics:

GP	G	A	TP	+/-	PIM	PP	SH	GW	GT	S	PCT
73	6	26	32	0	31	2	0	1	0	147	4.1

LAST SEASON

Acquired from Anaheim on July 6, 2002, with Jeff Friesen and Maxim Balmochnykh for Petr Sykora, Mike Commodore, J-F Damphousse and Igor Pohanka. Led Ducks defencemen in points for third consecutive season. Tied for second on Ducks in assists. Missed nine games with groin injury. Injury stopped his ironman streak at 363 games (at the time, second among active players in the league after Tony Amonte).

THE FINESSE GAME

Tverdovsky has Brian Leetch potential. Now that he's playing for a solid team for the first time in his eight-year NHL career, we may get to see Tverdovsky reach his peak. He's an explosive skater and he can carry the puck at high tempo. He works the point on the power play, utilizing a nice lateral slide along the blueline, and he kills penalties. He also sees his options and makes his decisions at lightning speed.

Tverdovsky is an impressive talent who passes the puck well and shoots bullets. He is clearly an "offenceman," but he has worked at improving his decision-making process. His defensive play is a lot less high-risk than it was his first few years in the league. It's an impressive development, because Tverdovsky has not had a veteran defenceman to mentor him along. Imagine what will happen when he gets to play alongside Scott Stevens.

He can still get lazy defensively, casually moving the puck around the wall or banging it off the glass. He prefers to grab the puck and go, or look for a streaking forward. He's among the best in the league

at the headman pass and he works exceptionally well in tandem with his speedy winger.

THE PHYSICAL GAME

Some of Tverdovsky's defensive weaknesses occur because he sometimes plays the puck instead of the man, or tries to poke-check without backing it up with his body. Physically, when he makes the right decision, he can eliminate the man, and he looks to be improving in this area by at least tying up his man.

He loves to play and is enthusiastic, durable and extremely competitive.

THE INTANGIBLES

If Tverdovsky had started his career with a team like the Devils, he might have been All-Star material. He will be part of a strong defence corps that has a good mix of steady, stay-at-home types who can anchor the riskier likes of Tverdovsky, Scott Niedermayer and Brian Rafalski.

PROJECTION

Expect a rejuvenated Tverdovsky, lots of first-unit power-play time, and a return to 50 points.

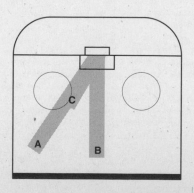

COLIN WHITE

Yrs. of NHL service: 2
Born: New Glasgow, N.S.; Dec. 12, 1977
Position: left defence
Height: 6-4
Weight: 210
Uniform no.: 5
Shoots: left

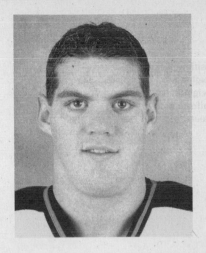

Career statistics:

GP	G	A	TP	PIM
176	5	23	28	328

1999-2000 statistics:

GP	G	A	TP	+/-	PIM	PP	SH	GW	GT	S	PCT
21	2	1	3	+3	40	0	0	1	0	29	6.9

2000-2001 statistics:

GP	G	A	TP	+/-	PIM	PP	SH	GW	GT	S	PCT
82	1	19	20	+32	155	0	0	1	0	114	0.9

2001-2002 statistics:

GP	G	A	TP	+/-	PIM	PP	SH	GW	GT	S	PCT
73	2	3	5	+6	133	0	0	0	0	81	2.5

LAST SEASON

Second NHL season. Led team in penalty minutes. Missed seven games with neck injuries. Missed one game due to personal reasons. Missed one game due to coach's decision.

THE FINESSE GAME

White isn't a very fast skater, but he has a long stride and is balanced. He has learned to play within his limits, which tends to keep him out of trouble. He can't go chasing better skaters around, nor can he make risky pinches. There are too many nights when it looks like White isn't learning from his mistakes.

White is a fearsome bodychecker. He has excellent size, which he uses to his full advantage. He is not agile enough to throw open-ice body bombs like teammate Scott Stevens, but along the wall and in front of the net he is punishing. He blocks shots and was used by the Devils on some penalty kills when their regulars needed a break.

White is a good passer who moves the puck quickly. He does not make many low-percentage plays. He has obviously been well-schooled in the Devils' system and uses the boards and his partner well.

White has a decent shot from the point, although he is not very slick with the puck along the blueline and makes some bad-percentage decisions that result in blocked shots or intercepted passes.

THE PHYSICAL GAME

An able and willing fighter, White is overly quick to jump to the aid of a teammate when no help is needed and the Devils have drawn a penalty, or to initiate or retaliate at any perceived slight. This is a diplomatic way of saying White is capable of taking some of the dumbest penalties on the team. He is easy to goad off

his game. White needs to learn that the threat of him snapping is more effective than actually going postal.

THE INTANGIBLES

White counts Dave Manson and Wendel Clark as his idols, and he plays with the toughness and the mean streak those two athletes possessed. He just needs to get smarter.

PROJECTION

White will be given every chance to regain his spot among the team's top four defencemen. He is poised to take over the role of the aging Ken Daneyko, but White needs to develop more consistency.

ANDREI ZYUZIN

Yrs. of NHL service: 5
Born: Ufa, Russia; Jan. 21, 1978
Position: left defence
Height: 6-1
Weight: 210
Uniform no.: 7
Shoots: left

Career statistics:

GP	G	A	TP	PIM
226	16	37	53	244

1998-1999 statistics:

GP	G	A	TP	+/-	PIM	PP	SH	GW	GT	S	PCT
25	3	1	4	+5	38	2	0	0	0	44	6.8

1999-2000 statistics:

GP	G	A	TP	+/-	PIM	PP	SH	GW	GT	S	PCT
34	2	9	11	-11	33	0	0	0	0	47	4.3

2000-2001 statistics:

GP	G	A	TP	+/-	PIM	PP	SH	GW	GT	S	PCT
64	4	16	20	-8	76	2	1	1	1	92	4.3

2001-2002 statistics:

GP	G	A	TP	+/-	PIM	PP	SH	GW	GT	S	PCT
47	1	4	5	-5	31	1	0	0	0	61	1.6

LAST SEASON

Acquired from Tampa Bay on November 9, 2001, for Josef Boumedienne, Sascha Go, and the rights to Anton But. Missed four games with shoulder injury. Missed three games with bruised foot. Missed 25 games due to coach's decision.

THE FINESSE GAME

Zyuzin is an offensive-minded defenceman, with the kind of speed and anticipation that should prevent him from being too much of a liability on defence. He could well prove to be the kind of player who can dictate the tempo of a game, or break it wide open with one end-to-end rush, like Brian Leetch. At the moment, he doesn't seem to possess the exceptional lateral movement along the blueline that sets Leetch apart from most of his NHL brethren, but Zyuzin has a big upside.

He doesn't take his offensive chances blindly; he knows what the score is. He takes a chance when his team needs a goal. And when he needs to stay back on defence, he will. He will also get burned once in awhile, but he makes smart choices.

The young Russian is a fast skater with quick acceleration and balance. He handles the puck well at a high pace and can either pass or shoot. He's a smart playmaker, but one who will not pass up a golden scoring opportunity. He has a hard point shot and will become a good power-play quarterback.

THE PHYSICAL GAME

Zyuzin is not a physical player. He has adequate size but will need a streak of Chris Chelios-like aggressiveness to make the best use of his ability. He does have a desire to excel, and if it means stepping up his game physically, he will probably be able to make that transition. He plays with a lot of energy.

THE INTANGIBLES

Zyuzin could not have asked for a better situation than to be traded to a strong defensive team with a respected Russian assistant coach (Hall-of-Famer Slava Fetisov). Fetisov was fired before the season was out and Zyuzin proved to be a high-risk disaster. The potential is still there, and at least Zyuzin will get a fresh start with new coach Pat Burns.

PROJECTION

Zyuzin will have to earn his ice time on a veteran team, but the Devils' off-season acquisition of Oleg Tverdovsky may mean Zyuzin's New Jersey days are numbered. He should score 25 points in a full-time role, if he gets one.

NEW YORK ISLANDERS

Players' Statistics 2001-2002

POS.	NO.	PLAYER	GP	G	A	PTS	+/-	PIM	PP	SH	GW	GT	S	PCT
C	79	ALEXEI YASHIN	78	32	43	75	-3	25	15		5		239	13.4
R	37	MARK PARRISH	78	30	30	60	10	32	9	1	6		162	18.5
C	27	MICHAEL PECA	80	25	35	60	19	62	3	6	5	1	168	14.9
C	17	SHAWN BATES	71	17	35	52	18	30	1	4	4	1	150	11.3
R	21	MARIUSZ CZERKAWSKI	82	22	29	51	-8	48	6		6	1	169	13.0
L	15	BRAD ISBISTER	79	17	21	38	1	113	4		2		142	12.0
L	12	OLEG KVASHA	71	13	25	38	-4	80	2		3		119	10.9
D	4	ROMAN HAMRLIK	70	11	26	37	7	78	4	1	1		169	6.5
D	3	ADRIAN AUCOIN	81	12	22	34	23	62	7		1		232	5.2
D	29	KENNY JONSSON	76	10	22	32	15	26	2	1			107	9.4
C	38	DAVE SCATCHARD	80	12	15	27	-4	111	3	1	4		117	10.3
C	11	KIP MILLER	37	7	17	24	2	6	2		1		52	13.5
C	13	CLAUDE LAPOINTE	80	9	12	21	-9	60	3				74	12.2
D	8	DICK TARNSTROM	62	3	16	19	-12	38				1	59	5.1
C	55	JASON BLAKE	82	8	10	18	-11	36			1		136	5.9
L	10	MATS LINDGREN	59	3	12	15	0	16			1		35	8.6
D	28	DARREN VAN IMPE	67	3	8	11	12	59	2		1		60	5.0
D	33	ERIC CAIRNS	74	2	5	7	-2	176			1		34	5.9
R	20	STEVE WEBB	60	2	4	6	0	104					31	6.4
D	45	MARKO KIPRUSOFF	27		6	6	0	4					17	
D	24	*RADEK MARTINEK	23	1	4	5	5	16			1		25	4.0
R	25	JURAJ KOLNIK	7	2		2	-2		1				10	20.0
D	6	KEN SUTTON	21		2	2	-5	8					22	
D	36	EVGENY KOROLEV	17		2	2	0	6					9	
D	2	BRANISLAV MEZEI	24		2	2	2	12					4	
L	16	*RAFFI TORRES	14		1	1	2	6					9	
R	14	ALEXANDER KHARITONOV	5				-1	4					5	
R	18	JIM CUMMINS	12				-6	31					3	
D	41	RAYMOND GIROUX	2				-1	2					2	
D	7	KEVIN HALLER	1				-1	2					2	
C	56	JASON PODOLLAN	1				0	2					1	
R	46	MARKO TUOMAINEN	1				-1							
L	51	DAVE ROCHE	1				0							
D	39	RAY SCHULTZ	2				-1	5						
C	28	JASON KROG	2				0							
G	30	GARTH SNOW	25				0	14						
G	35	CHRIS OSGOOD	66				0	10						
G	1	RICK DIPIETRO					0							

GP = games played; G = goals; A = assists; PTS = points; +/- = goals-for minus goals-against while player is on ice; PIM = penalties in minutes; PP = power-play goals; SH = shorthanded goals; GW = game-winning goals; GT = game-tying goals; S = no. of shots; PCT = percentage of goals to shots; * = rookie

ARRON ASHAM

Yrs. of NHL service: 3
Born: Portage La Prairie, Man.; Apr. 13, 1978
Position: right wing
Height: 5-11
Weight: 209
Uniform no.: 45
Shoots: right

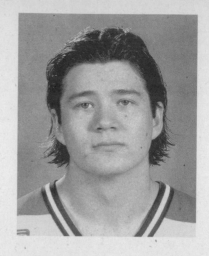

Career statistics:

GP	G	A	TP	PIM
121	11	9	20	138

1998-1999 statistics:

GP	G	A	TP	+/-	PIM	PP	SH	GW	GT	S	PCT
7	0	0	0	-4	0	0	0	0	0	5	0.0

1999-2000 statistics:

GP	G	A	TP	+/-	PIM	PP	SH	GW	GT	S	PCT
33	4	2	6	-7	24	0	1	1	0	29	13.8

2000-2001 statistics:

GP	G	A	TP	+/-	PIM	PP	SH	GW	GT	S	PCT
46	2	3	5	-9	59	0	0	0	0	32	6.3

2001-2002 statistics:

GP	G	A	TP	+/-	PIM	PP	SH	GW	GT	S	PCT
35	5	4	9	+7	55	0	0	0	0	30	16.7

LAST SEASON

Acquired from Montreal on June 22, 2002, with a fifth-round draft pick for Mariusz Czerkawski. Appeared in 24 games with Quebec (AHL), scoring 9-14-23 with 36 PIM. Missed two games due to personal reasons.

THE FINESSE GAME

Asham is a gritty forward who makes space for himself by his willingness to play a fierce game. He isn't big, but he is always willing to fight and lets his opponents know it. He has good hands for either scrapping or scoring.

Although his natural position is centre, Asham is a better right wing. He doesn't see the ice well and isn't a good passer. His job is to disturb the defencemen into making mistakes and then make a beeline for the net for rebounds and screens. He is strong along the boards.

Asham has terrific hockey sense and the skating speed to compete at the NHL level. He is usually in the right place at the right time.

THE PHYSICAL GAME

He doesn't just throw himself about wildly: Asham knows when to hit and when to take the edge off. He plays a smart forechecking game and doesn't go head-hunting. Experience is only going to make him a more dangerous and more valuable role player.

THE INTANGIBLES

Asham reminds some onlookers of a young Mike Keane. He was inspired by playing with a former Hab, Shayne Corson, whose combination of toughness and scoring touch make him the perfect role model for Asham. Asham lacks Corson's size, but is undeterred by the disadvantage in any given match-up. The Islanders recognized their need for additional toughness after losing a rugged series with Toronto, and Asham should fill that need.

PROJECTION

Asham could provide 15 goals along with a high-energy game.

ADRIAN AUCOIN

Yrs. of NHL service: 7
Born: Ottawa, Ont.; July 3, 1973
Position: right defence
Height: 6-2
Weight: 210
Uniform no.: 3
Shoots: right

Career statistics:

GP	G	A	TP	PIM
448	62	104	166	332

1998-1999 statistics:

GP	G	A	TP	+/-	PIM	PP	SH	GW	GT	S	PCT
82	23	11	34	-14	77	18	2	3	1	174	13.2

1999-2000 statistics:

GP	G	A	TP	+/-	PIM	PP	SH	GW	GT	S	PCT
57	10	14	24	+7	30	4	0	1	0	126	7.9

2000-2001 statistics:

GP	G	A	TP	+/-	PIM	PP	SH	GW	GT	S	PCT
73	4	24	28	+5	45	2	0	0	0	159	2.5

2001-2002 statistics:

GP	G	A	TP	+/-	PIM	PP	SH	GW	GT	S	PCT
81	12	22	34	+23	62	7	0	1	0	232	5.2

LAST SEASON

Led team in plus-minus. Led team defencemen in scoring. Second on team in shots. Third on team in power-play goals. Missed one game with heel injury.

THE FINESSE GAME

Aucoin is a mobile, agile skater who moves well with the puck. He doesn't have breakaway speed, but he jumps alertly into the play. On the power play, he smartly switches off with a forward to cut in deep, and he has good hands for shots in-tight. He also has a good point shot and is very intelligent with his shot selection.

Once considered strictly an offensive defencemen, Aucoin has worked hard to improve the defensive side of his game. He puts his finesse skills to great use as a defender. He's among the league's best one-on-one in open ice. Even a shifty puck carrier like Pavel Bure has trouble getting past Aucoin on a mano-a-mano rush. Aucoin doesn't fall for the deke, he keeps his feet moving and his body aligned, and simply pokes the puck away. He makes it look so easy against the game's elite forwards.

Aucoin developed into the Islanders' most valuable weapon on the power play. He is a very good point man, with lateral movement along the blueline and a quick, accurate one-timer. He also kills penalties.

THE PHYSICAL GAME

Aucoin is a strong, good-sized defenceman who often plays smaller. Aucoin isn't a big hitter, and along the board may fail to stick and pin his man. He has no mean streak to speak of; opponents know he can be pushed around and they take advantage of that. What Aucoin does do well is position his body effectively to cut down on passing lanes in the defensive zone.

Aucoin is in top physical condition and can handle a lot of minutes (he was second in the league to Chris Pronger with an average of 28:53 minutes per game). Paired most often with Kenny Jonsson, Aucoin often handled duties against the other team's top line.

THE INTANGIBLES

Aucoin logged a mind-boggling 40:13 of ice time in a February 2002 game against Florida. Let's just say the Isles know how to get their money's worth out of a player. The workload probably took its toll on Aucoin late in the season and his offence suffered. Just because Aucoin can handle those excessive minutes doesn't mean he should.

PROJECTION

We called for 30 points for Aucoin last season, and he should be in the 30-40 range again.

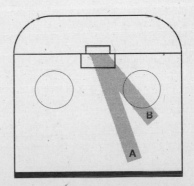

ERIC CAIRNS

Yrs. of NHL service: 6
Born: Oakville, Ont.; June 27, 1974
Position: left defence
Height: 6-6
Weight: 230
Uniform no.: 33
Shoots: left

Career statistics:

GP	G	A	TP	PIM
274	6	21	27	740

1998-1999 statistics:

GP	G	A	TP	+/-	PIM	PP	SH	GW	GT	S	PCT
9	0	3	3	+1	23	0	0	0	0	2	0.0

1999-2000 statistics:

GP	G	A	TP	+/-	PIM	PP	SH	GW	GT	S	PCT
67	2	7	9	-5	196	0	0	0	0	55	3.6

2000-2001 statistics:

GP	G	A	TP	+/-	PIM	PP	SH	GW	GT	S	PCT
45	2	2	4	-18	106	0	0	0	0	21	9.5

2001-2002 statistics:

GP	G	A	TP	+/-	PIM	PP	SH	GW	GT	S	PCT
74	2	5	7	-2	176	0	0	1	0	34	5.9

LAST SEASON

Led team in penalty minutes. Missed five games with strained oblique muscle. Missed one game with rib injury. Missed two games due to NHL suspension.

THE FINESSE GAME

It is natural to think a player as big as Cairns would be clumsy, but he has some smarts with the puck and enough skill to skate the puck out of the defensive zone. Occasionally he can beat a forechecker, but Cairns knows better than to make a habit of that. He doesn't have great foot speed and can get caught flat-footed.

With the puck, Cairns favours backhand moves that allow him to use his body to shield the puck from defenders. He is content to get the puck deep in the zone and let the forwards do the offensive work, but his point shot is accurate when he elects to use it. Out of his own zone, he makes an accurate outlet pass.

Although not a great skater, Cairns turns pretty smoothly and makes up for any shortcomings in speed by using his size and reach. He may look like someone who can be beaten easily to the outside, but he generally does a nice job of angling a puck carrier to less dangerous ice. Cairns works every off-season to improve his footwork.

THE PHYSICAL GAME

Cairns is a willing fighter and likes playing policeman if any opponent starts taking liberties with his teammates. He likes the big hits and mean rubouts, but does a pretty good job of avoiding the cheap hooking and holding penalties big defencemen always seem to get against smaller, quicker forwards. He has become a legitimate NHL fighter and one who doesn't need to prove himself anymore at every challenge, which means he can concentrate more on actually playing.

THE INTANGIBLES

If injuries hadn't struck him so hard, Cairns' improved game would have been more noticeable. He has become a solid No. 5 defenceman, which appears to be his niche, and the Isles have developed the right depth at that position to let him settle into his role.

PROJECTION

Cairns will never be a star and he isn't going to score much, but he has made himself into a decent NHL defenceman. He's still a project, and he will forever be a player who has to work at his game on a daily basis. His size, strength and reach, sensibly packaged and deployed, are a commodity in the NHL. If he plays his cards right he can have a good career as a dependable stay-at-home, and as a partner for the offensive guy who's going to be up-ice all night.

ROMAN HAMRLIK

Yrs. of NHL service: 10
Born: Gottwaldov, Czech Republic; Apr. 12, 1974
Position: left defence
Height: 6-2
Weight: 215
Uniform no.: 4
Shoots: left

Career statistics:

GP	G	A	TP	PIM
719	101	270	371	830

1998-1999 statistics:

GP	G	A	TP	+/-	PIM	PP	SH	GW	GT	S	PCT
75	8	24	32	+9	70	3	0	0	0	172	4.7

1999-2000 statistics:

GP	G	A	TP	+/-	PIM	PP	SH	GW	GT	S	PCT
80	8	37	45	+1	68	5	0	0	1	180	4.4

2000-2001 statistics:

GP	G	A	TP	+/-	PIM	PP	SH	GW	GT	S	PCT
76	16	30	46	-20	92	5	1	4	0	232	6.9

2001-2002 statistics:

GP	G	A	TP	+/-	PIM	PP	SH	GW	GT	S	PCT
70	11	26	37	+7	78	4	1	1	0	169	6.5

LAST SEASON

Led team defencemen in points for second consecutive season. Tied for third on team in shots. Missed 12 games with knee injuries.

THE FINESSE GAME

Hamrlik is better defensively than some people think, and not as good offensively as some other people think. He has turned into a solid two-way defenceman whose game doesn't have many valleys or peaks.

He can handle marathon ice time and has the desire to dominate a game. He has all the tools. He is a fast, strong skater — forwards and backwards.

A mobile defenceman with a solid shot and good passing skills, Hamrlik is not creative. But he knows how to outsmart and not just overpower attackers. He loves to get involved offensively, despite not having elite skills. He has an excellent shot with a quick release. He could be smarter about taking some velocity off his shot in order to get a less blockable shot through.

Hamrlik has learned to make less risky plays in his own zone. He makes a great first pass out of the zone. Defensively, he runs into problems when he is trying to move the puck out of his zone and when he is forced to handle the puck on his backhand, but that is about the only way the opposition can cope with him.

THE PHYSICAL GAME

Hamrlik is aggressive and likes physical play, though he is not a huge, splashy hitter. He usually keeps himself in good condition and can handle a lot of minutes.

THE INTANGIBLES

Knee injuries nagged Hamrlik from late November on. The Isles seem to be a little disenchanted with him, and he could be moved.

PROJECTION

Hamrlik should be a 15-goal, 40-point scorer.

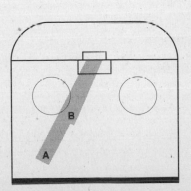

BRAD ISBISTER

Yrs. of NHL service: 5
Born: Edmonton, Alberta; May 7, 1977
Position: right wing
Height: 6-4
Weight: 227
Uniform no.: 15
Shoots: right

Career statistics:

GP	G	A	TP	PIM
292	70	67	137	420

1998-1999 statistics:

GP	G	A	TP	+/-	PIM	PP	SH	GW	GT	S	PCT
32	4	4	8	+1	46	0	0	2	0	48	8.3

1999-2000 statistics:

GP	G	A	TP	+/-	PIM	PP	SH	GW	GT	S	PCT
64	22	20	42	-18	100	9	0	1	1	135	16.3

2000-2001 statistics:

GP	G	A	TP	+/-	PIM	PP	SH	GW	GT	S	PCT
51	18	14	32	-19	59	7	1	4	0	129	13.9

2001-2002 statistics:

GP	G	A	TP	+/-	PIM	PP	SH	GW	GT	S	PCT
79	17	21	38	+1	113	4	0	2	0	142	12.0

LAST SEASON

Second on team in penalty minutes. Missed three games with back injury.

THE FINESSE GAME

Isbister is not creative, but he fits in well in a strong forechecking scheme because he plays up and down his left wing. He is a solid skater with straightaway speed and quickness. He has excellent acceleration from the blueline in, and he cuts to the net.

A decent passer when he has a little time, his hand skills are a shade below average. Unlike more creative players, he tends not to see more than one option. His goals will come from driving to the net.

With better hands and a quicker shot, Isbister could be a power forward in the making. He certainly tries to play like a power forward, and those do take a little longer to develop, which may be why the Islanders are being so patient.

THE PHYSICAL GAME

Isbister is strong, able to fend off a defender with one arm and keep going. He protects the puck well. He is an enthusiastic forechecker and likes to be the first man in. He will take or make a hit to make a play happen. He has an aggressive nature and will aggravate a lot of players by making them eat glass. He has to be more consistent in his effort on a nightly basis.

THE INTANGIBLES

O.K., maybe next year will be the breakthrough? Isbister had a disappointing season in the midst of the great Islander revival, but GM Mike Milbury continues to resist trade offers. So far.

PROJECTION

Isbister needs to step up his game and his production to around 25 goals.

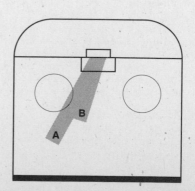

KENNY JONSSON

Yrs. of NHL service: 8
Born: Angelholm, Sweden; Oct. 6, 1974
Position: left defence
Height: 6-3
Weight: 195
Uniform no.: 29
Shoots: left

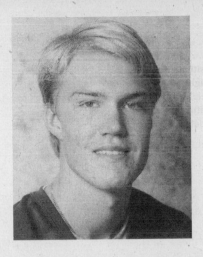

Career statistics:

GP	G	A	TP	PIM
536	50	162	212	252

1998-1999 statistics:

GP	G	A	TP	+/-	PIM	PP	SH	GW	GT	S	PCT
63	8	18	26	-18	34	6	0	0	0	91	8.8

1999-2000 statistics:

GP	G	A	TP	+/-	PIM	PP	SH	GW	GT	S	PCT
65	1	24	25	-15	32	1	0	0	0	84	1.2

2000-2001 statistics:

GP	G	A	TP	+/-	PIM	PP	SH	GW	GT	S	PCT
65	8	21	29	-22	30	5	0	0	0	91	8.8

2001-2002 statistics:

GP	G	A	TP	+/-	PIM	PP	SH	GW	GT	S	PCT
76	10	22	32	+15	26	2	1	0	0	107	9.4

LAST SEASON

Missed two games with concussion. Missed two games with flu. Missed one game with neck strain. Missed one game with quad injury.

THE FINESSE GAME

Jonsson is not overly creative, nor is he a risk taker. He reads the ice and passes the puck very well. He makes a good first pass out of the zone, but he will also bank it off the boards if that's the safer play. He doesn't shoot for the home-run pass on every shift, but will recognize the headman play when it's there.

Jonsson moves the puck up and plays his position. He always makes sure he has somebody beaten before he makes a pass. He can be used in almost every game situation. He kills penalties, works the point on the power play, plays four-on-four and is used in the late stages of a period or a game to protect a lead. Jonsson is not elite in any one role, but he is very good in many of them. He's reliable and coachable.

Jonsson is a talented skater, big and mobile, yet tends to leave himself open after passes and gets nailed.

THE PHYSICAL GAME

Jonsson is smart and plays with an edge. He and Adrian Aucoin were almost exclusively matched up night after night against the opposition's top line and were seldom outplayed. The knock on him earlier in his career was that he was a bit soft and didn't like to play through traffic, but that has changed. He competes hard every night and in the hard areas of the ice. He can handle all the minutes he gets, and was among the league leaders with 25:33 average minutes per game last season.

THE INTANGIBLES

A year after losing the captaincy, Jonsson emerged as a quiet leader on the improved Islanders. He seemed much happier in the shadow of more high-profile players, but his underrated contributions on and off the ice cannot be overlooked. While he isn't a true No. 1 defenceman, he is a solid No. 2 on his best nights and even a No. 3 when he's just a little off.

PROJECTION

Another serious concussion, this one suffered in the playoffs, had the Isles worried enough during the off-season to scramble for defensive depth. Head injuries are cumulative, and there are enough red flags regarding his health that should concern general managers as well as pool players.

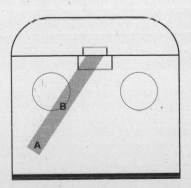

OLEG KVASHA

Yrs. of NHL service: 4
Born: Moscow, Russia; July 26, 1978
Position: left wing
Height: 6-5
Weight: 215
Uniform no.: 12
Shoots: right

Career statistics:

GP	G	A	TP	PIM
279	41	67	108	205

1998-1999 statistics:

GP	G	A	TP	+/-	PIM	PP	SH	GW	GT	S	PCT
68	12	13	25	+5	45	4	0	2	1	138	8.7

1999-2000 statistics:

GP	G	A	TP	+/-	PIM	PP	SH	GW	GT	S	PCT
78	5	20	25	+3	34	2	0	0	0	110	4.5

2000-2001 statistics:

GP	G	A	TP	+/-	PIM	PP	SH	GW	GT	S	PCT
62	11	9	20	-15	46	0	0	0	0	118	9.3

2001-2002 statistics:

GP	G	A	TP	+/-	PIM	PP	SH	GW	GT	S	PCT
71	13	25	38	-4	80	2	0	3	0	119	10.9

LAST SEASON

Missed five games with knee injury. Missed two games with shoulder injury. Missed four games due to coach's decision.

THE FINESSE GAME

Kvasha has tremendous speed and great hands. He can make a lot of things happen with the puck in full stride. He can also play centre, and he brings a centre's vision to the left wing. He has terrific hockey sense and vision. He anticipates well and sees holes a split second before they open.

With big-time skills, Kvasha has to improve his play away from the puck. He never seems to put himself in the right position at the right time, and his defensive lapses usually mean he ends up riding the bench in a tight game.

Kvasha could use his shot more. He has an excellent wrist shot that is his best weapon.

THE PHYSICAL GAME

With his strength and good size, Kvasha will drive to the net. He is not above crashing the goalie. But he can be intimidated, and on those nights he is way too big and talented to be as invisible as he tries to be.

THE INTANGIBLES

Who is the real Oleg Kvasha? The slacker forward who was booed every time he touched the puck? Or the guy who showed up to play in the postseason? Even the motivated Kvasha was only able to score a single assist in seven playoff games. Kvasha has probably worn out his welcome already on the Island, although he may have bought himself a second chance with that two-goal performance against the Rangers during the late-season stretch run.

PROJECTION

We know what Kvasha is capable of. He has the skill level to be a 20-goal, 50-point player. Like everyone else, we're waiting for that "click" where his game falls neatly into place.

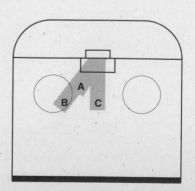

CLAUDE LAPOINTE

Yrs. of NHL service: 11
Born: Lachine, Que.; Oct. 11, 1968
Position: centre
Height: 5-9
Weight: 181
Uniform no.: 13
Shoots: left

Career statistics:

GP	G	A	TP	PIM
757	114	167	281	653

1998-1999 statistics:

GP	G	A	TP	+/-	PIM	PP	SH	GW	GT	S	PCT
82	14	23	37	-19	62	2	2	1	0	134	10.4

1999-2000 statistics:

GP	G	A	TP	+/-	PIM	PP	SH	GW	GT	S	PCT
76	15	16	31	-22	60	2	1	3	0	129	11.6

2000-2001 statistics:

GP	G	A	TP	+/-	PIM	PP	SH	GW	GT	S	PCT
80	9	23	32	-2	56	1	1	1	1	94	9.6

2001-2002 statistics:

GP	G	A	TP	+/-	PIM	PP	SH	GW	GT	S	PCT
80	9	12	21	-9	60	0	3	0	0	74	12.2

LAST SEASON

Third on team in shorthanded goals. Missed two games with flu.

THE FINESSE GAME

Lapointe is one of those useful veteran forwards who will always find a spot in a lineup because of his intelligence, yet he'll always be worried about his job because he doesn't do anything special.

He drives to the front of the net, knowing that that's where good things happen. He has good acceleration and quickness with the puck, plus decent hand skills to make things work down low. He isn't blessed with great vision, but he doesn't take unnecessary chances, either, and can be used in clutch situations.

Quick and smart, Lapointe gets a breakaway every other game, but he doesn't have the hands to finish off his chances. He is heady and aggressive. As a low draft pick (234th overall in 1988), he has always had to fight for respect. His effort is what has kept him around this long.

Lapointe was used as a checking-line winger, where he can make use of his speed. He is a very effective penalty killer and is strong on defensive-zone draws.

THE PHYSICAL GAME

Small but solidly built, Lapointe uses his low centre of gravity and good balance to bump people much bigger than he is; he surprises some by knocking them off the puck. He doesn't quit and is dogged in the corners and in front of the net. He is gritty and hard-working.

THE INTANGIBLES

Lapointe is used as a checker, an energy guy, a penalty killer and on face-offs. He doesn't score many goals but the ones he does score tend to be big. He is an excellent team man.

PROJECTION

Lapointe is a role-playing forward who can get 10 goals and play 13-15 hard minutes every night.

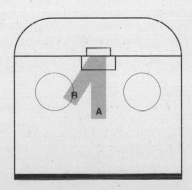

RADIM MARTINEK

Yrs. of NHL service: 0
Born: Havlicko Brod, Czech Republic
Position: defence
Height: 6-0
Weight: 196
Uniform no.: 24
Shoots: right

Career statistics:

GP	G	A	TP	PIM
23	1	4	5	16

2001-2002 statistics:

GP	G	A	TP	+/-	PIM	PP	SH	GW	GT	S	PCT
23	1	4	5	+5	16	0	0	1	0	25	4.0

LAST SEASON

Missed 59 games due to knee injury.

THE FINESSE GAME

Martinek is a blue-chip prospect. He is rock-solid defensively, and is confident in his finesse skills. Martinek was not afraid to jump up into the play from his first shift in his first NHL game.

Martinek is smart. He is a good passer, making the first smooth move out of the zone, or he can carry it himself. He's not a great skater, but he's NHL-calibre.

Martinek is only average-sized, but he holds up physically against the game's best power forwards.

THE PHYSICAL GAME

Martinek can play against other teams' top lines on a nightly basis. He is strong on his skates and he patrols his own end of the ice with authority. Martinek clears out space in front of his net. He competes hard, every night, every shift.

THE INTANGIBLES

Because he was lost to injury, Martinek's contribution to the Islanders' impressive start — which was essential to them getting into the playoffs — was just about forgotten. Assuming he is able to recover completely from his surgery, Martinek will be among the Isles' top four defencemen.

PROJECTION

If the first quarter of his season is any indication, look for big things, and maybe 20 points, when Martinek comes back.

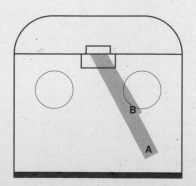

CHRIS OSGOOD

Yrs. of NHL service: 8
Born: Peace River, Alta.; Nov. 26, 1972
Position: goaltender
Height: 5-10
Weight: 175
Uniform no.: 35
Catches: left

Career statistics:

GP	MIN	GA	SO	GAA	A	PIM
455	26217	1056	34	2.42	12	89

1998-1999 statistics:

GP	MIN	GAA	W	L	T	SO	GA	S	SAPCT	PIM
63	3691	2.42	34	25	4	3	149	1654	.910	8

1999-2000 statistics:

GP	MIN	GAA	W	L	T	SO	GA	S	SAPCT	PIM
53	3148	2.40	30	14	8	6	126	1349	.907	18

2000-2001 statistics:

GP	MIN	GAA	W	L	T	SO	GA	S	SAPCT	PIM
52	2834	2.69	25	19	4	1	127	1310	.903	8

2001-2002 statistics:

GP	MIN	GAA	W	L	T	SO	GA	S	SAPCT	PIM
66	3743	2.50	32	25	6	4	156	1727	.910	10

LAST SEASON

Recorded 30 or more wins for fifth time in career. Missed two games with wrist injury.

THE PHYSICAL GAME

Osgood is a small goalie, and he gets into trouble when he stops challenging shooters and stays too deep in his net. When Osgood is playing well, he plays his angles well, textbook-style. But Osgood has a streak in him where he relies on his reflexes too much. While his reaction time is excellent, he tends to lose the puck in scrambles around (especially behind) his net and ends up looking foolish on wraparounds.

Osgood has a superb glove and he's tough to beat high. His problems arise when he loses his concentration and his angles, and fails to square himself to the shooter. On nights when he's on, he controls his rebounds well and doesn't have to scramble for too many second or third shots. His lateral movement is very good.

Osgood can handle the puck; in fact, he scored a goal and had four assists last year. He also uses his stick effectively to poke pucks off attackers' sticks around the net. He's no Martin Brodeur, however, and he tends to get overambitious.

THE MENTAL GAME

Osgood had some truly abysmal games in his first season with the Islanders. He also stole some points for a franchise that was in transition from laughing-stock to playoff qualifiers. The Isles almost always let him battle his way through.

Playing behind an evolving team was more of a challenge than backstopping the defensively sound Detroit Red Wings, but Osgood appreciated the chance to be an undisputed No. 1 goalie and was one of the key reasons why the Isles made the playoffs for the first time in eight years.

THE INTANGIBLES

Osgood has played on two Cup winners, but there are still a lot of other goalies we'd pick ahead of him if we needed to win a big one. However, he was the perfect pickup for the Islanders (who plucked him off the waiver wire just before the 2001-02 season started).

PROJECTION

Another 30-win season is probably in the cards, but the Isles may stumble a little through the first half of the season — teams who make the playoffs for the first time after a long absence tend to suffer a little hangover the next year. Team defence and Osgood's totals may reflect that.

MARK PARRISH

Yrs. of NHL service: 4
Born: Edina, Minn. Feb. 2, 1977
Position: right wing
Height: 5-11
Weight: 191
Uniform no.: 37
Shoots: right

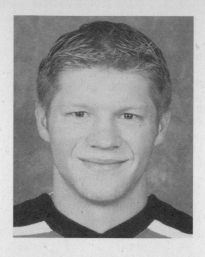

Career statistics:

GP	G	A	TP	PIM
302	97	74	171	124

1998-1999 statistics:

GP	G	A	TP	+/-	PIM	PP	SH	GW	GT	S	PCT
73	24	13	37	-6	25	5	0	5	1	129	18.6

1999-2000 statistics:

GP	G	A	TP	+/-	PIM	PP	SH	GW	GT	S	PCT
81	26	18	44	+1	39	6	0	3	0	152	17.1

2000-2001 statistics:

GP	G	A	TP	+/-	PIM	PP	SH	GW	GT	S	PCT
70	17	13	30	-27	28	6	0	3	0	123	13.8

2001-2002 statistics:

GP	G	A	TP	+/-	PIM	PP	SH	GW	GT	S	PCT
78	30	30	60	+10	32	9	1	6	0	162	18.5

LAST SEASON

Led team in shooting percentage. Tied for team lead in game-winning goals. Second on team in goals with career high. Tied for second on team in points with career high. Career high in assists. Second on team in power-play goals. Missed four games with rib injury.

THE FINESSE GAME

Parrish enjoyed a breakthrough season last year. With his good outside speed and reads, Parrish is able to wiggle past such top one-on-one defenders as Brian Leetch for scoring chances. He is a goal-scorer by skill and by nature. He goes to the net hard because he knows he has to score to stay in the lineup.

Parrish has terrific hands and a great shot, and he has started thinking like a finisher. He will get a lot of first-unit power-play time. He does some of his best work around the front of the net. He loves to score.

Parrish started the season with eight goals in four games and ended it on an 0-for-9 streak. That is pretty much Parrish's pattern, and he needs to snap out of it to take his place among the league's top goal-scorers. He is just 25 and the next few seasons could see that maturity blossom.

THE PHYSICAL GAME

Parrish doesn't have great size but he doesn't avoid the high-traffic areas. He is not afraid of anything or anybody. Parrish works in all of the dirty areas in the attacking zone, and not just around the net, either. He will absorb a blow just to chip the puck in safely rather than make a high-risk play. His defensive awareness has improved. The Isles even used him on the occasional penalty-killing shift, and he scored his first career shorthanded goal.

THE INTANGIBLES

Parrish could be moved to centre in the absence of Michael Peca, but he is far more comfortable and effective with the move to right wing. Unfortunately, he will miss Peca as his set-up man — the line of Parrish, Peca and Shawn Bates was the Isles' best last season.

He is developing into a quiet leader and character player, so with the right attitude he can be a huge asset for the Isles. Parrish is still developing a goal-scorer's confidence, and remains a streaky, slumping player. He scored 16 of his 30 goals in the first 23 games of the season. Not being picked for the U.S. Olympic team seemed to take a little air out of his balloon. His playoffs weren't impressive.

PROJECTION

Last season we said 30 goals would not be a shock for Parrish. That total was only a shock because his hot start should have meant 40. Don't expect that number this year, though. Unless Parrish develops more consistency, a small slip back into the mid-20s in goals is more likely.

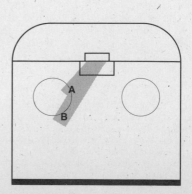

MICHAEL PECA

Yrs. of NHL service: 6
Born: Toronto, Ont.; March 26, 1974
Position: centre
Height: 5-11
Weight: 190
Uniform no.: 27
Shoots: right

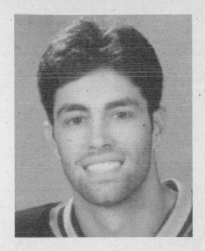

Career statistics:

GP	G	A	TP	PIM
480	127	162	289	446

1998-1999 statistics:

GP	G	A	TP	+/-	PIM	PP	SH	GW	GT	S	PCT
82	27	29	56	+7	81	10	0	8	1	199	13.6

1999-2000 statistics:

GP	G	A	TP	+/-	PIM	PP	SH	GW	GT	S	PCT
73	20	21	41	+6	67	2	0	3	0	144	13.9

2000-2001 statistics:

Did not play in NHL

2001-2002 statistics:

GP	G	A	TP	+/-	PIM	PP	SH	GW	GT	S	PCT
80	25	35	60	+19	62	3	6	5	1	168	14.9

LAST SEASON

Won 2002 Selke Trophy. Second in NHL and led team in shorthanded goals. Second on team in plus-minus. Second on team in shooting percentage. Tied for second on team in assists, points and game winning goals. Third on team in goals. Missed two games with a concussion.

THE FINESSE GAME

Everyone knew about Peca's leadership abilities when he arrived on Long Island last season. What might have come as a surprise was his skill level.

Of course, it helps that everything Peca does, he does with intensity, which only enhances his talent. Peca is a strong, sure skater who plays every shift as if a pink slip will be waiting on the bench if he slacks off. He's good with the puck in traffic and has the timing and the nice hands to create time and space for his linemates. He does a lot of the little things — especially when forechecking — that create turnovers and scoring chances. His goals come from his quickness and his effort. He challenges anyone for the puck.

The Islanders gave Peca more rein offensively than he had in his years in Buffalo. While he will never be a 100-point guy, Peca seldom looks out of place playing with or against the elite-level players in the league. His hustle and attitude have earned him his NHL job and league-wide respect. Peca thinks the game well and can be used in all situations.

Peca creates breakaway chances with his reads and anticipation. He is smart at disrupting plays and knows what to do once he has control of the puck.

THE PHYSICAL GAME

What is most impressive about Peca's first season with the Isles is that he got off to a hot start — he scored their first goal of the season — and never let up until Toronto's Darcy Tucker cheap-shotted him in

the playoffs. For a player to do that after sitting out a season (in a contract dispute with Buffalo in 2000-01) is a testament to Peca's determination.

Peca plays much bigger than his size. He's gritty and honest, and is always trying to add more weight. He has a tough time even keeping an extra five pounds on, and with all of the ice time he gets (he averaged 20:13 last season), he can wear down. Although he lacks the size to match up with some of the league's bigger forwards, he is tireless in his pursuit and effort.

He's among the best open-ice hitters in the league. Peca launches successful strikes against bigger players because of his timing, balance and leg strength. He will also drop the gloves and go after even the biggest toe. He is prickly and in-your-face, although opponents are less impressed with his diving skills.

THE INTANGIBLES

Peca found the perfect fit as the No. 2 centre behind Alexei Yashin on Long Island. However, his recuperation from reconstructive knee surgery will likely cost him the opening half of this season. The Isles will miss his leadership on and off the ice.

PROJECTION

We pegged Peca for 50 points last season, which he surpassed. Unfortunately, the knee rehab means we won't see him at his best again until next season. Still, he's a player to keep in mind as a late-season pickup for your pool since he is bound to come back as dedicated as ever in the stretch drive to the playoffs.

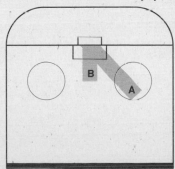

DAVE SCATCHARD

Yrs. of NHL service: 5
Born: Hinton, Alta.; Feb. 20, 1976
Position: centre
Height: 6-2
Weight: 220
Uniform no.: 38
Shoots: right

Career statistics:

GP	G	A	TP	PIM
384	71	81	152	647

1998-1999 statistics:

GP	G	A	TP	+/-	PIM	PP	SH	GW	GT	S	PCT
82	13	13	26	-12	140	0	2	2	0	130	10.0

1999-2000 statistics:

GP	G	A	TP	+/-	PIM	PP	SH	GW	GT	S	PCT
65	12	18	30	-3	117	0	1	1	0	128	9.4

2000-2001 statistics:

GP	G	A	TP	+/-	PIM	PP	SH	GW	GT	S	PCT
81	21	24	45	-9	114	4	0	5	1	176	11.9

2001-2002 statistics:

GP	G	A	TP	+/-	PIM	PP	SH	GW	GT	S	PCT
80	12	15	27	-4	111	3	1	4	0	117	10.3

PROJECTION

We thought Scatchard would become a consistent 20-goal scorer but he barely made half that.

LAST SEASON

Third on team in penalty minutes. Missed two games due to coach's decision.

THE FINESSE GAME

Scatchard can play a third-line centre's role and brings a little offensive touch to the job. He has a long reach and uses it well around the net as well as defensively. He is not creative, but produces most of his scoring chances by taking the puck to the net. His goals come from effort. He needs to take more shots. He does not have an NHL release.

Scatchard is an admirer of former Vancouver teammate Mark Messier, and their games have some similarities, though Scatchard will never become the dominating force Messier was. Scatchard can play centre or either wing. He is developing into a sound two-way forward.

Scatchard is a good skater with a quick first step. He also has decent hands. He likes to forecheck and churn up turnovers.

THE PHYSICAL GAME

Scatchard needs to build more upper-body strength. He likes to play an aggressive game. He will take a hit to make a play and he protects the puck well. He will also get involved, but he needs a little more muscle to back up the game he is willing to play.

THE INTANGIBLES

Scatchard will be one of the guys asked to pick up some of the slack with Michael Peca missing the first few months of the season.

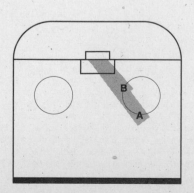

JASON WIEMER

Yrs. of NHL service: 8
Born: Kimberley, B.C.; Apr. 14, 1976
Position: left wing/centre
Height: 6-1
Weight: 220
Uniform no.: 28
Shoots: left

Career statistics:

GP	G	A	TP	PIM
521	71	77	148	1071

1998-1999 statistics:

GP	G	A	TP	+/-	PIM	PP	SH	GW	GT	S	PCT
78	8	13	21	-12	177	1	0	1	0	128	6.3

1999-2000 statistics:

GP	G	A	TP	+/-	PIM	PP	SH	GW	GT	S	PCT
64	11	11	22	-10	120	2	0	3	0	104	10.6

2000-2001 statistics:

GP	G	A	TP	+/-	PIM	PP	SH	GW	GT	S	PCT
65	10	5	15	-15	177	3	0	1	1	76	13.2

2001-2002 statistics:

GP	G	A	TP	+/-	PIM	PP	SH	GW	GT	S	PCT
70	11	20	31	-4	178	5	1	1	0	115	9.6

LAST SEASON

Acquired from Florida on July 2, 2002, for Branislav Mezei. Third on Panthers in penalty minutes and shooting percentage. Missed five games with concussion. Missed seven games due to suspension.

THE FINESSE GAME

The Isles pursued Wiemer for several reasons. With captain Michael Peca expected to miss several months of the season, there will be a leadership void. And one thing GM Mike Milbury learned from the playoffs is that his team needed a toughness upgrade. Wiemer's seven-game suspension for high-sticking noted Isles' tormentor Darcy Tucker? A bonus.

Wiemer has the build and the touch for standing in the traffic areas and picking pucks out of scrambles. He also has a touch of mean that merits him some room and time to execute. His release has improved, but he does not have an NHL-calibre shot that will make him a power forward who can post big numbers. Wiemer has to grind out his goals, and is willing to.

He does the dirty work in the corners, but Wiemer needs to play with some skilled linemates because he doesn't have the finesse or creativity to make any pretty plays. He can finish off what someone with more vision opens up for him, however.

Wiemer's major shortcoming is his skating, but it is not enough of a problem to prevent him from becoming an impact player. He is very strong and well balanced for work around the net. He relies on his strength and his reach. He is good-enough two-way player who can be given a checking assignment to shadow a star centre. He can be a physical force and go toe-to-toe with guys like Ed Jovanovski. And he is used on the power play and to kill penalties.

THE PHYSICAL GAME

Wiemer relishes body contact and initiates checks to intimidate. He is very strong and can hit to hurt. He drives to the net and pushes defenders back; he isn't shy about dropping his gloves or raising his elbows. He functions as the grinder; he will scrap along the boards and in the corners for the puck. He can complement almost any linemate. Wiemer is passionate, plays with an edge, and makes his teammates braver. Wiemer suffered a season-ending concussion, but the Islanders were assured by the medical tests and decided to go ahead with the deal.

THE INTANGIBLES

Wiemer is extremely valuable two-way forward. He has had the misfortune to play on poor teams and has only made one postseason appearance (back in 1995). Players like Wiemer make their reputation in the playoffs, and if the Isles get back there, his grit and leadership will be prized. Wiemer is dependable and rarely takes a shift off. He can be put on the ice to protect a lead or help his team tie a game up late.

PROJECTION

Wiemer will probably score in the 15-goal range as he continues in his third-line role and picks up some second-unit power-play time.

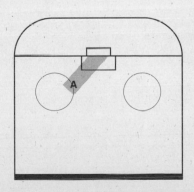

ALEXEI YASHIN

Yrs. of NHL service: 8
Born: Sverdlovsk, Russia; Nov. 5, 1973
Position: centre
Height: 6-3
Weight: 225
Uniform no.: 79
Shoots: right

Career statistics:

GP	G	A	TP	PIM
582	250	316	566	247

1998-1999 statistics:

GP	G	A	TP	+/-	PIM	PP	SH	GW	GT	S	PCT
82	44	50	94	+16	54	19	0	5	1	337	13.1

1999-2000 statistics:

Missed NHL season.

2000-2001 statistics:

GP	G	A	TP	+/-	PIM	PP	SH	GW	GT	S	PCT
82	40	48	88	+10	30	13	2	10	1	263	15.2

2001-2002 statistics:

GP	G	A	TP	+/-	PIM	PP	SH	GW	GT	S	PCT
78	32	43	75	-3	25	15	0	5	0	239	13.4

LAST SEASON

Led team in goals, assists, points, power-play goals and shots. Tied for second on team in game-winning goals. Third on team in shooting percentage. Tied for eighth in NHL in power-play points (30). Missed four games with groin injury.

THE FINESSE GAME

Yashin's skills are world class — on par with those of any other player of his generation. He has great hands and size. As he stickhandles in on the rush, he can put the puck through the legs of two or three defenders en route to the net. He has to learn, though, that he can go directly to the net and not wait for the defence to come to him so he can dazzle by using their legs as croquet wickets.

Yashin doesn't have pure breakaway speed, but he is shifty, powerful and balanced. He doesn't utilize his teammates well. He wants the puck a lot and has to play with unselfish linemates. He is at his best with the extra open ice that the power play provides.

Yashin isn't a flashy skater, but he has drawn comparisons to Ron Francis with his quiet effectiveness, and he is spectacular at times. He doesn't go all-out every shift, though, and on those occasions it looks like he's either pacing himself or he's fatigued. Because it looks as if he isn't trying, when things go poorly for him people assume he's loafing. His protracted contract battles of the past have also made the critics quick to attack. He was among the Isles' MVPs last season.

THE PHYSICAL GAME

Yashin is big and rangy and he protects the puck well. He has stepped up his desire to play through checks and pays the price in traffic. He is also smart and skilled enough to avoid unnecessary wallops. Because he has a long fuse, Yashin was once thought of as a timid player. He may be chilly outside, but last season Yashin burned with a desire to prove himself. He needs to maintain that intensity.

THE INTANGIBLES

Yashin posted a 75-point season even though the Islanders never found compatible wingmen for him (one of the reasons why Mariusz Czerkawski was shipped to Montreal). Playing with one defensive-minded winger would help. What will hurt is Michael Peca's anticipated half-season absence. It will increase the checking attention on Yashin.

PROJECTION

It should be the 80-point range again for Yashin, although there will be more pressure both from checkers and from fans, since the Isles will be expected to make the playoffs again this season and to take another step forward. The Islanders are no longer a novelty act and Yashin is a major part of their renaissance.

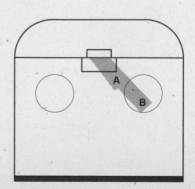

NEW YORK RANGERS

Players' Statistics 2001-2002

POS.	NO.	PLAYER	GP	G	A	PTS	+/-	PIM	PP	SH	GW	GT	S	PCT
C	88	ERIC LINDROS	72	37	36	73	19	138	12	1	4		196	18.9
R	9	PAVEL BURE	68	34	35	69	-5	62	12	1	2	1	287	11.8
R	14	THEOREN FLEURY	82	24	39	63	0	216	7		5		267	9.0
D	2	BRIAN LEETCH	82	10	45	55	14	28	1		3		202	4.9
C	93	PETR NEDVED	78	21	25	46	-8	36	6	1	3	1	175	12.0
L	19	MARTIN RUCINSKY	75	11	27	38	8	42	3		2		128	8.6
R	20	RADEK DVORAK	65	17	20	37	-20	14	3	3	1		210	8.1
D	23	VLADIMIR MALAKHOV	81	6	22	28	10	83	1				145	4.1
C	17	REM MURRAY	80	8	19	27	-4	18		2	1	1	98	8.2
D	3	TOM POTI	66	2	23	25	-10	44	2		1		109	1.8
L	26	ANDREAS JOHANSSON	70	14	10	24	6	46	3		1		108	13.0
R	10	SANDY MCCARTHY	82	10	13	23	-8	171	1		3		90	11.1
C	11	MARK MESSIER	41	7	16	23	-1	32	2		2		69	10.1
D	34	BRYAN BERARD	82	2	21	23	-1	60					132	1.5
R	36	MATTHEW BARNABY	77	8	13	21	-10	214			1		69	11.6
C	37	*MIKAEL SAMUELSSON	67	6	10	16	10	23	1	2	1		94	6.4
D	33	DAVE KARPA	75	1	10	11	-9	131			1		53	1.9
L	8	MICHAL GROSEK	15	3	2	5	-3	12					23	13.0
D	24	SYLVAIN LEFEBVRE	41		5	5	-3	23					20	
D	22	TOMAS KLOUCEK	52	1	3	4	-2	137					21	4.8
D	5	DALE PURINTON	40		4	4	4	113					11	
L	21	STEVE MCKENNA	54	2	1	3	0	144	1		1		17	11.8
C	29	ROMAN LYASHENKO	19	2		2	2						16	12.5
C	39	TRENT WHITFIELD	25		1	1	-2	28					15	
D	25	*PETER SMREK	8		1	1	-7	4					2	
R	38	*RICO FATA	10				-2						8	
L	47	*BARRETT HEISTEN	10				-4	2					7	
R	27	JASON DAWE	1				-1						1	
R	13	RICHARD SCOTT	5				0	5					1	
D	4	*MIKE MOTTAU	1				0							
G	35	MIKE RICHTER	55				0	4						
G	40	JOHAN HOLMQVIST	1				0							
G	42	JASON LABARBERA					0							
G	31	DANIEL BLACKBURN	31				0	10						

GP = games played; G = goals; A = assists; PTS = points; +/- = goals-for minus goals-against while player is on ice; PIM = penalties in minutes; PP = power-play goals; SH = shorthanded goals; GW = game-winning goals; GT = game-tying goals; S = no. of shots; PCT = percentage of goals to shots; * = rookie

MATTHEW BARNABY

Yrs. of NHL service: 9
Born: Ottawa, Ont.; May 4, 1973
Position: right wing
Height: 6-0
Weight: 189
Uniform no.: 36
Shoots: left

Career statistics:

GP	G	A	TP	PIM
552	74	114	188	1958

1998-1999 statistics:

GP	G	A	TP	+/-	PIM	PP	SH	GW	GT	S	PCT
62	6	16	22	-12	177	1	0	3	0	79	7.6

1999-2000 statistics:

GP	G	A	TP	+/-	PIM	PP	SH	GW	GT	S	PCT
64	12	12	24	+3	197	0	0	3	0	80	15.0

2000-2001 statistics:

GP	G	A	TP	+/-	PIM	PP	SH	GW	GT	S	PCT
76	5	8	13	-10	265	1	0	0	0	67	7.5

2001-2002 statistics:

GP	G	A	TP	+/-	PIM	PP	SH	GW	GT	S	PCT
77	8	13	21	-10	214	0	0	1	0	69	11.6

LAST SEASON

Acquired from Tampa Bay on December 12, 2001, for Zdeno Ciger. Second on team in penalty minutes.

THE FINESSE GAME

Barnaby's offensive skills are minimal. He gets some room because of his reputation, and that buys him a little time around the net to get a shot away. He is utterly fearless and dives right into the thick of the action, going for loose pucks. But he has no hands — for scoring goals, that is.

No one hires Barnaby for his scoring touch. His game is marked by his fierce intensity. He hits anyone, but especially loves going after the other teams' big names. He is infuriating to play against.

He skates well enough not to look out of place and is strong and balanced on his feet. He will do anything to win. If he could develop a better scoring touch he would start reminding people of Dale Hunter.

THE PHYSICAL GAME

Barnaby is a human bobblehead doll. A little breeze from an opponents' stick and Barnaby's head snaps back to try to draw a penalty.

Barnaby brings a lot of energy to the game; considering his size, it's a wonder he survives the season. He has to do some cheap stuff to survive, which makes him an even more irritating opponent. Big guys especially hate him because it's a no-win when a big bruiser takes on the poor underdog Barnaby. But he's so obnoxious they just can't help it.

THE INTANGIBLES

There was many a night last season when Barnaby was one of the Rangers' best forwards. He shouldn't be playing on a second line, hard though he may try. He simply lacks the offensive instincts. But he has a knack for stirring up loose pucks as well as trouble, and loves the game so much that you can seldom fault his effort.

He was thrilled with the trade — all eight of his goals came in his 48 games with the Rangers.

PROJECTION

Barnaby needs to be a little less selfish about his antics and then he would become a lot more valuable. We don't expect him to change his style now. He is capable of another 20-point, 200-penalty-minute season.

PAVEL BURE

Yrs. of NHL service: 11
Born: Moscow, Russia; Mar. 31, 1971
Position: right wing
Height: 5-10
Weight: 189
Uniform no.: 10
Shoots: left

Career statistics:

GP	G	A	TP	PIM
663	418	331	749	468

1998-1999 statistics:

GP	G	A	TP	+/-	PIM	PP	SH	GW	GT	S	PCT
11	13	3	16	+3	4	5	1	0	1	44	29.5

1999-2000 statistics:

GP	G	A	TP	+/-	PIM	PP	SH	GW	GT	S	PCT
74	58	36	94	+25	16	11	2	14	0	360	16.1

2000-2001 statistics:

GP	G	A	TP	+/-	PIM	PP	SH	GW	GT	S	PCT
82	59	33	92	-2	58	19	5	8	3	384	15.4

2001-2002 statistics:

GP	G	A	TP	+/-	PIM	PP	SH	GW	GT	S	PCT
68	34	35	69	-5	62	12	1	2	1	287	11.8

LAST SEASON

Acquired from Florida on March 18, 2002, with a second-round draft pick in exchange for Igor Ulanov, Filip Novak, first- and second-round draft picks in 2002 and a fourth-round draft pick in 2003. Led team in shots. Tied for team lead in power-play goals. Second on team in goals and points. Missed 14 games due to injury.

THE FINESSE GAME

Bure needs to play with linemates who move the puck to him quickly and let him do the work. Bure is a self-ish player, in the positive sense of the word. He is a gifted scorer, so he should shoot and not look for a pass. Let his assists come from rebounds off the goalies' pads or teammates recovering one of his bullet shots off the glass. Bure averages four shots on goal per game and six to eight that whistle wide.

Goalies never know when Bure's shot is going to come. He keeps his legs churning and the shot is on net before the keeper knows it. He does not telegraph his shot by breaking stride, and it's an awesome sight. He has great balance and agility; he moves equally well both with the puck and without it. Bure is always lurking and looking for the headman pass.

The Russian Rocket's quickness — and his control of the puck at supersonic speed — means anything is possible. He intimidates with his skating, driving back defenders who must play off him or risk being deked out of their skates at the blueline. He opens up tremendous ice for his teammates and will leave a drop pass or, more often, try to do it himself.

Bure doesn't do much defensively. When he is going through a slump he doesn't do the other little things that can make a player useful until the scoring

starts to kick in again. He is a shorthanded threat because of his speed and anticipation. He is one of the best breakaway scorers in the league. His explosive skating comes from his thick, powerful thighs, which look like a speed skater's.

THE PHYSICAL GAME

Bure has a little nasty edge to him, and will make solid hits for the puck, though he doesn't apply himself as enthusiastically in a defensive role. He has to play a reckless game to drive to the net and score goals. He takes a lot of punishment getting there and that's what makes him vulnerable to injuries. He can log a lot of ice time and averaged 23 minutes per game last season.

THE INTANGIBLES

When Bure is interested, as he was after the deal to the Rangers, he is one of the most dynamic players in the game. Bure scored 20 points in 12 games with the Rangers. New coach Bryan Trottier doesn't figure to throw a harness over him, so Bure will be free to keep doing his thing.

PROJECTION

Bure now has a better supporting cast than he's had in many recent seasons. He could flirt with the 60-goal, 100-point range and may even return to the playoffs for only the second time since 1995.

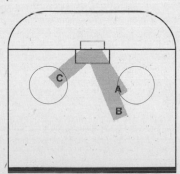

RADEK DVORAK

Yrs. of NHL service: 7
Born: Tabor, Czech Republic; Mar. 9, 1977
Position: left wing
Height: 6-1
Weight: 194
Uniform no.: 20
Shoots: right

Career statistics:

GP	G	A	TP	PIM
529	128	171	299	162

1998-1999 statistics:

GP	G	A	TP	+/-	PIM	PP	SH	GW	GT	S	PCT
82	19	24	43	+7	29	0	4	0	0	182	10.4

1999-2000 statistics:

GP	G	A	TP	+/-	PIM	PP	SH	GW	GT	S	PCT
81	18	32	50	+5	16	2	1	1	0	157	11.5

2000-2001 statistics:

GP	G	A	TP	+/-	PIM	PP	SH	GW	GT	S	PCT
82	31	36	67	+9	20	5	2	3	0	230	13.5

2001-2002 statistics:

GP	G	A	TP	+/-	PIM	PP	SH	GW	GT	S	PCT
65	17	20	37	-20	14	3	3	1	0	210	8.1

LAST SEASON

Third on team in shots. Missed 14 games with knee injury.

THE FINESSE GAME

Dvorak has exceptional speed and is among the fastest skaters in the Eastern Conference. He bursts down the wing and will mix up the defence by sometimes driving wide and sometimes cutting through the middle. He takes the puck with him at a high tempo and creates off the rush.

Dvorak seemed poised to put all of those ingredients together after scoring 31 goals in 2000-01. Instead, the off-season trade of linemate Jan Hlavac (in the Eric Lindros deal) destroyed whatever chemistry and confidence he had developed, and both he and linemate Petr Nedved were simply abysmal.

Dvorak lacks a true goal-scorer's mentality. He tends to over-pass. He has become a more complete player by adding defensive awareness to his game. Dvorak is very conscientious. He is a fine penalty killer because of his speed and anticipation.

THE PHYSICAL GAME

Dvorak has very strong legs, which power his explosive skating. While he is not a hitter, he will fight for the puck on the forecheck, and he's not a bit intimidated by physical play.

THE INTANGIBLES

For a player who showed every sign of developing into a solid two-way forward, Dvorak's team-worst -20 was inexcusable.

PROJECTION

Dvorak regressed instead of progressed last season. The knee injury was no excuse — it happened late in the season — and it's tough to predict what will become of him. He's a sure bet to get 20, but if he should turn into a good fit with Eric Lindros and Pavel Bure, he could net 40. Dvorak certainly has the speed to click with Bure, assuming he is able to make a full recovery from his knee injury.

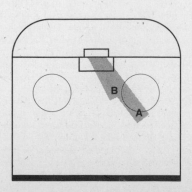

THEOREN FLEURY

Yrs. of NHL service: 14
Born: Oxbow, Sask.; June 29, 1968
Position: right wing / centre
Height: 5-6
Weight: 180
Uniform no.: 14
Shoots: right

Career statistics:

GP	G	A	TP	PIM
1030	443	612	1055	1763

1998-1999 statistics:

GP	G	A	TP	+/-	PIM	PP	SH	GW	GT	S	PCT
75	40	53	93	+26	86	8	3	5	2	301	13.3

1999-2000 statistics:

GP	G	A	TP	+/-	PIM	PP	SH	GW	GT	S	PCT
80	15	49	64	-4	68	1	0	1	0	246	6.1

2000-2001 statistics:

GP	G	A	TP	+/-	PIM	PP	SH	GW	GT	S	PCT
62	30	44	74	0	122	8	7	3	0	238	12.6

2001-2002 statistics:

GP	G	A	TP	+/-	PIM	PP	SH	GW	GT	S	PCT
82	24	39	63	0	216	7	0	5	0	267	9.0

LAST SEASON

Led Rangers in penalty minutes and game-winning goals. Second on Rangers in assists, power-play goals and shots. Third on Rangers in goals and points. One of three Rangers to appear in all 82 games.

THE FINESSE GAME

Fleury's well-publicized off-ice problems made their way onto the ice last season. He was simply an out-of-control player. He always brought a great deal of energy, but no sooner would he do something to help his team (score a goal, set up a linemate) then he would do something to hurt the Rangers. The latter usually involved taking hotheaded, pointless penalties.

Fleury always has his legs churning, and he draws penalties by driving to the net. He has a strong wrist shot that he can get away from almost anywhere. He can score even if he is pulled to his knees.

He is an effective penalty killer, blocking shots and getting the puck out along the boards. And he is poised and cool with the puck under attack, holding it until he finds an opening instead of just firing blindly. His hand quickness makes him effective on draws, and he takes offensive-zone draws.

THE PHYSICAL GAME

Fleury can take a hit and not get knocked down because he is so solid and has a low centre of gravity. He uses his stick liberally and will take a lot of penalties sticking up for himself and his teammates. The abuse over a long season tends to wear him down, yet Fleury is remarkably durable.

THE INTANGIBLES

The Rangers traded Fleury's rights to San Jose just before the free agent market. He was unsigned through the first flurry of signings and may find trouble latching on to another team. For a little guy, he sure carries around a lot of baggage.

PROJECTION

Fleury is high-risk, but he can score 65-70 points if all is right with his world.

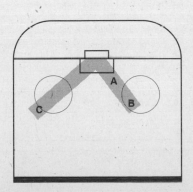

BOBBY HOLIK

Yrs. of NHL service: 12
Born: Jihlava, Czech Republic; Jan. 1, 1971
Position: centre
Height: 6-4
Weight: 230
Uniform no.: 16
Shoots: right

Career statistics:

GP	G	A	TP	PIM
878	240	311	551	954

1998-1999 statistics:

GP	G	A	TP	+/-	PIM	PP	SH	GW	GT	S	PCT
78	27	37	64	+16	119	5	0	8	0	253	10.7

1999-2000 statistics:

GP	G	A	TP	+/-	PIM	PP	SH	GW	GT	S	PCT
79	23	23	46	+7	106	7	0	4	1	257	8.9

2000-2001 statistics:

GP	G	A	TP	+/-	PIM	PP	SH	GW	GT	S	PCT
80	15	35	50	+19	97	3	0	3	0	206	7.3

2001-2002 statistics:

GP	G	A	TP	+/-	PIM	PP	SH	GW	GT	S	PCT
81	25	29	54	+7	97	6	0	3	2	270	9.3

LAST SEASON

Signed as a free agent on July 1, 2002. Led Devils in shots. Tied for second on Devils in goals and power-play goals. Third on Devils in points and penalty minutes. Missed one game due to suspension.

THE FINESSE GAME

Few players combine brute strength and skill as well as Holik does. Holik is somewhat limited as a creative playmaker because he lacks vision. He plays a fairly straightforward power game and needs to play with wingers who do the same. He does not play well when forced to carry the puck. His best formula is to dump-and-chase, cycle and create off the forecheck.

Holik has a terrific shot, a bullet drive he gets away quickly from a rush down the left side. He has great hands for working in-tight, in traffic and off the backhand. On the backhand, Holik uses his bulk to obscure the vision of his defenders, protecting the puck and masking his intentions. He has a fair wrist shot.

He's a powerful skater with good balance, but lacks jump and agility. Once he starts churning, though, Holik can get up a good head of steam. He is more responsible defensively, although he is seldom used to kill penalties. He ranked ninth in the NHL in face-offs (54.51 per cent) last season. When he doesn't win a draw cleanly, he almost always ties up his opposing number and prevents him from getting involved in the play.

THE PHYSICAL GAME

Holik is just plain big. And mean. He's a serious hitter who can hurt and who applies his bone-jarring body checks at the appropriate times. He takes some bad penalties, and can be easily frustrated when he feels he is being hooked and held and the opposition isn't penalized. Holik plays with a smirk that is absolutely infuriating. Holik plays at his best when he is given a checking assignment to focus on, especially if he is matched against another physical centre.

THE INTANGIBLES

Holik signed a lucrative five-year, $45 million (US) free-agent deal with the Rangers. How will he mesh with new players in a new environment? Holik is blunt and plain-spoken, and cares more about winning than making friends. This will come as a great shock to the rest of the Rangers.

PROJECTION

Expect another 20-25 goals and 50 points from Holik. If Eric Lindros can stay healthy, this will be one of the best one-two centre duos in the game.

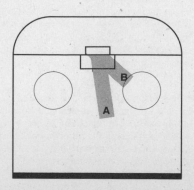

DARIUS KASPARAITIS

Yrs. of NHL service: 10
Born: Elektrenai, Lithuania; Oct. 16, 1972
Position: right defence
Height: 5-11
Weight: 212
Uniform no.: 11
Shoots: left

Career statistics:

GP	G	A	TP	PIM
648	21	108	129	1119

1998-1999 statistics:

GP	G	A	TP	+/-	PIM	PP	SH	GW	GT	S	PCT
48	1	4	5	+12	70	0	0	0	0	32	3.1

1999-2000 statistics:

GP	G	A	TP	+/-	PIM	PP	SH	GW	GT	S	PCT
73	3	12	15	-12	146	1	0	1	0	76	3.9

2000-2001 statistics:

GP	G	A	TP	+/-	PIM	PP	SH	GW	GT	S	PCT
77	3	16	19	+11	111	1	0	0	0	81	3.7

2001-2002 statistics:

GP	G	A	TP	+/-	PIM	PP	SH	GW	GT	S	PCT
80	2	12	14	0	142	0	0	0	0	81	2.5

LAST SEASON

Signed as free agent by N.Y. Rangers on July 2, 2002. Acquired by Colorado on March 19, 2002, from Pittsburgh for Rick Berry and Ville Nieminen. Second on Avs in penalty minutes.

THE FINESSE GAME

Kasparaitis is a strong, powerful skater and he can accelerate in all directions. You can run but you can't hide from this defenceman, who accepts all challenges. He is aggressive in the neutral zone, sometimes overly so, stepping up to break up a team's attack when he would be better to back off.

He has the skills to occasionally get involved in the offence, although it's not Kasparaitis's concern or his strength. He will make a sharp outlet pass and then follow up into the play. He also has good offensive instincts, moves the puck well and, if he plays on his off-side, will open up his forehand for the one-timer. He concentrates heavily on the defensive and physical part of his game, and would be blissfully happy going through the season without a point if he could wreak havoc elsewhere.

Kasparaitis has infectious enthusiasm, which is an inspiration to the rest of his team. He's highly competitive.

THE PHYSICAL GAME

It's always borderline interference with Kasparaitis, who uses his stick liberally, waiting three or four seconds after a victim has gotten rid of the puck to apply the lumber. Cross-check, butt-end, high stick — through the course of a season Kasparaitis will usually illustrate all of the stick infractions.

His timing isn't always the best, and he has to think about the good of the team rather than indulging in his own vendettas. Kasparaitis is legitimately tough. It doesn't matter whose name is on back of the jersey — Tkachuk, Modano, Yashin — he will goad the stars and the heavyweights equally. He yaps, too, and is as irritating as a car alarm at 3 a.m.

THE INTANGIBLES

Kasparaitis is probably a good No. 4 but he will be a No. 3 (and maybe even a No. 2) with the Rangers. His brief stay in Colorado wasn't the biggest success. Kasparaitis is thrilled to return to the New York area (he played for the Islanders and will be a fan favourite at Madison Square Garden).

PROJECTION

Chalk up another 100 PIM and maybe 20 points.

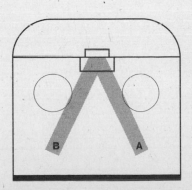

TOMAS KLOUCEK

Yrs. of NHL service: 2
Born: Prague, Czech.; Mar.7, 1980
Position: left defence
Height: 6-2
Weight: 205
Uniform no.: 22
Shoots: left

Career statistics:

GP	G	A	TP	PIM
95	2	7	9	211

2000-2001 statistics:

GP	G	A	TP	+/-	PIM	PP	SH	GW	GT	S	PCT
43	1	4	5	-3	74	0	0	0	0	22	4.6

2001-2002 statistics:

GP	G	A	TP	+/-	PIM	PP	SH	GW	GT	S	PCT
52	1	3	4	-2	137	0	0	0	0	21	4.8

LAST SEASON

Second NHL season. Appeared in nine games with Hartford (AHL), scoring 0-2-2 with 27 PIM. Missed 13 games due to coach's decision. Missed five games recovering from knee surgery. Missed two games with back spasms. Missed one game with knee injury.

THE FINESSE GAME

Kloucek reads the play well and makes a good enough first pass to show that he can be an everyday top four defenceman. What sets Kloucek apart is his fearsome and fearless physical play. But simply walloping people isn't enough to keep a player in uniform.

He is still a little young with the puck at times. He will get panicky and throw the puck away under pressure, but that appears to be a factor of inexperience. Kloucek is so eager to strut his stuff when he gets a shift that he has a tendency to try to do too much. Once he relaxes, his game will flow much more effortlessly.

His skating is NHL calibre. Kloucek is the kind of defenceman who can develop into an excellent complement for the most highly skilled defender on the team.

THE PHYSICAL GAME

Kloucek returned from reconstructive knee surgery ahead of schedule and completely assured in his hitting. Kloucek is still young and learning what he needs to do to be a full-time NHL player. He is so big and strong that he has the ability to change the tempo of a game just with his hitting. Kloucek needs to curb his reckless hitting, because even some of his clean checks are mistaken by referees for penalties.

THE INTANGIBLES

There was one set of rules for veteran defencemen on the Rangers last season, and another for youngsters like Kloucek. The vets were allowed to blunder and coast and seldom missed a shift, while Kloucek got the hook and rode the bench if he took a single bad penalty. It was hardly a confidence-building season.

If the Rangers had done a better job of helping Kloucek develop, they might not have needed spend the money on free agent Darius Kasparaitis.

PROJECTION

None of Kloucek's contributions are offensive. He is a tough, physical defenceman who should benefit from the addition of Jim Schoenfeld to the coaching staff. He will start the season in the Rangers' top six.

BRIAN LEETCH

Yrs. of NHL service: 14
Born: Corpus Christi, Tex.; Mar. 3, 1968
Position: left defence
Height: 6-1
Weight: 190
Uniform no.: 2
Shoots: left

Career statistics:

GP	G	A	TP	PIM
1021	215	700	915	481

1998-1999 statistics:

GP	G	A	TP	+/-	PIM	PP	SH	GW	GT	S	PCT
82	13	42	55	-7	42	4	0	1	0	184	7.1

1999-2000 statistics:

GP	G	A	TP	+/-	PIM	PP	SH	GW	GT	S	PCT
50	7	19	26	-16	20	3	0	2	1	124	5.6

2000-2001 statistics:

GP	G	A	TP	+/	PIM	PP	SH	GW	GT	S	PCT
82	21	58	79	-18	34	10	1	3	1	241	8.7

2001-2002 statistics:

GP	G	A	TP	+/-	PIM	PP	SH	GW	GT	S	PCT
82	10	45	55	+14	28	1	0	3	0	202	4.9

LAST SEASON

Fourth in NHL and led team defencemen in points. Led team in assists. Second on team in plus-minus. Tied for third on team in game-winning goals. One of four Rangers to appear in all 82 games.

THE FINESSE GAME

Leetch is a premier passer who sees the ice clearly, identifies the passing option on the move and hits his target with a forehand or backhand pass. He is terrific at picking passes out of the air and keeping clearing passes from getting by him at the point.

He has a fine first step that sends him close to top speed almost instantly. He can be posted at the point, then see an opportunity to jump into the play down low and bolt into action. His anticipation is superb. He seems to be thinking about five seconds ahead of everyone else. He instantly makes a transition from defence to offence, and always seems to make the right decision to pass or skate with the puck.

Leetch has a remarkable knack for getting his point shot through traffic and to the net. He even uses his eyes to fake. He is adept at looking and/or moving in one direction, then passing the opposite way.

He smartly jumps into holes to make the most of an odd-man rush, and he is more than quick enough to hop back on defence if the puck goes the other way. Leetch has astounding lateral movement, leaving forwards completely out of room when it looked like there was open ice to get past him. He uses this as a weapon on offence to open up space for his teammates.

Leetch has a range of shots. He'll use a slapper from the point, usually through a screen because it won't overpower any NHL goalie, but he'll also use a wrist shot from the circle. He is gifted with the one-on-one moves that help him wriggle in front for 10-footers on the forehand or backhand, and he has worked on one-timers from close to the net.

THE PHYSICAL GAME

Not a thumping hitter, Leetch is still capable of taking the body. He competes for the puck and is a first-rate penalty killer. He block shots. Leetch's major problem is overwork. The Rangers did cut down his ice time to 25:51 (eighth in the NHL, but down four minutes per game from the previous season). Shaving another minute or two off that would be beneficial.

THE INTANGIBLES

Leetch has never felt completely comfortable with a partner since Jeff Beukeboom was forced into retirement in 1999. He is paired most often with the high-risk Vladimir Malakhov, but the Rangers would get the elite Leetch back if they could find him the right stay-at-home guy.

PROJECTION

Playing a full season with Pavel Bure on the power play should boost Leetch's points back into the 70-point range.

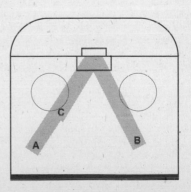

ERIC LINDROS

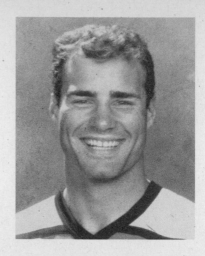

Yrs. of NHL service: 8
Born: London, Ont.; Feb. 28, 1973
Position: centre
Height: 6-4
Weight: 236
Uniform no.: 88
Shoots: right

Career statistics:

GP	G	A	TP	PIM
558	327	405	732	1084

1998-1999 statistics:

GP	G	A	TP	+/-	PIM	PP	SH	GW	GT	S	PCT
71	40	53	93	+35	120	10	1	2	3	242	16.5

1999-2000 statistics:

GP	G	A	TP	+/-	PIM	PP	SH	GW	GT	S	PCT
55	27	32	59	+11	83	10	1	2	1	187	14.4

2000-2001 statistics:

Did not play in NHL

2001-2002 statistics:

GP	G	A	TP	+/-	PIM	PP	SH	GW	GT	S	PCT
72	37	36	73	+19	138	12	1	4	0	196	18.9

LAST SEASON

Tied for ninth in NHL in goals. Led team in goals, points, plus-minus and shooting percentage. Tied for team lead in power-play goals. Second on team in game-winning games. Third on team in assists. Missed four games with knee injury. Missed four games with concussion. Missed two games with bruised foot.

THE FINESSE GAME

The Rangers tried to sugarcoat things by calling Lindros's mid-season concussion "minor," but when a player has had as many "major" concussions in his career as Lindros, no head injury is trivial. Lindros, who had found his stride after missing the entire 2000-01 season due to a combination of the Scott Stevens-inflicted playoff concussion and waiting for the Flyers to trade his rights, was never the same after the late December hit last season.

Lindros is not the physical presence he once was. He can't afford to be. He is still big enough and skilled enough to demand a lot of room on the ice. He has a very good passing touch, which is underrated, and a shot that weighs a ton. Lindros has the balance and soft hands to control the puck in extremely tight quarters and make those nimble moves at the high speed he reaches quickly. That said, it remains more his nature to muscle the puck to a teammate or to the front of the net, and to let his strength do most of the work — because strength remains the watchword of his game.

To offset the torque his arms can generate, the stick Lindros uses has an extremely firm shaft with only a slight curve to the blade. That helps on face-offs, adds velocity to his wrist and snap shots and

makes his backhand shot a significant weapon, both for its speed and its accuracy to the upper corners from close range.

THE PHYSICAL GAME

The addition of Bobby Holik will lessen the checking pressure on Lindros, but the notion that a player this big needs a bodyguard is absurd. Lindros can best help himself by keeping his head up. You would have thought he would have learned by now, but Lindros still looks down at his feet when he is steaming across the blueline, a perfect vulnerable position for another crushing blow.

THE INTANGIBLES

Lindros had a few weeks last season where he was as dominant as any player in the NHL.

PROJECTION

Lindros is likely to be a point-a-game player for a team that will be offensive-minded under new head coach Bryan Trottier. The key will be how many healthy games he gets to play.

ROMAN LYASHENKO

Yrs. of NHL service: 3
Born: Murmansk, Russia; May 2, 1979
Position: centre
Height: 6-0
Weight: 189
Uniform no.: 29
Shoots: right

Career statistics:

GP	G	A	TP	PIM
137	14	9	23	55

1999-2000 statistics:

GP	G	A	TP	+/-	PIM	PP	SH	GW	GT	S	PCT
58	6	6	12	-2	10	0	0	1	0	51	11.8

2000-2001 statistics:

GP	G	A	TP	+/-	PIM	PP	SH	GW	GT	S	PCT
60	6	3	9	-1	45	0	0	1	0	48	12.5

2001-2002 statistics:

GP	G	A	TP	+/-	PIM	PP	SH	GW	GT	S	PCT
19	2	0	2	-2	0	0	0	0	0	16	12.5

LAST SEASON

Acquired from Dallas on March 12, 2002, with Martin Rucinsky for Manny Malhotra and Barrett Heisten. Appeared in 58 games with Utah (AHL), scoring 11-25-36 with 37 PIM.

THE FINESSE GAME

Lyashenko is a defence-first player, but he also has the kind of offensive skills that allow him to fill in alongside first-line players.

Lyashenko is all smoothness. He has good vision and hand skills. He is progressing quickly as an NHL player, though he did not see much offensive ice time last season.

He will become a complete player who can work the second-unit power play, kill penalties and take key face-offs. He can check the other teams' top lines and add some offensive punch.

THE PHYSICAL GAME

Lyashenko plays a solid game and takes the body well, though he is not a physical force. He fights hard for the puck and will not back down from battles along the boards.

THE INTANGIBLES

The Rangers never seemed to know what to make of Lyashenko once they got him, even though they had no checking centres and that role could have been filled nicely by him. Instead, Lyashenko was shuffled down to the fourth line. New coach Bryan Trottier might recognize Lyashanko's assets. He is the kind of role player who can come up big.

The problem for Lyashenko in New York is the acquisition of Bobby Holik, which moves Lyashenko further down the depth chart at centre.

PROJECTION

The Rangers either need to find a third-line role for Lyashenko or move him. He is capable of scoring 50 points in a full-time role.

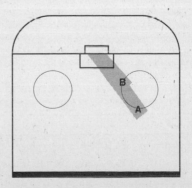

VLADIMIR MALAKHOV

Yrs. of NHL service: 10
Born: Ekaterinburg, Russia; Aug. 30, 1968
Position: left defence
Height: 6-4
Weight: 230
Uniform no.: 23
Shoots: left

Career statistics:

GP	G	A	TP	PIM
550	76	225	301	564

1998-1999 statistics:

GP	G	A	TP	+/-	PIM	PP	SH	GW	GT	S	PCT
62	13	21	34	-7	77	8	0	3	0	143	9.1

1999-2000 statistics:

GP	G	A	TP	+/-	PIM	PP	SH	GW	GT	S	PCT
24	1	4	5	+1	23	1	0	1	0	18	5.6

2000-2001 statistics:

GP	G	A	TP	+/-	PIM	PP	SH	GW	GT	S	PCT
3	0	2	2	0	4	0	0	0	0	6	0.0

2001-2002 statistics:

GP	G	A	TP	+/-	PIM	PP	SH	GW	GT	S	PCT
81	6	22	28	+10	83	1	0	0	0	145	4.1

LAST SEASON

Tied for third on team in plus-minus. Career high in games played. Missed one game with flu.

THE FINESSE GAME

For most of last season, Malakhov rose to the level that he had long hinted he was capable of. That Malakhov did it after needing a year off to recover from reconstructive knee surgery is phenomenal.

Malakhov has an absolute bullet of a shot; one of the hardest shot in the league. He rifles off a one-timer or shoots on the fly, and has outstanding offensive instincts for both shooting and playmaking. He moves the puck and jumps into the play alertly.

Malakhov is so talented he never looks like he's trying hard. Some nights he's not. He seems discouraged at times when things aren't going smoothly. If he tries a few plays early in a game that don't work, you might as well put him on the bench for the rest of the night. If he has a few good shifts early, especially offensively, odds are he'll be one of the three stars.

Defensively, Malakhov is in love with the poke-check, and uses his long reach to cut down passing lanes. Malakhov can be used on both special teams. He is a mobile skater, with good agility and balance. He has a huge stride, and is fast but not necessarily agile. He can be easily turned the wrong way by a shifty attacker.

THE PHYSICAL GAME

Malakhov is a big guy and when he is inspired, he sticks and pins his man. He has a little bit of a mean streak. He doesn't fight often, but he is capable of winning a bout when he does get fired up. Malakhov

blocks shots willingly. He averaged just under 23 minutes of ice time last season and wore down a bit in the final months, which is understandable given his comeback from the knee injury.

THE INTANGIBLES

Maybe it just took 10 NHL seasons for Malakhov to "get it." Now the question is whether this enigmatic defenceman can put together consecutive impressive seasons. He partnered the hard-working Brian Leetch most of last season. Maybe that teammate's work ethic rubbed off.

PROJECTION

A duplication of last season's effort would get Malakhov closer to the 40-point mark.

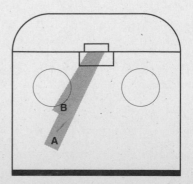

MARK MESSIER

Yrs. of NHL service: 23
Born: Edmonton, Alta.; Jan. 18, 1961
Position: centre
Height: 6-1
Weight: 210
Uniform no.: 11
Shoots: left

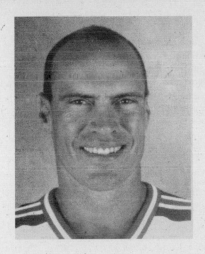

Career statistics:

GP	G	A	TP	PIM
1602	658	1146	1804	1838

1998-1999 statistics:

GP	G	A	TP	+/-	PIM	PP	SH	GW	GT	S	PCT
59	13	35	48	-12	33	4	2	2	0	97	13.4

1999-2000 statistics:

GP	G	A	TP	+/-	PIM	PP	SH	GW	GT	S	PCT
66	17	37	54	-15	30	6	0	4	0	131	13.0

2000-2001 statistics:

GP	G	A	TP	+/-	PIM	PP	SH	GW	GT	S	PCT
82	24	43	67	-25	89	12	3	2	0	131	18.3

2001-2002 statistics:

GP	G	A	TP	+/-	PIM	PP	SH	GW	GT	S	PCT
41	7	16	23	-1	32	2	0	2	0	69	10.1

LAST SEASON

Missed 38 games with shoulder injury and surgery.

THE FINESSE GAME

Messier is strong on his skates: he changes directions, pivots, bursts into open ice and, when his game is at its strongest, does it all with or without the puck. He still has tremendous acceleration and a powerful burst of straightaway speed, which is tailor-made for killing penalties and scoring shorthanded goals — even if he cheats into the neutral zone, looking for a breakaway pass, too often.

Messier's shot of choice is a wrister off the back ("wrong") foot from the right-wing circle, which is where he always seems to gravitate. It's a trademark, and it still fools many a goalie. He also makes as much use of the backhand, for passing and shooting, as any other North American player in the league. He will weave to the right-wing circle, fake a pass to the centre, get the goalie to cheat away from the post, then flip a backhand under the crossbar. He shoots from almost anywhere and is unpredictable in his shot selection when the back-foot wrister is not available.

Messier has always been better at making the utmost use of his teammates, rather than trying one-on-one moves. His hallmark is his bottomless determination to win, which prevents his more skilled but less brave cohorts from faltering. He just drags them right to the front lines with him. Defensively, Messier has become a liability.

THE PHYSICAL GAME

The Messier mean streak is legendary, but less frequently evident. He is a master of the pre-emptive strike, the elbows or stick held teeth-high when a checker is coming towards him.

THE INTANGIBLES

There are few better big-game players in NHL history than Messier, but the past is the past.

PROJECTION

Messier is at best a third-line forward. It's just a question of whether this great player can mentally accept a part-time role.

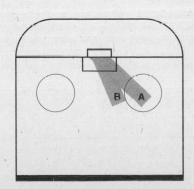

PETR NEDVED

Yrs. of NHL service: 11
Born: Liberec, Czech Republic; Dec. 9, 1971
Position: centre
Height: 6-3
Weight: 195
Uniform no.: 93
Shoots: left

Career statistics:

GP	G	A	TP	PIM
730	255	321	576	500

1998-1999 statistics:

GP	G	A	TP	+/-	PIM	PP	SH	GW	GT	S	PCT
56	20	27	47	-6	50	9	1	3	0	153	13.1

1999-2000 statistics:

GP	G	A	TP	+/-	PIM	PP	SH	GW	GT	S	PCT
76	24	44	68	+2	40	6	2	4	0	201	11.9

2000-2001 statistics:

GP	G	A	TP	+/-	PIM	PP	SH	GW	GT	S	PCT
79	32	46	78	+10	54	9	1	5	0	230	13.9

2001-2002 statistics:

GP	G	A	TP	+/-	PIM	PP	SH	GW	GT	S	PCT
78	21	25	46	-8	36	6	1	3	1	175	12.0

LAST SEASON

Third on team in shooting percentage. Tied for third on team in game-winning goals. Missed four games due to concussion.

THE FINESSE GAME

When he gets in a slump, Nedved quickly reverts to his old bad habit of overpassing. He plays best with linemates who are well-schooled in European-style hockey, but too often he gets in the best position to shoot and instead forces a pass that is knocked down or picked off. Nedved makes use of time and space. He has an excellent wrist shot with a hair-trigger release and radar-like accuracy. He likes to go high on the glove side, picking the corner.

The Rangers occasionally use him as a power-play quarterback, which is all wrong. He lacks a heavy shot from the point and a shooter's confidence, and is better up front on the half-boards.

Tall but slightly built, he is good at handling the puck in traffic or in open ice at tempo. He sees the ice well and has a creative mind. Good on attacking-zone draws, Nedved knows his way around a face-off. He has good hand quickness and cheats well. On offensive-zone draws, he turns his body so that he's almost facing the boards. That's about it for his defensive contribution, though he can kill penalties because of his quickness and anticipation. Nedved frequently gets confused in his defensive assignments.

THE PHYSICAL GAME

Nedved took a giant step back last season after a year in which he did nearly everything the Rangers asked. He isn't as averse to contact as his reputation indicates, but he has to be motivated to pay the price and that certainly wasn't the case last season.

THE INTANGIBLES

On a team chock-full of underachivers, Nedved was the ringleader. Well, it was good to seem him lead the way in one category. Nedved was booed nearly every time he touched the puck, and now that he looks like the No. 3 (or 4) centre on the team after the addition of Bobby Holik, it's tough to think he will make much of an impact on the Rangers.

PROJECTION

Nedved needs a fresh start. He can score 60 points if he gets traded to the right team where he can be a No. 2 centre, but the Rangers will probably have to pick up part of his salary for that to happen. Nedved's trade value isn't very high after last season.

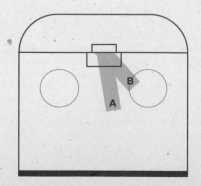

TOM POTI

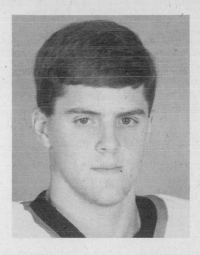

Yrs. of NHL service: 4
Born: Worcester, Mass.; Mar. 22, 1977
Position: left defence
Height: 6-3
Weight: 215
Uniform no.: 3
Shoots: left

Career statistics:

GP	G	A	TP	PIM
296	28	85	113	211

1998-1999 statistics:

GP	G	A	TP	+/-	PIM	PP	SH	GW	GT	S	PCT
73	5	16	21	+10	42	2	0	3	0	94	5.3

1999-2000 statistics:

GP	G	A	TP	+/-	PIM	PP	SH	GW	GT	S	PCT
76	9	26	35	+8	65	2	1	1	0	125	7.2

2000-2001 statistics:

GP	G	A	TP	+/-	PIM	PP	SH	GW	GT	S	PCT
81	12	20	32	-4	60	6	0	3	0	161	7.4

2001-2002 statistics:

GP	G	A	TP	+/-	PIM	PP	SH	GW	GT	S	PCT
66	2	23	25	-10	44	2	0	1	0	109	1.8

LAST SEASON

Acquired from Edmonton on March 19, 2002, with Rem Murray for Mike York and a fourth-round draft pick in 2002. Missed seven games with fractured finger.

THE FINESSE GAME

Poti is a good — but not great — "offenceman." He doesn't score enough points to compensate for his defensive lapses, which are major. If he fails to either up his production or cut down on his defensive miscues, he is going to be trouble to have in a lineup.

Early in his Edmonton career, Poti was likened to a young Paul Coffey. That comparison was never fair, and it looks like Poti will not become an elite offensive defenceman, but at least he has a good role model in New York in Brian Leetch.

Poti is a fine puckhandler and passer. He has good vision and can spring to teammates with headman passes. He carries the puck with speed and disguises his intentions. He is an excellent skater, who figures to fit in with what will probably be an uptempo team in New York under new coach Bryan Trottier. Poti uses a low shot from the point that isn't a rocket, so teammates can take advantage of it for tip-ins. He needs to work on his defence to become a better all-round player. He is intelligent and should keep developing.

THE PHYSICAL GAME

What don't we like? Well, Poti took a huge step back in Edmonton, despite a similar offensive style that the Rangers will try to copy. And Poti is soft. He has decent size but doesn't use it well. He is still adding some muscle and needs to throw his weight around a

bit more and add some grit to his game. He prefers to use his stick instead of his body to do the defensive work. He has to deal with a medical condition, a severe food allergy, which forces him to pay strict attention to his nutrition and condition. His effortless skating style helps him handle a lot of minutes.

Leetch, until he gets worn down late in a season, can play with an edge, block shots, and at least play the body. Poti needs to watch and learn.

THE INTANGIBLES

Poti scored 1-7-8 in 11 games after the trade and was pretty unimpressive, but we were in his corner when he broke in and we're willing to clean the slate. Poti probably figures in the Rangers' plans as a top four defenceman.

PROJECTION

Maybe a steal for GM Glen Sather, maybe a dud. We're going to think positive and project 40 points.

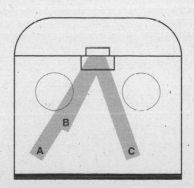

MIKE RICHTER

Yrs. of NHL service: 11
Born: Abingdon, Pa.; Sept. 22, 1966
Position: goaltender
Height: 5-11
Weight: 185
Uniform no.: 35
Catches: left

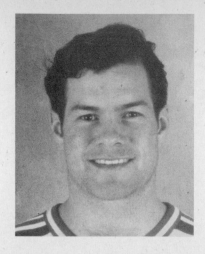

Career statistics:

GP	MIN	GA	SO	GAA	A	PIM
653	37489	1806	24	2.89	8	34

1998-1999 statistics:

GP	MIN	GAA	W	L	T	SO	GA	S	SAPCT	PIM
68	3878	2.63	27	30	8	4	170	1898	.910	0

1999-2000 statistics:

GP	MIN	GAA	W	L	T	SO	GA	S	SAPCT	PIM
61	3622	2.87	22	31	8	0	173	1815	.905	4

2000-2001 statistics:

GP	MIN	GAA	W	L	T	SO	GA	S	SAPCT	PIM
45	2635	3.28	20	21	3	0	144	1343	.893	0

2001-2002 statistics:

GP	MIN	GAA	W	L	T	SO	GA	S	SAPCT	PIM
55	3195	2.95	24	26	4	2	157	1675	.906	4

LAST SEASON
Missed nine games with fractured temporal bone.

THE PHYSICAL GAME
Richter is strong in every area of goalie fundamentals except for one that almost every young goalie is adept at: puck handling. Puck exchanges with his defencemen are often laughable and, at times, life-threatening, because Richter simply cannot decide whether to leave the puck behind the net or try a cute little pass to help the cause. The results are usually calamitous. Either there is a turnover for an easy goal or some defenceman, trying to find Richter's pass in his feet, gets creamed from behind by a forechecker. Richter would be far better off just staying in the paint.

Richter uses his stick for poke-checks in one-on-one battles, but still doesn't use it enough as a pass-blocking tool. Too often, he concedes the pass across the crease and relies on his explosive lateral movement to make a quick save he wouldn't have to make at all if he merely prevented the puck from reaching the shooter.

Nonetheless, Richter is agile, flexible and athletic, and boasts exceptional post-to-post quickness. Quick reflexes allow him to reach second-chance shots off rebounds or one-timers off odd-man rushes.

He rarely gets beat on the low corners. Shooters beat him high on the glove side or on slam-dunks to the weak side after he has overplayed an angle. He gets a whopping percentage of the first shots. While he catches more pucks now and holds onto them more, he still fumbles a little too often for comfort.

THE MENTAL GAME
Richter may be the most patient one-on-one goalie in the NHL. Confident and fluid, he simply lets himself make whatever save is necessary. If that results in him losing his stick and at least one of his gloves, no problem.

Uncanny at finding the puck through traffic, Richter is able to make stops on close-range shots off passes from behind the net. Similarly, when the puck is moving from point to point, he stays focused, stays crouched, sees the puck and stays with it. He tends to lose his concentration on long shots, and gets beaten every now and then by a ridiculous goal.

THE INTANGIBLES
The Rangers were wisely cautious in spacing Richter's starts in the first half of the season as he recovered from left knee surgery. His season-ending injury was the result of a shot taken off his mask, just another in a streak of bad breaks for Richter.

After some dithering, the Rangers decided to re-sign the free agent goalie in July. He is an ideal character guy to help 19-year-old backup goalie Dan Blackburn progress.

PROJECTION
Richter will enter the season as the Rangers' No. 1 goalie, and might be yielding more starts to Blackburn. The Rangers desperately want to make the playoffs, however, which means they might be inclined to play Richter more and experiment with the kid less. A conservative prediction is 25 wins.

OTTAWA SENATORS

Players' Statistics 2001-2002

POS.	NO.	PLAYER	GP	G	A	PTS	+/-	PIM	PP	SH	GW	GT	S	PCT
R	11	DANIEL ALFREDSSON	78	37	34	71	3	45	9	1	4	2	243	15.2
C	14	RADEK BONK	82	25	45	70	3	52	6	2	5		170	14.7
R	18	MARIAN HOSSA	80	31	35	66	11	50	9	1	4	1	278	11.1
R	9	MARTIN HAVLAT	72	22	28	50	-7	66	9		6	1	145	15.2
C	28	TODD WHITE	81	20	30	50	12	24	4		1		147	13.6
L	15	SHAWN MCEACHERN	80	15	31	46	9	52	5		3		196	7.7
L	20	MAGNUS ARVEDSON	74	12	27	39	27	35			1		121	9.9
D	6	WADE REDDEN	79	9	25	34	22	48	4	1	1		156	5.8
C	12	MIKE FISHER	58	15	9	24	8	55		3	4		123	12.2
D	3	ZDENO CHARA	75	10	13	23	30	156	4	1	2		105	9.5
L	26	BENOIT BRUNET	61	9	14	23	-3	12	1	1	3		72	12.5
D	4	CHRIS PHILLIPS	63	6	16	22	5	29	1		1		103	5.8
D	5	SAMI SALO	66	4	14	18	1	14	1	1	2		122	3.3
D	23	KAREL RACHUNEK	51	3	15	18	7	24	1		2		55	5.4
R	25	*CHRIS NEIL	72	10	7	17	5	231	1				56	17.9
C	36	JUHA YLONEN	80	4	11	15	-11	10		1			97	4.1
L	33	CHRIS HERPERGER	72	4	9	13	4	43					81	4.9
D	7	CURTIS LESCHYSHYN	79	1	9	10	-5	44					59	1.7
D	27	RICARD PERSSON	34	2	7	9	3	42					35	5.7
R	17	BILL MUCKALT	70		8	8	-3	46					73	
R	16	JODY HULL	24	2	2	4	0	6			1		12	16.7
D	34	SHANE HNIDY	33	1	1	2	-10	57					34	2.9
C	21	STEVE MARTINS	14	1		1	1	4					11	9.1
R	10	*TONI DAHLMAN	10		1	1	-1						5	
L	52	*CHRIS BALA	6		1	1	1						2	
L	13	PETR SCHASTLIVY	1		1	1	1							
D	29	JOEL KWIATKOWSKI	11				5	12					9	
R	39	*JOSH LANGFELD	1				0	2					5	
G	40	PATRICK LALIME	61				0	19						
G	35	JANI HURME	25				0	17						
G	1	SIMON LAJEUNESSE	1				0							
G	31	MARTIN PRUSEK	1				0							

GP = games played; G = goals; A = assists; PTS = points; +/- = goals-for minus goals-against while player is on ice; PIM = penalties in minutes; PP = power-play goals; SH = shorthanded goals; GW = game-winning goals; GT = game tying goals; S = no. of shots; PCT = percentage of goals to shots; * = rookie

DANIEL ALFREDSSON

Yrs. of NHL service: 7
Born: Grums, Sweden; Dec. 11, 1972
Position: right wing
Height: 5-11
Weight: 195
Uniform no.: 11
Shoots: right

Career statistics:

GP	G	A	TP	PIM
474	160	250	410	193

1998-1999 statistics:

GP	G	A	TP	+/-	PIM	PP	SH	GW	GT	S	PCT
58	11	22	33	+8	14	3	0	5	0	163	6.7

1999-2000 statistics:

GP	G	A	TP	+/-	PIM	PP	SH	GW	GT	S	PCT
57	21	38	59	+11	28	4	2	0	0	164	12.8

2000-2001 statistics:

GP	G	A	TP	+/-	PIM	PP	SH	GW	GT	S	PCT
68	24	46	70	+11	30	10	0	3	1	206	11.7

2001-2002 statistics:

GP	G	A	TP	+/-	PIM	PP	SH	GW	GT	S	PCT
78	37	34	71	+3	45	9	1	4	2	243	15.2

LAST SEASON

Led team in goals and points. Tied for ninth in NHL in goals with career high. Tied for team lead in power-play goals and shooting percentage. Second on team in shots. Third on team in assists. Tied for third on team in game-winning goals. Missed four games with hip injury.

THE FINESSE GAME

Considering that Alfredsson hasn't played with a No. 1 centre most of his career in Ottawa, he has compiled some pretty remarkable numbers. Even when Alexei Yashin was with the Sens, Alfredsson wasn't always on his line.

Alfredsson's release is hair-trigger, and he has one of the best shots in the league. He also has a solid work ethic; he didn't make it to the NHL by being on cruise control. Alfredsson has to work for his space. One of the reasons why he is so good on the power play is because of his work in open ice. Alfredsson can work the power play off the half-boards but the Senators frequently use him at the point. He has excellent vision and hands. He can be quiet an entire game and then kill a team with two shots.

Alfredsson likes to play a puck-control game and needs to work with other forwards who will distribute the puck. Alfredsson is well schooled in the defensive aspects of the game, and he works diligently along the wall. He is a constant shorthanded threat when killing penalties because of his speed and anticipation. There are few better players in the league one-on-one or on the breakaway. He has reduced the curve of his blade a bit for improved puck control.

THE PHYSICAL GAME

Alfredsson has a very thick and powerful lower body to fuel his skating. He is fearless and takes a lot of abuse to get into the high-scoring areas. He will skate up the wall and cut to the middle of the ice. He might get nailed by the off-side defenceman, but on the next rush he will try it again. He won't be scared off, and on the next chance he may get the shot away and in.

Alfredsson was able to stay pretty healthy last season after averaging only 59 games played over the previous four seasons.

THE INTANGIBLES

The Senators took care of one pending headache when they wrapped up Alfredsson's new contract (he was a restricted free agent) early in the summer. Teammates respect Alfredsson for his work ethic; he is a leader by example.

PROJECTION

Alfredsson is a point-a-game player.

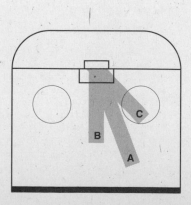

MAGNUS ARVEDSON

Yrs. of NHL service: 5
Born: Karlstad, Sweden; Nov. 25, 1971
Position: left wing
Height: 6-2
Weight: 198
Uniform no.: 20
Shoots: left

Career statistics:

GP	G	A	TP	PIM
313	76	97	173	181

1998-1999 statistics:

GP	G	A	TP	+/-	PIM	PP	SH	GW	GT	S	PCT
80	21	26	47	+33	50	0	4	6	0	136	15.4

1999-2000 statistics:

GP	G	A	TP	+/-	PIM	PP	SH	GW	GT	S	PCT
47	15	13	28	+4	36	1	1	4	1	91	16.5

2000-2001 statistics:

GP	G	A	TP	+/-	PIM	PP	SH	GW	GT	S	PCT
51	17	16	33	+23	24	1	2	4	0	79	21.5

2001-2002 statistics:

GP	G	A	TP	+/-	PIM	PP	SH	GW	GT	S	PCT
74	12	27	39	+27	35	0	0	1	0	121	9.9

LAST SEASON

Second on team in plus-minus. Missed five games with groin injury. Missed two games with a concussion.

THE FINESSE GAME

Arvedson has great speed and is strong on the puck. He hasn't been much of a scorer coming up to the NHL and that isn't about to change now. Arvedson has a good shot but he doesn't use it enough. He is unselfish and will usually look to set up a teammate. He is an accurate shooter when he does fire.

Arvedson has some offensive upside, but he just doesn't seem interested in pushing the envelope. He is good and smart enough to play on one of the top two lines, maybe in a defensive-minded, Jere Lehtinen type of role, although he is probably best suited to play on a third line.

He is good enough defensively that he was a Selke Trophy candidate in only his second NHL season. He kills penalties and can be used as a checking centre.

THE PHYSICAL GAME

Arvedson is big and strong and able to handle the rigours of an NHL schedule. He can handle a checking assignment to cover the top players, kill penalties and contribute offensively.

THE INTANGIBLES

Arvedson was able to stay fairly healthy last season, although the December concussion may have been a factor in his inconsistent second-half play.

PROJECTION

Arvedson could score 20 goals if he stays healthy.

RADEK BONK

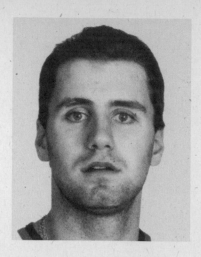

Yrs. of NHL service: 8
Born: Krnov, Czech Republic; Jan. 9, 1976
Position: centre
Height: 6-3
Weight: 210
Uniform no.: 14
Shoots: left

Career statistics:

GP	G	A	TP	PIM
553	118	183	301	299

1998-1999 statistics:

GP	G	A	TP	+/-	PIM	PP	SH	GW	GT	S	PCT
81	16	16	32	+15	48	0	1	6	0	110	14.5

1999-2000 statistics:

GP	G	A	TP	+/-	PIM	PP	SH	GW	GT	S	PCT
80	23	37	60	-2	53	10	0	5	1	167	13.8

2000-2001 statistics:

GP	G	A	TP	+/-	PIM	PP	SH	GW	GT	S	PCT
74	23	36	59	+27	52	5	2	3	0	139	16.5

2001-2002 statistics:

GP	G	A	TP	+/-	PIM	PP	SH	GW	GT	S	PCT
82	25	45	70	+3	52	6	2	5	0	170	14.7

LAST SEASON

Led team in assists and shorthanded goals. Second on team in points and game-winning goals. Third on team in goals. Career highs in goals and points. Only Senator to appear in all 82 games.

THE FINESSE GAME

Considering the flaws in his game — his lack of foot speed being the biggest thing holding him back — Bonk is a competent No. 2 centre. The problem is the Senators employ him as a No. 1. You have to give Bonk high marks for trying, and you can't blame him when he is bested because of the talent gap.

Bonk's skating is fine when he gets a good head of steam up, but he doesn't explode in his first two strides (the way Joe Sakic does, for example). Bonk can't utilize his skills when he can't accelerate away from stick-checks. His skating is the primary reason why he has not been able to be an impact scorer in the NHL as he was in the minors.

Bonk is a puck magnet; the puck always seems to end up on his stick in the slot. He scores the majority of his goals from work in-tight, getting his stick free. He has a heavy shot but doesn't have a quick release. He is a smart and creative passer and plays well in advance of his years, with a great deal of poise.

Defensively, Bonk keeps improving. He is decent on face-offs, and can be used to kill penalties because of his anticipation. He is a poor-man's Bobby Holik when he plays with a little edge.

THE PHYSICAL GAME

Although Bonk has good size, he does not show signs of becoming a power forward. He is aggressive only in pursuit of the puck. He goes into the corners and wins many one-on-one battles because of his strength and hand skills. He can lose his cool and will take the occasional bad penalty.

THE INTANGIBLES

Bonk has overachieved for so long now that he's taken for granted, but given how hard Bonk had to work to get this good, he deserves a lot of credit.

PROJECTION

We underestimated Bonk by about 10 points last year. His totals will be assist-heavy. Maybe another 70-point season is in the offing, but we still think 60 is his magic number.

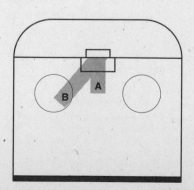

ZDENO CHARA

Yrs. of NHL service: 5
Born: Trencin, Slovakia; Mar. 18, 1977
Position: right defence
Height: 6-9
Weight: 255
Uniform no.: 3
Shoots: left

Career statistics:

GP	G	A	TP	PIM
306	16	36	52	503

1998-1999 statistics:

GP	G	A	TP	+/-	PIM	PP	SH	GW	GT	S	PCT
59	2	6	8	-8	83	0	1	0	0	56	3.6

1999-2000 statistics:

GP	G	A	TP	+/-	PIM	PP	SH	GW	GT	S	PCT
65	2	9	11	-27	57	0	0	1	1	47	4.3

2000-2001 statistics:

GP	G	A	TP	+/-	PIM	PP	SH	GW	GT	S	PCT
82	2	7	9	-27	157	0	1	0	0	83	2.4

2001-2002 statistics:

GP	G	A	TP	+/-	PIM	PP	SH	GW	GT	S	PCT
75	10	13	23	+30	156	4	1	2	0	105	9.5

LAST SEASON

Led team and fifth in NHL in plus-minus. Second on team in penalty minutes. Career highs in goals, assists and points. Missed four games with flu. Missed three games with left shoulder injury.

THE FINESSE GAME

For a player of his height, Chara is very well-coordinated. He has worked on his foot speed which enables him to get in a better position for his checks. Chara's number of hits has risen because he is able to line up players and stay in motion. If he is out of position at all, his hits are sure to be called high sticks and elbows, for the simple reason that he is so much taller than everyone else — their faces just happen to be in the wrong place. By keeping his hands down and his feet moving, Chara can avoid taking needless penalties. He can also register a more jarring legal check.

Chara moves the puck well but he has a tendency to admire his passes, like a baseball player waiting to break into a slow home-run jog around the bases. This leaves him open to hits when he is off balance.

With his long arms, long stick and long body, Chara made a daunting screen up front on the power play, where the Senators often used him.

THE PHYSICAL GAME

Chara is solid, with a good centre of gravity that is rare to find in a player of his altitude. Players simply bounce off him. He goes through phases when he loses his edge, though. When he starts getting those high-sticking calls he has a tendency to back down for a while. He doesn't mind a good scrap, and he has a long reach. He has handled assignments against other teams' top lines. He loves to hit, and for the second straight season was among the NHL leaders in that department.

THE INTANGIBLES

Chara is often his own worst enemy because he demands so much of himself. He has a great reputation as a gamer, and as a kid who is coachable and willing to work to improve his game. At six-foot-nine, he is the tallest defenceman in NHL history. He and Chris Phillips worked well together last season as Ottawa's top defensive pair.

PROJECTION

Even with the power-play time, Chara is a 25-point player. Add to that a triple-digit PIM total, almost guaranteed, and he's a nice pickup for pool players whose categories include penalty minutes.

MIKE FISHER

Yrs. of NHL service: 3
Born: Peterborough, Ont.; June 5, 1980
Position: centre
Height: 6-0
Weight: 193
Uniform no.: 12
Shoots: right

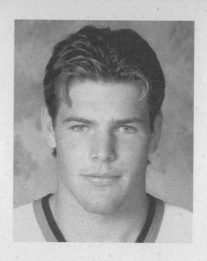

Career statistics:

GP	G	A	TP	PIM
150	26	26	52	116

1999-2000 statistics:

GP	G	A	TP	+/-	PIM	PP	SH	GW	GT	S	PCT
32	4	5	9	-6	15	0	0	1	0	49	8.2

2000-2001 statistics:

GP	G	A	TP	+/-	PIM	PP	SH	GW	GT	S	PCT
60	7	12	19	-1	46	0	0	3	0	83	8.4

2001-2002 statistics:

GP	G	A	TP	+/-	PIM	PP	SH	GW	GT	S	PCT
58	15	9	24	+8	55	0	3	4	0	123	12.2

LAST SEASON

Tied for third on team in game-winning goals. Missed 19 games with right shoulder separation. Missed one game with left shoulder injury.

THE FINESSE GAME

None of Fisher's skills are elite, but he has a very good all-round game and is rapidly developing into a very reliable centre.

Fisher is a good skater. He puts his speed and agility to work on a smart forechecking game; he is well-balanced and shifty on his feet. He possesses good instincts and intelligence; he reads plays well in all zones.

Fisher is developing into a keen penalty killer because of his speed and anticipation. His chief offensive asset is that of a playmaker. He plays a good puck-control game and creates time and space for his linemates with his patience with the puck. He has a deft passing touch. Fisher started getting goal-hungry last season and that was a good thing. He doesn't have a great shot. His scoring chances come from his desire and his willingness to drive to the front of the net. Fisher's work pays off with some close-range goals.

THE PHYSICAL GAME

Amid a finesse-laden lineup in Ottawa, Fisher stands out because of his willingness to play a physical game. He plays an in-your-face style and uses speed as an aggressive weapon. He wins most of his battles for loose pucks. He has decent size but is still growing. Fisher is very competitive and will sacrifice his body to make a play. Unfortunately, he has been banged up in each of the last three seasons.

THE INTANGIBLES

Fisher is developing into a very sound third-line centre.

PROJECTION

It seems whenever Fisher gets on a roll, he gets put back on the shelf again with another injury. We wouldn't bank on Fisher for much more than 60 games, and 30 points, until he gets past the injury bug.

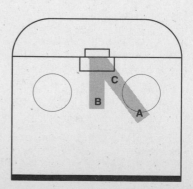

MARTIN HAVLAT

Yrs. of NHL service: 2
Born: Mlada Boleslav, Czech Republic; Apr. 19, 1981
Position: right wing
Height: 6-1
Weight: 178
Uniform no.: 9
Shoots: left

Career statistics:

GP	G	A	TP	PIM
145	41	51	92	86

2000-2001 statistics:

GP	G	A	TP	+/-	PIM	PP	SH	GW	GT	S	PCT
73	19	23	42	+8	20	7	0	5	0	133	14.3

2001-2002 statistics:

GP	G	A	TP	+/-	PIM	PP	SH	GW	GT	S	PCT
72	22	28	50	-7	66	9	0	6	1	145	15.2

LAST SEASON

Led team in game-winning goals. Career highs in goals, assists and points. Tied for team lead in power-play goals and shooting percentage. Third on team in penalty minutes. Missed 10 games with groin injuries.

THE FINESSE GAME

Havlat is an excellent, speedy skater with a huge reserve of confidence. He has superb one-on-one moves, and can leave far more experienced players in a tangle as he dipsy-doodles past them.

Havlat could develop along Claude Lemieux lines, thanks to the way he plays with an edge. He is a catalyst, and plays the game hard both ways. He has the hand skills to back up his brash style. He tends to score big, clutch goals. Havlat is grating enough to goad even smart players into taking a retaliatory penalty. To rub it in, Havlat will go out and score on the power play.

A creative player, Havlat also combines well with his teammates rather than trying to make everything a solo effort.

THE PHYSICAL GAME

Havlat is average-sized but plays much bigger. He is game-tough.

THE INTANGIBLES

Havlat's second half of the season was compromised by his groin injury, which recurred after the Olympics (when he played for the Czech Republic). It might have been the reason for his disappointing playoffs.

PROJECTION

Havlat would have hit the 25-goal mark were it not for his injuries. We fully expect him to reach 30.

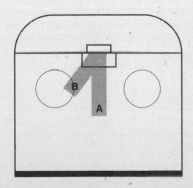

MARIAN HOSSA

Yrs. of NHL service: 4
Born: Stara Lubovna, Slovakia; Jan. 12, 1979
Position: right wing
Height: 6-1
Weight: 199
Uniform no.: 18
Shoots: left

Career statistics:

GP	G	A	TP	PIM
306	107	121	228	163

1998-1999 statistics:

GP	G	A	TP	+/-	PIM	PP	SH	GW	GT	S	PCT
60	15	15	30	+18	37	1	0	2	2	124	12.1

1999-2000 statistics:

GP	G	A	TP	+/-	PIM	PP	SH	GW	GT	S	PCT
78	29	27	56	+5	32	5	0	4	0	240	12.1

2000-2001 statistics:

GP	G	A	TP	+/-	PIM	PP	SH	GW	GT	S	PCT
81	32	43	75	+19	44	11	2	7	0	249	12.9

2001-2002 statistics:

GP	G	A	TP	+/-	PIM	PP	SH	GW	GT	S	PCT
80	31	35	66	+11	50	9	1	4	1	278	11.1

LAST SEASON

Led team in shots. Tied for team lead in power-play goals. Second on team in goals. Third on team in points. Tied for third on team in game-winning goals. Missed one game with knee injury. Missed one game with flu.

THE FINESSE GAME

Hossa is a pure goal-scorer, with excellent hands and the kind of instincts that cannot be taught or drilled into a player. He is nothing short of brilliant on the attack, and destined to be a great, great scorer. His ability to finish is without equal in his age group.

Hossa is a swift and mobile skater, always dangerous one-on-one. There are some similarities between him and fellow Slovak, Ziggy Palffy. Hossa works hard in the offensive zone, but needs to work on his defensive game and his play without the puck. He also needs to be more consistent in his effort. He is used to kill penalties and is a shorthanded threat.

Hossa works well down low, has keen hockey sense, excellent vision, size and skating ability. This guy is the complete offensive package.

THE PHYSICAL GAME

Hossa uses his size well — better in the offensive zone than the rest of the ice. He isn't shy about physical play at all. But Ottawa is a very soft team and he gets bounced around a lot more than he should. Hossa sees a lot of ice time (averaging 18:29 last season) and he tends to wear down a little late in the season.

THE INTANGIBLES

Hossa is still going through some growing pains but he is ready to hit his best stride very soon.

PROJECTION

Hossa is going to keep improving his goal total, year by year, until he wins the Rocket Richard trophy. We thought he would get a little closer to 40 last season, so we'll ask for it from him this year.

PATRICK LALIME

Yrs. of NHL service: 6
Born: St. Bonaventure, Que.; July 7, 1974
Position: goaltender
Height: 6-3
Weight: 185
Uniform no.: 40
Catches: left

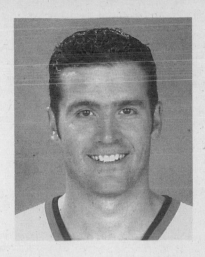

Career statistics:

GP	MIN	GA	SO	GAA	A	PIM
198	11286	469	20	2.49	2	25

1999-2000 statistics:

GP	MIN	GAA	W	L	T	SO	GA	S	SAPCT	PIM
38	2038	2.33	19	14	3	3	79	834	.905	4

2000-2001 statistics:

GP	MIN	GAA	W	L	T	SO	GA	S	SAPCT	PIM
60	3607	2.35	36	19	5	7	141	1640	.914	2

2001-2002 statistics:

GP	MIN	GAA	W	L	T	SO	GA	S	SAPCT	PIM
61	3583	2.48	27	24	8	7	148	1521	.903	19

LAST SEASON
Tied for second in NHL in shutouts.

THE PHYSICAL GAME
Lalime plays an almost classic stand-up style and has very good technique. His reflexes aren't great, so he is careful to make the best use of his height and take away the angle.

Even when he faces a barrage of shots, Lalime never looks like he is getting panicky. Like Martin Brodeur, Lalime plays behind a solid defence, and he probably doesn't get the credit he deserves. He isn't the best puckhandler, but he is adequate.

Lalime struggled with consistency last season, which led to some benchings, which led to more inconsistency. Lalime bears up well under the crease-crashing that has become epidemic, and he doesn't get off his game. He has a temper, though, and he will come out swinging when he's had enough.

THE MENTAL GAME
Season No. 2 as Ottawa's No. 1 goalie did not go smoothly. Maybe Lalime felt threatened by Jani Hurme, who wants his job. It's different than having a veteran backup goalie who understands he is there to start 15-20 games in a support role.

THE INTANGIBLES
Lalime is good enough for now, but he is not among the game's elite goalies and there is serious doubt that he will be. For the Senators to become a serious Cup contender, Lalime will either have to be replaced or will have to take his game to a level we haven't seen yet. But people have always doubted Lalime, and he has usually erased those doubts.

PROJECTION
Lalime holds the top goalie job for now but that might not last the season if he gets off to a slow start. Lalime didn't make it to the 30-win mark last season. It's quite possible he won't this season either, and you might want to downscale him to 25-27 wins.

CURTIS LESCHYSHYN

Yrs. of NHL service: 14
Born: Thompson, Man.; Sept. 21, 1969
Position: left defence
Height: 6-1
Weight: 220
Uniform no.: 7
Shoots: left

Career statistics:

GP	G	A	TP	PIM
923	45	155	200	635

1998-1999 statistics:

GP	G	A	TP	+/-	PIM	PP	SH	GW	GT	S	PCT
65	2	7	9	-1	50	0	0	0	0	35	5.7

1999-2000 statistics:

GP	G	A	TP	+/-	PIM	PP	SH	GW	GT	S	PCT
53	0	2	2	-19	14	0	0	0	0	31	-

2000-2001 statistics:

GP	G	A	TP	+/-	PIM	PP	SH	GW	GT	S	PCT
65	2	7	9	+5	19	1	0	1	0	51	3.9

2001-2002 statistics:

GP	G	A	TP	+/-	PIM	PP	SH	GW	GT	S	PCT
79	1	9	10	-5	44	0	0	0	0	59	1.7

PROJECTION

Leschyshyn will barely reach double digits in points.

LAST SEASON

Missed two games with flu. Missed one game with back injury.

THE FINESSE GAME

Leschyshyn has average skills for a defensive defenceman. He has very slow feet, though he is balanced and strong in a containment game. His passes are soft, but he has a rather low panic point and will try to lug it out himself — not the best option given his limited skills.

He has a nice point shot. It's low and accurate and Leschyshyn gets it away quickly, but it's not elite enough to warrant any significant power-play time. He knows the importance of getting the shot on target, though. He'd rather take a little velocity off the puck to make sure his aim is true.

Leschyshyn is not overly creative and is wholly defence-oriented. His reads are excellent.

THE PHYSICAL GAME

Leschyshyn is aerobically fit. He provides consistency and strong defensive-zone coverage, though he's rather passive and doesn't use his size well. But he does make efficient take-outs to eliminate his man, and doesn't run around the ice trying to pound people. He competes harder in some games than others.

THE INTANGIBLES

Ottawa has a strong but young defence, and Leschyshyn couldn't be in a better situation. He is a third-pair defencemen, which suits his talent level, and provides steadiness and a voice of experience.

CHRIS PHILLIPS

Yrs. of NHL service: 5
Born: Fort McMurray, Alta.; Mar. 9, 1978
Position: left defence
Height: 6-3
Weight: 215
Uniform no.: 4
Shoots: left

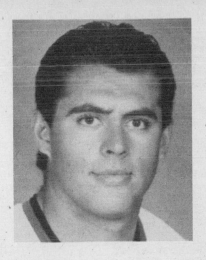

Career statistics:

GP	G	A	TP	PIM
307	21	56	77	169

1998-1999 statistics:

GP	G	A	TP	+/-	PIM	PP	SH	GW	GT	S	PCT
34	3	3	6	-5	32	2	0	0	0	51	5.9

1999-2000 statistics:

GP	G	A	TP	+/-	PIM	PP	SH	GW	GT	S	PCT
65	5	14	19	+12	39	0	0	1	0	96	5.2

2000-2001 statistics:

GP	G	A	TP	+/-	PIM	PP	SH	GW	GT	S	PCT
73	2	12	14	+8	31	2	0	0	0	77	2.6

2001-2002 statistics:

GP	G	A	TP	+/-	PIM	PP	SH	GW	GT	S	PCT
63	6	16	22	+5	29	1	0	1	0	103	5.8

LAST SEASON

Missed 15 games with elbow injury. Missed three games with shoulder injury. Missed one game due to coach's decision.

THE FINESSE GAME

Phillips is a very good skater for his size. He has all of the attributes (decent speed, lateral mobility, balance and agility), and he skates well backwards and has a small turning radius. Carrying the puck doesn't slow him down much. He is skilled enough to be used up front in a pinch, although it confused his development as a younger player.

Phillips still has trouble making defensive reads, probably from the time the Senators switched him between wing and defence. His future is as a blueliner, and he played that position steadily last season.

He will never post Ray Bourque numbers, but Phillips can handle Bourque-like ice time. He has a feel for the offensive part of the game. He joins the attack intelligently and has a hard shot from the point, as well as a good wrist shot when he goes in deep. He is not a great skater: he has a short stride and is not fluid. He doesn't move the puck well and lacks vision.

THE PHYSICAL GAME

There are very few question marks about Phillips's honest brand of toughness. He is solidly built and likes to hit, and just has to learn to do so more consistently. He is mobile enough to catch a defender and drive with his legs to pack a wallop in his checks.

THE INTANGIBLES

Phillips was partnered with Zdeno Chara. The duo saw most of the action against other teams' top lines.

PROJECTION

Phillips had injury problems again, but when he was healthy, he demonstrated that he has taken the next step in becoming a top-four NHL defencemen. Estimate about 30 points from him.

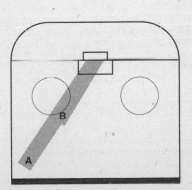

WADE REDDEN

Yrs. of NHL service: 6
Born: Lloydminster, Sask.; June 12, 1977
Position: left defence
Height: 6-2
Weight: 205
Uniform no.: 6
Shoots: left

Career statistics:

GP	G	A	TP	PIM
472	51	147	198	268

1998-1999 statistics:

GP	G	A	TP	+/-	PIM	PP	SH	GW	GT	S	PCT
72	8	21	29	+7	54	3	0	1	1	127	6.3

1999-2000 statistics:

GP	G	A	TP	+/-	PIM	PP	SH	GW	GT	S	PCT
81	10	26	36	-1	49	3	0	2	1	163	6.1

2000-2001 statistics:

GP	G	A	TP	+/-	PIM	PP	SH	GW	GT	S	PCT
78	10	37	47	+22	49	4	0	0	0	159	6.3

2001-2002 statistics:

GP	G	A	TP	+/-	PIM	PP	SH	GW	GT	S	PCT
79	9	25	34	+22	48	4	1	1	0	156	5.8

PROJECTION

Redden's production was off, which might have something to do with concentrating more on his defence. Not a bad thing, since Redden was starting to tilt too much to the offensive part of the game. His scoring range should be 40 points.

LAST SEASON

Led team defencemen in points for third consecutive season. Third on team in plus-minus. Missed three games with flu.

THE FINESSE GAME

Redden is a good skater who can change gears swiftly and smoothly, and his superb rink vision enables him to get involved in his team's attack. He has a high skill level. His shot is hard and accurate and he is a patient and precise passer; his ability to move the puck is one of his best assets.

Redden was mature when he broke into the game. He is smart and his level rises with the level of competition. His poise is exceptional.

Redden's work habits and attitude are thoroughly professional. He is a player who is willing to learn in order to improve his game.

THE PHYSICAL GAME

Redden is not a big hitter, and the coaching staff has to continually ride him to finish his checks. What he lacks in aggressiveness he makes up for with his quietly competitive nature. He can handle a lot of ice time (he averaged 25:09 minutes last season). He plays an economical game without a lot of wasted effort, and he is durable and can skate all night long. He would move up a step if he dished it out instead of just taking it. Redden has a very long fuse.

THE INTANGIBLES

Redden has a laid-back nature, but he raises his game when something is on the line.

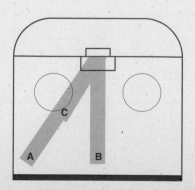

SAMI SALO

Yrs. of NHL service: 4
Born: Turku, Finland; Sept. 2, 1974
Position: right defence
Height: 6-3
Weight: 215
Uniform no.: 5
Shoots: right

Career statistics:

GP	G	A	TP	PIM
195	19	50	69	50

1998-1999 statistics:

GP	G	A	TP	+/-	PIM	PP	SH	GW	GT	S	PCT
61	7	12	19	+20	24	2	0	1	0	106	6.6

1999-2000 statistics:

GP	G	A	TP	+/-	PIM	PP	SH	GW	GT	S	PCT
37	6	8	14	+6	2	3	0	1	0	85	7.1

2000-2001 statistics:

GP	G	A	TP	+/-	PIM	PP	SH	GW	GT	S	PCT
31	2	16	18	+9	10	1	0	0	0	61	3.3

2001-2002 statistics:

GP	G	A	TP	+/-	PIM	PP	SH	GW	GT	S	PCT
66	4	14	18	+1	14	1	1	2	0	122	3.3

LAST SEASON

Missed six games with right hand injury. Missed six games with back spasms. Missed one game with flu. Missed three games with groin injury.

THE FINESSE GAME

Salo is highly skilled. He is also highly vulnerable.

Salo has very quick feet and good mobility, which, combined with his long reach, make him hard to beat one-on-one. He also possesses an extremely hard shot. He likes to get involved offensively, and steps up into the play alertly. He is still growing into his NHL job and as he gains confidence, his offensive contributions will increase. He will eventually develop into a regular on the point on the first power-play unit.

Salo has good hands for passing or receiving the puck, and he makes a crisp first pass out of the zone. He has a good head for the game, and is calm with the puck under pressure. He reads plays well and moves the puck without mistakes. The epitome of a low-risk defenceman, he is a classic crunch-time defenceman for protecting a lead.

Salo has quickly established himself as a top-four defenceman on a solid team.

THE PHYSICAL GAME

Salo won't punish anyone. He is more of a positional defenceman who will ride guys out. He has good size but is not physical.

THE INTANGIBLES

Three consecutive seasons interrupted by injuries are red flags. If he weren't so banged up, Salo would start getting a lot more recognition around the league. Now the question is if Salo will remain healthy enough to make the impact he ought to.

PROJECTION

A healthy Salo will flirt with the 40-point mark this season.

JASON SPEZZA

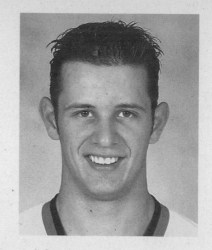

Yrs. of NHL service: 0
Born: Mississauga, Ont.; June 13, 1983
Position: centre
Height: 6-2
Weight: 214
Uniform no.: n.a.
Shoots: right

Career statistics:

GP	G	A	TP	PIM
161	109	173	282	118

2001-2002 junior statistics:

GP	G	A	TP	PIM
53	42	63	105	42

LAST SEASON

Will be entering first NHL season. Appeared in 27 games with Windsor (OHL), scoring 19-26-45. Appeared in 26 games with Belleville (OHL), scoring 23-37-60. Third in OHL in points.

THE FINESSE GAME

There is no denying Spezza has NHL talent. The question, as is it with all young players, is how long it will take before all of the pieces fall into place.

He has been compared to Pierre Turgeon for his playmaking ability and, like Turgeon in his early days, Spezza has a tendency to melt a little under pressure.

Spezza has slick moves and a big shot, but he would rather make the pass. He will have to learn to mix up his play selection. He can toast a defender one-on-one. Spezza needs to improve his defensive play and his skating.

THE PHYSICAL GAME

Spezza has good size, but don't look for him to get involved. He could be a future Lady Byng winner.

THE INTANGIBLES

Spezza has been under intense scrutiny since he was 16, and he hasn't always handled it well. Spezza was in contention for a job with the Senators until late in training camp in 2001, and it affected his play when he was sent back to junior. Spezza didn't revive his season until he was traded to Belleville.

Ottawa is willing to add young players to the lineup when they are ready to step in. The Sens have a desperate need at centre and have a job waiting if Spezza proves he wants it.

PROJECTION

Spezza will be given every chance to win a job in training camp. If he wins it, a 15-goal, 30-assist rookie year would not surprise.

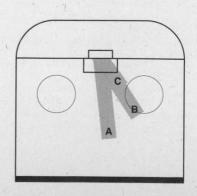

SHAUN VAN ALLEN

Yrs. of NHL service: 7
Born: Calgary, Alta.; Aug. 29, 1967
Position: centre
Height: 6-1
Weight: 204
Uniform no.: 27
Shoots: left

Career statistics:

GP	G	A	TP	PIM
643	70	155	225	335

1998-1999 statistics:

GP	G	A	TP	+/-	PIM	PP	SH	GW	GT	S	PCT
79	6	11	17	+3	30	0	1	0	0	47	12.8

1999-2000 statistics:

GP	G	A	TP	+/-	PIM	PP	SH	GW	GT	S	PCT
75	9	19	28	+20	37	0	2	4	0	75	12.0

2000-2001 statistics:

GP	G	A	TP	+/-	PIM	PP	SH	GW	GT	S	PCT
59	7	16	23	+5	16	0	2	3	0	51	13.7

2001-2002 statistics:

GP	G	A	TP	+/-	PIM	PP	SH	GW	GT	S	PCT
73	8	13	21	0	26	0	1	1	0	48	16.7

PROJECTION

Van Allen is likely to be on the move again. He is a role player who can be useful in the right spot. His optimum production is 30 points.

LAST SEASON

Acquired from Dallas on November 20, 2001, with Donald Audette for Martin Rucinsky and Benoit Brunet. Missed four games with wrist injury.

THE FINESSE GAME

Van Allen always posted huge numbers in the minors, but like so many minor-league scoring stars he cannot transfer his touch to the big leagues. The flaw in Van Allen's case is his skating. It is marginally NHL calibre, and it forced him to change his profile from that of an offensive player to a defensive one.

When Van Allen does accomplish something offensively, it's because of his intelligence and hard work. He is a very good face-off man. If he controls the draw in the offensive zone, he knows how to set up an attack.

Van Allen has become something of a power-play specialist. He seldom plays a poor game because his intensity level is usually high.

THE PHYSICAL GAME

Van Allen's solid defensive play is enhanced by his work ethic. He's not a banger but he will get in the way. He seldom forgets what it takes for him to keep a job in the NHL.

THE INTANGIBLES

Van Allen didn't get much playing time in the first two months after the deal. His future with the Habs seems dim.

PHILADELPHIA FLYERS

Players' Statistics 2001-2002

POS.	NO.	PLAYER	GP	G	A	PTS	+/-	PIM	PP	SH	GW	GT	S	PCT
C	77	ADAM OATES	80	14	64	78	-4	28	3		1		102	13.7
C	97	JEREMY ROENICK	75	21	46	67	32	74	5		3		167	12.6
L	12	SIMON GAGNE	79	33	33	66	31	32	4	1	7		199	16.6
R	8	MARK RECCHI	80	22	42	64	5	46	7	2	4		205	10.7
L	10	JOHN LECLAIR	82	25	26	51	5	30	4		6	1	220	11.4
C	25	KEITH PRIMEAU	75	19	29	48	-3	128	5		3		151	12.6
D	5	KIM JOHNSSON	82	11	30	41	12	42	5		1		150	7.3
R	14	JUSTIN WILLIAMS	75	17	23	40	11	32			1	1	162	10.5
L	87	DONALD BRASHEAR	81	9	23	32	-8	199	1		2		107	8.4
C	39	MARTY MURRAY	74	12	15	27	10	10	1	1	2		109	11.0
C	20	JIRI DOPITA	52	11	16	27	9	8	3		2		79	13.9
L	26	RUSLAN FEDOTENKO	78	17	9	26	15	43		1	3		121	14.1
D	37	ERIC DESJARDINS	65	6	19	25	-1	24	2	1			117	5.1
D	2	ERIC WEINRICH	80	4	20	24	27	26			2		102	3.9
D	3	DANIEL MCGILLIS	75	5	14	19	17	46	2		1		147	3.4
D	6	CHRIS THERIEN	77	4	10	14	16	30		2	3		105	3.8
L	19	PAUL RANHEIM	79	5	4	9	5	36	1				75	6.7
D	22	LUKE RICHARDSON	72	1	8	9	18	102					65	1.5
L	29	TODD FEDORUK	55	3	4	7	-2	141					21	14.3
R	17	BILLY TIBBETTS	42	1	6	7	-16	178			1		48	2.1
D	24	CHRIS MCALLISTER	42		5	5	-7	113					26	
R	92	RICK TOCCHET	14		2	2	-2	28					10	
R	55	*PAVEL BRENDL	8	1		1	-1	2					6	16.7
R	18	*TOMAS DIVISEK	3	1		1	1				1		3	33.3
C	15	JARROD SKALDE	1				0	2					5	
D	42	*BRUNO ST. JACQUES	7				4	2					4	
L	23	GUILLAUME LEFEBVRE	3				-1						3	
L	11	VACLAV PLETKA	1				0						2	
D	15	JOHN SLANEY	1				2						1	
R	21	JESSE BOULERICE	3				-1	5					1	
G	35	NEIL LITTLE	1				0	10						
G	33	BRIAN BOUCHER	41				0	4						
G	32	ROMAN CECHMANEK	46				0	10						

GP = games played; G = goals; A = assists; PTS = points; +/- = goals-for minus goals-against while player is on ice;
PIM = penalties in minutes; PP = power-play goals; SH = shorthanded goals; GW = game-winning goals; GT =
game-tying goals; S = no. of shots; PCT = percentage of goals to shots; * = rookie

PAVEL BRENDL

Yrs. of NHL service: 0
Born: Opocno, Czech Rep.; Mar. 23, 1981
Position: right wing
Height: 6-0
Weight: 204
Uniform no.: 55
Shoots: right

Career statistics:

GP	G	A	TP	PIM
8	1	0	1	2

2001-2002 statistics:

GP	G	A	TP	+/-	PIM	PP	SH	GW	GT	S	PCT
8	1	0	1	-1	2	0	0	0	0	6	16.7

LAST SEASON

Appeared in 64 games with Philadelphia (AHL), scoring 15-22-37 with 22 PIM.

THE FINESSE GAME

When you start throwing the name Mike Bossy around as a comparison point for a young player, you know how special he might be, and what a heavy burden of expectation he is shouldering. Toss in the fact that he was traded in a package for Eric Lindros, and it's no wonder Brendl struggled in his first season in Philadelphia.

One scout said that three things happen when Brendl shoots the puck: he misses the net, he hits the goalie or he scores. In other words, the goalie is virtually helpless and finds it almost impossible to make the save unless Brendl's shot finds him.

Brendl has a heavy wrist and slap shot. His skating is a sticking-point, though. He is strong and balanced on his skates but his foot speed is suspect. Brendl also isn't the game's most advanced defensive player. But neither was Bossy when he was drafted.

THE PHYSICAL GAME

Brendl has excellent size and the desire to take the puck to the net in traffic. He is poised under fire and can shoot or make a play in a throng of defenders. Brendl is still getting used to the notion that the guys who bounced off him in junior are smaller and not as strong as the pros who will now try to stop him on a nightly basis.

Brendl has a history of being extremely lax in his conditioning. The Flyers seem to think they have that problem licked, but we'll see in training camp.

THE INTANGIBLES

It's way too early to give up on a 20-year-old with this much potential. Brendl showed some positive signs in last year's training camp but then sprained his ankle and finished the year in the minors. That's not such a bad thing. Brendl is one kid who needs to grasp the notion of earning a job, rather than having one handed to him.

PROJECTION

Even an improved Brendl will face a battle for a job among a veteran-heavy Flyers team. Still, the Flyers have made room for a kid who proves he belongs (case in point: Simon Gagne). If Brendl can break in with 15 goals, that would be a positive first step.

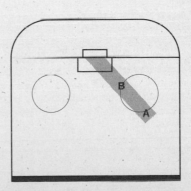

ROMAN CECHMANEK

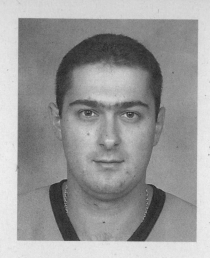

Yrs. of NHL service: 2
Born: Gottwaldov, Czech Republic, Mar. 2, 1971
Position: goaltender
Height: 6-3
Weight: 200
Uniform no.: 32
Catches: left

Career statistics:

GP	MIN	GA	SO	GAA	A	PIM
105	6034	204	14	2.03	1	14

2000-2001 statistics:

GP	MIN	GAA	W	L	T	SO	GA	S	SAPCT	PIM
59	3431	2.01	35	15	6	10	115	1464	.921	4

2001-2002 statistics:

GP	MIN	GAA	W	L	T	SO	GA	S	SAPCT	PIM
46	2603	2.05	24	13	6	4	89	1131	.921	10

LAST SEASON

Second in NHL in goals-against average. Tied for third in NHL in save percentage. Missed 13 games with sprained ankle. Missed one game due to sinus infection.

THE PHYSICAL GAME

Cechmanek is limited in his lateral movement. Teams who play an east-west game can jerk him from post to post and find an opening. It also appears he doesn't always know where the puck is after he makes the initial save. Cechmanek overchallenges, often seeming to come out to the top of the circle, and it's a wonder he knows where the net is behind him. He probably just figures that anything shot towards him, he's going to be able to reach. He's a big sucker.

Cechmanek's biggest asset (pun intended) is his sheer size. He takes up a lot of the net, and when he squares to the shooter, there is very little daylight for even the most gifted sniper to find.

Cechmanek covers the bottom half of the net as well as any goalie in the league. He is the only goalie who intentionally plays pucks off his head. OK, his head is protected by a helmet, but it's still weird.

He's more difficult to beat in-close: he slides his paddle along the ice to close holes. But he will allow bad long-range goals. His tendency to drop quickly makes him vulnerable to high shots on the corners; you'll see teams coming over the blueline and firing shots on him from above the circles.

THE MENTAL GAME

Cechmanek hates to lose, and on his best nights he plays a very focused game. But when things are going badly, Cechmanek is quick to pull up stakes rather than battle on.

THE INTANGIBLES

Only midway into what was a shaky sophomore season, the Flyers foolishly signed Cechmanek to a contract extension. Goaltending is the one position the Flyers have not gotten right during GM Bobby Clarke's reign. Cechmanek blew up in spectacular fashion in the playoffs, yelling at his teammates, who couldn't wait to see him get back on a plane to the Czech Republic. The Flyers traded away his pal, Jiri Dopita, which doesn't bode well.

PROJECTION

It's hard to see Cechmanek finishing the season with the Flyers as their No. 1 goalie. As long as he sticks around, he'll get his share of wins because the Flyers will likely play a sound defensive style under new coach Ken Hitchcock.

ERIC DESJARDINS

Yrs. of NHL service: 14
Born: Rouyn, Que.; June 14, 1969
Position: right defence
Height: 6-1
Weight: 200
Uniform no.: 37
Shoots: right

Career statistics:

GP	G	A	TP	PIM
971	123	384	507	638

1998-1999 statistics:

GP	G	A	TP	+/-	PIM	PP	SH	GW	GT	S	PCT
68	15	36	51	+18	38	6	0	2	0	190	7.9

1999-2000 statistics:

GP	G	A	TP	+/-	PIM	PP	SH	GW	GT	S	PCT
81	14	41	55	+20	32	8	0	4	1	207	6.8

2000-2001 statistics:

GP	G	A	TP	+/-	PIM	PP	SH	GW	GT	S	PCT
79	15	33	48	-3	50	6	1	4	1	187	8.0

2001-2002 statistics:

GP	G	A	TP	+/-	PIM	PP	SH	GW	GT	S	PCT
65	6	19	25	-1	24	2	1	0	0	117	5.1

LAST SEASON

Missed 12 games with broken finger. Missed three games with back injury and bursitis of left elbow. Missed two games with back strain.

THE FINESSE GAME

Desjardins is a competent two-way defenceman. He has the puckhandling skills and poise to beat the first forechecker and carry the puck out of the defensive zone. He makes accurate breakout passes and has enough savvy to keep the play simple, gain the redline and dump the puck deep in attacking ice if no other option is available. He makes the smart, safe play all the time.

Stable and capable enough to handle power-play duty, Desjardins is wise enough to realize only the ultra-elite overpower NHL goalies with point shots. Although he has a strong one-timer, his slap shot is not always accurate. He is much more dangerous offensively when he uses his wrist shot, or simply flips deflectable pucks toward the net.

A fine skater with light, agile feet and a small turning radius, Desjardins goes up-ice well with the play, keeping the gap to the forwards small and remaining in good position to revert to defence if there is a turnover. A long reach helps him challenge puck carriers to make plays more quickly, change their minds or shoot from a lower-percentage angle. He keeps his stick active while killing penalties, sweeping it on the ice to contest passing lanes and intercept pucks.

THE PHYSICAL GAME

Desjardins is particularly effective when penalty killing in front of the net. He immobilizes the opponent's stick first, then ties up the body — which separates him from the huge percentage of defence-men who are satisfied to do one or the other, but not both. He plays a hard game more than a punishing one, but uses his strength in more subtle ways to gain position in front of both goals. On offence, he will venture to the corners from time to time and will beat his check to the front of the net after winning a battle for the puck. Desjardins is quietly tough, but he is not big enough to survive the ice time he is consistently given. The Flyers did cut him back to 22 minutes of average ice time last season but he still struggled.

THE INTANGIBLES

Desjardins's stock has plummeted in Philadelphia. It wouldn't be a shock if the Flyers moved him, and he would make a nice No. 3 or 4 defenceman with a fresh start. A quiet leader on-ice and in the dressing room, Desjardins plays a clean, controlled game and rarely takes stupid penalties. He always seems to be where he is most needed, does not panic and does not fight. He is steady and professional and easy to underappreciate.

PROJECTION

Desjardins gives a lot of steady minutes, and if he can get through a season without the kind of injuries that nagged him last year, he could again get into the 40-point neighbourhood.

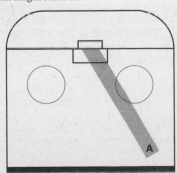

SIMON GAGNE

Yrs. of NHL service: 3
Born: Ste. Foy, Que.; Feb. 29, 1980
Position: centre/left wing
Height: 6-0
Weight: 190
Uniform no.: 12
Shoots: left

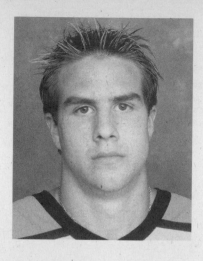

Career statistics:

GP	G	A	TP	PIM
228	80	93	173	72

1999-2000 statistics:

GP	G	A	TP	+/-	PIM	PP	SH	GW	GT	S	PCT
80	20	28	48	+11	22	8	1	4	0	159	12.6

2000-2001 statistics:

GP	G	A	TP	+/-	PIM	PP	SH	GW	GT	S	PCT
69	27	32	59	+24	18	6	0	7	1	191	14.1

2001-2002 statistics:

GP	G	A	TP	+/-	PIM	PP	SH	GW	GT	S	PCT
79	33	33	66	+31	32	4	1	7	0	199	16.6

LAST SEASON

Led team in goals, game-winning goals and shooting percentage. Third in league and second on team in plus-minus. Third on team in points and shots. Career highs in goals, assists and points in third NHL season. Missed two games with bruised shoulder. Missed one game with virus.

THE FINESSE GAME

Gagne is one of those rare young players who has improved steadily from the first season he broke into the league. He just keeps getting better with seldom a stumble.

Gagne is an effortless skater who can be as effective in the closing shifts of the game, when his team is desperate for a goal, as he is in the opening minutes. He doesn't seem to tire. Sleek and fluid, with seamless changes of direction and pace, he can carry the puck without slowing one whit. He plays a strong puck-control game and is one of those puck magnets — he always seems to be involved in the play with the puck.

Gagne is an unselfish player, and works best when teamed with pure finishers. He can score on his own, too, and is a natural goal scorer with an excellent wrist shot. He is outstanding on the power play. He always has his head up and senses his best options. Gagne has improved his defensive game immensely as he made the transition from centre to left wing.

THE PHYSICAL GAME

Gagne will get his body in the way but he is not a physical player. He has some problems when the Flyers are facing a team that is big and strong. Gagne also started to tire and wear down late in the season. As this is likely to become an annual problem for him, he will need to devote himself to fitness and conditioning year-round.

THE INTANGIBLES

Scouts who told us that Gagne would prove to be the best player of the strong rookie crop of 2000 obviously knew what they were talking about. Gagne was a success on a line with Jeremy Roenick and Justin Williams, a line that is likely to stay intact barring any major personnel upheavals.

PROJECTION

Gagne is legit and will continue to see a lot of prime power-play ice time. We predicted 30 goals for him last season. He could easily improve on that to the 35-40 goals range.

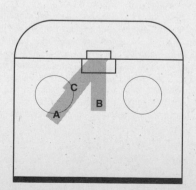

MICHAL HANDZUS

Yrs. of NHL service: 4
Born: Banska Bystrica, Slovakia; Mar. 11, 1977
Position: centre
Height: 6-5
Weight: 210
Uniform no.: 16
Shoots: left

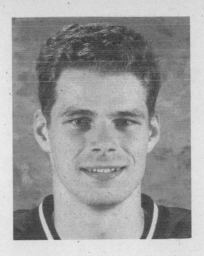

Career statistics:

GP	G	A	TP	PIM
272	58	88	146	141

1998-1999 statistics:

GP	G	A	TP	+/-	PIM	PP	SH	GW	GT	S	PCT
66	4	12	16	-9	30	0	0	0	0	78	5.1

1999-2000 statistics:

GP	G	A	TP	+/-	PIM	PP	SH	GW	GT	S	PCT
81	25	28	53	+19	44	3	4	5	1	166	15.1

2000-2001 statistics:

GP	G	A	TP	+/-	PIM	PP	SH	GW	GT	S	PCT
46	14	18	32	+16	33	3	3	2	0	72	19.4

2001-2002 statistics:

GP	G	A	TP	+/-	PIM	PP	SH	GW	GT	S	PCT
79	15	30	45	-8	34	3	1	1	0	94	16.0

LAST SEASON

Acquired from Phoenix on June 12, 2002, for Brian Boucher and a third-round draft pick. Second on Coyotes in shooting percentage. Tied for third on Coyotes in assists. Missed three games with groin injury.

THE FINESSE GAME

Handzus is so defensively smart that he is the first forward his team can throw out to kill a penalty when a team is two men down. He is very dependable and has a tremendous work ethic.

Handzus has some offensive skill with a big-league shot, and needs to stop thinking purely like a Selke Trophy candidate. Handzus is big (six-foot-five), though still a little weedy. His skating is his primary drawback. It is probably adequate for the NHL, but if he works harder to improve he can become an effective player. He has good balance but needs to add a bit of quickness.

Handzus likes to pass a little too much. He needs to take the puck to the net and chase down rebounds. He needs a little more greed in his game.

Handzus's skills and hockey sense allow him to play in all game situations. He can develop into a solid all-round centre with an emphasis on his offensive skills.

THE PHYSICAL GAME

Handzus needs to fill out just a little, but he has gotten much stronger. He can hold off a defender with one arm and still take a shot or make a pass. He doesn't mind the physical game at all. He has the stamina to handle a lot of ice time. He is not very aggressive and will have to decide how badly he wants an NHL job, and be willing to pay a higher price.

THE INTANGIBLES

Handzus was on the move again. Philadelphia might not appreciate his lack of an edge, but they will like his defensive smarts.

PROJECTION

Handzus can be a steady 30-assist, 50-point player and is a very good two-way centre.

KIM JOHNSSON

Yrs. of NHL service: 3
Born: Malmo, Sweden; Mar. 16, 1976
Position: left defence
Height: 6-1
Weight: 178
Uniform no.: 5
Shoots: left

Career statistics:

GP	G	A	TP	PIM
233	22	66	88	128

1999-2000 statistics:

GP	G	A	TP	+/-	PIM	PP	SH	GW	GT	S	PCT
76	6	15	21	-13	46	1	0	1	0	101	5.9

2000-2001 statistics:

GP	G	A	TP	+/-	PIM	PP	SH	GW	GT	S	PCT
75	5	21	26	-3	40	4	0	0	0	104	4.8

2001-2002 statistics:

GP	G	A	TP	+/-	PIM	PP	SH	GW	GT	S	PCT
82	11	30	41	+12	42	5	0	1	0	150	7.3

LAST SEASON

Led team defencemen in points. Tied for second on team in power-play goals. Career highs in goals, assists and points. One of two Flyers to appear in all 82 games.

THE FINESSE GAME

Johnsson is a mobile skater and puck mover. Never underestimate the value of a defender who does the job of getting the puck out of his zone so efficiently; it keeps the opposition from setting up and reduces the strain on his goaltender.

When Johnsson is playing with confidence, as he did much of last season, he eagerly joins the rush. Johnsson works the point on the first power-play unit. He has a good shot from the point. It is not overpowering, but he releases it quickly and he keeps it low and on net. He is not afraid to venture into the circles because he knows his skating can help him recover and prevent odd-man rushes against. He brings a little cockiness to his game that makes him try some creative plays. Where Johnsson must improve most is in his play without the puck.

Quite reliable defensively, Johnsson plays his position well and makes smart defensive reads. He has a long reach for making sweep and poke checks and tying up an opponent's stick. If he continues to work on the defensive part of his game, he could become a poor man's Nick Lidstrom.

THE PHYSICAL GAME

Just average size, Johnsson is not very physical or aggressive, and he needs to get stronger. His lack of strength around his net is a drawback, and he must work on playing firmer in his own end.

THE INTANGIBLES

It is pretty damning that Johnsson couldn't beg his way into the Rangers' lineup in 2000-01. It is also pretty damning on the Flyers' part that he went from No. 7 or 8 in New York to No. 1 in Philadelphia after arriving in the trade for the rights to Eric Lindros. Is Johnsson that good or were the other Flyers defencemen that bad?

PROJECTION

Johnsson made major progress to become a 40-point scorer, but we don't see him moving into much better company than that. He is a very good offensive defenceman, but not an elite one.

JOHN LECLAIR

Yrs. of NHL service: 11
Born: St. Albans, VT; July 5, 1969
Position: left wing
Height: 6-3
Weight: 226
Uniform no.: 10
Shoots: left

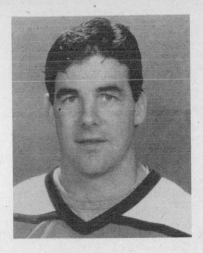

Career statistics:

GP	G	A	TP	PIM
763	341	337	678	361

1998-1999 statistics:

GP	G	A	TP	+/-	PIM	PP	SH	GW	GT	S	PCT
76	43	47	90	+36	30	16	0	7	3	246	17.5

1999-2000 statistics:

GP	G	A	TP	+/-	PIM	PP	SH	GW	GT	S	PCT
82	40	37	77	+8	36	13	0	7	2	249	16.1

2000-2001 statistics:

GP	G	A	TP	+/-	PIM	PP	SH	GW	GT	S	PCT
16	7	5	12	+2	0	3	0	2	0	48	14.6

2001-2002 statistics:

GP	G	A	TP	+/-	PIM	PP	SH	GW	GT	S	PCT
82	25	26	51	+5	30	4	0	6	1	220	11.4

LAST SEASON

Led team in shots. Second on team in goals and game-winning goals. One of two Flyers to appear in all 82 games.

THE FINESSE GAME

You rarely find a player who shoots as often as LeClair does and who has such a good shooting percentage. Most snipers waste a lot of shots, and high-percentage shooters are most selective. LeClair combines the two by working to get into the highest-quality scoring areas and using a terrific shot with a quick release.

A team can defend against LeClair all night long, then lose position on him once and the puck is in the net. He knows his job is to score goals and he doesn't let up — from the opening whistle to the final second of the game.

He is big enough to post up in front and drive through the melees for all the rebounds, deflections and garbage goals his teammates can create. He also has enough power in his skating and confidence in his strength to cut in from the wing and drive to the net. But the left wing's attributes as a scorer far outweigh his abilities as a puckhandler. If the puck were a football, you could imagine him putting it under his arm, lowering his head and ramming it across the goal line.

THE PHYSICAL GAME

LeClair may be the strongest man in the NHL and is nearly impossible to push off the puck legally. He wants to win the puck, wants the puck in the net and will use every ounce of his strength to try to put it there. He always draws the attention of at least one

defender, but accepts his role willingly. Because of a long reach and a big body, LeClair is able to place himself between the puck and the defender. When he has a defender under each arm behind the net, he will happily kick the puck to the front.

The frequent disappointment is that LeClair, who puts so much into winning the puck behind the goal line, doesn't really have the deft touch to make a smooth relay to someone who might be driving to the net. His passing skills are dubious, his puckhandling skills erratic. Teams try to neutralize him by forcing him to carry the puck and make plays.

For all his size and positioning, LeClair isn't a true power forward. He lacks the mean streak around the net that the elite power forwards possess. LeClair is more like Dave Andreychuk. You can hack and whack him, but as his low PIM totals suggest, he rarely fights back.

THE INTANGIBLES

LeClair finally got to enjoy a healthy season after his back problems of two seasons ago, but he is clearly not the 50-goal scorer he once was.

PROJECTION

Lower your expectations and pencil LeClair in for 25-30 goals instead of 40 to 50.

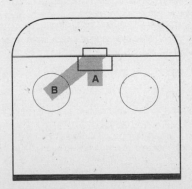

DANIEL MCGILLIS

Yrs. of NHL service: 6
Born: Hawkesbury, Ont.; July 1, 1972
Position: left defence
Height: 6-2
Weight: 230
Uniform no.: 3
Shoots: left

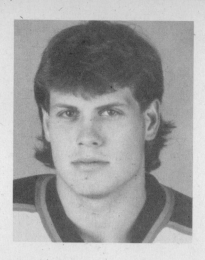

Career statistics:

GP	G	A	TP	PIM
456	48	136	184	409

1998-1999 statistics:

GP	G	A	TP	+/-	PIM	PP	SH	GW	GT	S	PCT
78	8	37	45	+16	61	6	0	4	0	164	4.9

1999-2000 statistics:

GP	G	A	TP	+/-	PIM	PP	SH	GW	GT	S	PCT
68	4	14	18	+16	55	3	0	1	0	128	3.1

2000-2001 statistics:

GP	G	A	TP	+/-	PIM	PP	SH	GW	GT	S	PCT
82	14	35	49	+13	86	4	0	4	0	207	6.8

2001-2002 statistics:

GP	G	A	TP	+/-	PIM	PP	SH	GW	GT	S	PCT
75	5	14	19	+17	46	2	0	1	0	147	3.4

LAST SEASON

Missed six games with back injury. Missed one game with groin injury.

THE FINESSE GAME

The arrival of Kim Johnsson and Eric Weinrich to the Flyers' defence corps helped alleviate some of the pressure McGillis might have felt to duplicate his 2000-01 season, when he led the team's defencemen in points. That is not McGillis's game.

True, that was the case in college. McGillis was an offensive defenceman at Northeastern, but his skills were not elite enough to develop into an "offence-man," so McGillis has applied himself to the defensive aspects of the game. The result is that he can provide point production with an edge. McGillis does have a wicked hard point shot, but he is better at playing a hard game.

Not a quick skater, McGillis is strong and agile enough for his size. He uses his finesse skills in a defensive role — sweep-checks, poke-checks — but needs to improve his reads. He is a fearless shot-blocker and is consistently among the team leaders in that department.

THE PHYSICAL GAME

McGillis steps up and challenges, and he's a big, big hitter. He's not afraid to go after the stars. He has also developed a very sly nasty streak. Even two referees can't catch him in the act. He is quickly becoming a disliked, and not necessarily respected, opponent.

THE INTANGIBLES

McGillis still has to become more reliable defensively, and the coaching change to Ken Hitchcock should help in that department. Hitchcock liked having crunching defenders when he was with Dallas. He is sure to appreciate what McGillis can do.

PROJECTION

McGillis dropped to more realistic numbers last season, but it's significant to note that even though his offence tailed off, his plus-minus improved. He should score in the 25-point range.

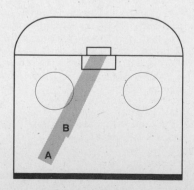

KEITH PRIMEAU

Yrs. of NHL service: 12
Born: Toronto, Ont.; Nov. 24, 1971
Position: centre
Height: 6-5
Weight: 220
Uniform no.: 25
Shoots: left

Career statistics:

GP	G	A	TP	PIM
766	239	305	544	1362

1998-1999 statistics:

GP	G	A	TP	+/-	PIM	PP	SH	GW	GT	S	PCT
78	30	32	62	+8	75	9	1	5	1	178	16.9

1999-2000 statistics:

GP	G	A	TP	+/-	PIM	PP	SH	GW	GT	S	PCT
23	7	10	17	+10	31	1	0	1	0	51	13.7

2000-2001 statistics:

GP	G	A	TP	+/-	PIM	PP	SH	GW	GT	S	PCT
71	34	39	73	+17	76	11	0	4	1	165	20.6

2001-2002 statistics:

GP	G	A	TP	+/-	PIM	PP	SH	GW	GT	S	PCT
75	19	29	48	-3	128	5	0	3	0	151	12.6

LAST SEASON

Tied for second on team in power-play goals. Missed four games with rib injuries. Missed three games with knee injury.

THE FINESSE GAME

The situation in Philadelphia seemed tailor-made for Primeau. Eric Lindros departed, Jeremy Roenick was signed and the Flyers looked to have a happy 1-2 punch up the middle. Primeau responded with his worst goal production since 1993.

Maybe it's because Primeau should really be a left wing and he keeps ending up on teams intent on using him at centre. He is effective there because of his size and skating, but he doesn't have the good playmaking skills, vision or sense to make the most of the centre-ice position. He doesn't have the puck on his stick much, nor does he use his wingers well or establish much chemistry.

Primeau's assets — his strength, his speed, his work along the boards — would serve him much better as a winger. There is less contact in the middle, and he limits himself by thinking more like a scorer than a power forward.

Primeau has a huge stride with a long reach. A left-handed shot, he will steam down the right side, slide the puck to his backhand, get his feet wide apart for balance, then shield the puck with his body and use his left arm to fend off the defenceman before shovelling the puck to the front of the net. He's clever enough to accept the puck at top speed and, instead of wondering what to do with it, make a move.

Primeau has worked hard at all aspects of his game and can be used in almost any role, including penalty killing and four-on-four play.

THE PHYSICAL GAME

It's not that Primeau doesn't like to hit, because he does. When he plays with a little bit of an edge he can dominate for a period or an entire game. He has a fiery temper and can lose control. Emotion is a desirable quality, but he has become too valuable a player to spend too much time in the penalty box. He can't be overly tame, either. He needs to wig out once in a while to scare people. Primeau has acquired considerable presence.

THE INTANGIBLES

Unless the Flyers acquire another centre in the off-season, Primeau looks destined to play the middle again. He is also a good candidate to be dealt.

PROJECTION

We're not sure which direction Primeau's career is heading in, but the signs aren't optimistic, and we would downgrade him to a 50-point guy.

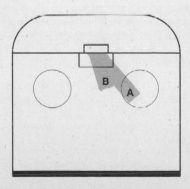

MARK RECCHI

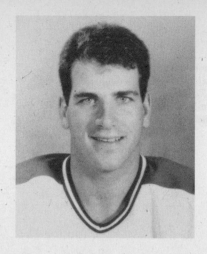

Yrs. of NHL service: 13
Born: Kamloops, B.C.; Feb. 1, 1968
Position: right wing
Height: 5-10
Weight: 185
Uniform no.: 8
Shoots: left

Career statistics:

GP	G	A	TP	PIM
1012	410	664	1074	698

1998-1999 statistics:

GP	G	A	TP	+/-	PIM	PP	SH	GW	GT	S	PCT
71	16	37	53	-7	34	3	0	2	0	171	9.4

1999-2000 statistics:

GP	G	A	TP	+/-	PIM	PP	SH	GW	GT	S	PCT
82	28	63	91	+20	50	7	1	5	1	223	12.6

2000-2001 statistics:

GP	G	A	TP	+/-	PIM	PP	SH	GW	GT	S	PCT
69	27	50	77	+15	33	7	1	8	0	191	14.1

2001-2002 statistics:

GP	G	A	TP	+/-	PIM	PP	SH	GW	GT	S	PCT
80	22	42	64	+5	46	7	2	4	0	205	10.7

LAST SEASON

Led team in power-play goals and shorthanded goals. Second on team in shots. Third on team in goals, assists and game-winning goals. Missed two games due to suspension for an elbowing incident.

THE FINESSE GAME

Recchi is one of the top small players in the game. He's a feisty and relentless worker in the offensive zone. He busts into open ice, finding the holes almost before they open, and excels at the give-and-go. His vision and patience with the puck make him the ideal man to find in open ice on the power play. Recchi can play the point and is dangerous off the right wing halfboards with his unerring ability to find John LeClair or Simon Gagne parked at the left side of the crease.

Recchi can score goals, too. He has a dangerous shot from the off-wing. Although he is not as dynamic as Maurice Richard, he likes to use the Richard cutback while rifling a wrist shot back across. It's heavy, it's on net and it requires no backswing. He follows his shot to the net for a rebound. He has excellent hands, vision and anticipation for any scoring opportunity.

Recchi has worked hard to improve his defensive play. He kills penalties well because he hounds the point men aggressively and knocks the puck out of the zone. Then he heads off on a breakaway or forces the defender to pull him down. He is one of the game's smartest players.

He isn't a pretty skater but he always keeps his feet moving. While other players are coasting,

Recchi's blades are in motion, and he draws penalties. He is ready to spring into any play. He is a puck magnet. He protects the puck well, keeping it close to his feet.

THE PHYSICAL GAME

Recchi gets chopped at because he doesn't hang around the perimeter. He accepts the punishment to get the job done. He is a solid player with a low centre of gravity, and he is tough to knock off the puck.

THE INTANGIBLES

Recchi is an unselfish player and team leader. If his points continue to fall off, he will have to continue to do the little things that can help his team win hockey games. His strong work ethic just continues to intensify.

PROJECTION

It's hard to tell if age or the sag in production from his usual linemate Leclair was most to blame for Recchi's drop-off. He still gets a lot of power-play time, but Recchi may no longer be the point-a-game player he has been for most of his career.

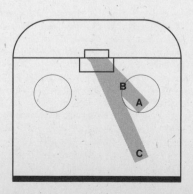

JEREMY ROENICK

Yrs. of NHL service: 13
Born: Boston, Mass.; Jan. 17, 1970
Position: centre
Height: 6-1
Weight: 207
Uniform no.: 97
Shoots: right

Career statistics:

GP	G	A	TP	PIM
983	429	585	1014	1208

1998-1999 statistics:

GP	G	A	TP	+/-	PIM	PP	SH	GW	GT	S	PCT
78	24	48	72	+7	130	4	0	3	0	203	11.8

1999-2000 statistics:

GP	G	A	TP	+/-	PIM	PP	SH	GW	GT	S	PCT
75	34	44	78	+11	102	6	3	12	1	192	17.7

2000-2001 statistics:

GP	G	A	TP	+/-	PIM	PP	SH	GW	GT	S	PCT
80	30	46	76	-1	114	13	0	7	1	192	15.6

2001-2002 statistics:

GP	G	A	TP	+/-	PIM	PP	SH	GW	GT	S	PCT
75	21	46	67	+32	74	5	0	3	0	167	12.6

LAST SEASON

Second in league and led team in plus-minus. Second on team in assists and points. Tied for second on team in power-play goals. Missed seven games with sprained knee.

THE FINESSE GAME

Although he is slowing down by a half-step, Roenick still commands a lot of attention on the ice, drawing away defenders to open up ice for his teammates. He has good acceleration and can turn quickly, change directions or burn a defender with outside speed. A defenceman who plays aggressively against him will be left staring at the back of Roenick's jersey as he skips by en route to the net. He has to be forced into the high-traffic areas, where his lack of size and strength are the only things that derail him.

Roenick is tough to handle one-on-one. He won't make the same move or take the same shot twice in a row. He has a variety of shots and can score from almost anywhere on the ice. He can rifle a wrist shot from 30 feet away, or else wait until the goalie is down and lift in a backhand from in-tight. He has a drag-and-pull move to his backhand that is highly deceptive, and it also keeps the goalie guessing because he is able to show a backhand but pull it quickly to his forehand once he has frozen the goalie.

Roenick is no longer a 90-point player, but he has improved defensively to become a much better two-way centre.

THE PHYSICAL GAME

Roenick remains one of the peskier centres to play against. He can take some stupid penalties. They are nearly all of the aggressive ilk — smashing people into the boards, getting his elbows up — and he never backs down. He plays through pain and is highly competitive. Roenick plays with passion and with such a headlong style that injuries are routine.

THE INTANGIBLES

Roenick should have been the missing ingredient in Philadelphia, but the team chemistry failed to evolve and the Flyers were again a first-round playoff failure. Roenick was the stand-up guy in the room and the go-to guy on the ice. Now there is an issue of how well he will get along with new coach Ken Hitchcock. Bonus points for kissing teammate Mark Recchi on the bench during Toronto's homophobic "Kiss Cam" segment on the Air Canada Centre's video scoreboard.

PROJECTION

Expect Roenick to score around 70 points and again be one of the Flyers' core players.

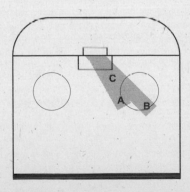

CHRIS THERIEN

Yrs. of NHL service: 8
Born: Ottawa, Ont.; Dec. 14, 1971
Position: left defence
Height: 6-5
Weight: 235
Uniform no.: 6
Shoots: left

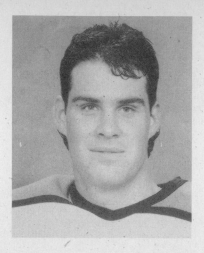

Career statistics:

GP	G	A	TP	PIM
583	27	111	138	463

1998-1999 statistics:

GP	G	A	TP	+/-	PIM	PP	SH	GW	GT	S	PCT
74	3	15	18	+16	48	1	0	0	0	115	2.6

1999-2000 statistics:

GP	G	A	TP	+/-	PIM	PP	SH	GW	GT	S	PCT
80	4	9	13	+11	66	1	0	1	0	126	3.2

2000-2001 statistics:

GP	G	A	TP	+/-	PIM	PP	SH	GW	GT	S	PCT
73	2	12	14	+22	48	1	0	0	0	103	1.9

2001-2002 statistics:

GP	G	A	TP	+/-	PIM	PP	SH	GW	GT	S	PCT
77	4	10	14	+16	30	0	2	3	0	105	3.8

LAST SEASON

Tied for team lead in shorthanded goals. Missed five games with concussion and bruised shoulder.

THE FINESSE GAME

Although not particularly quick, Therien is a fluid skater for his size and has average offensive instincts. He handles the puck well and looks to move it as his first option, but he can skate it out of the defensive zone and make a crisp pass while in motion. If that option is not available, he keeps it simple and bangs the puck off the boards.

Good balance allows Therien to maximize his size when, rather than use the typical big-man play and slide on the ice, he takes a stride, drops to one knee and keeps his stick flat on the ice — making himself a larger and wider obstacle.

Therien doesn't have much lateral speed, but he is a strong, straight-ahead skater who can get up-ice in a hurry. He also has enough offensive sense that he can play the point on the power play on the second unit.

THE PHYSICAL GAME

Therien uses his reach to good advantage. He can dominate, and physically punishes opposing forwards in front of the net in penalty-killing situations. Extremely alert away from the puck, he dedicates himself to gaining body position and making sure his man doesn't get it.

Therien knows big defencemen can be penalty magnets, but he keeps much of his game within the rules. He keeps the elbows down, and plays an effective, clean physical game. Therien has low PIM totals for a player as involved in hitting as he is. When he hits along the boards or battles in the corners, he tends to lower his body position and use his weight to smear an opponent along the boards. Other big defencemen are too upright in those situations or try to use their arms to pin opponents, which isn't as effective. Therien makes his heft and bulk work for him.

THE INTANGIBLES

Therien is a top-four defenceman in Philadelphia and handles a lot of ice time, but he will never be a dominating rearguard. He needs to play with a mobile defenceman. He is a bit exposed when he doesn't get to play with a fluid partner. Therien needs to be motivated at times.

PROJECTION

Therien's offensive instincts do not translate into points because he usually takes only one or two shots per game. He tends to score big goals when he does score, though. He plays fairly mistake-free hockey and has channelled his enthusiasm into dogged, effective play, making him a key contributor. He is a fairly typical journeyman who would be better off as a No. 5 defenceman than a top-four.

ERIC WEINRICH

Yrs. of NHL service: 12
Born: Roanoke, Va.; Dec. 19, 1966
Position: right defence
Height: 6-1
Weight: 213
Uniform no.: 2
Shoots: left

Career statistics:

GP	G	A	TP	PIM
921	63	269	332	687

1998-1999 statistics:

GP	G	A	TP	+/-	PIM	PP	SH	GW	GT	S	PCT
80	7	15	22	-25	89	4	0	1	1	119	5.9

1999-2000 statistics:

GP	G	A	TP	+/-	PIM	PP	SH	GW	GT	S	PCT
77	4	25	29	+4	39	2	0	0	0	120	3.3

2000-2001 statistics:

GP	G	A	TP	+/-	PIM	PP	SH	GW	GT	S	PCT
82	7	24	31	-9	44	3	0	2	1	109	6.4

2001-2002 statistics:

GP	G	A	TP	+/-	PIM	PP	SH	GW	GT	S	PCT
80	4	20	24	+27	26	0	0	2	0	102	3.9

LAST SEASON

Third on team in plus-minus. Missed two games with shoulder injury.

THE FINESSE GAME

Weinrich's skating is above average. He accelerates quickly and has good straightaway speed, though he doesn't have great balance for pivots or superior leg drive for power. He has improved his skating but he is not sturdy on his feet. He jumps into the rush; still, he needs to get his shots through from the point.

Shooting and passing hard, he is strong on the puck. Weinrich usually sees second power-play unit time with the Flyers. He has a low, accurate shot that he gets away quickly. He will not gamble down low, but will sometimes sneak into the top of the circle for a one-timer. Weinrich's composure with the puck in all zones has improved with experience. He is an outstanding penalty killer and shot-blocker.

Weinrich plays better with an offensive-minded partner. He used to be pegged as a more offensive defenceman, but as he has matured, his finesse skills have become more valuable on the defensive side of the puck. He is more useful when he is the support player who can move the puck up and shift into the play. Weinrich is a steady influence for a younger defenceman.

THE PHYSICAL GAME

A good one-on-one defender, Weinrich has reached an age (36 this season) where he needs to watch his minutes. If the Flyers can keep him around 18-20 minutes, they will probably get another solid season out of this smart and likeable veteran.

Although not a soft player (a criticism that dogged him early in his career), Weinrich is not mean by any stretch of the imagination. He will stand up for himself or a teammate, and won't get pushed around. His experience playing with Chris Chelios in Chicago taught him to battle hard and he has incorporated that into his game.

THE INTANGIBLES

An excellent team player in both performance and temperament, Weinrich proved to be one of the better free agent signings of 2001. The Flyers could use another one like him. Weinrich is probably better suited at this stage of his career to be a No. 4 or 5 defencemen, but he figures to be in the Flyers' top three again this season.

PROJECTION

Weinrich should again score in the 25-point range.

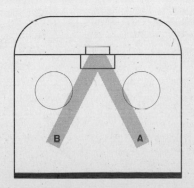

PHOENIX COYOTES

Players' Statistics 2001-2002

POS.	NO.	PLAYER	GP	G	A	PTS	+/-	PIM	PP	SH	GW	GT	S	PCT
C	11	DAYMOND LANGKOW	80	27	35	62	18	36	6	3	2	1	171	15.8
C	8	DANIEL BRIERE	78	32	28	60	6	52	12		5	1	149	21.5
R	19	SHANE DOAN	81	20	29	49	11	61	6		2		205	9.8
D	27	TEPPO NUMMINEN	76	13	35	48	13	20	4		6		117	11.1
C	16	MICHAL HANDZUS	79	15	30	45	-8	34	3	1	1		94	16.0
C	17	LADISLAV NAGY	74	23	19	42	6	50	5		5		187	12.3
L	49	BRIAN SAVAGE	77	20	21	41	-13	38	9		4	1	164	12.2
R	22	CLAUDE LEMIEUX	82	16	25	41	-5	70	4	1	3		174	9.2
D	55	DANNY MARKOV	72	6	30	36	-7	67	4		1		103	5.8
R	12	MIKE JOHNSON	57	5	22	27	14	28	1	2			73	6.8
D	23	PAUL MARA	75	7	17	24	-6	58	2			1	112	6.3
C	36	*KRYSTOFER KOLANOS	57	11	11	22	6	48			5		81	13.6
L	32	BRAD MAY	72	10	12	22	11	95	1		3	1	105	9.5
R	28	LANDON WILSON	47	7	12	19	4	46	1				100	7.0
D	15	RADOSLAV SUCHY	81	4	13	17	25	10	1				49	8.2
D	2	TODD SIMPSON	67	2	13	15	20	152					51	3.9
D	4	OSSI VAANANEN	76	2	12	14	6	74		1			41	4.9
L	44	ANDREI NAZAROV	77	6	5	11	5	215					56	10.7
C	10	DENIS PEDERSON	48	2	6	8	-4	51					42	4.8
D	5	DRAKE BEREHOWSKY	57	2	6	8	0	60			1		38	5.3
R	29	*BRANKO RADIVOJEVIC	18	4	2	6	1	4			1		19	21.0
C	18	SEBASTIEN BORDELEAU	20	1	4	5	-2	10					28	3.6
C	26	MIKE SULLIVAN	42	1	2	3	-3	16					28	3.6
L	24	*DARCY HORDICHUK	34	1	1	2	-5	141					8	12.5
C	45	*JASON JASPERS	4		1	1	-1	4					1	
D	37	DAN FOCHT	8				0	11					5	
C	20	WYATT SMITH	10				-5						4	
R	14	TYLER BOUCK	7				-1	4					3	
L	31	JEAN-GUY TRUDEL	3				0	2					1	
D	38	*MARTIN GRENIER	5				0	5					1	
G	1	SEAN BURKE	60				0	14						
G	42	ROBERT ESCHE	22				0	16						
G	40	PATRICK DESROCHERS	5				0	2						

GP = games played; G = goals; A = assists; PTS = points; +/- = goals-for minus goals-against while player is on ice; PIM = penalties in minutes; PP = power-play goals; SH = shorthanded goals; GW = game-winning goals; GT = game-tying goals; S = no. of shots; PCT = percentage of goals to shots; * = rookie

TONY AMONTE

Yrs. of NHL service: 11
Born: Hingham, Mass.; Aug. 2, 1970
Position: right wing
Height: 6-0
Weight: 200
Uniform no.: 10
Shoots: left

Career statistics:

GP	G	A	TP	PIM
861	352	372	724	603

1998-1999 statistics:

GP	G	A	TP	+/-	PIM	PP	SH	GW	GT	S	PCT
82	44	31	75	0	60	14	3	8	0	256	17.2

1999-2000 statistics:

GP	G	A	TP	+/-	PIM	PP	SH	GW	GT	S	PCT
82	43	41	84	+10	48	11	5	2	1	260	16.5

2000-2001 statistics:

GP	G	A	TP	+/-	PIM	PP	SH	GW	GT	S	PCT
82	35	29	64	-22	54	9	1	3	1	256	13.7

2001-2002 statistics:

GP	G	A	TP	+/-	PIM	PP	SH	GW	GT	S	PCT
82	27	39	66	+11	67	6	1	4	0	232	11.6

LAST SEASON

Signed as free agent by Phoenix on July 12, 2002. Second on Blackhawks in goals and shots. Third on Blackhawks in points. Tied for third on Blackhawks in power-play goals. One of five Blackhawks to appear in all 82 games. Holds current NHL ironman streak with 410 games played.

THE FINESSE GAME

Amonte is blessed with exceptional speed and acceleration. His timing is accurate and his anticipation keen. He has good balance and he can carry the puck at a pretty good clip, though he is more effective when streaking down the wing and getting the puck late. Playing on the left side leaves his forehand open for one-timers, but Amonte is equally secure on the right wing, which gives the Coyotes options in how to utilize him. He's been called a young Yvan Cournoyer for the way he uses his speed to drive wide around the defence to the net. His speed intimidates.

Amonte has a quick release on his wrist shot. He likes to go top shelf, just under the crossbar, and he can also go to the backhand shot or a wrist shot off his back foot, like a fadeaway jumper in basketball. He is a top power-play man, since he is always working himself into open ice. He is better utilized down low on a power play than on the point. An accurate shooter, and one who takes a lot of shots, Amonte is also creative in his playmaking. He passes very well and is conscious of where his teammates are; he usually makes the best percentage play. He has confidence in his shot and wants the puck when the game is on the line.

Offensively, Amonte is a smart player away from the puck. He sets picks and creates openings for his teammates. He is an aggressive penalty killer and a shorthanded threat.

THE PHYSICAL GAME

Amonte's speed and movement keep him out of a lot of trouble zones, but he will also drive to the front of the net and take punishment there if that's the correct play. He loves to score, he loves to help his linemates score, and although he is outweighed by a lot of NHL defencemen, he is seldom outworked. He's intense and is not above getting chippy and rubbing his glove in someone's face. Amonte plays through pain, as evidenced by his ironman streak.

Amonte takes a lot of abuse and plays through the checks. He seldom takes bad retaliatory penalties. He just keeps his legs driving and draws calls with his nonstop skating.

THE INTANGIBLES

His pending free agency and trade talk were a continuing distraction for Amonte in his last season in Chicago, but he still stayed focused well enough to help them make the playoffs. He will be asked to be a leader on a young team again in Phoenix, but it is a hungry team and looks like a nice fit.

PROJECTION

Expect Amonte to be energized by the move to Arizona, and he could return to 90-point territory. Amonte is the kind of guy who will want to prove he's worth the Coyotes' investment.

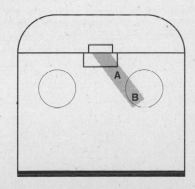

DRAKE BEREHOWSKY

Yrs. of NHL service: 10
Born: Toronto, Ontario; Jan. 3, 1972
Position: right defence
Height: 6-2
Weight: 225
Uniform no.: 5
Shoots: right

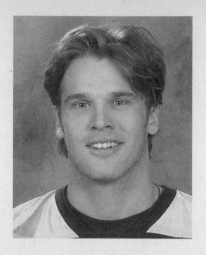

Career statistics:

GP	G	A	TP	PIM
486	30	92	122	754

1998-1999 statistics:

GP	G	A	TP	+/-	PIM	PP	SH	GW	GT	S	PCT
74	2	15	17	-9	140	0	0	0	0	79	2.5

1999-2000 statistics:

GP	G	A	TP	+/-	PIM	PP	SH	GW	GT	S	PCT
79	12	20	32	-4	87	5	0	1	0	102	11.8

2000-2001 statistics:

GP	G	A	TP	+/-	PIM	PP	SH	GW	GT	S	PCT
80	7	19	26	-9	121	4	0	1	0	107	6.5

2001-2002 statistics:

GP	G	A	TP	+/-	PIM	PP	SH	GW	GT	S	PCT
57	2	6	8	0	60	0	0	1	0	38	5.3

PROJECTION

Berehowsky has been counted out before. He will have to battle for his ice time in Phoenix, but he can probably get about 12-13 minutes a game and around 20 points.

LAST SEASON

Acquired from Vancouver on December 28, 2001, with Denis Pederson for Todd Warriner, Trevor Letowski, Tyler Bouck and a third-round draft pick in 2003.

THE FINESSE GAME

Expansion rescues some players from the NHL's junk drawer, and Berehowsky was salvaged by the Nashville Predators. His career nearly ended by a knee injury, he had to fight his way back into the league by playing in such places as San Antonio before earning a full-time role with the Predators. He has since been on the move to Vancouver and now Phoenix, where he may find a numbers crunch.

Berehowsky's foot speed is not great, but he has good hands for a big guy. He logs a lot of ice time and gets significant power-play time by default. He rates average in most categories.

He will probably be a fifth or sixth defenceman on most teams with Phoenix. He picked up some playing time after Danny Markov's injury but it will be a battle for him to get into the top four.

THE PHYSICAL GAME

Berehowsky is strong and tough and loves to mix it up. He plays with a lot of confidence and fire.

THE INTANGIBLES

Berehowsky is serious about the game. He gets to the rink early and prepares himself well. He nearly lost his NHL career, which is why he appreciates it more than many young players. He is a good character player who has persevered.

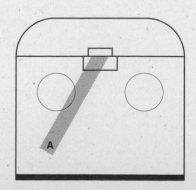

DANIEL BRIERE

Yrs. of NHL service: 4
Born: Gatineau, Que.; Oct. 6, 1977
Position: centre
Height: 5-10
Weight: 181
Uniform no.: 8
Shoots: left

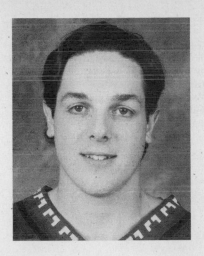

Career statistics:

GP	G	A	TP	PIM
190	53	47	100	96

1998-1999 statistics:

GP	G	A	TP	+/-	PIM	PP	SH	GW	GT	S	PCT
64	8	14	22	-3	30	2	0	2	0	90	8.9

1999-2000 statistics:

GP	G	A	TP	+/-	PIM	PP	SH	GW	GT	S	PCT
13	1	1	2	0	0	0	0	0	1	9	11.1

2000-2001 statistics:

GP	G	A	TP	+/-	PIM	PP	SH	GW	GT	S	PCT
30	11	4	15	-2	12	9	0	1	0	43	25.6

2001-2002 statistics:

GP	G	A	TP	+/-	PIM	PP	SH	GW	GT	S	PCT
78	32	28	60	+6	52	12	0	5	1	149	21.5

LAST SEASON

Led NHL in shooting percentage. Led team in goals and power-play goals. Second on team in points. Tied for second on team in game-winning goals. Career highs in goals, assists and points. Missed one game with back spasms. Missed three games due to coach's decision.

THE FINESSE GAME

Briere is a pure goal-scorer, but what has turned him from a career minor leaguer to a bona fide major leaguer is his willingness to add other elements to his game instead of simply relying on his great shot. Briere kills penalties, wins draws (he was the Coyotes' best face-off man at over 51 per cent) and works hard to get to loose pucks.

He has a great release on an accurate shot, but Briere's chief asset is as a playmaker. He is dynamite on the power play, with the extra space allowing him the extra half-second of time to make a play. He uses his time and space wisely. He has a great passing touch with the puck, plus terrific hockey sense and vision. He knows how to play this game.

Briere is an excellent, shifty skater, which serves him well in the offensive zone since players are forced to restrain him rather than hit him. Defensively, he has to use his skating and his hand skills to survive. He's outmuscled in any physical match-ups. The big knock on Briere is his lack of defensive awareness, but his plus-minus was respectable.

THE PHYSICAL GAME

Briere devoted his 2001 off-season to better physical conditioning, and it paid off with a career year. Briere couldn't have a better inspirational teammate than Claude Lemieux. Briere has to play with an edge, even if he is on the small side. Scott Gomez, who was tutored by Lemieux in New Jersey, isn't that much bigger than Briere, but is much harder to play against.

THE INTANGIBLES

Briere was available off the waiver wire, and a lot of GMs have to be kicking themselves because Briere suddenly "gets it." Maybe it was being benched three times in mid-season. Maybe Briere realized he was running out of chances. Whatever the reason, it appears that Briere has brought all the necessary elements of his game together.

PROJECTION

We pegged Briere for 25 goals last season and he exceeded that. He should become a consistent 30-goal scorer.

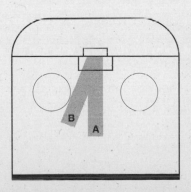

SEAN BURKE

Yrs. of NHL service: 14
Born: Windsor, Ont.; Jan. 29, 1967
Position: goaltender
Height: 6-4
Weight: 210
Uniform no.: 1
Catches: left

Career statistics:

GP	MIN	GA	SO	GAA	A	PIM
693	39551	1979	31	3.00	21	274

1998-1999 statistics:

GP	MIN	GAA	W	L	T	SO	GA	S	SAPCT	PIM
59	3402	2.66	21	24	14	3	151	1624	.907	27

1999-2000 statistics:

GP	MIN	GAA	W	L	T	SO	GA	S	SAPCT	PIM
7	418	2.58	2	5	0	0	18	208	.913	2

2000-2001 statistics:

GP	MIN	GAA	W	L	T	SO	GA	S	SAPCT	PIM
62	3644	2.27	25	22	13	4	138	1766	.922	16

2001-2002 statistics:

GP	MIN	GAA	W	L	T	SO	GA	S	SAPCT	PIM
60	3587	2.29	33	21	6	5	137	1711	.920	14

LAST SEASON

Career high in wins and shutouts. Recorded 20 or more wins for seventh time in career. Missed 10 games with groin injuries. Missed one game with flu.

THE PHYSICAL GAME

Burke is a big goalie and when he is on his game, he challenges the shooter well and comes out to the top of his crease. He worked extensively with a goalie coach and has learned to make the game easier on himself. Burke is much better technically now than at any other point in his career.

Burke handles the puck well. He is confident and active on the dump-ins. He gives his defencemen a chance to handle the puck more easily and break out of the zone with less effort.

Burke fills up the net and is very quick for a net-minder of his size. He has a quick glove hand, but when he gets into slumps he will drop it and give the shooter the top corner over his left shoulder.

THE MENTAL GAME

Burke had to work very hard to win a full-time role again in the NHL and he takes nothing for granted. At 35, he is in the best physical shape of his career, and that has made him more mentally relaxed as well. He doesn't have to ask his body to respond to a play — he simply trusts that it will.

Burke is smarter and mellower but still highly competitive.

THE INTANGIBLES

Burke was the Coyotes' MVP for the second consecutive season. Phoenix might be a little worried about him losing an edge — they acquired Brian Boucher from Philadelphia during the off-season — but Burke probably has one peak year left to give.

PROJECTION

Phoenix played better than expected in front of Burke, and if he hadn't been injured, he would have been among the league's leaders in victories. He is capable of another 30-win season.

SHANE DOAN

Yrs. of NHL service: 7
Born: Halkirk, Alta.; Oct. 10, 1976
Position: right wing
Height: 6-2
Weight: 223
Uniform no.: 19
Shoots: right

Career statistics:

GP	G	A	TP	PIM
487	94	131	225	455

1998-1999 statistics:

GP	G	A	TP	+/-	PIM	PP	SH	GW	GT	S	PCT
79	6	16	22	-5	54	0	0	0	0	156	3.8

1999-2000 statistics:

GP	G	A	TP	+/-	PIM	PP	SH	GW	GT	S	PCT
81	26	25	51	+6	66	1	1	4	0	221	11.8

2000-2001 statistics:

GP	G	A	TP	+/-	PIM	PP	SH	GW	GT	S	PCT
76	26	37	63	0	89	6	1	6	1	220	11.8

2001-2002 statistics:

GP	G	A	TP	+/-	PIM	PP	SH	GW	GT	S	PCT
81	20	29	49	+11	61	6	0	2	0	205	9.8

LAST SEASON

Led team in shots. Third on team in points. Missed one game with sprained ankle.

THE FINESSE GAME

Doan's game is speed. He is fast and strong, and forechecks aggressively and intelligently along the wall and in the corners. He intimidates with his skating because he gets in on a defenceman fast. Once he gains control of the puck he finds the open man in front of the net. He isn't overly creative, but will thrive on the dump-and-chase play, where he can just skate on his wing and race for the puck.

Doan has acceptable wrist and slap shots and has gained a great deal of confidence in using them. That has elevated his game. He has stopped thinking purely like a checker and drives to the net instead of turning away from the play.

Doan sees first-unit power-play time and is given plenty of responsibility to score. It's not really his game, and Tony Amonte's arrival may relieve some of that pressure. Doan is better as a No. 2 winger. He is an excellent penalty killer and adds a huge dimension to his game when he gets in a scoring groove.

THE PHYSICAL GAME

Doan is strong and a very good body checker. He seems to have a mean streak lurking under his exterior. He will lay some hard hits on people. He plays with a little edge but doesn't take many bad penalties.

THE INTANGIBLES

Doan seemed to suffer from the departure of Jeremy Roenick, and was never in sync with the other Phoenix centres, who are more finesse-oriented than Roenick. That made his goal production somewhat disappointing, but it really wasn't that off the mark. People look at Doan's size and speed and want 40 goals from him, but it's not going to happen.

Not many forwards score 25 goals and play as well defensively and physically as Doan. He is well-respected by teammates and coaches and could be a future captain of the Coyotes — or another NHL team. Doan has pretty high trade value and the Coyotes are always looking to balance the budget.

PROJECTION

Doan can develop into a Jere Lehtinen type of forward who can consistently score 25 goals a season.

KRYSTOFER KOLANOS

Yrs. of NHL service: 1
Born: Calgary, Alta.; July 27, 1981
Position: centre
Height: 6-3
Weight: 203
Uniform no.: 36
Shoots: right

Career statistics:

GP	G	A	TP	PIM
57	11	11	22	48

2001-2002 statistics:

GP	G	A	TP	+/-	PIM	PP	SH	GW	GT	S	PCT
57	11	11	22	+6	48	0	0	5	0	81	13.6

LAST SEASON

First NHL season. Led NHL rookies in game-winning goals. Missed 22 games with a concussion. Missed three games due to coach's decision.

THE FINESSE GAME

Kolanos may turn into a special kind of goal-scorer. He is one of those players that always seems to attract the puck. He knows where the play is going to go and anticipates. Most importantly, Kolanos wants the puck when the game is on the line.

Kolanos made the jump right out of college with an impressive training camp in 2001. He scored the overtime goal that won the NCAA title for Boston College. His confidence had to carry him through his first test — getting a contract with the Coyotes.

Kolanos will develop into a very good second-line centre. He is smart and has very good hand skills. His skating is NHL calibre. Kolanos played on a line with Shane Doan and Ladislav Nagy and was fifth among the league's rookie scorers at the time of his injury.

THE PHYSICAL GAME

Kolanos clearly wasn't the same player when he returned in March after his concussion. He scored only one goal in the final 10 games, and appeared in only two games in the playoffs. He has decent size, but wasn't a very aggressive player even before the injury.

THE INTANGIBLES

Kolanos had a shot at Calder Trophy consideration until his season was ruined by a concussion. The Coyotes were impressed enough with what they saw to feel comfortable trading away the more experienced centre Michal Handzus.

PROJECTION

We'll look for 15-20 goals and 15-20 assists from Kolanos over a full second season, which would be a good step forward (or in his case, back).

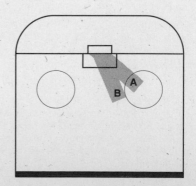

DAYMOND LANGKOW

Yrs. of NHL service: 6
Born: Edmonton, Alberta; Sept. 27, 1976
Position: centre
Height: 5-11
Weight: 180
Uniform no.: 11
Shoots: left

Career statistics:

GP	G	A	TP	PIM
462	95	155	250	278

1998-1999 statistics:

GP	G	A	TP	+/-	PIM	PP	SH	GW	GT	S	PCT
78	14	19	33	-8	39	4	1	2	0	149	9.4

1999-2000 statistics:

GP	G	A	TP	+/-	PIM	PP	SH	GW	GT	S	PCT
82	18	32	50	+1	56	5	0	7	0	222	8.1

2000-2001 statistics:

GP	G	A	TP	+/-	PIM	PP	SH	GW	GT	S	PCT
71	13	41	54	+12	50	3	0	2	0	190	6.8

2001-2002 statistics:

GP	G	A	TP	+/-	PIM	PP	SH	GW	GT	S	PCT
80	27	35	62	+18	36	6	3	2	1	171	15.8

LAST SEASON

Led team in points and shorthanded goals. Tied for team lead in assists. Second on team in goals. Third on team in plus-minus, power-play goals and shooting percentage. Career highs in goals and points. Missed two games with fractured toe.

THE FINESSE GAME

Langkow's primary drawback is his size. Yet small men can succeed in the NHL, and it appears Langkow could be one of them, especially if the Coyotes get just a little bigger to support him. He has terrific hockey sense, which is probably his chief asset, along with his stickhandling ability and shot. He is a fine passer with good vision, and he is patient with the puck. He is not shy about shooting and possesses an effective wrist shot and slap shot.

Langkow has good speed, spies his options quickly and works hard. He knows what's going to happen before it does, which is the mark of an elite playmaker. He will harass opponents on the forecheck and create turnovers. Langkow is a solid two-way forward and likes to play in a system with aggressive forechecking. His defensive awareness is above average, but his face-off ability is less than average.

THE PHYSICAL GAME

Langkow is a spunky, fast, in-your-face kind of player. He has some sandpaper in his game, which gives him an edge over other small forwards who only rely on their finesse skills. He doesn't mind aggravating people, and he'll throw punches at far bigger men. He won't be intimidated and does his scoring in the trenches despite getting hit. He has a high pain threshold.

THE INTANGIBLES

Langkow and Daniel Briere up the middle is a pretty small 1-2 punch and Langkow handled a lot of minutes (averaging 19:10). Langkow shows all the signs of being one of those indispensable forwards that other teams dislike playing against. He has a disappointing playoffs record.

PROJECTION

While Langkow is best suited as a third-line forward, he's destined to be a top six in Phoenix for the foreseeable future. He is a solid 25-goal, 60-point player.

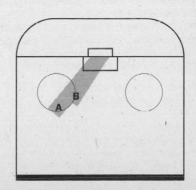

CLAUDE LEMIEUX

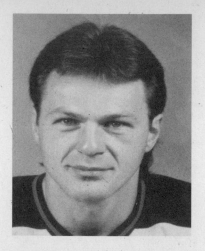

Yrs. of NHL service: 18
Born: Buckingham, Que.; July 16, 1965
Position: right wing
Height: 6-1
Weight: 226
Uniform no.: 22
Shoots: right

Career statistics:

GP	G	A	TP	PIM
1129	371	394	765	1712

1998-1999 statistics:

GP	G	A	TP	+/-	PIM	PP	SH	GW	GT	S	PCT
82	27	24	51	0	102	11	0	8	1	292	9.2

1999-2000 statistics:

GP	G	A	TP	+/-	PIM	PP	SH	GW	GT	S	PCT
83	20	27	47	-3	90	7	0	3	0	257	7.8

2000-2001 statistics:

GP	G	A	TP	+/-	PIM	PP	SH	GW	GT	S	PCT
46	10	16	26	+1	58	2	0	1	0	99	10.1

2001-2002 statistics:

GP	G	A	TP	+/-	PIM	PP	SH	GW	GT	S	PCT
82	16	25	41	-5	70	4	1	3	0	174	9.2

LAST SEASON

Only Coyote to appear in all 82 games. Third on team in shots.

THE FINESSE GAME

Lemieux is a shooter, a disturber, a force. He loves the puck, wants the puck, needs the puck and is sometimes obsessed with the puck. When he is struggling, that selfishness hurts the team. But when he gets into his groove, everyone is happy to stand back and let him roll.

When Lemieux is on, he rocks the house. He has a hard slap shot and shoots well off the fly. He is not afraid to jam the front of the net for tips and screens and will battle for loose pucks. He has great hands for close-in shots. But there are fewer nights like that now for Lemieux, who turned 37 during the off-season, so he has wisely concentrated on other areas. He is defensively responsible and can kill penalties. He can also take face-offs, since he will work hard to tie up the opposing man on the draw.

What hasn't changed about Lemieux is that his value increases once the regular season ends. If the Coyotes improve just a bit more this season, fans could yet see vintage Lemieux in the postseason.

THE PHYSICAL GAME

Lemieux is strong, with good skating balance and great upper-body and arm power. He is very tough along the boards and in traffic in front of the net, out-duelling many bigger opponents because of his fierce desire. Because he is always whining and yapping, the abuse he takes is often ignored, but it's not unusual to find him with welts across his arms and cuts on his

face. His satisfaction comes from knowing that his opponent usually looks even worse.

Of course, Lemieux also infuriates opponents by goading them into dropping their gloves — then he turtles. He will gleefully inform you that he's a lover, not a fighter.

THE INTANGIBLES

Even the Lemieux magic couldn't help the Coyotes progress in the playoffs. Despite the prickly image he projects as a player, Lemieux is a surprisingly good guy to have around to help bring younger kids along. The rookies and sophs on the Coyotes will benefit from another season playing with this winner.

PROJECTION

Lemieux is purely a third-line player now, but he can still play an important role and score 15-20 goals. Time is running out on him now, and this could be his last season to howl. We don't expect him to go quietly.

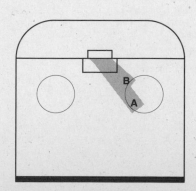

PAUL MARA

Yrs. of NHL service: 3
Born: Ridgewood, NJ; Sept. 7, 1979
Position: left defence
Height: 6-4
Weight: 210
Uniform no.: 23
Shoots: left

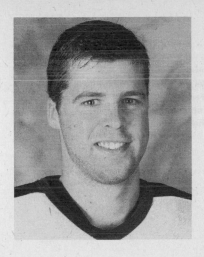

Career statistics:

GP	G	A	TP	PIM
192	21	43	64	185

1998-1999 statistics:

GP	G	A	TP	+/-	PIM	PP	SH	GW	GT	S	PCT
1	1	1	2	-3	0	1	0	0	0	1	100.0

1999-2000 statistics:

GP	G	A	TP	+/-	PIM	PP	SH	GW	GT	S	PCT
54	7	11	18	-27	73	4	0	1	0	78	9.0

2000-2001 statistics:

GP	G	A	TP	+/-	PIM	PP	SH	GW	GT	S	PCT
62	6	14	20	-16	54	2	0	1	0	78	7.7

2001-2002 statistics:

GP	G	A	TP	+/-	PIM	PP	SH	GW	GT	S	PCT
75	7	17	24	-6	58	2	0	0	1	112	6.3

LAST SEASON

Career highs in assists and points. Tied career high in goals. Missed five games with bruised foot. Missed two games with bruised wrist.

THE FINESSE GAME

Mara is primarily an offensive defenceman. His point shot is a weapon not because of its velocity — he is no Al MacInnis — but because he gets it away quickly and keeps it low and on net. He creates chances for tip-ins and scrambles off his rebounds. He can run a power play.

Mobile for his size, Mara's skating is quite smooth and powerful. He is also one of those efficient skaters who can stay as strong late in the game as he was on his first few shifts.

He has good vision and is an excellent passer. He is also quick to move the puck out of his zone and will jump up and join the rush. Mara is fairly advanced defensively for a young player, and has become more reliable, which means Phoenix will continue to use him in more crunch-time situations. Mara's progress has been steady. He has good hockey intelligence.

THE PHYSICAL GAME

Mara makes take-outs, but he is not a punishing hitter. He is tall but lean, and needs to fill out more because he will need more strength to compete in the trenches. Mara was not in the best of shape when he arrived from Tampa Bay in a trade (in 2001 in the Nikolai Khabibulin deal), but Phoenix stresses conditioning for its players (look what it did for Daniel Briere) and Mara has improved in this department.

THE INTANGIBLES

Mara has moved into the top four of the Coyotes defence corps. He will see a lot of prime ice time, especially on the power play.

PROJECTION

Mara finally was able to enjoy a fairly healthy season. He came close to the 30 points we predicted for him last season, and the way he has developed, an improvement to 30 or 35 points would not come as a surprise.

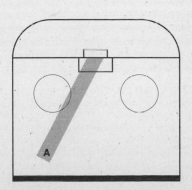

DANIIL MARKOV

Yrs. of NHL service: 5
Born: Moscow, Russia; July 11, 1976
Position: left defence
Height: 6-1
Weight: 190
Uniform no.: 55
Shoots: left

Career statistics:

GP	G	A	TP	PIM
272	15	66	81	204

1998-1999 statistics:

GP	G	A	TP	+/-	PIM	PP	SH	GW	GT	S	PCT
57	4	8	12	+5	47	0	0	0	1	34	11.8

1999-2000 statistics:

GP	G	A	TP	+/-	PIM	PP	SH	GW	GT	S	PCT
59	0	10	10	+13	28	0	0	0	0	38	-

2000-2001 statistics:

GP	G	A	TP	+/-	PIM	PP	SH	GW	GT	S	PCT
59	3	13	16	+6	34	1	0	2	0	49	6.1

2001-2002 statistics:

GP	G	A	TP	+/-	PIM	PP	SH	GW	GT	S	PCT
72	6	30	36	-7	67	4	0	1	0	103	5.8

LAST SEASON

Tied for third on team in plus-minus. Career highs in goals, assists and points. Missed 10 games with fractured bone in foot.

THE FINESSE GAME

Markov was paired last season with another young defenceman, Paul Mara, and they are a terrific duo to see in action. Markov is pretty sound positioning-wise, and he is a good skater. Markov has become a lot smarter about recognizing his offensive chances — he loves that part of the game — and is lower-risk defensively.

Markov makes a good first pass. Once he gets the puck he is looking to go up-ice for a play, which not all defencemen do, and a stick-to-stick pass gets him out of trouble. His frequent injuries kept him from getting in a real groove.

Markov has added an edge to his game, rather than just relying on his skills. He can be as irritating as teammate Claude Lemieux, and he will plow over an opponent (or a referee) in his pursuit of the puck. His enthusiasm is contagious. His teammates love playing with him because of his zest for the game.

THE PHYSICAL GAME

Markov isn't very big but he brings a little edge and a little chippiness to his game. He's a bit brash and cocky. He has some grit and steps up his game in big spots. Markov tends to get hit with a nagging injury season after season.

His teammates and coach appreciate Markov's toughness. In a November game against Columbus, Markov took a puck in the face, suffered a broken nose and cuts around his left eye. Even though his team had a three-goal lead, Markov shrugged off the pain and returned to action even though only 10 minutes remained in the game.

THE INTANGIBLES

When Markov suffered a broken foot late in the season, it pretty much ended the Coyotes' hopes to do anything in the playoffs. He has become that important to the team. Markov is a key component of a team that traded away its older stars and is building a competitive young squad. He is a leader by example.

PROJECTION

Markov stepped up in both points and overall play. If he stays healthy all season, look for 40 points from this fully evolved defenceman.

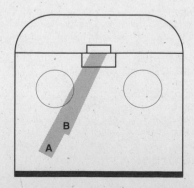

LADISLAV NAGY

Yrs. of NHL service: 2
Born: Preslov, Slovakia; June 1, 1979
Position: centre
Height: 5-11
Weight: 194
Uniform no.: 17
Shoots: left

Career statistics:

GP	G	A	TP	PIM
131	33	32	65	74

1999-2000 statistics:

GP	G	A	TP	+/-	PIM	PP	SH	GW	GT	S	PCT
11	2	4	6	+2	2	1	0	0	0	15	13.3

2000-2001 statistics:

GP	G	A	TP	+/-	PIM	PP	SH	GW	GT	S	PCT
46	8	9	17	-2	22	2	0	2	0	64	12.5

2001-2002 statistics:

GP	G	A	TP	+/-	PIM	PP	SH	GW	GT	S	PCT
74	23	19	42	+6	50	5	0	5	0	187	12.3

PROJECTION

A 30-goal season is not that far off for Nagy. It might even be this season.

LAST SEASON

Second on team in shots. Tied for second on team in game-winning goals. Third on team in goals. Missed seven games with knee injury. Missed one game with bruised shoulder.

THE FINESSE GAME

Nagy is a very skilled player. He has great hands and a good sense for the game.

Nagy's overall speed is just about average but what sets him apart is his initial burst of quickness, cheetah-like, for the first 10 feet. He jumps into holes and reads the openings very well. Nagy is good at taking the puck to the net with his quickness and his deft touch.

Nagy has a confidence to him, almost a cockiness, which good scorers have to have. He is creative and willing to try moves that other players either can't do or would hesitate to even attempt. Nagy is not afraid to shoot the puck or walk off the half-boards on a power play.

Nagy hasn't been used to kill penalties but he could learn to become a shorthanded threat if he applies himself there.

THE PHYSICAL GAME

Nagy is on the small side and does not play a physical game, although he is by no means a perimeter player. You will find Nagy playing in traffic.

THE INTANGIBLES

Nagy has a tremendous offensive upside. Being able to play on a line with Tony Amonte — whether full-time or on the power play — will open up some ice for Nagy. Nagy is one of the players Phoenix received in exchange for Keith Tkachuk in 2001.

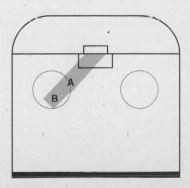

ANDREI NAZAROV

Yrs. of NHL service: 8
Born: Chelyabinsk, Russia; May 22, 1974
Position: left wing
Height: 6-5
Weight: 234
Uniform no.: 44
Shoots: right

Career statistics:

GP	G	A	TP	PIM
477	49	69	118	1143

1998-1999 statistics:

GP	G	A	TP	+/-	PIM	PP	SH	GW	GT	S	PCT
62	7	9	16	-4	73	0	0	2	1	71	9.9

1999-2000 statistics:

GP	G	A	TP	+/-	PIM	PP	SH	GW	GT	S	PCT
76	10	22	32	+3	78	1	0	1	0	110	9.1

2000-2001 statistics:

GP	G	A	TP	+/-	PIM	PP	SH	GW	GT	S	PCT
79	2	4	6	-23	229	0	0	0	0	63	3.2

2001-2002 statistics:

GP	G	A	TP	+/-	PIM	PP	SH	GW	GT	S	PCT
77	6	5	11	+5	215	0	0	0	0	56	10.7

LAST SEASON

Acquired from Boston on January 25, 2002, for a fifth-round draft choice in 2002. Led Coyotes in penalty minutes. Missed three games due to coach's decision.

THE FINESSE GAME

Nazarov isn't overly creative with the puck, but with his size, does he have to be? This giant has decent hand skills around the net, though he does have some trouble fishing out loose pucks from his feet in goal-mouth scrambles, presumably because his head is so far from the ice it's tough to see.

The biggest improvement in Nazarov's game is in his skating. He can handle some second-line and second-unit power-play time with assurance. He is not at his best handling the puck for long and is insecure if forced to rush with it. Defenders brave enough to venture close have a relatively easy time stripping it from him because the puck is so far from his feet. He plops himself in front of the net on power plays and creates a wall that is nearly impossible for the goalie to see around. Nazarov needs to play with linemates who will get him the puck. He has decent hands and can shoot.

Nazarov is smart and understands the game well. He is aware of his limitations and won't try to do too much. He has an obvious love for the game.

THE PHYSICAL GAME

When he first broke into the league with San Jose, he quickly developed a reputation as a scary-mean player. He is a good, hard, physical player, but he isn't the sort who goes looking to hurt people. Nazarov is just so big and strong that the injuries kind of happen. He'll fight when he has to, and his long reach makes him tough for even some of the league's best brawlers to cope with. He will protect his teammates and provide an emotional spark.

THE INTANGIBLES

Nazarov is with his sixth NHL team in a very short span. It seems that no one can quite contain this bull in the china shop style. Nazarov is raw and rough. He certainly gets a lot of room to work on his puck-handling skills.

PROJECTION

Forget points. Although Nazarov will continue to work on being a better player to get ice time, his value lies in your fantasy league with a category for PIM. A sensational year for him would be 10 goals.

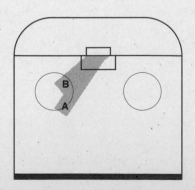

TEPPO NUMMINEN

Yrs. of NHL service: 14
Born: Tampere, Finland; July 3, 1968
Position: left defence
Height: 6-2
Weight: 199
Uniform no.: 27
Shoots: right

Career statistics:

GP	G	A	TP	PIM
1020	102	402	504	375

1998-1999 statistics:

GP	G	A	TP	+/-	PIM	PP	SH	GW	GT	S	PCT
82	10	30	40	+3	30	1	0	0	2	156	6.4

1999-2000 statistics:

GP	G	A	TP	+/-	PIM	PP	SH	GW	GT	S	PCT
79	8	34	42	+21	16	2	0	2	0	126	6.3

2000-2001 statistics:

GP	G	A	TP	+/-	PIM	PP	SH	GW	GT	S	PCT
72	5	26	31	+9	36	1	0	2	0	109	4.6

2001-2002 statistics:

GP	G	A	TP	+/-	PIM	PP	SH	GW	GT	S	PCT
76	13	35	48	+13	20	4	0	6	0	117	11.1

LAST SEASON

Led team defencemen in points for fifth consecutive season. Tied for sixth among NHL defencemen in points. Tied for team lead in assists. Missed six games with fractured foot.

THE FINESSE GAME

The "all-underrated" team tag has become kind of a cliché now. Suffice it to say that Numminen does have the flashy numbers or playing style to merit Norris Trophy consideration, but is just a notch below the game's elite defencemen.

Smart and reserved, Numminen's agility and anticipation make him look much faster than he is. A graceful skater with a smooth change of direction, he never telegraphs what he is about to do. His skating makes him valuable on the first penalty-killing unit. He will not get caught out of position and is seldom bested one-on-one.

If he is under pressure, Numminen is not afraid to give up the puck on a dump-and-chase, rather than force a neutral-zone play. He works best with a partner with some offensive savvy. Otherwise, he takes too much of the offensive game on himself, and his plays look forced. He would rather dish off than rush with the puck, and he is a crisp passer, moving the puck briskly and seldom overhandling it. He is terrific at making the first pass to move the puck out of the zone.

Numminen is not a finisher. He joins the play but doesn't lead it. Most of his offence is generated from point shots or passes in-deep. He works the right point on the power play. He is uncannily adept at keeping the puck in at the point, frustrating opponents who try to clear it out around the boards. He intentionally shoots the puck wide for tip-ins by his surehanded forwards. He is not afraid to pinch, either.

THE PHYSICAL GAME

For a scrawny guy, Numminen plays an acceptable physical game, and he plays hurt. He can be intimidated and doesn't scare attackers, who will attempt to drive through him to the net. Opponents get a strong forecheck on him to neutralize his smart passing game. He'll employ his body as a last resort, but would rather use his stick and gain the puck. He is even-tempered and not at all nasty. He averaged close to 24 minutes per game last season and faced other teams' top lines night after night. At 34, that's a bit taxing, and the Coyotes need to trim his minutes.

THE INTANGIBLES

Surely it would have helped this steady defenceman's cause if he had played for some successful teams, but earning paycheques in Winnipeg and Phoenix failed to do much to raise Numminen's profile. He is respected throughout the league, though. No NHL team would hesitate to take him and put him on its top pair.

PROJECTION

Numminen is a complete, if not elite, defenceman and capable of again scoring 45 points.

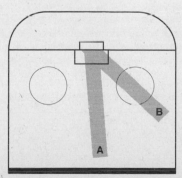

DENIS PEDERSON

Yrs. of NHL service: 6
Born: Prince Albert, Sask.; Sept. 10, 1975
Position: centre / left wing
Height: 6-2
Weight: 205
Uniform no.: 10
Shoots: right

Career statistics:

GP	G	A	TP	PIM
392	53	65	118	359

1998-1999 statistics:

GP	G	A	TP	+/-	PIM	PP	SH	GW	GT	S	PCT
76	11	12	23	-10	66	3	0	1	0	145	7.6

1999-2000 statistics:

GP	G	A	TP	+/-	PIM	PP	SH	GW	GT	S	PCT
47	6	5	11	-6	18	0	0	1	0	56	10.7

2000-2001 statistics:

GP	G	A	TP	+/-	PIM	PP	SH	GW	GT	S	PCT
61	4	8	12	0	65	0	1	3	0	70	5.7

2001-2002 statistics:

GP	G	A	TP	+/-	PIM	PP	SH	GW	GT	S	PCT
48	2	6	8	-4	51	0	0	0	0	42	4.8

LAST SEASON

Acquired from Vancouver on December 28, 2001, with Drake Berehowsky for Todd Warriner, Trevor Letowski, Tyler Bouck and a third-round draft choice in 2003. Missed 11 games with fractured sternum. Missed seven games with hip pointer.

THE FINESSE GAME

Pederson is an intelligent hockey player who has the potential to develop into a solid two-way forward, but we just don't know if he is going to reach that potential. Pederson's development has been constantly interrupted by injuries, and there may just come a point where it stalls completely.

Pederson's skills aren't elite level, but he makes the most of all of his abilities with his hockey sense. He shows some heady flashes of playmaking and is alert around the net for loose pucks. Most of his goals come from hard work around the cage, not pretty rushing plays.

On the power play, he uses his size down low and crashes the net. He works well in traffic, and has nice hands for picking the puck out of a tangle of skates and sticks. Pederson is a puck magnet because he gives a second and third effort. He has a decent array of shots, including a backhand and a wrist shot, the latter being his best weapon.

Pederson can play centre or wing. Centre is his natural position and he is happier there, but he needs to be put in one position and left there. Moving him around just seems to confuse him.

Very good defensively, Pederson can be used to kill penalties.

THE PHYSICAL GAME

Pederson is strong and competes hard for the puck. He has a little bit of a mean streak in him, enough to keep his opponents on their toes, and he will come unglued once in awhile. But for the most part he is a disciplined player and does not take lazy penalties. He protects the puck well with his body.

Still gaining in size and strength, Pederson should have the goods to compete against any team's power forwards on a nightly basis, though he has been absurdly susceptible to nagging injuries.

THE INTANGIBLES

Pederson is highly regarded for his leadership qualities, but it's hard for a player to lead when he always seems to be in the trainer's room. Pederson is on his third team in the last three years. He is a player who tends to be very hard on himself, which doesn't make things any easier for him because of all the bad breaks he has had.

PROJECTION

Pederson should be a 20-goal, checking-line forward, but the chance he can stay healthy for a full season in order to attain those numbers is doubtful.

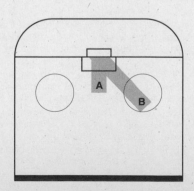

BRIAN SAVAGE

Yrs. of NHL service: 8
Born: Sudbury, Ont.; Feb. 24, 1971
Position: centre / left wing
Height: 6-2
Weight: 193
Uniform no.: 49
Shoots: left

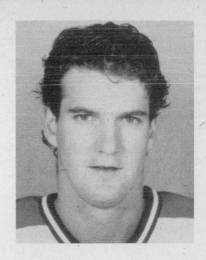

Career statistics:

GP	G	A	TP	PIM
491	161	136	297	233

1998-1999 statistics:

GP	G	A	TP	+/-	PIM	PP	SH	GW	GT	S	PCT
54	16	10	26	-14	20	5	0	4	1	124	12.9

1999-2000 statistics:

GP	G	A	TP	+/-	PIM	PP	SH	GW	GT	S	PCT
38	17	12	29	-4	19	6	1	5	0	107	15.9

2000-2001 statistics:

GP	G	A	TP	+/-	PIM	PP	SH	GW	GT	S	PCT
62	21	24	45	-13	26	12	0	1	0	172	12.2

2001-2002 statistics:

GP	G	A	TP	+/-	PIM	PP	SH	GW	GT	S	PCT
77	20	21	41	-13	38	9	0	4	1	164	12.2

LAST SEASON

Acquired from Montreal on January 25, 2002, with a third-round draft choice in 2002 or 2003 and future considerations for Sergei Berezin. Second on Coyotes in power-play goals. Missed four games with wrist injury. Missed two games with hip injury.

THE FINESSE GAME

Savage lacks the creativity and vision for playing centre (he suffers from a bit of tunnel vision), but his experience as a centre helps him as a left wing. He has a quick release and is accurate with his shot. He feasts from the hash marks in and seldom passes up a shot to make a play. He needs to play with a centre to get him the puck. Savage has excellent outside speed.

A streaky scorer, Savage doesn't bring much to the game when he isn't scoring. Rather than working harder through the dry spells, he lets the slumps slow him down. Then it becomes a vicious cycle, where it's hard for him to get ice time to break out of it.

Savage has quick hands for picking up the puck and for working on face-offs. He's a good skater. Defensively he remains a liability, mostly because of his inconsistent effort.

THE PHYSICAL GAME

He doesn't use his body well and can be intimidated playing a daunting team. He is strong on his skates and he has decent size. He needs to compete more.

THE INTANGIBLES

Savage was a disappointment in Phoenix, scoring only 6-6-12 in the 30 games after the trade, and he followed that up with an uninspiring playoffs. Savage has worked so hard to resume his NHL career, coming back from a career-threatening neck injury in 1999-2000. We'd like to give him the benefit of the doubt and chalk it up to him being negatively affected by the move from Montreal. If that's the case, Savage has to shake it off. He will have to prove himself in training camp with winning a top six spot.

PROJECTION

Savage still has the goods to be a 30-goal scorer, but it's starting to look like 20-25 will be his niche now.

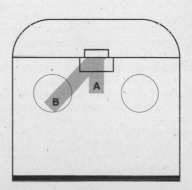

OSSI VAANANEN

Yrs. of NHL service: 2
Born: Vantaa, Finland; Aug. 18, 1980
Position: left defence
Height: 6-5
Weight: 205
Uniform no.: 4
Shoots: left

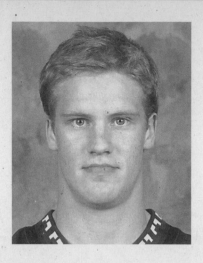

Career statistics:

GP	G	A	TP	PIM
157	6	24	30	164

2000-2001 statistics:

GP	G	A	TP	+/-	PIM	PP	SH	GW	GT	S	PCT
81	4	12	16	+9	90	0	0	2	0	69	5.8

2001-2002 statistics:

GP	G	A	TP	+/-	PIM	PP	SH	GW	GT	S	PCT
76	2	12	14	+6	74	0	1	0	0	41	4.9

LAST SEASON

Second NHL season. Tied career high in assists. Missed six games with bruised shoulder.

THE FINESSE GAME

In only his sophomore season, Vaananen was among the Coyotes' top defencemen in ice time and less-glamorous departments like hits and blocked shots.

Most of what Vaananen does well occurs in his own end of the ice. He blocks shots, takes away passing lanes and clears out the front of his net. He is big and strong and sturdy on his skates. If he is guilty of anything, it is nights when he tries to do too much.

Vaananen is a smart player and a quick study. He has never been a scorer at any level of his development, and it isn't going to happen in the NHL. He digs in around his own net, though, and is gritty in all the right areas. He moves the puck very well.

THE PHYSICAL GAME

Vaananen has good size and strength and plays a zesty game. He is tall and has a very long reach for tying up attackers. He handles a lot of ice time (averaging just over 20 minutes last season). Once he got into the lineup after opening night he was impossible to pry off the ice. He doesn't take many bad penalties. He plays hard and clean.

Vaananen has added a few pounds (about 10-12) since his rookie year but it's not likely he'll get overly bulky.

THE INTANGIBLES

Vaananen is part of a very solid Phoenix defence core that has a nice blend of veteran leadership (Teppo Numminen and Todd Simpson), finesse (Danny Markov) and youth (Paul Mara and Vaananen). He hasn't taken a backwards step yet.

PROJECTION

Vaananen is colourful and just plain fun to watch. He will never score many points, but his effort is consistent.

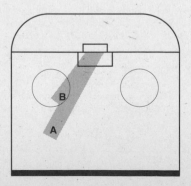

PITTSBURGH PENGUINS

Players' Statistics 2001-2002

POS.	NO.	PLAYER	GP	G	A	PTS	+/-	PIM	PP	SH	GW	GT	S	PCT
R	27	ALEXEI KOVALEV	67	32	44	76	2	80	8	1	3	2	266	12.0
C	38	JAN HRDINA	79	24	33	57	-7	50	6		6		115	20.9
C	20	ROBERT LANG	62	18	32	50	9	16	5	1	3		175	10.3
R	95	ALEXEI MOROZOV	72	20	29	49	-7	16	7		3		162	12.4
C	22	RANDY ROBITAILLE	58	14	23	37	-23	33	5		1		121	11.6
C	66	MARIO LEMIEUX	24	6	25	31	0	14	2				75	8.0
D	28	MICHAL ROZSIVAL	79	9	20	29	-6	47	4		4		89	10.1
L	10	VILLE NIEMINEN	66	11	16	27	-1	38	1		5		83	13.3
C	16	*KRIS BEECH	79	10	15	25	-25	45	2				126	7.9
C	17	*TOBY PETERSEN	79	8	10	18	-15	4	1	1			116	6.9
L	33	DAN LACOUTURE	82	6	11	17	-19	71		1			77	7.8
C	14	MILAN KRAFT	68	8	8	16	-9	16	1		2	1	103	7.8
R	18	SHEAN DONOVAN	61	8	7	15	-21	44	1		2		82	9.8
L	9	JEFF TOMS	52	9	5	14	-9	14	2			1	84	10.7
D	5	JANNE LAUKKANEN	47	6	7	13	-18	28	3		1		66	9.1
D	7	ANDREW FERENCE	75	4	7	11	-12	73	1			1	82	4.9
C	15	WAYNE PRIMEAU	33	3	7	10	-1	18		1			28	10.7
R	24	IAN MORAN	64	2	8	10	-11	54			1		94	2.1
C	82	MARTIN STRAKA	13	5	4	9	3		1		1		33	15.1
C	26	KENT MANDERVILLE	38	3	5	8	3	12					43	7.0
D	3	JAMIE PUSHOR	76		8	8	-13	84					60	
D	8	HANS JONSSON	53	2	5	7	-12	22	2				37	5.4
L	25	KEVIN STEVENS	32	1	4	5	9	25					34	2.9
D	23	JOHN JAKOPIN	19		4	4	2	42					3	
R	37	*TOM KOSTOPOULOS	11	1	2	3	-1	9					8	12.5
D	2	*JOSEF MELICHAR	60		3	3	-1	68					46	
D	4	MIKE WILSON	21	1	1	2	-12	17					14	7.1
D	6	*RICK BERRY	70		2	2	-3	81					49	
L	29	KRZYSZTOF OLIWA	57		2	2	-5	150					31	
R	72	*ERIC MELOCHE	23	1		1	-7	8					29	
C	41	*SHANE ENDICOTT	4		1	1	-1	4					2	
G	1	JOHAN HEDBERG	66				0	22						
G	30	J-SEBASTIEN AUBIN	21				0								

GP = games played; G = goals; A = assists; PTS = points; +/- = goals-for minus goals-against while player is on ice; PIM = penalties in minutes; PP = power-play goals; SH = shorthanded goals; GW = game-winning goals; GT = game-tying goals; S = no. of shots; PCT = percentage of goals to shots; * = rookie

KRIS BEECH

Yrs. of NHL service: 1
Born: Salmon Arm, B.C.; Feb. 5, 1981
Position: centre
Height: 6-3
Weight: 180
Uniform no.: 16
Shoots: left

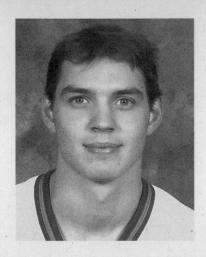

Career statistics:

GP	G	A	TP	PIM
83	10	15	25	47

2000-2001 statistics:

GP	G	A	TP	+/-	PIM	PP	SH	GW	GT	S	PCT
4	0	0	0	-2	2	0	0	0	0	0	0.0

2001-2002 statistics:

GP	G	A	TP	+/-	PIM	PP	SH	GW	GT	S	PCT
79	10	15	25	-25	45	2	0	0	0	126	7.9

LAST SEASON

First NHL season. Missed three games due to coach's decision.

THE FINESSE GAME

Beech is a six-foot-three centre who can skate (right there, a good formula for future success). Comparisons to Jean Ratelle and maybe even Jean Béliveau will abound because of Beech's size, grace, reach and playmaking ability. He is an excellent skater, widely considered the best skater among the top draft prospects of 1999. He also has good anticipation. Combine that with an explosive first step and you get a hint of what an offensive force Beech could become.

A playmaker first, Beech has a quick release on his wrist shot and a low, hard, accurate slapper. He will need to play with a big winger who likes to drive to the net so Beech can get the puck through. His defensive game needs a lot more work. He had the worst plus-minus on a team that had a lot of bad minuses. He can score goals, but those will come because he knows where to position himself rather than because of his offensive strength.

Beech needs to learn the two-way game and become better on draws.

THE PHYSICAL GAME

Beech needs to fill out. He is a little weedy, and while he was able to compete physically in junior, he will have to get a little stronger to do so at the NHL level. Part of that will come as he matures, but he will also need time with a strength coach. He plays with a little edge. If you push him, he'll whack you.

THE INTANGIBLES

He proved he wasn't ready yet for the NHL in his brief stint with the Caps at the start of the season. Beech is probably the first player Penguins fans will see in their lineup who comes to the team as the result of the Jagr trade. That tag will never escape him, and Beech is going to have to learn to deal with it.

The No. 2 role behind Mario Lemieux is wide open in training camp (especially after Martin Straka's off-season back injury, suffered during weight training).

PROJECTION

Beech is being rushed in Pittsburgh, and he'll have to sink or swim. He will be much heavier on assists than goals, and may score in the 40-point range — more if he gets the second-line role.

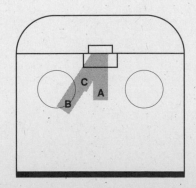

RICK BERRY

Yrs. of NHL service: 1
Born: Brandon, On.; Nov. 4, 1978
Position: defence
Height: 6-2
Weight: 210
Uniform no.: 6
Shoots: left

Career statistics:

GP	G	A	TP	PIM
89	0	6	6	119

2001-2002 statistics:

GP	G	A	TP	+/-	PIM	PP	SH	GW	GT	S	PCT
70	0	2	2	-3	81	0	0	0	0	49	0.0

LAST SEASON

Acquired from Colorado on March 19, 2002, with Ville Nieminen for Darius Kasparaitis.

THE FINESSE GAME

Berry has some really top-notch finesse skills, and he applies them almost exclusively to the defensive part of the game.

Berry is a very good skater, forward and back. He has good lateral mobility and is quite agile. He makes a good first pass out of the defensive zone, or he can skate the puck out himself and get a rush started. Berry won't pinch or gamble too deep into the offensive zone, even though he is such a good skater he could scramble back and recover defensively.

Berry has good hockey sense and a pretty good point shot. He could be involved more in the attack as he becomes more comfortable. Right now he seems more intent on learning his defensive positioning, and that's not a bad thing. It will give him a better foundation for what looks like a bright future.

THE PHYSICAL GAME

Berry is a good-sized defenceman who relishes the physical part of the game. Because he is such a good skater, he can generate some good leg drive for his hits. Berry has a naturally aggressive streak.

THE INTANGIBLES

Every year Penguins GM Craig Patrick auctions off one of his kids and seems to end up with a prized prospect from someone else's organization. This time, it's Berry, who should easily fit into Pittsburgh's top four (maybe even top two) on defence. He has very good leadership qualities.

PROJECTION

Berry hasn't been much of a scorer at any level. More than 20 points would be a pleasant surprise.

SHEAN DONOVAN

Yrs. of NHL service: 7
Born: Timmins, Ont.; Jan. 22, 1975
Position: right wing
Height: 6-3
Weight: 210
Uniform no.: 18
Shoots: right

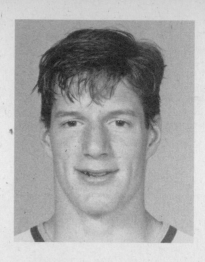

Career statistics:

GP	G	A	TP	PIM
471	62	61	123	311

1998-1999 statistics:

GP	G	A	TP	+/-	PIM	PP	SH	GW	GT	S	PCT
68	7	12	19	+4	37	1	0	1	0	81	8.6

1999-2000 statistics:

GP	G	A	TP	+/-	PIM	PP	SH	GW	GT	S	PCT
51	5	7	12	-17	26	1	0	1	0	66	7.6

2000-2001 statistics:

GP	G	A	TP	+/-	PIM	PP	SH	GW	GT	S	PCT
63	12	11	23	-14	47	1	3	1	0	93	12.9

2001-2002 statistics:

GP	G	A	TP	+/-	PIM	PP	SH	GW	GT	S	PCT
61	8	7	15	-21	44	1	0	2	0	82	9.8

LAST SEASON

Claimed off waivers from Atlanta on March 15, 2002. Missed two games with lacerated elbow.

THE FINESSE GAME

Donovan has big-league speed but lacks the hand skills to make the best use of it. His quickness and powerful stride allow him to shift directions with agility. And he doesn't waste energy. He knows where he is supposed to be positioned and reads plays well. He has good anticipation, which stamps him as a strong penalty killer, though he is not a shorthanded scoring threat yet because of his lack of moves on a breakaway.

Donovan may never be a great point producer because of his lack of scoring or playmaking touch. For the second straight season he showed fatal lapses in effort and, as a result, was a healthy scratch down the stretch and into the playoffs. He could earn a steady job as a third-line checking winger, but has to become more consistent in his nightly effort. He isn't fazed by facing some of the league's better wingers, and has the skating ability to shadow almost anyone.

THE PHYSICAL GAME

Donovan is always busy making hits; he brings a lot of energy to a game when he is in the mood. He doesn't have much of a mean streak but shows an occasional willingness to agitate. He needs to get under his opponents' skin a little more. He takes the body but doesn't punish people. He is well-conditioned and has good stamina. He doesn't get pushed off the puck easily.

THE INTANGIBLES

A player with Donovan's kind of speed can have a comfortable, 10-year NHL career, but he'll only be successful if he can add more scoring and intensity. He has few games when he is a real presence, and that's the tease. Donovan scored 2-1-3 in 13 games after the joining the Penguins.

PROJECTION

All speed, no finish. He is a long shot to get much more than 25 points.

JOHAN HEDBERG

Yrs. of NHL service: 1
Born: Leksand, Sweden, May 5, 1973
Position: goaltender
Height: 5-11
Weight: 178
Uniform no.: 1
Catches: left

Career statistics:

GP	MIN	GA	SO	GAA	A	PIM
75	4422	202	6	2.74	1	22

2000-2001 statistics:

GP	MIN	GAA	W	L	T	SO	GA	S	SAPCT	PIM
9	545	2.64	7	1	1	0	24	253	.905	0

2001-2002 statistics:

GP	MIN	GAA	W	L	T	SO	GA	S	SAPCT	PIM
66	3877	2.75	25	34	7	6	178	1851	.904	22

LAST SEASON
Set a team record by appearing in 66 games.

THE PHYSICAL GAME
Hedberg is a classic butterfly goalie. He has very good reflexes, moves well laterally across the crease and has a quick glove hand. He stays square to the shooters and, while he will occasionally allow a bad-angle goal, he doesn't beat himself often.

A little too aggressive at the start of his NHL career, Hedberg would charge out of his net thinking he could play pucks in the slot. In his first full NHL season, he learned to play a more conservative style. It doesn't help him that the Penguins are not very solid defensively. Often, Hedberg will have to do too much to help his defence out.

Hedberg is pretty good with his stick, moving the puck and using his stick to break up passes around the crease. He is very level-headed and doesn't get flustered under pressure. Hedberg freezes the puck a lot for draws. His centres are good on face-offs, and his defencemen have trouble moving the puck, so Hedberg likes to settle things down. The NHL has been talking about a crackdown on this, and if delay of game penalties start being called more tightly on goalies, Hedberg could run into some problems.

THE MENTAL GAME
Hedberg has assumed the role and the demeanour of a No. 1 goalie. He wants to play with the game and the season on the line. While he is not an elite level goalie, he is just a notch below the NHL netminding stars, and he was a terrific pickup by the Penguins at the 2001 trade deadline (from San Jose with Bobby Dollas for Jeff Norton).

THE INTANGIBLES
Hedberg had to wait a long time to get his NHL break (at age 28) and he does not take winning the job lightly. He plays with an upbeat attitude. His team-mates want to play hard in front of him, and he gives them a chance to win every night.

PROJECTION
Last year we said Hedberg would do well to get 25-28 wins, and he just made it to 25. The Penguins' season hinges on Mario Lemieux. If the big guy is healthy, Hedberg could get 28 wins or more. Otherwise, 25 would again be ambitious.

JAN HRDINA

Yrs. of NHL service: 4
Born: Hradec Kralove, Czech Republic; Feb. 5, 1976
Position: centre
Height: 6-0
Weight: 200
Uniform no.: 38
Shoots: right

Career statistics:

GP	G	A	TP	PIM
309	65	123	188	181

1998-1999 statistics:

GP	G	A	TP	+/-	PIM	PP	SH	GW	GT	S	PCT
82	13	29	42	-2	40	3	0	2	0	94	13.8

1999-2000 statistics:

GP	G	A	TP	+/-	PIM	PP	SH	GW	GT	S	PCT
70	13	33	46	+13	43	3	0	1	0	84	15.5

2000-2001 statistics:

GP	G	A	TP	+/-	PIM	PP	SH	GW	GT	S	PCT
78	15	28	43	+19	48	3	0	1	1	89	16.9

2001-2002 statistics:

GP	G	A	TP	+/-	PIM	PP	SH	GW	GT	S	PCT
79	24	33	57	-7	50	6	0	6	0	115	20.9

LAST SEASON

Led team in game-winning goals and shooting percentage. Third in NHL in shooting percentage. Second on team in goals, assists and points. Third on team in power-play goals. Career highs in goals and points. Missed two games with back injury. Missed one game with flu.

THE FINESSE GAME

Hrdina is a highly skilled centre whom the Pens have allowed to mature gradually through the minor-league ranks. He does everything well. He is a very good skater with the ability to shift gears and directions effortlessly. He doesn't shoot enough, but when he does he has a quick and accurate wrist shot. It would be a terrific weapon if he used it more often, but Hrdina is more likely to be guilty of overpassing the puck.

Hrdina is a highly intelligent player in all areas, and it looked like he was going to settle into a comfort zone where he would be a strictly defensive forward. Injuries and player movements have forced him to keep up the offensive side of his game as well. In Mario Lemieux's absence, Hrdina often functioned as the Pens' No. 1 centre last season.

That top role is asking too much of him, but Hrdina has fine offensive sense and touch, although he doesn't shoot enough. He is also versatile enough to play centre or left wing.

THE PHYSICAL GAME

Hrdina is slightly less than average height but he has a wide body. He fights for the puck and is tough to knock off his feet. He is excellent on draws. Not only does he have quick hands, he is able to tie up the opposing centre's stick, and he uses his feet. He cheats a bit on draws, but usually gets away with it.

THE INTANGIBLES

The role of No. 2 centre is going to be up for grabs in training camp, assuming Lemieux comes back healthy. Hrdina will have to earn it.

PROJECTION

Hrdina approached the 60-point range that is probably his top end. There is no reason why he can't repeat it.

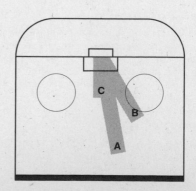

HANS JONSSON

Yrs. of NHL service: 2
Born: Jarved, Sweden; Aug. 2, 1973
Position: left defence
Height: 6-1
Weight: 202
Uniform no.: 8
Shoots: left

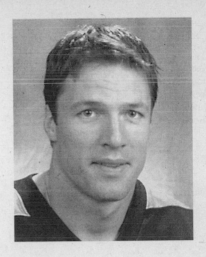

Career statistics:

GP	G	A	TP	PIM
179	9	34	43	56

1999-2000 statistics:

GP	G	A	TP	+/-	PIM	PP	SH	GW	GT	S	PCT
68	3	11	14	-5	12	0	1	1	0	49	6.1

2000-2001 statistics:

GP	G	A	TP	+/-	PIM	PP	SH	GW	GT	S	PCT
58	4	18	22	+11	22	2	0	0	0	44	9.1

2001-2002 statistics:

GP	G	A	TP	+/-	PIM	PP	SH	GW	GT	S	PCT
53	2	5	7	-12	22	2	0	0	0	37	5.4

LAST SEASON

Missed 14 games with broken foot. Missed eight games with broken finger. Missed one game with shoulder injury. Missed six games due to coach's decision.

THE FINESSE GAME

Jonsson has very good puck skills. He has an unbelievable shot when he uses it. He either does not have much confidence in his shot or else he is not very aggressive offensively, because it could be a bigger weapon for him. He loses a lot of power-play time because the Pens opt to go with a five-man forward unit.

He's not very aggressive defensively either. Jonsson will make the take-outs but not the big hits, even though he has good size and is fairly strong. He uses his skills and smarts in a defensive capacity.

Jonsson is a good skater and uses body position, poke-checks and the like in his own zone.

THE PHYSICAL GAME

Jonsson battled a lot of nagging injuries for the second straight season and he isn't very physical. It would move him up if he developed more of a mean streak, but it doesn't seem to be part of his makeup and that aspect of a game is almost impossible to force on someone. It's like a scoring touch: either a player has it or he doesn't. Jonsson is a little on the timid side.

THE INTANGIBLES

Jonsson has continued to regress after a promising first season.

PROJECTION

Jonsson needs to decide how much he really wants an NHL career. Even on a defensively thin team, Jonsson is looking like a bubble guy. He needs to score more than 25 points to be a factor.

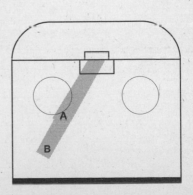

ALEXEI KOVALEV

Yrs. of NHL service: 10
Born: Togliatti, Russia; Feb. 24, 1973
Position: right wing
Height: 6-1
Weight: 215
Uniform no.: 27
Shoots: left

Career statistics:

GP	G	A	TP	PIM
693	241	317	558	766

1998-1999 statistics:

GP	G	A	TP	+/-	PIM	PP	SH	GW	GT	S	PCT
77	23	30	53	+2	49	6	1	5	0	191	12.0

1999-2000 statistics:

GP	G	A	TP	+/-	PIM	PP	SH	GW	GT	S	PCT
82	26	40	66	-3	94	9	2	4	1	254	10.2

2000-2001 statistics:

GP	G	A	TP	+/-	PIM	PP	SH	GW	GT	S	PCT
79	44	51	95	+12	96	12	2	9	1	307	14.3

2001-2002 statistics:

GP	G	A	TP	+/-	PIM	PP	SH	GW	GT	S	PCT
67	32	44	76	+2	80	8	1	3	2	266	12.0

LAST SEASON

Led team in goals, assists, points, power-play goals and shots. Second on team in plus-minus. Third on team in penalty minutes. Missed 13 games with knee injury and surgery. Missed two games with hip injury.

THE FINESSE GAME

You don't often see hands or feet as quick as Kovalev's on a player of his size. He has the dexterity, puck control, strength, balance and speed to beat the first forechecker coming out of the zone or the first line of defence once he crosses the attacking blueline. He is one of the few players in the NHL agile and balanced enough to duck under a check at the sideboards and maintain possession of the puck. Exceptional hands allow him to make remarkable moves, but his hockey thought process doesn't always allow him to finish them off well. Kovalev has a deceptive wrist shot with a lightning release.

On many occasions, Kovalev's slithery moves don't do enough offensive damage. Sometimes he overhandles, then turns the puck over. Too many times, he fails to get the puck deep. He hates to surrender the puck even when dump-and-chase is the smartest option, and as a result he causes turnovers at the blueline and has to chase any number of opposition breakaways to his team's net. Everytime Kovalev seems rid of these bad habits, they come sneaking back into his game. At least they appear less frequently and seem to do less damage.

Kovalev played the right point for the Penguins on the power play last season. He is better on the half-boards.

THE PHYSICAL GAME

The chippier the game, the happier Kovalev is; he'll bring his stick up and wade into the fray. He can be sneaky dirty. He'll run goalies over and try to make it look as if he was pushed into them by a defender. He's so strong and balanced on his skates that when he goes down, odds are it's a dive. At the same time, he absorbs all kinds of physical punishment, legal and illegal, and rarely receives the benefit of the doubt from the referees.

Kovalev has very good size and is a willing hitter. He likes to make highlight-reel hits that splatter people. Because he is such a strong skater, he is very hard to knock down unless he's leaning. He makes extensive use of his edges because he combines balance and a long reach to keep the puck well away from his body, and from a defender's. But there are moments when he seems at a 45-degree angle and then he can be nudged over.

THE INTANGIBLES

Kovalev's salary situation will probably have the Penguins shopping him again for prospects. Fortunately for the Pens, two solid seasons by this once-mystifying player gives him an all-time high trade value.

PROJECTION

We downgraded Kovalev to a 75-point prediction after his record 2000-01 year, but it was more the absence of Lemieux and Kovalev's injuries than any decline in Kovalev's talent or effort that did the damage. He has clearly made his mark as a point a game player now.

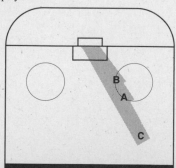

MILAN KRAFT

Yrs. of NHL service: 2
Born: Plzen, Czech.; Jan. 17, 1980
Position: centre
Height: 6-2
Weight: 176
Uniform no.: 14
Shoots: right

Career statistics:

GP	G	A	TP	PIM
110	15	15	30	24

2000-2001 statistics:

GP	G	A	TP	+/-	PIM	PP	SH	GW	GT	S	PCT
42	7	7	14	-6	8	1	1	1	1	63	11.1

2001-2002 statistics:

GP	G	A	TP	+/-	PIM	PP	SH	GW	GT	S	PCT
68	8	8	16	-9	16	1	0	2	1	103	7.8

LAST SEASON

Appeared in eight games with Wilkes-Barre (AHL), scoring 4-4-8 with 10 penalty minutes. Missed three games due to coach's decision.

THE FINESSE GAME

Kraft has a high skill level. He is a good skater, not an outstanding one, but there is no doubt he can compete at the NHL level. Kraft's primary asset is his stick-handling. He is a good playmaker, but needs to take more shots to make his game less predictable. He will work best with a finishing winger who likes to get the puck late. In his stints with the Pens, Kraft often played on the third or fourth lines. He needs to be a top six forward to maximize his potential.

His biggest weakness is draws. Kraft was just brutal on face-offs early in his NHL stint. He has learned to keep his hands lower on his stick and get into a better crouch, and he has improved somewhat. He still needs a lot of work in that department, however. He needs to improve his overall defence as well.

THE PHYSICAL GAME

Kraft needs to get stronger, especially if he is going to be handling the anticipated amount of ice time this season. He is rangy and needs to develop a more muscular frame.

THE INTANGIBLES

There is a spot among the top six forwards waiting for Kraft, but he has yet to put all the pieces of his game together to prove he belongs.

PROJECTION

It's a Catch-22 (or Catch-14) for Kraft. He needs to score to play on one of the top two lines, but in order to play on one of the top two lines, he had better score at least 20 goals this season.

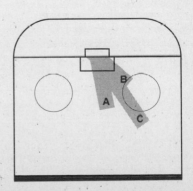

JANNE LAUKKANEN

Yrs. of NHL service: 7
Born: Lahti, Finland; Mar. 19, 1970
Position: left defence
Height: 6-1
Weight: 194
Uniform no.: 5
Shoots: left

Career statistics:

GP	G	A	TP	PIM
388	20	93	113	327

1998-1999 statistics:

GP	G	A	TP	+/-	PIM	PP	SH	GW	GT	S	PCT
50	1	11	12	+18	40	0	0	0	0	46	2.2

1999-2000 statistics:

GP	G	A	TP	+/-	PIM	PP	SH	GW	GT	S	PCT
71	2	18	20	+17	67	1	0	0	0	81	2.5

2000-2001 statistics:

GP	G	A	TP	+/-	PIM	PP	SH	GW	GT	S	PCT
50	3	17	20	+9	34	0	0	0	0	58	5.2

2001-2002 statistics:

GP	G	A	TP	+/-	PIM	PP	SH	GW	GT	S	PCT
47	6	7	13	-18	28	3	0	1	0	66	9.1

LAST SEASON

Missed 21 games recovering from knee surgery. Missed 14 games due to coach's decision.

THE FINESSE GAME

Laukkanen's hockey sense is about average, but his courage, will to win and character are all very much above average. He is one of the defencemen that coaches want on the ice in the last minutes of the game because he will rarely lose a battle. He will do anything to win.

Skating is Laukkanen's best physical asset, but that has been compromised by his off-season knee surgery in 2001. He has learned to shift gears smoothly. He will never be a big point producer, though, because he doesn't have a great shot. His hands are pretty good for passing, however. He makes an alert first pass out of the zone and can spot a breaking forward for a home-run pass. He earns some power-play time because he is poised with the puck.

Laukkanen kills penalties aggressively and intelligently.

THE PHYSICAL GAME

Laukkanen is a brave defenceman who will block shots and battle defensively, even though he is much smaller than most NHL heavyweight forwards.

THE INTANGIBLES

Laukkanen lost 51 games to injury the past two seasons. Recovery from knee surgery often takes a full season, so maybe last season should just be considered a washout. The Penguins need Laukkanen to return to his old competitive self, but there is no guarantee that will happen. He was a "healthy" scratch down the stretch as the Penguins were battling to make the playoffs, not an encouraging sign.

PROJECTION

When healthy, Laukkanen is a solid, if not elite, two-way defenceman who could score 25-30 points. He's 32 now, though, and the chance for a full-scale comeback appears to be small.

MARIO LEMIEUX

Yrs. of NHL service: 15
Born: Montreal, Que.; Oct. 5, 1965
Position: centre
Height: 6-4
Weight: 220
Uniform no.: 66
Shoots: right

Career statistics:

GP	G	A	TP	PIM
812	654	947	1601	769

2000-2001 statistics:

GP	G	A	TP	+/-	PIM	PP	SH	GW	GT	S	PCT
43	35	41	76	+15	18	16	1	5	0	171	20.5

2001-2002 statistics:

GP	G	A	TP	+/-	PIM	PP	SH	GW	GT	S	PCT
24	6	25	31	0	14	2	0	0	0	75	8.0

LAST SEASON

Missed 54 games with hip injury, surgery and rest for ailment.

THE FINESSE GAME

It probably seems like sacrilege to criticize Lemieux — especially in Canada. After all, the big guy did save a franchise (at least twice) and his comeback in 2000-01 lifted hockey out of its doldrums. But Lemieux's pursuit of Olympic gold, at the cost of his health and his team's performance, couldn't have been too rewarding for Penguins season-ticket holders.

When healthy, Lemieux is sneaky-good. He can seem to be no factor in a game for 58 minutes and then beat a team with two plays, whether it is a creative assist or one of his heavy and deceptive shots. Lemieux looks like he is cruising, but his first step to the puck is so huge and effortless that he can still make defencemen look silly by controlling the puck and then swooping around them. Step up to challenge Lemieux when he is carrying the puck, and he will use his long reach to pull the puck through a defender's legs. Back off him, and he will use the open ice to wheel tightly and put the puck on the tape of the breaking teammate.

Even though it appears he is slowing the game down to a molasses pace, Lemieux can do everything at a high tempo. He has spectacular vision, hands and grace, and is one of the rare athletes still capable of dominating a game completely.

Discipline-minded Dallas coach Ken Hitchcock says he would have no trouble having Lemieux on his team. "He's the best defensive player in the league," Hitchcock said. "He always has the puck."

THE PHYSICAL GAME

Lemieux managed to score more than a point a game with a bum hip in his limited performance last season. He needs to come back at full strength but play fewer minutes. It can't be an easy decision for the coaching staff to keep Lemieux on the bench, though, not when he's the owner and the rest of the Penguins' lineup has been depleted by the recent departures of Jaromir Jagr, Robert Lang and Darius Kasparaitis.

THE INTANGIBLES

It's not an Olympic year. So expect Lemieux, 37, to pace himself by sitting out around 20 games in hopes of getting his team into the playoffs.

PROJECTION

Figure Lemieux to play in about 60 games and score about 80 points if he can come back from this latest health crisis.

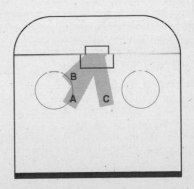

STEVE MCKENNA

Yrs. of NHL service: 5
Born: Toronto, Ont.; Aug. 21, 1973
Position: left wing
Height: 6-8
Weight: 255
Uniform no.: 23
Shoots: left

Career statistics:

GP	G	A	TP	PIM
245	8	11	19	611

1998-1999 statistics:

GP	G	A	TP	+/-	PIM	PP	SH	GW	GT	S	PCT
20	1	0	1	-3	36	0	0	0	0	12	8.3

1999-2000 statistics:

GP	G	A	TP	+/-	PIM	PP	SH	GW	GT	S	PCT
46	0	5	5	+3	125	0	0	0	0	14	0.0

2000-2001 statistics:

GP	G	A	TP	+/-	PIM	PP	SH	GW	GT	S	PCT
54	1	1	2	-4	119	0	0	0	0	19	5.3

2001-2002 statistics:

GP	G	A	TP	+/-	PIM	PP	SH	GW	GT	S	PCT
54	2	1	3	0	144	1	0	1	0	17	11.8

LAST SEASON

Signed as free agent by Pittsburgh on July 12, 2002. Appeared in three games with Hartford (AHL), scoring 0-0-0 with 11 PIM. Missed 14 games due to coach's decision.

THE FINESSE GAME

McKenna is all rough edges, but it has been a long-term project for this lifetime defenceman to be converted into a mostly physical left wing. He sticks his nose in and plays hard.

He plays mainly on the fourth line at even strength, although McKenna sees the occasional shift with better players, who play a little bolder with him around. He can be used up front on the power play, with moderate impact.

McKenna's skating is a drawback, but he has good lower-body strength and works hard. He's been progressing steadily and has a solid work ethic. His game isn't pretty but he thinks the game pretty well. He just needs his feet and hands to react quickly enough for the NHL level. When he has the time, he knows what to do with the puck and can make a play.

McKenna has good leadership qualities. He is a heart-and-soul player.

THE PHYSICAL GAME

McKenna is as tough as he is tall. He has a long reach. He will take on anybody, and, most often, he'll win. He's a serious pugilist who always sticks up for his teammates. He's a hard 255 pounds, has a mean streak and can deliver punishing hits. Be afraid. Be very afraid.

THE INTANGIBLES

McKenna needs to be able to stay on his skates in order to be an effective enforcer. The Penguins need his toughness, but he isn't skilled enough to get much ice time on a team with Pittsburgh's offensive style. The Pens must like him, because they reacquired him.

PROJECTION

In a best-case scenario, he'll score 15 goals by scaring people away and getting enough room and time to bang in loose pucks, but 15 points is more logical, along with triple-digit penalty minutes.

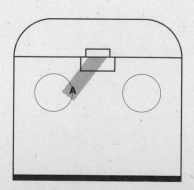

JOSEF MELICHAR

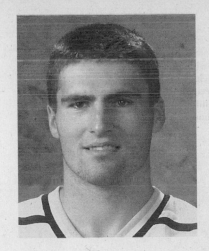

Yrs. of NHL service: 1
Born: Ceske-Budjovice, Czech Republic; Jan. 20, 1979
Position: defence
Height: 6-3
Weight: 198
Uniform no.: 2
Shoots: left

Career statistics:

GP	G	A	TP	PIM
78	0	5	5	89

2001-2002 statistics:

GP	G	A	TP	+/-	PIM	PP	SH	GW	GT	S	PCT
60	0	3	3	-1	68	0	0	0	0	46	0.0

LAST SEASON

First full NHL season. Missed 21 games with shoulder injuries. Missed one game with bruised hip.

THE FINESSE GAME

Melichar is one of the best defensive prospects of his age group. He is big and thick and solid. Think of the Devils' Colin White with better skating ability and you have an idea the kind of foundation defenceman Melichar can evolve into. He can move his feet and move the puck.

He plays well at both ends of the ice. For now, Melichar's game is weighted heavily on the defensive side. It's clear he wants to develop that part of his game first. He was a decent scorer at the junior level, but not in the minors, and it's not likely he will have much of an offensive impact.

Physically, you'll know Melichar is around. He and Rick Berry are going to make it a little tougher for teams to get two points off the Pens next season.

THE PHYSICAL GAME

Melichar is a rugged hitter. He should annually be Pittsbugh's leader in blocked shots and hits. Melichar is good-sized and he's strong. He will be asked to handle a lot of ice time.

THE INTANGIBLES

Melichar has the makings of a top two defenceman. His shoulder injury is the only concern at this point. Other than that, he gets a green light.

PROJECTION

Melichar is not likely to score more than 20 points next season.

ALEXEI MOROZOV

Yrs. of NHL service: 5
Born: Moscow, Russia; Feb. 16, 1977
Position: right wing
Height: 6-1
Weight: 196
Uniform no.: 95
Shoots: left

Career statistics:

GP	G	A	TP	PIM
349	59	85	144	58

1998-1999 statistics:

GP	G	A	TP	+/-	PIM	PP	SH	GW	GT	S	PCT
67	9	10	19	+5	14	0	0	0	0	75	12.0

1999-2000 statistics:

GP	G	A	TP	+/-	PIM	PP	SH	GW	GT	S	PCT
68	12	19	31	+12	14	0	1	0	0	101	11.9

2000-2001 statistics:

GP	G	A	TP	+/-	PIM	PP	SH	GW	GT	S	PCT
66	5	14	19	-8	6	0	0	1	0	72	6.9

2001-2002 statistics:

GP	G	A	TP	+/-	PIM	PP	SH	GW	GT	S	PCT
72	20	29	49	-7	16	7	0	3	0	162	12.4

LAST SEASON

Second on team in power-play goals. Third on team in goals, shots and shooting percentage. Career highs in goals, assists and points. Missed nine games with shoulder injuries; one game due to coach's decision.

THE FINESSE GAME

With a very sneaky, deceptive selection of shots, Morozov looks like he will be a big-goal scorer — in terms of importance, if not numbers. He tries to be too cute and make the extra play instead of shooting, but once he learns to use his hard and accurate shot to his advantage, he will be extremely effective. He is a good stickhandler and has a good sense of timing with his passes.

Morozov was a gangly, awkward player who took some time to develop and grow into his body. Now the Penguins are reaping the rewards. The team plays a European, puck-moving style that suits Morozov.

Morozov became a little more selfish last season, taking more shots, and that paid off with power-play ice time. Morozov has a very quick release on his shot and a high degree of accuracy.

THE PHYSICAL GAME

Morozov is a little on the stringy side, but he's still growing and will probably fill out into a solid winger. He'll never be confused with a power forward, though the Penguins are a little shy on size up front and need him to be more of a presence.

THE INTANGIBLES

The Penguins' wait finally paid off. We said last season that Morozov had to come up with 20 goals or the Pens would move on. He did, and now he can be the No. 2 right wing behind Alexei Kovalev, although he can also play the left side on the top line, which he did frequently last season.

PROJECTION

Morozov is definitely a guy to have on your roster if you're playing the New Jersey Devils. He scored four of his 20 goals against Martin Brodeur and company last season and has 12 career goals against N.J. in 24 regular-season games.

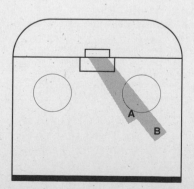

VILLE NIEMINEN

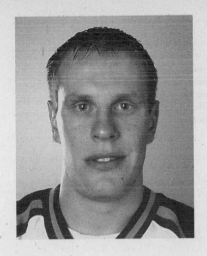

Yrs. of NHL service: 2
Born: Tampere, Finland; Apr. 6, 1977
Position: left wing
Height: 6-0
Weight: 200
Uniform no.: 10
Shoots: left

Career statistics:

GP	G	A	TP	PIM
117	25	24	49	76

1999-2000 statistics:

GP	G	A	TP	+/-	PIM	PP	SH	GW	GT	S	PCT
1	0	0	0	0	0	0	0	0	0	2	0.0

2000-2001 statistics:

GP	G	A	TP	+/-	PIM	PP	SH	GW	GT	S	PCT
50	14	8	22	+8	38	2	0	3	0	68	20.6

2001-2002 statistics:

GP	G	A	TP	+/-	PIM	PP	SH	GW	GT	S	PCT
66	11	16	27	-1	38	1	0	5	0	83	13.3

PROJECTION

Niememen should score 15 goals in a third- or fourth-line role.

LAST SEASON

Acquired from Colorado on March 19, 2002, with Rick Berry for Darius Kasparaitis. Second on Penguins in game-winning goals and shooting percentage.

THE FINESSE GAME

Nieminen is a spunky guy with not a lot of offensive upside. He isn't a very fast skater. Although he is strong on his skates, it takes him a while to get in gear.

Nieminen has had some shining moments, though. He was a terrific role player for Colorado in the 2001 run to the Stanley Cup. His effort, production and ice time, declined last season until he was included in the rent-a-player trade for Kasparaitis.

Nieminen was a good goal-scorer in the minors, but he doesn't have the quickness to be very productive at the NHL level. Any of his goals will come from turnovers and digging around the net. Desire seems to be the biggest issue.

THE PHYSICAL GAME

Nieminen needs to do a better job of emulating two of his favourite players, Wendel Clark and Esa Tikkanen. He is on the small, stocky side, but he is also a high-energy guy who can forecheck and annoy the opposition. On his best nights, that's exactly what happens. Nieminen needs to work on his conditioning — and just work. Period.

THE INTANGIBLES

Pittsburgh could certainly use a player with an edge, but Nieminen didn't seem too thrilled with the trade that took him away from a contender. Nieminen scored just 1 2 3 in 13 games with the Pens.

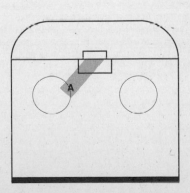

JAMIE PUSHOR

Yrs. of NHL service: 6
Born: Lethbridge, Alta.; Feb. 11, 1973
Position: right defence
Height: 6-3
Weight: 218
Uniform no.: 3
Shoots: right

Career statistics:

GP	G	A	TP	PIM
427	10	43	53	570

1998-1999 statistics:

GP	G	A	TP	+/-	PIM	PP	SH	GW	GT	S	PCT
70	1	2	3	-20	112	0	0	0	0	75	1.3

1999-2000 statistics:

GP	G	A	TP	+/-	PIM	PP	SH	GW	GT	S	PCT
62	0	8	8	0	53	0	0	0	0	27	-

2000-2001 statistics:

GP	G	A	TP	+/-	PIM	PP	SH	GW	GT	S	PCT
75	3	10	13	+7	94	0	1	0	0	64	4.7

2001-2002 statistics:

GP	G	A	TP	+/-	PIM	PP	SH	GW	GT	S	PCT
76	0	8	8	-13	84	0	0	0	0	60	0.0

LAST SEASON

Acquired from Columbus on March 15, 2002, for a fourth-round draft pick in 2003. Third on Penguins in penalty minutes.

THE FINESSE GAME

Pushor is totally unspectacular, but he is steady defenceman who has paid his dues. He is remarkably calm and consistent.

Pushor is a good skater with average speed and acceleration and above-average balance. He won't rush the puck up-ice, but he will make the smart first pass to get it out of the zone.

He reads plays well defensively. He was a bubble guy in a couple of stronger organizations and was obviously well-schooled in his spare time. He uses his range to take away passing lanes and force attackers to the boards. He blocks shots. He does the dirty work along the boards and in the corners. He knows his size is what got him to the NHL and it's his willingness to use his strength that will keep him there.

Pushor doesn't get involved much offensively because he lacks the hand skills and vision. He will not push his way in much beyond the blueline.

THE PHYSICAL GAME

Although strong on his skates and strong along the wall, Pushor is not overly aggressive. He has good size and can be a solid hitter. Once in a while he gets carried away with his checking and steps up to make risky open-ice hits in the neutral zone. He became much more of a battler in his toe-to-toe match-ups with big players. Pushor fights when he has to and sticks up for teammates, who seem to think the world

of him. Pushor averaged around 19 minutes per game with the Pens.

THE INTANGIBLES

Pushor needs the assurance that came with knowing he would be in the lineup every night, instead of worrying that one mistake would cost him a long stint in the press box. He is more relaxed and confident; he's having fun, playing hard and leading by example.

PROJECTION

He won't compile points or massive penalty minutes, but Pushor will play a steady, stay-at-home style.

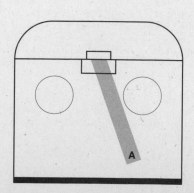

MICHAL ROZSIVAL

Yrs. of NHL service: 3
Born: Vlasim, Czech.; Sept. 3, 1978
Position: right defence
Height: 6-1
Weight: 200
Uniform no.: 28
Shoots: right

Career statistics:

GP	G	A	TP	PIM
184	14	41	55	121

1999-2000 statistics:

GP	G	A	TP	+/-	PIM	PP	SH	GW	GT	S	PCT
75	4	17	21	+11	48	1	0	1	0	73	5.5

2000-2001 statistics:

GP	G	A	TP	+/-	PIM	PP	SH	GW	GT	S	PCT
30	1	4	5	+3	26	0	0	0	0	17	5.9

2001-2002 statistics:

GP	G	A	TP	+/-	PIM	PP	SH	GW	GT	S	PCT
79	9	20	29	-6	47	4	0	4	0	89	10.1

LAST SEASON

Led team defencemen in points. Career highs in goals, assists and points. Third on team in game-winning goals. Missed two games with groin injury. Missed one game due to coach's decision.

THE FINESSE GAME

While Rozsival isn't a No. 1 defenceman, he is a poised, low-risk blueliner who afforded the Penguins a measure of stability last season.

Rozsival ranks "good" in a number of skill areas: skating, passing, playmaking and hockey sense. He is a strong skater and is tough to beat one-on-one.

Rozsival's development was delayed by a knee injury in 1998-99. It seemed to set back his confidence, but his skating recovered well.

THE PHYSICAL GAME

Rozsival doesn't play with much of an edge. He plays a containment game, and is not much of a hitter. Rozsival is good-sized and pretty strong and needs to assert himself more. Maybe playing with a guy like Rick Berry all season will help.

THE INTANGIBLES

Rozsival would make a nice second- or third-pair defenceman on a number of teams. Pittsburgh is stretched so thin at the position that he will be asked again to overachieve in the top-pair role.

PROJECTION

Rozsival would be hard-pressed to exceed last year's point totals by much. It really looks like 30 points is about his max.

MARTIN STRAKA

Yrs. of NHL service: 10
Born: Plzen, Czech Republic; Sept. 3, 1972
Position: centre
Height: 5-10
Weight: 176
Uniform no.: 82
Shoots: left

Career statistics:

GP	G	A	TP	PIM
616	164	294	458	240

1998-1999 statistics:

GP	G	A	TP	+/-	PIM	PP	SH	GW	GT	S	PCT
80	35	48	83	+12	26	5	4	4	1	177	19.8

1999-2000 statistics:

GP	G	A	TP	+/-	PIM	PP	SH	GW	GT	S	PCT
71	20	39	59	+24	26	3	1	2	0	146	13.7

2000-2001 statistics:

GP	G	A	TP	+/-	PIM	PP	SH	GW	GT	S	PCT
82	27	68	95	+19	38	7	1	4	1	185	14.6

2001-2002 statistics:

GP	G	A	TP	+/-	PIM	PP	SH	GW	GT	S	PCT
13	5	4	9	+3	0	1	0	1	0	33	15.1

LAST SEASON

Missed 47 games with broken leg. Missed four games with broken orbital/sinus bone. Missed 18 games with re-break in leg.

THE FINESSE GAME

Things don't get much tougher for a player than they did last season for Straka. He kicked off the season with nine points in 11 games, then broke his leg. He played in one game after that injury, and was hit in the face. He came back one game from the broken face, and reinjured his broken leg.

It was devastating for Straka, who had been coming off a career year. Straka has elite skills that he applies with the work ethic of a third-line grinder. The only thing that keeps him from being in the same class as a Jaromir Jagr or Pavel Bure is his shot, which isn't in the same class as his skating or hockey sense. Most of his goals come from breakaways, where Straka uses his speed, or by pouncing on loose pucks and rebounds.

He plays the left point on the power play (the Pens often used a five-man forward unit after Mario Lemieux came out of retirement) not because of his shot, but because of his heady puck movement.

Straka can do a lot of things. He is a water bug with imagination. He makes clever passes that always land on the tape and give the recipient time to do something with the puck. He draws people to him and creates open ice for his linemates, or he intimidates with his speed to hurry the defender into a giveaway.

Straka doesn't have the outside speed to burn defenders, but creates space for himself with his wheeling in tight spaces. He has good balance and is tough to knock off his feet, even though he's not big. Not a great defensive player, Straka is effective in five-on-five situations. He is a perpetual threat.

THE PHYSICAL GAME

Straka is small and avoids corners and walls, and has to be teamed with more physical linemates to give him some room. He needs to learn to protect the puck better with his body and buy some time. The beating he took last season may cost him speed and agility and could affect him mentally as well.

THE INTANGIBLES

Straka can play centre or left wing, and did his best playing on the left side.

PROJECTION

It's usually best to take a wait-and-see strategy with players who have been through the wringer like Straka was last season. We really hope he bounces back. Straka's numbers will always be assist-heavy. If he is healthy, he's a point-a-game player.

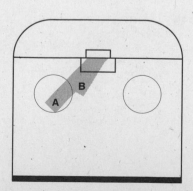

SAN JOSE SHARKS

Players' Statistics 2001-2002

POS.	NO.	PLAYER	GP	G	A	PTS	+/-	PIM	PP	SH	GW	GT	S	PCT
R	11	OWEN NOLAN	75	23	43	66	7	93	8	2	2	1	217	10.6
C	25	VINCENT DAMPHOUSSE	82	20	38	58	8	60	7	2	4	1	172	11.6
R	8	TEEMU SELANNE	82	29	25	54	-11	40	9	1	8		202	14.4
C	18	MIKE RICCI	79	19	34	53	9	44	5	2			115	16.5
C	12	PATRICK MARLEAU	79	21	23	44	9	40	3		5		121	17.4
L	17	SCOTT THORNTON	77	26	16	42	11	116	6		5		144	18.1
L	19	MARCO STURM	77	21	20	41	23	32	4	3	5		174	12.1
R	24	NIKLAS SUNDSTROM	73	9	30	39	7	50		1		1	74	12.2
D	20	GARY SUTER	82	6	27	33	13	57	3		1	1	174	3.5
L	9	ADAM GRAVES	81	17	14	31	11	51	1	3	1		139	12.2
D	7	BRAD STUART	82	6	23	29	13	39	2		2		96	6.3
R	13	TODD HARVEY	69	9	13	22	16	73			1		66	13.6
R	28	*MATT BRADLEY	54	9	13	22	22	43			2		63	14.3
D	27	BRYAN MARCHMENT	72	2	20	22	22	178					68	2.9
D	10	MARCUS RAGNARSSON	70	5	15	20	4	44	2		3		68	7.3
D	5	*JEFF JILLSON	48	5	13	18	2	29	3		2		47	10.6
D	2	MIKE RATHJE	52	5	12	17	23	48	4				56	8.9
D	22	SCOTT HANNAN	75	2	12	14	10	57			1		68	2.9
L	32	STEPHANE MATTEAU	55	7	4	11	4	15	1	1			43	16.3
R	15	ALEXANDER KOROLYUK	32	3	7	10	2	14			1		49	6.1
C	16	MARK SMITH	49	3	3	6	-1	72			1		40	7.5
D	23	SHAWN HEINS	17		2	2	1	24					20	
D	3	STEVE BANCROFT	5		1	1	-2	2					5	
R	50	HANNES HYVONEN	6				-2						4	
R	26	MIKE CRAIG	2				0	2					2	
G	35	EVGENI NABOKOV	67				0	14						
G	29	VESA TOSKALA	1				0							
G	37	MIIKKA KIPRUSOFF	20				0	4						

GP = games played; G = goals; A = assists; PTS = points; +/- = goals-for minus goals-against while player is on ice;
PIM = penalties in minutes; PP = power-play goals; SH = shorthanded goals; GW = game-winning goals; GT =
game-tying goals; S = no. of shots; PCT = percentage of goals to shots; * = rookie

VINCENT DAMPHOUSSE

Yrs. of NHL service: 16
Born: Montreal, Que.; Dec. 17, 1967
Position: centre
Height: 6-1
Weight: 200
Uniform no.: 25
Shoots: left

Career statistics:

GP	G	A	TP	PIM
1214	397	706	1103	1058

1998-1999 statistics:

GP	G	A	TP	+/-	PIM	PP	SH	GW	GT	S	PCT
77	19	30	49	-4	50	6	2	3	0	190	10.0

1999-2000 statistics:

GP	G	A	TP	+/-	PIM	PP	SH	GW	GT	S	PCT
82	21	49	70	+4	58	3	1	1	1	204	10.3

2000-2001 statistics:

GP	G	A	TP	+/-	PIM	PP	SH	GW	GT	S	PCT
45	9	37	46	+17	62	4	0	3	0	101	8.9

2001-2002 statistics:

GP	G	A	TP	+/-	PIM	PP	SH	GW	GT	S	PCT
82	20	38	58	+8	60	7	2	4	1	172	11.6

LAST SEASON

Second on team in assists, points and power-play goals. One of four Sharks to appear in all 82 games.

THE FINESSE GAME

Cool in-tight, Damphousse has a marvellous backhand shot he can roof; he creates opportunities low by shaking and faking checkers with his skating. He likes to set up behind the net to make plays. Goalies need to be on the alert when Damphousse is on the attack because he is unafraid to take shots from absurd angles. He just likes to get a shot on net and get the goalie and defence scrambling. It's an effective tactic.

Damphousse shows poise with the puck. Although he is primarily a finisher, he has become less selfish playing with Owen Nolan. His puck control and passing touch are superb. He's a superb player in four-on-four situations. He has sharp offensive instincts and is good in traffic.

He won't leave any vapour trails with his skating in open ice, but Damphousse is quick around the net, especially with the puck. His lack of foot speed isn't as much of a detriment in San Jose because they have some skaters who can drive the defence back and give Damphousse more time and space for his shot. He has exceptional balance to hop through sticks and checks. In open ice he uses his weight to shift and change direction, making it appear as if he's going faster than he is — and he can juke without losing the puck while looking for his passing and shooting options.

THE PHYSICAL GAME

Damphousse uses his body to protect the puck, but he is not much of a grinder and loses most of his one-on-one battles. He has to be supported by physical linemates who will get him the puck. He'll expend a great deal of energy in the attacking zone, but little in his own end of the ice, though he is more diligent about this in crunch times.

A well-conditioned athlete who can handle long shifts and lots of ice time, Damphousse has a pretty high pain threshold. He is not shy about using his stick.

THE INTANGIBLES

Nolan's quiet season affected Damphousse.

PROJECTION

Damphousse may not be a point-a-game player again. We'll downgrade our expectations to 60 points.

ADAM GRAVES

Yrs. of NHL service: 14
Born: Toronto, Ont.; Apr. 12, 1968
Position: left wing
Height: 6-0
Weight: 205
Uniform no.: 9
Shoots: left

Career statistics:

GP	G	A	TP	PIM
1070	320	278	598	1192

1998-1999 statistics:

GP	G	A	TP	+/-	PIM	PP	SH	GW	GT	S	PCT
82	38	15	53	-12	47	14	2	7	0	239	15.9

1999-2000 statistics:

GP	G	A	TP	+/-	PIM	PP	SH	GW	GT	S	PCT
77	23	17	40	-15	14	11	0	4	0	194	11.9

2000-2001 statistics:

GP	G	A	TP	+/-	PIM	PP	SH	GW	GT	S	PCT
82	10	16	26	-16	77	1	0	1	0	136	7.3

2001-2002 statistics:

GP	G	A	TP	+/-	PIM	PP	SH	GW	GT	S	PCT
81	17	14	31	+11	51	1	3	1	0	139	12.2

LAST SEASON

Tied for third on team in shorthanded goals. Missed one game with back injury.

THE FINESSE GAME

While his timing has eroded, Graves remains a short-game player who scores a high percentage of his goals off deflections, rebounds and slam dunks. A shot from the top of the circle is a long-distance effort for him. He favours the wrist shot; his rarely used slap shot barely exists. He is much better when working on instinct because, when he has time to make plays, he will outthink himself.

Although not very fast in open ice and something of an awkward skater, Graves's balance and strength are good and he can get a few quick steps on a rival. He is smart with the puck. He protects it with his body and is strong enough to fend off a checker with one arm and shovel the puck to a linemate with the other. He needs to play on a line with scorers, because he is a grinder first, a scorer second. He will drive to the net to screen the goalie and dig for rebounds, so he needs to play with someone who shoots to make the most of his efforts.

Graves is a former centre who can step in on draws. He is an intelligent penalty killer.

THE PHYSICAL GAME

Graves is a role player. It is a job he accepts willingly. He is great with young players and veterans alike. He is never critical of a teammate. He is as loyal as a St. Bernard, but he can play like a junkyard dog.

THE INTANGIBLES

Graves may have just enough left to help get the Sharks past their playoff frustrations and on to the finals. On those nights when the points aren't coming, Graves never hurts his club and finds other ways to contribute. He's a frequent winner of "Players' Player" awards, such is the respect he has earned. Off the ice, the absurdly modest Graves is one of the genuine good guys.

PROJECTION

Graves should score in the 30-point range.

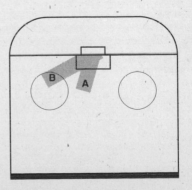

TODD HARVEY

Yrs. of NHL service: 8
Born: Hamilton, Ont.; Feb. 17, 1975
Position: right wing
Height: 6-0
Weight: 200
Uniform no.: 13
Shoots: right

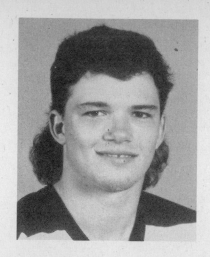

Career statistics:

GP	G	A	TP	PIM
485	79	109	188	806

1998-1999 statistics:

GP	G	A	TP	+/-	PIM	PP	SH	GW	GT	S	PCT
37	11	17	28	-1	72	6	0	2	1	58	19.0

1999-2000 statistics:

GP	G	A	TP	+/-	PIM	PP	SH	GW	GT	S	PCT
71	11	7	18	-11	140	2	0	0	0	90	12.2

2000-2001 statistics:

GP	G	A	TP	+/-	PIM	PP	SH	GW	GT	S	PCT
69	10	11	21	+6	72	1	0	2	0	66	15.1

2001-2002 statistics:

GP	G	A	TP	+/-	PIM	PP	SH	GW	GT	S	PCT
69	9	13	22	+16	73	0	0	1	0	66	13.6

LAST SEASON

Missed 10 games with shoulder injury. Missed three games with knee injury.

THE FINESSE GAME

Harvey's skating is rough. In fact, it's pretty choppy, and as a result he lacks speed. To make up for that, he has good anticipation and awareness. He's clever and his hands are very good. When Harvey gets the puck, he plays it with patience and strength. He is not a legitimate first-line player, but he can fit in with skilled players if asked because of his effort, but only on a short-term basis.

The goals Harvey gets are ugly ones. He works the front of the net with grit. He goes to the net and follows up shots with second and third efforts. He always has his feet moving and has good hand-eye coordination. He doesn't have the greatest shot, but he battles to get into the prime scoring areas.

Harvey needs to play big every night to maximize his abilities, but he also has to become smarter in picking his spots. It's not going to do his career any good to spend half the season in the trainer's room.

THE PHYSICAL GAME

Harvey's talent level rises when he gets more involved. He's not big enough to be a legitimate NHL heavyweight, but he doesn't back down from challenges. When he's at his best, he gets inside other people's jerseys and heads.

THE INTANGIBLES

Harvey can be an effective, chippy fourth-liner and get spot power-play duty. He tends to get dinged up and miss 10-15 games a season.

PROJECTION

Harvey can play energetic shifts, be annoying and, if he stays in one piece, score 10 to 15 goals.

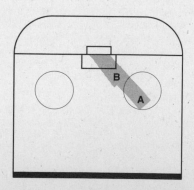

JEFF JILLSON

Yrs. of NHL service: 1
Born: Providence, RI; July 24, 1980
Position: right
Height: 6-3
Weight: 220
Uniform no.: 5
Shoots: right

Career statistics:

GP	G	A	TP	PIM
48	5	13	18	29

2001-2002 statistics:

GP	G	A	TP	+/-	PIM	PP	SH	GW	GT	S	PCT
48	5	13	18	+2	29	3	0	2	0	47	10.6

LAST SEASON

First NHL season. Appeared in 27 games with Cleveland (AHL), scoring 2-13-15 with 45 PIM.

THE FINESSE GAME

Jillson took advantage of Mike Rathje's protracted contract hassle to make a favourable first impression. Once Rathje returned, however, it was too tough for Jillson to crack a very solid top four and he was sent back to the minors.

Jillson can become a solid two-way defenceman. He won't be an elite scoring defenceman, but he will eagerly get involved in the attack. Jillson is a righthanded shot, a valuable asset that should help the San Jose power play get even better. He will cheat down to the circles for a one-timer or a slapshot.

Jillson needs to improve his skating, especially his foot speed, in order to become a full-timer. He also needs to improve his decision-making, which should evolve with more experience. He has improved at making the first pass out of the zone and tying up opposing players' sticks in the defensive zone. Jillson appears coachable and willing to learn from mistakes.

THE PHYSICAL GAME

Jillson took the college route to the NHL, which is unusual for a player with his kind of ferocious game. He is very competitive, and can be taken off his game when he gets too fired up.

THE INTANGIBLES

Jillson left college (University of Michigan) early to get a jump start on his pro career. If the Sharks don't re-sign veteran Gary Suter, Jillson has a shot at earning a third-pair job.

PROJECTION

If Jillson makes the big squad, he will see power-play time and should improve to 30-35 points.

PATRICK MARLEAU

Yrs. of NHL service: 5
Born: Swift Current, Sask.; Sept. 15, 1979
Position: centre
Height: 6-2
Weight: 210
Uniform no.: 12
Shoots: left

Career statistics:

GP	G	A	TP	PIM
396	97	116	213	136

1998-1999 statistics:

GP	G	A	TP	+/-	PIM	PP	SH	GW	GT	S	PCT
81	21	24	45	+10	24	4	0	4	1	134	15.7

1999-2000 statistics:

GP	G	A	TP	+/-	PIM	PP	SH	GW	GT	S	PCT
81	17	23	40	-9	36	3	0	3	0	161	10.6

2000-2001 statistics:

GP	G	A	TP	+/-	PIM	PP	SH	GW	GT	S	PCT
81	25	27	52	+7	22	5	0	6	0	146	17.1

2001-2002 statistics:

GP	G	A	TP	+/-	PIM	PP	SH	GW	GT	S	PCT
79	21	23	44	+9	40	3	0	5	0	121	17.4

Sharks averted a contract hassle by re-signing Marleau soon after the season ended. Marleau is so polished, it's easy to forget he's just 23 years old.

PROJECTION

Marleau hit the 25 goals we predicted for him last season. He should score about the same, but expect his assists to be up, thanks to Selanne.

LAST SEASON

Tied for second on team in game-winning goals. Missed three games due to coach's decision.

THE FINESSE GAME

Because of Marleau's quickness and intelligence, some scouts have described him as a bigger version of Paul Kariya. Marleau has great first- and second-step acceleration, with an extra gear.

Marleau plays an advanced offensive game; his defensive game is developing. He should become a high-level, two-way centre. He pounces on a loose puck and is a scoring threat every time he has it. His offensive reads are outstanding. He anticipates plays and has excellent hands. He is a terrific finisher as well as a fine playmaker. He has a quick release with an accurate touch, and will become a valuable power-play weapon.

Marleau had a sluggish start, and didn't start competing harder on a consistent basis until the last quarter of the season. Marleau still needs to work on that as well as his face-offs.

THE PHYSICAL GAME

Marleau is an imposing athlete. He skates through his checks and when he hits you, you know it. He has a thick build. He does not go looking to run people, but he will battle to get into traffic for the puck. He will take a check to make a play.

THE INTANGIBLES

Marleau finished the season strong, with 11 goals in the last 12 games, and followed that with a solid play-offs. Just in time for salary negotiations, too. The

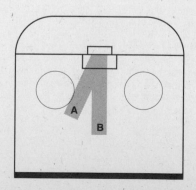

EVGENI NABOKOV

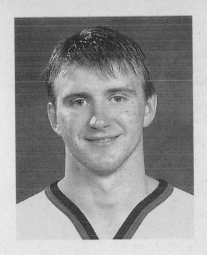

Yrs. of NHL service: 2
Born: Ust-Kamenogorsk, Kazakhstan; July 25, 1975
Position: goaltender
Height: 6-0
Weight: 200
Uniform no.: 35
Catches: left

Career statistics:

GP	MIN	GA	SO	GAA	A	PIM
144	8015	299	14	2.24	5	22

1999-2000 statistics:

GP	MIN	GAA	W	L	T	SO	GA	S	SAPCT	PIM
11	414	2.17	2	2	1	1	15	166	.910	0

2000-2001 statistics:

GP	MIN	GAA	W	L	T	SO	GA	S	SAPCT	PIM
66	3700	2.19	32	21	7	6	135	1582	.915	8

2001-2002 statistics:

GP	MIN	GAA	W	L	T	SO	GA	S	SAPCT	PIM
67	3901	2.29	37	24	5	7	149	1818	.918	14

LAST SEASON

Third in NHL in wins. Tied for second in NHL in shutouts. Career high in wins.

THE PHYSICAL GAME

The most impressive skill Nabokov has is his recovery. When he does drop down into a butterfly, it seems like his pads never stay on the ice long, if at all. He goes into a textbook butterfly, but is back on his feet and in his stance immediately. It's one of the quickest moves in the game.

His glove is always perfectly positioned, like one of those goalies in a tabletop hockey game. Nabokov's glove isn't noisy. He's not flapping it all over the place. He makes the tough gloves saves look easy, unlike some goalies who give even a routine save a flourish. What might be a Statue of Liberty save for Patrick Roy is a simple snap of the glove and hold for a face-off for Nabokov. Nabokov's glove is always cocked and ready. He is very consistent.

Nabokov scored a (power play!) goal last season and his play with the puck has improved, but it still remains one of the weaker parts of his game.

THE MENTAL GAME

Nabokov is very coachable and, despite still practising his English, he integrated himself well with his teammates. They seem to like playing for him and want to play hard in front of him. He was very comfortable by the end of the season and confident in his abilities. Nabokov doesn't need to showboat. He is that good, and that's good enough for the Sharks.

THE INTANGIBLES

Nabokov looks like he has staying power. It helps having one of the best goalie coaches in the business, Warren Strelow, to help prevent Nabokov from collapsing into bad habits. It's amazing how many teams refuse to invest in proper support for their goaltenders, given how essential the position is to a team's success.

One red flag: Nabokov had another disappointing playoffs (2.61 GAA).

PROJECTION

Nabokov fell one win short of our goal of 38 wins. We think he'll improve to 40.

OWEN NOLAN

Yrs. of NHL service: 12
Born: Belfast, N. Ireland; Sept. 22, 1971
Position: right wing
Height: 6-1
Weight: 210
Uniform no.: 11
Shoots: right

Career statistics:

GP	G	A	TP	PIM
775	301	332	633	1383

1998-1999 statistics:

GP	G	A	TP	+/-	PIM	PP	SH	GW	GT	S	PCT
78	19	26	45	+16	129	6	2	3	1	207	9.2

1999-2000 statistics:

GP	G	A	TP	+/-	PIM	PP	SH	GW	GT	S	PCT
78	44	40	84	-1	110	18	4	6	2	261	16.9

2000-2001 statistics:

GP	G	A	TP	+/-	PIM	PP	SH	GW	GT	S	PCT
57	24	25	49	0	75	10	1	4	1	191	12.6

2001-2002 statistics:

GP	G	A	TP	+/-	PIM	PP	SH	GW	GT	S	PCT
75	23	43	66	+7	93	8	2	2	1	217	10.6

LAST SEASON

Led team in assists, points and shots. Second on team in power-play goals. Third on team in goals and penalty minutes. Missed four games with back injury. Missed one game with groin injury. Missed one game with leg injury.

THE FINESSE GAME

Nobody knows where Nolan's shot is headed, except Nolan. A pure shooter with good hands, he rips one-timers from the circle with deadly speed and accuracy. Vincent Damphousse is so terrific as a set-up man that he has Nolan thinking like a pure finisher. Nolan needs to be selfish.

He has an amazing knack for letting the puck go at just the right moment. Nolan has a little move in-tight to the goal with a forehand-to-backhand, and around the net he is about as good as anyone in the game. On the power play, he is just about unstoppable.

Nolan is a strong skater with good balance and fair agility. He is quick straight-ahead but won't split the defence when carrying the puck. He's better without the puck, driving into open ice for the pass and quick shot. Defensively, he has improved tremendously, though it is still not his strong suit.

THE PHYSICAL GAME

Nolan is as strong as a bull and since he's capable of snapping at any time, opponents are wary of him.

THE INTANGIBLES

Nolan just hasn't been the same guy since serving an 11-game suspension in 2000-01 for sucker-punching Grant Marshall. He should be a physical force and a big-time goal-scorer.

PROJECTION

Nolan again disappointed in the goals department, registering a decline for the third straight year. He would be hard to recommend for more than 30 with that trend.

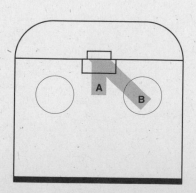

MARCUS RAGNARSSON

Yrs. of NHL service: 7
Born: Ostervala, Sweden; Aug. 13, 1971
Position: left defence
Height: 6-1
Weight: 215
Uniform no.: 10
Shoots: left

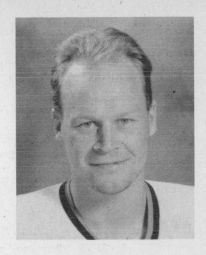

Career statistics:

GP	G	A	TP	PIM
494	27	118	145	362

1998-1999 statistics:

GP	G	A	TP	+/-	PIM	PP	SH	GW	GT	S	PCT
74	0	13	13	+7	66	0	0	0	0	87	0.0

1999-2000 statistics:

GP	G	A	TP	+/-	PIM	PP	SH	GW	GT	S	PCT
63	3	13	16	+13	38	0	0	0	0	60	5.0

2000-2001 statistics:

GP	G	A	TP	+/-	PIM	PP	SH	GW	GT	S	PCT
68	3	12	15	+2	44	1	0	0	0	74	4.1

2001-2002 statistics:

GP	G	A	TP	+/-	PIM	PP	SH	GW	GT	S	PCT
70	5	15	20	+4	44	2	0	3	0	68	7.3

PROJECTION

Ragnarsson's offensive game has more upside, but he has found a comfort zone and won't score much more than 25 points.

LAST SEASON

Missed 12 games with broken finger.

THE FINESSE GAME

Ragnarsson has a lot of poise, plus hand skills and skating ability. He has quick feet and he moves the puck well. He makes a good first pass and some good decisions at the blueline to get the puck through. He is so calm he seems just about bomb-proof.

Ragnarsson controls a lot of the breakouts for San Jose and he makes smart choices in the neutral zone. He is given a lot of responsibility on the power play, and while he is not in the elite class of quarterbacks, he has a decent, if not outstanding, point shot and is not afraid to shoot.

Defensively, Ragnarsson uses his body positionally to take up space, but isn't much of a hitter. He lets his partner Mike Rathje do that. But if opposing forwards don't want to attack Rathje's side, they will attack Ragnarsson's, and he has to be prepared.

THE PHYSICAL GAME

Built solidly, Ragnarsson will play a physical game, though finesse is his forte. He can handle a lot of ice time, and led the team with an average of 22:36.

THE INTANGIBLES

Ragnarsson and steady partner Rathje face the opponents' top lines night after night, but Ragnarsson doesn't seem to play as well paired with anyone else.

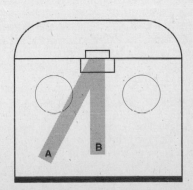

MIKE RATHJE

Yrs. of NHL service: 9
Born: Mannville, Alta.; May 11, 1974
Position: left defence
Height: 6-5
Weight: 245
Uniform no.: 2
Shoots: left

Career statistics:

GP	G	A	TP	PIM
509	18	89	107	345

1998-1999 statistics:

GP	G	A	TP	+/-	PIM	PP	SH	GW	GT	S	PCT
82	5	9	14	+15	36	2	0	1	0	67	7.5

1999-2000 statistics:

GP	G	A	TP	+/-	PIM	PP	SH	GW	GT	S	PCT
66	2	14	16	-2	31	0	0	0	0	46	4.3

2000-2001 statistics:

GP	G	A	TP	+/-	PIM	PP	SH	GW	GT	S	PCT
81	0	11	11	+7	48	0	0	0	0	89	0.0

2001-2002 statistics:

GP	G	A	TP	+/-	PIM	PP	SH	GW	GT	S	PCT
52	5	12	17	+23	48	4	0	0	0	56	8.9

THE INTANGIBLES

The cornerstone of the Sharks' blueline, Rathje has become a franchise defenceman.

PROJECTION

Rathje can get 25 points and keep other teams' forward lines off the board.

LAST SEASON

Tied for team lead in plus-minus. Missed two games with knee injury. Missed 28 games due to a contract dispute.

THE FINESSE GAME

A stay-at-home type, Rathje has great quickness for a player his size. He is a lot like Ken Morrow, the kind of player who is so quiet that you have to watch him every game to appreciate how good he is. He is strong enough to play against the league's power forwards and quick enough to deal with skilled, faster players. Rathje is routinely matched up against other teams' top lines (with his usual partner Marcus Ragnarsson) and just as routinely smothers them.

Rathje has the ability to get involved in the attack, but is prized primarily for his defence. He combines his lateral mobility with a good low shot, to get the puck on the net without being blocked.

With great poise, Rathje helps get the puck out of the zone quickly. He can either carry the puck out and make a smart headman pass, then follow the play, or make the safe move and chip the puck out along the wall.

THE PHYSICAL GAME

Rathje has good size and he's adding more muscle. He plays with controlled aggression. He has a little bit of mean in him, and he likes to hit. He has unbelievable strength and good mobility for his size. His penalty minutes look low because he plays hard without taking bad penalties. Rathje doesn't hit with Scott Stevens-like force, but he is well-respected by opponents.

MIKE RICCI

Yrs. of NHL service: 12
Born: Scarborough, Ont.; Oct. 27, 1971
Position: centre
Height: 6-0
Weight: 190
Uniform no.: 18
Shoots: left

Career statistics:

GP	G	A	TP	PIM
868	215	313	528	808

1998-1999 statistics:

GP	G	A	TP	+/-	PIM	PP	SH	GW	GT	S	PCT
82	13	26	39	+1	68	2	1	2	1	98	13.3

1999-2000 statistics:

GP	G	A	TP	+/-	PIM	PP	SH	GW	GT	S	PCT
82	20	24	44	+14	60	10	0	5	0	134	14.9

2000-2001 statistics:

GP	G	A	TP	+/-	PIM	PP	SH	GW	GT	S	PCT
81	22	22	44	+3	60	9	2	4	0	141	15.6

2001-2002 statistics:

GP	G	A	TP	+/-	PIM	PP	SH	GW	GT	S	PCT
79	19	34	53	+9	44	5	2	0	0	115	16.5

LAST SEASON

Third on team in assists and shooting percentage. Most points since 1992-93. Missed two games with shoulder injury. Missed one game with back injury.

THE FINESSE GAME

Ricci looks like he shaves with a cheese grater. He usually has a black eye or stitches. Some of his teeth have been missing since the Reagan administration. His is the face of old-school hockey.

Ricci is a top-flight two-way forward. He has good hand skills, combined with his hockey sense and a tireless work ethic. He always seems to be in the right place, poised to make the right play. He sees his passing options well and is patient with the puck. He can rifle it as well. Ricci has a good backhand shot that is a useful weapon in tight.

Ricci's major flaw is his lack of foot speed. It prevented him from being more of an offensive force, but Ricci has long been an efficient forechecker and he never seems that out of place among his NHL brethren because he wants to get from Point A to Point B more than a lot of other guys do.

Very slick at face-offs, Ricci has good hand speed and hand-eye coordination for winning draws outright. He will battle to tie up the opposing centre and use his feet to kick the puck to a teammate. Ricci is a determined penalty killer. He pressures the points and blocks shots, and he has excellent anticipation. Ricci is a checking forward with some offensive capabilities.

THE PHYSICAL GAME

Ricci is annoying to play against. He will antagonize and draw penalties. Ricci will fearlessly accept checking assignments against other team's top lines and star players. He isn't huge but he is big and sturdy. It's not unusual to see him cutting to the front of the net and dragging a defender like a big floppy anchor. He will play hurt. Ricci keeps himself in good condition and can handle a lot of ice time.

THE INTANGIBLES

Ricci is a character guy and a team leader who is part of the core of the Sharks. He considers it his job to make sure the kids are comfortable and is well-respected by the veterans. He is upbeat off the ice and his versatility is a plus. Ricci has long been a favourite of this publication and he is one of our foxhole guys.

PROJECTION

Ricci exceeded our prediction by 13 points. So let's ask him for 50 points this time.

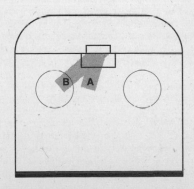

TEEMU SELANNE

Yrs. of NHL service: 10
Born: Helsinki, Finland; July 3, 1970
Position: right wing
Height: 6-0
Weight: 204
Uniform no.: 8
Shoots: right

Career statistics:

GP	G	A	TP	PIM
719	408	447	855	273

1998-1999 statistics:

GP	G	A	TP	+/-	PIM	PP	SH	GW	GT	S	PCT
75	47	60	107	+18	30	25	0	7	1	281	16.7

1999-2000 statistics:

GP	G	A	TP	+/-	PIM	PP	SH	GW	GT	S	PCT
79	33	52	85	+6	12	8	0	6	2	236	14.0

2000-2001 statistics:

GP	G	A	TP	+/-	PIM	PP	SH	GW	GT	S	PCT
73	33	39	72	-7	36	12	0	7	1	233	14.2

2001-2002 statistics:

GP	G	A	TP	+/-	PIM	PP	SH	GW	GT	S	PCT
82	29	25	54	-11	40	9	1	8	0	202	14.4

LAST SEASON

Led team in goals, power-play goals and game-winning goals. Second on team in shots. Third on team in points. One of four Sharks to appear in all 82 games.

THE FINESSE GAME

Selanne has Porsche Turbo speed. He gets down low and then simply explodes past defencemen, even when starting from a standstill. He gets tremendous thrust from his legs and has quick feet. Acceleration, balance, change of gears, it's all there.

Everything you could ask for in a shot is there as well. He employs all varieties of attacks and is equally comfortable on either wing. He can collect a pass at top speed while barely breaking stride.

Selanne is constantly in motion. If his first attempt is stopped, he'll pursue the puck behind the net, make a pass and circle out again for a shot. He is almost impossible to catch and is tough to knock down because of his balance. He will set up on the off-wing on the power play and can score on the backhand. His shot is not especially hard, but it is quick and accurate.

He doesn't just try to overpower with his skating, Selanne also outwits opponents. He has tremendous hockey instincts and vision, and is as good a playmaker as a finisher. He has a reputation for being selfish with the puck.

THE PHYSICAL GAME

Teams set out to bump and grind Selanne from the first shift, and he has to fight his way through the junk. When the referees are slow on the whistle, he takes matters into his own hands, usually with his stick. He is one of the toughest players in the league, European or otherwise. He is big and uses his strength along the wall, but he takes a beating.

THE INTANGIBLES

Selanne took a pay cut to stay with the Sharks. Don't worry — he's not on food stamps. But the choice does say something about his faith in the team and his ability to help them attain the next level (i.e., playoff success).

PROJECTION

Selanne is unlikely to reach the 50-goal mark again, or even 40. But anything over 30 would be impressive.

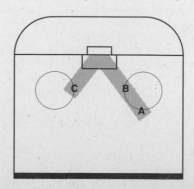

BRAD STUART

Yrs. of NHL service: 3
Born: Rocky Mountain House, Alta.; Nov. 6, 1979
Position: left defence
Height: 6-2
Weight: 210
Uniform no.: 7
Shoots: left

Career statistics:

GP	G	A	TP	PIM
241	21	67	88	127

1999-2000 statistics:

GP	G	A	TP	+/-	PIM	PP	SH	GW	GT	S	PCT
82	10	26	36	+3	32	5	1	3	0	133	7.5

2000-2001 statistics:

GP	G	A	TP	+/-	PIM	PP	SH	GW	GT	S	PCT
77	5	18	23	+10	56	1	0	2	1	119	4.2

2001-2002 statistics:

GP	G	A	TP	+/-	PIM	PP	SH	GW	GT	S	PCT
82	6	23	29	+13	39	2	0	2	0	96	6.3

LAST SEASON

One of four Sharks to appear in all 82 games.

THE FINESSE GAME

Stuart is an offensive-minded defenceman. His primary asset is his ability to make a smart first pass. He gets the puck out of the zone intelligently and quickly and opens up the rink for the Sharks. He finds the open man. He plays the point on the first power-play unit.

Stuart is a powerful skater. He is speedy and mobile and can lead a rush or join the attack as the trailer. He is a good one-on-one defender. Poised and smart, he will soon have the ability to dominate games with his skating and puck possession.

His defensive reads overall are good, although he is still learning. He is intelligent and will work to better his game. Stuart has started applying his skills more to the defensive part of the game, which will be the next step towards making him an all-around defenceman.

THE PHYSICAL GAME

Well-conditioned, Stuart is a natural at playing hysically. He is strong along the wall and in front of the net and doesn't take bad penalties. He can (and does) handle a lot of ice time.

THE INTANGIBLES

Stuart still struggles a bit with confidence and inconsistency, but for the most part the sophomore jinx skipped right over him. He is going to keep getting better. He will be one of the Sharks' top three defencemen.

PROJECTION

Stuart will be among the league's defencemen scoring leaders within the next few years. We would like to see him move into the 40-point range this season.

MARCO STURM

Yrs. of NHL service: 5
Born: Dingolfing, Germany; Sept. 8, 1978
Position: left wing
Height: 6-0
Weight: 195
Uniform no.: 19
Shoots: left

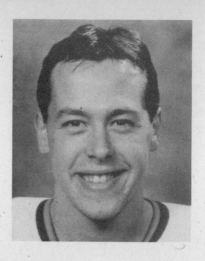

Career statistics:

GP	G	A	TP	PIM
384	73	95	168	174

1998-1999 statistics:

GP	G	A	TP	+/-	PIM	PP	SH	GW	GT	S	PCT
78	16	22	38	+7	52	3	2	3	2	140	11.4

1999-2000 statistics:

GP	G	A	TP	+/-	PIM	PP	SH	GW	GT	S	PCT
74	12	15	27	+4	22	2	4	3	0	120	10.0

2000-2001 statistics:

GP	G	A	TP	+/-	PIM	PP	SH	GW	GT	S	PCT
81	14	18	32	+9	28	2	3	5	0	153	9.1

2001-2002 statistics:

GP	G	A	TP	+/-	PIM	PP	SH	GW	GT	S	PCT
77	21	20	41	+23	32	4	3	5	0	174	12.1

LAST SEASON

Tied for team lead in plus-minus and shorthanded goals. Tied for second on team in game-winning goals. Tied for third on team in shots. Career high in goals. Missed two games with hand injury. Missed two games with elbow injury. Missed one game with flu.

THE FINESSE GAME

Sturm may be the best all-round player on the Sharks, although his offence still lags a bit behind his defence. A versatile skater who can play all three forward positions, Sturm doesn't require a lot of maintenance. He knows where to be without the puck.

He is also a fine skater with smooth acceleration. Sturm has good hands for stickhandling and shooting (which he needs to do more of). He is still young and developing confidence in his shot and the desire to score will be the next step in his evolution.

Sturm is extremely intelligent and hardworking. He is not afraid to block shots. He is going to be the kind of player who scores important goals and makes key plays that determine the outcome of games. He is the third-liner playing on a first or second line, and he could give the Sharks what Jere Lehtinen gives the Dallas Stars.

THE PHYSICAL GAME

Sturm is not big but he competes every night. He is chippy and feisty, and plays bigger than he is.

THE INTANGIBLES

The most complete, reliable forward on the team, Sturm hasn't produced the way the Sharks had hoped, especially for a player who sees so much ice time. Still, San Jose quickly re-signed him after he became a restricted free agent at the end of the season.

PROJECTION

Sturm will probably score in the 20-goal range and provide an outstanding all-round game, and he has more offensive upside.

386

NIKLAS SUNDSTROM

Yrs. of NHL service: 7
Born: Ornskoldsvik, Sweden; June 6, 1975
Position: right wing
Height: 6-0
Weight: 190
Uniform no.: 24
Shoots: left

Career statistics:

GP	G	A	TP	PIM
549	96	192	288	178

1998-1999 statistics:

GP	G	A	TP	+/-	PIM	PP	SH	GW	GT	S	PCT
81	13	30	43	-2	20	1	2	3	0	89	14.6

1999-2000 statistics:

GP	G	A	TP	+/-	PIM	PP	SH	GW	GT	S	PCT
79	12	25	37	+9	22	2	1	2	3	90	13.3

2000-2001 statistics:

GP	G	A	TP	+/-	PIM	PP	SH	GW	GT	S	PCT
82	10	39	49	+10	28	4	1	0	0	100	10.0

2001-2002 statistics:

GP	G	A	TP	+/-	PIM	PP	SH	GW	GT	S	PCT
73	9	30	39	+7	50	0	1	0	1	74	12.2

PROJECTION

Sundstrom will stay on the third line in San Jose, given the team's depth up front. He can score 10 to 15 goals in that role, with about 40 assists.

LAST SEASON

Missed nine games with knee injuries.

THE FINESSE GAME

Sundstrom is a defensive forward who possesses some finishing capabilities. As a scorer, he is opportunistic, but he doesn't have the feel for goal scoring or the drive to pay the price around the net.

A deceptively fast skater with good balance and a strong stride, Sundstrom plays a smart game and does a lot of subtle things well.

A puck magnet, he applies his skills to the defensive game. He reads plays very well, is aware defensively and always makes the safe decision. And when he forechecks, especially when killing penalties, he usually comes up with the puck in a one-on-one battle.

THE PHYSICAL GAME

Sundstrom will not get much bigger and has to stay strong. He is persistent and consistently physical. One of the Swede's talents is lifting an opponent's blade to steal the puck. He absorbs far more punishment than he dishes out (since he doesn't punish anybody).

THE INTANGIBLES

Because he doesn't throw big hits or make flashy plays on the ice, and because he is almost constantly smiling off of it, Sundstrom gets taken lightly a lot more than he should. He is committed to playing, and playing well. He is also committed to winning, and is enormously respected in the dressing room.

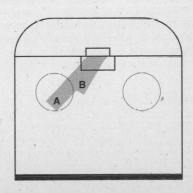

SCOTT THORNTON

Yrs. of NHL service: 12
Born: London, Ont.; Jan. 9, 1971
Position: left wing
Height: 6-3
Weight: 216
Uniform no.: 17
Shoots: left

Career statistics:

GP	G	A	TP	PIM
644	100	95	195	1126

1998-1999 statistics:

GP	G	A	TP	+/-	PIM	PP	SH	GW	GT	S	PCT
47	7	4	11	-2	87	1	0	1	1	56	12.5

1999-2000 statistics:

GP	G	A	TP	+/-	PIM	PP	SH	GW	GT	S	PCT
65	8	6	14	-12	108	1	0	1	0	83	9.6

2000-2001 statistics:

GP	G	A	TP	+/-	PIM	PP	SH	GW	GT	S	PCT
73	19	17	36	+4	114	4	0	1	1	159	11.9

2001-2002 statistics:

GP	G	A	TP	+/-	PIM	PP	SH	GW	GT	S	PCT
77	26	16	42	+11	116	6	0	5	0	144	18.1

LAST SEASON

Led team in shooting percentage. Second on team in goals and shots. Career highs in goals, assists and points. Tied for second on team in game-winning goals. Missed three games with back injury. Missed one game with wrist injury. Missed one game due to coach's decision.

THE FINESSE GAME

Thornton matches up against just about any forward in the league when it comes to winning puck battles. He makes a forceful left wing on the Sharks' third line, and can also handle power-play time.

He has played centre and can be used on face-offs, although he plays left wing most of the time. If Thornton doesn't win a draw outright, he uses his muscle to tie up the opponent and work the puck to a teammate.

He uses his toughness to get rid of a defender, then has good hands when he works in-tight to get his scoring chances. Thornton is by no means a sniper, and even though he has concentrated more on the defensive aspects of the game, he is able to convert a scoring chance when it presents itself. He was a scorer at the junior level, although he doesn't have an NHL release.

Thornton is not an overly fast skater, but he's no plodder. He is strong and balanced on his feet and hard to knock off the puck. He is alert positionally. If one of his defencemen goes in deep on the attack, Thornton will be the forward back covering for him.

THE PHYSICAL GAME

Thornton is a big, solid, smart, defensive forward — a young Joel Otto, but with better mobility.

THE INTANGIBLES

Thornton will never be a major point producer, but he will fill a steady checking role or act as a safety valve for more offence-minded linemates. He adds toughness to a skilled San Jose lineup and also has a touch.

PROJECTION

Thornton went right past the 20-goal mark that we thought was his ceiling. Thornton is thinking of himself as a goal-scorer. Well, so can we. How about another 25?

ST. LOUIS BLUES

Players' Statistics 2001-2002

POS.	NO.	PLAYER	GP	G	A	PTS	+/-	PIM	PP	SH	GW	GT	S	PCT
R	38	PAVOL DEMITRA	82	35	43	78	13	46	11		10		212	16.5
L	7	KEITH TKACHUK	73	38	37	75	21	117	13		7	1	244	15.6
C	39	DOUG WEIGHT	61	15	34	49	20	40	3		1		131	11.4
D	44	CHRIS PRONGER	78	7	40	47	23	120	4	1	3		204	3.4
D	2	AL MACINNIS	71	11	35	46	3	52	6		4	1	231	4.8
L	61	CORY STILLMAN	80	23	22	45	8	36	6		4		140	16.4
R	48	SCOTT YOUNG	67	19	22	41	11	26	5		1		210	9.1
R	19	SCOTT MELLANBY	64	15	26	41	-5	93	8		2		137	10.9
C	13	RAY FERRARO	76	14	23	37	-30	74	4		1	1	99	14.1
R	10	DALLAS DRAKE	80	11	15	26	8	87	1	3	2		116	9.5
D	29	ALEXANDER KHAVANOV	81	3	21	24	9	55					87	3.5
L	25	SHJON PODEIN	64	8	10	18	2	41		1	2		67	11.9
R	21	JAMAL MAYERS	77	9	8	17	9	99	1				105	8.6
C	32	MIKE EASTWOOD	71	7	10	17	-2	41			2		60	11.7
L	9	TYSON NASH	64	6	7	13	2	100			1		66	9.1
L	17	*SERGEI VARLAMOV	52	5	7	12	4	26					83	6.0
D	27	BRYCE SALVADOR	66	5	7	12	3	78	1		2		37	13.5
C	15	DANIEL CORSO	41	4	7	11	3	6	1		2		25	16.0
D	43	*MIKE VAN RYN	48	2	8	10	10	18			1		52	3.8
D	37	JEFF FINLEY	78		6	6	12	30					39	
R	34	REED LOW	58		5	5	-3	160					25	
R	42	*MARK RYCROFT	9		3	3	0	4					14	
D	4	MARC BERGEVIN	30		3	3	6	2					13	
D	47	RICHARD PILON	8		2	2	-1	9					3	
C	33	ERIC BOGUNIECKI	8		1	1	-2	4					10	
D	46	CHRISTIAN LAFLAMME	8		1	1	3	4					6	
L	6	TED DONATO	5				-5	4					2	
D	5	*BARRET JACKMAN	1				0						1	
C	26	*JUSTIN PAPINEAU	1				-2							
G	40	FRED BRATHWAITE	25				0							
G	35	BRENT JOHNSON	58				0	2						
G	30	REINHARD DIVIS	1				0							

GP = games played; G = goals; A = assists; PTS = points; +/- = goals-for minus goals-against while player is on ice; PIM = penalties in minutes; PP = power-play goals; SH = shorthanded goals; GW = game-winning goals; GT = game-tying goals; S = no. of shots; PCT = percentage of goals to shots; * = rookie

PAVOL DEMITRA

Yrs. of NHL service: 8
Born: Dubnica, Slovakia; Nov. 29, 1974
Position: right wing/centre
Height: 5-11
Weight: 203
Uniform no.: 38
Shoots: left

Career statistics:

GP	G	A	TP	PIM
407	157	211	368	120

1998-1999 statistics:

GP	G	A	TP	+/-	PIM	PP	SH	GW	GT	S	PCT
82	37	52	89	+13	16	14	0	10	1	259	14.3

1999-2000 statistics:

GP	G	A	TP	+/-	PIM	PP	SH	GW	GT	S	PCT
71	28	47	75	+34	8	8	0	4	0	241	11.6

2000-2001 statistics:

GP	G	A	TP	+/-	PIM	PP	SH	GW	GT	S	PCT
44	20	25	45	+27	16	5	0	5	0	124	16.1

2001-2002 statistics:

GP	G	A	TP	+/-	PIM	PP	SH	GW	GT	S	PCT
82	35	43	78	+13	46	11	0	10	0	212	16.5

LAST SEASON

Led NHL in game-winning goals. Tied for seventh in NHL in points. Led team in assists, points and shooting percentage. Second on team in goals and power-play goals. Only Blue to appear in all 82 games.

THE FINESSE GAME

Demitra had to adjust to playing in a new position — centre — full-time. He struggled with it at first, especially on face-offs, but he finished the season around 48 per cent on his draws and was comfortable in the role. Even though teams were able to key on him in Doug Weight's absence, Demitra continued to battle and succeed.

Demitra's speed makes things happen. He has great moves one-on-one, and he finds a way to get in the holes. He has good stick skills and loves to shoot. He can really find the top of the net, especially with his one-timer. He is well-versed at picking the top corners, and he can do it at speed.

Demitra is a creative and exceptional puckhandler, with a quick, deceptive shot. He's not shy about letting the puck go. He likes to drag the puck into his skates and then shoot it through a defenceman's legs. The move gets the rearguard to move up a little bit, and Demitra gets it by him on net.

Coming in off his right (off) side, Demitra will move to the middle on his forehand and throw the puck back against the grain. He needs to work on his puck-protection skills. Sometimes he exposes the puck too much and what should be a scoring chance for him gets knocked away. Defensively, he's reliable.

THE PHYSICAL GAME

Demitra is not very big but he has built up his body over the past several years. He is very competitive and durable. He can take the heat and the ice time.

THE INTANGIBLES

Credit linemate Keith Tkachuk with some of Demitra's success. Demitra is by nature a modest and reserved player, but Tkachuk urged Demitra to step up and be a leader. They meshed in playing styles as well, after an adjustment period. Tkachuk demands the puck, and they feed off of one another. Demitra has arrived as an NHL star. He wants to succeed and appears to be willing to pay the price to succeed in the NHL. He is a pretty low-maintenance star, too.

PROJECTION

Demitra can repeat as a 35-goal, 80-point scorer. We'd go higher if Chris Pronger was not going to be away half the year.

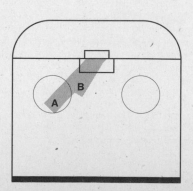

DALLAS DRAKE

Yrs. of NHL service: 10
Born: Trail, B.C.; Feb. 4, 1969
Position: right wing
Height: 6-1
Weight: 187
Uniform no.: 10
Shoots: left

Career statistics:

GP	G	A	TP	PIM
663	133	235	368	616

1998-1999 statistics:

GP	G	A	TP	+/-	PIM	PP	SH	GW	GT	S	PCT
53	9	22	31	+17	65	0	0	3	0	105	8.6

1999-2000 statistics:

GP	G	A	TP	+/	PIM	PP	SH	GW	GT	S	PCT
79	15	30	45	+11	62	0	2	5	0	127	11.8

2000-2001 statistics:

GP	G	A	TP	+/-	PIM	PP	SH	GW	GT	S	PCT
82	12	29	41	+18	71	2	0	3	0	142	8.4

2001-2002 statistics:

GP	G	A	TP	+/-	PIM	PP	SH	GW	GT	S	PCT
80	11	15	26	+8	87	1	3	2	0	116	9.5

LAST SEASON

Led team in shorthanded goals. Missed one game with knee injury. Missed one game due to coach's decision.

THE FINESSE GAME

Drake is best suited to a third-line role, and he knows it even though in the past he has played with some top-line guys. In a pinch, Drake can be used to play with more highly skilled players. Because he is so involved and so intelligent, he is better than the average grinder. He is an aggressive forechecker, strong along the boards and in front of the net. He's not huge, but he sure plays big. He doesn't stand in and take a bashing, but he'll jump in and out of traffic to fight for the puck or bounce in on rebounds.

Quick and powerful in his skating, Drake will get outmuscled but not outhustled. His scoring chances come in-deep. Drake doesn't have great hands. He needs to bang around for his pucks.

He shouldn't start thinking like a scorer, though — he has to keep doing the same dirty things that got him this far. He is the kind of player needed in a championship mix. Drake is an excellent penalty killer and is always a threat.

THE PHYSICAL GAME

Drake gets noticed because he runs right over people. He is limited by his size, but he will give a team whatever he's got. He's feisty enough to get the other team's attention, and he works to keep himself in scoring position. He has a mean streak.

THE INTANGIBLES

Drake is at his best at crunch time — in the closing minutes of a game, in a playoff stretch drive, in the postseason. If he isn't putting points on the board, he is disrupting the other team's attack. Drake is all heart.

PROJECTION

Drake provides 12-15 goals a season, reliable defence and an edge.

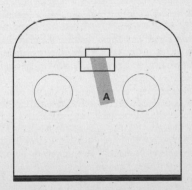

RAY FERRARO

Yrs. of NHL service: 18
Born: Trail, B.C.; Aug. 23, 1964
Position: centre
Height: 5-10
Weight: 180
Uniform no.: 13
Shoots: left

Career statistics:

GP	G	A	TP	PIM
1258	408	490	898	1288

1998-1999 statistics:

GP	G	A	TP	+/-	PIM	PP	SH	GW	GT	S	PCT
65	13	18	31	0	59	4	0	4	0	84	15.5

1999-2000 statistics:

GP	G	A	TP	+/-	PIM	PP	SH	GW	GT	S	PCT
81	19	25	44	-33	88	10	0	3	0	170	11.2

2000-2001 statistics:

GP	G	A	TP	+/-	PIM	PP	SH	GW	GT	S	PCT
81	29	47	76	-11	91	11	0	2	0	172	16.9

2001-2002 statistics:

GP	G	A	TP	+/-	PIM	PP	SH	GW	GT	S	PCT
76	14	23	37	-30	74	4	0	1	1	99	14.1

LAST SEASON

Acquired from Atlanta on March 18, 2002, for a fourth-round draft pick in 2002.

THE FINESSE GAME

Ferraro excels at the short game. From the bottoms of the circles in, he uses his quickness and hand skills to work little give-and-go plays through traffic.

A streaky player, when he is in the groove he plays with great concentration and hunger around the net. He is alert to not only his first, but also his second and third options, and he makes a rapid play selection. His best shot is his wrister from just off to the side of the net, which is where he likes to work on the power play. He has good coordination and timing for deflections.

Ferraro's skating won't win medals. He has a choppy stride and lacks rink-long speed, but he shakes loose in a few quick steps and maintains his balance well. Handling the puck does not slow him down.

Defensively, Ferraro has improved tremendously and is no longer a liability. In fact, he's a pretty decent two-way centre, though the scales still tip in favour of his offensive ability. He has particularly improved in his defensive work down low. He's good on face-offs.

THE PHYSICAL GAME

Ferraro is on the small side but is deceptively strong. Many players aren't willing to wade in to the areas where they will get crunched, and he will avoid those situations when he can. But if it's the right play, he will take the abuse and whack a few ankles. At 37, he is still a fit athlete.

THE INTANGIBLES

Ferraro's hopes for a Cup run were dashed when St. Louis was knocked out in the second round — and Ferraro scored no goals in 10 games in his first post-season appearance since 1998. He was a free agent after the season.

PROJECTION

Ferraro scored six goals in 15 regular season games with the Blues, showing he can still put the puck in the net, but without knowing where (or if) he'll end up playing, a guess would only be a guess. He can still score 20 goals if he finds a cozy spot.

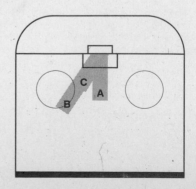

BRENT JOHNSON

Yrs. of NHL service: 2
Born: Farmington, Mich.; Mar. 12, 1977
Position: goaltender
Height: 6-2
Weight: 200
Uniform no.: 35
Catches: left

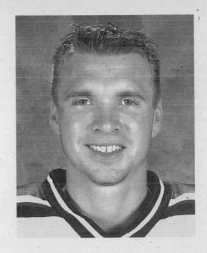

Career statistics:

GP	MIN	GA	SO	GAA	A	PIM
89	5235	190	9	2.18	4	4

1998-1999 statistics:

GP	MIN	GAA	W	L	T	SO	GA	S	SAPCT	PIM
6	286	2.10	3	2	0	0	10	127	.921	0

2000-2001 statistics:

GP	MIN	GAA	W	L	T	SO	GA	S	SAPCT	PIM
31	1744	2.17	19	9	2	4	63	676	.907	2

2001-2002 statistics:

GP	MIN	GAA	W	L	T	SO	GA	S	SAPCT	PIM
58	3491	2.18	34	20	4	5	127	1293	.902	2

LAST SEASON

Fifth in NHL in wins with career high. Career high in shutouts.

THE PHYSICAL GAME

This was Johnson's first season as the No. 1 goalie in St. Louis. There were some bumps, but overall Johnson gave the Blues fairly sound technical goaltending all season along.

He loves to handle the puck. Johnson is good at it, and almost looks like he's enjoying it (as Martin Brodeur does), and he makes smart decisions with it. Johnson will make the occasional "Oops!" play up the middle that gets picked off, but he never seems to lose his confidence in his ability to move the puck. Johnson communicates well with the defencemen, who appreciate the fact that they don't have to race back to get the puck all the time. Johnson has learned to use the boards and the glass and move the puck past the forecheck. It's a great asset.

Johnson plays a butterfly style similar to the way Tom Barrasso (another American goalie) did. He is tall and that style keeps a lot of his torso in the net and in the way of the puck. Johnson can get wrapped up in the action and when he does, he tends to overchallenge shooters.

THE MENTAL GAME

Johnson has matured a lot as a goalie and as an individual. The jury is still out on whether he is going to be among the best goalies in the league.

THE INTANGIBLES

The Blues tried to hold the No. 1 role away from Johnson as long as they could, but the 2001 trade of Roman Turek to Calgary forced the issue, and the young player responded well by winning the battle with Fred Brathwaite for the job. Johnson was very strong down the stretch for the Blues and had a great first-round series against Chicago. Against Detroit, though, Johnson had something of a meltdown. It might have had to do with the added pressure (as if he needed any) of playing against his hometown Red Wings. Or, it simply could have been because the Red Wings were just that much better than everyone else, as they proved by winning the Cup.

The issue in the off-season was whether or not the Blues wanted to stick with Johnson, or go for a free agent veteran goalie, of which there were many good ones available. The Blues are sticking with the kid in the hope that in three or four years he will be among the elite. The only way Johnson will get better is to keep going into the fire.

PROJECTION

St. Louis will have a little tougher time defensively in Chris Pronger's absence, but 30 wins should be within Johnson's reach.

ALEXANDER KHAVANOV

Yrs. of NHL service: 2
Born: Moscow, Russia; Jan 30, 1972
Position: defence
Height: 6-2
Weight: 190
Uniform no.: 29
Shoots: left

Career statistics:

GP	G	A	TP	PIM
155	10	37	47	107

2001-2002 statistics:

GP	G	A	TP	+/-	PIM	PP	SH	GW	GT	S	PCT
81	3	21	24	+9	55	0	0	0	0	87	3.5

LAST SEASON

Missed one game due to coach's decision.

THE FINESSE GAME

Khavanov is a very skilled player who doesn't get rattled with the puck. He came to North America as an older player (this will be his third season and he is 30 years old), so he was pretty poised when he stepped in.

What Khavanov is lacking is a sense of urgency. Khavanov should be rushing the puck more, dictate the play and get more involved. Khavanov was frustrated by his lack of ice time last season, but he did little to earn it, and it was a vicious cycle.

The Blues used Khavanov on the right side, both out of need and because with his ability, he was one of the players who was capable of handling the switch (not all defencemen can). He was a bit unhappy with that, as he prefers playing the left side.

THE PHYSICAL GAME

Khavanov is tall but a little on the light side. He can handle 22 minutes a game but there were games last season where he only saw 10 or 12.

THE INTANGIBLES

Khavanov didn't make the impact the Blues had hoped last season due to personal concerns (his girlfriend had difficulty getting out of Russia to come to the U.S.). That seemed to weigh on his mind a lot. He needs to get his act back together for this season.

PROJECTION

The Blues need every hand on deck in Pronger's absence. If Khavanov can earn back his ice time, he should be a 35-point player.

AL MACINNIS

Yrs. of NHL service: 20
Born: Inverness, N.S.; July 11, 1963
Position: right defence
Height: 6-2
Weight: 209
Uniform no.: 2
Shoots: right

Career statistics:

GP	G	A	TP	PIM
1333	324	880	1204	1444

1998-1999 statistics:

GP	G	A	TP	+/-	PIM	PP	SH	GW	GT	S	PCT
82	20	42	62	+33	70	11	1	2	2	314	6.4

1999-2000 statistics:

GP	G	A	TP	+/-	PIM	PP	SH	GW	GT	S	PCT
61	11	28	39	+20	34	6	0	7	0	245	4.5

2000-2001 statistics:

GP	G	A	TP	+/-	PIM	PP	SH	GW	GT	S	PCT
59	12	42	54	+23	52	6	1	3	0	218	5.5

2001-2002 statistics:

GP	G	A	TP	+/-	PIM	PP	SH	GW	GT	S	PCT
71	11	35	46	+3	52	6	0	4	1	231	4.8

LAST SEASON

Tenth among NHL defencemen in points. Second on team in shots. Tied for third on team in game-winning goals. Missed four games with ankle injury. Missed three games with back spasms. Missed three games with bruised foot; one game due to coach's decision.

THE FINESSE GAME

What makes MacInnis's shot so good is that he knows the value of a change-up, and he changes his shot according to the situation. From the point, he will try to keep his shot low. It will be a screaming shot if he thinks he can beat the goalie cleanly, but he will take a few m.p.h. off it if there are teammates there to tip the shot. If he dances to the top of the circles or closer, MacInnis will go top-shelf. And as much as he likes to shoot, he will also fake a big wind-up, which freezes the defenders, then make a quick slap-pass to an open teammate. There aren't too many better defencemen than MacInnis on the power play.

MacInnis knows when to jump into the play and when to back off. He can start a rush with a rink-wide pass, then be quick enough to burst up-ice and be in position for a return pass. Even when he merely rings the puck off the boards he's a threat, since there is so much on the shot the goaltender has to be careful to stop it. MacInnis has a hard shot even when he's moving backwards.

He skates well with the puck. MacInnis is not very agile, but he gets up to speed in a few strides and can hit his outside speed to beat a defender one-on-one. He will gamble and is best paired with a defensively alert partner, though he has improved his defensive play and is very smart against a two-on-one.

THE PHYSICAL GAME

MacInnis uses his finesse skills in a defensive posture, always looking for the counterattack. He reads defences alertly, and positions himself to tie up attackers rather than try to knock them down. In his own way, he is a tough competitor who will pay the price to win.

THE INTANGIBLES

With Chris Pronger in the lineup last season, MacInnis averaged close to 27 minutes a night. That is likely to increase due to Pronger's expected long absence, but increasing MacInnis's ice time will hurt the Blues in the long run. He will be 39 this season, and fatigue has a way of making players more susceptible to injury. The Blues can ill afford to have both of their veteran blueliners out of the lineup at the same time.

PROJECTION

Doug Weight didn't mesh as well as might be expected in his first season with the Blues, meaning MacInnis's numbers didn't hit the lofty 75-point heights we had imagined for him. We'll lower the target to 60 points, which would still be a terrific season.

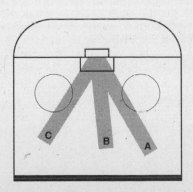

JAMAL MAYERS

Yrs. of NHL service: 4
Born: Toronto, Ont.; Oct. 24, 1974
Position: centre / right wing
Height: 6-0
Weight: 212
Uniform no.: 21
Shoots: right

Career statistics:

GP	G	A	TP	PIM
273	28	37	65	348

1998-1999 statistics:

GP	G	A	TP	+/-	PIM	PP	SH	GW	GT	S	PCT
34	4	5	9	-3	40	0	0	0	0	48	8.3

1999-2000 statistics:

GP	G	A	TP	+/-	PIM	PP	SH	GW	GT	S	PCT
79	7	10	17	0	90	0	0	0	0	99	7.1

2000-2001 statistics:

GP	G	A	TP	+/-	PIM	PP	SH	GW	GT	S	PCT
77	8	13	21	-3	117	0	0	0	0	132	6.1

2001-2002 statistics:

GP	G	A	TP	+/-	PIM	PP	SH	GW	GT	S	PCT
77	9	8	17	+9	99	0	1	0	0	105	8.6

LAST SEASON

Missed four games with groin injury. Missed one game with bruised foot.

THE FINESSE GAME

Mayers was often used at centre last season, but it is not his best position. He is good on face-offs (52.56 per cent last season), but he is a better winger and more controlled as a winger. He gets too busy on the ice as a centre. When he comes in off the wing and forechecks, the defenceman doesn't have time to move the puck. Whether Mayers hits him or not, he is on the puck so quickly that the defender is hurried into throwing the puck around the boards or making another mistake. Mayers has to keep reminding himself that he can really rush a play on the forecheck.

Speed is his biggest asset. Now Mayers is starting to learn how to position himself. Sometimes it is tough for a player with his energy and his speed to do anything but charge around full-tilt. Sometimes he has to slow down and get the other player into an angle or into a pocket to close him out instead of going right at him, and Mayers has begun to recognize that.

Mayers doesn't have a great scoring touch. He has to work hard for a goal by driving to the net. Mayers sometimes thinks he can play a finesse game. He can't.

As Mayers has matured, the Blues have given him increasing responsibility. He killed some penalties last season (scoring a shorthanded goal) and will probably do more this year.

THE PHYSICAL GAME

Mayers is a solidly built player and dedicates himself to conditioning year-round. He is really fit, and if his game develops to where he gets more ice time (he averaged 11:35 last season), he can take it. Mayers loves the physical part of the game. He is a willing and powerful hitter.

THE INTANGIBLES

Mayers has a lot of confidence, sometimes too much. He will try things that are beyond his talent level, and while you can't blame a guy who aspires higher, players last a long time in this league when they come to terms with their limitations and understand how to tailor their game. If Mayers sticks to what he does best, he will continue to grow and be effective.

PROJECTION

Mayers may increase to 25-30 points but his top end isn't much higher than that.

SCOTT MELLANBY

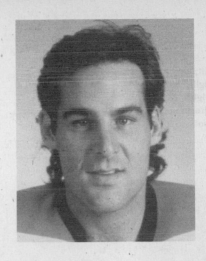

Yrs. of NHL service: 16
Born: Montreal, Que,; June 11, 1966
Position: right wing
Height: 6-1
Weight: 205
Uniform no.: 19
Shoots: right

Career statistics:

GP	G	A	TP	PIM
1143	300	382	682	2109

1998-1999 statistics:

GP	G	A	TP	+/-	PIM	PP	SH	GW	GT	S	PCT
67	18	27	45	+5	85	4	0	3	3	136	13.2

1999-2000 statistics:

GP	G	A	TP	+/-	PIM	PP	SH	GW	GT	S	PCT
77	18	28	46	+14	126	6	0	2	1	134	13.4

2000-2001 statistics:

GP	G	A	TP	+/-	PIM	PP	SH	GW	GT	S	PCT
63	11	10	21	-13	71	3	0	0	0	95	11.6

2001-2002 statistics:

GP	G	A	TP	+/-	PIM	PP	SH	GW	GT	S	PCT
64	15	26	41	-5	93	8	0	2	0	137	10.9

LAST SEASON

Third on team in power-play goals. Missed 12 games with broken jaw. Missed four games for personal reasons. Missed two games due to coach's decision.

THE FINESSE GAME

Not having a great deal of speed or agility, Mellanby generates most of his effectiveness in tight spaces, where he can use his size. On the power play, he sets up below the hash marks for a one-timer. He works for screens and tips. He doesn't have many moves, but he can capitalize on a loose puck with some good hands in-tight. Goals don't come naturally to him; however, he's determined and pays the price in front of the net.

Mellanby has developed a quicker release and more confidence in his shot, but still needs to shoot more, since he is quite accurate with his shot.

He has become more of a two-way player in his golden years, though he no longer sees many penalty-killing shifts. He is not much of a shorthanded threat. He lacks the speed and scoring instincts to convert turnovers into dangerous chances. His skating was never his strong suit and he has become slower, but he will still give his best effort on a nightly basis.

THE PHYSICAL GAME

Mellanby forechecks aggressively, using his body well to hit and force mistakes in the attacking zone. He engages in one-on-one battles in tight areas and tries to win his share. He is also willing to mix it up and take penalties of aggression. He seldom misses an opportunity to rub his glove in an opponent's face.

He's very strong along the boards and uses his feet when battling for the puck.

THE INTANGIBLES

Mellanby adds leadership to the Blues. He has played through pain, both physical and personal. Mellanby is a gamer, and this might be his final NHL season. He had an outstanding playoffs.

PROJECTION

Mellanby was a steady 15- to 20-goal scorer the past few seasons when healthy. He will probably still get enough ice time in St. Louis to approach those numbers.

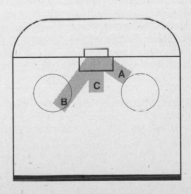

TYSON NASH

Yrs. of NHL service: 3
Born: Edmonton, Alta.; Mar. 11, 1975
Position: left wing
Height: 6-0
Weight: 186
Uniform no.: 9
Shoots: left

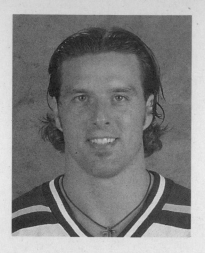

Career statistics:

GP	G	A	TP	PIM
189	18	23	41	365

1998-1999 statistics:

GP	G	A	TP	+/-	PIM	PP	SH	GW	GT	S	PCT
2	0	0	0	-1	5	0	0	0	0	1	0.0

1999-2000 statistics:

GP	G	A	TP	+/-	PIM	PP	SH	GW	GT	S	PCT
66	4	9	13	+6	150	0	1	1	0	68	5.9

2000-2001 statistics:

GP	G	A	TP	+/-	PIM	PP	SH	GW	GT	S	PCT
57	8	7	15	+8	110	0	1	0	0	113	7.1

2001-2002 statistics:

GP	G	A	TP	+/-	PIM	PP	SH	GW	GT	S	PCT
64	6	7	13	+2	100	0	0	1	0	66	9.1

LAST SEASON

Missed four games recovering from abdominal surgery. Missed two games with elbow injury. Missed seven games with hip pointer. Missed one game with broken nose. Missed five games due to coach's decision.

THE FINESSE GAME

Nash underwent reconstructive knee surgery in the 2001 off-season, as well as operations on two sports hernias. Nash was unable to work out much during the summer, and started off the year well behind the rest of the skaters and just never caught up.

This was highly frustrating for a player like Nash, because he couldn't make things happen the way he likes to, or anticipate. Nash is a forechecking force, and agitator. But by losing a step, Nash couldn't get in on his man, or do anything if he did get there.

Nash is a high-energy player who can lift the bench and the building with his effort. He lacks the skill level to rise above much more than a fourth-line role, but boy, does he try.

THE PHYSICAL GAME

Nash played through pain in his knee all season, often limping into the building. It was obvious that his recovery wasn't complete, and it severely limited his ability to be effective. The frustration boiled over into taking bad penalties. The season was pretty much a complete wash.

THE INTANGIBLES

This will be a season for Nash to get back to full steam, if he is able to. He will be anxious to prove himself.

PROJECTION

Nash's point totals will never be very high. He might break 20 over a full season. He is pretty much a safe bet for triple digit PIM totals.

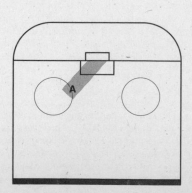

SHJON PODEIN

Yrs. of NHL service: 10
Born: Rochester, Minn.; Mar. 5, 1968
Position: left wing
Height: 6-2
Weight: 200
Uniform no.: 25
Shoots: left

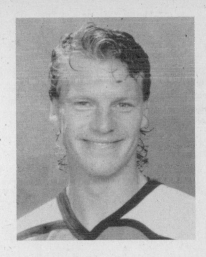

Career statistics:

GP	G	A	TP	PIM
631	96	100	196	411

1990-1999 statistics:

GP	G	A	TP	+/-	PIM	PP	SH	GW	GT	S	PCT
55	3	6	9	-5	24	0	0	0	0	75	4.0

1999-2000 statistics:

GP	G	A	TP	+/-	PIM	PP	SH	GW	GT	S	PCT
75	11	8	19	+12	29	0	1	3	0	104	10.6

2000-2001 statistics:

GP	G	A	TP	+/-	PIM	PP	SH	GW	GT	S	PCT
82	15	17	32	+7	68	0	0	3	0	137	10.9

2001-2002 statistics:

GP	G	A	TP	+/-	PIM	PP	SH	GW	GT	S	PCT
64	8	10	18	+2	41	0	1	2	0	67	11.9

LAST SEASON

Acquired from Colorado for Mike Keane on February 11, 2002.

THE FINESSE GAME

Podein is a labourer. He works hard, loves his job and uses his size well. He started out as a centre, but he is better suited as a winger because his hands aren't great and his passing skills are average at best. He is happiest in a dump-and-chase game, where he can use his straightaway speed to bore in on the puck carrier. Podein's work ethic makes him a mainstay on the Blues' first penalty-killing unit.

A mucker, Podein is not a fancy scorer. He gets most of his goals from digging around the net for rebounds and loose pucks. He doesn't have particularly good hockey sense, but he is determined.

Podein is not an agile skater but he is sturdy for work along the boards, and he can work up a pretty good head of steam. Just don't ask him to turn.

THE PHYSICAL GAME

Podein is antagonistic, with a bit of a mean streak, and he tends to be a bit careless with his stick. He can take bad penalties because of that tendency.

THE INTANGIBLES

Podein plays well on a checking line. He is a high-energy player and a penalty killer who can lift the bench with a strong shift. He has taken a long route to the NHL and works to stay here. He won't have trouble finding work anywhere as a role player if the Blues decide to go younger at the position. Almost every NHL team looks for a guy like Podein at the trade deadline for a playoff run. It didn't work for the Blues last season, however.

PROJECTION

In his defensive role, Podein can pop in 10 to 15 goals a season.

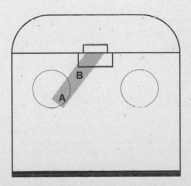

CHRIS PRONGER

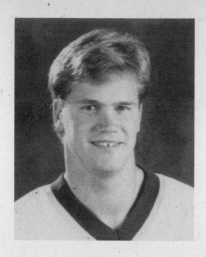

Yrs. of NHL service: 9
Born: Dryden, Ont.; Oct. 10, 1974
Position: left defence
Height: 6-6
Weight: 220
Uniform no.: 44
Shoots: left

Career statistics:

GP	G	A	TP	PIM
637	79	263	342	1000

1998-1999 statistics:

GP	G	A	TP	+/-	PIM	PP	SH	GW	GT	S	PCT
67	13	33	46	+3	113	8	0	0	0	172	7.6

1999-2000 statistics:

GP	G	A	TP	+/-	PIM	PP	SH	GW	GT	S	PCT
79	14	48	62	+52	92	8	0	3	2	192	7.3

2000-2001 statistics:

GP	G	A	TP	+/-	PIM	PP	SH	GW	GT	S	PCT
51	8	39	47	+21	75	4	0	0	1	121	6.6

2001-2002 statistics:

GP	G	A	TP	+/-	PIM	PP	SH	GW	GT	S	PCT
78	7	40	47	+23	120	4	1	3	0	204	3.4

LAST SEASON

Led team defencemen in points. Tied for eighth among NHL defencemen in points. Led team in plus-minus. Second on team in assists and penalty minutes. Missed one game with wrist injury. Missed one game due to coach's decision. Missed two games due to suspension.

THE FINESSE GAME

Pronger is lanky with a powerful skating stride for angling his man to the boards for a take-out. He blends his physical play with good offensive instincts and skills. His skating is so fluid and his strides so long and efficient that he looks almost lazy, but he is faster than he looks and covers a lot of ground.

He also handles the puck well when skating and is always alert for passing opportunities. Pronger's vision shows in his work on the power play. He patrols the point smartly, using a low, tippable shot. Like many tall defencemen, he doesn't get his slap shot away quickly, but he compensates with a snap shot that he uses liberally. He has good enough hands for a big guy and the Blues occasionally use him up front on the power play.

Pronger not only jumps into the rush, he knows when to, which is an art. He'll back off if the opportunity is not there. Playing with Al MacInnis, one of the game's great offensive defencemen, has helped Pronger in this area. He makes unique plays that make him stand out, great breakout passes and clever feeds through the neutral zone. He is also wise enough to dump-and-chase rather than hold on to the puck and force a low-percentage pass. He focuses more on his defensive role, but there is a considerable upside to his offence.

Disciplined away from the puck and alert defensively, Pronger shows good anticipation, going where the puck is headed before it's shot there. He is very confident with the puck in his own end. His defensive reads are excellent.

THE PHYSICAL GAME

Pronger finishes every check with enthusiasm and shows something of a nasty streak with his stick. He makes his stand between the blueline and the top of the circle, forcing the forward to react. His long reach helps to make that style effective. He also uses his stick and reach when killing penalties.

Pronger can handle a lot of ice time, and the Blues sure give it to him. He led the NHL with 29:28 average ice time last season.

THE INTANGIBLES

Pronger is expected to be out until December with wrist and knee surgery. He is one of the top defenders in the game and the Blues will be struggling in his absence.

PROJECTION

Pronger's absence would make him a midseason pickup for pool players, and it's always best to take a wait and see attitude with guys who have to try to step into the midseason pace.

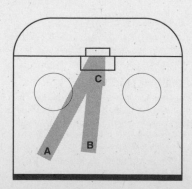

BRYCE SALVADOR

Yrs. of NHL service: 2
Born: Brandon, Man.; Feb. 11, 1976
Position: defence
Height: 6-2
Weight: 215
Uniform no.: 27
Shoots: left

Career statistics:

GP	G	A	TP	PIM
141	7	15	22	147

2001-2002 statistics:

GP	G	A	TP	+/-	PIM	PP	SH	GW	GT	S	PCT
66	5	7	12	+3	78	1	0	2	0	37	13.5

LAST SEASON

Missed eight games due to a concussion. Missed seven games with rib injury. Missed one game with chest injury.

THE FINESSE GAME

Salvador could become a poor man's Kevin Lowe. At his best, he is a steady, stay-at-home type of defender and he likes the physical part of the game. He will never be the kind of big open-ice hitter like Scott Stevens, another player he has been compared to, but it would be fine with the Blues if he learns to block shots, kill penalties and bulldoze the front of the cage the way Stevens does. After all, Stevens was a member of the Blues — for one season.

Salvador has enough dedicated players around him on defence, particularly Chris Pronger, that he doesn't have to look far to find a solid example to follow. Salvador won't be a Pronger-type of player, since he lacks the finesse skills to get as involved offensively. He has an okay shot from the point and makes some pretty smart reads, so he's not a total waste on the power play, when he merits second-unit assignments. Salvador's feet are pretty good. He is a decent skater with good balance and isn't easy to beat one-on-one.

Consistency is the quality that eludes Salvador. Last season he would have five good games, and the coaches would go, "I think he's got it," only to watch Salvador fall back into another lull. If Salvador can develop that dependability, he will draw the top defensive assignments against other team's No. 1 lines. At least that is what the Blues hope.

THE PHYSICAL GAME

Salvador is not overly aggressive but he can play a very in-your-face style of game. He needs to do that more often, but it doesn't seem to come naturally. He needs to make it tougher for teams to wrest two points from the Blues. Salvador is fairly tall and solidly built. He suffered a concussion late in the season but seemed to recover.

THE INTANGIBLES

The door is open for Salvador this season, and not just the one to the penalty box. Training camp will be the place to prove that he can step into the top four and help the Blues survive Pronger's half-season absence. We may also find out if Salvador's career survives.

PROJECTION

Salvador won't get a lot of points, but if he starts earning upwards of 20 minutes a game, he could surprise with 25 points.

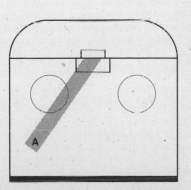

CORY STILLMAN

Yrs. of NHL service: 7
Born: Peterborough, Ont.; Dec. 20, 1970
Position: left wing
Height: 6-0
Weight: 194
Uniform no.: 61
Shoots: left

Career statistics:

GP	G	A	TP	PIM
485	135	152	287	234

1998-1999 statistics:

GP	G	A	TP	+/-	PIM	PP	SH	GW	GT	S	PCT
76	27	30	57	+7	38	9	3	5	1	175	15.4

1999-2000 statistics:

GP	G	A	TP	+/-	PIM	PP	SH	GW	GT	S	PCT
37	12	9	21	-9	12	6	0	3	1	59	20.3

2000-2001 statistics:

GP	G	A	TP	+/-	PIM	PP	SH	GW	GT	S	PCT
78	24	28	52	-8	51	10	0	4	0	174	13.8

2001-2002 statistics:

GP	G	A	TP	+/-	PIM	PP	SH	GW	GT	S	PCT
80	23	22	45	+8	36	6	0	4	0	140	16.4

LAST SEASON

Second on team in shooting percentage. Third on team in goals. Tied for third on team in game-winning goals. Missed two games with knee injury.

THE FINESSE GAME

A natural centre, Stillman brings a pivot's playmaking ability to the wing. He's intelligent and has sound hockey instincts, but doesn't have that extra notch of speed an elite player at the NHL level needs. Since he's not very big (which hampers his odds of playing centre), he needs every advantage he can get.

Stillman has a good enough point shot to be used on the power play. He can beat a goalie with his shot from just inside the blueline. He has good hands and a keen understanding of the game. He possesses great patience and puckhandling skills, and is efficient in small areas. He has the potential to become an effective player if he is supported by gifted forwards.

A goal scorer, Stillman possesses a kind of selfishness that is intrinsic to good scorers. He wants the puck, and he wants to shoot it. He creates off the forecheck, not with his size but with his anticipation. Stillman's major flaw is his lack of consistency.

THE PHYSICAL GAME

Stillman is thick and sturdy enough to absorb some hard hits. He is not overly aggressive but will protect the puck.

THE INTANGIBLES

Stillman has worked hard to be an NHL player. He is not an overwhelming player, just a useful sort. Until the Blues get a little deeper on the left side, Stillman will probably be the No. 2 left wing behind Keith Tkachuk and should get his share of ice time.

PROJECTION

Stillman can score in the 20- to 25-goal range.

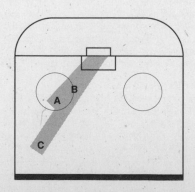

KEITH TKACHUK

Yrs. of NHL service: 10
Born: Melrose, Mass.; Mar. 28, 1972
Position: left wing
Height: 6-2
Weight: 225
Uniform no.: 7
Shoots: left

Career statistics:

GP	G	A	TP	PIM
725	367	339	706	1639

1998-1999 statistics:

GP	G	A	TP	+/-	PIM	PP	SH	GW	GT	S	PCT
68	36	32	68	+22	151	11	2	7	1	258	14.0

1999-2000 statistics:

GP	G	A	TP	+/-	PIM	PP	SH	GW	GT	S	PCT
50	22	21	43	+7	82	5	1	1	0	183	12.0

2000-2001 statistics:

GP	G	A	TP	+/-	PIM	PP	SH	GW	GT	S	PCT
76	35	44	79	+3	122	17	0	5	2	271	12.9

2001-2002 statistics:

GP	G	A	TP	+/-	PIM	PP	SH	GW	GT	S	PCT
73	38	37	75	+21	117	13	0	7	1	244	15.6

LAST SEASON

Led team and tied for seventh in NHL in goals. Led team in power-play goals and shots. Second on team in points, plus-minus and game-winning goals. Third on team in assists, penalty minutes and shooting percentage. Missed eight games with thigh injury. Missed one game due to suspension.

THE FINESSE GAME

In front of the net Tkachuk will bang and crash, but he also has soft hands for picking pucks out of skates and flicking strong wrist shots. He can also kick at the puck with his skates without going down. He has a quick release. He looks at the net, not down at the puck on his stick, and finds the openings. He has a great feel for the puck. From the hash marks in, he is one of the most dangerous forwards in the NHL. Eliminating the man-in-the-crease rule has increased his effectiveness and his production because the trenches are where he does his best work. He doesn't just stand in the slot, either, but moves in and out.

Tkachuk has improved his one-step quickness and agility. He is powerful and balanced, and often drives through bigger defencemen. Because of his size and strength, he is frequently used to take draws, and it's a rare face-off where the opposing centre doesn't end up getting smacked by him.

THE PHYSICAL GAME

Volatile and mean as a scorpion, Tkachuk takes bad penalties. And since he has a reputation around the league for getting his stick up and retaliating for hits with a quick rabbit-punch to the head, referees keep a close eye on him. Tkachuk needs to stay on the ice. He can be tough without buying a time-share in the penalty box.

Tkachuk can dictate the physical tempo of a game with his work in the corners and along the boards. He comes in hard with big-time hits on the forecheck.

THE INTANGIBLES

Tkachuk has had trouble succeeding in St. Louis since they depleted their corps of centres to get him in a trade from Phoenix. He finally developed some good chemistry with Pavol Demitra, and finished up strong.

PROJECTION

Tkachuk had to play through trade rumours last season, and will probably have to do so again. We predicted 75 points for Tkachuk last season (bingo) and will do it again this year.

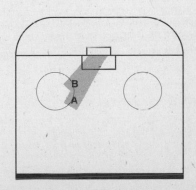

MIKE VAN RYN

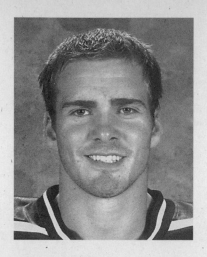

Yrs. of NHL service: 1
Born: London, Ont.; May 14, 1979
Position: right defence
Height: 6-1
Weight: 190
Uniform no.: 43
Shoots: right

Career statistics:

GP	G	A	TP	PIM
49	2	8	10	18

2000-2001 statistics:

GP	G	A	TP	+/-	PIM	PP	SH	GW	GT	S	PCT
1	0	0	0	-2	0	0	0	0	0	1	0.0

2001-2002 statistics:

GP	G	A	TP	+/-	PIM	PP	SH	GW	GT	S	PCT
48	2	8	10	+10	18	0	0	1	0	52	3.8

LAST SEASON

Missed two games due to coach's decision. Appeared in 24 games with Worcester (AHL), scoring 2-8-10 with 18 PIM.

THE FINESSE GAME

Van Ryn has spent part of the last two seasons in the minors, and when he rejoined the Blues in December, he was ready to stick. He played a strict defensive role while with Worcester, and that helped Van Ryn gain a lot of confidence. He understands the defensive aspect of the game better. Van Ryn was such a dominant skater that in junior, he was able to rush the puck all the time and outskate other players. When he got to the pro level, he found that players could angle him off. He wasn't able to have much success until he learned the give and go.

Playing alongside Chris Pronger was the next step in his development. Pronger helped settle Van Ryn down, and he held his high level of play from the minors for a long stretch. When he was asked to sit a few nights and study the game from the press box, he didn't sulk. He studied the opposition's forechecks and came back and played well again.

Van Ryn saw only light special teams duty last night to help ease him into the NHL game, but he is likely to see more of that this year because of Pronger's expected half-season absence. Van Ryn has a low, hard, accurate shot from the point and mixes things up with some slick passing. He is smart, patient and reads plays well. He saw more penalty killing time later in the season. Van Ryn is learning to read situations well.

THE PHYSICAL GAME

Van Ryn is still filling out to NHL size. He has an aggressive streak in him. He willingly clears out the front of his net and just has to get a little stronger for those wars. He's an intense player.

THE INTANGIBLES

Van Ryn will be asked to step up into the top four on a full-time basis with Pronger recovering from surgery. So far he has risen to the challenges the Blues have given him, but this will be a severe test.

PROJECTION

Van Ryn could score 20 points and will continue to develop all aspects of his game.

DOUG WEIGHT

Yrs. of NHL service: 11
Born: Warren, Mich.; Jan. 21, 1971
Position: centre
Height: 5-11
Weight: 200
Uniform no.: 39
Shoots: left

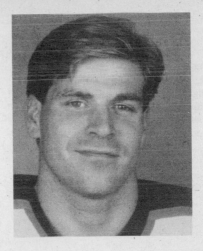

Career statistics:

GP	G	A	TP	PIM
767	195	501	696	645

1998-1999 statistics:

GP	G	A	TP	+/-	PIM	PP	SH	GW	GT	S	PCT
43	6	31	37	-8	12	1	0	0	1	79	7.6

1999-2000 statistics:

GP	G	A	TP	+/-	PIM	PP	SH	GW	GT	S	PCT
77	21	51	72	+6	54	3	1	4	0	167	12.6

2000-2001 statistics:

GP	G	A	TP	+/-	PIM	PP	SH	GW	GT	S	PCT
82	25	65	90	+12	91	8	0	3	2	188	13.3

2001-2002 statistics:

GP	G	A	TP	+/-	PIM	PP	SH	GW	GT	S	PCT
61	15	34	49	+20	40	3	0	1	0	131	11.4

LAST SEASON

Third on team in points and plus-minus. Missed 22 games with torn pelvic muscle and knee injury. Missed one game due to coach's decision.

THE FINESSE GAME

Weight carried — pardon the pun — the weight of the St. Louis hockey world at the start of the season, when he was healthy. By season's end, he could barely walk. Weight tried to make it a point to play as if he had to prove every night he was worth every dollar of his new contract with the Blues, instead of playing his natural fluid game.

Playmaking is Weight's strong suit. He has good vision and passes well to either side. His hands are soft and sure. He has quick and accurate wrist and snap shots. He handles the puck well in traffic, is strong on the puck and creates a lot of scoring chances. Weight is an outstanding one-on-one player, but doesn't have to challenge all the time. He will trail the play down the right wing (his preferred side) and jump into the attack late. On the power play, Weight does his best work off the right-wing half-boards. He always seems to find a passing seam.

Weight won't win many footraces, but he keeps his legs pumping and he often surprises people on the rush who think they had him contained only to see him push his way past. He frequently draws penalties. He has decent quickness, good balance and a fair change of direction. Every asset Weight owns is enhanced by his competitive nature. Even when he isn't scoring, he is making other players around him better.

Weight has improved his defensive play slightly; he is an offensive Doug Risebrough. Weight's point production is amazingly consistent. He seldom slumps. Last season was an aberration.

THE PHYSICAL GAME

Weight's injury, a torn muscle in his pubic bone area, meant he couldn't do a thing late in the season. Even though he tried to come back, he didn't have much to give physically because of the injury.

Weight shows flashes of grit but doesn't bring it to the ice every night, maybe because he gets banged up so easily. Still, he is built like a fire hydrant, and on the nights he's on he hits with enthusiasm, finishing every check. He initiates and annoys. Weight has a mean streak when riled. He's also a bit of a trash talker, yapping and playing with a great deal of spirit. He has worked on his strength and conditioning and can handle a lot of ice time. He is strong on his skates and hard to knock off the puck.

THE INTANGIBLES

Weight didn't adjust well in his first season in St. Louis. He was accustomed to being a leader on a young team in Edmonton. In St. Louis, there are more veterans and strong personalities. Weight needs to relax. He doesn't have to lead or be the spotlight guy every night. He needs to put less pressure on himself.

PROJECTION

We would expect a strong bounce-back season for Weight, although the absence of Chris Pronger will cost the Blues in overall quality of team play. Weight should rebound to the 75-point range, assuming he is healthy.

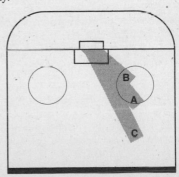

TAMPA BAY LIGHTNING

Players' Statistics 2001-2002

POS.	NO.	PLAYER	GP	G	A	PTS	+/-	PIM	PP	SH	GW	GT	S	PCT
C	19	BRAD RICHARDS	82	20	42	62	-18	13	5			1	251	8.0
C	20	VACLAV PROSPAL	81	18	37	55	-11	38	7		2		166	10.8
L	25	DAVE ANDREYCHUK	82	21	17	38	-12	109	9	1	5		161	13.0
C	4	VINCENT LECAVALIER	76	20	17	37	-18	61	5		3	1	164	12.2
C	26	MARTIN ST. LOUIS	53	16	19	35	4	20	6	1	2	2	105	15.2
D	7	BEN CLYMER	81	14	20	34	-10	36	4		2		151	9.3
D	13	PAVEL KUBINA	82	11	23	34	-22	106	5	2	3		189	5.8
L	33	FREDRIK MODIN	54	14	17	31	0	27	2		4	1	141	9.9
D	22	DAN BOYLE	66	8	18	26	-16	39	3		1	1	99	8.1
L	18	ZDENO CIGER	56	12	13	25	-15	26	1		3		92	13.0
R	24	SHANE WILLIS	80	11	13	24	-8	30	2			1	155	7.1
L	36	ANDRE ROY	65	7	9	16	-2	211					66	10.6
L	41	*JIMMIE OLVESTAD	74	3	11	14	3	24					99	3.0
R	28	SHELDON KEEFE	39	6	7	13	-11	16			1	2	52	11.5
D	5	JASSEN CULLIMORE	78	4	9	13	-1	58			1		84	4.8
D	21	CORY SARICH	72		11	11	-4	105					55	
C	27	TIM TAYLOR	48	4	4	8	-2	25		1			50	8.0
R	15	*NIKITA ALEXEEV	44	4	4	8	-9	8	1		1		47	8.5
D	2	STAN NECKAR	77	1	7	8	-18	24		1			38	2.6
C	46	*MARTIN CIBAK	26	1	5	6	-6	8					22	4.6
L	11	CHRIS DINGMAN	44		5	5	-10	103					41	
D	3	GRANT LEDYARD	53	1	3	4	-5	12					27	3.7
C	9	BRIAN HOLZINGER	23	1	2	3	-4	4					20	5.0
D	44	NOLAN PRATT	46		3	3	-4	51					38	
L	34	GORDIE DWYER	26		2	2	-4	60					6	
D	55	*JOSEF BOUMEDIENNE	4	1		1	-2	6					1	100.0
D	43	MATHIEU BIRON	36				-16	12					35	
D	6	*SASHA GOC	11				-2						4	
L	17	*RYAN TOBLER	4				-2	5					1	
L	29	*DIMITRY AFANASENKOV	5				-1						1	
R	54	*GAETAN ROYER	3				-1	2						
D	11	*KRISTIAN KUDROC	2				0							
G	35	NIKOLAI KHABIBULIN	70					0	6					
G	31	DIETER KOCHAN	5					0						
G	1	EVGENY KONSTANTINOV						0						

GP = games played; G = goals; A = assists; PTS = points; +/- = goals-for minus goals-against while player is on ice; PIM = penalties in minutes; PP = power-play goals; SH = shorthanded goals; GW = game-winning goals; GT = game-tying goals; S = no. of shots; PCT = percentage of goals to shots; * = rookie

DMITRI AFANASENKOV

Yrs. of NHL service: 1
Born: Arkhangelsk, Russia; May 12, 1980
Position: left wing
Height: 6-2
Weight: 200
Uniform no.: 29
Shoots: right

Career statistics:

GP	G	A	TP	PIM
14	1	1	2	4

2000-2001 statistics:

GP	G	A	TP	+/-	PIM	PP	SH	GW	GT	S	PCT
9	1	1	2	+1	4	0	0	0	0	8	12.5

2001-2002 statistics:

GP	G	A	TP	+/-	PIM	PP	SH	GW	GT	S	PCT
5	0	0	0	-1	0	0	0	0	0	1	0.0

LAST SEASON

Will be entering first full NHL season. Appeared in 46 games with Grand Rapids (AHL) scoring 5-7-12 with 6 PIM.

THE FINESSE GAME

Afanasenkov is considered a pure goal-scorer. Once he is over the blueline, he wants the puck and he knows what to do with it — he is extremely creative and loves to shoot. He is a right-handed shot, but, like so many Europeans, can play the left wing. This opens up his forehand to the centre of the ice for one-timers. He is also a smart playmaker. He plays a good puck-control game.

A powerful skater, Afanasenkov can go end-to-end with the puck. He is deceptively quick, and skating with the puck doesn't slow him down. He has excellent vision and good hockey sense. Afanasenkov should be a natural on the power play.

THE PHYSICAL GAME

Afanasenkov is strong along the boards and in front of the net. He doesn't initiate but he doesn't back down.

THE INTANGIBLES

Afanasenkov has spent two seasons in the minors and adapting to North America. Tampa Bay is still holding out the hope that he can step in this season. He was actually considered a better prospect than Brad Richards, although the Lightning have probably adjusted their thinking on that assessment.

PROJECTION

Afanasenkov may be more a two-way player than the sniper the Lightning originally hoped. If he makes the team, could score 10 to 15 goals in his first season.

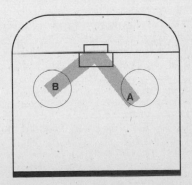

NIKITA ALEXEEV

Yrs. of NHL service: 1
Born: Murmansk, Russia; Dec. 27, 1981
Position: right wing
Height: 6-5
Weight: 215
Uniform no.: 15
Shoots: left

Career statistics:

GP	G	A	TP	PIM
44	4	4	8	8

2001-2002 statistics:

GP	G	A	TP	+/-	PIM	PP	SH	GW	GT	S	PCT
44	4	4	8	-9	8	1	0	1	0	47	8.5

LAST SEASON

Appeared in 35 games with Springfield (AHL), scoring 5-9-14 with 16 PIM.

THE FINESSE GAME

Alexeev is big, strong and skilled. His skating is average, but he has good size and great, soft hands and should be able to find a home on one of Tampa Bay's top two lines.

Alexeev was rushed to the pros before he was really ready, but sometimes bad teams don't believe they have any other option. At least it looked like Alexeev will survive. His confidence doesn't appear irreparably harmed.

Alexeev has a lot of offensive upside. Like many young players, he needs to bring a more consistent effort to the rink every night. He has the tools to become a dominant player.

THE PHYSICAL GAME

Alexeev is six-foot-five but he has none of the clumsiness or lack of coordination that sometimes afflicts big kids. He needs to get stronger. Alexeev isn't very physical. People see this hulking player and assume he will be tossing guys aside with one arm, but it's not in his nature. Alexeev will have to pick his physical game up a notch — he can't be effective playing a perimeter game.

THE INTANGIBLES

The Lightning envision Alexeev as a linemate for Vincent Lecavalier. Alexeev needs to adopt a more serious approach to his job. He missed the plane on one recall from the minors, and after he arrived, Tampa Bay sent him right back as punishment.

PROJECTION

Three or four seasons down the road, Alexeev will be scoring 25 goals. We'll look for 15 from him this season.

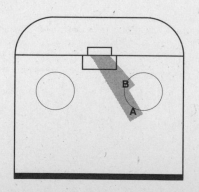

MATHIEU BIRON

Yrs. of NHL service: 3
Born: Lac-St. Charles, Que.; Aug. 29, 1980
Position: right defence
Height: 6-6
Weight: 212
Uniform no.: 43
Shoots: right

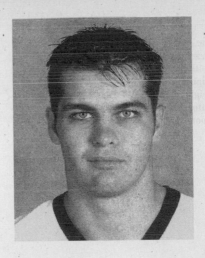

Career statistics:

GP	G	A	TP	PIM
110	4	5	9	62

1999-2000 statistics:

GP	G	A	TP	+/-	PIM	PP	SH	GW	GT	S	PCT
60	4	4	8	-13	38	2	0	2	0	70	5.7

2000-2001 statistics:

GP	G	A	TP	+/-	PIM	PP	SH	GW	GT	S	PCT
14	0	1	1	+2	12	0	0	0	0	10	0.0

2001-2002 statistics:

GP	G	A	TP	+/-	PIM	PP	SH	GW	GT	S	PCT
36	0	0	0	-16	12	0	0	0	0	35	0.0

LAST SEASON

Appeared in 35 games with Springfield (AHL), scoring 4-9-13 with 16 penalty minutes.

THE FINESSE GAME

Biron has all of the desired skills in a young NHL defenceman. He skates well for a big guy. He has a long, smooth stride with good acceleration, and he's tight in his turns.

He has an excellent shot. He has a nice touch with the puck for passing or shooting, but has to improve his speed in moving the puck, yet not be hasty. He is still guilty of some ghastly giveaways. He was a scorer at the junior level and should develop more poise and confidence with the puck. He could be involved on the Lightning's second power-play unit.

THE PHYSICAL GAME

Biron has picked up his hitting. He has good size and needs to make the most of it. He is well-balanced and hard to knock off his feet. He has to initiate more, but he is very at home when the hitting picks up. He needs to develop more lower-body strength to pack a bigger wallop in his checks.

THE INTANGIBLES

Biron was probably force-fed a little too much before he was capable of handling an NHL job with the Islanders when they were still a pretty dismal team. Biron has a good attitude that doesn't seem to have been permanently scarred by some of his struggles with his first organization. He struggled last season trying to find a niche on the Lightning.

PROJECTION

Big defencemen take longer to graduate. Biron will be worth the wait. He needs to learn defence first, but he has good offensive upside and could score in the 20-point range.

BEN CLYMER

Yrs. of NHL service: 3
Born: Edina, Minn.; Apr. 11, 1978
Position: right defense/centre
Height: 6-1
Weight: 195
Uniform no.: 7
Shoots: right

Career statistics:

GP	G	A	TP	PIM
164	21	27	48	144

1999-2000 statistics:

GP	G	A	TP	+/-	PIM	PP	SH	GW	GT	S	PCT
60	2	6	8	-26	87	2	0	0	0	98	2.0

2000-2001 statistics:

GP	G	A	TP	+/-	PIM	PP	SH	GW	GT	S	PCT
23	5	1	6	-7	21	3	0	0	0	25	20.0

2001-2002 statistics:

GP	G	A	TP	+/-	PIM	PP	SH	GW	GT	S	PCT
81	14	20	34	-10	36	4	0	2	0	151	9.3

LAST SEASON

Career highs in goals, assists and points.

THE FINESSE GAME

Clymer is a defenceman who has been converted to a checking-line winger by the Lightning, with surprisingly good results.

Good size and decent skating ability made him a high second-round draft pick by the Boston Bruins in 1997. When the Bruins failed to sign him, Tampa Bay nabbed him as a free agent in 1999. He struggled on defence at the NHL level, so the Lightning tried their experiment. Last season, Clymer played almost exclusively up front after being switched back and forth in the previous season.

Clymer has a strong stride and good speed. He has good-enough offensive skills that he can create something offensively when he forces a turnover. Clymer has little trouble with defensive-zone coverage, but draws (he played centre) were a big problem.

THE PHYSICAL GAME

Clymer plays with an edge. One of his idols is Chris Chelios, and Clymer can play with a similar mean streak. He is a willing hitter and his skating gives him the ability to crunch.

THE INTANGIBLES

Clymer is eager to play in the NHL, so he readily accepted the challenge of changing roles. He also gives the team versatility: he can be switched back to defence in an emergency.

PROJECTION

Clymer can continue to chip in 15 goals in a third-line role.

JASSEN CULLIMORE

Yrs. of NHL service: 8
Born: Simcoe, Ont.; Dec. 4, 1972
Position: left defence
Height: 6-5
Weight: 235
Uniform no.: 5
Shoots: left

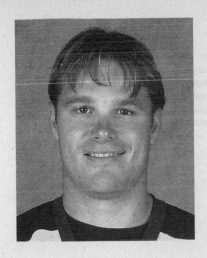

Career statistics:

GP	G	A	TP	PIM
417	16	39	55	415

1998-1999 statistics:

GP	G	A	TP	+/-	PIM	PP	SH	GW	GT	S	PCT
78	5	12	17	-22	81	1	1	1	0	73	6.8

1999-2000 statistics:

GP	G	A	TP	+/-	PIM	PP	SH	GW	GT	S	PCT
46	1	1	2	-12	66	0	0	0	0	23	4.3

2000-2001 statistics:

GP	G	A	TP	+/-	PIM	PP	SH	GW	GT	S	PCT
74	1	6	7	-6	80	0	0	0	0	56	1.8

2001-2002 statistics:

GP	G	A	TP	+/-	PIM	PP	SH	GW	GT	S	PCT
78	4	9	13	-1	58	0	0	1	0	84	4.8

PROJECTION

Cullimore is completely keyed on using his finesse skills on defence, so 12-15 points would be a safe and conservative bet.

LAST SEASON

Missed one game with hip injury. Missed one game with thigh injury.

THE FINESSE GAME

Cullimore is big and rangy, and a good skater for his size. He jumps smartly into the play, using a big stride and a big reach. He makes smart pinches and doesn't gamble too often.

He is a good enough skater to hustle back if he does make a mistake in judgement. Cullimore is a good passer but not creative. He will to chip the puck off the boards if that's the right play, but he is also ready to break a forward with a smooth outlet pass.

Cullimore is intelligent and diligent in his approach to the game. He will always be after the coaches to analyze plays. Cullimore is not a top-pair defenceman, but in Tampa Bay he routinely draws the checking assignments against other team's top forward line.

THE PHYSICAL GAME

Not big or mean but determined, Cullimore takes his man out effectively in front of the net. He gets good leg drive to power his checks. He blocks a lot of shots.

THE INTANGIBLES

Cullimore does not take his job for granted and he will be one of Tampa Bay's top four (actually, top two) defencemen as well as one of the team's leaders.

BRIAN HOLZINGER

Yrs. of NHL service: 7
Born: Parma, Ohio; Oct. 10, 1972
Position: centre
Height: 5-11
Weight: 190
Uniform no.: 9
Shoots: right

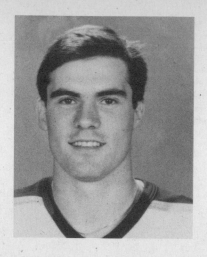

Career statistics:

GP	G	A	TP	PIM
459	85	127	212	291

1998-1999 statistics:

GP	G	A	TP	+/-	PIM	PP	SH	GW	GT	S	PCT
81	17	17	34	+2	45	5	0	2	0	143	11.9

1999-2000 statistics:

GP	G	A	TP	+/-	PIM	PP	SH	GW	GT	S	PCT
73	10	20	30	-3	51	1	2	2	0	104	9.6

2000-2001 statistics:

GP	G	A	TP	+/-	PIM	PP	SH	GW	GT	S	PCT
70	11	25	36	-9	64	3	0	2	0	87	12.6

2001-2002 statistics:

GP	G	A	TP	+/-	PIM	PP	SH	GW	GT	S	PCT
23	1	2	3	-4	4	0	0	0	0	20	5.0

LAST SEASON

Missed one game due to coach's decision. Missed 58 games with shoulder injury and surgery.

THE FINESSE GAME

Holzinger has a fine touch down low, and patience with the puck to find the open passing lane. He needs to work with a big grinder on one wing, because he is too small to do much work effectively in the corners. He is not as gritty as a number of smaller forwards and plays too much on the perimeter.

He's not a natural scorer but Holzinger has some speed, which he needs to learn to use to his advantage on a more consistent basis. He is crafty and deceptively quick.

The key to Holzinger's development will be adding the little things to his game that make a complete player. He has to ask himself how he can contribute if he's not scoring. He can play, but can he win? He has a lot of raw talent, but at the moment he's an open-ice break player. He has a lot of hockey sense and may be adaptable. His defence has improved. Holzinger needs to improve on draws.

THE PHYSICAL GAME

Holzinger will have to work for his open ice in the NHL. He is neither very big nor very strong. Strength and conditioning work must figure in his summer-vacation plans again, and every season for as long as he wants to stay in the NHL. He has a little bit of an edge to his game, and has to play gritty.

THE INTANGIBLES

Holzinger is too small to play a third-line checking role, but hasn't made a good enough impression in Tampa Bay to win a top-six forward job. His shoulder problems last season were another stumbling block.

PROJECTION

Holzinger is not an impact player — not even on a team as weak as the Lightning. If he gets the playing time, he could score 30 points, but it's likely to occur elsewhere.

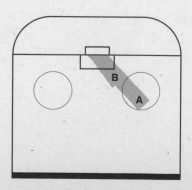

NIKOLAI KHABIBULIN

Yrs. of NHL service: 8
Born: Sverdlovsk, Russia; Jan. 13, 1973
Position: goaltender
Height: 6-1
Weight: 195
Uniform no.: 35
Catches: left

Career statistics:

GP	MIN	GA	SO	GAA	A	PIM
72	4019	159	7	2.37	8	74

1998-1999 statistics:

GP	MIN	GAA	W	L	T	SO	GA	S	SAPCT	PIM
63	3657	2.13	32	23	7	8	130	1681	.923	8

1999-2000 statistics:

Missed NHL season.

2000-2001 statistics:

GP	MIN	GAA	W	L	T	SO	GA	S	SAPCT	PIM
2	123	2.93	1	1	0	0	6	69	.913	0

2001-2002 statistics:

GP	MIN	GAA	W	L	T	SO	GA	S	SAPCT	PIM
70	3896	2.36	24	32	10	7	153	1914	.920	6

LAST SEASON

Fifth in NHL in save percentage. Tied for second in NHL in shutouts.

THE PHYSICAL GAME

Khabibulin is a butterfly-style goalie who positions himself like a shortstop. He gets down low and always gets his body behind the shot, and he stays on his feet and moves with the shooter. He may perform the best split-save in the league: it's stunningly graceful and athletic, and his legs look about five feet long. He leaves only the tiniest five-hole because he also gets the paddle of his stick down low across the front of the crease. Shooters have to go upstairs on him, but he doesn't give away a lot of net high.

Solid in his fundamentals, Khabibulin plays well out on the top of his crease, which is unusual for Russian goalies, who tend to stay deep in their net. He is aggressive but patient at the same time, and waits for the shooter to commit first. He could still improve his puckhandling. He has an excellent glove hand.

Khabibulin needs to have his minutes watched closely. He tends to break down sharply with too much activity. If Tampa Bay ever makes it into the playoffs, Khabibulin can't arrive overused.

THE MENTAL GAME

Khabibulin is able to maintain a strong attitude despite a lack of offensive support.

THE INTANGIBLES

If they had made the playoffs, Khabibulin would have given Montreal's Jose Theodore keen competition for the Hart Trophy. He was that dominant.

PROJECTION

Khabibulin is terrific, but he's still backstopping a bad team. He'll do well to get 25 wins, most of which he will earn on his own.

PAVEL KUBINA

Yrs. of NHL service: 4
Born: Vsetin, Czech Republic; Sept. 10, 1979
Position: right defence
Height: 6-4
Weight: 230
Uniform no.: 13
Shoots: right

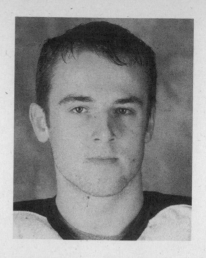

Career statistics:

GP	G	A	TP	PIM
299	40	74	114	404

1998-1999 statistics:

GP	G	A	TP	+/-	PIM	PP	SH	GW	GT	S	PCT
68	9	12	21	-33	80	3	1	1	1	119	7.6

1999-2000 statistics:

GP	G	A	TP	+/-	PIM	PP	SH	GW	GT.	S	PCT
69	8	18	26	-19	93	6	0	3	0	128	6.3

2000-2001 statistics:

GP	G	A	TP	+/-	PIM	PP	SH	GW	GT	S	PCT
70	11	19	30	-14	103	6	1	1	0	128	8.6

2001-2002 statistics:

GP	G	A	TP	+/-	PIM	PP	SH	GW	GT	S	PCT
82	11	23	34	-22	106	5	2	3	0	189	5.8

PROJECTION

Kubina fell a point shy of the 35 points we projected for him last season, and we expect the same output this season.

LAST SEASON

Led team in shorthanded goals. Second on team in shots. Third on team in assists and penalty minutes. Tied for third on team in game-winning goals. One of three Lightning players to appear in all 82 games.

THE FINESSE GAME

Kubina is one of the most exciting young defence prospects in the league. He stumbled a bit last season, but Tampa Bay maintains a lot of confidence in him. If he makes a mistake (and he does), the Lightning will put him right back out to keep learning.

Kubina isn't a great skater. He is big and somewhat upright in his stance, and he takes short strides. He lacks lateral quickness, though he has shown improvement. He is very strong on his skates.

The key to his game is his passing. He has fair offensive instincts, though he doesn't have a good shot. And he gets significant power-play time. His puck skills and his composure are advanced for such an inexperienced player. He receives a lot of ice time and a lot of responsibility, often facing other teams' top lines, and he has grown with the challenges. Kubina is Tampa Bay's best shot-blocker.

THE PHYSICAL GAME

Kubina has good size and he uses it well. He has a bit of an edge to him. All in all, a solid package.

THE INTANGIBLES

As part of the Lightning's top defence pair, Kubina is going to get a heavy workload again this season. He has to be nagged to keep at his conditioning and to work on his off-ice habits. He averaged a team-high 23:39 of ice time last season.

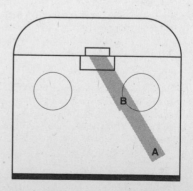

VINCENT LECAVALIER

Yrs. of NHL service: 4
Born: Ile Bizard, Que.; Apr. 21, 1980
Position: centre
Height: 6-4
Weight: 205
Uniform no.: 4
Shoots: left

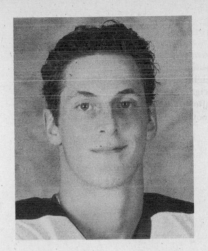

Career statistics:

GP	G	A	TP	PIM
306	81	102	183	193

1998-1999 statistics:

GP	G	A	TP	+/-	PIM	PP	SH	GW	GT	S	PCT
82	13	15	28	-19	23	2	0	2	1	125	10.4

1999-2000 statistics:

GP	G	A	TP	+/-	PIM	PP	SH	GW	GT	S	PCT
80	25	42	67	-25	43	6	0	3	1	166	15.1

2000-2001 statistics:

GP	G	A	TP	+/-	PIM	PP	SH	GW	GT	S	PCT
68	23	28	51	-26	66	7	0	3	0	165	13.9

2001-2002 statistics:

GP	G	A	TP	+/-	PIM	PP	SH	GW	GT	S	PCT
76	20	17	37	-18	61	5	0	3	1	164	12.2

LAST SEASON

Tied for second on team in goals. Tied for third on team in game-winning goals. Missed four games with ankle injury. Missed two games in contract dispute.

THE FINESSE GAME

Lecavalier's puck skills are everything they were advertised to be when the Lightning drafted him first overall in 1998. He is an elite playmaker. His passing skills are world class, and he has gained more confidence in his moves, even making daring spin-o-ramas. Like Wayne Gretzky and Mario Lemieux, the two great centres with whom he has been compared, Lecavalier will invent moves lesser players don't even dare dream of. His linemates have to be constantly aware that he can get the puck to them at any time.

Like many young players, Lecavalier will need to focus on his defensive play, but he has a good foundation for that already and should be an apt pupil. He is a shifty skater who can catch a defenceman flat-footed. His speed is major league. He can burst to the outside with the puck and beat a defenceman one-on-one.

Lecavalier has played centre and wing in Tampa and hasn't shone in either position.

THE PHYSICAL GAME

A tall, skinny kid who has to keep working in the weight room in order to do battle against the league's heavyweights, Lecavalier has worked with a personal trainer. He has a nasty streak in him, and is just as quick to answer a hit with a whack of the stick.

THE INTANGIBLES

So he isn't the next Michael Jordan. When is he going to become the first Vincent Lecavalier? Yeah, he was rushed to the NHL, and yeah, he isn't playing with great stock. But he will be entering his fourth NHL season now and it's time to step up. No matter what Lecavalier's issues are, getting outplayed on a nightly basis by Dave Andreychuk should embarrass him.

Lecavalier missed training camp and the first two games of the season in a contract dispute, which didn't help his cause.

PROJECTION

We've been expecting more of Lecavalier. If he doesn't score 70 points this season, it might be time to reconsider his future.

FREDRIK MODIN

Yrs. of NHL service: 6
Born: Sundsvall, Sweden; Oct. 8, 1974
Position: left wing
Height: 6-4
Weight: 220
Uniform no.: 33
Shoots: left

Career statistics:

GP	G	A	TP	PIM
427	106	105	211	184

1998-1999 statistics:

GP	G	A	TP	+/-	PIM	PP	SH	GW	GT	S	PCT
67	16	15	31	+14	35	1	0	3	1	108	14.8

1999-2000 statistics:

GP	G	A	TP	+/-	PIM	PP	SH	GW	GT	S	PCT
80	22	26	48	-26	18	3	0	5	0	167	13.2

2000-2001 statistics:

GP	G	A	TP	+/-	PIM	PP	SH	GW	GT	S	PCT
76	32	24	56	-1	48	8	0	4	0	217	14.8

2001-2002 statistics:

GP	G	A	TP	+/-	PIM	PP	SH	GW	GT	S	PCT
54	14	17	31	0	27	2	0	4	1	141	9.9

PROJECTION

Modin has all the makings of a consistent 30-goal scorer.

LAST SEASON

Second on team in game-winning goals. Missed 26 games with wrist injury. Missed two games with charley horse.

THE FINESSE GAME

Modin's shot is so heavy that it can physically knock the breath out of even the most well-padded goalie. He is dangerous as soon as he crosses the blueline.

Modin needs to take more shots. He should be close to 300 shots over a full season, but he still looks to pass too much.

He clicks beautifully with rookie centre Brad Richards. In the past, Modin was always looking to set up a shooter, but now Richards looks to set Modin up. If Modin plays with Richards again this season, that positive trend should continue.

Modin has a bit of a knock-kneed skating style and isn't pretty to watch, but he has NHL-calibre speed and is strong on his skates. He is fairly aware defensively.

THE PHYSICAL GAME

Modin has a powerful upper body for muscling through plays when he has a notion to, though he will still drift once in awhile. On nights when he gets it into his head to play a physical game, he drives to the net with better intent and is far more effective. He has very good size and could be developing into a bona fide power forward.

THE INTANGIBLES

His wrist injury was a serious blow to the Lightning last season. He should be on Tampa Bay's top line.

JIMMIE OLVESTAD

Yrs. of NHL service: 1
Born: Stockholm, Sweden; Feb. 16, 1980
Position: left wing
Height: 6-1
Weight: 194
Uniform no.: 41
Shoots: left

Career statistics:

GP	G	A	TP	PIM
74	3	11	14	24

2001-2002 statistics:

GP	G	A	TP	+/-	PIM	PP	SH	GW	GT	S	PCT
74	3	11	14	+3	24	0	0	0	0	99	3.0

LAST SEASON

First NHL season. Second on team in plus-minus. Missed five games due to coach's decision. Missed three games with shoulder injury.

THE FINESSE GAME

Olvestad is still a very young forward who is going to continue to go through some growing pains.

He is primarily a checking winger who doesn't have a great deal of offensive upside. His major problem is that he isn't big enough or strong enough to handle a third-line role on a full-time basis. He will simply be overwhelmed by most of the NHL's power forwards.

Olvestad has worked hard and earned his ice time in Tampa Bay. He is a swift skater. He saw a lot of penalty-killing duty, but can the Lightning really afford to keep him around as a specialist?

THE PHYSICAL GAME

Olvestad is pretty stringy. He just isn't constructed for NHL warfare.

THE INTANGIBLES

Olvestad can't be faulted on his effort. Too bad his work ethic can't be grafted onto some bigger players.

PROJECTION

It would be surprising to see Olvestad score much more than 20 points.

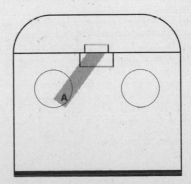

VACLAV PROSPAL

Yrs. of NHL service: 5
Born: Ceske-Budejovice, Czech Republic; Feb. 17, 1975
Position: centre
Height: 6-2
Weight: 195
Uniform no.: 20
Shoots: left

Career statistics:

GP	G	A	TP	PIM
387	66	149	215	183

1998-1999 statistics:

GP	G	A	TP	+/-	PIM	PP	SH	GW	GT	S	PCT
79	10	26	36	+8	58	2	0	3	0	114	8.8

1999-2000 statistics:

GP	G	A	TP	+/-	PIM	PP	SH	GW	GT	S	PCT
79	22	33	55	-2	40	5	0	4	0	204	10.8

2000-2001 statistics:

GP	G	A	TP	+/-	PIM	PP	SH	GW	GT	S	PCT
74	5	24	29	-1	22	1	0	0	0	136	3.7

2001-2002 statistics:

GP	G	A	TP	+/-	PIM	PP	SH	GW	GT	S	PCT
81	18	37	55	-11	38	7	0	2	0	166	10.8

LAST SEASON

Second on team in assists, points and power-play goals. Third on team in shots. Missed one game with flu.

THE FINESSE GAME

Prospal has a power-play weapon, and it's not an overpowering shot: it's his ability to thread the puck through penalty killers to an open man.

He loves to score (his wrist shot and one-timers are accurate) and make plays. He had to learn to play without the puck, and he succeeded. His defensive game has also improved. He thinks the game well and is an unselfish player. Last season he was probably too unselfish. Prospal needs to shoot more and be less predictable.

The only rap on Prospal is his skating ability, but it's NHL calibre and his view of the ice and his hockey sense compensate for any lack of pure speed. Prospal is very good on face-offs.

THE PHYSICAL GAME

Prospal is tall but lean and needs a little more muscle for one-on-one battles. Right now he gives the impression of being a little smaller than he is, but he's an eager player who will get involved. However, he doesn't always do this on a nightly basis.

THE INTANGIBLES

Consistency has always eluded Prospal. Tampa Bay is so thin up front that his job security isn't threatened for the time being.

PROJECTION

Prospal is a legitimate 20-goal scorer, and he rebounded from a dreadful 2000-01 to have a decent season in Tampa Bay.

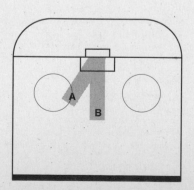

BRAD RICHARDS

Yrs. of NHL service: 2
Born: Montague, P.E.I.; May 2, 1980
Position: centre/left wing
Height: 6-0
Weight: 170
Uniform no.: 19
Shoots: left

Career statistics:

GP	G	A	TP	PIM
164	41	83	124	27

2000-2001 statistics:

GP	G	A	TP	+/-	PIM	PP	SH	GW	GT	S	PCT
82	21	41	62	-10	14	7	0	3	0	179	11.7

2001-2002 statistics:

GP	G	A	TP	+/-	PIM	PP	SH	GW	GT	S	PCT
82	20	42	62	-18	13	5	0	0	1	251	8.0

LAST SEASON

Led team in assists, points and shots. Tied for second on team in goals. One of three Lightning players to appear in all 82 games.

THE FINESSE GAME

Nothing about Richards' game is outstanding. He is only average size, isn't a dazzling skater and doesn't have great hands. But what Richards possesses is a Mario Lemieux-like ability to slow the game down to his own pace. He certainly isn't the next Lemieux, but he is deceptive and calm with his playmaking, and that fools a lot of people.

Richards is a very smart player. To compare him to another great player, Wayne Gretzky, Richards seems to think the game on a completely different level. He is calm and poised.

Richards needs to work on his defensive game and face-offs, but he has shown a willingness to rise to any challenge.

THE PHYSICAL GAME

He needs to get stronger. Richards continues to work in the off-season to better his upper-body strength. He is willing to scrap along the boards for the puck. Richards also needs to continue to improve his skating. He is a fit player and can handle a lot of minutes (he led Tampa Bay forwards in ice time with 19:47). Richards finished the season strong, too. He was better than a point-a-game player after the Olympic break.

THE INTANGIBLES

The only problem with Richards is that there is only one of him. Richards upgrades the level of any wingers who get to play alongside him. A lot of people thought it was Lecavalier who made Richards look so good in junior. It might have been just the opposite.

PROJECTION

Richards scored 62 points on a bad team last season. Tampa Bay isn't going to get much better. Richards is.

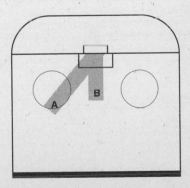

CORY SARICH

Yrs. of NHL service: 3
Born: Saskatoon, Sask.; Aug. 16, 1978
Position: right defence
Height: 6-3
Weight: 193
Uniform no.: 21
Shoots: right

Career statistics:

GP	G	A	TP	PIM
208	1	25	26	288

1998-1999 statistics:

GP	G	A	TP	+/-	PIM	PP	SH	GW	GT	S	PCT
4	0	0	0	+3	0	0	0	0	0	2	0.0

1999-2000 statistics:

GP	G	A	TP	+/-	PIM	PP	SH	GW	GT	S	PCT
59	0	6	6	-6	77	0	0	0	0	69	0.0

2000-2001 statistics:

GP	G	A	TP	+/-	PIM	PP	SH	GW	GT	S	PCT
73	1	8	9	-25	106	0	0	1	0	66	1.5

2001-2002 statistics:

GP	G	A	TP	+/-	PIM	PP	SH	GW	GT	S	PCT
72	0	11	11	-4	105	0	0	0	0	55	0.0

LAST SEASON

Career highs in points and assists. Missed four games with shoulder injury. Missed two games with knee injury. Missed one game with concussion.

THE FINESSE GAME

Sarich is a stay-at-home defenceman who should develop into an extremely steady and reliable bedrock for the Tampa Bay defence. He has NHL skating ability, with decent lateral movement, pivots and balance. He moves the puck very well. Being big and strong and being able to get the puck out of the zone quickly and safely already has Sarich ahead of some NHL veteran defencemen.

Sarich does not get involved in the attack. He knows his game is defence. There isn't much fancy about him.

Sarich plays like things are happening too fast around him. Either he hasn't adjusted to the NHL pace or he isn't learning from his mistakes or his reads are not as advanced as they should be.

THE PHYSICAL GAME

Sarich has pro size and a mean streak, but he lost some of his aggression last season. The concussion (which occurred in October) may have been a factor. His skating is powerful enough to help him line up opponents for some pretty big hits. He has to be careful not to go running out of position looking for his checks, though.

THE INTANGIBLES

Sarich is in a tough spot on a weak Tampa Bay team, but he should have improved more. He joined a team that needed him, and while he didn't regress, he didn't show the kind of progress we would like to see in a player his age. This could be a critical year for him.

PROJECTION

Sarich will probably not put many more than 15 points on the board.

ALEXANDER SVITOV

Yrs. of NHL service: 0
Born: Omsk, Russia; Nov. 3, 1982
Position: centre
Height: 6-3
Weight: 198
Uniform no.: n.a.
Shoots: left

Career statistics:

GP	G	A	TP	PIM
60	11	9	20	162

2001-2002 European statistics:

GP	G	A	TP	PIM
3	0	1	1	2

LAST SEASON

Appeared in 3 games with Omsk (Russia), scoring
0-1-1 with 2 PIM.

THE FINESSE GAME

A battle for Svitov's rights prevented the highly
skilled centre from playing in his native Russia last
season. Tampa Bay would love to negotiate through
the murky waters of international hockey and get him
in North America under the Lightning's control, but
that may be easier said than done.

Svitov was probably ready to step into the NHL
when he was drafted in 2001. He is projected as a top-
two centre. Svitov's game is well-rounded. There isn't
much missing from his game. He can skate, shoot,
pass, backcheck, forecheck and win draws.

He will be able to kill penalties, block shots and
jam up front on the power play.

THE PHYSICAL GAME

Svitov is a power player with a nasty streak. He
reminds a lot of scouts of Bobby Holik. The Lightning
could use a player like that. What team couldn't?

THE INTANGIBLES

When Svitov did get to play — in the World Junior
Championships for Russia — he was a force. He only
scored 2-1-3 in five games, but was dominating just
the same.

PROJECTION

Svitov might be a year removed from playing in the
big league.

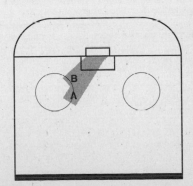

SHANE WILLIS

Yrs. of NHL service: 2
Born: Edmonton, Alta.; June 13, 1977
Position: right wing
Height: 6-1
Weight: 195
Uniform no.: 24
Shoots: right

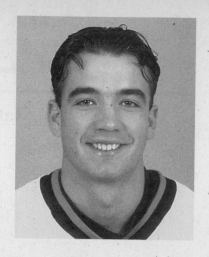

Career statistics:

GP	G	A	TP	PIM
162	31	37	68	75

1998-1999 statistics:

GP	G	A	TP	+/-	PIM	PP	SH	GW	GT	S	PCT
7	0	0	0	-2	0	0	0	0	0	1	0.0

1999-2000 statistics:

GP	G	A	TP	+/-	PIM	PP	SH	GW	GT	S	PCT
2	0	0	0	-1	0	0	0	0	0	1	-

2000-2001 statistics:

GP	G	A	TP	+/-	PIM	PP	SH	GW	GT	S	PCT
73	20	24	44	-6	45	9	0	6	0	172	11.6

2001-2002 statistics:

GP	G	A	TP	+/-	PIM	PP	SH	GW	GT	S	PCT
80	11	13	24	-8	30	2	0	0	1	155	7.1

LAST SEASON

Acquired from Carolina on March 5, 2002, with Chris Dingman for Kevin Weekes. Missed three games with back injury.

THE FINESSE GAME

Willis's shot is almost legendary. He has a wicked slap shot from the point — it's a rocket. He gets it away quickly and he's accurate. He's not shy about using it, either.

Willis also has terrific speed. It took a while for the rest of his game to catch up with his skating and his shot. Willis needed to learn the defensive part of the game and he still needs to improve his play away from the puck, although he has improved greatly.

He has very good offensive hockey sense.

THE PHYSICAL GAME

Willis is fair-sized but not really big and strong. His physical play waned after the concussion he absorbed from a Scott Stevens hit in the 2001 playoffs.

THE INTANGIBLES

Willis is back with the team that originally drafted him (in 1995), but he was a much more subdued player. He was 4-3-7 in 21 games with the Lightning after the trade — not exactly tearing up the gulf.

PROJECTION

With that howitzer shot of his, Willis has 30-goal potential. Looks like 20 will be his next stepping-stone.

TORONTO MAPLE LEAFS

Players' Statistics 2001-2002

POS.	NO.	PLAYER	GP	G	A	PTS	+/-	PIM	PP	SH	GW	GT	S	PCT
C	13	MATS SUNDIN	82	41	39	80	6	94	10	2	9	2	262	15.6
C	16	DARCY TUCKER	77	24	35	59	24	92	7		5		124	19.4
R	89	ALEXANDER MOGILNY	66	24	33	57	1	8	5		4		188	12.8
R	19	MIKAEL RENBERG	71	14	38	52	11	36	4		3		130	10.8
C	21	ROBERT REICHEL	78	20	31	51	7	26	1		3		152	13.2
L	7	GARY ROBERTS	69	21	27	48	-4	63	6	2	2	1	122	17.2
R	14	JONAS HOGLUND	82	13	34	47	11	26	1	1	4		199	6.5
D	24	BRYAN MCCABE	82	17	26	43	16	129	8		1		157	10.8
D	15	TOMAS KABERLE	69	10	29	39	5	2	5		3	1	85	11.8
C	39	TRAVIS GREEN	82	11	23	34	13	61	3		2		119	9.2
L	27	SHAYNE CORSON	74	12	21	33	11	120		1	1		111	10.8
R	28	TIE DOMI	74	9	10	19	3	157			2		93	9.7
D	36	DMITRY YUSHKEVICH	55	6	13	19	14	26	3				79	7.6
C	18	ALYN MCCAULEY	82	6	10	16	10	18		1	1		95	6.3
R	10	GARRY VALK	63	5	10	15	2	28					80	6.3
D	25	JYRKI LUMME	66	4	9	13	8	22	1	2	1		73	5.5
D	4	CORY CROSS	50	3	9	12	11	54			1		39	7.7
D	8	AKI BERG	81	1	10	11	14	46					66	1.5
R	26	PAUL HEALEY	21	3	7	10	7	2					29	10.3
D	2	WADE BELAK	63	1	3	4	2	142					47	2.1
D	29	*KAREL PILAR	23	1	3	4	3	8					32	3.1
R	22	*ALEXEI PONIKAROVSKY	8	2		2	2				1		8	25.0
C	11	NIK ANTROPOV	11	1	1	2	-1	4					12	8.3
D	44	ANDERS ERIKSSON	34		2	2	-1	12					31	
C	20	*JEFF FARKAS	6		2	2	1	4					3	
D	3	MARC MORO	15				-3	25					7	
L	43	NATHAN DEMPSEY	3				1						3	
C	37	DONALD MACLEAN					0							
L	33	BOB WREN	1					1						
G	30	TOM BARRASSO	38				0	4						
G	31	CURTIS JOSEPH	51				0	10						
G	35	COREY SCHWAB	30				0	2						
G	30	SEBASTIEN CENTOMO	1				0							

GP = games played; G = goals; A = assists; PTS = points; +/- = goals-for minus goals-against while player is on ice; PIM = penalties in minutes; PP = power-play goals; SH = shorthanded goals; GW = game-winning goals; GT = game-tying goals; S = no. of shots; PCT = percentage of goals to shots; * = rookie

ED BELFOUR

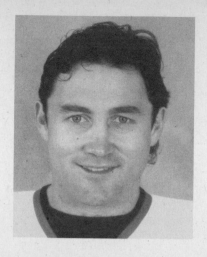

Yrs. of NHL service: 12
Born: Carman, Man.; Apr. 21, 1965
Position: goaltender
Height: 5-11
Weight: 192
Uniform no.: 20
Catches: left

Career statistics:

GP	MIN	GA	SO	GAA	A	PIM
735	42328	1743	58	2.47	24	320

1998-1999 statistics:

GP	MIN	GAA	W	L	T	SO	GA	S	SAPCT	PIM
61	3536	1.99	35	15	9	5	117	1373	.915	26

1999-2000 statistics:

GP	MIN	GAA	W	L	T	SO	GA	S	SAPCT	PIM
62	3620	2.10	32	21	7	4	127	1571	.919	10

2000-2001 statistics:

GP	MIN	GAA	W	L	T	SO	GA	S	SAPCT	PIM
63	3687	2.34	35	20	7	8	144	1508	.905	4

2001-2002 statistics:

GP	MIN	GAA	W	L	T	SO	GA	S	SAPCT	PIM
60	3467	2.65	21	27	11	1	153	1458	.895	12

LAST SEASON

Signed as free agent by Toronto on July 2, 2002. Lowest single-season win total since 1996-97.

THE PHYSICAL GAME

Belfour's style relies more on athleticism than technique. He is always on his belly, his side, his back. He has taken over from the retired Dominik Hasek as the best goalie with the worst style in the NHL.

He has great instincts and reads the play well. Belfour plays in an inverted-V form, giving the five-hole but usually taking it away from the shooter with his quick reflexes. He is very aggressive and often comes so far out of his crease that he gets tangled with his own defenders and runs interference on opponents. He knows he is well-padded and is not afraid to use his body, though injuries have made him less aggressive than in the past. In fact, Belfour uses his body more than his stick or glove, and that is part of his problem. He tries to make the majority of saves with his torso, making the routine saves more difficult.

Belfour tends to keep his glove low. The book on him is to shoot high, but that's the case with most NHL goalies — and a lot of NHL shooters have trouble picking that spot. He sometimes gives up bad rebounds, but his defence is so good and so quick they will swoop in on the puck before the opposition gets a second or third whack.

He has a lot of confidence and an impressive ability to handle the puck, though he sometimes overdoes it. He uses his body to screen when handling the puck for a 15-foot pass, and often sets picks for his forwards.

THE MENTAL GAME

Belfour is such a battler, such a competitor. Sometimes he goes overboard, but it's easier to cool an athlete off than fire him up. His teammates believe in him fully, and he has supreme confidence, even arrogance, in his abilities. Off the ice is another issue. Belfour has clashed with his coaches in the past in Dallas and probably will again with the Maple Leafs. The media scrutiny is far more intense in Toronto and it may be a factor in whether or not Belfour can maintain an even keel.

THE INTANGIBLES

In last year's *HSR* we said that when Belfour's downturn came, it would come quickly. The Maple Leafs are betting last year was an aberration. We are not so sure.

PROJECTION

Belfour should improve over his 21 wins, but 30 isn't the lock it once was.

AKI-PETTERI BERG

Yrs. of NHL service: 7
Born: Turku, Finland; July 28, 1977
Position: left defence
Height: 6-3
Weight: 215
Uniform no.: 8
Shoots: left

Career statistics:

GP	G	A	TP	PIM
374	9	48	57	250

1998-1999 statistics:
Did not play in NHL

1999-2000 statistics:

GP	G	A	TP	+/-	PIM	PP	SH	GW	GT	S	PCT
70	3	13	16	-1	45	0	0	0	0	70	4.3

2000-2001 statistics:

GP	G	A	TP	+/-	PIM	PP	SH	GW	GT	S	PCT
59	3	4	7	-3	45	3	0	1	0	43	7.0

2001-2002 statistics:

GP	G	A	TP	+/-	PIM	PP	SH	GW	GT	S	PCT
81	1	10	11	+14	46	0	0	0	0	66	1.5

LAST SEASON

Third on team in plus-minus. Missed one game due to injury.

THE FINESSE GAME

Berg has a pleasing combination of offensive and defensive skills. His skating is topnotch. He has a powerful stride with great mobility and balance. And he gets terrific drive from perfect leg extension and deep knee bends.

He sees the ice well and has excellent passing skills. His skating ability and his ability to make the first pass out of the zone are solid. Berg jumps into the play and moves to open ice. He handles the puck well, but probably lacks the vision and creativity to be a first-unit power-play quarterback. He does have some offensive upside and could develop into a solid two-way defenceman.

Berg has improved defensive-zone reads, but he still needs the coaching staff to stay on his case.

THE PHYSICAL GAME

Berg is big and strong, and has the mobility to lay down some serious open-ice checks. He is almost the same size as former Kings teammate Rob Blake, and Berg is capable of the same style of punishing checks that Blake and Scott Stevens have doled out. Berg, though, hasn't shown the same taste for hitting that Blake and Stevens do, and he has to be constantly ridden to use his size and strength. Berg is not tough.

THE INTANGIBLES

Berg qualifies as a reclamation project and he seems to be rebuilding his career after a bad experience in Los Angeles. He is nicely slotted as a No. 4 in Toronto and his game should continue to grow.

PROJECTION

Berg can, and should, score 20 points as his ice time and responsibility increases.

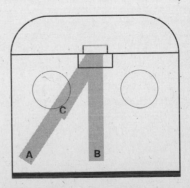

SHAYNE CORSON

Yrs. of NHL service: 16
Born: Barrie, Ont.; Aug. 13, 1966
Position: left wing
Height: 6-1
Weight: 202
Uniform no.: 27
Shoots: left

Career statistics:

GP	G	A	TP	PIM
1093	261	407	668	2279

1998-1999 statistics:

GP	G	A	TP	+/-	PIM	PP	SH	GW	GT	S	PCT
63	12	20	32	-10	147	7	0	4	0	142	8.5

1999-2000 statistics:

GP	G	A	TP	+/-	PIM	PP	SH	GW	GT	S	PCT
70	8	20	28	-2	115	2	0	1	0	121	6.6

2000-2001 statistics:

GP	G	A	TP	+/-	PIM	PP	SH	GW	GT	S	PCT
77	8	18	26	+1	189	0	0	2	0	102	7.8

2001-2002 statistics:

GP	G	A	TP	+/-	PIM	PP	SH	GW	GT	S	PCT
74	12	21	33	+11	120	0	1	1	0	111	10.8

LAST SEASON

Missed give games with shoulder injury. Missed three games with back injury.

THE FINESSE GAME

Corson makes a lot of things happen by overpowering people around the net. He has surprising scoring ability for a player who is considered a mucker. People give him an extra foot or two because of his muscle, which allows him extra time to pick up loose pucks out of scrums and jam his shots in-tight or lift them over a goalie's stick. He has become more of a defensive force now.

Corson scores a lot of rebound goals if he plays on a line with people who throw the puck to the net, because he will go barrelling in for it. He's free to play that style more on left wing than at centre, but he also has some nice playmaking abilities when put in the middle. He won't do anything too fancy, but he is intelligent enough to play a basic short game. He can win draws outright on his backhand.

He is a powerful skater, but is not very fast or agile. Corson has good balance for his work along the boards, and has all the attributes of a power forward. He does his dirty work in front of the net for screens and deflections, and has the hands to guide hard point shots. He is wildly inaccurate with any shots that aren't at close range, so on nights when he is not winning the duels around the net he is a nonfactor. From 8 to 10 feet around the net, he can't be moved when he puts his mind to it.

Corson has also developed into a player who willingly applies himself to the defensive side of the game. In the playoffs, he will be given an assignment like checking the other team's top centre and go at it like a demon.

THE PHYSICAL GAME

Corson succeeds by fighting for his ice in the slot area. He takes an absolute beating around the net, setting screens and distracting the goalie to allow teammates to get good scoring chances. He creates second-chance opportunities for himself and his teammates because he is tremendous along the wall. He has grit and plays tough and hard every shift. He is dangerous because of his short fuse. Opponents never know when he will go off; since he's strong and can throw punches, few people want to be around when he does. He inspires fear. He hits to hurt and is so unpredictable he earns himself plenty of room on the ice.

THE INTANGIBLES

Corson was an important addition both on and off the ice for the Leafs.

PROJECTION

At 36, Corson could still have a few productive seasons left, but he isn't a big goals or points man anymore. His top end is about 40 points.

TOM FITZGERALD

Yrs. of NHL service: 14
Born: Melrose, Mass.; Aug. 28, 1968
Position: right wing / centre
Height: 6-1
Weight: 191
Uniform no.: 12
Shoots: right

Career statistics:

GP	G	A	TP	PIM
891	124	161	285	627

1998-1999 statistics:

GP	G	A	TP	+/-	PIM	PP	SH	GW	GT	S	PCT
80	13	19	32	-18	48	0	0	1	0	180	7.2

1999-2000 statistics:

GP	G	A	TP	+/-	PIM	PP	SH	GW	GT	S	PCT
82	13	9	22	-18	66	0	3	1	0	119	10.9

2000-2001 statistics:

GP	G	A	TP	+/-	PIM	PP	SH	GW	GT	S	PCT
82	9	9	18	-5	71	0	2	2	0	135	6.7

2001-2002 statistics:

GP	G	A	TP	+/-	PIM	PP	SH	GW	GT	S	PCT
78	8	12	20	-7	39	0	2	0	0	125	6.4

LAST SEASON

Signed as free agent by Toronto on July 16, 2002. Acquired by Chicago on March 13, 2002, from Nashville for a fourth-round draft pick in 2003 and future considerations. Led Blackhawks in short-handed goals. Missed three games with rib injury, ending consecutive games-played streak at 246.

THE FINESSE GAME

Fitzgerald is a defensive specialist, a checker and penalty killer who elevates his game with clutch performances.

He is quick and uses his outside speed to take the puck to the net. He doesn't shoot often. He doesn't have the fastest release and a goalie can usually adjust himself in time despite Fitzgerald's foot speed. He isn't very creative. Fitzgerald's chances emerge from his hard work digging around the net.

Fitzgerald is versatile and can be used as a centre or right wing. He is more effective on the wing. He is only average on draws. His hands aren't very quick and he tends to be overwhelmed by bigger centres.

THE PHYSICAL GAME

Fitzgerald is gritty and wiry-strong. He has fairly good size and he uses it along the boards and in front of the net. Although he's a pesky checker who gets people teed off, his own discipline keeps him from taking many cheap penalties. He gives his team some bang and pop and energy, and he finishes his checks. He is durable, handles a lot of minutes, and is a tough guy to keep out of the lineup. When Fitzgerald misses a game because of injury, you know he's really hurt.

THE INTANGIBLES

Fitzgerald's role as changed. In Nashville, he was asked to not only help build an expansion team on the ice, but to be the frontman and help win over a city that was new to the game. He fulfilled both of those jobs admirably. He is back to being a role player on a largely veteran team of stars in a hockey-crazed city. We're not sure where he will fit in the Leafs' pecking order, but we have always admired Fitzgerald's character and believe he can only help Toronto.

PROJECTION

Fitzgerald brings effort, not points. If he gets third-line duty with Toronto, he can score around 25 points.

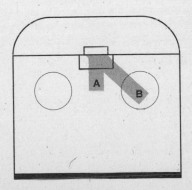

AARON GAVEY

Yrs. of NHL service: 7
Born: Sudbury, Ont.; Feb. 22, 1974
Position: centre
Height: 6-2
Weight: 200
Uniform no.: 44
Shoots: left

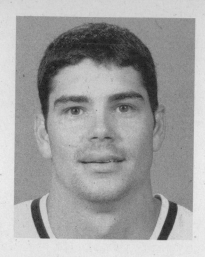

Career statistics:

GP	G	A	TP	PIM
350	41	49	90	270

1998-1999 statistics:

GP	G	A	TP	+/-	PIM	PP	SH	GW	GT	S	PCT
7	0	0	0	-1	10	0	0	0	0	4	0.0

1999-2000 statistics:

GP	G	A	TP	+/-	PIM	PP	SH	GW	GT	S	PCT
41	7	6	13	0	44	1	0	2	0	39	17.9

2000-2001 statistics:

GP	G	A	TP	+/-	PIM	PP	SH	GW	GT	S	PCT
75	10	14	24	-8	52	1	0	2	0	100	10.0

2001-2002 statistics:

GP	G	A	TP	+/-	PIM	PP	SH	GW	GT	S	PCT
71	6	11	17	-21	38	1	0	0	0	75	8.0

PROJECTION

Gavey will be slotted in a defensive role and isn't likely to score more than 10 goals, 20 points.

LAST SEASON

Signed as free agent by Toronto on July 24, 2002. Missed three games with facial laceration. Missed two games with flu. Missed two games with fractured left foot. Missed four games due to coach's decision.

THE FINESSE GAME

Gavey is a poor-man's Ian Laperriere. He is a two-way centre (he can also play either wing) who plays intelligent defence and has some offensive ability. His major drawback is his lack of foot speed, but he has worked very hard to turn himself into a decent player.

Everything Gavey does is rough around the edges. His main strength is on face-offs. He can be relied upon to battle for key draws in the defensive zone.

Gavey has a very good shot, a strong wrist or snap. He reads plays well and is very intelligent.

THE PHYSICAL GAME

Gavey has filled out to NHL size and is strong for battles along the wall and on face-offs. He is always running into people, and running over people.

THE INTANGIBLES

Gavey has gone through four organizations (Tampa Bay, Calgary, Dallas and Minnesota), without making much of an impression. He is a useful enough player because he tries hard and brings a lot of energy to every shift. He will be a depth player with Toronto.

TRAVIS GREEN

Yrs. of NHL service: 10
Born: Castlegar, B.C.; Dec. 20, 1970
Position: centre
Height: 6-2
Weight: 200
Uniform no.: 39
Shoots: right

Career statistics:

GP	G	A	TP	PIM
718	159	232	391	524

1998-1999 statistics:

GP	G	A	TP	+/-	PIM	PP	SH	GW	GT	S	PCT
79	13	17	30	-7	81	3	1	2	0	165	7.9

1999-2000 statistics:

GP	G	A	TP	+/-	PIM	PP	SH	GW	GT	S	PCT
78	25	21	46	-4	45	6	0	2	1	157	15.9

2000-2001 statistics:

GP	G	A	TP	+/-	PIM	PP	SH	GW	GT	S	PCT
69	13	15	28	-11	63	3	0	0	0	113	11.5

2001-2002 statistics:

GP	G	A	TP	+/-	PIM	PP	SH	GW	GT	S	PCT
82	11	23	34	+13	61	3	0	2	0	119	9.2

LAST SEASON

One of five Maple Leafs to appear in all 82 games.

THE FINESSE GAME

Green deserves a lot of credit for reinventing himself as a hockey player. Considered a pure scorer in minor and junior league, Green was taken in hand several years ago by Islanders minor-league coach Butch Goring — whose defensive play was a key factor in all four of the team's Stanley Cups — and he added a completely new dimension to Green's game. Green's keen defensive awareness and ability to win draws make him a valuable third-line centre. Green's game has made almost a complete 180, though, since his offensive contributions continue to dwindle.

Green is on the ice in the waning seconds of the period or the game to protect a lead. His skating is flawed. He can stop pushing and stop moving so there's no glide to him, and his skating really falls off. He has decent balance and agility with some quickness, though he lacks straight-ahead speed.

He controls the puck well. He plays more of a finesse game than a power game. An unselfish player, Green passes equally well to either side. He sees the ice well, but he has a very heavy shot. His release is sluggish, which he why he was never the scorer at the NHL level that he was in the minors. His goals are usually the result of sheer effort, not natural ability.

Green is good on face-offs. He has quick hands and he uses his body to tie up an opponent, enabling his linemates to skate in for the puck.

THE PHYSICAL GAME

Green has good size and is competitive, but hockey courage doesn't come naturally to him. He talks himself into going into the corners and around the net, knowing he has to get to dirty areas to produce. He uses his body to get in the way. He wants to be on the ice and has learned to pay the price to be there.

THE INTANGIBLES

Green's skating is what keeps him from ascending to a higher level, keeping him from playing alongside topnotch players. His perceived lack of fire is another reason why he is frequently changing addresses.

PROJECTION

Green is a third line player who can give around 10-15 goals and 30 points.

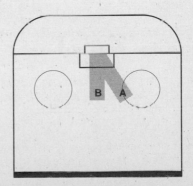

JONAS HOGLUND

Yrs. of NHL service: 6
Born: Hammaro, Sweden; Aug. 29, 1972
Position: right wing
Height: 6-3
Weight: 215
Uniform no.: 14
Shoots: right

Career statistics:

GP	G	A	TP	PIM
466	104	126	230	100

1998-1999 statistics:

GP	G	A	TP	+/-	PIM	PP	SH	GW	GT	S	PCT
74	8	10	18	-5	16	1	0	0	1	122	6.6

1999-2000 statistics:

GP	G	A	TP	+/-	PIM	PP	SH	GW	GT	S	PCT
82	29	27	56	-2	10	9	1	3	0	215	13.5

2000-2001 statistics:

GP	G	A	TP	+/-	PIM	PP	SH	GW	GT	S	PCT
82	23	26	49	+1	14	5	0	5	2	196	11.7

2001-2002 statistics:

GP	G	A	TP	+/-	PIM	PP	SH	GW	GT	S	PCT
82	13	34	47	+11	26	1	1	4	0	199	6.5

LAST SEASON

Second on team in shots. Third on team in assists. Tied for third on team in game-winning goals. One of five Maple Leafs to appear in all 82 games. Has appeared in 253 consecutive games.

THE FINESSE GAME

Hoglund is a natural goal-scorer. Every time he gets the puck he has a chance to score. The trick is to encourage him to shoot more, and instil an intense drive. He has a good, hard slap shot and half-wrister. So why doesn't he score more? Even though he had 199 shots on goal last season, his skill level is high enough that he should have around 250. Instead, Hoglund looks for the pass almost every time. He lacks a goal-scorer's mentality but he has a goal-scorer's tools. Goal-scorers have a confidence, almost an arrogance, about them, and Hoglund lacks that.

Hoglund has adapted well to North American hockey in his defensive and positional play. Play along the boards was a new concept to him, but he was unafraid of getting involved.

Hoglund skates well for a big man. He's no speed skater, but his skating is NHL calibre.

THE PHYSICAL GAME

Hoglund is a big guy but doesn't play a physical game. He has a long reach, which he uses instead of his body to try to win control of the puck or slow down an opponent. He's getting used to the idea of hitting. Still, he has to get better at it. When he does, his whole game perks up.

THE INTANGIBLES

If the Leafs hadn't learned early on that Gary Roberts was going to be lost for most of the season because of surgery on both of his shoulders, Hoglund would not have been re-signed. Toronto will move him if they get any kind of sensible offer.

PROJECTION

Hoglund has 30-goal ability, 15-goal results. No wonder teams get fed up with him.

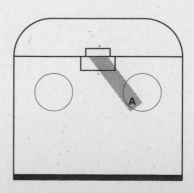

TOMAS KABERLE

Yrs. of NHL service: 4
Born: Rakovnik, Czech Republic; Mar. 2, 1978
Position: left defence
Height: 6-2
Weight: 200
Uniform no.: 15
Shoots: left

Career statistics:

GP	G	A	TP	PIM
290	27	119	146	62

1998-1999 statistics:

GP	G	A	TP	+/-	PIM	PP	SH	GW	GT	S	PCT
57	4	18	22	+3	12	0	0	2	0	71	5.6

1999-2000 statistics:

GP	G	A	TP	+/-	PIM	PP	SH	GW	GT	S	PCT
82	7	33	40	+3	24	2	0	0	0	82	8.5

2000-2001 statistics:

GP	G	A	TP	+/-	PIM	PP	SH	GW	GT	S	PCT
82	6	39	45	+10	24	0	0	1	0	96	6.3

2001-2002 statistics:

GP	G	A	TP	+/-	PIM	PP	SH	GW	GT	S	PCT
69	10	29	39	+5	2	5	0	3	1	85	11.8

LAST SEASON

Missed 12 games in contract dispute. Missed one game due to coach's decision.

THE FINESSE GAME

Kaberle brings all the skills expected of a good European defenceman and combines them with a taste for the North American style of play. It's an impressive package. Kaberle has not joined the NHL's elite corps of defencemen, and he might never, but he is a solid No. 2 as Bryan McCabe's partner.

One of the things that keeps Kaberle from being even more productive is his hesitation with the puck on the point. He will often hold up and look for a play instead of taking the shot. Penalty killers know they can press him aggressively.

Kaberle is a mobile skater who makes a smart first pass — he's an excellent puck-moving defenceman. He is always looking to join the rush, and he likes to create offence. He can get too fancy at times when he should be making the simple play instead, and will occasionally get into trouble in his own zone because of that tendency.

Kaberle is still learning and has already made great strides. His panic point is a lot higher than it was. He is poised and seldom gives up the puck under pressure.

THE PHYSICAL GAME

Kaberle comes to compete hard every night. He needs to get a little bigger and stronger to improve his play around the net, but he's still young and growing, and physical maturity will come. Kaberle faces a lot of the opposing team's top lines every night.

THE INTANGIBLES

Kaberle is a solid top four on anyone's team and he is in the upper tier of the second pairings in the league, with the potential to improve that status. He could develop along Scott Niedermayer-like lines — which is to say he will never be a star, and should remain just a notch below the league's elite offensive defencemen. Kaberle missed the start of last season in a contract dispute and it made for a slow start to his season.

PROJECTION

Over a full season, Kaberle should break into 50-point territory for the first time.

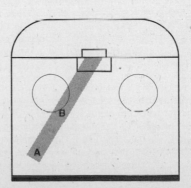

BRYAN MCCABE

Yrs. of NHL service: 7
Born: St. Catharines, Ont.; June 8, 1975
Position: left defence
Height: 6-1
Weight: 210
Uniform no.: 24
Shoots: left

Career statistics:

GP	G	A	TP	PIM
558	54	139	193	1041

1998-1999 statistics:

GP	G	A	TP	+/-	PIM	PP	SH	GW	GT	S	PCT
69	7	14	21	-11	120	1	2	0	0	98	7.1

1999-2000 statistics:

GP	G	A	TP	+/-	PIM	PP	SH	GW	GT	S	PCT
79	6	19	25	-8	139	2	0	2	0	119	5.0

2000-2001 statistics:

GP	G	A	TP	+/-	PIM	PP	SH	GW	GT	S	PCT
82	5	24	29	+16	123	3	0	2	0	159	3.1

2001-2002 statistics:

GP	G	A	TP	+/-	PIM	PP	SH	GW	GT	S	PCT
82	17	26	43	+16	129	8	0	1	0	157	10.8

LAST SEASON

Led team defencemen in points. Career highs in goals, assists and points. Second on team in plus-minus and power-play goals. Third on team in penalty minutes. One of five Maple Leafs to appear in all 82 games.

THE FINESSE GAME

McCabe's offensive upside gave the Maple Leafs the confidence to trade Danny Markov to Phoenix prior to the 2001-02 season. McCabe inherited most of Markov's power-play time on the first unit and took full advantage. McCabe has a heavy, major-league slap shot.

McCabe is an unorthodox skater with a bit of a hitch. He doesn't have a fluid, classic stride. He is okay going from his right to his left, but suspect going from his left to his right. When he has the puck or is jumping into the play he has decent speed, but his lack of mobility defensively is one of his flaws. He is hesitant in his own zone when reading the rush and will get caught.

He also doesn't have great puck-moving skills, which is a tremendous defect for a defenceman. His passes don't go tape-to-tape. They go off the glass, or down the rink for an icing, or worse, are picked off by a defender. He kills penalties well and blocks shots.

THE PHYSICAL GAME

McCabe is willing to drop his gloves and can handle himself in a bout, though it's not a strong part of his game. He is strong but not mean. McCabe understands that the physical part of the game is a major element of his success. McCabe is in good physical condition and was among the team leaders in ice time (24:34).

THE INTANGIBLES

Toronto's 2000 trade for McCabe (from Chicago for Alexander Karpovtsev and a draft pick) was daytime robbery. McCabe played well after the deal and topped himself last season. McCabe is not an elite defenceman but he is not far below that. McCabe had a big playoffs going up against other team's top lines.

PROJECTION

McCabe blew right past our 25-point projection. This is a new player now, and McCabe should score consistently in the 40-point range.

ALEXANDER MOGILNY

Yrs. of NHL service: 13
Born: Khabarovsk, Russia; Feb. 18, 1969
Position: right wing
Height: 5-11
Weight: 200
Uniform no.: 89
Shoots: left

Career statistics:

GP	G	A	TP	PIM
846	420	478	898	402

1998-1999 statistics:

GP	G	A	TP	+/-	PIM	PP	SH	GW	GT	S	PCT
59	14	31	45	0	58	3	2	1	1	110	12.7

1999-2000 statistics:

GP	G	A	TP	+/-	PIM	PP	SH	GW	GT	S	PCT
59	24	20	44	+3	20	5	1	1	2	161	14.9

2000-2001 statistics:

GP	G	A	TP	+/-	PIM	PP	SH	GW	GT	S	PCT
75	43	40	83	+10	43	12	0	7	0	240	17.9

2001-2002 statistics:

GP	G	A	TP	+/-	PIM	PP	SH	GW	GT	S	PCT
66	24	33	57	+1	8	5	0	4	0	188	12.8

LAST SEASON

Tied for second on team in goals. Third on team in points and shots. Tied for third on team in game-winning goals. Missed 16 games with back injuries.

THE FINESSE GAME

When he is healthy and in a groove, skating is the basis of Mogilny's game. He has a burst of speed from a standstill and hits his top speed in just a few strides. When he streaks down the ice, there is a good chance you'll see something new, something you didn't expect. He is unbelievably quick.

Mogilny's anticipation sets him apart from players who are merely fast. He is about as good a player as there is in the league at the transition game. He waits for a turnover and a chance to get a jump on the defenceman, with a preferred move to the outside. He's not afraid to go inside either, so a defenceman intent on angling him to the boards could just as easily get burned inside.

Mogilny can beat you in so many ways. He has a powerful and accurate wrist shot from the tops of the circles in. He shoots without breaking stride. He can work a give-and-go that is a thing of beauty. He one-times with the best of them. And everything is done at racehorse speed. The game comes easy to Mogilny.

THE PHYSICAL GAME

Mogilny intimidates with his speed but will also add a physical element. He has great upper-body strength and will drive through a defender to the net. His back problems were a drag on his season, but he still managed to be third on the Leafs in scoring.

THE INTANGIBLES

Mogilny was one of the Leafs' best forwards in the playoffs, a complete reversal from his woeful 2001 postseason.

PROJECTION

If Mogilny stays healthy this season, he could easily return to the 40-goal ranks.

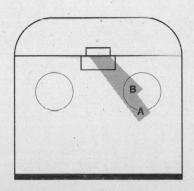

KAREL PILAR

Yrs. of NHL service: 0
Born: Prague, Czech Republic; Dec. 23, 1977
Position: defence
Height: 6-3
Weight: 207
Uniform no.: 29
Shoots: right

Career statistics:

GP	G	A	TP	PIM
23	1	3	4	8

2001-2002 statistics:

GP	G	A	TP	+/-	PIM	PP	SH	GW	GT	S	PCT
23	1	3	4	+3	8	0	0	0	0	32	3.1

LAST SEASON

Will be entering first full NHL season. Appeared in 52 games with St. John's (AHL), scoring 10-14-24 with 26 PIM.

THE FINESSE GAME

Pilar is a big defenseman whose chief asset is his puck-moving ability. But even at that, he's not elite. He takes a little too much time making the outlet pass. Pilar is still adjusting to the faster NHL pace.

His skating is bit awkward for this level, making it tough for him to jump into the play, which is something he really likes to do. He was a purely offensive defenceman in the Czech League but it's unlikely he will succeed in the NHL as that kind of player. He needs to learn to use his finesse skills in a defensive role and improve his play away from the puck.

THE PHYSICAL GAME

Pilar had good leg drive and lower body strength to generate power into his checks. He won't be a big open-ice hitter, and he's not very assertive. He has a lot less physical presence than a player of his size should exhibit.

THE INTANGIBLES

Toronto was planning on auditioning Pilar for a top four role this season, but the acquisition of Robert Svehla is likely to relegate him to the third pair. It's likely that is his niche anyway.

PROJECTION

Pilar should see second-unit power-play time and get his share of points 20 to 25 — but nothing he does excites us much.

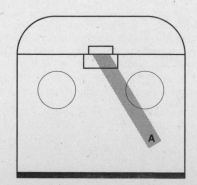

ROBERT REICHEL

Yrs. of NHL service: 9
Born: Litvinov, Czech Republic; June 25, 1971
Position: centre
Height: 5-10
Weight: 185
Uniform no.: 21
Shoots: left

Career statistics:

GP	G	A	TP	PIM
78	20	31	51	26

1998-1999 statistics:

GP	G	A	TP	+/-	PIM	PP	SH	GW	GT	S	PCT
83	26	43	69	-13	54	8	1	4	1	236	11.0

1999-2000 statistics:

Did not play in NHL.

2000-2001 statistics:

Did not play in NHL

2001-2002 statistics:

GP	G	A	TP	+/-	PIM	PP	SH	GW	GT	S	PCT
78	20	31	51	+7	26	1	0	3	0	152	13.2

LAST SEASON

Missed two games with back spasms. Missed two games with knee injury.

THE FINESSE GAME

Reichel's strength is as a playmaker. He thinks "pass" first and needs to play on a line with a pure finisher. He is one of those gifted passers who can make a scoring opportunity materialize when there appears to be no hole; his wingers have to be alert because the puck will find its way to their tape. He has great control of the puck in open ice or in scrums.

Reichel will certainly take the shot when he's got it, but he won't force a pass to someone who is in a worse scoring position than he is. He has an explosive shot with a lot of velocity on it. He pursues loose pucks in front and wheels around to the back of the net to look for an open teammate. He is good in traffic.

At least that's how Reichel plays when things are going well. He's just as likely to go into a slump or a pout, and he doesn't add much to a team when he isn't piling up points. He's moody and is just as inclined to sulk as he is to go on a scoring streak.

THE PHYSICAL GAME

Reichel is small but sturdy. He is not a big fan of contact and there are some who question his hockey courage. He's not a player other teams are afraid to play against. He is well-conditioned and can handle a lot of ice time.

THE INTANGIBLES

Reichel is a costly bomb. We've long questioned his desire and motivation and don't think he can be part of the core of any team wanting to be a champion. Not convinced? Will zero goals in 18 playoff games last season convince you? He is the opposite of clutch.

PROJECTION

Reichel is skilled and can get 50 points.

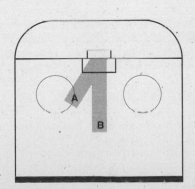

MIKAEL RENBERG

Yrs. of NHL service: 7
Born: Pitea, Sweden; May 5, 1972
Position: right wing
Height: 6-2
Weight: 218
Uniform no.: 19
Shoots: left

Career statistics:

GP	G	A	TP	PIM
535	164	240	404	286

1998-1999 statistics:

GP	G	A	TP	+/-	PIM	PP	SH	GW	GT	S	PCT
66	15	23	38	+5	18	6	0	2	0	154	9.7

1999-2000 statistics:

GP	G	A	TP	+/-	PIM	PP	SH	GW	GT	S	PCT
72	10	25	35	-1	32	3	0	1	0	122	8.2

2000-2001 statistics:

Did not play in NHL

2001-2002 statistics:

GP	G	A	TP	+/-	PIM	PP	SH	GW	GT	S	PCT
71	14	38	52	+11	36	4	0	3	0	130	10.8

LAST SEASON

Second on team in assists. Missed 11 games due to injuries.

THE FINESSE GAME

Renberg has a long, strong stride and excellent balance, but only average speed. Anticipation is the key that gives him a head start on the defence.

He drives to the net, and is strong enough to shrug off a lot of checks, or even shovel a one-handed shot or pass if one arm is tied up. He likes to come in on the off-wing, especially on the power play, and snap a strong shot off his back foot. He sees the ice well and is always looking for a teammate he can hit with a pass. Playing with Mats Sundin made him want to become even more of a set-up guy than a finisher, since he was always looking for his partner instead of scoring himself.

Renberg's best shots are his quick-release wristers or snaps with little backswing. He is defensively aware and is a solid two-way forward who can be on the ice in almost any situation.

THE PHYSICAL GAME

Renberg doesn't fight, but he is extremely strong, has a nasty streak and likes to hit hard. He won't be intimidated. Since he isn't a great skater, his adjustment to the smaller ice surfaces actually helped his game.

THE INTANGIBLES

Renberg made a nice complementary player with Sundin, but we still don't think of him as a true first-line winger.

PROJECTION

Renberg failed to come anywhere close to the 25 goals we projected for him last season. We have to assume this is the new path Renberg has chosen, so adjust his prediction to 15 goals, 40 assists.

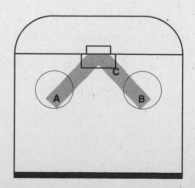

GARY ROBERTS

Yrs. of NHL service: 15
Born: North York, Ont.; May 23, 1966
Position: left wing
Height: 6-1
Weight: 200
Uniform no.: 7
Shoots: left

Career statistics:

GP	G	A	TP	PIM
943	364	386	750	2251

1998-1999 statistics:

GP	G	A	TP	+/-	PIM	PP	SH	GW	GT	S	PCT
77	14	28	42	+2	178	1	1	4	0	138	10.1

1999-2000 statistics:

GP	G	A	TP	+/-	PIM	PP	SH	GW	GT	S	PCT
69	23	30	53	-10	62	12	0	1	0	150	15.3

2000-2001 statistics:

GP	G	A	TP	+/-	PIM	PP	SH	GW	GT	S	PCT
82	29	24	53	+16	109	8	2	3	0	138	21.0

2001-2002 statistics:

GP	G	A	TP	+/-	PIM	PP	SH	GW	GT	S	PCT
69	21	27	48	-4	63	6	2	2	1	122	17.2

LAST SEASON

Tied for first on team in shorthanded goals. Second on team in shooting percentage. Missed 10 games with rib injury.

THE FINESSE GAME

Soft hands, tough cookie.

Roberts has excellent hands and terrific instincts around the net. He works hard for loose pucks and, when he gets control, doesn't waste time trying anything fancy. As soon as the puck is on his blade, it's launched towards the net. He shoots by instinct and is not very creative. His rule is: throw the puck at the front of the net and see what happens. Roberts seldom shoots wildly. He works to get into a high-quality scoring area and he almost always makes goalies work for their saves.

Roberts is not an agile skater. He can beat the defender one-on-one on the occasional rush, powered by his strong stride and his ability to handle the puck at a fair clip.

He sees the ice well and will spot an open teammate for a smart pass. He forechecks intelligently and creates turnovers with his persistent work. An excellent penalty killer, he anticipates well and turns mistakes into shorthanded scoring chances.

THE PHYSICAL GAME

Roberts makes his living around the net and in the corners. Despite a neck injury that almost ended his career, Roberts added an element of fearless, inspirational hockey, that the Leafs had been so sorely lacking. They will miss his presence this season.

THE INTANGIBLES

Roberts underwent surgery on both of his shoulders during the off-season and should be gone until after the All-Star break. You might wonder why a 36-year-old guy would bother to try to come back from that ordeal. That is pretty much what Roberts is about.

PROJECTION

It will be a victory just for Roberts to make it back to the NHL. If his contribution comes, it will be in the playoffs (when he was simply the Leafs' best player last season).

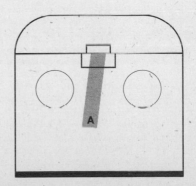

MATS SUNDIN

Yrs. of NHL service: 12
Born: Bromma, Sweden; Feb. 13, 1971
Position: centre
Height: 6-4
Weight: 220
Uniform no.: 13
Shoots: right

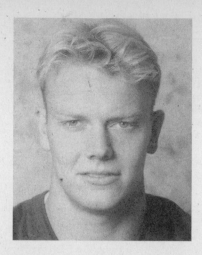

Career statistics:

GP	G	A	TP	PIM
930	397	545	942	759

1998-1999 statistics:

GP	G	A	TP	+/-	PIM	PP	SH	GW	GT	S	PCT
82	31	52	83	+22	58	4	0	6	0	209	14.8

1999-2000 statistics:

GP	G	A	TP	+/-	PIM	PP	SH	GW	GT	S	PCT
73	32	41	73	+16	46	10	2	7	0	184	17.4

2000-2001 statistics:

GP	G	A	TP	+/-	PIM	PP	SH	GW	GT	S	PCT
82	28	46	74	+15	76	9	0	6	1	226	12.4

2001-2002 statistics:

GP	G	A	TP	+/-	PIM	PP	SH	GW	GT	S	PCT
82	41	39	80	+6	94	10	2	9	2	262	15.6

LAST SEASON

Tied for second in NHL in goals and game-winning goals. Led team in assists and points for fourth consecutive season. Led team in goals, power-play goals, game-winning goals and shots. Tied for team lead in shorthanded goals. One of five Maple Leafs to appear in all 82 games.

THE FINESSE GAME

Sundin is a big skater who looks huge, as he uses an ultralong stick that gives him a broad wingspan. For a big man he is an agile skater, and his balance has improved. He has good lower-body strength, supplying drive for battles along the boards. He's evasive, and once he is on the fly he is hard to stop. He is less effective when carrying the puck. His best play is to get up a head of steam, jump into the holes and take a quick shot.

Sundin plays centre but attacks from the off (left) wing, where he can come off the boards with speed. He protects the puck along the wall and makes it hard for people to reach in without taking him down for a penalty. He gets the puck low in his own end; people can move to him right away, and he has to move the puck. If a checker stays with him, Sundin can't get the puck back.

Sundin can take bad passes in stride, either kicking an errant puck up onto his stick or reaching behind to corral it. He isn't a clever stickhandler. His game is power and speed. He doesn't look fast, but he has ground-eating strides that allow him to cover in two strides what other skaters do in three or four. He is quick, too, and can get untracked in a heartbeat.

Sundin's shot is excellent. He can use a slap shot, one-timer, wrister or backhand. The only liability to his reach is that he will dangle the puck well away from his body and he doesn't always control it, which makes him vulnerable to a poke-check when he is in open ice. He has developed into one of the league's better face-off men and was sixth in that category last season with a 57.75 percentage.

THE PHYSICAL GAME

Sundin is big and strong. He has shown better attention to off-ice work to improve his strength. His conditioning is excellent — he can skate all night. He has even shown a touch of meanness, but mostly with his stick.

THE INTANGIBLES

Sundin always looks like he's ready to bust out, and last year's numbers were impressive. He has just never had the right supporting cast to make him a winner.

PROJECTION

Sundin had his typically fine regular season — 40 goals, 80 points is his norm — but was injured in the playoffs with a broken bone in his hand.

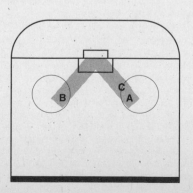

ROBERT SVEHLA

Yrs. of NHL service: 7
Born: Martin, Slovakia; Jan. 2, 1969
Position: right defence
Height: 6-1
Weight: 210
Uniform no.: 24
Shoots: right

Career statistics:

GP	G	A	TP	PIM
573	61	229	290	603

1998-1999 statistics:

GP	G	A	TP	+/-	PIM	PP	SH	GW	GT	S	PCT
80	8	29	37	-13	83	4	0	0	1	157	5.1

1999-2000 statistics:

GP	G	A	TP	+/-	PIM	PP	SH	GW	GT	S	PCT
82	9	40	49	+23	64	3	0	1	0	143	6.3

2000-2001 statistics:

GP	G	A	TP	+/-	PIM	PP	SH	GW	GT	S	PCT
82	6	22	28	-8	76	0	0	0	0	121	5.0

2001-2002 statistics:

GP	G	A	TP	+/-	PIM	PP	SH	GW	GT	S	PCT
82	7	22	29	-19	87	3	0	0	0	119	5.9

LAST SEASON

Acquired from Florida on July 17, 2002, for Dmitry Yushkevich. Tied for second on Panthers in goals. One of two Panthers to appear in all 82 games. Has appeared in 300 consecutive games.

THE FINESSE GAME

Svehla is among the best in the NHL at the lost art of the sweep-check. If he does lose control of the puck, and an attacker has a step or two on him on a break-away, he has the poise to dive and use his stick to knock the puck away without touching the man's skates.

He is a terrific skater. No one, not even Jaromir Jagr, can beat Svehla wide, because he skates well backwards and laterally. He plays a quick transition. He is among the best NHL defencemen one-on-one in open ice. He pinches aggressively and intelligently and makes high-risk plays. Unfortunately for the Panthers, he gambles too often in his own zone. Svehla also has the uncanny knack of making a change at the worst time. But then he is off the ice, so his plus-minus doesn't suffer. Because of his skating, Svehla is an effective open-ice hitter.

Svehla works on the first power play, moving to the left point. He uses a long wrist shot from the point to make sure the puck will get through on net. When he kills penalties, he makes safe plays off the boards.

THE PHYSICAL GAME

Svehla is not that strong or naturally aggressive, but he competes. He gets into the thick of things by battling along the wall and in the corners for the puck. He is not a huge checker, but he pins his man and doesn't allow him back into the play. He is in peak condition and needs little recovery time between shifts, so he can handle a lot of ice time.

THE INTANGIBLES

Svehla completely lost interest in the game last season, prompting his retirement in June. Toronto has a bizarre interest in acquiring players who quit on the NHL (Robert Reichel, Mikael Renberg), and while Svehla's farewell lasted all of 35 days, you'd think the Leafs would start concentrating on guys who actually want to stay here. It looks like Svehla will join Bryan McCabe and Tomas Kaberle in the top three and upgrade the Maple Leafs defence.

PROJECTION

Svehla is capable of a 50-point season when he is motivated.

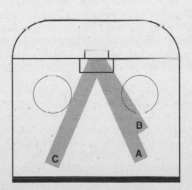

DARCY TUCKER

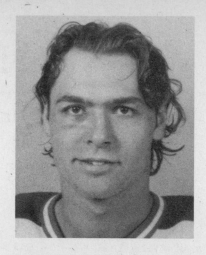

Yrs. of NHL service: 6
Born: Castor, Alberta; Mar. 15, 1975
Position: centre
Height: 5-11
Weight: 185
Uniform no.: 16
Shoots: left

Career statistics:

GP	G	A	TP	PIM
468	96	134	230	828

1998-1999 statistics:

GP	G	A	TP	+/-	PIM	PP	SH	GW	GT	S	PCT
82	21	22	43	-34	176	8	2	3	0	178	11.8

1999-2000 statistics:

GP	G	A	TP	+/-	PIM	PP	SH	GW	GT	S	PCT
77	21	30	51	-12	163	1	2	5	0	138	15.2

2000-2001 statistics:

GP	G	A	TP	+/-	PIM	PP	SH	GW	GT	S	PCT
82	16	21	37	+6	141	2	0	4	0	122	13.1

2001-2002 statistics:

GP	G	A	TP	+/-	PIM	PP	SH	GW	GT	S	PCT
77	24	35	59	+24	92	7	0	5	0	124	19.4

LAST SEASON

Led team in plus-minus and shooting percentage. Second on team in points, power-play goals and game-winning goals. Tied for second on team in goals. Third on team in power-play goals. Career highs in goals, assists and points. Missed three games with concussion. Missed two games due to suspension.

THE FINESSE GAME

Tucker is a pesky forward with a scoring touch. He brings an offensive awareness that enhances his role as a third-line checking centre. He has decent hands, and a knack for scoring big goals.

Like Tomas Holmstrom, Tucker is a player who is wasted on a non-playoff team. Tucker is the kind of player to keep no matter what his points are just to have on hand for a pressure game. He is just the kind of role player who needs a specific assignment. Every night he brings a level of intensity to his game that supplements — and some might suggest, surpasses — his talent.

Tucker was a scorer in junior (137 points in his last year at Kamloops of the WHL) and the minors (93 points with Fredericton of the AHL in 1995-96). His major drawback is that he lacks big-league speed. He is a good forechecker who will hound the puck carrier, and he can do something with the puck once it's on his stick. He is good on draws and will tie up his opposing centre. He will block shots. He will fill the water bottles. Whatever it takes to win, Tucker is there.

THE PHYSICAL GAME

Tucker crossed the line when he went from being an annoying, pesky guy to a cheap shot artists (Exhibit A: Tucker's knee-hunting hit on the Islanders' Mike Peca in the playoffs). Maybe the change stemmed from Tucker being on the receiving end (a concussion courtesy of Florida's Jason Wiemer) early in the season. In a nice ironic twist, the Islanders traded for Wiemer in the off-season.

THE INTANGIBLES

Tucker's got spunk. He cares. He wants to make his team better. Like Claude Lemieux, Tucker is able to take some of the heat off the other players in the room by handling media attention.

PROJECTION

When a player like Tucker produces close to 60 points the way he did last season, that is something special. We don't expect him to duplicate the points, but he will the effort. He should provide 45-50 points, assuming he doesn't become a victim again.

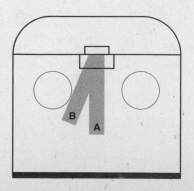

VANCOUVER CANUCKS

Players' Statistics 2001-2002

POS.	NO.	PLAYER	GP	G	A	PTS	+/-	PIM	PP	SH	GW	GT	S	PCT
L	19	MARKUS NASLUND	81	40	50	90	22	50	8		6	1	302	13.3
L	44	TODD BERTUZZI	72	36	49	85	21	110	14		3		203	17.7
C	7	BRENDAN MORRISON	82	23	44	67	18	26	6		4		183	12.6
C	25	ANDREW CASSELS	53	11	39	50	5	22	7		1		64	17.2
D	55	ED JOVANOVSKI	82	17	31	48	-7	101	7	1	3	1	202	8.4
C	16	TREVOR LINDEN	80	13	24	37	-5	71	3		2		141	9.2
C	33	HENRIK SEDIN	82	16	20	36	9	36	3		1	1	78	20.5
D	2	MATTIAS OHLUND	81	10	26	36	16	56	4	1	3		193	5.2
C	24	MATT COOKE	82	13	20	33	4	111	1		2		103	12.6
L	22	DANIEL SEDIN	79	9	23	32	1	32	4		2		117	7.7
L	17	JAN HLAVAC	77	16	15	31	9	18	1		3	1	132	12.1
C	10	TREVOR LETOWSKI	75	9	16	25	4	19	1				108	8.3
D	3	BRENT SOPEL	66	8	17	25	21	44	1		3		116	6.9
R	26	TRENT KLATT	34	8	7	15	9	10	2	1	3		67	11.9
D	14	SCOTT LACHANCE	81	1	10	11	15	50					48	2.1
C	13	ARTEM CHUBAROV	51	5	5	10	-3	10			3		73	6.8
D	28	BRYAN HELMER	40	5	5	10	10	53	2		1	1	43	11.6
L	37	JARKKO RUUTU	49	2	7	9	-1	74					37	5.4
L	15	TODD WARRINER	32	2	7	9	1	20					28	7.1
C	9	HAROLD DRUKEN	27	4	4	8	-1	6	1		2		33	12.1
D	4	*JUSTIN KURTZ	27	3	5	8	-4	14	2				30	10.0
D	23	MURRAY BARON	61	1	6	7	8	68					38	2.6
D	34	JASON STRUDWICK	44	2	4	6	4	96					13	15.4
R	29	HERBERT VASILJEVS	18	3	2	5	0	2	2				17	17.6
L	18	STEVE KARIYA	3		1	1	-2	2						
D	5	*BRYAN ALLEN	11				1	6					4	
L	27	*MIKE BROWN	15				1	72					2	
R	38	*BRAD LEEB	2				1						1	
D	6	*ALEXEI TEZIKOV	2				2							
G	30	MARTIN BROCHU	6				0							
G	39	DAN CLOUTIER	62				0	20						
G	1	PETER SKUDRA	23				0	2						
G	31	ALFIE MICHAUD					0							
G	35	ALEXANDER AULD	1				0							

GP = games played; G = goals; A = assists; PTS = points; +/- = goals-for minus goals-against while player is on ice; PIM = penalties in minutes; PP = power-play goals; SH = shorthanded goals; GW = game-winning goals; GT = game-tying goals; S = no. of shots; PCT = percentage of goals to shots; * = rookie

BRYAN ALLEN

Yrs. of NHL service: 1
Born: Kingston, Ont.; Aug. 21, 1980
Position: left defence
Height: 6-4
Weight: 215
Uniform no.: 5
Shoots: left

Career statistics:

GP	G	A	TP	PIM
17	0	0	0	6

2000-2001 statistics:

GP	G	A	TP	+/-	PIM	PP	SH	GW	GT	S	PCT
6	0	0	0	0	0	0	0	0	0	2	0.0

2001-2002 statistics:

GP	G	A	TP	+/-	PIM	PP	SH	GW	GT	S	PCT
11	0	0	0	+1	6	0	0	0	0	4	0.0

LAST SEASON

Appeared in 68 games with Manitoba (AHL), scoring 7-18-25 with 121 PIM.

THE FINESSE GAME

Allen combines size and mobility in a package that has taken a little longer to develop due to injuries in the first few years of his career.

Allen had the chance to turn pro at 18 with the Canucks, but decided instead to return to junior. That is usually the smartest choice, but Allen (who was drafted one spot behind Brad Stuart in 1998) ran into serious injuries along the way.

Allen's skating is very good for a player of his size. Although he lacks lateral mobility, his leg drive allows him to unleash some solid checks. He doesn't have a great shot and lacks the vision that would help him more offensively, but he is a decent passer. Allen is poised and patient with the puck. He plays a stay-at-home defensive style.

THE PHYSICAL GAME

Sturdy and strong, Allen lacks the mean streak that comes naturally to the game's punishing hitters. He will work hard along the boards and around the net with take-out hits. He's Derian Hatcher minus the snarl.

THE INTANGIBLES

Allen seems finally ready to challenge for a top-four role. The Canucks don't want to keep him here as a third-pair defencemen, which means he had better show up in training camp hungry for a top spot. Vancouver moved Drake Berehowsky and cut Scott Lachance and Jason Strudwick loose, which would seem to indicate room is being opened up for Allen.

PROJECTION

If Allen wins a job, he won't score much. Barely into double digits would be the extent of it.

TODD BERTUZZI

Yrs. of NHL service: 7
Born: Sudbury, Ont.; Feb. 2, 1975
Position: left wing
Height: 6-3
Weight: 235
Uniform no.: 44
Shoots: left

Career statistics:

GP	G	A	TP	PIM
477	135	166	301	645

1998-1999 statistics:

GP	G	A	TP	+/-	PIM	PP	SH	GW	GT	S	PCT
32	8	8	16	-6	44	1	0	3	0	72	11.1

1999-2000 statistics:

GP	G	A	TP	+/-	PIM	PP	SH	GW	GT	S	PCT
80	25	25	50	-2	126	4	0	2	0	173	14.5

2000-2001 statistics:

GP	G	A	TP	+/-	PIM	PP	SH	GW	GT	S	PCT
79	25	30	55	-18	93	14	0	3	0	203	12.3

2001-2002 statistics:

GP	G	A	TP	+/-	PIM	PP	SH	GW	GT	S	PCT
72	36	49	85	+21	110	14	0	3	0	203	17.7

LAST SEASON

Third in NHL in points. Eighth in NHL in assists. Tied for sixth in NHL in power-play points (30). Led team in power-play goals and shooting percentage. Second on team in goals, assists, points, penalty minutes and shots. Tied for second on team in plus-minus. Tied for third on team in game-winning goals. Career highs in goals, assists and points. Missed 10 games due to suspension.

THE FINESSE GAME

One of the biggest success stories of the season was Bertuzzi's dazzling development into a premier power forward. The talent was always there, just shimmering below the surface, but Bertuzzi's maturity and a good mix of players around him brought all of the ingredients together.

For a big man, he's quick and mobile, and he's got a soft pair of hands to complement his skating. With the puck, Bertuzzi can walk over people. He is effective in the slot area, yet he's also creative with the puck and can make some plays. He can find people down low and make things happen on the power play. Bertuzzi has keen offensive instincts.

Bertuzzi has physically dominating skills, but he doesn't have great vision. He has a tendency to roam all over the ice and doesn't think the game well. What he won't become is a physical, tough, aggressive fighter. It's not in his makeup, but he can be an energetic player. He has worked on his defensive game and went from -18 in 2000-01 to +21 this season.

THE PHYSICAL GAME

Bertuzzi often wanders around and doesn't finish his checks with authority. He's a solid physical specimen who shows flashes of aggression and an occasional mean streak, but he really has to be pushed and aggravated to reach a boiling point. Then again, there will be games where he snaps completely and takes either bad aggressive penalties or peculiarly lazy ones — or draws a lengthy suspension.

THE INTANGIBLES

Bertuzzi needs to be handled gently by the coaching staff, with an arm around his shoulder and a kick to the butt administered at the right times. He is now a top-line player with the Canucks, and should gain confidence from that. He's also a fan favourite. Bertuzzi earned over $1 million (US) in performance bonuses and salary upgrades last season. Let's hope that money wasn't the only reason and the consistency Bertuzzi exhibited last year was no illusion.

PROJECTION

Bertuzzi might have had a shot at 40 goals if he hadn't missed 10 games.

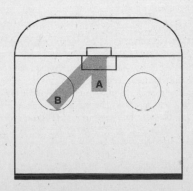

MIKE BROWN

Yrs. of NHL service: 1
Born: Surrey, B.C.; Apr. 27, 1979
Position: left wing
Height: 6-5
Weight: 230
Uniform no.: 27
Shoots: left

Career statistics:

GP	G	A	TP	PIM
16	0	0	0	77

2000-2001 statistics:

GP	G	A	TP	+/-	PIM	PP	SH	GW	GT	S	PCT
1	0	0	0	0	5	0	0	0	0	1	0.0

2001-2002 statistics:

GP	G	A	TP	+/-	PIM	PP	SH	GW	GT	S	PCT
15	0	0	0	+1	72	0	0	0	0	2	0.0

LAST SEASON

Appeared in 31 games with Syracuse (AHL), scoring 7-9-16 with 155 penalty minutes.

THE FINESSE GAME

Brown was part of the package that came to the Canucks in return for Pavel Bure in 1999. The two players couldn't be more different.

Brown is all brawn, but since pure goons are pretty much dinosaurs in today's NHL, Brown has continued to hone the other aspects of his game — while getting a good deal of space, we might add. He is an intense competitor, and does what it takes to win, whether it's throwing a punch, forechecking like a freight train or, yes, even scoring a goal.

Brown has deceptively good hands for a player of his style, and some deceptively good moves. In a few more years, he may be able to do what Chris Simon does for the Washington Capitals.

He will never be an NHL sniper, and he is going to have to work for his goals. For that matter, he is going to have to work hard for his job.

THE PHYSICAL GAME

Brown has added more than 40 pounds since his draft year. He's a mean, nasty hitter who won't back down from a challenge.

THE INTANGIBLES

Brown is the heir apparent to the former Canucks bruiser, Donald Brashear.

PROJECTION

Brown could make his way onto the fourth line and he'll make some of his teammates a little bolder. His PIM totals could be triple digits, but don't expect many points at first.

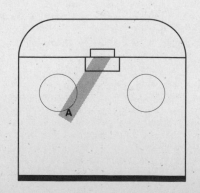

ANDREW CASSELS

Yrs. of NHL service: 12
Born: Bramalea, Ont.; July 23, 1969
Position: centre
Height: 6-1
Weight: 185
Uniform no.: 25
Shoots: left

Career statistics:

GP	G	A	TP	PIM
847	174	452	626	340

1998-1999 statistics:

GP	G	A	TP	+/-	PIM	PP	SH	GW	GT	S	PCT
70	12	25	37	-12	18	4	1	3	0	97	12.4

1999-2000 statistics:

GP	G	A	TP	+/-	PIM	PP	SH	GW	GT	S	PCT
79	17	45	62	+8	16	6	0	1	0	109	15.6

2000-2001 statistics:

GP	G	A	TP	+/-	PIM	PP	SH	GW	GT	S	PCT
66	12	44	56	+1	10	2	0	1	0	104	11.5

2001-2002 statistics:

GP	G	A	TP	+/-	PIM	PP	SH	GW	GT	S	PCT
53	11	39	50	+5	22	7	0	1	0	64	17.2

LAST SEASON

Tied for third on Canucks in power-play goals. Missed eight games with concussion. Missed 20 games with knee injury.

THE FINESSE GAME

When it comes to hockey smarts, Cassels is a member of Mensa. He is an intelligent player with terrific hockey instincts, who knows when to recognize passing situations, when to move the puck and who to move it to. He has a good backhand pass in traffic and is almost as good on his backhand as his forehand.

Cassels just hates to shoot. He won't do it much, and although he has spent a great deal of time practising it, his release is just not NHL calibre. He needs to play with a finisher. He has quick hands, though, and can swipe a shot off a bouncing puck in midair. He doesn't always fight through checks to get the kind of shots he should.

A mainstay on both specialty teams, Cassels has improved on draws. He backchecks and blocks shots. He has good speed but lacks one-step quickness. He has improved his puckhandling at a high tempo.

THE PHYSICAL GAME

To complement his brains, Cassels needs brawn. He does not force his way through strong forechecks and traffic around the net. He tends to get nicked up and run down late in the season or during a tough stretch.

THE INTANGIBLES

Cassels is 33 and was on the free agent market during the off-season. He would be a useful pickup for a team looking for a set-up guy on a No. 2 line.

PROJECTION

Cassels was a No. 1 centre for a time in Vancouver and overachieved. He can score 50 assist-heavy points in the right situation.

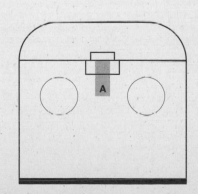

DAN CLOUTIER

Yrs. of NHL service: 3
Born: Mont-Laurier, Que.; Apr. 22, 1976
Position: goaltender
Height: 6-1
Weight: 182
Uniform no.: 39
Catches: left

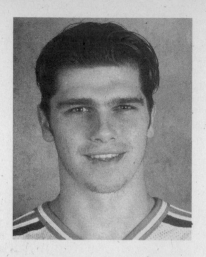

Career statistics:

GP	MIN	GA	SO	GAA	A	PIM
188	9561	455	8	2.86	0	64

1998-1999 statistics:

GP	MIN	GAA	W	L	T	SO	GA	S	SAPCT	PIM
22	1097	2.68	6	8	3	0	49	570	.914	2

1999-2000 statistics:

GP	MIN	GAA	W	L	T	SO	GA	S	SAPCT	PIM
52	2492	3.49	9	30	3	0	145	1258	.885	29

2000-2001 statistics:

GP	MIN	GAA	W	L	T	SO	GA	S	SAPCT	PIM
40	1919	2.43	7	19	8	1	96	889	.892	4

2001-2002 statistics:

GP	MIN	GAA	W	L	T	SO	GA	S	SAPCT	PIM
62	3502	2.43	31	22	5	7	142	1440	.901	20

LAST SEASON

Career high in wins. Missed nine games with ankle injury.

THE PHYSICAL GAME

Cloutier is an athletic, stand-up goalie — surprising in an era of so many Patrick Roy butterfly clones. He doesn't have the reflexes to excel with a less technical style.

He follows the play well and squares his body to the shooter. He will learn to play his angles better with more NHL experience, but he has good size to take away a lot of the net from the shooter.

Cloutier's skills are still a little raw. He doesn't control his rebounds well off his pads, and his stick-handling could use work. But he is an eager student who would benefit from a veteran backup goalie and a quality goalie coach.

THE MENTAL GAME

Cloutier is combative and emotional. He has to learn to channel his aggression better, because it often gets the best of him. The fight in him extends to his desire to succeed at the NHL level. He is as competitive on the ice as he is easygoing off it.

Cloutier will have to be able to shake off the memory of the 100-foot goal by Nicklas Lidstrom that turned the playoff series against Detroit. His playoff GAA was 3.52, which isn't very encouraging.

THE INTANGIBLES

Vancouver showed little interest in signing one of the veteran free agent goalies available during the off-season. Either the Canucks are convinced Cloutier is up to the task, or they need to stay on budget and figure he's just good enough.

PROJECTION

Cloutier is not an elite No. 1 goalie. He earned 31 wins last season and is good for that number again.

HAROLD DRUKEN

Yrs. of NHL service: 3
Born: St. John's, Nfld.; Jan. 26, 1979
Position: centre
Height: 6-0
Weight: 205
Uniform no.: 9
Shoots: left

Career statistics:

GP	G	A	TP	PIM
115	26	28	54	30

1999-2000 statistics:

GP	G	A	TP	+/-	PIM	PP	SH	GW	GT	S	PCT
33	7	9	16	+14	10	2	0	0	0	69	10.1

2000-2001 statistics:

GP	G	A	TP	+/-	PIM	PP	SH	GW	GT	S	PCT
55	15	15	30	+2	14	6	0	3	0	82	18.3

2001-2002 statistics:

GP	G	A	TP	+/-	PIM	PP	SH	GW	GT	S	PCT
27	4	4	8	-1	6	1	0	2	0	33	12.1

LAST SEASON

Appeared in 11 games with Manitoba (AHL), scoring 2-9-11 with 4 PIM. Missed 11 games with ankle injury. Missed remainder of season with shoulder surgery in January.

THE FINESSE GAME

A point-a-game player at the minor-league level, Druken is never likely to achieve that level of production in the NHL. He is very offensive-minded, however, and has some attractive skills. He has a nose for the net and earned some power-play time on the second unit. He has excellent offensive instincts and is an opportunistic scorer.

He doesn't have great speed, but Druken doesn't look out of place and can compete. He has worked hard on the defensive part of his game, which was considered a major liability. He forechecks diligently and intelligently.

Druken can play centre or wing and could build a 10-year career if he keeps doing what he's doing. He will not look out of place with the more highly skilled forwards on the Canucks.

THE PHYSICAL GAME

Druken is not very tall but he is solid. He displays some grit, and he wants to keep an NHL job. He has to make sure to maintain his conditioning.

THE INTANGIBLES

Injuries derailed Druken last season.

PROJECTION

Druken will be pencilled in as a fourth-line player, but he is versatile and his skills will allow him to fill in here and there when injuries strike. He could score 30 points again in a part-time role.

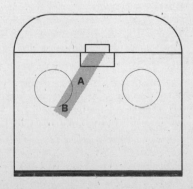

JAN HLAVAC

Yrs. of NHL service: 3
Born: Prague, Czech Republic; Sept. 20, 1976
Position: left wing
Height: 6-0
Weight: 185
Uniform no.: 17
Shoots: left

Career statistics:

GP	G	A	TP	PIM
223	63	74	137	54

1999-2000 statistics:

GP	G	A	TP	+/-	PIM	PP	SH	GW	GT	S	PCT
67	19	23	42	+3	16	6	0	2	0	134	14.2

2000-2001 statistics:

GP	G	A	TP	+/-	PIM	PP	SH	GW	GT	S	PCT
79	28	36	64	+3	20	5	0	6	0	195	14.4

2001-2002 statistics:

GP	G	A	TP	+/-	PIM	PP	SH	GW	GT	S	PCT
77	16	15	31	+9	18	1	0	3	1	132	12.1

LAST SEASON

Acquired from Philadelphia on December 17, 2001, with a third-round draft pick for Donald Brashear and a sixth-round draft pick. Tied for third on team in game-winning goals.

THE FINESSE GAME

Where did this guy's game go? He was a disaster in Philadelphia (seven goals in 31 games) before being moved to Vancouver. Despite a heavy European influence there, Hlavac did not find a comfortable role.

Hlavac is capable of being a dynamic, top-level scorer. Hlavac is a good stickhandler who can move the puck at a high tempo. He has good anticipation and acceleration. He is occasionally guilty of over-handling the puck. Hlavac has a good scoring touch and needs to shoot more.

Hlavac forechecks intelligently and creates plays off the turnovers. He is a very good passer and play-maker and has good defensive awareness.

THE PHYSICAL GAME

Hlavac is strong on his skates, even though he isn't very big. He has a quiet toughness to him.

THE INTANGIBLES

Maybe being traded twice in six months, and being removed from his Rangers linemates Petr Nedved and Radek Dvorak, with whom he had so much success in 2000-01, rattled Hlavac. He has lost all confidence in his game.

PROJECTION

Maybe Hlavac's 28-goal season in New York was a fluke. We would downgrade him to 20 goals until proven otherwise.

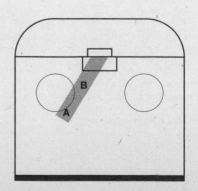

ED JOVANOVSKI

Yrs. of NHL service: 7
Born: Windsor, Ont.; June 26, 1976
Position: left defence
Height: 6-2
Weight: 210
Uniform no.: 55
Shoots: left

Career statistics:

GP	G	A	TP	PIM
520	65	150	215	850

1998-1999 statistics:

GP	G	A	TP	+/-	PIM	PP	SH	GW	GT	S	PCT
72	5	22	27	-9	126	1	0	1	0	109	4.6

1999-2000 statistics:

GP	G	A	TP	+/-	PIM	PP	SH	GW	GT	S	PCT
75	5	21	26	-3	54	1	0	1	0	109	4.6

2000-2001 statistics:

GP	G	A	TP	+/-	PIM	PP	SH	GW	GT	S	PCT
79	12	35	47	-1	102	4	0	2	2	193	6.2

2001-2002 statistics:

GP	G	A	TP	+/-	PIM	PP	SH	GW	GT	S	PCT
82	17	31	48	-7	101	7	1	3	1	202	8.4

LAST SEASON

Led team defencemen in points for third consecutive season. Tied for fifth among NHL defencemen in points. Third on team in penalty minutes and shots. Tied for third on team in power-play goals and game-winning goals. Career highs in goals and points. One of four Canucks to appear in all 82 games.

THE FINESSE GAME

Jovanovski started playing hockey later than most NHLers. His skating will always be his most prominent flaw, although he has worked hard to improve and it doesn't hold him back anymore. He can get up to full steam and streak through the neutral zone like a freight train. He sure isn't pretty, but he's powerful.

Strong on his feet with a dynamic stride, Jovanovski is quicker than most big men, perhaps because of early soccer training, and he can use his feet to move the puck if his stick is tied up. His powerful hitting is made more wicked because he gets so much speed and leg drive. He can make plays, too. He gets a little time because his speed forces the opposition to back off, and he has a nice passing touch.

Jovanovski can also score, and he has become more confident. He has an excellent point shot and good vision of the ice for passing. He is developing along the lines of a Scott Stevens, a defenceman who can dominate in all zones. Jovanovski still gives the impression of being more raw than polished, which means he could get even better.

THE PHYSICAL GAME

Jovanovski is among the best open-ice hitters in the NHL. He hits to hurt. Because of his size and agility, he's able to catch people right where he wants them. They aren't dirty hits, but they're old-time hockey throwbacks, administered by a modern-sized defenceman.

He has to continue to play smarter. Jovanovski can still be diverted from his game by smaller, peskier players. He is so easy to distract that this must be at the top of every team's game plan against the Canucks.

THE INTANGIBLES

Jovanovski has become a big-time, crunch-time player.

PROJECTION

We projected Jovanovski as a potential 50-point scorer last season and he came very close. He could do it this time.

TREVOR LETOWSKI

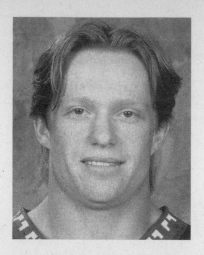

Yrs. of NHL service: 3
Born: Thunder Bay, Ont.; Apr. 5, 1977
Position: centre
Height: 5-10
Weight: 176
Uniform no.: 10
Shoots: right

Career statistics:

GP	G	A	TP	PIM
248	37	53	90	73

1998-1999 statistics:

GP	G	A	TP	+/-	PIM	PP	SH	GW	GT	S	PCT
14	2	2	4	+1	2	0	0	0	0	8	25.0

1999-2000 statistics:

GP	G	A	TP	+/-	PIM	PP	SH	GW	GT	S	PCT
82	19	20	39	+2	20	3	4	3	0	125	15.2

2000-2001 statistics:

GP	G	A	TP	+/-	PIM	PP	SH	GW	GT	S	PCT
77	7	15	22	-2	32	0	1	3	0	110	6.4

2001-2002 statistics:

GP	G	A	TP	+/-	PIM	PP	SH	GW	GT	S	PCT
75	9	16	25	+4	19	1	0	0	0	108	8.3

LAST SEASON

Acquired from Phoenix on December 28, 2001, with Todd Warriner, Tyler Bouck and a third-round draft pick in 2003 for Drake Berehowsky and Denis Pederson.

THE FINESSE GAME

Letowski is a shorthanded specialist. He is a small centre with good quickness. He devoted himself to the defensive aspects of the game even as a junior, which probably accounts for his low draft position (174th overall in 1996), though he did have seasons of 99 and 108 points after his draft year. After paying his dues in the minors, he has turned into one of those nifty little forwards who could find an NHL job with any team.

Letowski has good anticipation and makes excellent reads in his forechecking. He pressures the points on the power play to harry them into making bad passes, which he can then convert into shorthanded scoring chances. He is an opportunistic scorer with soft hands and a good, patient shot. He is average on face-offs.

If Vancouver doesn't get much deeper up front, Letowksi could see some second-unit power-play time, as he did in his strong rookie season.

THE PHYSICAL GAME

Letowski has a big heart in a small frame. He is very competitive and not shy about going after the puck in the corners, though he lacks the strength for one-on-one battles.

THE INTANGIBLES

Letowksi needed a change of scenery after a contract battle in Phoenix in 2000-01. He took off after the deal and finished up with a solid second half.

PROJECTION

If Letowski plays this season the way he did after the trade, he will get quality ice time and score 20 goals.

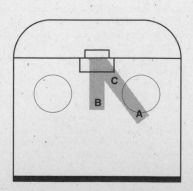

TREVOR LINDEN

Yrs. of NHL service: 14
Born: Medicine Hat, Alta.; Apr. 11, 1970
Position: centre / right wing
Height: 6-4
Weight: 211
Uniform no.: 16
Shoots: right

Career statistics:

GP	G	A	TP	PIM
1008	316	421	737	775

1998-1999 statistics:

GP	G	A	TP	+/-	PIM	PP	SH	GW	GT	S	PCT
82	18	29	47	-14	32	8	1	1	0	167	10.8

1999-2000 statistics:

GP	G	A	TP	+/-	PIM	PP	SH	GW	GT	S	PCT
50	13	17	30	-3	34	4	0	3	0	87	14.9

2000-2001 statistics:

GP	G	A	TP	+/-	PIM	PP	SH	GW	GT	S	PCT
69	15	22	37	0	60	6	0	3	0	126	11.9

2001-2002 statistics:

GP	G	A	TP	+/-	PIM	PP	SH	GW	GT	S	PCT
80	13	24	37	-5	71	3	0	2	0	141	9.2

LAST SEASON

Acquired from Washington on November 10, 2001, with a second-round draft pick for a first-round pick in 2002 and a third-round pick in 2003.

THE FINESSE GAME

Not a graceful skater, Linden at times looks awkward, and he's not as strong on his skates as a player of his size should be. Despite his heavy feet, his agility is satisfactory, but he lacks first-step quickness and doesn't have the all-out speed to pull away from a checker. He has a big turning radius.

Linden has improved his release, but it is not quick. He has a long reach, although unlike, say, Dave Andreychuk's (who is built along similar lines), his short game is not as effective as it should be.

Linden is a well-rounded player who can kill penalties, work on the power play and is very sound at even strength. Linden is unselfish and makes quick, safe passing decisions that help his team break smartly up the ice, often creating odd-man rushes. He has improved tremendously in his defensive coverage. He is very good on face-offs.

Linden can play centre or right wing and is better on the wing.

THE PHYSICAL GAME

Linden is big but doesn't always play tough, and so doesn't make good use of his size. He will attack the blueline and draw the attention of both defencemen, but will pull up rather than try to muscle through and earn a holding penalty. There are people he should nullify who still seem able to get away from him. He does not skate through the physical challenges along the boards. When he plays big, he is a big, big player.

If only he would keep his feet moving, Linden would be so much more commanding. Instead, he can be angled off the play fairly easily because he will not battle for better ice.

When Linden is throwing his weight around, he drives to the net and drags a defender or two with him, opening up a lot of ice for his teammates. He creates havoc in front of the net on the power play, planting himself for screens and deflections. When the puck is at the side boards, he's smart enough to move up higher, between the circles, forcing the penalty killers to make a decision. If the defenceman on that side steps up to cover him, space will open behind the defenceman; if a forward collapses to cover him, a point shot will open up.

THE INTANGIBLES

Linden is a character guy and a reliable performer. His return to Vancouver was motivated by his wife, who was unhappy in Washington.

PROJECTION

Linden's numbers are declining. He will get 12 to 15 goals and 35 to 40 points.

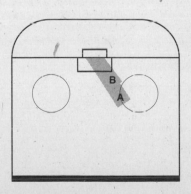

BRENDAN MORRISON

Yrs. of NHL service: 4
Born: North Vancouver, B.C.; Aug. 12, 1975
Position: centre
Height: 5-11
Weight: 190
Uniform no.: 7
Shoots: left

Career statistics:

GP	G	A	TP	PIM
307	64	147	211	104

1998-1999 statistics:

GP	G	A	TP	+/-	PIM	PP	SH	GW	GT	S	PCT
76	13	33	46	-4	18	5	0	2	0	111	11.7

1999-2000 statistics:

GP	G	A	TP	+/-	PIM	PP	SH	GW	GT	S	PCT
56	7	28	35	+12	18	2	0	1	0	96	7.3

2000-2001 statistics:

GP	G	A	TP	+/-	PIM	PP	SH	GW	GT	S	PCT
82	16	38	54	+2	42	3	2	3	3	179	8.9

2001-2002 statistics:

GP	G	A	TP	+/-	PIM	PP	SH	GW	GT	S	PCT
82	23	44	67	+18	26	6	0	4	0	183	12.6

LAST SEASON

Second on team in game-winning goals. Third on team in goals, assists and points. Tied for third on team in shooting percentage. Career highs in goals, assists and points. One of four Canucks to appear in all 82 games.

THE FINESSE GAME

Morrison's hockey sense and vision are outstanding. He is exceptional on the power play, where he can use his best assets. Vancouver upgraded him to the top line between Todd Bertuzzi and Markus Naslund last season. Morrison isn't a true No. 1 NHL centre.

Morrison has a world of confidence in his abilities, almost to the point of cockiness, and he will try some daring and creative moves. He has soft hands for passing and he uses a selection of deceptively heavy and accurate shots. He can work low on the power play or at the point, and he sees all of his options quickly. He doesn't panic and is poised with the puck.

He is a strong skater, with balance, quickness, agility and breakaway speed. Morrison has no trouble with NHL speed, except when it comes to defensive decisions, although he is adjusting. Morrison is a quick and savvy penalty killer.

THE PHYSICAL GAME

Small but wise enough to stay out of trouble, Morrison has wiry strength for playing in the high-traffic areas. He loves to create plays from behind the net. He plays with a little edge to him that shows he will not be intimidated. He is strong on his skates and tough to knock off balance.

THE INTANGIBLES

Morrison was headed to salary arbitration in the off-season and had career numbers to take with him. We're not sold on Morrison as a first-line centre but he did nothing wrong last year. Vancouver opted not to re-sign Andrew Cassels after the season, which means they are convinced of Morrison's readiness for the role.

PROJECTION

Morrison surpassed the 60 points we projected for him last season. Assuming he retains the top centre spot, he should score between 65-70 points.

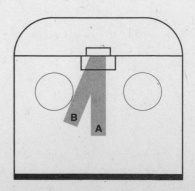

MARKUS NASLUND

Yrs. of NHL service: 9
Born: Örnsköldsvik, Sweden; July 30, 1973
Position: left wing
Height: 5-11
Weight: 195
Uniform no.: 19
Shoots: left

Career statistics:

GP	G	A	TP	PIM
630	207	234	441	403

1998-1999 statistics:

GP	G	A	TP	+/-	PIM	PP	SH	GW	GT	S	PCT
80	36	30	66	-13	74	15	2	3	1	205	17.6

1999-2000 statistics:

GP	G	A	TP	+/-	PIM	PP	SH	GW	GT	S	PCT
82	27	38	65	-5	64	6	2	3	1	271	10.0

2000-2001 statistics:

GP	G	A	TP	+/-	PIM	PP	SH	GW	GT	S	PCT
72	41	34	75	-2	58	18	1	5	0	277	14.8

2001-2002 statistics:

GP	G	A	TP	+/-	PIM	PP	SH	GW	GT	S	PCT
81	40	50	90	+22	50	8	0	6	1	302	13.3

LAST SEASON

Second in NHL in points. Tied for fourth in NHL in assists. Fifth in NHL in goals, shots and power-play points (31). Led team in goals, assists, points, plus-minus, game-winning goals and shots. Second on team in power-play goals and shooting percentage. Career highs in assists and points.

THE FINESSE GAME

Naslund is Vancouver's most skilled player and is among the NHL's elite. As good as his numbers are, Naslund is a better two-way player than he is given credit for. This is a player who can be relied upon in the closing minutes of the game, either to make a big play that results in a goal, or to protect a lead.

Naslund is a pure sniper. He has excellent snap and wrist shots and can score in just about every way imaginable, including the backhand in-tight. He has quick hands and an accurate touch. He needs to play with people who will get him the puck, although he has become far more aggressive and consistent in his puck pursuit. He is a jitterbug on the ice and can keep up with the fastest linemates. He is also confident with the puck, and loves to toast defencemen with an inside-outside move.

A lot was expected of Naslund early in his career. He started out in the Pittsburgh system and bounced around in the minors before finding his niche with the Canucks and especially with Todd Bertuzzi on Vancouver's top line.

THE PHYSICAL GAME

Naslund has good conditioning habits and is a tireless worker. He is not a major physical presence, but he makes something of a pest out of himself. Naslund recovered well from a badly broken leg that required surgery and ended his 2000-01 season prematurely.

THE INTANGIBLES

Being named captain meant a great deal to Naslund, and he wears the "C" well. The next step Naslund (and the rest of the Canucks) must take is performing well in the playoffs.

PROJECTION

A healthy Naslund is a sure bet for 40 goals.

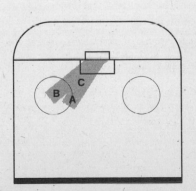

MATTIAS OHLUND

Yrs. of NHL service: 5
Born: Pitea, Sweden; Sept. 9, 1976
Position: left defence
Height: 6-2
Weight: 220
Uniform no.: 2
Shoots: left

Career statistics:

GP	G	A	TP	PIM
339	38	111	149	285

1998-1999 statistics:

GP	G	A	TP	+/-	PIM	PP	SH	GW	GT	S	PCT
74	9	26	35	-19	83	2	1	1	0	129	7.0

1999-2000 statistics:

GP	G	A	TP	+/-	PIM	PP	SH	GW	GT	S	PCT
42	4	16	20	+6	24	2	1	1	0	63	6.3

2000-2001 statistics:

GP	G	A	TP	+/-	PIM	PP	SH	GW	GT	S	PCT
65	8	20	28	-16	46	1	1	4	0	136	5.9

2001-2002 statistics:

GP	G	A	TP	+/-	PIM	PP	SH	GW	GT	S	PCT
81	10	26	36	+16	56	4	1	3	0	193	5.2

LAST SEASON

Tied for third on team in game-winning goals. Career highs in goals and points. Missed one game with flu.

THE FINESSE GAME

Ohlund seems completely recovered from his eye injury. If Ohlund isn't seeing the ice well, then he is fooling a lot of people

Ohlund has a high skill level and a big body to go with it. He is a lovely, fluid skater with splendid agility for his size. He's very confident with the puck. Because of his skating and his reach, he is difficult to beat one-on-one. He isn't fooled by dekes, either. He plays the crest and maintains his position.

A good power-play player from the right point, Ohlund gets first-unit power-play time. He uses an effective, short backswing on his one-timer. He makes a sharp first pass out of the defensive zone, and gets involved in the attack by moving up into the rush (but he won't get caught deep very often).

THE PHYSICAL GAME

Ohlund is big and powerful. He is assertive, won't be intimidated and finishes his checks. He clears out the front of the net and works the boards and corners. For a player considered to be a finesse defenceman, he plays an involved game. He has an iron constitution and can handle a lot of ice time.

THE INTANGIBLES

Ohlund has fought to come back from a career-threatening eye injury and surgery, so his development has been delayed. He was healthy last season and at 26 is just coming into his prime.

PROJECTION

Ohlund will score 35-40 points as a very good all-around defenceman.

DANIEL SEDIN

Yrs. of NHL service: 2
Born: Ornskoldsvik, Sweden; Sept. 26, 1980
Position: left wing
Height: 6-1
Weight: 200
Uniform no.: 22
Shoots: left

Career statistics:

GP	G	A	TP	PIM
154	29	37	66	56

2000-2001 statistics:

GP	G	A	TP	+/-	PIM	PP	SH	GW	GT	S	PCT
75	20	14	34	-3	24	10	0	3	0	127	15.8

2001-2002 statistics:

GP	G	A	TP	+/-	PIM	PP	SH	GW	GT	S	PCT
79	9	23	32	+1	32	4	0	2	0	117	7.7

LAST SEASON
Missed two games with sprained knee.

THE FINESSE GAME
This is supposed to be the finisher of the pair of Sedin twins, but Daniel struggled last season, off 11 goals from the previous season. Sedin needed back surgery in the 2001 off-season, and that might have been a major factor in the slump.

Sedin has outstanding hockey sense. He is one of those natural goal-scorers to whom shooting and shot selection is a reflex. He doesn't have to think about where the puck is going. He knows what he is going to do with it before it's on his stick. He moves the puck quickly. He has very good hockey vision and intelligence. Primarily an offensive player, he needs to improve on his defensive duties.

Daniel is fast and strong on his skates. Although he is a shooter first, he also has good playmaking skills. He was often taken off his brother's line last season, which had to affect him since the two have always played so well together.

THE PHYSICAL GAME
Daniel's immediate need will be to beef up. The stats say he is 200 pounds, but that seems generous. Considering the size of the typical NHL defenceman these days, he needs some upper-body work for the battles in the trenches.

THE INTANGIBLES
Sedin's back surgery didn't force him to miss any playing time, but it's a concern that it could be a chronic problem he has simply learned to live with.

PROJECTION
We anticipated a decline in Sedin's numbers, but not as steep as this. Unless Sedin shows some spark in training camp, pool players would be wise to steer clear.

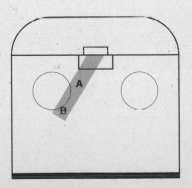

HENRIK SEDIN

Yrs. of NHL service: 2
Born: Ornskoldsvik, Sweden; Sept. 26, 1980
Position: centre
Height: 6-2
Weight: 200
Uniform no.: 33
Shoots: left

Career statistics:

GP	G	A	TP	PIM
164	25	40	65	74

2000-2001 statistics:

GP	G	A	TP	+/-	PIM	PP	SH	GW	GT	S	PCT
82	9	20	29	-2	38	2	0	1	0	98	9.2

2001-2002 statistics:

GP	G	A	TP	+/-	PIM	PP	SH	GW	GT	S	PCT
82	16	20	36	+9	36	3	0	1	1	78	20.5

LAST SEASON

Career highs in goals and points. One of four Canucks to appear in all 82 games.

THE FINESSE GAME

Henrik the playmaker, is be better suited to the NHL style of play than his twin Daniel, the scorer. He's a little bigger than his brother, and a little grittier. He doesn't have a great, soft touch with the puck, but he works hard to complete his plays.

Sedin showed a better finishing touch last season, which is important to develop. If he becomes too shot-shy, then opposing defences can always sag off him and wait for him to try to force a pass to one of his wingers. He hasn't played with the most gifted snipers on the team, which may have given him the motivation to shoot.

Sedin is a very good, powerful skater, though he doesn't have great acceleration, and he will need to work on his footwork. His defensive game is advanced, but he will need to continue to improve his work on draws. He has very good hockey sense. Sedin saw more penalty-killing shifts last season.

THE PHYSICAL GAME

Henrik has NHL size and NHL temperament. Feisty by nature, the physical side of the game comes naturally to him. He is solid on his skates and well-balanced.

THE INTANGIBLES

Sedin started off slowly (not unusual for a sophomore) but had a decent second half. His twin brother struggled, which may have also affected Henrik negatively. The two played on the same line in their rookie year, but they were often broken up last year.

PROJECTION

Sedin showed the progress we expected of him when he came close to hit the assist-heavy 40 points we anticipated in his second season. If he moves up as the No. 2 centre, his production should show a bump.

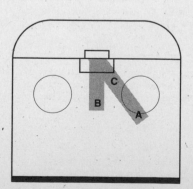

BRENT SOPEL

Yrs. of NHL service: 2
Born: Calgary, Alta.; Jan. 7, 1977
Position: defence
Height: 6-1
Weight: 185
Uniform no.: 3
Shoots: right

Career statistics:

GP	G	A	TP	PIM
141	15	31	46	70

1998-1999 statistics:

GP	G	A	TP	+/-	PIM	PP	SH	GW	GT	S	PCT
5	1	0	1	-1	4	1	0	0	0	5	20.0

1999-2000 statistics:

GP	G	A	TP	+/-	PIM	PP	SH	GW	GT	S	PCT
18	2	4	6	+9	12	0	0	1	0	11	18.2

2000-2001 statistics:

GP	G	A	TP	+/-	PIM	PP	SH	GW	GT	S	PCT
52	4	10	14	+4	10	0	0	1	0	57	7.0

2001-2002 statistics:

GP	G	A	TP	+/-	PIM	PP	SH	GW	GT	S	PCT
66	8	17	25	+21	44	1	0	3	0	116	6.9

LAST SEASON

Tied for second on team in plus-minus. Tied for third on team in game-winning goals.

THE FINESSE GAME

Sopel is well on his way to becoming a reliable top-four defenceman with the Canucks. Last year was a big step up for him, and he grew into the job.

Sopel is a good skater. He skates well backwards and has good lateral movement. He makes a firm outlet pass, or if he has to, he can skate the puck out of his own zone.

Sopel has good hockey sense. He doesn't get panic-stricken under pressure.

THE PHYSICAL GAME

Sopel has good size but certainly isn't too big by today's standards. He is stronger than he looks. Sopel has added about 15 pounds since his draft year (1995). Sopel is a containment hitter. He doesn't make big open-ice checks, but he will keep his man tied up in the corners, along the wall or in front of the net.

THE INTANGIBLES

Sopel's favourite player growing up was Mathieu Schneider, and Sopel resembles Schneider in more than a few ways. He is developing into a defenceman who won't be flashy, but at the end of the night you'll realize he did a lot more things to help his team win than some of the stars.

PROJECTION

Sopel has some offensive upside. He could be a 30-point scorer this season.

WASHINGTON CAPITALS

Players' Statistics 2001-2002

POS.	NO.	PLAYER	GP	G	A	PTS	+/-	PIM	PP	SH	GW	GT	S	PCT
R	68	JAROMIR JAGR	69	31	48	79	0	30	10		3		197	15.7
R	12	PETER BONDRA	77	39	31	70	-2	80	17	1	8	1	333	11.7
D	55	SERGEI GONCHAR	76	26	33	59	-1	58	7		2		216	12.0
R	10	ULF DAHLEN	69	23	29	52	-5	8	7		4	1	141	16.3
R	9	DAINIUS ZUBRUS	71	17	26	43	5	38	4		3		138	12.3
C	13	ANDREI NIKOLISHIN	80	13	23	36	-1	40	1				143	9.1
L	17	CHRIS SIMON	82	14	17	31	-8	137	1		1	1	121	11.6
R	8	DMITRI KHRISTICH	61	9	12	21	2	12	3		2		54	16.7
C	11	JEFF HALPERN	48	5	14	19	-9	29			4		74	6.8
C	20	GLEN METROPOLIT	35	1	16	17	1	6					52	1.9
D	2	KEN KLEE	68	8	8	16	4	38	2		3		85	9.4
L	33	BENOIT HOGUE	58	7	8	15	-5	37			1		42	16.7
D	3	SYLVAIN COTE	70	3	11	14	-15	26	1		2		101	3.0
L	22	STEVE KONOWALCHUK	28	2	12	14	-2	23					36	5.6
D	4	FRANTISEK KUCERA	56	1	13	14	7	12					67	1.5
L	18	*MATT PETTINGER	61	7	3	10	-8	44	1		1		73	9.6
D	19	BRENDAN WITT	68	3	7	10	-1	78					81	3.7
C	36	COLIN FORBES	38	5	3	8	-2	15		1	1		49	10.2
R	14	JOE SACCO	65		7	7	-13	51					57	
D	24	ROB ZETTLER	49	1	4	5	3	56					28	3.6
R	51	*STEPHEN PEAT	38	2	2	4	-1	85					11	18.2
D	58	*JEAN-FRANCOIS FORTIN	36	1	3	4	-1	20					24	4.2
L	23	*IVAN CIERNIK	29	1	3	4	0	6					23	4.3
D	6	CALLE JOHANSSON	11	2		2	-4	8			1		18	11.1
D	40	*NOLAN YONKMAN	11	1		1	3	4					7	14.3
R	48	*CHRIS CORRINET	8		1	1	-4	6					8	
D	38	TODD ROHLOFF	16		1	1	-2	14					6	
R	27	CHRIS FERRARO	1		1	1	0						4	
R	28	PETER FERRARO	4		1	1	-1						3	
D	57	DEAN MELANSON	4			1		4					6	
C	41	*BRIAN SUTHERBY	7				-3	2					3	
D	34	*JAKUB CUTTA	2				-3						2	
D	46	*MICHAEL FARRELL	8				-1						1	
D	39	PATRICK BOILEAU	2				-1	2						
G	1	CRAIG BILLINGTON	17				0							
G	37	OLAF KOLZIG	71				0	8						
G	31	COREY HIRSCH					0							
G	35	SEBASTIEN CHARPENTIE	2				0							

GP = games played; G = goals; A = assists; PTS = points; +/- = goals-for minus goals-against while player is on ice; PIM = penalties in minutes; PP = power-play goals; SH = shorthanded goals; GW = game-winning goals; GT = game-tying goals; S = no. of shots; PCT = percentage of goals to shots; * = rookie

PETER BONDRA

Yrs. of NHL service: 12
Born: Luck, Ukraine; Feb. 7, 1968
Position: right wing
Height: 6-1
Weight: 205
Uniform no.: 12
Shoots: left

Career statistics:

GP	G	A	TP	PIM
831	421	313	734	605

1998-1999 statistics:

GP	G	A	TP	+/-	PIM	PP	SH	GW	GT	S	PCT
66	31	24	55	-1	56	6	3	5	1	284	10.9

1999-2000 statistics:

GP	G	A	TP	+/-	PIM	PP	SH	GW	GT	S	PCT
62	21	17	38	+5	30	5	3	5	0	187	11.2

2000-2001 statistics:

GP	G	A	TP	+/-	PIM	PP	SH	GW	GT	S	PCT
82	45	36	81	+8	60	22	4	8	0	305	14.7

2001-2002 statistics:

GP	G	A	TP	+/-	PIM	PP	SH	GW	GT	S	PCT
77	39	31	70	-2	80	17	1	8	1	333	11.7

LAST SEASON

Led NHL in power-play goals. Led team in goals, game-winning goals and shots. Second on team in points. Third on team in assists and penalty minutes. Second in NHL in shots. Tied for fourth in NHL in game-winning goals. Tied for seventh in NHL in goals. Missed five games with flu.

THE FINESSE GAME

Bondra is an explosive skater. He has a wide skating stance for balance, a deep knee bend and a powerful kick, like a sprinter out of the starting blocks. Bondra skates as fast with the puck as without it, and he wants the puck early. He cuts in on the off-wing and shoots in stride. He has a very good backhand shot and likes to cut out from behind the net and make things happen in-tight. He mixes up his shots. He will fire quickly — not many veteran European players have this good a slap shot — or drive in close, deke and wrist a shot.

At his best, Bondra is in the category of players you would pay to watch play. His speed is exceptional, and he makes intelligent offensive plays. He accelerates quickly and smoothly and drives defenders back because they have to play off his speed. If he gets hooked to the ice he doesn't stay down, but jumps back to his skates and gets involved in the play again, often after the defender has forgotten about him.

Bondra lives to score goals. He has a real scorer's mentality. But don't underestimate his defensive awareness. Bondra quickly grasped the concept that better defence helps his offence. That's not so odd when you think of the game in terms of gap control.

Bondra, with 33 shorthanded goals in the past eight seasons (although he scored only one last year), is a dangerous shorthanded threat. He makes opposing teams' power plays jittery because of his anticipation and breakaway speed, and he follows up his shots to the net and is quick to pounce on rebounds.

THE PHYSICAL GAME

Bondra isn't strong, but he will lean on people. He can't be intimidated.

THE INTANGIBLES

Where would the Caps have been without Bondra's play in the first half? He didn't have a centre after Adam Oates was traded. But the plan is to team him up with free agent acquisition Robert Lang.

PROJECTION

Bondra nearly hit 40 goals in what had to be a tough season. If he clicks with Lang, he might get 50 again.

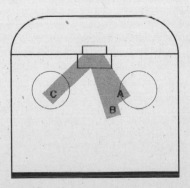

SYLVAIN COTE

Yrs. of NHL service: 18
Born: Quebec City, Que.; Jan. 19, 1966
Position: left defence
Height: 6-0
Weight: 190
Uniform no.: 3
Shoots: right

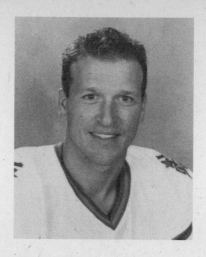

Career statistics:

GP	G	A	TP	PIM
1170	122	313	435	541

1998-1999 statistics:

GP	G	A	TP	+/-	PIM	PP	SH	GW	GT	S	PCT
79	5	24	29	+22	28	0	0	1	0	119	4.2

1999-2000 statistics:

GP	G	A	TP	+/-	PIM	PP	SH	GW	GT	S	PCT
76	8	27	35	+3	28	5	0	2	0	128	6.3

2000-2001 statistics:

GP	G	A	TP	+/-	PIM	PP	SH	GW	GT	S	PCT
68	7	11	18	-3	18	1	1	1	0	86	8.1

2001-2002 statistics:

GP	G	A	TP	+/-	PIM	PP	SH	GW	GT	S	PCT
70	3	11	14	-15	26	1	0	2	0	101	3.0

LAST SEASON

Missed five games with back injury. Missed seven games due to coach's decision.

THE FINESSE GAME

Cote is a solid two-way defenceman. He has good puckhandling skills and can make a pass to his forehand or backhand side with confidence. He overhandles the puck at times, especially in his defensive zone. When he gets into trouble he seems to struggle with his forehand clearances off the left-wing boards.

Carrying the puck does not slow Cote down. He can do everything in stride, and he can rush end to end. He is gifted in all skating areas: fine agility, good balance, quick stops and starts. He likes to bring the puck up on the power play. He gets a lot on his shot from the point, which causes rebounds, and it's the source of most of his assists.

Cote has decent hockey sense. He can lead a rush or come into the play as a trailer, but he knows enough not to force and to play more conservatively when the situation dictates. His skating covers up for most of his defensive lapses. His instincts lag well behind his skill level. He can be beaten one-on-one, but it takes a good player to do it.

THE PHYSICAL GAME

Although Cote doesn't have great size, he is a solid hitter who finishes his checks. He isn't mean, however, and will occasionally fall into the trap of playing the puck instead of the man.

THE INTANGIBLES

Cote's skill levels are beginning to erode slightly with age and wear and tear. He is on the bubble.

PROJECTION

Cote's ice time will decrease as Washington works younger defencemen into its lineup. It's unlikely he would score more than 20 points.

JEAN FRANCOIS FORTIN

Yrs. of NHL service: 1
Born: Laval, Que.; Mar. 15, 1979
Position: defence
Height: 6-2
Weight: 200
Uniform no.: 58
Shoots: right

Career statistics:

GP	G	A	TP	PIM
36	1	3	4	20

2001-2002 statistics:

GP	G	A	TP	+/-	PIM	PP	SH	GW	GT	S	PCT
36	1	3	4	-1	20	0	0	1	0	24	4.2

LAST SEASON

Appeared in 44 games with Portland (AHL), scoring 4-9-13 with 20 PIM. Missed two games with leg injury. Missed one game due to coach's decision.

THE FINESSE GAME

Fortin started the season in the minors but was able to stick with the Caps after his January promotion. What impressed the Caps most is Fortin's poise. He is not outstanding at any one thing. Fortin is just an effective package of all-around skill.

Fortin has good size. He handles the puck well with a good first pass. Fortin doesn't get too involved offensively, but he has decent hands and can make some plays. Fortin is seldom flustered with the puck. He doesn't get panicky.

Fortin saw some penalty-killing time late in the season and will probably earn more this year. Fortin can also get a little more involved in the scoring. He has a good shot from the point and doesn't use a big wind-up, so he gets it away efficiently.

THE PHYSICAL GAME

Fortin is a good-sized defenceman who is still learning about what it means to be a pro athlete — that is, to take care of conditioning and nutrition because he is now making a living at playing a game. He was frequently teamed up with Witt last season, and they made a pretty solid pair.

THE INTANGIBLES

Fortin was a relatively high draft pick (second round, 35th overall, in 1997), but he didn't take the easy road to the NHL. He has paid his dues in the minors (Portland, Richmond, Hampton Roads), and this is the payoff. He's 23 and still a little rough around the edges, but he was one of the few truly good things to happen to the Caps last season.

PROJECTION

Expect Fortin to gradually get more ice time. He could be a 20-point player in an expanded role.

SERGEI GONCHAR

Yrs. of NHL service: 8
Born: Chelyabinsk, Russia; Apr. 13, 1974
Position: left defence
Height: 6-2
Weight: 212
Uniform no.: 55
Shoots: left

Career statistics:

GP	G	A	TP	PIM
516	119	181	300	421

1998-1999 statistics:

GP	G	A	TP	+/-	PIM	PP	SH	GW	GT	S	PCT
53	21	10	31	+1	57	13	1	3	0	180	11.7

1999-2000 statistics:

GP	G	A	TP	+/-	PIM	PP	SH	GW	GT	S	PCT
73	18	36	54	+26	52	5	0	3	0	181	9.9

2000-2001 statistics:

GP	G	A	TP	+/-	PIM	PP	SH	GW	GT	S	PCT
76	19	38	57	+12	70	8	0	2	0	241	7.9

2001-2002 statistics:

GP	G	A	TP	+/-	PIM	PP	SH	GW	GT	S	PCT
76	26	33	59	-1	58	7	0	2	0	216	12.0

LAST SEASON

Led NHL defencemen in goals. Tied for NHL lead among defencemen in goals. Second on team in assists and shots. Third on team in goals and points. Tied for third on team in power-play goals. Missed five games with concussion.

THE FINESSE GAME

It's difficult to believe that Gonchar developed as a defensive defenceman in Russia. He sees the ice well and passes well, but he never put up any big offensive numbers before coming into the NHL. Now he ranks among the game's elite offensive defencemen.

Gonchar made the quick jump to becoming a complete player by adding offence. He becomes a little too involved with the offensive game, however, and will lapse into making high-risk passes. When the scoring slumps come, and they do, Gonchar needs to remember to do the other things to help his team win a game.

He jumps up into the play willingly and intelligently. Gonchar has a natural feel for the flow of a game and makes tape-to-tape feeds through people — even under pressure. He sees first-unit power-play time on the point and makes a first-rate quarterback. He plays heads-up. He doesn't have the blazing speed that some elite defencemen have when carrying the puck, but he will gain the zone with some speed. He is an excellent passer.

Gonchar's shot is accurate enough, but it won't terrorize any goalies. He doesn't push the puck forward and step into it like Al MacInnis. Most of the time he is content with getting it on the net, though he is not reluctant to shoot.

THE PHYSICAL GAME

Strong on his skates, Gonchar has worked hard on his off-ice conditioning. His defence is based more on reads and positional play than on a physical element. He is not an overly aggressive player. Teams like to target him early to scare him off his best effort.

THE INTANGIBLES

Gonchar's 85 goals are the most scored by any NHL defenceman during the past three seasons. Gonchar simply gets better every season.

PROJECTION

Gonchar is a consistent scorer in the 55- to 60-point range.

JEFF HALPERN

Yrs. of NHL service: 3
Born: Potomac, Maryland; May 3, 1976
Position: centre
Height: 5-11
Weight: 195
Uniform no.: 11
Shoots: right

Career statistics:

GP	G	A	TP	PIM
207	44	46	90	128

1999-2000 statistics:

GP	G	A	TP	+/-	PIM	PP	SH	GW	GT	S	PCT
79	18	11	29	+21	39	4	0	2	1	118	10.2

2000-2001 statistics:

GP	G	A	TP	+/-	PIM	PP	SH	GW	GT	S	PCT
80	21	21	42	+13	60	2	1	5	2	110	19.1

2001-2002 statistics:

GP	G	A	TP	+/-	PIM	PP	SH	GW	GT	S	PCT
48	5	14	19	-9	29	0	0	4	0	74	6.8

LAST SEASON

Missed 34 games with knee injury and surgery.

THE FINESSE GAME

Halpern is a very smart player without the puck. Halpern doesn't have great speed, but he is very aware positionally. He is the kind of guy you would like to have on the ice all night long. You never have to worry about him. He makes big plays.

Halpern is a reliable, low-risk forward at even strength. Halpern's job as a "goal preventer" is advanced for a rather inexperienced player.

Halpern can play centre or wing, though he's more effective in the middle. That's likely where the Caps would like to play him with Steve Konowalchuk.

Halpern used to be something of a liability on draws, but he studied Adam Oates when that face-off specialist was with the Caps and he has improved.

THE PHYSICAL GAME

Halpern isn't big, but he plays with a quiet kind of toughness.

THE INTANGIBLES

Halpern is locked in as the team's third-line centre. Halpern has continued to upgrade his game as his responsibilities intensify. A knee injury and surgery in mid-January ended his season.

PROJECTION

Halpern should continue to develop into a solid two-way centre, with emphasis on the checking side. He scored 21 goals in his rookie season, and if he can do that again, the Caps would be thrilled. Players coming back off knee surgery usually bear some watching, however. Halpern may not hit his best stride until a month or so into the season.

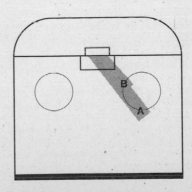

JAROMIR JAGR

Yrs. of NHL service: 12
Born: Kladno, Czech Republic; Feb. 15, 1972
Position: right wing
Height: 6-2
Weight: 234
Uniform no.: 68
Shoots: left

Career statistics:

GP	G	A	TP	PIM
875	470	688	1158	623

1998-1999 statistics:

GP	G	A	TP	+/-	PIM	PP	SH	GW	GT	S	PCT
81	44	83	127	+17	66	10	1	7	2	343	12.8

1999-2000 statistics:

GP	G	A	TP	+/-	PIM	PP	SH	GW	GT	S	PCT
63	42	54	96	+25	50	10	0	5	1	290	14.5

2000-2001 statistics:

GP	G	A	TP	+/-	PIM	PP	SH	GW	GT	S	PCT
81	52	69	121	+19	42	14	1	10	1	317	16.4

2001-2002 statistics:

GP	G	A	TP	+/-	PIM	PP	SH	GW	GT	S	PCT
69	31	48	79	0	30	10	0	3	0	197	15.7

LAST SEASON

Led team in assists, points and power-play goals. Second on team in goals and shooting percentage. Third on team in shots. Tied for fifth in NHL in points. Tied for ninth in NHL in assists. Missed six games with groin injury. Missed seven games with knee injuries.

THE FINESSE GAME

Jagr's exceptional skating and extraordinary ice time make him tough to shadow. Jagr is as close to a perfect skater as there is in the NHL. He keeps his body centred over his skates, giving him a low centre of gravity and making it tough for anyone to knock him off the puck. He has a deep knee bend, for quickness and power. His strokes are long and sure, and he has control over his body and exceptional lateral mobility. He dazzles with his footwork and handles the puck at high tempo. If he was affected by lower body injuries, as he was last season, Jagr's game is severely compromised. He can score, but he can't dominate the way he does when he's 100 per cent.

Jagr loves — and lives — to score. He's poetry in motion with his beautifully effortless skating style. And, with his Mario Lemieux-like reach, Jagr can dangle the puck while he's gliding and swooping. He fakes the backhand and goes to his forehand in a flash. He is also powerful enough to drag a defender with him to the net and push off a strong one-handed shot. He has a big slap shot and can drive it on the fly or fire it with a one-timer off a pass.

Not much of a team player, Jagr is the game's best offensive forward, and a diva too.

THE PHYSICAL GAME

Earlier in his career he could be intimidated physically — and he still doesn't like to get hit, but he's not as wimpy as he used to be. Playing on a line with Chris Simon eliminates some of the nonsense. Jagr is confident, almost cocky, and tough to catch. When he feels like it, anyway.

THE INTANGIBLES

Injuries, the lack of a compatible centre and general disinterest made Jagr merely a player in the first half. He picked up his game considerably after the Olympic break, as if he could carry the Caps into the playoffs by himself. It was too late and Jagr missed the postseason for the first time in his career. Jagr found some chemistry once Dainius Zubrus joined his line, but Zubrus isn't a natural centre and that probably isn't a long-term solution.

The Caps signed centre Robert Lang as a free agent but Lang may be used on a second line to play with Peter Bondra.

PROJECTION

Jagr didn't like missing the playoffs. There was a coaching change after the season and the Caps will have to regroup again. He is certainly capable of another 100-point season, and a sixth scoring title may be on his agenda.

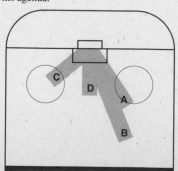

CALLE JOHANSSON

Yrs. of NHL service: 15
Born: Goteborg, Sweden; Feb. 14, 1967
Position: left defence
Height. 5-11
Weight: 200
Uniform no.: 6
Shoots: left

Career statistics:

GP	G	A	TP	PIM
1019	116	398	514	497

1998-1999 statistics:

GP	G	A	TP	+/-	PIM	PP	SH	GW	GT	S	PCT
67	8	21	29	+10	22	2	0	2	1	145	5.5

1999-2000 statistics:

GP	G	A	TP	+/-	PIM	PP	SH	GW	GT	S	PCT
82	7	25	32	+13	24	1	0	3	0	138	5.1

2000-2001 statistics:

GP	G	A	TP	+/-	PIM	PP	SH	GW	GT	S	PCT
76	7	29	36	+11	26	5	0	0	0	154	4.6

2001-2002 statistics:

GP	G	A	TP	+/-	PIM	PP	SH	GW	GT	S	PCT
11	2	0	2	-4	8	0	0	1	0	18	11.1

LAST SEASON

Missed 72 games with shoulder injury and surgery.

THE FINESSE GAME

Johansson has tremendous legs, notably big, strong thighs that generate the power for his shot and his explosive skating. He makes every move look easy. He is agile, mobile and great at moving up-ice with the play. Speed, balance and strength allow him to chase a puck behind the net, pick it up without stopping and make an accurate pass. He is confident, even on the backhand, and likes to have the puck in key spots.

Johansson is not an elite scorer, but he is smart offensively. He moves the puck with a good first pass, then has enough speed and instinct to jump up and be ready for a return pass. He keeps the gap tight as the play enters the attacking zone, which opens up more options: he is available to the forwards if they need him for offence, and closer to the puck if it is turned over to the opposition.

Johansson has a low, accurate shot that can be tipped. He is unselfish to a fault, often looking to pass when he should use his shot.

He has good defensive instincts and reads plays well. His skating gives him the confidence (maybe overconfidence) to gamble and challenge the puck carrier. He has a quick stick for poke- and sweep checks.

THE PHYSICAL GAME

Although not an aggressive player, Johansson is strong and knows what he has to do with his body in the defensive zone. This part of the game has not come naturally, but he has worked at it. He is not an impact player defensively, though he wins his share of the one-on-one battles because he gets so much power from his legs. He stays in good condition and can (and does) give a team a lot of minutes.

THE INTANGIBLES

Johansson was essential to Brendan Witt's emergence as an NHL force. He is one of the most underrated defencemen in the league and his absence was keenly felt by the Caps. Johansson may drop down to a No. 4 or even 5 as the younger defencemen develop, but the Caps want to keep him around. If Johansson's injury had affected his lower body, we would be more worried about his comeback at age 35.

PROJECTION

Johansson should produce around 30 points if healthy.

OLAF KOLZIG

Yrs. of NHL service: 6
Born: Johannesburg, South Africa; Apr. 9, 1970
Position: goaltender
Height: 6-3
Weight: 225
Uniform no.: 37
Catches: left

Career statistics:

GP	MIN	GA	SO	GAA	A	PIM
415	23784	1006	27	2.54	8	69

1998-1999 statistics:

GP	MIN	GAA	W	L	T	SO	GA	S	SAPCT	PIM
64	3586	2.58	26	31	3	4	154	1538	.900	19

1999-2000 statistics:

GP	MIN	GAA	W	L	T	SO	GA	S	SAPCT	PIM
73	4371	2.24	41	20	11	5	163	1957	.917	6

2000-2001 statistics:

GP	MIN	GAA	W	L	T	SO	GA	S	SAPCT	PIM
72	4279	2.48	37	26	8	5	177	1941	.909	14

2001-2002 statistics:

GP	MIN	GAA	W	L	T	SO	GA	S	SAPCT	PIM
71	4131	2.79	31	29	8	6	192	1977	.903	8

LAST SEASON

Second among NHL goalies in minutes played. Fourth season with 30 or more wins. Missed one game with sprained ankle. Missed one game with knee injury.

THE PHYSICAL GAME

Kolzig is a big butterfly goalie with sharp reflexes and good skating ability for a player of his size. Rather than just lumber around and let the puck hit him, however, he is active and positions himself well to block as much of the net as possible from the shooter. Kolzig is very good at controlling his rebounds. He still works at this skill almost daily during the season.

Kolzig is aggressive and consistent in his technical play. Although still not regarded as an elite NHL goalie, Kolzig is solidly among the second echelon and may soon move up to join the leaders.

He needs to improve his stickhandling. He could use his stick better to break up plays around the net.

The book on Kolzig is to go high, since he takes away the bottom of the net so well.

THE MENTAL GAME

Kolzig has matured so much. He can still be a bit of a hothead in the course of a game, but for the most part he stays relaxed and focused. He is a good influence in the dressing room and his teammates want to play hard in front of him. Bad goals or bad games don't haunt him. He always gives his team a chance to win, and he steals some games.

THE INTANGIBLES

Kolzig had a second consecutive season where he was just average. The Caps aren't likely to look elsewhere for goalie help just yet, and are counting on him to want to battle his way back to top form.

PROJECTION

Kolzig posted 31 wins for a team that was in disarray most of the season. If the team settles in front of him, Kolzig might get back up to 35 wins or more.

STEVE KONOWALCHUK

Yrs. of NIIL service: 10
Born: Salt Lake City, Utah; Nov. 11, 1972
Position: left wing
Height: 6-2
Weight: 207
Uniform no.: 22
Shoots: left

Career statistics:

GP	G	A	TP	PIM
610	131	180	311	548

1998-1999 statistics:

GP	G	A	TP	+/-	PIM	PP	SH	GW	GT	S	PCT
45	12	12	24	0	26	4	1	2	0	98	12.2

1999-2000 statistics:

GP	G	A	TP	+/-	PIM	PP	SH	GW	GT	S	PCT
82	16	27	43	+19	80	3	0	1	0	146	11.0

2000-2001 statistics:

GP	G	A	TP	+/-	PIM	PP	SH	GW	GT	S	PCT
82	24	23	47	+8	87	6	0	5	0	163	14.7

2001-2002 statistics:

GP	G	A	TP	+/-	PIM	PP	SH	GW	GT	S	PCT
28	2	12	14	-2	23	0	0	0	0	36	5.6

LAST SEASON

Missed 54 games with shoulder injury and surgery.

THE FINESSE GAME

Konowalchuk is a willing guy who plays any role asked of him. He's a digger who has to work hard for his goals, and an intelligent and earnest player who uses every ounce of energy on every shift. He is one of the Caps' most eager forecheckers.

There is nothing fancy about his offence. He just lets his shot rip and drives to the net. He doesn't have the moves and hand skills to beat a defender one-on-one, but he doesn't care; he'll go right through him. His release on his shot is improving.

Konowalchuk is reliable and intelligent defensively. On the draw, he ties up the opposing centre if he doesn't win the puck drop outright. He uses his feet along the boards as well as his stick. He's the kind of guy who does all the dirty work that makes the finesse players on his team look even prettier.

THE PHYSICAL GAME

Konowalchuk is very strong. He has some grit in him, too, and will aggravate opponents with his constant effort. He doesn't take bad penalties, but often goads rivals into retaliating. He is very fit and can handle a lot of ice time.

THE INTANGIBLES

Konowalchuk is a heart-and-soul guy. His absence (his injury occurred in October) was one of the reasons why the Caps got off to such a terrible start. By the time Konowalchuk returned, things had pretty much spun out of control. His nonstop intensity makes him one of the Caps' most gutsy leaders.

PROJECTION

Konowalchuk is a quality guy on the ice or in the dressing room, and he can score 20 to 25 goals.

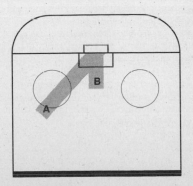

ROBERT LANG

Yrs. of NHL service: 9
Born: Teplice, Czech Republic; Dec. 19, 1970
Position: centre
Height: 6-2
Weight: 216
Uniform no.: 20
Shoots: right

Career statistics:

GP	G	A	TP	PIM
495	122	197	319	124

1998-1999 statistics:

GP	G	A	TP	+/-	PIM	PP	SH	GW	GT	S	PCT
72	21	23	44	-10	24	7	0	3	3	137	15.3

1999-2000 statistics:

GP	G	A	TP	+/-	PIM	PP	SH	GW	GT	S	PCT
78	23	42	65	-9	14	13	0	5	1	142	16.2

2000-2001 statistics:

GP	G	A	TP	+/-	PIM	PP	SH	GW	GT	S	PCT
82	32	48	80	+20	28	10	0	2	0	177	18.1

2001-2002 statistics:

GP	G	A	TP	+/-	PIM	PP	SH	GW	GT	S	PCT
62	18	32	50	+9	16	5	1	3	0	175	10.3

LAST SEASON

Signed as free agent with Washington on July 1, 2002. Led Penguins in plus-minus. Second on Penguins in shots. Third on Penguins in assists and points. Missed 18 games with broken hand. Missed two games with oral surgery.

THE FINESSE GAME

This move made it appear that superstar Jaromir Jagr had started playing GM, and that he asked for Lang to be signed. They might be friends, but they were seldom linemates in Pittsburgh. The plan going into the season is for Lang to be teamed up with Peter Bondra, not Jagr.

Lang has always given the impression that there is something left in his tank. It's not exactly the right quality for a first-line player, and with the kind of money the Caps just invested in him, they will be asking him to be a top six guy. Lang has never had very strong playoffs, for example, but for now the Caps will just ask him to get them into the postseason and worry about the rest later.

Lang is certainly not without skill. He has deceptive quickness and is very solid on his skates, along with great hands, great hockey sense and the ability to make plays on his forehand or backhand. Players on both wings have to be prepared for a pass that could materialize out of thin air or through a thicket of sticks and skates. Lang has the presence to draw defenders to him to open up ice for his linemates, and he makes good use of them.

Patient with the puck, Lang often holds on too long. He will always pass up a shot if he can make a

play instead. Lang is a smart penalty killer because of his anticipation. He lapses defensively at even strength, however.

THE PHYSICAL GAME

Lang will not take a hit to make a play, a glaring flaw for a front-line player. He has to show more willingness to initiate. He'll never trounce anyone, but he has to fight for the puck and fight through checks.

THE INTANGIBLES

Lang picked the right time to have a solid year, and landed a five-year, $25 million (US) free agent contract with Washington.

PROJECTION

Lang's top end is probably an assist-heavy 80 points. Whether he plays with Bondra or Jagr, he is likely to put up some big numbers.

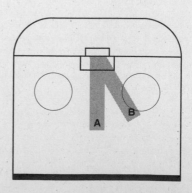

ANDREI NIKOLISHIN

Yrs. of NHL service: 8
Born: Vorkuta, Russia, March 25, 1973
Position: left wing / centre
Height: 6-0
Weight: 206
Uniform no.: 13
Shoots: left

Career statistics:

GP	G	A	TP	PIM
519	82	165	247	220

1998-1999 statistics:

GP	G	A	TP	+/-	PIM	PP	SH	GW	GT	S	PCT
73	8	27	35	0	28	0	1	1	0	121	6.6

1999-2000 statistics:

GP	G	A	TP	+/-	PIM	PP	SH	GW	GT	S	PCT
76	11	14	25	+6	28	0	2	2	0	98	11.2

2000-2001 statistics:

GP	G	A	TP	+/-	PIM	PP	SH	GW	GT	S	PCT
81	13	25	38	+9	34	4	0	2	1	145	9.0

2001-2002 statistics:

GP	G	A	TP	+/-	PIM	PP	SH	GW	GT	S	PCT
80	13	23	36	-1	40	1	0	0	0	143	9.1

LAST SEASON

Missed two games with leg injury.

THE FINESSE GAME

The biggest difference in Nikolishin's game over the past two seasons is his willingness to shoot more. He sees the ice well and is a gifted playmaker, but by taking more shots, his game is less predictable. He fits best with a finishing winger who can convert his slippery passes. He has become more of a defensive-minded forward, which means it's less likely he will earn a spot on the top two lines. He backchecks, blocks shots and kills penalties.

He does a great job on draws — no doubt learning from former teammate Adam Oates has helped him. Nikolishin studies his opponents well and reacts to them, winning a majority of his draws by countering what the other player is doing.

Nikolishin is a strong skater with a powerful stride, and he makes some of the tightest turns in the league. His great talent is puckhandling, but like many Europeans he tends to hold on to the puck too long and leave himself open for hits.

THE PHYSICAL GAME

Nikolishin is extremely strong on his skates and likes to work in the corners for the puck. He is tough to knock off balance and has a low centre of gravity. He has adapted smoothly to the more physical style of play in the NHL, and although he isn't very big, he will plow into heavy players while going for the puck. When he puts his mind to it, he is one of the tougher defensive forwards in the league.

THE INTANGIBLES

Nikolishin is popular with his teammates, both for his personality and his work habits. He is most effective when he isn't relied upon as one of the top two centres. As long as the Caps stay healthy, Nikolishin can be well-spotted in a part-time and penalty-killing role. He's a valuable player to have on hand.

PROJECTION

Nikolishin seems content to let his defensive game carry him. He has proven before that he can put up some numbers, but it's likely he'll stay in the 35-point range.

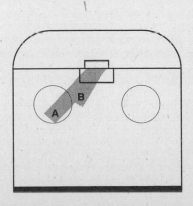

CHRIS SIMON

Yrs. of NHL service: 9
Born: Wawa, Ont.; Jan. 30, 1972
Position: left wing
Height: 6-4
Weight: 235
Uniform no.: 17
Shoots: left

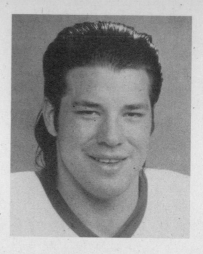

Career statistics:

GP	G	A	TP	PIM
456	96	109	205	1198

1998-1999 statistics:

GP	G	A	TP	+/-	PIM	PP	SH	GW	GT	S	PCT
23	3	7	10	-4	48	0	0	0	0	29	10.3

1999-2000 statistics:

GP	G	A	TP	+/-	PIM	PP	SH	GW	GT	S	PCT
75	29	20	49	+11	146	7	0	5	1	201	14.4

2000-2001 statistics:

GP	G	A	TP	+/-	PIM	PP	SH	GW	GT	S	PCT
60	10	10	20	-12	109	4	0	2	0	123	8.1

2001-2002 statistics:

GP	G	A	TP	+/-	PIM	PP	SH	GW	GT	S	PCT
82	14	17	31	-8	137	1	0	1	1	121	11.6

LAST SEASON

Led team in penalty minutes. Only Cap to appear in all 82 games.

THE FINESSE GAME

Staying healthy, and starting off the season without a holdout, sparked the return of Simon to the ranks of Washington's top two lines. Simon finished the season playing on the left side with Jaromir Jagr and Dainius Zubrus, and it was a good fit.

Simon made his reputation as a brawler, but he always has some moves where he dekes a defender and scores with an honest-to-goodness snap shot. Simon always gets a lot of room to move because of his fierce reputation, and once he has it, he knows what to do with it. He had to improve his skating to earn more ice time, and he has.

Simon has decent hands for a big guy, and most of his successes come in-tight. Now he has great confidence in his shot, so he isn't afraid to shoot from almost anywhere. He has improved the release on his shot — that extra room helps again — and he has a wicked slapper.

THE PHYSICAL GAME

As tough as they come, Simon has a wide streak of mean. The difference now is that he doesn't go looking for fights. He doesn't have to prove himself as a battler. He will pick his spots. Players never know when he is going to snap, which is pretty scary. He has already established himself as a player who can throw them when the time comes, but he isn't as easily goaded into going off with another team's fourth-liner. That's beneath him now. He unleashes some clean, mean shoulder hits on the forecheck.

THE INTANGIBLES

Simon is truly an inspiration for players with size and raw skill who want to make themselves into something more. In Simon's case, much more.

PROJECTION

Simon can chip in 15 goals and play bodyguard for Jagr.

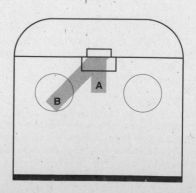

BRENDAN WITT

Yrs. of NHL service: 7
Born: Humboldt, Sask.; Feb. 20, 1975
Position: left defence
Height: 6-2
Weight: 226
Uniform no.: 19
Shoots: left

Career statistics:

GP	G	A	TP	PIM
427	15	34	49	665

1998-1999 statistics:

GP	G	A	TP	+/-	PIM	PP	SH	GW	GT	S	PCT
54	2	5	7	-6	87	0	0	0	0	51	3.9

1999-2000 statistics:

GP	G	A	TP	+/-	PIM	PP	SH	GW	GT	S	PCT
77	1	7	8	+5	114	0	0	0	0	64	1.6

2000-2001 statistics:

GP	G	A	TP	+/-	PIM	PP	SH	GW	GT	S	PCT
72	3	3	6	+2	101	0	0	0	0	87	3.5

2001-2002 statistics:

GP	G	A	TP	+/-	PIM	PP	SH	GW	GT	S	PCT
68	3	7	10	-1	78	0	0	0	0	81	3.7

PROJECTION

Witt hasn't reached his best level yet, but he's getting closer. One very positive sign is how much he continues to improve each year. Although he won't score a lot of points, he will get a lot of ice time.

LAST SEASON

Missed seven games with thumb injury. Missed two games with leg injury.

THE FINESSE GAME

Witt's skill level is high, if not elite, and he applies his abilities in his own zone. His skating is capable. He has worked to improve his agility, though his pivots and passing skills remain a bit rough. Still, he does not overhandle the puck, and by making simple plays he keeps himself out of serious trouble. He skates well backwards and has decent lateral mobility.

Witt gets involved somewhat in the attack, but the extent of his contribution is a hard point shot. He won't gamble low and can't run a power play. He won't ever be an offensive force.

One of the steadier, and sometimes scarier, players on the Caps' blueline, Witt is effective without being flashy. His game is maturing.

THE PHYSICAL GAME

A strong physical presence on the ice, Witt can get even stronger. He has added close to 10 pounds of needed muscle without losing any mobility. As a result, he loses fewer one-on-one battles. He blocks shots fearlessly, and is naturally aggressive and intimidating. He is a little too eager to fight and can be goaded into the box. Witt is a powerful hitter.

THE INTANGIBLES

As a co-captain with Steve Konowalchuk, Witt was (at 27) the youngest player in the league to wear the "C" last season. Witt has continued to mature slowly and steadily, and is one of the Caps' top two defencemen. Witt has yet to find his ideal defence partner.

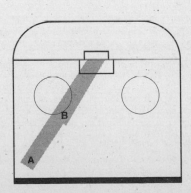

NOLAN YONKMAN

Yrs. of NHL service: 0
Born: Punnicht, Sask.; Apr. 1, 1981
Position: defence
Height: 6-5
Weight: 218
Uniform no.: 40
Shoots: right

Career statistics:

GP	G	A	TP	PIM
11	1	0	1	4

2001-2002 statistics:

GP	G	A	TP	+/-	PIM	PP	SH	GW	GT	S	PCT
11	1	0	1	+3	4	0	0	0	0	7	14.3

LAST SEASON

Appeared in 59 games with Portland (AHL), scoring 4-3-7 with 116 PIM.

THE FINESSE GAME

Yonkman is a big, big guy, and he's a gifted skater for his size. Yonkman's forward skating is as good as a lot of forwards around the league.

Yonkman is smart defensively and knows how to position himself to take up even more of the ice than his massive frame. Yonkman is strong on his stick and uses it well to eliminate passing lanes. He can be described as a better-skating Kjell Samuelsson, with more of an edge.

Yonkman is a low-risk defenceman. He makes the safe and easy play — banking the puck off the boards rather than gamble with a pass up the middle.

THE PHYSICAL GAME

Yonkman doesn't splatter people. He makes solid contact, but he plays more of a containment game than a power one. He takes up a lot of room on the ice and it's tough for opponents to get past him because he is also mobile. He doesn't play soft, exactly, but don't expect Scott Stevens-style hits from him.

Yonkman needed to add some muscle from his draft year (1999), and has put on 18 useful pounds since then. He is fit and will be ready to handle the extra minutes when the Caps start using him more.

THE INTANGIBLES

The Caps are hopeful that veteran Calle Johansson will return healthy this season and hope to have him ease Yonkman into the NHL battles. Yonkman played with another prized Caps prospect, Jakub Cutta, in the minors, and they are a Caps defence pair of the future. Yonkman made a positive impression in his 11-game stint with the Caps last season.

PROJECTION

Yonkman is purely a defensive defenceman and his point totals will barely be double-digits even after he graduates to a top-four role.

DAINIUS ZUBRUS

Yrs. of NHL service: 6
Born: Elektrenai, Lithuania; June 16, 1978
Position: right wing
Height: 6-4
Weight: 227
Uniform no.: 9
Shoots: left

Career statistics:

GP	G	A	TP	PIM
422	66	115	181	222

1998-1999 statistics:

GP	G	A	TP	+/-	PIM	PP	SH	GW	GT	S	PCT
80	6	10	16	-8	29	0	1	1	0	80	7.5

1999-2000 statistics:

GP	G	A	TP	+/-	PIM	PP	SH	GW	GT	S	PCT
73	14	28	42	-1	54	3	0	1	0	139	10.1

2000-2001 statistics:

GP	G	A	TP	+/-	PIM	PP	SH	GW	GT	S	PCT
61	13	13	26	-11	37	4	0	0	0	83	15.7

2001-2002 statistics:

GP	G	A	TP	+/-	PIM	PP	SH	GW	GT	S	PCT
71	17	26	43	+5	38	4	0	3	0	138	12.3

LAST SEASON

Second on team in plus-minus. Third on team in shooting percentage. Missed five games with groin injury. Missed five games with fractured right hand. Missed one game with bruised foot.

THE FINESSE GAME

Zubrus has the ability to be a big-time offensive threat, and playing with Jaromir Jagr might help him reach his peak. As a lefthanded shot, Zubrus, who can play centre, will be able to make forehand feeds to his streaking right winger. Zubrus plays the game in a north-south direction, goal line to goal line, rather than in the east-west fashion favoured by most imports. He is helped in this regard by a long stride that covers lots of ground. His puck control is impressive, as though the puck is on a very short rope that is nailed to his stick. His great ability is to control the puck down low and create scoring chances for himself and his teammates. He is not a natural goal-scorer.

Splendid acceleration is a key component of Zubrus's game. He is both confident in his skating and competent enough to burst between defencemen to take the most direct path to the net. He also features enough power and balance to control a sweep behind the net, pull in front and roof a backhand shot under the crossbar from close range.

Zubrus uses his edges well and is tough to knock off the puck. He is quite willing to zoom in off the wing, use his body to shield the puck from a defender and make something happen. The soft touch in his hands and the quick release of the puck shot complement the power in his legs.

Zubrus still has a way to go to become a complete player. He is a better player in his own zone than he was.

THE PHYSICAL GAME

Zubrus will fight his own battles. He uses his size to his advantage, finishes checks with authority and out-muscles as many people as he can. He's gritty in the corners and along the boards, and is adept at using his feet to control the puck if his upper body is tied up. He is a very strong one-on-one player.

THE INTANGIBLES

Zubrus tends to be rather self-involved and has to improve his work ethic. If he continues to play with Jagr, he will soon learn there is a league quota of only one diva per line.

PROJECTION

Zubrus has the ability, if not the desire, to be a 60-point scorer. His totals will be assist-heavy.

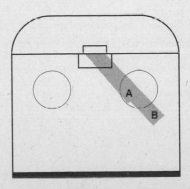

PLAYER INDEX